FRANKLINCOVEY

Style Guide™

FOR BUSINESS AND TECHNICAL COMMUNICATION

THIRD EDITION

Preface

Effective communication is simply good customer service. We serve our customers well by sharing relevant information quickly and efficiently. We fail to serve them when we give them information that is unclear, inaccurate, or irrelevant. These principles are valid for businesses, industries, and governmental agencies.

The aim of this third edition of the *FranklinCovey Style Guide* for Business and Technical Communication is to help you serve your customers and your coworkers in these ways:

- You will communicate information that people can understand and use.

- You will be complying with the best current styles and practices in business and technical communication.

- You will be saving time and money for your customers because they won't have to contend with misleading and unprofessional documents.

Communicate information that people can use.

In the workplace, information has value only if it is accessible, easy to understand, and relevant. Data and facts are not information until you communicate their relevance and importance to someone.

This *Style Guide* provides tips for making your message accessible, easy to understand, and relevant. As you consult the *Style Guide* sections on WRITING AND REVISING, ORGANIZATION, EMPHASIS, PAGE LAYOUT , and ONLINE DOCUMENTATION, you will find both process and format suggestions. You will also find new and colorful sections on GRAPHICS FOR DOCUMENTS. GRAPHICS FOR PRESENTATIONS, COLOR, CHARTS, MAPS, and PHOTOGRAPHS. These newly rewritten entries will help you prepare visually effective documents.

Comply with the best current styles and practices in business and technical communication.

In this *Style Guide*, we record and illustrate currently accepted stylistic conventions for written English. We label the conventions "rules," but they are not laws, and over time they will surely change just as the language is constantly changing. These rules are not always logical; they are rarely consistent; and they have many exceptions. But if you follow these rules, your writing will reflect the best current standards of business and technical communication.

Save time and money for your customers because they won't have to contend with misleading and unprofessional documents.

Effective business communication saves time and money. Cogent and persuasive business plans allow swift, logical management decisions. Analytic and well-crafted scientific reports support scientific dialogues and sound policy decisions. Well-designed and clearly written software manuals decrease customer service calls and prevent costly downtimes. Even short technical memos and routine letters are easier to read and clearer if they are well written.

Time and money are irreplaceable resources, and wise stewardship of them often means the difference between an organization's success and its failure. Effective business communication is one of the more important ways for you to improve your stewardship of scarce organizational resources.

We hope that this third edition of the *Style Guide* will be a valuable and cost-saving tool for all of you who wish to become more effective communicators.

FranklinCovey acknowledges Larry H Freeman for his efforts in compiling the FranklinCovey Style Guide. While many others contributed, Larry provided the knowledge and inspiration that created this valuable resource. We hope you will enjoy using it.

FranklinCovey offers tools and services for improving individual and organizational effectiveness through proven principles. We provide a broad range of products and training programs to help people achieve personal fulfillment and career satisfaction, and help institutions build highly skilled, high trust, high performance cultures. Above all, FranklinCovey supports individuals, families, and organizations in accomplishing what matters most to them. We teach them how to save time and to improve the quality of their communication.

FranklinCovey's client portfolio includes eighty-two of the Fortune 100 companies, more than two-thirds of the Fortune 500 companies, thousands of small and midsize companies, and government entities at local, state, and national levels.

FranklinCovey trains in excess of 750,000 participants annually. Implementation tools, including the Franklin Planner™ and a wide offering of audio and video tapes, books, and computer software programs, enable clients to retain and effectively utilize concepts and skills. These and other products carefully selected and endorsed by FranklinCovey are available in more than 130 FranklinCovey stores throughout North America and in several other countries.

For more information on FranklinCovey products and programs, call **1-800-599-0238** or visit our Web site at **www.franklincovey.com**.

Training and Products for Time and Life Management

* FOCUS: Achieving Your Highest Priorities
* Rethinking Stress™
* Project Management™

Leadership Training

* The 7 Habits of Highly Effective People®
* The 4 Roles of Leadership™
* Leadership Week™
* The 4 Disciplines of Execution™

Training for Effective Communication

* Building Trust™
* Writing Advantage®
* Presentation Advantage™
* Meeting Advantage™
* Technical Writing Advantage™

Training and Consulting Services

* Measurement and Assessment
* Certified Facilitation Workshops
* Sales Training

Three Workshop Options to Meet Your Training Needs

Public Workshops

Public workshops are perfect for individuals and organizations in any industry or profession. They are taught by expert FranklinCovey presenters in more than 350 cities in North America and in more than 40 countries worldwide. Call **1-800-735-1921** for public workshop schedules or visit our web site at **www.franklincovey.com**.

Custom On-Site Workshops

Experienced FranklinCovey presenters teach our workshops to your employees on site. These workshops can be customized to address the specific needs, challenges, and objectives of your organization or work team. Call **1-800-599-0238** for information about custom on-site workshops or visit us at **www.franklincovey.com**.

Internally Facilitated Workshops

We train one or more representatives from your organization to present FranklinCovey workshops to your employees. If your organization is already licensed to teach certain FranklinCovey workshops, representatives from your organization can qualify to teach new curricula through our certification process. Call **1-800-599-0238** for information about becoming a licensed FranklinCovey facilitator or visit us at **www.franklincovey.com**.

Contents

Alphabetical

Reference Glossary

Contents

Alphabetical

Model Documents

Contents

Topical

 Document Design

 Formats

 Graphics

 Model Documents

 Numbers

Parts of Speech

Contents

Topical

 Punctuation

 Sentence Style

 Skills/Processes

 Word Choice

Contents

Keyed Thematically to Stephen R. Covey's *The Seven Habits of Highly Effective People*®

This table of contents links Stephen Covey's seven habits with communication skills. For each habit, we list key communication skills and their page reference in the *Style Guide*. Just as the seven habits address both **personal** and **interpersonal issues**, effective communication is both personal and interpersonal. Personal skills begin with clear thinking, which helps produce well-conceived speech and well-designed documents. But neither speech nor documents are successful unless they effectively and ethically convey information to listeners and readers.

Reference
Glossary

Using the Reference Glossary

The Reference Glossary is designed and written to help writers and editors answer routine, yet important, questions about the preparation of business and technical documents. The alphabetical arrangement of the entries allows writers to answer questions easily and rapidly, often without having to search through the Index. The many illustrative phrases, words, and sentences make the various rules and suggestions practical and applicable to real-world situations.

Still, as with any reference book, users need to become familiar with what the Reference Glossary covers and what it doesn't cover. To assist new users, we make the following suggestions about using the Reference Glossary.

- Use the alphabetical arrangement to help you find where a specific topic is addressed. As with any alphabetical list, you may have to try a couple of titles before you find the information you want. If you cannot find a topic, refer to the Index (p. 423).

- After you have found the relevant entry, survey the listed rules or headings previewed in the shaded box at the beginning of the entry. Then turn to the rule or heading that appears to answer your question.

- Read the rule and accompanying text. Be sure to review any illustrative phrases or sentences because they will often help clarify the rule. Remember, also, that many of the rules are suggestions rather than legal requirements.

- Check to see if any notes follow the rule and its examples. Notes begin with the word NOTE and are numbered if there are several notes. Notes often include information about exceptions or options to the stated rule.

- Turn to other entries that are cross-referenced, especially if you still have questions that the entry has not answered. Cross-references have this format: See LETTERS and MEMOS.

- Don't be disappointed if you cannot find the answer to a question. No reference book can answer every question. To help answer difficult or obscure questions, experienced writers and editors usually have several recent references available. For a list of other references, see the entry entitled REFERENCES.

Abbreviations allow writers to avoid cumbersome repetition of lengthy words and phrases. They are a form of shorthand and are appropriate in technical and business writing, particularly in lists, tables, charts, graphs, and other visual aids where space is limited. See ACRONYMS.

Abbreviations

1. Eliminate periods in and after most abbreviations.

2. Use the same abbreviation for both singular and plural units of measurement.

3. Clarify an unfamiliar abbreviation by enclosing its unabbreviated form within parentheses following its first use in a document.

4. Do not abbreviate a unit of measurement unless it is used in conjunction with a number.

5. Do not abbreviate a title unless it precedes a name.

6. Spell out abbreviations that begin a sentence (except for abbreviated words that, by convention, are never spelled out, like *Mr.* and *Mrs.*).

7. Spell out rather than abbreviate words that are connected to other words by hyphens.

8. Do not abbreviate the names of months and days within normal text. Use the abbreviations in chronologies, notes, tables, and charts.

9. Avoid the symbol form of abbreviations except in charts, graphs, illustrations, and other visual aids.

10. Use a single period when an abbreviation ends a sentence.

1. Eliminate periods in and after most abbreviations.

Formerly, most abbreviations required periods. Today, the trend is to eliminate periods in and after abbreviations, especially in the abbreviated names of governmental agencies, companies, private organizations, and other groups:

AFL-CIO	AMA	CBS	DOE
FTC	IOOF	NFL	NLRB
OPEC	TVA	TWA	YWCA

NOTE 1: The abbreviations covered by this rule do not include informal ones such as *Dept.* and *Mgt.*, which use a final period but no periods between letters.

NOTE 2: By convention, some abbreviations still require periods:

A.D.	a.m.	B.C.	Dr.
e.g.	etc.	i.e.	Mr.
Mrs.	Ms.	p.m.	pp.
U.K.	U.S. (*or* USA)		

Retain the period, too, in abbreviations that spell normal words:

in., inches (*not* in)
no., number (*not* no)

A recent dictionary, such as *Webster's New Collegiate Dictionary,* is the best resource for determining if an abbreviation requires periods. See REFERENCES.

NOTE 3: Abbreviations with periods should be typed without spaces between letters and periods:

e.g. (*not* e. g.)
U.K. (*not* U. K.)

2. Use the same abbreviation for both singular and plural units of measurement.

When you abbreviate a unit of measurement, use the same symbol for both the singular and the plural forms:

6 lb and 1 lb
3 m and 1 m
20 ft and 1 ft
23.5 cm and 1.0 cm

If you spell out the abbreviated word, retain the plural when the number is greater than one:

15 kilometers and 1 kilometer
6.8 meters and 1 meter

3. Clarify an unfamiliar abbreviation by enclosing its unabbreviated form within parentheses following its first use in a document:

The applicant had insurance through CHAMPUS (Civilian Health and Medical Program of the Uniformed Services).

The alloy is hardened with 0.2 percent Np (neptunium). Adding Np before cooling alters the crystalline structure of manganese host alloys

NOTE 1: Some writers and editors prefer to cite the unabbreviated form of the word or words before the abbreviation. We believe that this practice can inhibit, rather than enhance, the reader's comprehension of the abbreviation:

The applicant had insurance through the Civilian Health and Medical Program of the Uniformed Services (CHAMPUS).

Abbreviations

The alloy is hardened with 0.2 percent neptunium (Np). Adding Np before cooling alters the crystalline structure of manganese host alloys.

NOTE 2: Do not use an unfamiliar abbreviation unless you plan to use it more than once in the same document.

4. Do not abbreviate a unit of measurement unless it is used in conjunction with a number:

Pipe diameters will be measured in inches.

but

Standard pipe diameter is 3 in.

———————

The dimensions of the property were recorded in both meters and feet.

but

The property is 88 ft by 130 ft.

The southern property line is 45.3 m.

5. Do not abbreviate a title unless it precedes a name:

The cardiac research unit comprises five experienced doctors.

but

Our program director is Dr. Royce Smith.

6. Spell out abbreviations that begin a sentence (except for abbreviated words that, by convention, are never spelled out, like *Mr.* and *Mrs.*):

Oxygen extraction will be accomplished at high temperatures.

not

O_2 extraction will be accomplished at high temperatures.

but

Ms. Jean MacIntyre will be responsible for modifying our subsea sensors.

7. Spell out rather than abbreviate words that are connected to other words by hyphens:

6-foot gap *(not* 6-ft)
12-meter cargo bay *(not* 12-m)
3.25-inch pipe *(not* 3.25-in.)

NOTE: The spelled-out form is preferred. The abbreviated form (as in *6-ft*) is common in some engineering documents, especially those with many numerical values. The hyphen is retained in the abbreviated form. See HYPHENS & FRACTIONS.

8. Do not abbreviate the names of months and days within normal text. Use the abbreviations in chronologies, notes, tables, and charts:

The facilities modernization plan is due January 1985. *(not* Jan 1985 *or* 1/85)

9. Avoid the symbol form of abbreviations except in charts, graphs, illustrations, and other visual aids:

55 percent *(not* 55%)
15 ft *(not* 15')
32.73 in. *(not* 32.73")

10. Use a single period when an abbreviation ends a sentence:

To head our laser redesign effort, we have hired the 1994 Nobel prize winner from the U.S.A. *(not* U.S.A..)

NOTE: If the clause or sentence ends with something other than a period, (e.g., comma, semicolon, colon, question mark, exclamation mark), then the other mark of punctuation follows the period at the end of the abbreviation:

Have we hired the 1994 Nobel prize winner from the U.S.A.?

If you plan to arrive by 6 p.m., you will not need to guarantee your reservation.

List of Abbreviations

Following is a short list of many common abbreviations for words and common measurements. For more complete lists of abbreviations, refer to *The Chicago Manual of Style* and to *Merriam-Webster's Collegiate Dictionary*. See REFERENCES.

In this listing, some abbreviations appear with periods, although the trend is to eliminate the periods (see rule 1). For example, *Ph.D.* appears with periods to assist writers and typists who wish to retain the periods, although many writers today prefer the increasingly more common *PhD* without periods.

In this listing, abbreviations printed without periods are ones that customarily appear without periods—for example, *HF* or *log*.

Abbreviations of Words and Phrases

AA, Alcoholics Anonymous
A.B. or B.A., bachelor of arts
abbr., abbreviation
abs., absolute; absent; absence; abstract
acct., account; accountant
A.D. *(anno Domini)*, in the year of the Lord
ADP, automated data processing
a.k.a., also known as
A.M. *(anno mundi)*, in the year of the world
A.M. or M.A., master of arts
a.m. *(ante meridiem)*, before noon
approx., approximately
Ave., avenue
a.w.l., absent with leave
a.w.o.l., absent without official leave

B.C., before Christ
bf., boldface
Bldg., building
B.Lit(t). or Lit(t).B., bachelor of literature
Blvd., boulevard
b.o., buyer's option
B.S. or B.Sc., bachelor of science

Ca. *(circa)*, about
ca, centiare
c. and s.c., caps and small caps
c.b.d., cash before delivery
cf. *(confer)*, compare or see
Co., company; country
c.o.d., cash on delivery; collect on delivery
COLA, cost-of-living adjustment

con., continued
Conus., continental United States
Corp., corporation
c.p., chemically pure
C.P.A., certified public accountant
cr., credit; creditor
Ct., court

d.b.a., doing business as
D.D., doctor of divinity
D.D.S., doctor of dental surgery; doctor of dental science
Dist. Ct., District Court
D.Lit(t). or Lit(t).D., doctor of literature
do. (ditto), the same
DP, displaced person
D.P.H , doctor of public health
D.P.Hy., doctor of public hygiene
dr., debtor
Dr., doctor; drive
D.V.M., doctor of veterinary medicine

E., east
EDP, electronic data processing
e.g. (exempli gratia), for example
e.o.m., end of month
et al. (et alii), and others
et seq. (et sequentia), and the following one
etc. (et cetera), and others

F., Fahrenheit, farad
f., female, force, forte, frequency
f., ff., and following page (pages)
f°, folio
f.o.b., free on board
4°, quarto

GDP, gross domestic product
GI, general issue; government issue
G.M.&S., general, medical, and surgical
Gov., governor
Govt., government
gr. wt., gross weight

HE, high explosive
HF, high frequency

ibid. (ibidem), in the same place
id. (idem), the same
ID, identification
i.e. (id est), that is
IF, intermediate frequency
Insp. Gen., Inspector General
IOU, I owe you
IQ, intelligence quotient

J.D. (juris doctor), doctor of laws
Jr., junior

Lat., latitude
LC, Library of Congress
lc., lowercase
liq., liquid
lf., lightface
LF, low frequency
LL.B., bachelor of laws
LL.D., doctor of laws
loc. cit. (loco citato), in the place cited
log, logarithm
long., longitude
Ltd., limited
Lt. Gov., lieutenant governor

M, money supply: M_1; M_{1B}; M_2
M., monsieur; MM., messieurs
m. (meridies), noon
M.D., doctor of medicine
memo, memorandum
MF, medium frequency
MIA, missing in action (plural, MIAs)
Mlle., mademoiselle
Mme., madam; Mmes., mesdames
mo., month
Mr., mister (plural, Messrs.)
Mrs., mistress
Ms., coined feminine title (plural, Mses.)
M.S., master of science
MS., manuscript; MSS., manuscripts
Msgr., monsignor
m.s.l., mean sea level

N., north
NA., not available; not applicable
NE., northeast
n.e.c., not elsewhere classified
n.e.s., not elsewhere specified
net wt., net weight
No., number; Nos., numbers
n.o.i.b.n., not otherwise indexed by name
n.o.p., not otherwise provided (for)
n.o.s., not otherwise specified
n.s.k., not specified by kind
n.s.p.f., not specifically provided for
NW., northwest

OK, OK'd, OK'ing, OK's
op. cit. (opere citato), in the work cited

PA, public address system
PAC, political action committee (plural, PACs)
Ph.B. or B.Ph., bachelor of philosophy
Ph.D. or D.Ph., doctor of philosophy
Ph.G., graduate in pharmacy
PIN, personal identification number
Pl., place; plural
p.m. (post meridiem), afternoon
P.O. Box (with number),
    but post office box (in general sense)
POW, prisoner of war (plural, POWs)
Prof., professor
pro tem (pro tempore), temporarily
P.S. (postscriptum), postscript; public school (with number)

QT, on the quiet

RAM, random-access memory
R&D, research and development
Rd., road
RDT&E, research, development, testing, and evaluation
Rev., reverend
RF, radio frequency
R.F.D., rural free delivery
RIF, reduction(s) in force; RIF'd, RIF'ing, RIF's
R.N., registered nurse
RR., railroad
Rt. Rev., right reverend
Ry., railway

S., south; Senate bill (with number)
S&L(s), savings and loan(s)
sc. (scilicet), namely (see also ss)

s.c., small caps
s.d. (sine die), without date
SE., southeast
2d, second; 3d, third
SHF, superhigh frequency
sic, thus
SOP, standard operating procedure
SOS, wireless distress signal
sp. gr., specific gravity
Sq., square (street)
Sr., senior
SS, steamship
ss (scilicet), namely (in law) (see also sc.)
St., Saint; Ste., Sainte; SS., Saints
St., street
STP, standard temperature and pressure
Supt., superintendent
Surg., surgeon
SW., southwest

T., Tbsp., tablespoon
T., township; Tps., townships
t., tsp., teaspoon
Ter., terrace
t.m., true mean
TV, television

uc., uppercase
UHF, ultrahigh frequency
U.S.A., United States of America
USA, U.S. Army
U.S. 40; U.S. No. 40; U.S. Highway No. 40

V. or vs. (versus), against
VAT, value-added tax
VCR, videocassette recorder
VHF, very high frequency
VIP, very important person
viz (videlicet), namely
VLF, very low frequency
VTR, videotape recorder

W., west
w.a.e., when actually employed
wf, wrong font
w.o.p., without pay

ZIP Code, Zone Improvement Plan Code (Postal Service)
ZIP+4, 9-digit ZIP Code

Abbreviations of Units of Measurement

A, ampere
Å, angstrom
a, are
a, atto (prefix, one-quintillionth)
aA, attoampere
abs, absolute (temperature and gravity)
ac, alternating current
AF, audiofrequency
Ah, ampere-hour
A/m, ampere per meter
AM, amplitude modulation
asb, apostilb
At, ampere-turn
at, atmosphere
atm, atmosphere
at wt, atomic weight

Abbreviations

au, astronomical unit
avdp, avoirdupois

b, born
B, bel
b, bit
bbl, barrel
bbl/d, barrel per day
Bd, baud
bd. ft., board foot
Bé, Baumé
Bev (obsolete); see GeV
Bhn, Brinell hardness number
bhp, brake horsepower
bm, beam
bp, boiling point
Btu, British thermal unit
bu, bushel

c, ¢, ct; cent(s)
c, centi (prefix, one-hundredth)
C, coulomb
c, cycle (radio)
°C, degree Celsius
cal, calorie (also: cal$_{IT}$, International Table; cal$_{th}$, thermochemical)
cc. (obsolete), use cm^3
cd, candela (obsolete: candle)
cd/in^2, candela per square inch
cd/m^2, candela per square meter
c.f.m. (obsolete), use ft^3/min
c.f.s. (obsolete), use ft^3/s
cg, centigram
c·h, candela-hour
Ci, curie
cL, centiliter
cm, centimeter
c/m, cycles per minute
cm^2, square centimeter
cm^3, cubic centimeter
cmil, circular mil
cp, candlepower
cP, centipoise
cSt, centistokes
cu ft (obsolete), use ft^3
cu in (obsolete), use in^3
cwt, hundredweight

D, darcy
d, day
d, deci (prefix, one-tenth)
d, pence
da, deka (prefix, 10)
dag, dekagram
daL, dekaliter
dam, dekameter
dam^2, square dekameter
dam^3, cubic dekameter
dB, decibel
dBu, decibel unit
dc, direct current
dg, decigram
dL, deciliter
dm, decimeter
dm^2, square decimeter
dm^3, cubic decimeter
dol, dollar
doz, dozen
dr, dram

dwt, deadweight tons
dwt, pennyweight
dyn, dyne

EHF, extremely high frequency
emf, electromotive force
emu, electromagnetic unit
erg, erg
esu, electrostatic unit
eV, electronvolt

°F, degree Fahrenheit
f, farad
f, femto (prefix, one-quadrillionth)
F, fermi (obsolete); use fm, femtometer
fc, footcandle
fL, footlambert
fm, femtometer
FM, frequency modulation
ft, foot
ft^2, square foot
ft^3, cubic foot
ftH$_2$O, conventional foot of water
ft·lb, foot-pound
ft·lbf, foot pound-force
ft/min, foot per minute
ft^2/min, square foot per minute
ft^3/min, cubic foot per minute
ft-pdl, foot poundal
ft/s, foot per second
ft^2/s, square foot per second
ft^3/s, cubic foot per second
ft/s^2, foot per second squared
ft/s^3, foot per second cubed

G, gauss
G, giga (prefix, one billion)
g, gram; acceleration of gravity
Gal, gal cm/s^2
gal, gallon
gal/min, gallons per minute
gal/s, gallons per second
Gb, gilbert
g/cm^3, gram per cubic centimeter
GeV, giga-electron-volt
GHz, gigahertz (gigacycle per second)
gr, grain; gross

h, hecto (prefix, 100)
H, henry
h, hour
ha, hectare
HF, high frequency
hg, hectogram
hl, hectoliter
hm, hectometer
hm^2, square hectometer
hm^3, cubic hectometer
hp, horsepower
hph, horsepower-hour
Hz, hertz (cycles per second)

id, inside diameter
ihp, indicated horsepower
in., inch
in^2, square inch
in^3, cubic inch
in/h, inch per hour
inH$_2$O, conventional inch of water
inHg, conventional inch of mercury

in-lb, inch-pound
in/s, inch per second

J, joule
J/K, joule per kelvin

K, kayser
K, Kelvin (degree symbol improper)
k, kilo (prefix, 1,000)
k, thousand (7k = 7,000)
kc, kilocycle; see also kHz (kilohertz), kilocycles per second
kcal, kilocalorie
keV, kilo-electron-volt
kG, kilogauss
kg, kilogram
kgf, kilogram-force
kHz, kilohertz (kilocycles per second)
kl, kiloliter
klbf, kilopound-force
km, kilometer
km^2, square kilometer
km^3, cubic kilometer
km/h, kilometer per hour
kn, knot (speed)
k , kilohm
kt, kiloton; carat
kv, kilovolt
kVa, kilovoltampere
kvar, kilovar
kw, kilowatt
kwh, kilowatt-hour

L, lambert
L, liter (also l)
lb, pound
lb ap, apothecary pound
lb avdp, avoirdupois pound
lbf, pound-force
lbf/ft, pound-force foot
lbf/ft^2, pound-force per square foot
lbf/ft^3, pound-force per cubic foot
lbf/in^2, pound-force per square inch
lb/ft, pound per foot
lb/ft^2, pound per square foot
lb/ft^3, pound per cubic foot
lct, long calcined ton
ldt, long dry ton
LF, low frequency
lin ft, linear foot
l/m, lines per minute
lm, lumen
lm/ft^2, lumen per square foot
lm/m^2, lumen per square meter
lm·s, lumen second
lm/W, lumen per watt
l/s, lines per second
l/s, liter per second
lx, lux

M, mega (prefix, 1 million)
M, million (3M = 3 million)
m, meter
m, milli (prefix, one-thousandth)
M$_1$, monetary aggregate
m^2, square meter
m^3, cubic meter
μ, micro (prefix, one-millionth)
μ, micron (obsolete); use μm, micrometer

mA, milliampere
µA, microampere
mbar, millibar
µbar, microbar
Mc, megacycle; *see also* MHz
(megahertz), megacycles per second
mc, millicycle; *see also* mHz (millihertz),
    millicycles per second
mcg, microgram *(obsolete); use* µg
mD, millidarcy
meq, milliquivalent
MeV, mega electron volts
mF, millifarad
µF, microfarad
mG, milligauss
mg, milligram
µg, microgram
Mgal/d, million gallons per day
mH, millihenry
µH, microhenry
mho, mho *(obsolete); use* S, siemens
MHz, megahertz
mHz, millihertz
mi, mile *(statute)*
mi², square mile
mi/gal, mile(s) per gallon
mi/h, mile per hour
mil, mil
min, minute *(time)*
µin, microinch
ml, milliliter
mm, millimeter
mm², square millimeter
mm³, cubic millimeter
mµ, *(obsolete); see* nm, nanometer
µm, micrometer
µm², square micrometer
µm³, cubic micrometer
µµ, micromicron *(use of compound
    prefixes is obsolete); use* pm, picometer
µµf, micromicrofarad *(use of compound
    prefixes is obsolete); use* pF
mmHg, conventional millimeter of
    mercury
µmho, micromho *(obsolete); use* µS,
    microsiemens
M , megohm
mo, month
mol, mole *(unit of substance)*
mol wt, molecular weight
mp, melting point

ms, millisecond
µs, microsecond
Mt, megaton
mV, millivolt
µV, microvolt
MW, megawatt
mW, milliwatt
µW, microwatt
MWd/t, megawatt-days per ton
Mx, maxwell

n, nano *(prefix, one-billionth)*
N, newton
nA, nanoampere
nF, nanofarad
nm, nanometer (millimicron, *obsolete*)
N·m, newton meter
N/m², newton per square meter
nmi, nautical mile
ns, nanosecond
N·s/m², newton second per square meter

Od, outside diameter
Oe, oersted *(use of* A/m, amperes per
    meter, *preferred)*
oz, ounce *(avoirdupois)*

p, pico *(prefix, one-trillionth)*
P, poise
Pa, pascal
pA, picoampere
pct, percent
pdl, poundal
pF, picofarad (micromicrofarad, *obsolete*)
pF, water-holding energy
pH, hydrogen-ion concentration
ph, phot; phase
pk, peck
p/m, parts per million
ps, picosecond
pt, pint
pW, picowatt

qt, quart
quad, quadrillion (10^{15})

°r, rankine
°R, roentgen
R, degree rankine
R, degree reaumur
rad, radian
rd, rad

rem, roentgen equivalent man
r/min, revolutions per minute
rms, root mean square
r/s, revolutions per second

s, second *(time)*
s, shilling
S, siemens
sb, stilb
scp, spherical candlepower
s·ft, second-foot
shp, shaft horsepower
slug, slug
sr, steradian
stet¹, standard cubic foot (feet)
Sus, saybolt universal second(s)

T, tera *(prefix, 1 trillion)*
Tft³, trillion cubic feet
T, tesla
t, tonne *(metric ton)*
tbsp, tablespoonful
thm, therm
ton, ton
tsp, teaspoonful
Twad, twaddell

u, (unified) atomic mass unit
UHF, ultrahigh frequency

V, volt
VA, voltampere
var, var
VHF, very high frequency
V/m, volt per meter

W, watt
Wb, weber
Wh, watt-hour
W/(m·K), watt per meter kelvin
W/sr, watt per steradian
W/(sr·m²), watt per steradian square
    meter

x, unknown quantity

yd, yard
yd², square yard
yd³, cubic yard
yr, year

Acronyms are abbreviations that are pronounced as words:

ALGOL (ALGOrithmic Language)

Amtrak (American Track)

ARAMCO (ARabian AMerican oil COmpany)

ASCII (American Standard Code for Information Interchange)

BASIC (Beginners' All-purpose Symbolic Instruction Code)

BIT *or* bit (BInary digiT)

CAD (Computer-Aided Design)

CAM (Computer-Aided Manufacturing)

DOS (Disk Operating System)

FORTRAN (FORmula TRANslator)

GUI (Graphical User Interface)

LAN (Local Area Network)

laser (Light Amplification by Stimulated Emission of Radiation)

loran (LOng-RAnge Navigation)

Nasdaq (National Association of Securities Dealers Automated Quotations)

NATO (North Atlantic Treaty Organization)

NOW (National Organization for Women)

Pepco (Potomac Electric Power Company)

PERT (Program Evaluation and Review Technique)

radar (RAdio Detecting And Ranging)

RAM (Random Access Memory)

SALT (Strategic Arms Limitation Treaty)

secant (SEparation Control of Aircraft by Nonsynchronous Techniques)

sonar (SOund NAvigation Ranging)

START (STrategic Arms Reduction Treaty)

UNICEF (United Nations International Children's Emergency Fund)

WAC (Womens Army Corps)

ZIP (Zone Improvement Plan)

Acronyms

1. When you introduce new or unfamiliar acronyms, use the acronym and then, in parentheses, spell out the name or expression.

2. Avoid overusing acronyms, especially if your readers are unlikely to be very familiar with them.

Acronyms may be written in all capitals if they form proper names. However, some acronyms are conventionally uppercase and lowercase:

> Amtrak   Nasdaq

The most common acronyms, those representing generic technical concepts rather than organizations or programs, are typically all lowercase:

> laser   radar   sonar

Some acronyms appear either in capitals or in lowercase:

> BIT *or* bit

See ABBREVIATIONS.

---

1. When you introduce new or unfamiliar acronyms, use the acronym and then, in parentheses, spell out the name or expression.

Our program fully complies with the provisions of STEP (the Supplemental Training and Employment Program). To implement STEP, however, we had to modify subcontracting agreements with four components suppliers.

NOTE: Some writers and editors prefer to introduce unfamiliar acronyms by first spelling out the component words and then placing the acronym in parentheses. We believe that readers should see the acronym first because that is how they will see it on later pages. See ABBREVIATIONS.

---

2. Avoid overusing acronyms, especially if your readers are unlikely to be very familiar with them.

Until readers learn to recognize and instantly comprehend an acronym (like *laser*), the acronym hinders reading. It creates a delay while the reader's mind recalls and absorbs the acronym's meaning. Therefore, you should be cautious about using acronyms, especially unfamiliar ones. Overloading a text with acronyms makes the text unreadable, even if you have previously introduced and explained the acronyms.

Acronyms are good shorthand devices, but use them judiciously. See SCIENTIFIC/TECHNICAL STYLE.

Active- and passive-voice sentences each convey actions. They differ in how they convey these actions by their different grammatical structures. Both types of sentences are good sentences, but you should use active-voice sentences when you can. Passive-voice sentences can seem weak-willed, indecisive, or evasive.

Active- and passive-voice sentences usually have three basic elements:

- The actor—the person or thing performing the action

- The action—the verb

- The receiver—the person or thing receiving the action

When the structure of the sentence has the actor in front of the action, the sentence is in the **active voice**:

> Australian companies manufacture millions of precision machine tools.

Companies is the actor; *manufacture* is the action; and *tools* receives the action. Because the actor comes before the action, the sentence is active. The subject of the sentence performs the action.

When the structure of the sentence has the receiver in front of the action, the sentence is in the **passive voice**:

> Millions of precision machine tools are manufactured by Australian companies.

In this sentence, the subject (*tools*) is not doing the manufacturing. The tools are being manufactured. They are being acted upon; they are receiving the action. Therefore, the subject—and the sentence—is passive.

Active/Passive

1. Prefer active sentences.

2. Use a passive sentence when you don't know or don't want to mention the actor.

3. Use a passive sentence when the receiver is more important than the actor.

4. Use a passive sentence when you need to form a smooth transition from one sentence to the next.

5. Do not use passive sentences to avoid using first person pronouns.

6. Make sentences active by turning the clause or sentence around.

7. Make sentences active by changing the verb.

8. Make sentences active by rethinking the sentence.

1. Prefer active sentences.

Active sentences are usually shorter and more dynamic than passive sentences. They generally have more impact and seem more "natural" because readers expect (and are accustomed to) the actor-action-receiver pattern. Active writing is more forceful and more self-confident.

Passive writing, on the other hand, can seem weak-willed, indecisive, or evasive. In passive sentences, the reader encounters the action before learning who performed it. In some passive sentences, the reader never discovers who performed the action. So passive sentences seem static.

Passive sentences are useful—even preferable—in some circumstances, but you should prefer active sentences.

When to Use Passives

2. Use a passive sentence when you don't know or don't want to mention the actor:

> The failure occurred because metal shavings had been dropped into the worm-gear housing.

> Clearly, the site had been inspected, but we found no inspection report and could not identify the inspectors.

In the first example above, a passive sentence is acceptable because we don't know who dropped the metal shavings into the housing. In the second example, we might know who inspected the site but don't want to mention names because the situation could be sensitive or politically charged.

3. Use a passive sentence when the receiver is more important than the actor.

The strongest part of most sentences is the opening. Therefore, the sentence element appearing first will receive greater emphasis than those elements appearing later in the sentence. For this reason, a passive sentence is useful when you wish to emphasize the receiver of the action:

> Cross-sectional analysis techniques—the most important of our innovations—are currently being tested in our Latin American Laboratory.
>
> Minimum material size or thickness requirements will then be established to facilitate recuperator weight, size, and cost estimates.

In both examples, we wish to emphasize the receiver of the action. Note how emphasis changes if we restructure the first example:

> The most important of our innovations (cross-sectional analysis techniques) is currently being tested in our Latin American Laboratory.
>
> Our Latin American Laboratory is currently testing the most important of our innovations—cross-sectional analysis techniques.
>
> Our Latin American Laboratory is currently testing cross-sectional analysis techniques—the most important of our innovations.

The emphasis in each sentence differs, depending on sentence structure. The first revision emphasizes *innovations*, and it is still a passive sentence. The last two revisions are active, and both stress *our Latin American Laboratory*.

The ending of a sentence is also emphatic (although not as emphatic as the beginning), so the sentence ending with *techniques* does place secondary emphasis on *techniques*. However, the best way to emphasize *cross-sectional analysis techniques* is by opening the sentence with that phrase.

4. Use a passive sentence when you need to form a smooth transition from one sentence to the next.

Occasionally, writers must arrange sentence elements so that key words appearing in both sentences are near enough to each other for readers to immediately grasp the connection between the sentences. In the example below, for instance, the writer needs to form a smooth transition between sentences by repeating the key words *work packages*:

> We will develop a simplified matrix of tasks that will include all budgetary and operational work packages. These work packages will be scheduled and monitored by individual program managers.

The second sentence is passive. It would be shorter and stronger as an active sentence:

> Individual program managers will schedule and monitor these work packages.

However, the active version does not connect as well with the previous sentence:

> We will develop a simplified matrix of tasks that will include all budgetary and operational work packages. Individual program managers will schedule and monitor these work packages.

For a brief moment, the second sentence seems to have changed the subject. Not until readers reach the end of the second sentence will they realize that both sentences deal with work packages. Therefore, making the second sentence passive creates a smoother transition and actually improves the passage. See TRANSITIONS.

Passives and First Person

5. Do not use passive sentences to avoid using first person pronouns.

Some writers use passives to avoid using first person pronouns (*I, me, we,* or *us*). These writers mistakenly believe that first person pronouns are inappropriate in business or technical writing. In fact, the first person is preferable to awkward or ambiguous passive sentences like the example below:

> It is recommended that a state-of-the-art survey be added to the initial redesign studies.

Who is recommending it? You? The customer? Someone else? And who is supposed to add the survey?

In the following sentences, things seem to be happening, but no one seems to be doing them:

> Cost data will be collected and maintained to provide a detailed history of the employee hours expended during the program. This tracking effort will be accomplished by the use of an established employee-hour accumulating system.

Writers who overuse the passive to avoid first person pronouns convey the impression that they don't want to accept the responsibility for their actions. This implication is why passive sentences can seem evasive even when the writer doesn't intend them to be.

Passive sentences allow you to eliminate the actor. In some cases, eliminating the actor is appropriate and desirable. In other cases (as in the previous examples), eliminating the actor creates confusion and doubt. Active versions of these examples, using first person pronouns, are much better:

> We recommend that the initial redesign studies include a state-of-the-art survey.

> Using our employee-hour accumulating system, we will collect and maintain cost data to provide a detailed history of the employee hours expended during the program.

How to Convert Passives

Technical and scientific writers generally use too many passives. They use them unnecessarily, often more from habit than choice. Converting unneeded passives to actives will strengthen the style of the document, making it appear crisper and more confident. The following guidelines present three techniques for converting passives to actives.

6. Make sentences active by turning the clause or sentence around:

> These methods are described in more detail in section 6.

> Section 6 describes these methods in more detail.

> A functional outline of the program is included in the Work Breakdown Structure (figure 1.1–2).

> The Work Breakdown Structure (figure 1.1–2) includes a functional outline of the program.

Brakes on both drums are activated as required by the control system to regulate speed and accurately position the launcher.

The control system activates brakes on both drums as required to regulate speed and accurately position the launcher.

After these requirements are identified, we will develop a comprehensive list of applicable technologies.

After identifying these requirements, we will develop a comprehensive list of applicable technologies.

---

7. Make sentences active by changing the verb:

> The solutions were achieved only after extensive development of fabrication techniques.

> The solutions occurred only after extensive development of fabrication techniques.

> The Gaussian elimination process can be thought of as a means of "decomposing" a matrix into three factors.

> The Gaussian elimination process "decomposes" a matrix into three factors.

> The Navy recuperator requirements are expected to bring added emphasis to structural integrity.

> The Navy recuperator requirements will probably emphasize structural integrity.

> Coalescence was always observed to start at the base of the column.

> Coalescence always started at the base of the column.

8. Make sentences active by rethinking the sentence:

> Special consideration must be given to structural mounting, heat exchanger shape, ducting losses, and ducting loads.

> Structural mounting, heat exchanger shape, ducting losses, and ducting loads are especially important.

> To ensure that a good alternate design approach is not overlooked, a comparison between plate-fin and tubular designs will be made during the proposed study program.

> Comparing plate-fin and tubular designs during the proposed study program will ensure that we thoughtfully consider alternate design approaches.

> This study will show what can be done to alleviate technology failure by selectively relaxing requirements.

> This study will show how selectively relaxing requirements can alleviate technology failure.

> It must be said, however, that while maximum results are gained by a design synthesis approach such as we propose, the area to be covered is so large that it will still be necessary to concentrate on the most important technologies and their regions of interest.

> Our proposed design-synthesis approach will yield maximum results. Nevertheless, the area of interest is very large. Concentrating on the most important technologies and their regions of interest will still be necessary.

Adjectives describe or modify nouns or pronouns. They typically precede nouns or follow either verbs of sense *(feel, look, sound, taste, smell)* or linking verbs *(be, seem, appear, become):*

> The slow process . . . *(or* The process is slow.)

> Warm weather . . . *(or* The weather seems warm.)

> The cautious superintendent . . . *(or* The superintendent became cautious.)

> The news seemed bad. *(not* badly, *which is an adverb)*

Adjectives also tell which one, what kind, or how many people or things are being discussed.

NOTE: As in the preceding examples, most adjectives potentially occur between an article and a noun (*a bad message*) or following a linking verb (*the message is bad*). In both of these positions, adjectives are describing a noun. Adjectives can also describe a pronoun:

> He is slow.
> They are ignorant.

Or less likely, but still possible:

> An arrogant somebody decided to speak up before the meeting ended.

Finally, an adjective may seem to describe a following adjective rather than the main noun in a phrase:

> low moral character
> pale yellow flowers

We consider *low* and *pale* to be adjectives that are describing or modifying *moral* and *yellow*. Optionally, *low* and *pale* might functionally be labeled adverbs. Native users of English still intuitively know that *low* and *moral* work together to describe *character*. For such users the grammatical terminology is unimportant.

Adjectives

1. Use adjectives, not adverbs, following verbs of sense *(feel, look, sound, taste, smell)* and linking verbs *(be, seem, appear, become).*

2. Use the comparative *(–er/more)* forms when comparing two people or things and the superlative *(–est/most)* forms when comparing more than two.

3. Avoid noun strings unless you are sure your readers know what each string means.

4. Arrange nouns used as adjectives in technical expressions so that the more general nouns are closest to the word they are modifying.

5. For the names of an organization or company modifying a noun, choose to use either a possessive form (with an apostrophe) or an unchanged descriptive form. Once you choose, stay with your choice throughout a document.

Adjectives and Adverbs

Adjectives and adverbs are similar. They both describe or modify other words, and they both can compare two or more things. Sometimes they appear in similar positions in sentences:

> Harry felt **cautious**. *(adjective)*

> Harry felt **cautiously** along the bottom of the muddy stream. *(adverb)*

> The guard remained **calm**. *(adjective)*

> The guard remained **calmly** at his post. *(adverb)*

> The car was **close** to the building. *(adjective)*

> The car came **close** to me. *(adverb)*

> The corporal watched the prisoner **closely**. *(adverb)*

NOTE: Not all adverbs end in *–ly* (for example, the adverbs *deep, fair, fast, long, wide*). Some forms can be both an adjective or an adverb (for example, *early* or *monthly*). Other adverbs have two forms: an *–ly* form and another form that is identical to the adjective (*deep/deeply, fair/fairly, hard/hardly, wide/widely.*) You can determine whether most words are adjectives by trying to put them in front of a noun. In the previous examples, *cautious Harry* and *the calm guard* both make sense, so *cautious* and *calm* are adjectives. In the third example, *close* is an adverb in the second context, but in the phrase *a close friend*, the word *close* is an adjective. See ADVERBS.

---

1. Use adjectives, not adverbs, following verbs of sense *(feel, look, sound, taste, smell)* and linking verbs *(be, seem, appear, become):*

> The engine sounded **rough**. *(not the adverb* roughly)

> The surface of the mirror felt **smooth**. *(not the adverb* smoothly)

> The programmer was **cautious** about saving each new electronic file.

but

> The programmer **cautiously** saved each new electronic file. *(adverb preceding the verb saved)*

The auditor appeared **eager** to assist our division.

but

The auditor volunteered **eagerly** to assist our division. *(adverb following the verb volunteered)*

See ADVERBS.

NOTE: *Harold felt badly because of the flu.* This use of *badly* is currently acceptable, especially in spoken English. The older parallel form with *bad* is still correct and widely used. *Harold felt bad because of the flu.* See *bad/badly* in WORD PROBLEMS.

Comparatives and Superlatives

Adjectives have different forms for comparing two objects (the comparative form) and comparing more than two objects (the superlative form):

> Our networking system is slower than the new WebWare system. *(Slower is the comparative form.)*
>
> The Gemini software package was the slowest one we surveyed. *(Slowest is the superlative form.)*
>
> Stocks are a likelier investment than bonds if long-term growth is the goal. *(or more likely)*
>
> Nissan's likeliest competitor in the suburban wagon market is General Motors. *(or most likely)*
>
> The 1997 budget is more adequate than the 1996 budget.
>
> The cooling provisions are the most adequate feature of the specifications.

NOTE: One-syllable words use *–er/–est* to form comparatives or superlatives. Two-syllable words use either *–er/–est* or *more/most*. Three-syllable words use *more/most*. A few adjectives have irregular comparative forms: *good (well), better, best; bad, worse, worst; many, more, most.*

2. Use the comparative *(–er/ more)* forms when comparing two people or things and the superlative *(–est/most)* forms when comparing more than two:

> Of the two designs, Boeing's seems more efficient.
>
> The Pinnacle Finance proposal is the most attractive. *(More than two options are implied, so the superlative is proper.)*
>
> Weekly deductions are the best method for financing the new hospital insurance plan.
>
> Weekly deductions are better than any other method for financing the new hospital insurance plan. *(The comparative better is used because the various options are being compared one by one, not as a group.)*

Nouns Used as Adjectives

Nouns often behave like adjectives, especially in complex technical phrases. Turning nouns into adjectives can reduce verbiage:

> percentage of error
> error percentage (the noun *error* becomes an adjective)
>
> reduction in weight
> weight reduction
>
> function of the liver
> liver function

Such nouns are useful because English often does not have an adjective form with the same meaning as the noun.

3. Avoid noun strings unless you are sure your readers know what each string means.

You should beware of noun strings, which are groups of nouns strung together as adjectives. Here is an example from an aircraft manual: *C-5A airframe weight calculation error percentage.* The first five words in this phrase are a noun string.

Such strings often cloud meaning. Breaking up noun strings clarifies the meaning: *percentage of error in calculating C-5A airframe weight.*

Although useful and often necessary, nouns used as adjectives in a noun string may be clear only to technically knowledgeable people:

> aluminum honeycomb edge panels

What is aluminum? The honeycomb, the edges, or the panels? Only a knowledgeable reader can tell for sure. Sometimes, the order of the words suggests an interpretation:

> aluminum edge honeycomb panels

From this phrase, we may expect the edges, and not the honeycomb, to be aluminum, but we still can't know for sure if *aluminum edge* and *honeycomb* equally modify *panels*, or if *aluminum edge* and *honeycomb* combine to become a single modifier of *panels*, or if *aluminum* modifies something called *edge honeycomb*:

> (aluminum + edge) + honeycomb panels
>
> *or*
>
> (aluminum + edge + honeycomb) panels
>
> *or*
>
> aluminum + (edge + honeycomb) panels

In alphabetical lists of parts, the main noun being modified must be listed first. Therefore, the modifying words appear afterwards, usually separated by commas. The modifying words are typically listed in reverse order, with the most general modifiers closest to the main noun:

> panels, honeycomb, aluminum edge
>
> *or*
>
> panels, edge, aluminum honeycomb
>
> *or*
>
> panels, aluminum edge honeycomb

Adjectives

A helpful technique for discovering or clarifying the structure of noun strings is to ask the question, *What kind?* Begin with the main noun being modified and proceed from there to build the string of modifying nouns:

> panels
>
> *What kind of panels?*
>
> honeycomb
>
> *What kind of honeycomb?*
>
> aluminum edge

In this case, we have assumed that *aluminum edge* describes a particular type of honeycomb. Because *aluminum* and *edge* jointly modify *honeycomb,* they act as one word. We usually show that two or more words are acting together as joint or compound modifiers by hyphenating them:

> aluminum-edge honeycomb panels

See HYPHENS.

---

4. Arrange nouns used as adjectives in technical expressions so that the more general nouns are closest to the word they are modifying:

> semiautomatic slat worm gear
>
> automatic slat worm gear
>
> semiautomatic strut backoff gear
>
> automatic strut backoff gear

NOTE 1: The structure of such phrases (as well as the logic behind this rule) appears in catalogued lists. You can display the structure by reversing the order of the noun string and using indentation to show levels of modification:

> gear
> > backoff
> > > automatic strut
> > > semiautomatic strut
> >
> > worm
> > > automatic slat
> > > semiautomatic slat

NOTE 2: Some technical writers and editors rarely use internal punctuation (either hyphens or commas) to separate nouns in noun strings. In many scientific and technical fields, hyphens that would normally connect parts of a unit modifier are eliminated:

> methyl bromide solution (*not* methyl-bromide solution)
>
> black peach aphid (*not* black-peach aphid *or* black peach-aphid)
>
> grey willow leaf beetle
>
> swamp black currant seedlings

Hyphens in many technical words are, however, very hard to predict: *horse-nettle* vs. *horseradish* or *devilsclaw* vs. *devils-paintbrush.* In instances where the first word is capitalized, the compound is often hyphenated: *China-laurel, Queen Annes-lace, Australian-pea,* etc. See HYPHENS.

NOTE 3: Commas are not used to separate nouns in noun strings. However, we use commas to separate true adjectives when the adjectives **equally** modify the same noun:

> grey, burnished, elliptical sphere
>
> sloppy, poorly written, inadequate proposal

See COMMAS.

---

5. For the names of an organization or company modifying a noun, choose to use either a possessive form (with an apostrophe) or an unchanged descriptive form. Once you choose, stay with your choice throughout a document.

For most organizations or companies, you can choose between two types of phrases:

Possessive form

> Shell's corporate benefit package
>
> General Motors' financial officer
>
> The Fitness Committee's recommendations

Descriptive (noun used as an adjective)

> The Shell corporate benefit package
>
> A General Motors financial officer
>
> The Fitness Committee recommendations

Both the possessive and the descriptive versions are acceptable. Some companies, however, have firm policies about which version to use in their documents. When a policy exists, a company frequently chooses to avoid the possessive form on the grounds that the company does not possess or own something.

NOTE 1: As in the descriptive phrases above, a common sign that the possessive is not appropriate is the use of *a, an,* or *the* before the organizational or company name. This practice is not 100 percent reliable as a sign because, as in the Fitness Committee example, an organization may have an attached *the* or *a/an* and still use the possessive.

NOTE 2: Deciding which form to use is especially difficult when the organizational or company name looks like a collection of individuals.

> Green, Hancock, Blaine, and Jestor
>
> Goodmark Consultants

In cases like the preceding, choose one pattern for your correspondence and stay with your choice:

> Green, Hancock, Blaine, and Jestor's acquittal rate is . . .
>
> Goodmark Consultants' fee structure is . . .
>
> *or*
>
> The Green, Hancock, Blaine, and Jestor acquittal rate is . . .
>
> The Goodmark Consultants fee structure is . . .

See AGREEMENT and APOSTROPHES.

Adverbs

Adverbs are modifiers that give the how, where, when, and extent of the action within a sentence. Most adverbs end in –ly, but some common adverbs do not: *so, now, later, then, well,* etc. Adverbs often modify the main verbs in sentences:

> The engineer **slowly** prepared the design plan. *(How?)*

> The supply ship moved **close** to the drilling platform. *(Where?)*

> They **later** surveyed all participants in the research project. *(When?)*

> The abdominal pain was **clearly** evident in all treatment groups. *(Extent?)*

Adverbs can also modify adjectives or other adverbs:

> Their proposal was **highly** entertaining.

> Costs were **much** lower than expected.

> The well was **so** deep that its costs became prohibitive.

> The board of directors cut costs **more** severely and **more** rapidly than we anticipated.

1. Place the adverbs *only, almost, nearly, merely,* and *also* as close as possible to the word they modify:

> The bank examiners looked at only five accounts. (*not* The bank examiners only looked at five accounts.)

> The engineer had almost finished the specifications. (*not* The engineer almost had finished the specifications.)

Adverbs and Adjectives

Adverbs and adjectives are quite similar. They each modify or describe other words, and they often appear in similar positions in sentences, but they have quite different meanings:

> The lab technician **carefully** smelled the sample. *(adverb)*

> The cheese smelled **bad**. *(adjective)*

> The Internet connection worked **badly** the first day. *(adverb)*

> Not knowing the language, they stayed **close** to the interpreter. *(adverb)*

> We **closely** studied the blueprints. *(adverb)*

> The election was so **close** that no one was a clear winner. *(adjective)*

---

2. Choose adverbs, not adjectives, to modify main verbs:

> Our accountants predicted **accurately** that cash flow would be a problem.

> The manager asked **quickly** for the up-to-date estimates.

> The test engineers calculated **roughly** the expected power.

NOTE 1: Some adverbs have two forms, one without the regular –ly and one with it: *close/closely, deep/deeply, late/lately, loud/loudly, quick/quickly, slow/slowly, wide/widely.* Sometimes the two adverbial forms have different meanings:

> We submitted the invoice **late**.

> We were involved **lately** in some takeover discussions.

> The loose flywheel moved very **close** to its housing.

> The flywheel is monitored **closely** during the trial run.

In other instances, the two forms mean almost the same thing, so the choice depends on personal preference or individual idiom (based on the surrounding words):

> Go **slow**. *vs.* Go **slowly**. *(Either form is correct.)*

> The evaluation team wanted to play **fair**. *(The phrase* play fairly *means the same but sounds a little stiff and overly formal.)*

> The evaluation team wanted to respond **fairly**. *(Fair* would sound awkward with the verb *respond.)*

See ADJECTIVES.

NOTE 2: Adjectives, not adverbs, follow verbs of sense (*feel, look, sound, taste, smell*) and linking verbs (*be, seem, appear, become*):

> The adhesive felt **cool** and **rubbery** when dry.

> The surface of the wing appeared **uneven**.

See *bad/badly* in WORD PROBLEMS.

Comparative and Superlative Forms

Adverbs, like adjectives, have different forms to show comparison of two things (the comparative form) and comparison of more than two things (the superlative form). The comparative uses an –er form or *more*, but not both; the superlative uses an –est or *most*, but not both.

> The counselor left sooner than expected. *(comparative)*

> The fluid returned more slowly to its original level. *(comparative)*

> They debated most successfully the wisdom of expanding into the West Coast market. *(superlative)*

> The most rapidly moving car turned out to be the new Ford high-performance model. *(superlative)*

NOTE 1: Some adverbs have irregular comparative and superlative forms: *well, better, best; badly, worse, worst; little, less, least; much, more, most.*

NOTE 2: See ADJECTIVES for a discussion of using –er or *more* for comparatives and –est or *most* for superlatives. The rules for adverbs are similar to those for adjectives.

Agreement is a basic grammatical rule of English. According to this rule, subjects of sentences must agree in number with their verbs:

The proposal was finished. (*not the plural* were finished)

She is the engineer who designed the valve. (*not the plural* are)

The boilers have become corroded. (*not the singular* has become)

They are our competitors on most major procurements. (*not the singular* is)

This rule also includes gender agreement (between pronouns and the persons or objects to which they refer):

Jane Swenson submitted her report. (The *pronoun* her *agrees with its antecedent* Jane Swenson.)

See NOUNS, PRONOUNS, and VERBS.

---

1. The subject of a sentence (nouns or pronouns) should agree in number with the sentence verb:

The investigator is analyzing the analgesic efficacy. (*singular noun and singular verb*)

The employees are discussing the benefit package. (*plural noun and plural verb*)

I am going to attend the international conference in June.

We are designing a light-sensitive monitoring system.

The Elements of Geometry is the basic textbook.

Our textbooks are usually translated into Russian, French, and German.

Midwest states normally include Kentucky and Missouri.

A list of Midwest states normally includes Kentucky and Missouri.

NOTE: A noun ending with an *–s* or *–es* is usually plural. A verb ending with an *–s* or *–es* is usually singular. *Employees* is plural. The verbs *is* and *includes* are both singular.

Agreement

1. The subject of a sentence (nouns or pronouns) should agree in number with the sentence verb.

2. Subjects connected by *and* require a plural verb.

3. Singular subjects connected by *either . . . or, neither . . . nor,* and *not only . . . but also* require a singular verb.

4. When used as a subject or as the modifier of the subject, *each, every, either, neither, one, another, much, anybody, anyone, everybody, everyone, somebody, someone, nobody,* and *no one* require singular verbs.

5. When used as a subject or as the modifier of a subject, *both, few, several, many,* and *other(s)* require plural verbs.

6. *All, any, more, most, none, some, one-half of, two-thirds of, a part of,* and *a percentage of* require either a singular or a plural verb, depending upon the noun they refer to.

7. Collective nouns and expressions with time, money, and quantities take a singular or a plural verb, depending upon their intended meaning.

8. Choose either a singular or plural verb for subjects that are organizational names, and then be consistent in all other contexts with the name.

Some verbs do not change their form to reflect singular and plural: *will include, included, had included, will have included,* etc. See NOUNS and VERBS.

Agreement problems sometimes occur because the subject of the sentence is not clearly singular or plural:

None of the crew is going to take leave.

or

None of the crew are going to take leave.

Both versions are correct. Some writers become confused, too, when the subject is separated from the verb by words or phrases that do not agree in number with the subject:

Only one of the issues we discussed is on the agenda for tomorrow's meeting.

Few aspects of the problem we are now facing are as clear as they should be.

The availability of rice, as well as of medical supplies, determines the life expectancy of a typical adult in Hong Kong.

Normal wear and tear, along with planned obsolescence, is the reason most automobiles provide only an average of 6.5 years of service.

The number of the subject must still agree with the verb even when following the verb:

What are your arguments for creating online access to the database?

There are five new pumps in the warehouse.

Discussed are the basic design flaws in the preliminary specifications and the lack of adequate detail in the drawings.

Finally, some noun subjects look plural because they end in –s or –ics, but they are still singular:

> Politics has changed drastically with the advent of television.
>
> The news from Algeria continues to be discouraging.
>
> Measles rarely occurs in adults.

2. Subjects connected by *and* require a plural verb:

> The ceiling panels and the fasteners have been fabricated.
>
> The software designer and the graphic artist agree that we should market the new instructional manual immediately.
>
> A personal computer and a photo copier are essential business tools today.

NOTE: Sometimes words connected by *and* become so closely linked that they become singular in meaning, thus requiring a singular verb:

> Bacon and eggs is my favorite breakfast.
>
> My name and address is on the inside cover.
>
> Simon & Schuster is an excellent publishing firm.

3. Singular subjects connected by *either . . . or, neither . . . nor,* and *not only . . . but also* require a singular verb:

> Either the post-operative therapy or the inflammation is causing the acute pain.
>
> Neither the district engineer nor the superintendent has approved the plans.
>
> Not only the cost but also the design is a problem.

NOTE: When one of a pair of subjects is plural, the verb agrees with the subject closest to it:

> Either the tail assembly or the wing struts are causing excessive fuel consumption.
>
> Either the wing struts or the tail assembly is causing excessive fuel consumption.

4. When used as a subject or as the modifier of the subject, *each, every, either, neither, one, another, much, anybody, anyone, everybody, everyone, somebody, someone, nobody,* and *no one* require singular verbs.

> Every proposal has been evaluated.
>
> Each engineer is responsible for the final proofing of engineering proposals.
>
> Everyone has received the pension information.
>
> Somebody was responsible for the drop in production.
>
> No one but the design engineer knows the load factors used in the calculations.

NOTE: Although words ending with *–one* and *–body* require a singular verb, sentences with such words often become awkward when a pronoun refers to those words:

> Everyone turns in his report on Monday.

Using the singular pronoun *his* maintains the agreement with the subject, but if the *everyone* mentioned includes women, the expression may be considered sexist. Some writers and editors argue that male pronouns *(he, his, him, himself)* are generic, that they refer to both males and females. Others maintain that this convention discriminates against women. Writers and editors who share this view prefer to include both men and women in their sentences:

> Everyone turns in his or her report on Monday.

Finally, some liberal editors argue that *everyone* implies a plurality, so the plural *their* becomes the acceptable pronoun. For example:

> Everyone turns in their reports on Monday.

The sexism problem is avoidable in most sentences simply by making the subject plural and eliminating such troublesome words as *everyone*:

> All engineers turn in their reports on Monday.

See PRONOUNS and BIAS-FREE LANGUAGE.

5. When used as a subject or as the modifier of a subject, *both, few, several, many,* and *others* require plural verbs:

> Both proposals were unsatisfactory.
>
> Several were available earlier this month.
>
> Few pipes were still in service.

6. *All, any, more, most, none, some, one-half of, two-thirds of, a part of,* and *a percentage of* require either a singular or a plural verb, depending upon the noun they refer to:

> All of the work has been assigned. *(singular)*
>
> All of the trees have been removed. *(plural)*

> Most sugar is now made from sugar beets.
>
> Most errors were caused by carelessness.

> Some of the report was written in an overly ornate style.
>
> Some design features were mandatory.

> One-half of the project has been completed.
>
> One-half of the pages have been proofed.

> A percentage of the room is for storage.
>
> A percentage of the employees belong to the company credit union.

7. Collective nouns and expressions with time, money, and quantities take a singular or a plural verb, depending upon their intended meaning:

The committee votes on pension policy when disputes occur. (Committee, *a collective noun, is considered singular. In British English* committee *is often used as a plural.*)

The committee do not agree on the interpretation of the mandatory retirement clause. (Committee, *a collective noun, is considered plural.*)

———————————

The audience was noisy, especially during the final act.

The audience were in their seats by 7:30 p.m.

———————————

Two years is the usual waiting period. (Two years *is an expression of time considered as a single unit.*)

The 2 years were each divided into quarters for accounting purposes. (Two years *is an expression of time considered as a plural of* year.)

———————————

Six dollars is the fee.

Six dollars were spread out on the counter.

———————————

Five liters is all the tank can hold.

Five liters of wine were sold before noon.

NOTE: Sometimes sentences with collective nouns become awkward because they seem both singular and plural. In such cases, rephrasing often helps:

Audience members were in their seats by 7:30 p.m.

8. Choose either a singular or plural verb for subjects that are organizational names, and then be consistent in all other contexts with the name.

Problems arise because organizational names often look plural even though they are the names of single organizations:

Kraus, Jones, and Blackstone

Franklin Covey

The Money Group

Thomas & Sons, Inc.

These names take a plural verb if you intend to stress the individual members or partners:

Kraus, Jones, and Blackstone have their law offices in the Tower Center Building.

Franklin Covey present training courses throughout the country.

The Money Group are uniquely qualified to advise you on your investments.

Thomas & Sons have been in business since 1950, and their reputation is unexcelled.

Otherwise, use a singular verb, which is the preferred pattern in business writing, probably because readers usually view an organization as a single entity:

Kraus, Jones, and Blackstone has signed a lease for a suite in the Tower Center Building.

Franklin Covey is a leading training firm, and its materials have won national awards.

The Money Group is licensed in Michigan, and its corporate offices are in Detroit.

Thomas & Sons has the city contract for all plumbing work.

NOTE 1: As in two of the examples with plural verbs, sentences with an organizational name often include a pronoun that refers back to the organization. If you have chosen a plural verb, this pronoun will be *they* or *them.* See NOUNS.

As in two of the examples with singular verbs, sentences often contain the singular pronoun *its* to refer back to the organization. See PRONOUNS.

NOTE 2: Often you must decide whether to use an apostrophe with an organizational name, as in contexts such as these:

Kraus, Jones, and Blackstone's personnel policy requires . . .

Franklin Covey's proposal includes . . .

The Money Group's line of credit exceeds . . .

Thomas & Sons' vans have . . .

An apostrophe is more common if you are considering the names plural. If you choose to make the names singular, then an apostrophe is usually unnecessary, especially if you precede the name with *a, an,* or *the*:

The Kraus, Jones, and Blackstone personnel policy requires . . .

A Franklin Covey proposal includes . . .

The Money Group line of credit exceeds . . .

The Thomas and Sons vans have . . .

Again, be consistent within a single document. Either use the possessive forms with their apostrophes or use descriptive forms without apostrophes. See ADJECTIVES, APOSTROPHES, and POSSESSIVES.

Apostrophes

Apostrophes signal omitted letters, possession, and the plural of letters and symbols. In possessive forms an apostrophe (') can appear with or without a following –s.

Apostrophes

1. Use apostrophes to signal omitted letters in a contraction.

2. Use apostrophes to show possession.

3. Use apostrophes to show the passage of time in certain stock phrases.

4. Use only the –s to form the plural of letters, signs, symbols, figures, acronyms, and abbreviations, unless the absence of the apostrophe would be confusing.

5. Distinguish between true possessives and merely descriptive uses of nouns (especially with company names).

1. Use apostrophes to signal omitted letters in a contraction:

It's not going to be easy. (It is not going to be easy.)

It won't be easy. (It will not be easy.)

We will coordinate with the manufacturer who's chosen to supply the semiconductors. (who is chosen)

NOTE: Use contractions in letters and memos to help establish an informal tone. Avoid contractions in more formal, edited documents. See CONTRACTIONS.

2. Use apostrophes to show possession:

Microsoft's design capabilities are world renowned.

The unit's most unique capability is its amplification of weak echoes.

• When the possessive word is singular, the apostrophe comes before the –s:

Rockwell International's process for budgeting is one of the most progressive in the industry.

The circuit's most unusual capability is its error detection and correction function.

• When the possessive word is singular and already ends with an –s, the apostrophe follows the –s and may itself be followed by another –s (although most writers prefer the apostrophe alone):

General Dynamics' (or Dynamics's) management proposal is very project specific.

Our project manager will be Dr. Martin Jones. Dr. Jones' (or Jones's) experience with laser refractors has made him a leader in the field.

• When the possessive word is plural and ends in –s, the apostrophe follows the –s:

The suppliers' requests are not unreasonable considering the amount of time required for fabrication.

We consider the states' environmental quality offices to be our partners in reclamation.

NOTE 1: Irregular plurals that do not end in –s require an 's:

The report on women's status in the executive community is due next Friday.

Materials for children's toys must conform to Federal safety standards.

NOTE 2: The possessive form of the pronoun it is its, not it's (it's is the contraction of it is or it has):

Possessive: Its products have over 10,000 hours of testing behind them.

Contraction: It's (It is) in the interests of economy and efficiency that we pursue atmospheric testing as well.

Similarly, the possessive form of who is whose, not who's. Who's is a contraction for who is or who has. See POSSESSIVES and who's/whose in WORD PROBLEMS.

3. Use apostrophes to show the passage of time in certain stock phrases:

a month's pay

an hour's time

4 days' work

3 years' study

5 years' experience

NOTE: Distinguish between the preceeding examples with apostrophes and the following unit modifiers with hyphens:

a 4-day work week

his 3-year study

See HYPHENS.

4. Use only the –s to form the plural of letters, signs, symbols, figures, acronyms, and abbreviations, unless the absence of the apostrophe would be confusing.

As in the following examples, the forms without apostrophes are preferred, but forms with apostrophes are acceptable:

The Xs indicate insertable material (or x's or X's but not xs)

All of our senior staff have PhDs. (or Ph.D.'s or Ph.D.s)

Simplex Pharmaceuticals coded all experimental drug runs with A's and I's. (not As or Is nor as or is)

Symmetek began making microchips in the 1990s. (or 1990's)

The tracer tests will be run on all APOs in Europe. (or APO's)

Apostrophes

The Bureau of Land Management has prepared three EAs (Environmental Assessments) for those grazing allotments. (*or* EA's)

In the following instances, the absence of the apostrophe produces confusing forms:

The manufacturer indicates fragile material by placing #'s in any of the last three positions in the transportation code.

Our risk management process is designed to eliminate the if's and but's.

---

5. Distinguish between true possessives and merely descriptive uses of nouns (especially with company names):

Exxon's response (possessive)
an Exxon response (descriptive)

General Motors' news release
(*or* a General Motors news release)
The General Motors sales staff

Franklin Coveys' proposal
Franklin Covey *Style Guide*

Verdi's first opera
an early Verdi opera

The teachers' testimony
A teacher guide
Teachers Guide
(*or* Teacher's Guide)
(*or* Teachers' Guide)

As in these examples, competing forms are common. The traditional use of the possessive (with an apostrophe) is less common today, especially with corporate names. See ADJECTIVES and AGREEMENT.

As in the examples with *teachers'/ teacher/teachers,* a number of options are possible. In *the teachers' testimony*, the possessive signals testimony from several different teachers.

The name for a guide for teachers is open to all sorts of possibilities. In *the teacher guide*, the noun *teacher* functions as an adjective, not a possessive. When both nouns are capitalized, the most common form is *Teachers Guide*. This form, without the apostrophe, would appear in titles and in news headlines (which often omit apostrophes). But notice that other options are possible (and correct).

The best advice is to decide for a single document whether you want to use a descriptive or possessive. Then be consistent throughout that document.

Appendices (often informally referred to as attachments) are more and more common in documents, especially those intended for busy peers, supervisors, and managers who do not have time to wade through pages of data and analysis. Appendices and attachments are acceptable (often desirable) in letters and memos as well as in reports.

The following types of information can and often do appear in appendices or attachments:

—Background data

—Case studies

—Computations

—Derivations

—Detailed component descriptions

—Detailed test results

—Excerpts from related research

—Histories

—Lengthy analyses

—Parts lists

—Photographs

—Raw data

—Sources of additional information

—Supporting letters and memos

—Tables of data

The word *appendix* has two acceptable plurals: *appendices* and *appendixes*. *Appendices* is still widely used by educated speakers and writers, but *appendixes* is growing in popularity because it follows the regular method for making English words plural. The style used by the U.S. Government is *appendixes*.

Appendices

1. Use appendices to streamline reports and memos that would otherwise be too lengthy.

2. Avoid making appendices a dumping ground for unnecessary information.

3. Number or letter appendices and attachments sequentially.

4. Refer to all appendices and attachments in the body of the document.

---

1. Use appendices to streamline reports and memos that would otherwise be too lengthy.

In business and technical reports and memos, assess your readers' need to know the background and analysis behind the relevant conclusions and recommendations.

Relevant conclusions and recommendations should appear very early in most business and technical reports, often as part of an executive summary. Busy readers can therefore receive a streamlined report of 8 to 10 pages (instead of the traditional formal report of 30 to 50 pages) with appendices containing appropriate background information, detailed results, and lengthy analyses. See SUMMARIES.

2. Avoid making appendices a dumping ground for unnecessary information.

Because the appendices are not part of the body of the report, some writers believe they have the license to include in the appendices every scrap of information they know about the subject. This practice leads to massive, often confusing appendices that discourage readers.

Would a knowledgeable reader need the information in the appendices to interpret the conclusions and recommendations? If so, then the appendices are justified. In writing your document, determine who the readers will be and ask yourself what additional information these readers will need to better understand your approach, analysis, results, conclusions, and recommendations.

One rule of thumb is that appendices should contain only information prepared for the project in question. Background information from files and tangential reports (general background information) should not appear in appendices. Often, readers know such background information anyway.

To summarize, if a reader needs certain information to understand a report, this information belongs in the body of a report. All other information belongs either in appendices or in backup files.

Appendices

3. Number or letter appendices and attachments sequentially.

Sequential numbering or lettering is essential: Appendix A, Appendix B, etc.; or Attachment 1, Attachment 2, etc. Numbers and letters are both correct, so either is acceptable. In longer documents, your choice may depend upon whether you have numbered or lettered the sections or chapters. If your sections or chapters are numbered, then use letters to label appendices. Conversely, if your sections or chapters are lettered, use numbers for the appendices. The system you use to label appendices should indicate a clear distinction between the appendices and the body of the document.

Typically, appendices are numbered in the order in which the references to them appear in the body of the report. So the first appendix mentioned in the report becomes appendix A (or appendix 1), the second one mentioned is appendix B (or appendix 2), and so on.

NOTE 1: As in the preceding sentence, you need not capitalize the initial *A* in appendix in ordinary text. Some authorities, however, prefer a capital: Appendix A. Choose one pattern and be consistent. See CAPITALS.

NOTE 2: Give each appendix or attachment a title. Referring to appendices or attachments only by number is not informative and can be confusing. In the text, refer to the appendix or attachment by both number and title.

4. Refer to all appendices and attachments in the body of the document.

Refer to all appendices or attachments in the body of the document so that readers know that the information within them is available.

Your references should be informative rather than cryptic. A cryptic reference (such as *See appendix C*) does not tell readers enough about the appended information. The following references are informative:

Particulate counts from all collection points in the study area appear in appendix C, Particulate Data.

Attachment 5, A Report on Reserve Faulting in the Boling Dome, provides further evidence of the complex faulting that may control production.

See appendix A (Prescription Trends During the 1970s) for further analysis of valium use and abuse since its introduction.

Articles are the simple structure words *a*, *an*, and *the*. These words always precede a following noun, but not every noun can accept both articles, and some nouns need neither of them. See NOUNS.

Common nouns that name countable things can use both *a/an* and *the* and have both a singular and a plural form:

a book (*singular indefinite*)
the book (*singular definite*)
the books (*plural*)

not

a books

Common nouns that name uncountable things are mass nouns. They have no plural forms, and they don't commonly accept *a* or *an*:

the rice/rice
the gold/gold

not

the rices
a rice
the golds
a gold

Some common nouns are both countable and uncountable (mass):

cake (*mass*)
a cake (*countable*)
the cake (*either mass or countable*)
cakes (*countable*)

_____

milk (*mass*)
a milk (*countable*)
the milk (*mass*)
milks (rare use—as in milk from cows, goats, horses, humans, etc.)

Proper nouns usually do not require articles:

Susan B. Anthony
Senator Robert Dole
Kansas City
Stone Mountain

but

The Mississippi River
The Great Lakes

A/An is the indefinite article because it points toward a single indefinite (unspecified) object:

Articles

1. Choose indefinite *a* or *an* to precede a singular countable noun.

2. Use definite *the* to precede (point out) either countable or mass nouns, both singular and plural.

3. Choose *a/an* and *the* (different pronunciations) to match the way an acronym is pronounced, not how it is spelled.

4. Alphabetize acronyms without using the customary article that would appear in the written-out titles.

5. For English as a Second Language (ESL) questions regarding articles, use a dictionary designed for ESL users.

A candle (*meaning* "any single candle")

An elephant (*meaning* "any single elephant")

The is the definite article because it points toward a definite (specified) object, either singular or plural:

The candle (*meaning* "one specific candle")

The candles (*meaning* "more than one specific candle")

The elephant (*meaning* "one specific elephant")

The elephants (*meaning* "more than one specific elephant")

_____

1. Choose indefinite *a* or *an* to precede a singular countable noun:

a tube
a leaf
a ring
an ear
an apple
an owl

NOTE 1: As in the above examples, the choice between *a* and *an* is based on the initial sound—not spelling—of the noun (or word) that follows the article. Words pronounced with a vowel sound require *an* (pronounced as in the initial sound of *ant*). Words pronounced with a consonant sound require *a* (pronounced as in the hesitation sound *uh*).

an amber leaf
an emerald ring
a good apple
a tiny owl

NOTE 2: Nouns beginning with *h* can potentially have either *a* or *an*. If the *h* is pronounced, as in *heap* or *hair*, *a* is correct:

a heap
a hair

If the *h* is silent (unpronounced), as in *honor* or *hour*, *an* is correct:

an honor
an hour

The word *history* has competing options. Most editors would routinely choose *a history* (not *an history*) as the written form. But speakers often use *an*, as in *an historical event*, perhaps because this *h* is nearly silent.

NOTE 3: *A/an* has an implied meaning of "one," so *a/an* could not precede the plurals of countable nouns. The plurals do not need any article, or *the* can precede them:

tubes/the tubes
ears/the ears
leaves/the leaves
apples/apples

_____

2. Use definite *the* to precede (point out) either countable or mass nouns, both singular and plural:

the engineer (singular countable)
the bee (singular countable)

the engineers (plural countable)
the bees (plural countable)

the butter (mass)
the air (mass)

NOTE 1: Although *the* in the above examples does not change its spelling, its pronunciation often changes just as *a/an* changes. Note, however, that native speakers of English do not always choose pronunciations that follow these rules. Sometimes they even reverse the rules, for emphasis.

When a vowel begins the following word, *the* is usually pronounced as the word *thee*:

the elevator
the almond tree

When a consonant begins the following word, *the* is pronounced as in the beginning of the word *thus*:

the director
the symposium

For emphasis, either *the director* or *the symposium* could begin with a *the* pronounced like *thee*.

As with *a/an*, in some words beginning with *h*, as with *historical*, either pronunciation of *the* is correct:

the historical profile (*with either pronunciation*)

NOTE 2: In all the above examples, using *the* points to a definite object or thing. This pointing function is, however, not as strong as in some other structure words—for example, in the demonstrative pronouns *this, that, these,* and *those.* See PRONOUNS. Using *the* points back to a prior sentence or phrase where the object or objects have been identified.

---

3. Choose *a/an* and *the* (different pronunciations) to match the way an acronym is pronounced, not how it is spelled:

a NEPA requirement

the NEPA requirement (*with the pronounced as in the beginning of* thus)— *for the National Environmental Policy Act (NEPA), which is pronounced as in a word, not by separate letters*

an NFL player

the NFL player (*pronounced as in* thee)— *for National Football League (NFL), which is pronounced letter by letter, not as a word*

an/the AFL-CIO publication

a/the DoD proposal

an/the MIS supervisor

a/the KUED television program

NOTE: Pronunciation also influences whether the article is needed or not. For example, with the *National Environmental Policy Act* (*NEPA*), the article *the* often drops when *NEPA* (pronounced as a word) appears in sentences:

NEPA requires that each agency . . .

A provision of NEPA is . . .

In either of these cases, the written-out version would include the article: *the National Environmental Policy Act.*

---

4. Alphabetize acronyms without using the customary article that would appear in the written-out titles:

CIA
GATT
NASA
SOP

NOTE 1: Each of these abbreviations would ordinarily use an article if written out:

the Central Intelligence Agency

the General Agreement on Tariffs and Trade

the National Aeronautics and Space Administration

NOTE 2: *SOP* illustrates the principle discussed in rule 3. The acronym—read letter by letter—begins with a vowel sound, so it would require *an* if an article is used with it. But the written-out version opens with a consonant sound, so it uses *a*:

a/the standard operating procedure

As in this example, the original words for an acronym may not require capitalization. See CAPITALS.

---

5. For English as a Second Language (ESL) questions regarding articles, use a dictionary designed for ESL users.

Articles are some of the most unpredictable words in English, despite their frequency. Most native speakers of English choose articles without thinking. A non-native English speaker has to work with rules. Unfortunately, the rules presented above have innumerable exceptions.

We recommend, therefore, A.S. Hornby's *Oxford Advanced Learner's Dictionary of Current English,* Fourth Edition (Oxford, England: Oxford University Press, 1989). See REFERENCES.

This excellent dictionary is designed especially for non-English-speaking users. As such, it has a wealth of examples and, in the case of articles, it marks nouns as countable (marked with a [C]) or uncountable (marked with a [U]).

For example, the simple noun *cover,* as discussed in this dictionary, has a variety of uses, some as a countable noun; others as an uncountable (mass) noun.

a cover on a typewriter [C]

design a front cover for the book [C]

provide cover from a storm [U]

a spy's cover (assumed identity) [U]

This dictionary also identifies special uses when a noun is only plural:

The covers on the bed [Plural only]

Finally, this dictionary lists special idioms, many of which either use or avoid articles, often without apparent logic:

under cover of darkness (*No article is used before* cover.)

Bias-free language is an increasingly important issue for business and technical writers and speakers. The list of forbidden words and phrases grows longer each week, and the legal penalties for violations are increasingly severe.

United States Federal laws and many state regulations mandate that an employee may not be discriminated against based on race, creed, sex, age, or national origin. These laws have various provisions, but penalties for violations apply both to individual employees and to their companies.

Cultural Awareness

Cultural awareness (rules 1, 2, 3, and 4), in the following discussion, covers language choices dealing with race, religion, physical status, social status, age, and national origins. Issues relating to gender are covered in a separate section (rules 5, 6, 7, 8, 9, and 10).

Many of the cultural awareness issues are changing social conventions. Writers and speakers should be constantly alert to changes in what is acceptable because words and phrases fall in and out of favor so rapidly. Also, as appropriate, check the status of terms in up-to-date dictionaries and other references. See REFERENCES.

---

1. Do not use words that unnecessarily identify a person's race, religion, physical status, social status, age, national origins, or gender.

In most instances, write documents giving people's names and, if appropriate, their job titles. Do not include, for example, references indicating that a person is a Native American, a Methodist, a woman,

Bias-Free Language

Cultural Awareness

1. Do not use words that unnecessarily identify a person's race, religion, physical status, social status, age, national origins, or gender.

2. Don't rely on the stereotypes often implied by the categorizations included in rule 1.

3. When appropriate, choose terms and designations that are neutral and acceptable to the group you are discussing.

4. Be sure to choose graphics—especially photographs—that fairly represent all groups and types of people within society.

Gender-Neutral Language

5. Use words that do not unnecessarily distinguish between male and female.

6. Avoid unnecessary uses of *he, him,* or *his* to refer back to such indefinite pronouns as *everyone, everybody, someone,* and *somebody.*

7. Avoid unnecessary uses of *he, him, his* or *she, her, hers* when the word refers to both males and females.

8. Avoid the traditional salutation *Gentlemen* if the organization receiving the letter includes males and females.

9. Do not substitute *s/he, he/she, hisorher,* or other such hybrid forms for standard personal pronouns.

10. Avoid demeaning or condescending gender terms for either females or males.

---

the user of a wheelchair, a vegetarian, nearly 65, or born in Puerto Rico.

These categorizations are irrelevant to any serious business discussion. They are also often insulting to the person referred to, especially if the category is being used as a short-hand way of implying something about the person.

For instance, mentioning someone's age can be a way of suggesting that the person is too close to retirement to be considered for a promotion or a special task team. This reference to the person's age is irrelevant, unfair, and likely illegal.

The golden rule is a good rule to follow when answering questions about cultural awareness. Would you appreciate someone identifying one or more traits about you if the trait had no relevance to the topic at hand? So, follow this rule: Treat others as you would want to be treated.

NOTE: In some contexts, such personal categorizations are appropriate for discussion and documentation. Census surveys routinely ask for such information. Or the Personnel Department for a company may develop survey information about employees to comply with Federal guidelines relating to Equal Employment Opportunity or Affirmative Action programs.

Usually personal information about any of these categories should be kept confidential.

2. Don't rely on the stereotypes often implied by the categorizations included in rule 1.

Stereotypes are a classic fault in logic because the stereotype for any group of people always fails when matched up to the traits for a single individual. Misuse of stereotypes is the basic reason why using group or category terms about an individual is wrong (see rule 1).

An argument based on stereotypes would be, for instance, that a specific auto mechanic was cheating you because all auto mechanics are crooks and out to gouge customers. Based on this stereotype, for example, people also make supposedly innocent jokes about the typical mechanic's shrug—a shrug implying that the mechanic doesn't have a clue as to what might be wrong with the car.

Neither the use of the stereotype nor the joke is innocent if you happen to be the mechanic in question. No legal issues are likely involved, but using a stereotype in this manner is probably offensive to the mechanic.

On the other hand, a serious assessment of a single auto mechanic would need to use facts and data about the individual. Such topics as the mechanic's rate of pay, quality of work, and solicitude for the customer are proper items for a company to document and discuss. They have nothing to do with the stereotype of the typical mechanic.

Stereotypes are common about any group of people who share a category or several categories:

Religions: Buddhist, Methodist, Latter-day Saint, Moslem, etc.

Race: Black, Native American, Latino, etc.

Age: retired, middle aged, yuppie, etc.

National Origin: French, Nigerian, Peruvian, Canadian, etc.

Professions: lawyer, doctor, banker, etc.

Sectional Origin: Southerner, Down Easter, Midwesterner, etc.

Physical Features: sightless, user of a wheelchair, diabetic, anorexic, etc.

Sexual Preference: heterosexual, homosexual, bisexual

Economic Status: homeless, fixed (or limited) income, well-to-do, etc.

Gender: female, male

A single individual can share more than a single category. For example, a middle-aged Nigerian female lawyer might be diabetic and on a fixed income. Given this complexity, which stereotypes apply? Probably none of them. And as noted above, most of them are irrelevant and likely illegal to mention in any business discussion or business document.

3. When appropriate, choose terms and designations that are neutral and acceptable to the group you are discussing.

News articles, research reports, and other serious documents properly and legally analyze and discuss data for various groups. Such discussions, which would not be based on stereotypes, include terms for a group or category of persons. These terms are, however, often the problem because they carry unfortunate echoes, and these echoes change rapidly.

For example, stylebooks for both the Associated Press and the United Press identify *blacks* as the term to choose when you need a category term for black Americans. *African-American* is also common. Some people now object to its use of the hyphen, which implies less than full status as an American. Even earlier, the terms *Negro* and *colored person* had seasons of use. Each of them collected negative echoes and fell out of favor.

When you choose any term for a group of people, be careful to choose the one that is most current and acceptable. If in doubt, don't assume that your choice makes no difference. Your choice may be insulting and even a legal issue.

For example, a recent court case on sexism included among other points, the assertion that the defendant called the women on his staff "girls." Of course, to wind up in court, he did much more than call them names. The moral is that the wrong word or phrase can be a costly mistake, especially to your reputation, if not to your pocketbook.

A second example comes from the terms dealing with people who have disabilities. Choose terms and phrases that do not emphasize the negative features of the disabilities, nor should the features be seen as more significant than they may be.

not these

crippled

blind

mentally defective

dumb

afflicted with MS

unfortunately has a speech problem

but these

> person who uses a wheelchair
>
> person without sight/partially sighted
>
> person with mental disability
>
> person unable to speak
>
> person with multiple sclerosis
>
> person with speech impediment

4. Be sure to choose graphics—especially photographs—that fairly represent all groups and types of people within society.

Both major graphics and incidental figures need to be balanced as to their representations of typical people. The graphics should not rely on either an overt or covert use of stereotyping. (See rule 2.)

A recent court case dealt with a realty firm that consistently pictured in advertisements middle-aged Caucasians who seemed to have money. In court, the firm was challenged with sending a signal that first-time black buyers would not be welcome. The realty firm lost.

Much the same sort of problem exists in training materials or procedures that present women in secretarial roles and men in managerial roles. Again, this is a covert reliance on stereotypes.

Finally, be sure that your representations of a racial or physical appearance do not accentuate facial features or dress to the point where the picture is more parody than reality.

Gender-Neutral Language

Gender signals are an integral part of our language. English from its earliest history has often marked words as either male or female (and even sometimes neuter). Pronouns are the commonest surviving

examples: *he, him, his* vs. *she, her, hers* vs. *it, its.* A number of nouns also have had different male and female forms: *waiter/waitress, stewardess/steward, heir/heiress, countess/count, host/hostess, actress/actor, usher/usherette.* And some words used for both genders seem to include only males: *mankind, layman, manpower,* and so on.

Many such distinctions, called gender distinctions, have become objectionable, especially in recent years with the debate about equal rights for women. So, many publishing firms and most writers routinely remove unnecessary and objectionable gender distinctions from published writing. This trend is the basis for the following rules, most of which require little effort from writers.

5. Use words that do not unnecessarily distinguish between male and female:

these	not these
flight attendant	stewardess
people, humans	mankind
work force	manpower
layperson	layman
employee	workman
heir	heiress
chair, chairperson	chairman
serving person or server	waitress

NOTE 1: The use of female forms such as *waitress* and *heiress* has declined. *Heir* now includes both male and female; *waiter* still has male echoes, but these may fade soon. The best advice is to be sensitive to this issue and avoid female designations.

NOTE 2: Historically the word *man* (especially used in compound words like *chairman* or *layman*) could include both males and females; its closest modern equivalent would be, for instance, the indefinite pronoun

one or *person.* This historical meaning has, however, been forgotten, so much so that many women now argue that they are silently being left out when compounds with *man* are used.

6. Avoid unnecessary uses of *he, him,* or *his* to refer back to such indefinite pronouns as *everyone, everybody, someone,* and *somebody.*

The problem sentences are often ones where the indefinite pronouns introduce a single person and then a later pronoun refers to that person:

> Everyone should take (his? her?) coat.
>
> Someone left (his? her?) report.

Unless we clearly know who *everyone* and *someone* refer to, we cannot pick the proper singular pronoun. We thus have to choose among several options:

—Make the sentences plural, if possible:

> All employees should take their coats.

—Remove the pronoun entirely:

> Someone left a (*or this*) report.

—Use both the male and female pronouns:

> Each employee should take his or her report.
>
> Someone left her or his report.

—Use the plural pronoun *their* (or maybe *they* or *theirs):*

> Each employee should take their coat.
>
> Someone left their report.

NOTE: This last option is fine for informal or colloquial speech, but many editors and writers would object to the use of the plural pronouns to refer back to the singular *everyone* and *someone.* See PRONOUNS and AGREEMENT.

Bias-Free Language

7. Avoid unnecessary uses of *he, him, his* or *she, her, hers* when the word refers to both males and females:

not these

A secretary should set her (his?) priorities each day.

The engineer opened her (his?) presentation with an overhead transparency.

A writer should begin his (her?) outline with the main point.

As with rule 6, writers have several options:

—Change the sentences to plurals:

Secretaries should set their priorities each day.

Writers should begin their outlines with the main point.

—Remove the pronouns:

The engineer began the presentation with an overhead transparency.

A secretary should set firm priorities each day.

NOTE: A third option is to use the phrase *his or her,* but this becomes clumsy in a text of any length, so it is better to use one of the two options given above.

---

8. Avoid the traditional salutation *Gentlemen* if the organization receiving the letter includes males and females.

Omit the salutation if your letter is to an organization, not to an individual. Your letter would then have an inside address, a subject line, followed by your text. This format is called a simplified letter. See LETTERS.

Whenever writing to people whose gender you don't know, use the title or the name without a title:

Dear Personnel Manager:

Dear G. L. Branson:

NOTE 1: We do not recommend *Ladies and Gentlemen* or *Gentlemen and Ladies.* The term *Ladies* (and maybe *Gentlemen*) seems old fashioned. Similarly, *Dear Sir or Madam* is old fashioned and overly formal.

NOTE 2: In recent years a number of unusual salutations have appeared. Avoid them:

Dear Gentlepersons:

Dear Gentlepeople:

Dear People:

Dear Folks:

See LETTERS.

---

9. Do not substitute *s/he, he/she, hisorher,* or other such hybrid forms for standard personal pronouns.

These hybrid forms are unpronounceable and are not universally accepted by English users, so avoid them. Instead, either remove pronouns or change the sentences to plurals, as suggested under rule 7.

Where you must use singular personal pronouns, use *he and she, his or her,* or *him and her.* Or as an option in longer documents, alternate between male and female pronouns.

10. Avoid demeaning or condescending gender terms for either females or males.

Gender terms such as *girls/gals* or *boys/guys* carry echoes of immaturity or irresponsibility. As such, they are condescending or, at the very least, humorous. So, do not use them in a business context, either in speech or writing.

For slightly different reasons, the more formal terms *ladies* and *gentlemen* have also become questionable.

The term *ladies* seems to belong to another era, when ladies wore white gloves, attended garden parties, and talked about the social scene. A lady of that era did not work nor worry about business.

The term *gentlemen* is not quite so demeaning, but it still has echoes of past formality.

Use *ladies* or *gentlemen* only in formal speech and probably only when people addressed are well over 30. Similarly, we recommend avoiding the old-fashioned letter salutation: *Ladies and Gentlemen.* See the note in rule 8.

The best advice is to be sensitive to the echoes or implications of your language. As a final example, the common phrase *man and wife* identifies only the sex of the man, but for the wife, both the sex and the marital role are marked. A better choice: *man and woman, husband and wife, woman and man,* or *wife and husband.*

Bibliographies appear at the end of chapters, articles, and books. Whatever the exact format, complete bibliographic entries include the name of the author, the title, and the full publication history (including the edition, the publisher or press, the city of publication, and the date of publication).

The forms of bibliographic entries vary greatly, depending on the professional background of the author, the profession's needs and traditions, the type of publication, and the publisher. The bibliographic form that we recommend represents a standard format useful for a variety of professions and publishers.

However, we advise you to find out the specific format requirements (including bibliographic format) of the publisher to whom you are submitting a document.

NOTE: In the following rules, the titles of publications in bibliographic entries are italicized. Underlining replaces italics when documents are typed or when italics is not available. See UNDERLINING and ITALICS.

Bibliographies

1. For a book, give the name of the author or authors, the date of publication, the full title, the volume number, the edition, the city of publication, and the publisher.

2. For a journal or a magazine article, give the name of the author or authors, the year of publication, the full title of the article (in quotation marks), the name of the journal or magazine, the volume, the month or quarter of publication, and the pages.

3. For electronic media, give the author, date, title, name of publication, and means of retrieving the information.

4. For unpublished material, give the author or authors, the title (in quotation marks), and as much of its history as available.

5. For public documents, give the country, state, county, or other government division, the full title, and complete publication information.

---

1. For a book, give the name of the author or authors, the date of publication, the full title, the volume number, the edition, the city of publication, and the publisher:

Book by one author

Dempster, Jacob B. 1982. *The Art of Fine Book Publishing.* New Haven: The Cottage Press, Inc.

Book by two authors

Gallo, George, and L. J. Lane. 1978. *Paper and Paper-Making.* Second Edition. Baltimore: The Freedom Press & Co.

Book by three authors

Green, H. J., Ellen Jacoby, and James Reed. 1976. *The Art of Graphic Illustration.* New Orleans: The Creole Community Press.

Book by more than three authors

Grundvik, K., et al. 1971. *The Evolution of the Printing Press.* Los Angeles: The Hispanic Press.

Book by one editor

Hough, R. William, ed. 1968. *Fine Lettering.* New York: Simon and Schuster.

Book by two editors

Millman, Howie J., and Fred Stein, eds. 1974. *Preparing Leather Book Covers.* Boston: J. L. Cabot and Sons Publishing.

Two volumes by an organization

Modern Language Association of America. 1974. *Scholarly Publishing In North America.* 2 vols. New Haven: The Classical Press.

Chapter of a book

Williams, Clive. 1979. "The Opacity of Ink." In *The Art of Printing,* edited by Jason Farnsworth. New York: Holt, Rinehart & Winston.

NOTE 1: In these entries, the date directly follows the name of the author or authors. This convention complements the author/date style of citations in the text. See CITATIONS.

In this style, the text of a document contains parenthetical references:

A 1981 study revealed that fleas transmit the virus (Babcock 1981). This study relied on two earlier studies (Duerdun 1976 and Abbott 1973).

or

A 1981 study revealed that fleas transmit the virus (Babcock). This study relied on two earlier studies (Duerdun 1976 and Abbott 1973).

Because the date of Babcock's study is already in the sentence, including the date in the citation is unnecessary.

NOTE 2: Publications in the humanities usually cite the publication date following the name of the publisher:

Smithson, Arthur J. *The History of Modern China.* New York: Simon and Schuster, 1976.

This bibliographic form complements the footnoting pattern of citations routinely used by most scholars in the humanities. For more information on this style, see *The Chicago Manual of Style,* 14th edition. See also FOOTNOTES.

Bibliographies

NOTE 3: Bibliographic entries in the physical and biological sciences often capitalize only the first word of the title:

Smithson, Arthur J. 1976. *The history of modern China.* New York: Simon and Schuster. [China *is capitalized because it is a proper noun.*]

2. For a journal or a magazine article, give the name of the author or authors, the year of publication, the full title of the article (in quotation marks), the name of the journal or magazine, the volume, the month or quarter of publication, and the pages:

Article by one author

Broward, Charles Evans. 1981. "Traveling the Southern California Desert." *UCLA Chronicle* 15 (Spring): 45–54.

Article by two authors

Calleston, Dwight R., and James Buchanan. 1976. "The Desert Tortoise: Its Vanishing Habitat." *The Californian* 7 (April): 23–28.

For articles with multiple authors, follow the example shown of the book format that deals with two or more authors:

Article appearing in more than one issue

Stevens, Harold, and Jason Drew. 1976. "The Family of Bighorn Sheep." *The Bighorn Sheep Newsletter* 8 (Fall) and 9 (Winter): 34–35, 28–31.

Article from a popular magazine

Trump, Josiah. 1969. "The Desert Indians." *Time,* December 12, 45–49.

Review of a published book

Williams, Ellen. 1980. Review of *Prospecting in the Southern Desert* by Amy Van Pol and James Freeman. *The Californian* (July): 24–31.

See QUOTATION MARKS.

NOTE 1: As with books, these entries cite the year of publication immediately after the name of the author or authors. In publications for the humanities, the date appears (with the month) after the volume of the journal or magazine:

Stillman, Wendy. "Photographing Desert Sunsets." *UCLA Chronicle* 15 (Spring 1981): 4–8.

NOTE 2: Some editors, especially in the biological and physical sciences, prefer to omit the quotation marks around the title of the article and to capitalize only the first word of the title:

Stillman, Wendy. 1981. Photographing desert sunsets. *UCLA Chronicle* 15 (Spring): 4–8.

3. For electronic media, give the author, date, title, name of publication, and means of retrieving the information.

Online article

Aziz, A., & Brooks, G. 1995. Pharmacokinetics of synthesized serotonin in fasted and non-fasted subjects. *Clinical Pharmaceutics* [Online serial]. Available FTP: *130.92.71.89* Directory: *pub/pharm* File: *clnphrm.95.9.25.serotonin*

Kimball, Lee. *Web Guide for Dummies.* 1996. Key word: *dummies http://www.dummies.com*

Online database

Survey of General-Obligation Bond Ratings [Electronic database]. 1995. New York, NY: D&F Bond Clearinghouse. Available ProfNet: *bndpfnt.unibas.ny* Directory: */archive_bnd/1995.volume.1*

Computer software

EasyChart [computer software]. 1995. Baltimore, MD: PlumStone Software.

NOTE 1: Describe the pathway to the information as precisely as possible. Indicate source or address, directory, and file or volume number.

NOTE 2: Electronic pathways change constantly; therefore, you might add key words by which to locate an address. Do not end a pathway description with a period, which will hamper retrieval if inadvertently used. Use lowercase and italics for pathway addresses in text.

4. For unpublished material, give the author or authors, the title (in quotation marks), and as much of its history as available:

Dissertation or thesis

Johnson, Dugdale. 1983. "The Habitat of the Desert Tortoise: Its Inter-Relationship with Man." D.Sc. diss., University of Southern California.

Professional paper

Rusk, Joan, and Elaine Yardley. 1980. "The Diseases of the Bighorn Sheep." Paper presented at the annual meeting of the Bighorn Sheep Society, Los Angeles, 24–26 May.

Personal communication

Turgott, Edward. 1983. Letter to the author, 31 May.

NOTE: The formats for other unpublished documents (television shows, radio shows, interviews, duplicated material, diaries, etc.) should supply as much bibliographic information as possible. The bibliographic form should allow readers to locate the document easily.

5. For public documents, give the country, state, county, or other government division, the full title, and complete publication information:

Iowa. State Assembly. Committee on Farm Commodities. 1974. *Report to the Farm Bureau on Corn Subsidies.* 45th Assembly, 2nd. sess.

U.S. Congress. House. Committee on Ways and Means. 1945. *Hearings on Import Duties on Shellfish.* 79th Cong., 1st sess.

U.S. Bureau of the Census. 1984. *Gross and Net Fishing Revenues, 1980.* Prepared by the Commerce Division in cooperation with the Commodity Division. Washington, D.C.: United States Government Printing Office.

Boldface type uses thicker and darker letters— for example, **boldface type** vs. normal type.

1. Use boldface type to emphasize key words and phrases and to complement the design and appearance of the page.

Integrate boldface into your overall design of the page or pages in your document. In particular, use boldface for the following key words and phrases:

—Titles of a book or chapter

—Headings and subheadings

—Listed items

—Steps in a procedure

—Rules or notes

—Subject lines (in letters and memos)

—Names or titles of graphics

—Titles or sections in an index

In each of these instances, the boldface type complements other emphasis techniques: placement, spacing, different type sizes, and the organization of content. See EMPHASIS and PAGE LAYOUT.

So, even without boldface type, the document would already be designed to emphasize major points and key words. Boldface just makes the items even more emphatic.

Boldface

1. Use boldface type to emphasize key words and phrases and to complement the design and appearance of the page.

2. Do not overuse boldface and do not use boldface randomly or in isolation from other emphasis techniques.

2. Do not overuse boldface and do not use boldface randomly or in isolation from other emphasis techniques.

Overusing boldface destroys its value and impact. Also, several lines of boldface or even a paragraph entirely in boldface can be more difficult to read than if it was in normal type.

Random and unplanned use of boldface occurs when, for example, a writer has written a paragraph and later decides to boldface a phrase or several words in the middle of the paragraph:

not this

During our recent audit of the Production Department, we identified a major problem arising from a **shortage of crucial fasteners**. The vendor who supplies fasteners often takes as long as 2 days to resupply our production line. When the production line fails to project ahead, **downtimes** can occur, often **as long as 2 days** while fasteners are in transit.

The writer of the preceding paragraph should have decided what she wanted to emphasize before writing the paragraph. The following is one possible rewrite, using an initial subheading for the major ideas:

Shortage of Fasteners (2-Day Delay)

During our audit, we discovered that the vendor for certain fasteners often required 2 days to resupply our line. Such delays would occur when workers on the production line failed to project accurately when they would need more fasteners.

Or as an option, the following sentence could replace the heading in the preceding example. In this case, no boldface would be necessary, although the phrase *up to 2 days* might be boldfaced.

Without crucial fasteners, downtimes on the production line can last for up to 2 days.

Brackets

Brackets are a pair of marks [ ] used to set off comments, corrections, or explanatory material. Although similar to parentheses, brackets do have different uses, as the following rules indicate. See PARENTHESES.

Brackets

1. Use brackets to insert comments or corrections in quoted material.

2. Use brackets to enclose parenthetical or explanatory material that occurs within material that is already enclosed within parentheses.

3. For mathematical expressions, place parentheses inside brackets inside braces inside parentheses.

4. No other marks of punctuation need to come before or after brackets unless the bracketed material has its own mark of punctuation or the overall sentence needs punctuation.

---

1. Use brackets to insert comments or corrections in quoted material:

"Your quoted price [$3,750] is far more than our budget allows."

"Our engineers surveyed the cite [site] for its suitability as a hardware assembly cite [site]."

See QUOTATIONS.

NOTE 1: In these examples, the brackets indicate that the material quoted did not have the information included within the brackets or was an error.

NOTE 2: A common use of brackets, especially in published articles, is to insert *sic* in brackets following an error:

"We studied the affect [sic] of the new design on production outputs."

Sic, borrowed from Latin, means "thus" or "so." It tells readers that the text quoted appears exactly as it did in the original, including the error. In the example above, the word preceding *[sic]* should have been *effect*.

2. Use brackets to enclose parenthetical or explanatory material that occurs within material that is already enclosed within parentheses:

We decided to reject the bid from Gulf Industries International. (Actually the bid [$58,000] was tempting because it was far below our estimate and because Gulf Industries usually does good work.)

See PARENTHESES.

NOTE: You can sometimes use dashes instead of the outer parentheses and then replace the brackets with parentheses:

this

The Board of Directors—or more accurately, a committee of the actual owners (Hyatt, Burke, and Drake)—are answerable to no one but themselves.

not this

The Board of Directors (or more accurately, a committee of the actual owners [Hyatt, Burke, and Drake]) are answerable to no one but themselves.

Some writers and editors consider the version without brackets preferable because having both parentheses and brackets in the same sentence can look clumsy and can be confusing. See DASHES.

3. For mathematical expressions, place parentheses inside brackets inside braces inside parentheses:

$(\{ [( )] \})$

See MATHEMATICAL NOTATION.

---

4. No other marks of punctuation need to come before or after brackets unless the bracketed material has its own mark of punctuation or the overall sentence needs punctuation:

this

The procedure was likely to be costly. (Actually, the cost [$38 per unit] included some of the research and development expenses.)

not this

The procedure was likely to be costly. (Actually, the cost, [$38 per unit], included some of the research and development expenses.)

British English is standard throughout the British Commonwealth of Nations (for example, Canada, Australia, Singapore) and among most English-speaking Africans, Asians, and Europeans. In former British colonies such as India, Pakistan, and Nigeria, British English is a common standard where many languages are spoken. American English is standard in the United States and among most English speaking Pacific Rim Asians.

Business English does not vary greatly from one country to another. However, American and British writing styles differ somewhat because of 400 years of geographical and cultural separation. Because American and British English are the main forms of English, this discussion focuses on the differences between them.

Writers addressing both cultures should avoid terms specific to each. For example, baseball terminology means little to British readers just as the language of cricket baffles Americans.

For complete guidance on British and American usage, see *Oxford Advanced Learner's Dictionary,* 4th edition (Oxford: Oxford University Press, 1992), and *The Economist Style Guide* (London: The Economist Books Ltd., 1993). For a glossary of words that differ in British and American usage, see *American English/English American,* 2nd edition (Bristol, England: Abson Books, 1982).

Choose between British or American usage depending on the needs and culture of the audience you are addressing. Be consistent about your choice. The following rules present the main traits of British English.

British English

1. Eliminate periods in and after most abbreviations.

2. Take care to make subjects agree with verbs.

3. Do not generally use commas before *and.*

4. Use a hyphen to separate a prefix ending with a vowel from a word beginning with the same vowel.

5. Use single quotation marks to mark off short quotations or sayings.

6. Take particular care to avoid gobbledygook in a British context.

7. Be aware of differences between British and American word choice, numbers, and spelling.

1. Eliminate periods in and after most abbreviations.

The trend to eliminate periods in abbreviations is even more marked in British than in American usage.

American	British
A.D.	AD
e.g.	eg
etc.	etc
i.e.	ie
Mrs.	Mrs

See ABBREVIATIONS.

2. Take care to make subjects agree with verbs.

Some nouns that are singular in American English are often treated as either plurals or singulars in Britain:

American

the government denies the rumor
the department is changing the policy

British

the government denies/deny the rumour
the department is/are changing the policy

See AGREEMENT.

3. Do not generally use commas before *and*:

Please revise the deadlines, budgets and specifications of the project.

Profits exceeded expectations and employment figures are up for the first quarter.

As in American usage, commas in British English are sometimes used to separate long, complete thoughts linked by a conjunction (*and, but, or, for, nor, so, yet*):

We had anticipated finishing product trials this month, but several important quality issues arose early and had to be dealt with.

See COMMAS.

4. Use a hyphen to separate a prefix ending with a vowel from a word beginning with the same vowel:

re-educate, pre-eminent, co-ordinate

This practice is now becoming less prevalent, but many Britons still hold to it.

See HYPHENS.

5. Use single quotation marks to mark off short quotations or sayings:

'We can deliver,' he said.

Double quotation marks are used to enclose quotations within quotations:

'It was Shakespeare who said, "To thine own self be true"'.

British English

Only the British observe this rule; in the USA and the Commonwealth, double quotation marks enclose quotations, while single quotation marks enclose quotations within quotations.

Although in enclosed by quotation marks in American English, commas and periods (full stops) usually appear outside the quotation marks in British English:

'We can deliver', he said.

Long quotations in British usage are usually indented as a block. See QUOTATIONS and QUOTATION MARKS.

---

6. Take particular care to avoid gobbledygook in a British context.

The British tend to be more economical and concise in their language than Americans are. Americans who are given to gobbledygook should take a lesson in British restraint.

American
This problem is an ongoing situation.

British
The problem continues.

American
The project team is violating accepted norms.

British
The project team is breaking the rules.

Sometimes Americans lengthen words, creating a pretentious effect to a British ear: *oblige* becomes *obligate*; *orient* becomes *orientate*; *need* becomes *necessitate*. See GOBBLEDYGOOK.

---

7. Be aware of differences between British and American word choice, numbers, and spelling.

The British and American vocabularies differ slightly. Some examples:

American	British
aluminum	aluminium
trunk (of a car)	boot
windshield	windscreen
thumbtack	drawing pin
freight train	goods train
elevator	lift
zip code	post code
fender	wing
highway	motorway
overpass	flyover
to mail	to post
a raise (in price)	a rise
gasoline	petrol
canned	tinned

Most technical terms are identical in British and American English.

Some words have different meanings: *homely* means "simple" or "comfortable" in British English, but "unattractive" in American English.

Some verb forms differ. Here are the main British forms for some common irregular verbs:

get, got, got (*instead of* gotten)
prove, proved, proved (*instead of* proven)
dive, dived (*instead of* dove), dived

British English uses –*t* instead of –*ed* with some verbs:

burn, burnt, burnt
leap, leapt, leapt
learn, learnt, learnt
spell, spelt, spelt

See VERBS.

Style

British writing and speaking style differs from American in terms of tone and pacing. Although generalizations are risky, usage experts generally agree that British style tends to be more impersonal and restrained, particularly in word choice. The American tendency to use hyperbolic language (*fantastic, excellent, terrific*) discomfits the British, as well as most Europeans.

Numbers

The terms for very large numbers differ in British and American usage:

American	British
one billion	one thousand million(s)
one trillion	one billion
one quadrillion	one thousand billion(s)
one quintillion	one trillion
one sextillion	one thousand trillion
one septillion	one quadrillion
one octillion	one thousand quadrillion
one nonillion	one quintillion
one decillion	one thousand quintillion

Spelling

For historical reasons, many British and American spellings differ. In the early 1800s the American lexicographer Noah Webster campaigned to simplify English spelling, and his influential dictionary led to American spelling patterns:

American	British
color	colour
candor	candour
labor	labour
center	centre
meter	metre
gray or grey	grey
defense	defence
mold	mould
check	cheque
traveling	travelling
counselor	counsellor
program	programme
tire	tyre
organize	organise/organize
analyze	analyse
paralyze	paralyse

Note that some words ending in –*ise* are the same for both British and Americans, for example:

advertise
compromise
exercise
premise
televise

Capitalization follows two basic rules—the first two rules cited below. Unfortunately, these two rules cannot begin to account for the number of exceptions and options facing writers who have to decide whether a word should be capitalized.

Because of the number of exceptions and options, this section includes many minor rules that supplement the two basic rules. Together, the basic and supplementary rules provide guidance, but you should also check an up-to date dictionary for additional guidance if the proper choice is still not clear. See REFERENCES.

Once you have decided whether to capitalize a word, record your decision in a list of editing reminders. Such a list will help you maintain consistent capitalization, especially if your document is long and complex. See EDITING AND PROOFREADING.

---

1. Capitalize the first letter of proper names—that is, those specific, one-of-a-kind names for a person, place, university or school, organization, religion, race, month or holiday, historic event, trade name, or titles of a person or of a document:

Capitals

1. Capitalize the first letter of proper names—that is, those specific, one-of-a-kind names for a person, place, university or school, organization, religion, race, month or holiday, historic event, trade name, or titles of a person or of a document.

2. Do not capitalize the first letter of common nouns—that is, those nouns that are general or generic.

3. Capitalize the first letter of the first word of sentences, quotations, and listed items (either phrases or sentences).

4. Capitalize the first letter of the names of directions when they indicate specific geographical areas. Do not capitalize the first letter of the names when they merely indicate a direction or a general or unspecified portion of a larger geographical area.

5. Capitalize the first letter of names for the Deity, names for the Bible and other sacred writings, names of religious bodies and their adherents, and names denoting the Devil.

6. Capitalize the first letter of the first word and all main words of headings and subheadings and of titles of books, articles, and other documents. Do not capitalize the first letter of the articles (*a, an,* and *the*), the coordinate conjunctions (*and, but, or, nor, for, so, yet*), or the short prepositions (*to, of,* etc.) unless they appear as the first word.

7. Capitalize in titles and headings the first letters of the initial word and of all later words in a hyphenated compound except for articles, short prepositions, and short conjunctions.

8. Capitalize the first letter of the geological names of eras, periods, systems, series, epochs, and ages.

9. In text, do not capitalize the first letter of a common noun used with a date, number, or letter merely to denote time or sequence.

10. Capitalize the first letter of proper nouns combined with common nouns, as in the names of plants, animals, diseases, and scientific laws or principles.

John F. Kennedy
Gail Anne Sawyer
Bill Gates
Jeanne Kirkpatrick
Henry Ford
Nancy Kassebaum
Sally

the Far East
China
the Eastern Shore (Maryland)
Massachusetts
Grove County
Baltimore City (or Baltimore)
United States of America
Lake Michigan
the Missouri River

the University of Utah
Western High School
the Golden Daycare Center

Shell Oil Company
the Prudential Life Insurance Co.
the American Legion
the Elks
the United Mine Workers
the Republican Party

Baptists
Judaism
Japanese
Hindus

May
September
Fourth of July
New Year's Day

the Reformation
World War I
Battle of Bull Run
the Crucifixion

Cyclone® (fence)
Xerox® copier
Band-Aids®
Kodak®
Coca-Cola®

Capitals

Mrs. Louise Lopez
Mr. Wing Phillips
Dr. Georgia Burke
Professor Robert Borson
Lieutenant Jeb Stuart

Handbook of Chemical Terms
The New York Times
The American Heritage Dictionary
"Time-Sharing" in *Training* magazine

See TITLES.

NOTE 1: In everyday English usage, the terms *capitalization* and *to capitalize* mean that only the initial letter of a word appears with a capital letter. So, rule 1 above would usually be clear to English speakers if written as follows: "Capitalize proper names . . . ." The expanded versions of rule 1 and the other rules in this discussion of capitals are intended to remove any ambiguities as to which letters in a word should be capitalized.

NOTE 2: As the many instances of lowercase *the* above indicate, *the* is usually not capitalized unless it has become part of the full official name:

The Hague
The Johns Hopkins University

NOTE 3: In lengthy proper names, conjunctions, short prepositions, and articles (*a, an,* and *the*) are not capitalized:

the Federal Republic of Germany
Johnson and Sons, Inc.
"Recovery of Oil in Plugged and Abandoned Wells"

See rule 6 in the following discussion.

NOTE 4: Capitalize the first letter of an individual's title only when it precedes the individual's proper name:

Professor George Stevens (*but* George Stevens, who is a professor . . .)

Captain Ellen Dobbs (*but* Ellen Dobbs, who is the captain of our company . . .)

President Henry Johnson (*but* Henry Johnson, president of Johnson Motors . . .)

See TITLES.

NOTE 5: Adjectives derived from proper names are capitalized only when the original sense is maintained:

a French word (*but* french fries)
Venetian art (*but* venetian blinds)

Even in these cases, dictionaries often differ; for instance, the current *American Heritage Dictionary* recommends *French fries* rather than the form preferred above. So, you often have to use your judgment. However, be consistent throughout a document.

2. Do not capitalize the first letter of common nouns—that is, those nouns that are general or generic:

a geologist
my accountant
the engineers
your secretary

a country
a planet
a river
north
the city

a trade school
college
high school
a holiday
the swing shift

a copier
the facial tissue

a foreman
my supervisor
the doctor

spring
fall

twentieth century
the thirties (*however,* the Gay Nineties)

See ARTICLES.

NOTE 1: One useful test to determine whether a noun is common is to ask if *a* or *an* does or can precede the noun in your context. If *a* or *an* makes sense before the noun, then the noun is common:

a pope (*but* the Pope)
an attorney
a U.S. senator

but

a President (*referring to any President of the United States*)

Because of special deference, the word *President* is always capitalized when it refers to any or all of the Presidents of the United States. This supersedes rule 2 above.

NOTE 2: Titles that follow a noun rather than precede it are not capitalized:

Theo Jones, who is our comptroller . . .
Betty Stevens, my secretary . . .
Rene Leon, who is a staff geophysicist . . .

NOTE 3: Common nouns separated from their proper nouns (or names) can occasionally be capitalized:

—Titles of high company officials, when the titles take the place of the officials' names:

We spoke to the President about the new labor policy.

The State Director has to sign before the plan goes into effect.

—Names of departments when they replace the whole name of the department:

We sent the letter to Accounting.

According to Maintenance, the pump had been replaced just last month.

—Names of countries, national divisions, governmental groups when the common noun replaces the full name (often in internal government correspondence):

From the beginning of the Republic, a balance of powers was necessary.

The State submitted a brief as a friend of the court.

The Department has a policy against overtime for employees at professional levels.

The House sent a bill to the Conference Committee.

—Names of close family members used in place of their proper names, especially in direct address:

Please understand, Mother, that I intend to pay my fair share.

Before leaving I spoke to Mother, Father, and Uncle George.

NOTE 4: Capitalize plural common nouns following two or more proper nouns unless the common nouns represent topographical features (such as lakes, rivers, mountains, oceans, and so on):

West and South High Schools
the Korean and Vietnam Wars
the State and Defense Departments

but

the Mississippi and Missouri rivers
the Wasatch and Uinta mountains
the Pacific and Indian oceans

---

3. Capitalize the first letter of the first word of sentences, quotations, and listed items (either phrases or sentences):

Researchers propose to complete eight projects this year.

The technical specifications stated: "All wing strut pins should have a 150 percent load factor."

The accountant discussed the following issues:

—Budget design
—Cost overruns
—Entry postings

NOTE: The first letter of a word following a colon or a dash within a sentence is often capitalized, although some editors prefer not to. A good rule of thumb is that full sentences and long quotations (usually sentences) begin with a capital letter after a colon or dash:

The Bible states: "The race is not to the swift."

We followed one principle: Short-term investments must be consistent with long-term goals.

or

We followed one principle—Short-term investments must be consistent with long-term goals.

4. Capitalize the first letter of the names of directions when they indicate specific geographical areas. Do not capitalize the first letter of the names when they merely indicate a direction or a general or unspecified portion of a larger geographical area:

the Deep South
the Midwest
the Near East
the North
the Northwest

blowing from the southeast
eastern Missouri
southern Italy
the northern Midwest
toward the south
traveling north

5. Capitalize the first letter of names for the Deity, names for the Bible and other sacred writings, names of religious bodies and their adherents, and names denoting the Devil:

Christ
God
He, Him
Messiah
Son of Man
the Almighty
Thee
Allah
Zeus

God's Word
the Good Book
the Old Testament
the Word
the Koran

Baha'is
a Lutheran
an Episcopalian
Episcopal Church
Lutheran Church
a Muslim
Buddhists

His Satanic Majesty
Satan
the Great Malevolence
Pluto

6. Capitalize the first letter of the first word and all main words of headings and subheadings and of titles of books, articles, and other documents. Do not capitalize the first letter of the articles (*a, an,* and *the*), the coordinate conjunctions (*and, but, or, nor, for, so, yet*), or the short prepositions (*to, of,* etc.) unless they appear as the first word:

"An Examination of Church-State Relations"
Declaration of Independence
MacUser
The Geology of East Texas
"The Greening of Panama" in *Scientific American*

See HEADINGS.

---

7. Capitalize in titles and headings the first letters of the initial word and of all later words in a hyphenated compound except for articles, short prepositions, and short conjunctions.

See rule 6 above.

A Report on Tin-Lined Acid Converters
Up-to Date Power-Driven Extraction Methodologies
State-of-the-Art Technology
Seventy-Five World Leaders as Voting Representatives

---

8. Capitalize the first letter of the geological names of eras, periods, systems, series, epochs, and ages:

Jurassic Period
Late Cretaceous
Little Willow
Paleozoic Era
Upper Triassic

NOTE 1: Unless they are part of a proper name, do **not** capitalize structural terms such as *arch, basin, formation, zone, field, pay, pool, dome, uplift, anticline, reservoir,* or *trend* when they combine with geological names:

Capitals

Cincinnati arch
Delaware basin
East Texas field
Ozark uplift

NOTE 2: Experts disagree about the capitalization of *upper, middle, lower* and *late, middle, early.* The following list from the *United States Government Printing Office Style Manual* (1984) provides the best summary of the difficult capitalization conventions in this technical area. Note that both *upper Oligocene* and *Upper Devonian* are correct, although the capitalization of *upper* is inconsistent:

Alexandrian
Animikie
Atoka
Cambrian:
  Upper, Late
  Middle, Middle
  Lower, Early
Carboniferous Systems
Cayuga
Cenozoic
Cincinnatian
Chester
Coahuila
Comanche
Cretaceous:
  Upper, Late
  Lower, Early
Des Moines
Devonian:
  Upper, Late
  Middle, Middle
  Lower, Early
Eocene:
  upper, late
  middle, middle
  lower, early
glacial:
  interglacial
  postglacial
  preglacial
Glenarm
Grand Canyon
Grenville
Guadalupe
Gulf
Gunnison River
Holocene
Jurassic:
  Upper, Late
  Middle, Middle
  Lower, Early
Keweenawan
Kinderhook
Leonard
Little Willow
Llano
Meramec
Mesozoic:
  pre-Mesozoic
  post-Mesozoic

Miocene:
  upper, late
  middle, middle
  lower, early
Mississippian:
  Upper, Late
  Lower, Early
Missouri
Mohawkian
Morrow
Niagara
Ochoa
Ocoee
Oligocene:
  upper, late
  middle, middle
  lower, early
Osage
Ordovician:
  Upper, Late
  Middle, Middle
  Lower, Early
Pahrump
Paleocene:
  upper, late
  middle, middle
  lower, early
Paleozoic
Pennsylvanian:
  Upper, Late
  Middle, Middle
  Lower, Early
Permian:
  Upper, Late
  Lower, Early
Pleistocene
Pliocene:
  upper, late
  middle, middle
  lower, early
Precambrian:
  upper
  middle
  lower
Quaternary
red beds
Shasta
Silurian:
  Upper, Late
  Middle, Middle
  Lower, Early
St. Croixan
Tertiary
Triassic:
  Upper, Late
  Middle, Middle
  Lower, Early
Virgil
Wolfcamp
Yavapai

NOTE 3: Topographical terms are usually capitalized, but the general terms *province* and *section* are not:

Hudson Valley
Interior Highlands
Middle Rocky Mountains
Ozark Plateaus
Uinta Basin

but

Navajo section
Pacific Border province

---

9. In text, do not capitalize the first letter of a common noun used with a date, number, or letter merely to denote time or sequence:

appendix A
collection 3
drawing 8
figure 5
page 45
paragraph 2
plate VI
section c
volume III

NOTE 1: The first letter of these common nouns should be capitalized if they appear in headings, titles, or captions: *Appendix A* or *Figure 5.*

NOTE 2: In these cases, *no., #,* or *No.* (for *Number*) is unnecessary:

Appendix A (*not* Appendix No. A)
page 45 (*not* page no. 45)
site 5 (*not* site #5)

NOTE 3: Some technical and scientific fields do capitalize a common noun used with a date, number, or letter. For example, The Society of Petroleum Engineers recommends in its *Style Guide* that writers observe the following style of capitalization in text:

Method 3
Sample 2
Table 4
Wells A22 and B7

---

10. Capitalize the first letter of proper nouns combined with common nouns, as in the names of plants, animals, diseases, and scientific laws or principles:

Boyle's law
Brittany spaniel
Cooper's hawk
Down's syndrome
Fremont silktassel
Gunn effect
Hodgkin's disease
Virginia clematis

Captions for graphics include the title and any explanatory material immediately under (or sometimes over) a graphic. Readers initially identify graphics using conventional references: *Figure 14, Map 3, Chart 16*, etc. However, readers' eyes need to be guided beyond mere identification.

Good captions are what guide readers not only to see but also to understand. Good captions both label graphics with titles and explain to readers what they are seeing and how to interpret the information captured in the graphic.

See GRAPHICS FOR DOCUMENTS and GRAPHICS FOR PRESENTATIONS. See also CHARTS, GRAPHS, ILLUSTRATIONS, MAPS, PHOTOGRAPHS, and TABLES.

Good captions are interpretive and informative. In some types of writing, such captions are even called "action captions" because they urge readers to make a decision or take an action.

A graphic and its caption should be clear and understandable without requiring readers to search for clarifying information in the text.

As an example, for some years now, *Scientific American* has used "stand alone" captions for their graphics. *Scientific American* has also discontinued even referencing graphics by title and number in their text. So a graphic in *Scientific American* does not have a label and title such as *Figure 4—A Peruvian Burial Site*. Instead, the caption begins by explaining and interpreting: *In a typical Peruvian burial site, the funereal jewelry signified . . . .*

Captions

1. Use interpretive captions whenever possible.

2. Avoid using short, often ambiguous, titles to replace interpretive captions.

3. Number figures and tables sequentially throughout the document, and place the number before the caption.

4. Use periods following interpretive captions but no punctuation following short captions that are not sentences.

5. Captions may appear below or above the visual, but be consistent throughout a document.

---

1. Use interpretive captions whenever possible.

Interpretive captions provide both a title and explanatory information (usually expressed in a complete sentence) to help readers understand the central point(s) that you want the graphic to convey:

Figure 4. Cabin-Temperature Control System. *Constant cabin temperature control is maintained by the system's modulated cabin sensor.*

Figure 23. Check Valve. *The risk of bad air entering the chamber is near zero because the check valve permits air flow in one direction only.*

Table 17. Air Intersect Data. *Only stations 23 and 45 experienced significant increases in CO levels during the study period.*

The figure 4 interpretive caption gives the title of the figure and then emphasizes that the cabin has a constant temperature—a benefit provided by the feature (modulated cabin sensor) described in the figure. The caption states clearly what the writer wants the reader to learn from the graphic.

The figure 23 interpretive caption gives the title and then tells the reader the principal message—that the check valve provides near-zero risk. Further, it states **how** the check valve provides near-zero risk.

The table 17 interpretive caption names the data in the table and then highlights significant data. By pointing out what is most important in the table, the caption helps the reader interpret the table, which might be very complex, and reinforces the major points that the writer will make in the text.

The following are additional examples of interpretive captions for figures and tables:

Figure 1. Axial-Flow Design. *The axial-flow design has the greatest performance potential.*

Figure 2. Life-Cycle Cost Projections. *General Framitz's design-to-cost strategy will guarantee low life-cycle costs.*

Figure 3. Project Management System. *Our project management software ensures maximum responsiveness to user requirements at all levels.*

Table 1. Population Impacts. *If population redistribution trends continue, the Southwest will exceed baseline figures by 1996.*

Table 2. Cost of Mitigation Measures. *The socioeconomic mitigation measures proposed are effective but very costly.*

Figure 4. Seasonal Streamflow Patterns. *Keta River and White Creek peak in mid-October during Snow Geese migration and provide the only suitable feeding and resting habitat within a radius of 150 miles.*

Table 3. Projections of New Jobs During the Next 10 Years. *Contrary to media opinion, the Thunder Basin Project will create—not destroy—jobs in the Sequaw Valley: at least 500 within the next 10 years.*

Figure 5. Test Results of Thermal Model 2. *Flame-envelope thermal Model 2 results in lower ambient temperatures but produces diffuse radiation.*

Figure 6. Limits of Multiplexer Design. The analog input multiplexer design limits components that are not included in self-testing to a few passive components.

NOTE: You can create interpretive captions without using complete sentences or a separate title—if the captions tell readers how to read and interpret the graphic:

Figure 14. Declining Production Through the 1980s

or

Figure 14. *Declining production through the 1980s*

In these examples (both acceptable versions of a caption), the title for the figure is combined with a phrase telling readers about the production trend during the 1980s. As the two examples illustrate, you can use either boldface type or italics to highlight the caption.

A longer version of the figure 14 caption would include a separate title and then add a complete sentence interpreting the figure:

Figure 14. Production (1980–1989). *Production declined steadily through the 1980s.*

Whether or not an interpretive caption is a complete sentence, it should provide a point of view on the graphic. It tells readers not only what the graphic is about but also what the graphic means.

2. Avoid using short, often ambiguous, titles to replace interpretive captions.

In the past, many technical and scientific documents used only short, simple titles (captions) for graphics.

Figure 3. A Horse

Figure 4. Schematic 23–A

In figure 3, surely a reader could see that the image was of a horse, so this title is worthless. The title should give some interpretive information: *Figure 3. A typical Arabian stallion in full gallop.*

Similarly, the title for figure 4 may be somewhat useful, especially if the figures include a number of different schematics. However, the writer probably should include information about how schematic 23–A relates to 23–B or how 23–A is different from 22.

Titles that provide minimum information are often so short and cryptic that they sound telegraphic:

Table 2. Problem Options

Table 14. Water and Soil Impacts

Telegraphic captions are only appropriate when the graphics are self-explanatory, thus requiring no interpretation. But even then, the telegraphic style can be confusing. In the above examples, for instance, are the table 2 options really problems, or are the options solutions to a single problem? Similarly, does table 14 include water impacts as well as soil impacts, or is the subject some sort of data about water and a separate presentation about impacts on soil types? As these examples illustrate, avoid telegraphic captions.

3. Number figures and tables sequentially throughout the document, and place the number before the caption.

Figures and tables should be numbered sequentially as they appear in the document. If you present an important figure or table twice, treat it as two separate visuals and number each according to its position in the sequence. See GRAPHICS FOR DOCUMENTS.

Figure and table numbers should be whole numbers: *Figure 1, Figure 2, Figure 3,* etc. If you are numbering graphics by chapter, then use an en dash to separate chapter number from graphics number: *Figure 14–2* (chapter 14, figure 2), *Table 2–8* (chapter 2, table 8). You can also use the decimal numbering system with an end dash to designate graphics numbers within a section of a report if the report's sections have been numbered decimally: *Figure 23.2–1* (section 23.2, figure 1), *Table 7.4–13* (section 7.4, table 13). If the graphic has several parts and you need to identify all parts, use parentheses and lowercase alphabetical characters to designate subparts: *Figure 34(a), Figure 34(b), Figure 34(c).* See DASHES.

NOTE 1: The style of punctuation for captions varies. Some editors prefer a colon or a period and a dash following the number. Some editors prefer no punctuation and leave three or four spaces between the number and the caption. Each version is acceptable.

Figure 14–2: Federal Shipbuilding and Repair Budget

Figure 14–2.—Federal Shipbuilding and Repair Budget

Figure 14–2   Federal Shipbuilding and Repair Budget

NOTE 2: In captions, the words *figure* and *table* should be capitalized. However, when you are referring to graphics in the text, even if you refer to a specific graphic, do not capitalize *figure* or *table* unless it begins a sentence:

> As shown in figure 33, . . .
>
> According to table 14.2–4, . . .
>
> *however*
>
> Figure 33 shows . . .
>
> Table 14.2–4 presents . . .

See CAPITALS.

4. Use periods following interpretive captions but no punctuation following short captions that are not sentences.

Interpretive captions are usually complete sentences and should therefore end with a period. Short captions, on the other hand, are like titles or headings and are normally not complete sentences, so they require no punctuation.

If you mix interpretive and telegraphic captions, end all of them with periods. See LISTS and PERIODS.

5. Captions may appear below or above the visual, but be consistent throughout a document.

Some graphics specialists argue that captions should always appear above graphics because a caption (which comes from the word *head*) ia like a title. Others argue that captions should always appear below graphics because the graphics are more important than the captions and placing captions below their graphics is more aesthetic. Still others argue that captions for tables should appear above tables but captions for figures should appear below figures.

When captions are used with slides and other projected visual aids, put the caption above the visual for better visibility. Captions placed at the bottom may be blocked by the heads of those seated in front. See GRAPHICS FOR PRESENTATIONS.

Be consistent. Treat tables no differently from figures. If you're going to place captions above or below graphics, then do so throughout your document.

Charts

Charts are some of the most valuable and frequently used types of graphics. Unfortunately, the term *chart* has different meanings for different people.

Webster's New Collegiate Dictionary defines *chart* as a map, table, graph, or diagram. That definition exemplifies the confusion many people have over the names of different types of graphics. Originally, *chart* meant a document, although most charts were maps. When maps were combined with tabular data (e.g., the mileage charts on modern road maps), *chart* came to mean a tabular or matrix display.

For the purposes of this *Style Guide*, charts are graphics that do not rely on numerical interpretations. These include **organizational charts**, **flow charts**, and **schedule charts**.

In contrast to charts, graphs are graphics that do rely on numerical interpretations, especially showing how one variable (such as time) relates to another variable (e.g., production or dollars). The graphics discussed in the GRAPHS entry include line (or coordinate) graphs, bar graphs, and circle (pie) graphs. In everyday language, however, bar graphs and pie graphs are often called bar charts and pie charts.

Don't let confusion between the terms *chart* and *graph* bother you. The best graphics are those that rapidly and effectively communicate their central ideas, regardless of what one might call them. See GRAPHS, GRAPHICS FOR DOCUMENTS, and GRAPHICS FOR PRESENTATIONS.

Charts

1. Use a flow chart, an organizational chart, or a schedule chart to help readers visualize easily the major points in a document.

2. Orient horizontally all letters, numbers, words, and phrases in headings, legends, and labels.

3. Number each chart sequentially, provide a title, and then add an informative caption to identify the purpose of the chart.

4. Place footnotes and source information below charts.

Organizational Charts

5. Use squares or rectangles to indicate divisions and subdivisions within the organization.

6. Structure an organizational chart from the top down.

7. Use solid lines between boxes to indicate direct relationships and dotted or dashed lines to indicate indirect relationships.

Flow Charts

8. Choose a standard system of symbols to indicate the types of activities and the control or transfer points.

9. Place the starting activity in the upper left corner of the chart and proceed to the right and down. Place the ending activity in the lower right corner of the chart.

10. Break large or complicated flow charts into smaller, simpler flow charts.

11. Use arrows to show the sequence or direction of flow within flow charts.

Schedule Charts

12. List activities in chronological order beginning at the top of the page and moving down.

13. Clearly label or identify the bars.

14. If appropriate, indicate milestones on the chart.

15. Use bar patterns to identify groups of related activities. If you do so, also include an explanation block or legend telling what the patterns represent.

1. Use a flow chart, an organizational chart, or a schedule chart to help readers visualize easily the major points in a document.

These charts should not be mere decoration. If they capture for readers the major points or themes in a document, they will be serving their intended purpose.

Remember that a chart is only as good as the effect it creates. Charts should communicate quickly and simply. They should be integrated with the text and should convey information more forcefully or dramatically than is possible in text.

In many documents, using one of these three charts will allow you to replace unnecessary text. A flow chart, for example, can be a very effective way to visualize the steps in a manufacturing process or in a political negotiation. A chart both replaces text and provides a visual road map that readers can use as they read dense and complicated text. A chart also helps readers recall or review what the document said.

If you can combine chart types to convey a rich, unusual, interesting, or dramatic message, then do so. You do not gain extra points for adhering strictly to some predetermined form. Let your purpose, readers, medium, data, and ideas dictate the form of chart (or other graphics) that would be most effective.

2. Orient horizontally all letters, numbers, words, and phrases in headings, legends, and labels.

All of the letters, numbers, and words on a chart should be readable from one reading perspective. Readers should not have to rotate the page to read different parts of a chart.

See the figures later in this discussion for examples of how to present letters, numbers, and words.

3. Number each chart sequentially, provide a title, and then add an informative caption to identify the purpose of the chart.

Charts and all other graphics are sequentially numbered and labeled as figures, so the numbering would be *Figure 1*, *Figure 2*, etc. Or, if the document has chapters, *Figure 1–1*, *Figure 1–2*, *Figure 1–3*, where the first number is the chapter number.

Following *Figure* and the number

comes the title of the chart:

Figure 3–1. Organizational Structure of the Finance Department

Then, provide an informative or interpretive caption to help readers understand the message of the chart:

Figure 3–1. Organizational Structure of the Finance Department. *Following the 1995 reorganization, all accounting personnel report to a single assistant departmental manager.*

See Captions.

4. Place footnotes and source information below charts.

Footnotes typically explain or clarify the information appearing in the entire chart or in one small part of it. Often, footnotes tell what the data apply to, where they came from, or how accurate they are:

[1]All project times are rounded up to full days.

[2]For the two regional offices only; the head office uses a different support organization.

[3]According to the National Stockmen's Council. The solid lines reflect the current policy for who reports to whom. The dotted lines reflect the earlier lines of authority, which still are important even though outdated.

The footnotes for each chart are numbered independently from footnotes in the text and from footnotes in other graphics. Begin with footnote 1 and proceed sequentially for that single graphic; for the next graphic, start the numbering again. Within the body of the chart, use superscripted footnote numbers. Place the footnote explanations (in numerical order) immediately below the chart and flush with the left margin. Repeat the superscripted footnote number and then provide the appropriate explanation, followed by a period.

If the chart covers more than one

page, place the appropriate footnotes with each page. If both a caption and footnote appear below a chart, place the footnotes after the caption.

If footnote numbers would be confusing in the body of the chart, use letters ([a], [b], [c], [d], etc.), asterisks (*, **, ***), or other symbols.

Source information may appear in footnotes if the referenced source provides only the data indicated by the footnote and not the data for the rest of the chart:

[4]From *The Wall Street Journal*, May 14, 1995.

[5]Source: U.S. Department of the Interior, Bureau of Land Management.

Source information may also appear within parentheses in the caption (regardless of where the caption appears) or within brackets under the caption if the caption appears ahead of the chart:

Figure 1. U.S. Aerospace Mergers and Acquisitions, 1960–1995 (U.S. Department of Commerce)

Figure 1. U.S. Aerospace Mergers and Acquisitions, 1960–1995

[U.S. Department of Commerce]

See Footnotes, Citations, and Intellectual Property.

Organizational Charts

Organizational charts depict the structure of an organization. These charts typically show the divisions and subdivisions of the organization; the hierarchy and relationship of the groups to one another; lines of control (responsibility and authority); and lines of communication and coordination. Organizational charts help readers visualize the structure of an organization and the relationships within it. Figure 1 is an example of an organizational chart showing how an engineering department is organized.

Charts

5. Use squares or rectangles to indicate divisions and subdivisions within the organization.

The conventional means of indicating divisions, subdivisions, groups, project teams, functional areas, etc., is to enclose the name of the organizational unit within a square or rectangle. Optionally, the squares can also contain the names of people filling the positions, but such a person-by-person chart for large organizations can be too long and complex, and it is quickly out of date because of transfers and reassignments.

You might distinguish between higher and lower units by changing the size of the rectangle or by changing its border (from boldface or thick lines representing upper-level units to thinner, normal lines representing lower-level units). In figure 1, for example, the box around the V.P. rectangle is a heavier ruled line.

6. Structure an organizational chart from the top down.

This rule reflects the way we read and our perception and understanding of organizational structure.

Readers of English read from left to right and from top to bottom. Therefore, an organizational chart should be structured from left to right and top to bottom. The left-to-right progression might or might not be useful, depending on the type of organization you are depicting. However, the top-to-bottom progression is always useful, simply because almost all organizations are based on a hierarchy.

Accordingly, you should display the structure of the organization in descending order of authority—with the highest authority or level at

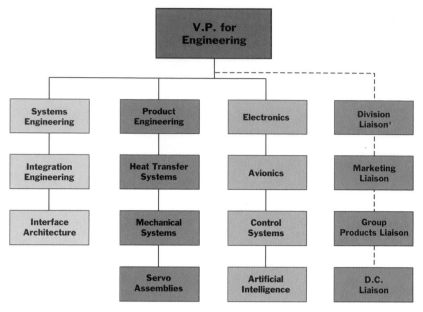

¹The acting manager of the Division Liaison Office is Frank Jason. He will return to the Public Affairs Office when a permanent manager is appointed.

Figure 1. Engineering Department Organization. *Besides those who report directly to her (shown in the boxes connected with solid lines), the Vice President oversees the Division Liaison office (shown in the boxes connected with dashed lines) to ensure that all lobbying in Washington, D.C., complies with Federal Acquisition Regulations.*

the top of the chart and the lowest authorities or levels at the bottom of the chart. This structure reflects the metaphor of top-down management and thus reinforces the readers' expectations about organizational structure.

If the organization you are describing does not operate on a top-down basis, be inventive and create an organizational display that does reflect the organization's operational style and structure. As in some of the recent discussions of quality circles or bottom-up activities, you might want to start with clusters of employees at the bottom of your chart, adding dotted lines showing how these employee clusters interact (see rule 7).

7. Use solid lines between boxes to indicate direct relationships and dotted or dashed lines to indicate indirect relationships.

Solid lines usually show direct lines of control. Dashed or dotted lines usually indicate lines of communication or coordination.

In figure 1, the dashed lines through the rectangles along the right side of the chart indicate that the Vice President for Engineering coordinates with the Division Liaison office and has lines of communication and coordination down through the Division Liaison organization, but the Vice President's direct authority extends only through Systems Engineering, Product Engineering, and Electronics.

Flow Charts

Flow charts depict a process. They show readers the parts of a process and how those parts are related. Processes include manufacturing systems (as shown in figures 2 and 3), decision-making processes within an organization, audit processes (with checks and balances), biological or physical processes (as shown in figure 4), or any other process that moves from a start to a finish.

8. Choose a standard system of symbols to indicate the types of activities and the control or transfer points.

Squares and rectangles typically indicate activities or steps in the process. In figure 2, for instance, the upper left rectangle represents "Ore Crushing," the first activity taking place in this ore processing system. The arrow linking this rectangle to the rectangle directly to the right indicates that, after being crushed, the ore undergoes a chemical bath.

The arrows indicate the sequence of activities in the process and show a chronological (and sometimes cause-and-effect) relationship between linked activities or control points.

Circles typically indicate control or transfer points. Control points are those points in the process where the activities are monitored, started, stopped, or in some other way controlled. Transfer points are those points where the sequence of activity leaves one flow chart and continues on to another. In figure 2, the two right-most circles indicate that the ore has been processed and is ready for packaging. To continue following the process, the reader must go to the packaging flow chart, which is shown in figure 3.

The "Pack" circles in figure 2 represent all of figure 3. Consequently, figure 2 is the more general flow chart. If "Ore Crushing" involved a series of steps, the writer could have turned the "Ore Crushing" symbol in figure 2 into a circle and then constructed another subordinate

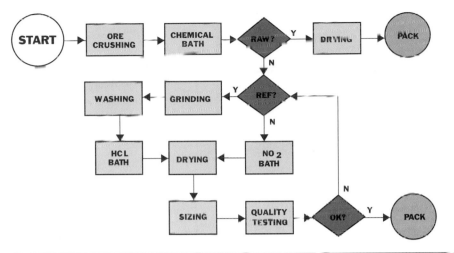

Figure 2. Ore Processing. *The quality and quantity of the ore is checked at three decision points, indicated by blue diamonds and Y (yes) and N (no) labels. Customers can opt to receive raw (semifinished) ore directly without additional refining or extra packaging.*

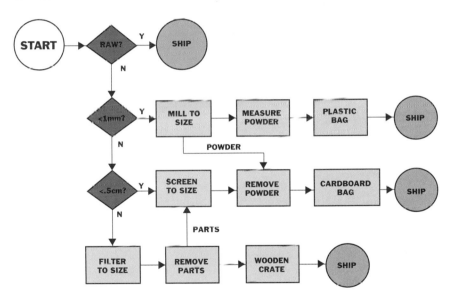

Figure 3. Packaging Options for Ore. *Customers can choose four packaging options. Raw (semifinished) ore is shipped in bulk by railway cars. Refined ore (in varying sizes) is shipped in three ways: (1) in sealed plastic bags, (2) in cardboard boxes, and (3) in wooden crates.*

flow chart (like figure 3) that represented all of the activities involved in crushing the ore.

Note that by putting all of the packaging activities into one subordinate flow chart, the writer has avoided significant repetition in figure 2.

Diamonds typically represent decision points. Often, as in figures 2 and 3, decisions are represented by

simple yes/no questions. Diamonds normally have three lines linking them to other symbols: one incoming line indicating what precedes the decision, one outgoing line indicating "yes," and the other outgoing line indicating "no."

The flow chart in figure 4 differs from figures 2 and 3. In figure 4, the boxes represent a conceptual sequence of possible effects, originating with the initial cause (the harvesting of a

Charts

Figure 4. Potential Effects of a Timber Harvest on Deer Populations. *The most positive scenario (the blue boxes) would increase the deer population. The other two scenarios (the brown boxes) would each decrease the deer population. Further analysis in the text would lead to a resolution between opposing scenarios. Note that the numbers on the boxes are for reference only, not to reflect the sequence of causes and effects.*

stand of Douglas-fir timber). Similar cause-and-effect figures would be possible throughout the physical and social sciences. For instance, in a social context, a flow chart might present the sequence of events if the government decided to subsidize automobiles with engines that did not use gasoline. Effects would flow through consumers to manufacturers, with possible feedback loops to government.

Other symbol systems for flow charts are possible, particularly in data processing and other specialized fields, such as architecture and electrical engineering. These symbols often have very specific meanings and have become traditional means of expression in particular scientific and technical applications. If you need to create flow charts for these specialized areas, consult appropriate trade journals and textbooks.

9. Place the starting activity in the upper left corner of the chart

and proceed to the right and down. Place the ending activity in the lower right corner of the chart.

Readers will expect the flow chart to begin in the upper left corner. Don't disappoint them. If possible, try to end the flow chart in the lower right corner.

10. Break large or complicated flow charts into smaller, simpler flow charts.

Flow charts that become too large or too complicated are unreadable as well as intimidating. To avoid repetition and to keep flow charts from becoming too long, break them into general (overview) charts and subordinate (component) charts.

After breaking up a flow chart, you must also decide just what parts of it to use in your document. Do your readers need the subordinate charts to understand your information, or

would the overall chart be sufficiently detailed?

In many instances, you can retain the overall chart in your document while putting the subordinate charts in an appendix or attachment. See Appendices.

11. Use arrows to show the sequence or direction of flow within flow charts.

Flow charts with activities or control points linked only by lines are often confusing. Place an arrow head on the end of the line to indicate the sequence or direction of flow (see figures 2 and 3).

Arrows are sometimes unnecessary. Notice in figure 4 that arrows are unnecessary because the flow is obviously from left to right; in addition, each square is numbered for easy reference and discussion.

Schedule Charts

Schedule charts are horizontal charts used to schedule tasks, projects, and programs.

Schedule charts are also called *time charts* or *timelines*. Other terms are also possible, especially to reflect some of the more sophisticated scheduling software. For example, critical path schedules are merely sophisticated schedule charts that link up to show whether items are concurrent or sequential.

Schedule charts help readers visualize a sequence of activity occurring over an extended period. They help readers see how sequential and concurrent activities are related to one another in time and how activities depend on one another for completion on schedule.

The horizontal (x) axis in schedule charts is always time. Time may be represented in decades, years, quarters, months, weeks, days, or hours. If necessary or helpful to readers, include more than one level of time on the x-axis (see figure 6). To make schedule charts easier to read, use vertical dotted or dashed lines to mark major time periods (see figures 5 and 6).

12.   List activities in chronological order beginning at the top of the page and moving down.

Schedule charts suggest strict chronology. Do not violate the

Figure 5. F27AF Production Schedule. *To shorten production time, we have scheduled each phase (shaded red) to begin before the prior phase is finished. These savings in time are possible because of our self-funded R&D work with the F27AF program.*

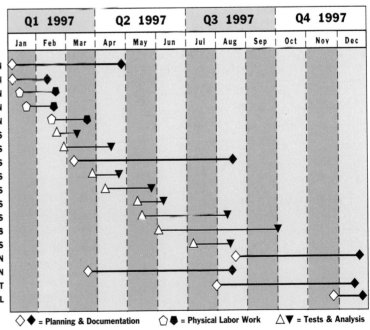

Figure 6. Schedule of Recombinant Tests and Documentation. *As the bars with the diamonds indicate, planning and documentation efforts are concurrent with the lab work (pentagons) and tests (triangles). As this schedule suggests, documentation should never be left until all the research work is finished.*

Charts

readers' expectation that the events listed from top to bottom along the vertical (y) axis will appear in chronological order.

13. Clearly label or identify the bars.

Always identify what each bar represents, either with a bar label along the left margin or with an explanation block (as in figure 5). Traditionally, the bar labels appear on the left side of the chart.

14. If appropriate, indicate milestones on the chart.

Milestones may be indicated with small circles, dots, or triangles. If you have reporting, control, or performance deadlines that constitute milestones for tracking and monitoring progress, then indicate them on the chart.

15. Use bar patterns to identify groups of related activities. If you do so, also include an explanation block or legend telling what the patterns represent.

Bar patterns (see the discussion of bar graphs in GRAPHS) can be used to indicate similar or identical activities that occur at different times. In figure 5, for instance, all airframe-production activities are shown with wave-patterned bars. The bars representing engine-production activities have a wide-left hatch pattern. These patterns enable readers to see how related activities fit within the whole sequence.

If you use bar patterns, always include an explanation block to the right or at the bottom of the chart.

Using colors as in figure 5 is increasingly desirable. Remember, however, that colors may not reproduce adequately in a black and white copy, so the patterns provide an additional tool for distinguishing between bars. See COLOR.

Citations (bibliographic entries) enable writers to identify in the text itself the sources of their information. The methods of citation vary, depending on the technical field and its traditions, the type of publication, and the publisher.

The method of citation that we recommend represents the standard convention in the physical sciences and engineering disciplines. However, if you are writing for a particular professional society or technical journal, you should follow its method of citation.

1. Enclose the author's name and the date of the publication in parentheses following the material quoted or the ideas referred to. Attach at the end of the text an alphabetical list of the cited works:

> One critic called the whole dispute a "galaxy of confusion" (Jameson 1976). In reply, the spokesman for the conservative wing rebutted Jameson point by point (S. Clarke 1977).

See BIBLIOGRAPHIES.

NOTE 1: This system, or some variation of it, is favored by physical and biological scientists, as well as many social scientists. Scholars in the humanities sometimes still use footnotes. See FOOTNOTES.

NOTE 2: An alternative method uses only numbers in the text, not the author's last name and date:

> One critic called the whole dispute a "galaxy of confusion" (1). In reply, the spokesman for the conservative wing rebutted Jameson point by point (2).

or

> One critic called the whole dispute a "galaxy of confusion" [1]. In reply, the spokesman for the conservative wing rebutted Jameson point by point [2].

The numbers appearing within parentheses or brackets are keyed to an unalphabetical list of sources at the end of the text.

NOTE 3: With only a few citations and if you want to omit the final alphabetical list, follow the footnote format within the text:

> Sinclair Jameson in *Age of Change* (New York: Freedom Press, 1993) called the whole dispute a "galaxy of confusion."

See FOOTNOTES.

2. Use a consistent format for citing the name of the author and the date of publication:

> (Jakobson 1994)
> (Bains and Fveslong 1993)
> (Federal Science Committee 1995)
> (Smithson, Haarke, and Bruppe 1991)
> (U.S. Department of Agriculture 1994)

NOTE: Some authors and journals prefer to place a comma between the author and the date:

> (Jakobson, 1994)

Another common variation is to include the page number or volume and page number following the date:

> (Jakobson 1994, 43–48)

The abbreviations *p.* and *pp.* (for *page* and *pages)* are unnecessary:

> (Bains and Eveslong 1993, 156)
> (Federal Science Committee 1995, 2:34–36)

In the last example, *2* is the volume number.

Whatever the format used, you should be consistent in your method of citation within the same document.

3. Include a full alphabetized list of cited sources following the article or chapter:

Book by one single author

> Bricke, Larry N. 1994. *Canadian Political Parties.* Toronto: New Country Press.

Book by two authors

> Campbell, Josiah, and Wallace Daugherly. 1996. *Conflict in the Provinces.* Edmonton, Alberta: The Royal Penny Press.

Journal or magazine article

> Mahoney, Edward G. 1993. "A Dissident's View of Canadian Politics." *The Political Review* 2:56–59.

NOTE 1: In these bibliographic entries, the date of publication comes immediately after the name of the author. In a common optional format, the date appears after the name of the publisher:

> Bricke, Larry N. *Canadian Political Parties.* Toronto: New Country Press, 1994.

See BIBLIOGRAPHIES.

NOTE 2: The titles may be underlined rather than italicized if italics is not available.

Cliches are worn-out phrases that were originally effective, even vivid:

innocent bystander
irony of fate
too funny for words
cool as a cucumber
moot point
far and wide

Such phrases are so common that writers and speakers use them habitually, without thinking. Their familiarity makes cliches convenient. So, when writers are struggling to express an idea, using a cliche becomes a tempting alternative to serious thought. See WORDY PHRASES.

The Origin of Cliches

The word *cliche* comes from French and is often still written with the French accent: *cliché*. Writers of English typically omit the accent mark because the word has been anglicized. See SPELLING.

Many cliches were originally metaphors and were therefore vivid. Their wittiness and sparkle made them memorable, so they were repeated often. However, the vividness of the original metaphor is dulled by repetition and the expression becomes a cliche.

The first person in medieval Europe to associate the concept of avoidance with the Black Death must have created a vivid image in listeners' minds. But today's users of the expression *to avoid it like the plague* experience little if any of the original effect. Today, the cliche means little. We've heard it too often.

Other cliches developed and survived because they sounded good:

bag and baggage

---

rack and ruin
not wisely but too well
snug as a bug in a rug
willy-nilly

The alliteration (repetition of consonants) and repetition of *bag* in the expression *bag and baggage* likely ensured the phrase's survival. Similarly, *willy-nilly* has survived so long that its original meaning has been lost: "whether you are willing or unwilling." Now *willy-nilly* implies haphazard or weak actions. The logical choice in its original meaning has faded. Now the cliche has more sound than substance.

---

1. Use cliches sparingly, if at all.

Writers would find eliminating **all** cliches a hard row to hoe. Reasonable cliches are fine in certain contexts, but the one in the preceding sentence is clearly inappropriate. The context of this discussion makes a cliche based on farm work ridiculous.

However, some cliches—in the right context—are valuable:

Following the testimony, the judge had to sift through 1,000 pages of unreadable and often contradictory testimony.

Here, the cliche of *sifting through* many pages is not objectionable. It is, in fact, a fine metaphor, given the circumstance to which it applies. In this case, the cliche does not clash with the context.

So one test of a cliche's acceptability is the degree to which it is relevant to the context in which it occurs and the extent to which it goes unnoticed. If the cliche does not call attention to itself, it is probably

acceptable. The moment a writer (or reader) knows the expression is a cliche, it is unacceptable in most contexts.

NOTE: Sometimes a cliche can be used to advantage if its meaning or phrasing allows the writer to play against the cliche itself, as in the following quote from Oscar Wilde:

"Truth is never pure, and rarely simple."

By rephrasing the cliche, Wilde asks readers to reexamine the cliche about *pure and simple truth*.

Some Common Cliches

English contains hundreds of cliches. The following list includes some of the more common ones currently in use:

A bad scene
a can of worms
acid test
active consideration
add insult to injury
agree to disagree
all things considered
all too soon
along these lines
among those present
ample opportunity
an end run
armed to the teeth
as a matter of fact
as the crow flies
at a loss for words
at one fell swoop
attached hereto
at this point in time
auspicious moment
avoid it like the plague
awaiting further orders

Back at the ranch
back to the drawing board
bag and baggage
bated breath
beat a hasty retreat
be at loggerheads
beginning of the end
benefit of the doubt
best-laid plans

better late than never
better left unsaid
beyond the shadow of a doubt
bite the bullet
bitter end
blissful ignorance
block out
bloody but unbowed
bolt from the blue
bone of contention
bottom line
bright and shining faces
broad daylight
brook no delay
brute force
budding genius
built-in safeguards
burning question
burning the midnight oil
busy as a bee
by leaps and bounds
by the same token

Calm before the storm
capacity crowd
cast a pall
casual encounter
chain reaction
charged with emotion
checkered career/past
cherished belief
chief cook and bottle washer
circumstances beyond my control
city fathers
civic wrath
clear as crystal/day
colorful display
come full circle
common/garden variety
confirming our conversation
conservative estimate
considered opinion
consigned to oblivion
conspicuous by its absence
contents noted
controlling factor
cool as a cucumber
crying need
curiously enough
cut a long story short
cut down in his prime

Dark horse
date with destiny
days are numbered
dazed condition
dead as a doornail
deadly earnest
deafening crash
deficits mount
deliberate falsehood
depths of despair
diamond in the rough
dig in your heels
discreet silence
do not hesitate to
doom is sealed

doomed to disappointment
dotted on the landscape
dramatic new move
drastic action
due consideration
dynamic personality

Each and every
easier said than done
eat, drink, and be merry
eloquent silence
eminently successful
enclosed herewith
engage in conversation
enjoyable occasion
entertaining high hopes of
epic struggle
equal to the occasion
errand of mercy
even tenor
exception that proves the rule
existing conditions
express one's appreciation
eyeball to eyeball

Failed to dampen spirits
fair sex
fall on bad times
fall on deaf ears
far and wide
far be it from me
far cry
fateful day
fate worse than death
feedback loop
feel free to
feel vulnerable
festive occasion
few and far between
few well-chosen words
fickle finger of fate
final analysis
fine-tune one's plans
finishing touches
fit as a fiddle
floral tribute
food for thought
fools rush in
foregone conclusion
foul play
from the sublime to the ridiculous

Gala occasion
generation gap
generous to a fault
gild the lily
give the green light to
glowing cheeks
go down the drain
goes without saying
goodly number
good team player
grateful acknowledgement
grave concern
green with envy
grim reaper
grind to a halt

Hale and hearty
hands across the sea
happy pair
hastily summoned
have the privilege
heartfelt thanks/appreciation
heart of the matter
heart's desire
heated argument
heave a sigh of relief
height of absurdity
herculean efforts
hook, line, and sinker
hook or crook
hope for the future
hope springs eternal
hot pursuit
how does that grab you?
hunker down
hurriedly retraced his steps

Ignominious retreat
ignorance is bliss
ill-fated
immaculately attired
immeasurably superior
impenetrable mystery
in close proximity
inextricably linked
infinite capacity
inflationary spiral
innocent bystander
in no uncertain terms
in our midst
in reference/regard to
in short supply
internecine strife
in the limelight
in the nick of time
in the same boat with
in the twinkling of an eye
in this day and age
into full swing
iron out the difficulty
irony of fate
irreducible minimum
irreparable/irreplaceable loss
it dawned on me

Just desserts
just for openers

Keep options open

Labor of love
lashed out at
last analysis
last but not least
last-ditch effort
leaps and bounds
leave no stone unturned
leaves much to be desired
leave up in the air
lend a helping hand
let well enough alone
like a bolt from the blue
limped into port
line of least resistance

Cliches

little woman
lit up like a Christmas tree
lock, stock, and barrel
logic of events
long arm of the law
long-felt need

Make good one's escape
man the barricades
marked contrast
masterpiece of understatement
matter of life and death
mecca for travelers
method to/in his madness
milk of human kindness
miraculous escape
moment of truth
momentous decision/occasion
monumental traffic jam
moot point
more in sorrow than in anger
more sinned against than sinning
more than meets the eye
more the merrier
motley crew

Narrow escape
nearest and dearest
needs no introduction
never a dull moment
never before in the history of
nipped in the bud
none the worse for wear
no sooner said than done
not wisely but too well

One and the same
ongoing dialogue
on more than one occasion
on unimpeachable authority
open secret
order out of chaos
other things being equal
outer directed
overwhelming odds
own worst enemy

Pales into insignificance
paralyzed with fright
paramount importance
part and parcel
patience of Job
pay the piper
peer group
pet peeve
pick and choose
pie in the sky
pinpoint the cause
pipe dream
place in the sun

play hardball
play it by ear
point with pride
poor but honest
powder keg
powers that be
pretty kettle of fish
pros and cons
proud heritage
proud possessor
pull one's weight

Rack and ruin
ravishing beauty
red-letter day
regrettable incident
reigns supreme
reliable source
remedy the situation
right on
riot-torn area
ripe old age
round of applause
rude habitation

Sadder but wiser
saw the light of day
scathing sarcasm
sea of faces
seat of learning
second to none
seething mass of humanity
select few
selling like hotcakes
shattering effect
shift into high gear
shot in the arm
sigh of relief
silence broken only by
silhouetted against the sky
simple life
skeleton in the closet
snug as a bug in a rug
social amenities
something hitting the fan
spectacular event
spirited debate
steaming jungle
stick out like a sore thumb
stick to one's guns
straight and narrow path
structure one's day
such is life
sum and substance
superhuman effort
supreme sacrifice
sweat of his brow
sweeping changes
sweet sixteen

Take the bull by the horns
take up the cudgels
telling effect
tender mercies
terror stricken
thanking you in advance
there's the rub
this day and age
those present
throw a monkey wrench
throw a party
throw caution to the winds
thrust of your report
thunderous applause
tie that binds
time immemorial
time of one's life
tongue in cheek
too funny for words
too numerous to mention
tough it out/through
tower of strength
trials and tribulations
trust implicitly
tumultuous applause

Uncharted seas
unprecedented situation
untimely end
untiring efforts
up tight

Vale of tears
vanish into thin air
viable alternative

Watery grave
wax eloquent/poetic
weaker sex
wear and tear
wend one's way
whirlwind tour
wide open spaces
words fail to express
word to the wise
work one's wiles
worse for wear
wrought havoc

X-ray vision/view

Yea verily yea
yeasty blend/mix
yellow journalism
yen for . . .
Young Turk

Zero hour
zest for life

Colons signal readers to keep reading because related thoughts or a list will follow. In this role, colons differ from periods, semicolons, and even commas, all of which signal a pause or even a full stop.

Colons

1. Colons link related thoughts, one of which must be capable of standing alone as a sentence.

2. Colons introduce lists or examples.

3. Colons separate hours from minutes, volumes from pages, and the first part of a ratio from the second.

4. Colons follow the salutation in a formal letter.

5. Colons separate titles from subtitles.

---

1. Colons link related thoughts, one of which must be capable of standing alone as a sentence.

Colons emphasize the second thought (unlike semicolons, which emphasize both thoughts equally, and dashes, which emphasize the break in the sentence and can emphasize the first thought).

Colons shift emphasis forward: They tend to make the second thought the most important part of the sentence. When such is the case, the colon indicates that explanation or elaboration follows:

> The Franklin Shipyard needed one thing to remain solvent: to win the Navy's supercarrier contract.

> The Franklin shipyard needed one thing to remain solvent: It had to win the Navy's supercarrier contract.

See CAPITALS.

NOTE: The two complete thoughts in the second example could also appear as two sentences:

> The Franklin Shipyard needed one thing to remain solvent. It had to win the Navy's supercarrier contract.

However, linking these thoughts with a colon emphasizes their close connection. Writing them as two sentences is less emphatic if the writer wishes to stress that the **one thing** Franklin needs is to win the contract.

2. Colons introduce lists or examples:

Our management development study revealed the need for greater monitoring during these crucial phases:

> 1. Initial organization
> 2. Design and development
> 3. Fabrication and quality control

The Mars Division's audit of field service personnel centers found the following general deficiencies:

> 1. Service personnel do not fully understand the new rebate policy.
> 2. Parts inventories are inadequate.
> 3. The centralized customer records are not operational, although the computer terminals have all been installed.

NOTE 1: A colon need not follow a heading or subheading that introduces a list. The heading itself is sufficient; a colon is redundant.

NOTE 2: The items listed do not require periods unless they are complete sentences. See LISTS.

3. Colons separate hours from minutes, volumes from pages, and the first part of a ratio from the second:

> The deadline is 3:30 p.m. on Friday.

> See *Government Architecture* 15:233.

> The ratio of direct to indirect costs is 1:1.45.

4. Colons follow the salutation in a formal letter:

> Dear Ms. Labordean:

> Dear President Crouch:

> Dear Clarence Johns:

See LETTERS.

5. Colons separate titles from subtitles:

> *Government Architecture: Managing Interface Specifications*

Color is important for all communication media: television, video games, photography, computer graphics, and print media (magazines, many books, and most major newspapers). In all media, color assists readers and viewers to acquire information. Without color, a magazine or a newsletter today seems outdated and even boring.

Color originates when an object emits or reflects different wavelengths of light. Light (as in a beam of sunlight) is made up of the colors of the spectrum. See figure 1. Light shining through a prism bends to a different degree depending on its wavelength, thus revealing all the different colors in the spectrum.

Color

1. Establish a color scheme and then add color standards to the project style sheet.

2. Use contrasting, bright colors to show opposing concepts or major changes; use shades or tints of one color to show minor variations.

3. Match your color choices to your goal or purpose in designing a document or making a presentation.

4. Remember that, on average, 10 percent of your readers may be color blind and that color perception varies greatly from individual to individual.

5. For more legibility, use a light background with dark text, and choose colors carefully.

6. Combine color tones and textures to improve legibility and understanding.

7. Avoid blue in documents if you want users to make black-and-white photocopies or xerographic copies.

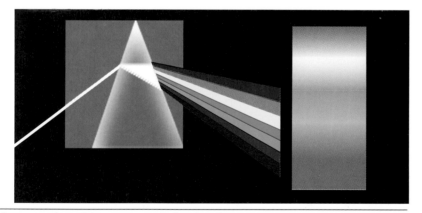

Figure 1. Colors of the Spectrum Displayed with a Prism. *As in this figure, the rainbow colors in a spectrum always appear in the same order.*

Additive color starts with light of three primary colors: red, green, and blue. Mixing light of these colors in equal amounts makes white light (imagine three overlapping colored spotlights in a darkened room). See figure 2. Changing the mixture produces any color. For example, equal parts of red and green light make yellow light; red and blue make magenta; and green and blue make cyan blue.

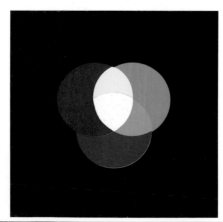

Figure 2. Colors of the Spectrum Displayed by Mixing Primary Light Colors. *Visualize multiple filters overlapping each other to produce different hues.*

1. Establish a color scheme and then add color standards to the project style sheet.

A style sheet for your document or presentation should include a color scheme, with text color(s), when or where they will be used, and background colors listed by topic, section, subject, or other logical grouping. For example, you might decide to use blue lettering for important rules and a light gray shaded background for quoted passages. See PAGE LAYOUT for examples of style sheets.

As you select colors, try to establish a color scheme that makes sense to potential readers. For example, if your readers are from the United States, green can suggest prosperity (as in money), yellow can suggest something transitional (as a declining houseplant), and red can show failure (as in red ink).

Many color associations are not universal, so avoid assuming that a certain color has a particular

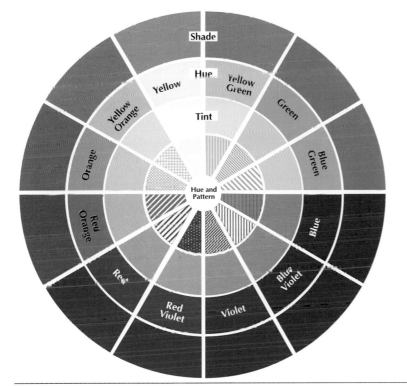

Figure 3. The Color Wheel. *This schematic presentation shows which colors are complementary (opposite) of each other and which are only minor shades and tints.*

Figure 4 displays three types of color combinations: complementary colors, split complementary colors, and harmonious colors.

Complementary colors are opposite one another on the color wheel. As the top row of figure 4 shows, yellow and violet are complementary colors. Other complementary pairs are blue and orange, or red and green. As complementary colors, yellow and violet contrast sharply, as shown in the middle box on the top row. Choosing a tint of yellow or a shade of violet leads to a less contrastive figure, as in the third box on that row.

Graphic artists often choose complementary colors because they have such high contrasts. But this choice must depend on the purpose of each graphic. Some graphics—

meaning. For example, in several Far Eastern countries, the color white is associated with death and mourning; in the United States, white is traditionally a sign of purity and innocence.

A color wheel is a basic diagram showing the relationships of colors, hues, shades, and tints, as well as complementary and harmonious relationships. A shade, sometimes called a chroma, is a darkened hue—the absence of light or the addition of black. A tint (the opposite of a shade) is a lightened hue—the increase of light or the addition of white.

The color wheel in figure 3 shows the relationship between hues, tints, and shades.

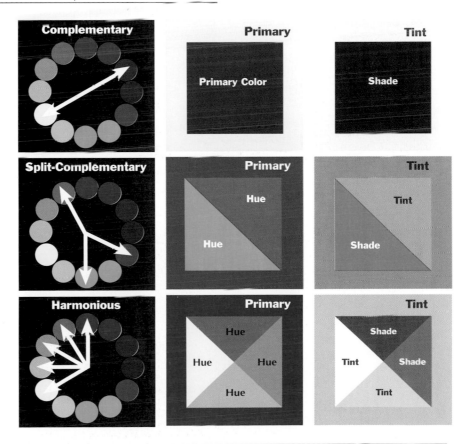

Figure 4. Complementary, Split-Complementary, and Harmonious Combinations. *The left-hand column shows how these three combinations are defined. The middle and right-hand columns demonstrate different combinations as they would appear in graphics.*

such as the advertising on a cereal box—need to catch a buyer's eye immediately, so high contrast is valuable. In other contexts—for instance, a presentation using overhead transparencies—complementary colors are often too bright, maybe even annoying.

Split-complementary colors are two colors positioned adjacent to a single color on the wheel. Their complement is opposite their adjacent color on the wheel. As the second row in figure 4 shows, red-orange is complementary to both blue and green. Split-complementary colors provide less contrast than complementary colors, but combinations of them are still bright, as the middle box on row two indicates. Using tints and shades will decrease the contrast, as shown in the third box on row two.

Harmonious colors lie between two primary colors on the color wheel. As figure 4 shows, the harmonious colors between red and yellow clearly relate to each other; thus they provide less contrast than either complementary or split-complementary combinations. Tints and shades will further decrease the low contrast between harmonious colors. Graphic artists use harmonious colors when they want to convey harmony or consistency within a graphic or a document.

3. Match your color choices to your goal or purpose in designing a document or making a presentation.

Which color combinations should you choose? No set answers exist. You have to assess the purpose of your graphic and your text. If you need to provide very bright, highly contrastive images, choose complementary or split-complementary colors, as explained

Figure 5. Road Signs. *Road signs use bright, contrasting color combinations to generate high visibility.*

in rule 2 above. Conversely, if your graphic or text needs to be more subtle, then choose tints, shades, or even harmonious combinations.

Figure 5 shows one use of high-contrast colors. On road signs, the goal is to use colors so vividly that no one can miss seeing the sign.

A more subtle use of color is desirable, however, in most business and technical documents and in the graphics for business or technical presentations. Figure 6 shows how three business graphs would look with different color combinations. As in this figure, you will likely find that you need to print sample graphics with different combinations because until you actually see the color version of

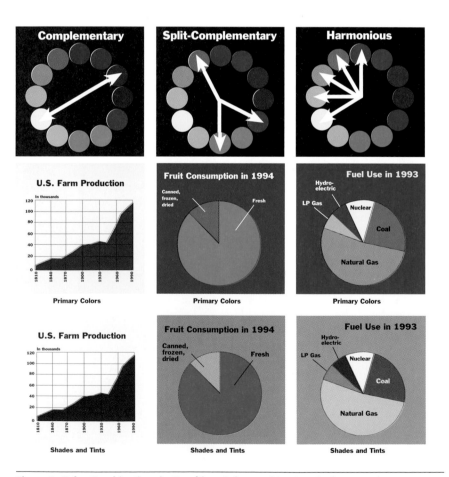

Figure 6. Color Combinations in Graphics. *Color combinations in the second row are bright and might be distracting. The bottom row shows more subdued combinations using tints and shades.*

something, you cannot judge what will be effective. Also, remember that the colors you see on a computer screen may not print accurately. You must often adjust colors to the parameters of the printer.

If possible, test your color combinations by asking colleagues to review actual versions of your materials. Do they find the combinations to be appropriate, given the intended use of the materials? What changes would they suggest?

After some experimentation and after comments from colleagues, you will be ready to settle on a color scheme that works for a particular project. This is the color scheme you should include in your project style sheet (see rule 1 above).

4. Remember that, on average, 10 percent of your readers may be color blind and that color perception varies greatly from individual to individual.

Red-green color blindness affects one in every 10 men, but is rare in women. Some color combinations are very difficult for color-blind men to interpret and should not be used. See Graphics for Presentations.

5. For more legibility, use a light background with dark text, and choose colors carefully.

Text in documents is usually printed in black ink on white paper because black ink generally costs less.

But color is useful to separate sections or emphasize important points. Using colored paper is an inexpensive way to add color. For example, the USDA Forest Service manual, which contains rules, procedures, and regulations governing Forest Service management activities, has traditionally used different colored papers for national, regional, and local sections of the manual.

Different combinations of text color and background vary widely in readability. Figure 7 on the next page shows some examples of colored text and backgrounds.

Remember that any of these examples may be less legible if you are using overhead transparencies, slides, a video screen, or a computer-driven projector. Test the circumstances. Stand halfway back in the audience. A person in the back receives about one-fourth the image quality you see halfway back. See Graphics for Presentations.

In computer-driven presentations, the high contrast of a dark background and light letters creates impact. However, to avoid losing its impact, this special effect should be used only for making major points.

6. Combine color tones and textures to improve legibility and understanding.

Tones and textures can make almost any graphic easier to understand. But you must choose carefully to ensure that the viewer interprets textural elements as you intend.

Use similar colors to bring together elements in groups. Black and white patterns are almost as effective as color in grouping elements.

When selecting colors and tones or textures for graphs, consider how the finished graphic will photocopy. You may want to use both color and texture to create a pleasing color graphic while ensuring improved legibility of a photocopy.

The purpose of textural elements, such as crosshatching, dots, or other shapes or lines, is to help the viewer's brain interpret edges and define shapes in a chart, graph, or illustration. Neighboring areas should not be too similar in color, brightness, or texture. See also Charts, Graphics for Documents, Graphics for Presentations, Graphs, Illustrations, Maps, and Page Layout.

7. Avoid blue in documents if you want users to make black-and-white photocopies or xerographic copies.

The human eye is more sensitive to blue than many copy machines, so some blue text may not copy well. You can reduce this problem by using blue-violet because most copiers are more sensitive to violet than blue.

Blue ink in many ballpoint pens is closer to blue-violet hue, and this color will permit notes to copy clearly.

However, special light blue pens are available to use when you want to make editorial marks that won't be seen by a copier.

Another strategy to make text difficult to copy is careful choice of text color and background color: black text on dark red paper will usually copy as all black; medium blue text on light blue paper will usually copy as all white, as will light blue on light gray paper.

Color

Color	Recommended	Not Recommended
Dk. Red	White, yellow, lt. yellow, lt. blue, lt. red, lt. green	Blue, green, black
Red	White, yellow, lt. yellow, lt. red, lt. orange, black	Brown, blue, green, orange
Med.Red	White, black, dk. blue, blue violet, dk. green	Brown, orange, yellow, red
Light Red	Black, dk. red, dk. blue, brown, blue violet, dk. green	White, yellow, lt. yellow, lt. blue
Dk. Brown	White, yellow, lt. yellow, lt. red, lt. green, lt. blue	Black, green, blue, dk. blue, red
Med. Brown	White, black, yellow, lt. yellow, lt. green, lt. blue, lt. red	Blue, green, red
Dk. Yellow	Black, yellow, White, lt. yellow	red, green, blue
Lt. Yellow	Black, red, dk. red, blue, dk. blue, dk. violet, dk. green, brown	lt. blue, lt. green, orange
Dk. Green	White, yellow, lt. yellow, lt. red, lt. blue	Black, brown, med. brown, red, blue
Green	White, yellow, lt. yellow, lt. red, black, lt. blue	Blue, red, violet, blue violet, dk. green, med. brown
Lt. Green	Black, White, brown, dk. blue, dk. green	lt. red, lt. blue, lt. yellow, med. brown
Dk. Blue	White, yellow, lt. yellow, lt. blue	Red, green, orange
Blue	White, yellow, lt. yellow, lt. red	Red, green, orange, violet
Lt. Blue	Black, yellow, dk. blue, violet	lt. red, lt. blue, lt. yellow
Black	White, yellow, lt. yellow, lt. blue, lt. red	Red, blue, green, violet

Figure 7. Colored Text on Different Colored Backgrounds. *The recommended combinations (middle column) still need to be verified in your particular context. Your printer or your paper may be just different enough to produce readability problems.*

Commas keep English sentences readable, especially long, involved sentences. Without commas, readers wouldn't know when to pause. But as the following rules show, correct placement of commas reflects the grammar and syntax of the language, not merely places to pause. See PUNCTUATION for information on mandatory and optional uses of commas.

Commas

1. Commas separate complete thoughts joined by these simple conjunctions: *and, but, or, for, nor, so, yet.*

2. Commas separate items in a series consisting of three or more words, phrases, or even whole clauses.

3. Commas separate long introductory phrases and clauses from the main body of a sentence.

4. Commas enclose parenthetical expressions.

5. Commas separate nonessential modifying and descriptive phrases and clauses from a sentence, especially those clauses beginning with *who, which,* or *that.*

6. Commas separate two or more adjectives that equally modify the same noun.

7. Commas separate items in dates and addresses.

8. Commas separate titles and degrees from names.

9. Commas follow the salutation in informal letters and the complimentary closing in all letters.

10. Commas enclose in text the names of people addressed.

11. Commas (or a comma and a semicolon) set off (enclose) the following transitional words and expressions when they introduce sentences or when they link two complete thoughts: *accordingly, consequently, for example, for instance, further, furthermore, however, indeed, nevertheless, nonetheless, on the contrary, on the other hand, then, thus.*

12. Commas, like periods, always go inside closing quotation marks. Commas go outside parentheses or brackets.

1. Commas separate complete thoughts joined by these simple conjunctions: *and, but, or, for, nor, so, yet:*

He was a Russian linguist in communications intelligence, and he has logged over 5,000 hours as a C-130 navigator in the Air Force.

Visophane has been marketed abroad since 1985, but it was not approved for the local market until May of last year because of insufficient clinical trials.

NOTE 1: You may omit this comma if both complete thoughts are short:

The chairman resigned and the company failed.

The simple conjunctions cited above are called coordinating conjunctions. When they link two complete thoughts, the resulting sentence is called a compound sentence. See CONJUNCTIONS, SENTENCES, and BRITISH ENGLISH.

NOTE 2: If you use any other transitional or connecting word (*however, furthermore, consequently,* and so on) to join two complete thoughts, use a semicolon. See SEMICOLONS and TRANSITIONS.

2. Commas separate items in a series consisting of three or more words, phrases, or even whole clauses:

Control Data's Integrated Support Software System provides compatibility between tools and workers, consistent tool interfaces, ease of learning, user friendliness, and expandability.

The user may also return to the control program to perform such other functions as database editing, special report generation, and statistical analyses.

The Carthage-Hines agreement contained provisions for testing the database, cataloguing the findings, creating a more user-friendly software package, and marketing any new software developed jointly.

NOTE 1: A comma separates the last two items in a series even though these items are linked by a conjunction (*and* in the above examples, but the rule applies for any conjunction). This comma was once considered optional, but the trend is to make it mandatory, especially in technical and business English. Leaving it out can cause confusion and misinterpretation. See PUNCTUATION and BRITISH ENGLISH.

Commas

NOTE 2: If all of the items in the series are linked by a simple conjunction, do not use commas:

> The user may also return to the control program to perform such other functions as database editing and special report generation and statistical analyses.

NOTE 3: In sentences containing a series of phrases or clauses that already have commas, use semicolons to separate each phrase or clause:

> Our legal staff prepared analyses of the Drury-Engels agreement, which we hoped to discontinue; the Hopkinson contract; and the joint leasing proposal from Shell, Mobil, and Amoco.

See CONJUNCTIONS and SEMICOLONS.

3. Commas separate long introductory phrases and clauses from the main body of a sentence:

> Although we are new to particle scan technology, our work with split-beam lasers gives us a solid experiential base from which to undertake this study.

> For the purposes of this investigation, the weapon will be synthesized by a computer program called RATS (Rapid Approach to Transfer Systems).

> Oil production was down during the first quarter, but when we analyzed the figures, we discovered that the production decline was due to only two of our eight wells.

NOTE 1: In the last example, the *when we analyzed* clause does not open the sentence, but it must still be separated from the main clause following it. It introduces the main thought of the last half of the sentence.

NOTE 2: If the introductory thought is short and no confusion will result, you can omit this comma:

> In either case the Carmichael procedure will be used to estimate the current requirements of the preliminary designs.

4. Commas enclose parenthetical expressions.

Parenthetical expressions are words or groups of words that are inserted into a sentence and are not part of the main thought of the sentence. These expressions describe, explain, or comment on something in the sentence, typically the word or phrase preceding the parenthetical expression:

> The transport will, according to our calculations, require only 10,000 feet of runway.

> The survey results, though not what we had predicted, confirm that the rate of manufacturer acceptance will exceed 60 percent.

Parentheses and dashes may also enclose parenthetical expressions. Use commas most of the time, but when you want to make the expression stand out, enclose it with parentheses (which are more emphatic than commas) or dashes—which are more emphatic than parentheses. See PARENTHESES and DASHES.

5. Commas separate nonessential modifying and descriptive phrases and clauses from a sentence, especially those clauses beginning with *who, which,* or *that*:

> These biocybernetic approaches, which merit further investigation, will improve performance of the man/machine interface.

In this sentence, *which merit further investigation* is not essential because the reader will already know which biocybernetic approaches the sentence refers to. The clause beginning with *which* is nonessential and could be left out:

> These biocybernetic approaches will improve performance of the man/machine interface.

If several biocybernetic approaches were listed, however, and if the writer needed to identify only those meriting further investigation, the clause would be essential, could not be left out, and would **not** take commas:

> Improving the performance of the man/machine interface meant identifying those biocybernetic approaches that merit further investigation.

The *that* in the preceding example commonly introduces essential clauses although *which* sometimes appears. See *that/which* in WORD PROBLEMS.

Modifying or descriptive clauses should always follow the words they modify. If they cannot be removed from the sentence without changing the meaning, they are essential and must not be separated by commas from the word they modify. If they can be removed, they are non-essential and must be separated by commas from the main thought in the sentence:

> *Essential:* She is the Dr. Gruber who developed analytical engine compressor stability models for NASA.

She is the Dr. Gruber does not make sense as an independent statement. The descriptive clause beginning with *who* is essential and therefore cannot be separated by a comma from *Gruber*.

> *Nonessential:* Our Design Team Leader will be Dr. Janet Gruber, who developed analytical engine compressor stability models for NASA.

Our Design Team Leader will be Dr. Janet Gruber does stand alone as a complete and independent thought. In this case, the descriptive clause beginning with *who* is nonessential. Separating it from *Gruber* with a comma shows that it is additional and nonessential information. Note that a comma would follow *NASA* if the sentence continued. See PRONOUNS for a discussion of relative pronouns.

6. Commas separate two or more adjectives that equally modify the same noun:

This design features an advanced, multidose oral therapy.

NOTE: If two or more adjectives precede a noun, however, and one adjective modifies another adjective—and **together** they modify the noun—you must use a hyphen:

They had designed a no-flow heat exchange.

A good test for determining whether two or more adjectives equally modify a noun is to insert *and* between them. If the resulting phrase makes sense, then the adjectives are equal, and you should use commas to replace the *ands:*

old and rusty pipe (*therefore,* old, rusty pipe)

however

old and rusty and steam pipe (*The* and *between* rusty *and* steam *makes no sense. Therefore, the phrase should be* old, rusty steam pipe.)

See HYPHENS and ADJECTIVES.

7. Commas separate items in dates and addresses:

The proposal was signed on March 15, 1996.

Contact Benson Pharmaceuticals, Lindsay, Indiana, for further information.

NOTE: A comma follows the day and the year when the month **and day** precede the year. However, when the date consists only of month and year, a comma is not necessary:

The final report will be due January 15, 1990, just a month before the board meeting.

but

The final report will be due in January 1997.

When the date appears in the day-month-year sequence, no commas are necessary:

The report is due 15 January 1997.

See PUNCTUATION.

8. Commas separate titles and degrees from names:

The chief liaison will be Roger Hillyard, Project Review Board Chairman.

Mary Sarkalion, PhD, will coordinate clinical studies.

Clinical studies will be the responsibility of Mary Sarkalion, PhD.

NOTE: When the degree or title appears in the middle of a sentence, commas must appear before and after it.

9. Commas follow the salutation in informal letters and the complimentary closing in all letters:

Dear Joan,

Sincerely,

See COLONS and LETTERS.

10. Commas enclose in text the names of people addressed:

So, Bob, if you'll check your records, we'll be able to adjust the purchase order to your satisfaction.

11. Commas (or a comma and a semicolon) set off (enclose) the following transitional words and expressions when they introduce sentences or when they link two complete thoughts: *accordingly, consequently, for example, for instance, further, furthermore, however, indeed, nevertheless, nonetheless, on the contrary, on the other hand, then, thus:*

Consequently, the primary difference between CDSP and other synthesis programs is development philosophy.

Synthesis programs are now common in industry; however, CDSP has several features that make it especially suitable for this type of study.

or

Synthesis programs are now common in industry; CDSP has, however, several features that make it especially suitable for this type of study.

See SEMICOLONS.

NOTE: A few of these transitional words (*however, thus, then, indeed*) are occasionally part of the main thought of the sentence and do not form an actual transition. When such is the case, omit the punctuation before and after the words:

However unreliable cross-section analysis may be, it is still the most efficient means of scaling mathematical models.

Thus translated, the decoded message can be used to diagram nonlinear relationships

12. Commas, like periods, always go inside closing quotation marks. Commas go outside parentheses or brackets:

The specifications contained many instances of the phrase "or equal," which is an attempt to avoid actually specifying significant features of a required product.

Thanks to this new NSAID (non-steroidal anti-inflammatory drug), post traumatic or postoperative conditions were significantly reduced.

NOTE: British usage places commas and periods inside or outside the quotation marks, depending on whether they are or are not part of the quotation. See SPACING, BRITISH ENGLISH, and QUOTATION MARKS.

Compound words are formed when two or more words act together. The compound may be written as a single word (with no space between the joined words), with a hyphen between the joined words, or with spaces between the joined words:

> footnote
> ourselves
> right-of-way
> 3-minute break
> delayed-reaction switch
> land bank loan
> parcel post delivery

The form of the compound varies with custom and usage as well as with the length of time the compound has existed.

Compound words usually begin as two or more separate, often unrelated words. When writers and speakers begin using the words together as nouns, verbs, adjectives, or adverbs, the compound generally has a hyphen or a space between words, depending on custom and usage. As the new compound becomes more common, the hyphen and space might drop, and the compound might be written as one word:

> on-site *has become* onsite
> co-operate *has become* cooperate
> rail road *has become* railroad
> auto body *has become* autobody

However, because of custom or usage, some compounds retain the hyphen or space between words:

> all-inclusive
> deep-rooted
> living room
> middle-sized
> re-cover *(to cover again)*
> re-create *(to create again)*
> rough-coat *(used as a verb)*
> sand-cast *(used as a verb)*
> satin-lined
> steam-driven
> sugar water
> summer school
> terra firma
> throw line
> under secretary

Because new compound words are continually appearing in the language

and because even familiar compounds might appear in different forms, depending on how they are used in a sentence, writers might have difficulty deciding which form of a compound to use. Recent dictionaries can often help by indicating how a word or compound has appeared previously.

However, for new compounds and for compounds not covered in dictionaries, use the principles of clarity and consistency, as well as the following guidelines, to select the form of the compound.

1. Write compounds as two words when the compounds appear with the words in their customary order and when the meaning is clear:

> test case   report card
> sick leave   barn door
> flood control   social security
> real estate   civil rights

NOTE 1: Many such combinations are so common that we rarely think of them as compounds (especially because they do not have hyphens and are written with spaces between words). In many cases, writing them as a single word would be ridiculous: *floodcontrol, realestate.*

NOTE 2: We continue to pronounce such compounds with fairly equal stress on the joined words, especially when one or more of the words has two or more syllables (as in *social security*).

2. Write compounds as single words (no spaces between joined words) when the first word of the compound receives the major stress in pronunciation:

> airplane
> cupboard
> doorstop
> dragonfly
> footnote
> nightclerk
> seaward
> warehouse

NOTE 1: The stress often shifts to the first word when that word has only one syllable, as in the preceding examples.

NOTE 2: Words beginning with the following prefixes are not true compounds. Such words are usually written without a space or a hyphen:

> *after*birth
> *Anglo*mania
> *ante*date
> *bi*weekly
> *by*law
> *circum*navigation
> *co*operate
> *contra*position
> *counter*case
> *de*energize
> *demi*tasse
> *ex*communicate
> *extra*curricular
> *fore*tell
> *hyper*sensitive
> *hypo*acid
> *in*bound
> *infra*red
> *inter*view
> *intra*spinal
> *intro*vert
> *iso*metric

macroanalysis
mesothorax
metagenesis
microphone
misspelling
monogram
multicolor
neophyte
nonneutral
offset
outback
overactive
overflow
pancosmic
paracentric
particoated
peripatetic
planoconvex
polynodal
postscript
preexist
proconsul
pseudoscientific
reenact
retrospect
semiofficial
stepfather
subsecretary
supermarket
thermocouple
transonic
transship
tricolor
ultraviolet
unnecessary
underflow

NOTE 3: Words ending with the following suffixes are not true compounds. Such words are usually written without a space or hyphen:

portable
coverage
operate
plebiscite
twentyfold
spoonful
kilogram
geography
manhood
selfish
meatless
outlet
wavelike
procurement
partnership
lonesome
homestead
northward
clockwise

3. Hyphenate compounds that modify or describe other words:

rear engine bracket
tool-and-die shop
two-phase engine-replacement program
down-to-cost model
two- or three-cycle process
4-year plan
20-day turn around
2- or 3-week vacation

See HYPHENS and ADJECTIVES.

NOTE 1: Such compounds are hyphenated only when they come before the word they modify. If the words forming the compound appear after the word they are describing, leave out the hyphens:

bracket for the rear engine (*but* rear-engine bracket)

a shop making tools and dies (*but* tool-and-die shop)

a program with two phases (*but* two-phase program)

NOTE 2: When the meaning is clear, such compound modifiers may not need hyphens:

sick leave policy
land management plan
life insurance company
per capita cost
production credit clause
speech improvement class

NOTE 3: Do not hyphenate if the first word of the compound modifier ends with *–ly*:

barely known problem
eminently qualified researcher
highly developed tests
gently sloping range

however

well-developed tests
well-known problem
well-qualified researcher

4. Treat compounds used as verbs as separate words:

to break down
to check out
to follow up
to get together
to go ahead
to know how
to run through
to shut down
to shut off
to stand by
to start up
to take off
to trade in

The parallel compound nouns are usually either written as one word or hyphenated:

breakdown
checkout
follow-up
get-together
go-ahead
know-how
run-through
shutdown
shutoff
standby
start-up
takeoff
trade-in

However, some verb phrases are identical to the compound noun form:

cross-reference (*both a noun and a verb*)

When in doubt, check your dictionary.

Conjunctions connect words, phrases, or clauses and at the same time indicate the relationship between them. Conjunctions include the simple coordinating conjunctions (*and, but, or, for, nor, so, yet*), the subordinate conjunctions (*because, since, although, when, if, so that,* etc.), the correlative conjunctions (*either . . . or, neither . . . nor, both . . . and*), and the conjunctive adverbs (*however, thus, furthermore,* etc.).

Coordinating Conjunctions

The simple coordinating conjunctions are *and, but, or, for, nor, so,* and *yet*. They often connect two independent clauses (complete thoughts):

> The program designer established the default settings, and the programmer built them into the system.

> Our proposal was a day late, but we were not eliminated from competition.

> The pump will have to be replaced, or we will continue to suffer daily breakdowns.

> We rejected his budget, yet he continued to argue that all contested items were justified.

See SENTENCES.

These simple connectors establish the relationship between the thoughts being coordinated:

—*And* shows addition
—*Or* shows alternative
—*Nor* shows negative alternative
—*But* and *yet* show contrast
—*For* and *so* show causality

NOTE 1: When you use a coordinating conjunction to connect two independent clauses or complete thoughts, place a comma before the conjunction, as in the sentences above. However, you may omit the comma when the two clauses are short and closely related. Also, a semicolon can replace both the comma and the conjunction. See SEMICOLONS and COMMAS.

Conjunctions

1. Ensure that in choosing *and* and *or* you select the conjunction that conveys exactly what you mean.

2. Occasionally, sentences can begin with a coordinating conjunction.

3. Do not use *and* or *but* before *which* (or *that, who, whose, whom, where*) unless you use a preceding parallel *which* (or *that, who, whose, whom, where*).

4. Subordinate conjunctions can begin sentences.

5. Distinguish between some subordinate conjunctions that have overlapping or multiple meanings (especially *because/since/as* and *while/although/as*).

6. Make the constructions following each coordinating conjunction parallel.

7. Use a semicolon before and a comma after conjunctive adverbs used to join two complete thoughts.

8. Use a comma following conjunctive adverbs at the beginning of a sentence.

NOTE 2: The conjunctions *and* and *or* (preceded by a comma) also connect the last two items in a series:

> The engineer designed an emergency exit door, a narrow outside stairway, and a concrete support pad.

> She requested full written disclosure, an apology, or financial compensation.

See COMMAS.

---

1. Ensure that in choosing *and* and *or* you select the conjunction that conveys exactly what you mean.

At first glance, *and* and *or* merely join two or more items, but they can and often do imply much more.

And

In the following sentences *and* does more than merely connect the ideas. What *and* implies is stated in parentheses following each example:

> He saw the accident, and he called the police. (*therefore*)

> My boss is competent, and David is not. (*contrast*)

> He changed the tire, and he replaced the hub cap. (*then*)

> Explain the cost savings, and I'll approve your proposal. (*condition*)

Or

The conjunction *or* usually means one of two possibilities:

> I want either a Ford or an Oldsmobile.

However, *or* sometimes has other, occasionally confusing, implications:

> The faulty part or the worm gear seemed to be causing our problem. (*Are the faulty part and the worm gear the same? Only knowledgeable readers would know for sure.*)

> Add to the bid, or I'll reject your offer. (*negative condition*)

> He began doing the schematics, or at least he appeared to be doing them. (*correction*)

See *AND/OR* IN WORD PROBLEMS.

2. Occasionally, sentences can begin with a coordinating conjunction.

This advice contradicts the rule that many of us learned in school: "Never begin a sentence with *and*." Some writers and editors still offer this advice, but most have now recognized that this so-called rule has no basis. Even Shakespeare began some of his sentences with coordinating conjunctions.

A coordinating conjunction at the beginning of a sentence links the sentence to the preceding sentence or paragraph. Sometimes, the linking is unnecessary:

> We objected to the proposal because of its length. And others felt that it had errors in its facts.

The *and* at the beginning of the second sentence is simply unnecessary. It adds nothing to the thought and may easily be omitted:

> We objected to the proposal because of its length. Others felt that it had errors in facts.

Using a conjunction to begin a sentence is not grammatically incorrect. Sometimes, it is good stylistic variation. But it tends to look and sound informal, so avoid this practice in formal documents.

3. Do not use *and* or *but* before *which* (or *that, who, whose, whom, where*) unless you use a preceding parallel *which* (or *that, who, whose, whom, where*):

> We explored the DeMarcus itinerary, which you explained in your letter but which you failed to mention in Saturday's meeting.
>
> The meetings should take place where we met last year or where we can arrange for equally good facilities.

The following sentence violates this principle. Consequently, it is awkward and nonparallel:

> The plans called for a number of innovative features, especially regarding extra insulation, and which should save us much in fuel costs. (*Deleting the* and *would solve the lack of parallelism in this sentence.*)

See PARALLELISM.

Subordinate Conjunctions

In contrast to the limited set of coordinating conjunctions, subordinate conjunctions are a varied and diverse group:

> after, although, as, because, before, if, once, since, that, though, until, when, where, while
>
> in that, so that, such that, except that, in order that, now (that), provided (that), supposing (that), considering (that), as far as, as long as, so long as, sooner than, rather than, as if, as though, in case
>
> if . . . (then)
> although . . . yet/nevertheless
> as . . . so
> more/–er/less . . . than
> as . . . as
> so . . . (that)
> such . . . as
> such . . . (that)
> no sooner . . . than
> whether . . . or (not)
> the . . . the

Subordinate conjunctions introduce subordinate clauses and phrases (dependent clauses and phrases that do not convey complete thoughts and are therefore not independent):

> After the engineer gave her talk
>
> Because of the voltage loss
>
> When the test results come in
>
> While still producing fluids
>
> In that you had already made the request
>
> Except that the procedure was costly
>
> Provided that you calculate the results
>
> As though it hadn't rained enough
>
> If we fail

> As aware as he is
>
> So expensive that it was prohibitive
>
> Whether or not you submit the report

These subordinate clauses and phrases must be attached to independent clauses (complete thoughts) to form sentences:

> After the engineer gave her talk, several colleagues had questions.
>
> In that you had already made the request, we decided to omit the formal interview.
>
> If we fail, the project stops. (*or* If we fail, then the project stops.)
>
> As aware as he is, he must be sensitive to the personnel problems.

See SENTENCES.

NOTE 1: A subordinate clause or phrase that opens a sentence should be followed by a comma. The preceding sentences illustrate this rule. See COMMAS.

NOTE 2: When the subordinate clause or phrase follows the independent clause or main thought of the sentence, no commas are necessary:

> The experiment failed because of the voltage loss.
>
> We would have denied the request except that the procedure was so costly.
>
> We wondered whether you would turn in your report.

NOTE 3: Occasionally, the subordinate clause or phrase interrupts the main clause and must have commas on both sides of it to indicate where the clause or phrase appears:

> The President and the Joint Chiefs of Staff, after receiving the latest aerial reconnaissance photos of the area, decided on a naval blockade of all ports.
>
> Our budgetary problems, regardless of the Madiera Project expense, would have taken care of themselves if the prime rate hadn't gone up three points.

Conjunctions

4. Subordinate conjunctions can begin sentences:

> When the test results come in, we'll have to analyze them carefully.

> Because the project manager was unfamiliar with the budget codes, we failed to expense the costs of fabrication.

NOTE: The old school rule "Never begin a sentence with *because*" was and remains a bad rule. You may begin a sentence with *because* as long as the dependent clause it introduces is followed by an independent clause or complete thought.

---

5. Distinguish between some subordinate conjunctions that have overlapping or multiple meanings (especially *because/since/as* and *while/although/as*).

Avoid using *since* and *as* to mean "because":

> Because the Leiper Project failed, several engineers were reassigned to electro-optics. (*not* Since the project failed . . .)

> Because we had ample supplies, no new batteries were ordered. (*not* As we had ample supplies . . .)

Avoid using *while* and *as* to mean "although":

> Although many employees begin work at 8 a.m., others begin at 7 a.m. (*not* While many employees begin work at 8 a.m. . . .)

> Although the value of the test results declined, we still felt we could meet the deadline. (*not* As the value of the test results declined . . .)

Correlative Conjunctions

Correlative conjunctions are pairs of coordinating conjunctions:

> both . . . and
> either . . . or
> neither . . . nor
> not only . . . but also

6. Make the constructions following each coordinating conjunction parallel:

> The committee was interested in both real estate holdings and stock investments. (*not . . . both in real estate holdings and the stock investments.*)

> The investigation revealed that either the budget was inaccurate or our records had gaps. (*not The investigation revealed either that the budget was inaccurate or our records had gaps.*)

NOTE: Faulty parallelism problems occur when the same phrase structure or word patterns do not occur after each coordinating conjunction:

> He was aware that not only was the pipe too small but also that the pipe supports were made of aluminum instead of stainless steel.

This sentence is confusing because the two *that*'s are not parallel. The first *that* comes before *not only*, and the second *that* comes after *but also*. A parallel version of the sentence is much smoother:

> He was aware not only that the pipe was too small but also that the pipe supports were made of aluminum instead of stainless steel.

See PARALLELISM.

Conjunctive Adverbs

Conjunctive adverbs are adverbs that function as conjunctions, typically by connecting independent clauses or complete thoughts. Usually, a semicolon appears along with the conjunctive adverb. The most common conjunctive adverbs are *accordingly, also, besides, consequently, further, furthermore, hence, however, moreover, nevertheless, otherwise, then, therefore, thus,* and *too.* See TRANSITIONS.

NOTE: Conjunctive adverbs and the accompanying semicolons lengthen sentences and convey a heavy, formal tone. If possible, replace conjunctive adverbs with *and, but, or, for, nor, so,* and *yet.*

7. Use a semicolon before and a comma after conjunctive adverbs used to join two complete thoughts:

> Motherboard assembly is a lengthy production process; however, the individual assembly steps must still be tightly controlled.

> Increasing pressure in the T-valves is potentially dangerous; nevertheless, we will not be able to monitor effluent discharge without increasing the pressure.

See SEMICOLONS and COMMAS.

NOTE: You can omit the comma following the conjunctive adverb if the sentence is short:

> I think; therefore I am.

---

8. Use a comma following conjunctive adverbs at the beginning of a sentence:

> Therefore, I am recommending that Pharmaco reconsider the baseline scores for the principal efficacy parameters.

> However, sulfur compounds might not be the answer either.

NOTE 1: You may omit this comma if the sentence is short:

> Thus the plan failed.

NOTE 2: If the adverb appears at the beginning of the sentence but does not behave as a conjunction, it is part of the sentence and cannot be followed by a comma:

> Then the seam split at the forward discharge valve, and the boiler lost pressure rapidly.

> Regardless of how we examined the problem, we could not resolve the fundamental dispute between the software designers and the copyright holders.

See COMMAS.

Contractions are words formed by joining two words and dropping letters. An apostrophe marks the dropped letters:

cannot
can't

we are
we're

there is
there's

Contractions

1. Use contractions to establish a personal, informal tone.

2. Don't confuse contractions with possessive pronouns.

1. Use contractions to establish a personal, informal tone.

Contractions are not appropriate for very formal or ceremonial documents such as contracts or legal notices. However, contractions lead to a conversational, friendly tone in most other business correspondence. Contractions are common in electronic mail (E-mail) messages because they cut the amount of screen space required.

> We're excited that you'll be joining our sales force!

> It's been a long time since you've come to see us.

See Letters, Tone, and *contractions* in Word Problems.

2. Don't confuse contractions with possessive pronouns.

Writers often confuse contractions, which require apostrophes, with possessive pronouns, which need no apostrophes:

> *It's* (it is) a regulatory issue.

> The company lost *its* lease.

> *There's* (there is) no time to waste.

> The contract is *theirs* if they want it.

Watch out for these pronouns commonly mistaken for contractions:

hers, *not* her's
yours, *not* your's
ours, *not* our's
theirs, *not* their's

Distinguish between:

it's (it is)
its (belonging to it)

you're (you are)
your (belonging to you)

they're (they are)
their (belonging to them)

See Apostrophes and Pronouns.

Dashes

Dashes are excellent devices for emphasizing key material and for setting off explanatory information in a sentence. They can also be used to indicate where each item in a list begins and to separate paragraph headings from succeeding text. See HEADINGS, LISTS, and PUNCTUATION.

Dashes primarily appear as an em dash—meaning that the dash is about as wide as the letter "m." Dashes also appear as an en dash, which is as wide as a letter "n." The en dash has only a few uses:

> 1959–1960
> Appendix D–2
> pages 120–122

Most word processing software programs have a special code for dashes so that dashes appear as a solid line, not two separate hyphens. Using this code makes your text appear to be typeset, not typed on an old-fashioned typewriter. When you use a dash between two words, leave no space on either side of the dash. See SPACING.

NOTE: Traditionally, hyphens are even shorter than en dashes, but many software programs have the same code for hyphens and en dashes. See HYPHENS.

1. Dashes link introductory or concluding thoughts to the rest of the sentence.

Dashes linking thoughts emphasize the break in the sentence. Dashes often make the first thought the most important part of the sentence:

> Winning the Navy's supercarrier contract—that's what the Franklin Shipyard needed to remain solvent.

Dashes

1. Dashes link introductory or concluding thoughts to the rest of the sentence.

2. Dashes interrupt a sentence for insertion of thoughts related to, but not part of, the main idea of the sentence.

3. Dashes emphasize explanatory information enclosed in a sentence.

4. Dashes link particulars to a following summary statement.

Dashes can act like colons, however, and throw emphasis to the last part of the sentence:

> We subjected the design to rigorous testing—but to no avail because stress, we discovered, was not the problem.

Often, the information following the dash clarifies, explains, or reinforces what came before the dash:

> We consider our plan bold and unusual—bold because no one has tried to approach the problem from this angle, unusual because it's not how one might expect to use laser technology.

Dashes can also link otherwise complete sentences:

> The technical problem was **not** the design of the filter—the problem was poor quality assurance.

2. Dashes interrupt a sentence for insertion of thoughts related to, but not part of, the main idea of the sentence:

> Octoronase had been undergoing clinical tests—all these were done abroad—for 3 years before the patients were withdrawn from the trial.

In this example, parentheses could replace the dashes; with parentheses, the sentence becomes slightly less emphatic. See PARENTHESES.

3. Dashes emphasize explanatory information enclosed in a sentence:

> Two of Barnett's primary field divisions—Industrial Manufacturing and Product Field Testing—will supervise the construction and implementation of the prototype.

In this example, commas or parentheses could replace the dashes. The commas would not be as emphatic as dashes; the parentheses would be more emphatic than commas, but less emphatic than dashes. See PARENTHESES and COMMAS.

4. Dashes link particulars to a following summary statement:

> Reliability and trust—this is what Bendix has to offer.

> Developing products that become the industry standard, minimizing the risk of failure, and controlling costs through aggressive management—these have become the hallmarks of our reputation.

Decimal numbers are a linear way to represent fractions based on multiples of 10. The decimal *0.45* represents the following fraction:

45/100

See FRACTIONS.

The decimal point (period) is the mark dividing the whole number on the left from the decimal fraction on the right:

504.678

In some countries, writers use a comma for the decimal point:

504,678

1. Use figures for all decimals and do not write the equivalent fractions:

4.5 (*not* 4 ⁵/10)

0.356 (*not* ³⁵⁶/1000)

0.5 (*not* ⁵/10)

0.4690 (*not* ⁴⁶⁹⁰/10,000)

2. If the decimal does not have a whole number, insert a zero before the decimal point:

0.578 (*not* .578)
0.2 (*not* .2)

NOTE: This rule has a few exceptions, including:

Colt .45
A batting average of .345
A probability of *p* =.07

Decimals

1. Use figures for all decimals and do not write the equivalent fractions.

2. If the decimal does not have a whole number, insert a zero before the decimal point.

3. Retain the zero after the decimal point or at the end of the decimal number only if the zero represents exact measurement (or a significant digit).

4. Use spaces but not commas to separate groups of three digits in the decimal fraction.

5. In columns, line up the decimal points.

6. Do not begin a sentence with a decimal number.

3. Retain the zero after the decimal point or at the end of the decimal number only if the zero represents exact measurement (or a significant digit):

0.45 *or* 0.450
28.303 *or* 28.3030

NOTE: Also retain the final zero in a decimal if the zero results from the rounding of the decimal:

23.180 for 23.1789 (*if the decimal number is supposed to be rounded to three digits in the decimal fraction*)

4. Use spaces but not commas to separate groups of three digits in the decimal fraction.

In the metric system, the decimals may be broken into groups of three digits by inserting spaces:

56.321 677 90
707.004 766 321

but 567.4572 (*not* 567.457 2)

You can use commas to separate groups of three digits that appear in the whole number part of the decimal:

56,894.65
500,067.453 467

However, do not use commas to separate groups of three digits in the decimal fraction:

4.672 34 (*not* 4.672,34)

2344.000 567 (*not* 2344.000,567)

See METRIC SYSTEM.

5. In columns, line up the decimal points:

56
0.004
115.9
56.24445
0.6

NOTE: Whole numbers without decimals (e.g., *56* above) do not require a decimal point.

6. Do not begin a sentence with a decimal number:

this

The timer interrupts the processor 14.73 times a second.

not this

14.73 times a second the timer interrupts the processor.

See NUMBERS.

Editors, writers, secretaries, reviewers, typesetters, proofreaders, printers—those people who work with documents—must have a system for indicating changes to a text.

The standard system of editing and proofreading symbols (listed in most dictionaries) is far more complex than most of us need because it includes symbols that were developed to allow copy-editors, typesetters, printers, and others involved in publishing to make minute corrections to a text about to be printed.

The editing and proofreading symbols listed in rule 1 constitute a simplified set of the standard symbols. This simplified set addresses the needs of most business and technical writers who must communicate suggestions and editorial corrections to writers, reviewers, or secretaries in a business environment. If you need the complete set of proofreading symbols, see *The Chicago Manual of Style,* 14th edition, or the *United States Government Printing Office Style Manual.*

The example under rule 1 illustrates the simplified method of editing and proofreading a printed piece of text. This example also follows the rules cited below.

Editing and Proofreading

1. Use consistent proofreading symbols to indicate changes or corrections to text.

2. Use marginal marks to indicate corrections made within lines.

3. Use different colors of ink for different proofreadings (either by the same person or several people).

4. Keep a list of editorial or proofreading decisions so you can be consistent and so you can summarize for the writer the changes you routinely make.

5. Follow effective proofreading strategies.

---

1. Use consistent proofreading symbols to indicate changes or corrections to text.

ℓ	Delete or take out.
∧	Insert a phrase, word, or punctuation mark.
∿	Transpose letters, words, or phrases.
⊐	Move to the right.
⊏	Move to the left.
≡	Use capital letter(s).
/	Use lower case letter(s).
◡	Close up a space.
#	Add a space.
¶	Make a new paragraph.

NOTE 1: Professional proofreaders sometimes use a different symbol in the margin than they use in the text. For instance, the # sign in the margin indicates that a space should be added. In text a slash mark indicates where the space should be added:

\# The incorrect/proposal

NOTE 2: In addition to the proofreading symbols shown above, some reviewers also use the symbol *sp* to indicate a spelling error. Most editors would correct a spelling error by inserting, deleting, or transposing letters, but if the reviewer wants the author to make the corrections, then indicating spelling errors with *sp* is helpful.

Original

Writers and Secrtaries of word processing specailists have to agree on what to use when editing and proofreading draft materials. without such an agreement, and a consistent convention, erros creep in and quality writing is impossible.

Corrected

Writers and secretaries or word processing specialists have to agree on what symbols to use when editing and proofreading draft materials.

Without such an agreement, errors creep in and quality writing is impossible.

2. Use marginal marks to indicate corrections made within lines.

Changes to a text are sometimes difficult to see, particularly those changes made in pencil or black ink, which readers may have trouble distinguishing from surrounding print. To highlight changes or corrections, you should use a red or green pencil for changes. Even the change in color is sometimes difficult to see, however, particularly for color-blind reviewers.

So indicate changes by marking the change within the line but also using marginal marks to show that a change appears on the line beside the mark. Professional proofreaders use marginal proofreading symbols to highlight changes, but even a simple check mark or an *X* can be effective in catching the reader's eye.

Be consistent, whether you use standard marginal proofreading symbols or simply a checkmark to indicate that a change has occurred in the line beside the checkmark.

3. Use different colors of ink for different proofreadings (either by the same person or several people).

A text going through multiple revisions can become difficult to decipher if the different revisions are not somehow indicated. A very good system is to change the color of the reviewer's or proofreader's pencil (as in the example below).

The first reviewer might indicate changes with a blue pencil, the second reviewer with a red pencil, the third with a green pencil, and so on. The color of the suggestion thus

indicates when and by whom the suggestion was made. This system is particularly effective during peer or group review.

4. Keep a list of editorial or proofreading decisions so you can be consistent and so you can summarize for the writer the changes you routinely make.

The list of editorial or proofreading decisions is sometimes called an editorial style sheet. Writers themselves sometimes develop it, or they wait for an editor or proofreader to develop one. The earlier it can be developed, the better.

Items on this list would include all decisions about punctuation, capitalization, spelling, or word

An Example of Multiple Proofreadings

usage. To illustrate, a proofreader working with the preceding example could make these sorts of decisions:

Grayson plant (*not* Grayson Plant)

MOGO (*not* Mogo)

Comma in a series precedes and: propane, butane, and gasoline

TransState Pipeline Co. (*not* Company)

TPS (TransState Pipeline Co.) *rather than* TransState Pipeline Co. (TPS)

NOTE: As the above examples suggest, some language decisions about a document are not clearly right or wrong. Instead, an editor or proofreader has to pick the preferred form and then stay with that choice throughout the document. See STYLE and PUNCTUATION.

5. Follow effective proofreading strategies.

To ensure the effectiveness of your document and to protect your image and your organization's, you should proofread every document. Documents differ in importance, however, and require different proofreading strategies. See WRITING AND REVISING.

When hurried or faced with a low-priority document, read through the document once, paying special attention to important points such as headings, topic sentences of paragraphs, visuals, and captions.

For more important documents, consider some of these proofreading strategies.

- **Check format.** Does the document look good—with uniform spacing, heading styles, lists? Are emphasis techniques (boldface, italics, etc.) consistently applied?

- **Check content.** Is the information correct? For example, if the invitation says the meeting is on Monday, June 15, will the meeting actually take place then? And does June 15 really fall on a Monday? Are figures such as dollar amounts or percentages correct? Do you find facts contradicted from one page to another?

- **Check for errors.** Although a spell checker will flag spellings it does not recognize, you must decide if words are spelled correctly for the context (for example, *their* vs. *there*). Double-check spelling of names. Question every capitalization, punctuation, word division. Note that typographical errors often occur in groups. Question every number and add up figures to make sure sums are accurate.

For particularly important documents, consider these strategies:

- **Read backwards** so the content does not distract you from watching for errors.

- **Read aloud** so you slow your reading speed and are more alert to flaws in grammar and sense.

- **Read in groups.** For long, complex documents, some readers can mark changes on the text or look up words or facts while another reads aloud. This strategy has the advantages of getting more than one viewpoint and speeding up the work.

Electronic mail (also called E-mail, e-mail, or email) is the exchange of messages using computers linked on a network. One person writes a message and then sends it to one or more readers. Often, hard (printed) copies of the message won't even exist because both the sender of the message and the readers will delete the message from the system without printing a hard copy.

(**Voice mail** is similar to electronic mail and is also becoming popular. See the end of this entry for a discussion of voice mail.)

Millions of people now use electronic mail. The number of individual messages is staggering even today, and estimates suggest that by the year 2000 electronic messages will annually total move than 60 billion worldwide.

Many E-mail users are unsure how to write in this relatively new medium. E-mail invites spontaneity—what some have called "written speech"—unhampered by old notions of etiquette, unguarded, casual, and personal in tone. At the same time, businesses own their E-mail networks and have a serious interest in ensuring that they are used in productive ways. For E-mail, you should adopt a conversational, businesslike tone. See TONE.

Some networks exist to serve subscribers with special-interest sites—for example, medical practitioners who want access to a medical database, or financial analysts who want financial information. Increasingly, the Internet is expanding and absorbing these special-interest sites.

Electronic Mail

1. Choose electronic mail when you want to communicate information rapidly and when the information is better conveyed by computer than by phone or hard (printed) copy.

2. Write an eye-catching entry (subject) line.

3. Preview key content up front and limit your document to one screen (page) if possible.

4. Review and revise (as necessary) your file before sending it to readers.

5. Signal clearly the end of your message.

Voice Mail

6. Be sure to identify yourself and give your listener the date, time, and your phone number.

7. Think before you speak.

8. Speak clearly and repeat important information.

Many managers see electronic mail reducing phone calls and eliminating unnecessary paperwork. They foresee a totally electronic office, one without files and files of hard copies. They also see more efficient and more rapid decision making.

Other managers see the problems associated with electronic mail. The main one is the problem of poor or incomplete documentation. Unless companies or agencies keep an accurate record of internal decision making, they will be unable to explain and defend their decisions.

As they increasingly rely on electronic mail, companies and agencies will need comprehensive guidelines about what needs to be retained in company files (electronic or hard copies) and what can be deleted or destroyed. Remember, also, that deleted files can often be retrieved for review. See MANAGING INFORMATION.

A second problem is that electronic mail will not prevent mis-under-standings and erroneous messages. A written message is neither better nor less ambiguous just because it is in electronic form. For instance, electronic mail may be less efficient than discussions on the phone because electronic mail does not permit the instantaneous feedback possible in a phone call.

Despite some problems with its use, electronic mail is part of today's high-tech business world. It is now a valuable tool, and it will become even more valuable as employees learn how best to use its strengths and avoid its weaknesses.

Using Electronic Mail Efficiently

---

1. Choose electronic mail when you want to communicate information rapidly and when the information is better conveyed by computer than by phone or hard (printed) copy.

Electronic mail is especially efficient when the persons you want to contact are unavailable. Electronic mail allows you to send the message

Electronic Mail

so that it will be available when the recipients return to their computers.

Electronic mail is also valuable when the data or information would be inconvenient to deliver over the phone. For instance, several names, addresses, and phone numbers are time consuming to dictate over the phone. Hard copy is, of course, an option, but hard copy might take several days to arrive if it has to go by outside mail or even through an internal mail system. A fax is another option, but it often requires the sender and receiver to go to fax stations somewhere else in their buildings.

Use the phone when you want to get immediate feedback or response to your message. For instance, if you have a request or if your message requires extra tact and the personal touch, use the phone. The computer screen can seem cold and unfeeling, for example, when the writer has to send unpleasant or negative messages.

Use hard (printed) copies when you want to keep a record of your message. For example, you might want to summarize a meeting where important departmental decisions were made. A second example would be personnel decisions, which potentially become part of an employee's personnel file. In either case, of course, you could write the document using electronic mail and then print a hard copy for your files.

2. Write an eye-catching entry (subject) line.

Make sure your entry line will stand out from a long list of entry lines that appear on the reader's screen. As electronic mail becomes more popular, more and more entries will confront a reader who calls up a list of electronic mail files. If your entry line doesn't catch a reader's attention, your file might not even be opened!

Write entry lines that get your message across in a few words:

> *this*
>
> —Scoping Meeting Nov. 9 at 10 p.m.
> —Cost Overruns of 20% on A-345 Prototype
> —Please Sign Divisional Budget by July 5
>
> *not this*
>
> —Scoping Meeting
> —Cost Overruns
> —Divisional Budget

See HEADINGS.

3. Preview key content up front and limit your document to one screen (page) if possible.

Electronic mail readers do not like being forced to scroll through several screens. Present your main points quickly, and preview the remaining content so readers will know what is coming.

If possible, limit your document to one screen (page).

Work toward the principle of "no surprises." A reader opening an electronic mail file and looking at the first page (screen) should know both the main point of the message and the content to follow. Whenever possible, design this one screen using emphasis techniques, such as lists, headings, and single-sentence paragraphs. See EMPHASIS.

this

We propose increasing the division's supplemental budget for July by $5,000 to account for cost overruns on the XYZ project. Here is why we are making this proposal:

1. Increased labor rates required from January through June and their projection into July

2. Several additional fact-finding trips projected during July

3. Increased managerial interest in XYZ

not this

As you know, during the recent managerial coordination meeting (June 15), the subject of XYZ came up. Concerns expressed included the timing of the project, especially work during July. Also, the engineering representatives indicated that several extra trips might be necessary during July . . . .

See ORGANIZATION and EMPHASIS.

For longer documents, consider writing a separate executive summary for the first page (screen) and then including other data as necessary. In many cases, the executive summary might be sufficient by itself, with the background or supporting data merely referenced or transmitted in hard copy to follow up the electronic version. See SUMMARIES.

4. Review and revise (as necessary) your file before sending it to readers.

The immediacy of electronic mail is both its strength and its weakness. Although readers can get the message almost as fast as if it were given by phone (or fax), the message itself might profit from review, both for errors and undesirable content. See WORD PROCESSING.

Depending on your potential readers, take time to clean up your document. A few errors will detract from the message; many errors will destroy your credibility and the impact of your message.

If possible, use your computer's spellchecker, but remember that a spellchecker will not identify wrong words (for example, *there* instead of *their*).

With hard (printed) copies—especially those written with heat and anger—a cooling period has always been desirable. Consider allowing a cooling period before you send certain electronic files to recipients. Give yourself at least one day to reconsider your message. Often you will change the message, and sometimes you may even decide not to send it.

5. Signal clearly the end of your message.

Readers resent being left hanging or scrolling to an empty screen, wondering if they have missed something.

End most documents in two clear ways. First, conclude with a brief summary or review of the content. You might restate a request or a deadline, or you might even list again the reasons for your request.

Second, give your documents a quick complimentary close— *Sincerely, Thanks, See you Thursday,* etc., plus your name (or initials). See LETTERS and MEMOS.

Using Voice Mail Efficiently

Voice mail (voice messaging) is becoming a popular alternative to electronic mail. The main benefits of voice mail are to avoid "telephone tag" and to get your message across quickly and efficiently.

A voice mail system connects your telephone to a computer that digitizes and stores telephone messages on a magnetic disk. Such a system does much more than standard telephone-answering machines: It can assign a date and time to each message, distribute the message to many receivers, page receivers, and redirect messages when receivers are not available at a particular location. It may also tell you if your message has been picked up or not.

Even though many companies have their own voice mail system, the service is also available by subscription. A voice mail service will issue you a telephone number, which then lets you send messages to any number of users with a single call.

6. Be sure to identify yourself and give your listener the date, time, and your phone number.

Don't assume that your listener will recognize your voice; also, not every system will automatically record the date, time, and your phone number.

7. Think before you speak.

Take a minute before dialing to review mentally your main points and your intent in making the call— perhaps even jot a list of points to cover. Unless you do one or both of these things, you are likely to ramble and to confuse your listener. Rambling is a problem if you are limited in the time you have to record your message.

8. Speak clearly and repeat important information.

Misunderstandings are inevitable, so work to reduce them in your recorded messages. Speak clearly and slightly slower than you would normally. As necessary, spell out difficult words—for example, people's names or the names of places—because names often have unusual spellings. Technical terms and associated numbers are also easy for a listener to confuse.

Repetition of meeting times, deadlines, and other important details is a courtesy. You might, for example, conclude by repeating your key request or recommendation, including any associated date or meeting time. See REPETITION.

Ellipses

Ellipses consist of three periods (. . .) separated by single spaces and preceded and followed by a single space. Ellipses indicate omissions, primarily in quoted material. See QUOTATIONS.

Ellipses are the opposite of brackets, which indicate insertions in quoted material. See BRACKETS.

Ellipses

1. Use an ellipsis within quoted material to indicate omissions of words, sentences, or paragraphs.

2. Do **not** use an ellipsis to omit words if such omissions change the meaning or intent of the original quotation.

3. Do **not** use an ellipsis to open or close a quotation if the quotation is clearly only part of an original sentence.

4. Use a line of periods to indicate that one or more entire lines of text are omitted.

5. Use an ellipsis to indicate omitted material in mathematical expressions.

6. Use an ellipsis to indicate faltering speech.

---

1. Use an ellipsis within quoted material to indicate omissions of words, sentences, or paragraphs:

"Labor costs . . . caused an operating loss for January of nearly $10,000."

Original: Labor costs, which our executive committee has been studying, caused an operating loss for January of nearly $10,000.

"No tax increases for 1996 . . . will occur."

Original: No tax increases for 1996 in personal withholding will occur.

NOTE 1: If omitted material comes at the beginning of a sentence, the quoted material opens with an ellipsis, especially if the material appears to be a complete sentence:

" . . . the printed budget will remain unchanged."

Original: Despite a few inconsistencies, the printed budget will remain unchanged.

NOTE 2: If the omitted material comes at the end of a sentence, the quoted material ends with an ellipsis plus the ending punctuation of the sentence:

"The Department of Energy denied our request for an energy subsidy . . . . "

Original: The Department of Energy denied our request for an energy subsidy even though we felt our request would be cost effective.

NOTE 3: If one or more sentences are omitted following a complete sentence, retain the ending

punctuation for the sentence followed by an ellipsis:

"The submittee adjourned at noon. . . . Shortly after they reconvened, the Majority Leader requested that they adjourn until the following Monday."

2. Do *not* use an ellipsis to omit words if such omissions change the meaning or intent of the original quotation:

"Chairman James Aubrey indicated that financing the debt load would . . . seriously undermine efforts to recover delinquent loans."

Original: Chairman James Aubrey indicated that financing the debt load would not detract from or seriously undermine efforts to recover delinquent loans.

3. Do *not* use an ellipsis to open or close a quotation if the quotation is clearly only part of an original sentence:

this

We discussed the "three legal loopholes" mentioned in the last Supreme Court decision on school busing.

not this

We discussed the " . . . three legal loopholes . . . " mentioned in the last Supreme Court decision on school busing.

4. Use a line of periods to indicate that one or more entire lines of text are omitted:

Friends, Romans, countrymen, lend me your ears;

I come to bury Caesar, not to praise him.

. . . .

He was my friend, faithful and just to me:

NOTE: The line of periods does not tell a reader how much was omitted. The writer is responsible for retaining the intent and meaning of the original material.

5. Use an ellipsis to indicate omitted material in mathematical expressions:

$a_1, a_2, \ldots, a_n$

$1 + 2 + \ldots + n$

See MATHEMATICAL NOTATION.

6. Use an ellipsis to indicate faltering speech:

I protest . . . or maybe I should only suggest that you have made a mistake.

I wonder . . . perhaps . . . if . . . that is a wise choice.

Emphasis includes any techniques writers use to make their messages both readable and unambiguous. Readers must immediately see your major point or points, and rereading should be unnecessary if you have designed your document using proper emphasis techniques.

Every misleading sentence or disputed fact represents a waste of time and money in today's technical society. Organizations cannot afford ambiguous procedures, unclear memos, and inconclusive reports.

Textual options and a rich and varied vocabulary become liabilities when writers need to remove ambiguities. The traditional academic essay or scholarly paper is often inefficient and unproductive precisely because it deliberately includes multiple meanings and different interpretations.

A well-designed, emphasis-driven document forces every reader to come away with the same message. A simple example would be the instructions for assembling an exercise bike. Every customer assembling the bike should be 100 percent successful. No calls to the bike company's customer service center should be necessary, and the final bike should have no unfastened parts or other unsafe features.

Successful world-of work documents have a 100 percent usability rating! See PROJECT MANAGEMENT.

Use the following format and emphasis principles to help you generate your initial content. Your intended format should guide your content. You will be writing to fit the format, not imposing a format on content that is already created. See WRITING AND REVISING.

Emphasis

1. Control your readers' eyes by controlling the position and appearance of your ideas.

2. Open with important ideas.

3. Subordinate minor ideas.

4. Repeat important ideas.

5. (Optional) Close with repetition of important points.

6. Use space and page design to highlight important ideas.

7. Use headings and lists to highlight important ideas.

8. Use graphics to emphasize important ideas.

9. Use single-sentence paragraphs to emphasize important ideas.

10. Use typographical features and color to emphasize words and ideas.

1. Control your readers' eyes by controlling the position and appearance of your ideas.

Effective writing is document design, not the spinning out of words and phrases. Effective writing is a visual activity, not an oral/aural one.

Yes, writing begins with and relies on the oral/aural resources of language, but these resources must be presented in an emphatic manner. Proper emphasis techniques will help guarantee that readers take one and only one meaning from a passage.

Writers achieve emphasis in documents by working with position and appearance.

Position refers to the placement of words within a sentence, paragraph, or section. Language, both written and oral, moves from word to word, so the order and sequence of language is important even if it is not always speedy or efficient.

Appearance refers to the visual presentation of ideas and to the physical character of the words or ideas—for example, page layout, spacing, indentation, boldface type, underlining, type size, type style, color, and production quality. See PAGE LAYOUT and GRAPHICS FOR DOCUMENTS.

2. Open with important ideas.

The beginnings of documents, sections, paragraphs, and sentences are the most visible and memorable parts of any document. Make the first page, the first line, the major subheading count by using them to record important ideas. Lead from important ideas, not up to them. See ORGANIZATION.

Test each document, section, paragraph, or sentence. The opening page, the opening paragraph, the opening sentence, and the opening words should capture the most important ideas. If they don't, you will have misled your reader. Or at the very least, you will be forcing

Emphasis

your reader to read and reread your information. The more rereading you require, the more ambiguous your document will be.

Emphasize your most important ideas by placing them in opening positions.

3. Subordinate minor ideas.

Arrange your document so that minor ideas receive less emphasis than major ones. Minor ideas should receive both less time and space than major ones. Minor ideas should not appear in headings, in graphics, or in boldface.

Place minor ideas in the middle of documents, paragraphs, and sentences. This will happen automatically if you have followed rule 2 above, which tells you to open with major ideas. See ORGANIZATION.

And in some cases, minor ideas need only be referenced because they should not appear in the document. These referenced ideas become part of the legal record or organizational documentation. See APPENDICES.

Minor ideas include backup data and their interpretation; lengthy analyses leading up to conclusions; routine explanations of your methodology; summaries of prior research; and any other peripheral information.

4. Repeat important ideas.

Repetition helps readers remember earlier messages as new words and ideas appear. Repetition signals important ideas and guarantees that readers remember the ideas. See REPETITION.

However, repetition can be either ineffective or effective.

Ineffective repetition states the same thing over and over again. Students often use ineffective repetition because they are trying to fill pages and to generate a certain number of words. They may write a dozen sentences, each saying they had an exciting summer vacation!

Effective repetition occurs when the design of a document repeats important ideas. The title, subject line, and major headings introduce major ideas. Graphics and accompanying captions further illustrate these same ideas. And if you include an executive summary, it will present the highlights of these ideas. See SUMMARIES.

Each mention of a major idea should use the same wording and the same technical data, such as acreage or the annual output. This type of deliberate repetition means that the most important ideas should be 100 percent unambiguous and consistent each time they appear.

Effective repetition is one indication that a document has been carefully designed and well edited.

5. (Optional) Close with repetition of important points.

This rule is optional because the visual nature of documents has decreased the role of the closing section, the closing paragraph, or the closing sentence.
See ORGANIZATION and REPETITION.

Some documents still may require closings that repeat important points. Letters and memos quite often should end with a repetition

of the requested meeting, the follow-up action, or other activity. Textbooks usually wrap up chapters with a final summary, which is often identical to the chapter overview that begins the chapter.

Of course, oral language still relies on the final statement, the final word. In oral presentations, speakers must lead up to their clincher idea, their major point, their most memorable phrase. This emphasis technique has become unnecessary in most well-designed documents.

6. Use space and page design to highlight important ideas.

Make your page design, especially its open spaces, support and reinforce your important ideas. See PAGE LAYOUT and GRAPHICS FOR DOCUMENTS.

Initially, readers visually perceive the overall appearance, not the details. They derive a general impression of your intent and your content before they ever begin reading sentence by sentence.

If readers scan your first page, what should they see? If you've designed the page well, the title and major headings have the important ideas, and these are always set off by surrounding space. Perhaps the page has a graphic on it, with an interpretive caption; this graphic should also present important ideas.

Make sure, however, that your pages are not so cluttered and busy that the important ideas are lost.

7. Use headings and lists to highlight important ideas.

Writing today is increasingly less linear and sequential. Passages of language do move word by word, but the use of headings and lists means that the sequence of words is not always the primary tool for conveying meaning.

Headings and lists are schematic ways of presenting bits of information so readers can select what they read. Readers using headings and lists can easily skip and scan your document for crucial content, and they often will not even read the entire document unless they need to. See HEADINGS and LISTS.

8. Use graphics to emphasize important ideas.

Graphics are increasingly important. Today's readers expect, even demand, that well-designed documents use graphics. See GRAPHICS FOR DOCUMENTS and GRAPHICS FOR PRESENTATIONS.

The availability of graphics software has revolutionized routine reports and other everyday documents. Readers are now accustomed to seeing bar graphs, illustrations, and other common graphics. What was innovative some years ago in *USA Today* is now commonplace in many world-of-work documents and business presentations.

9. Use single-sentence paragraphs to emphasize important ideas.

Paragraphs are increasingly less important as ways of organizing ideas. In particular, a document with a sequence of long paragraphs is not very readable even if the paragraphs are well written and the language interesting. Most of the time such a document is a costly waste of time. See PARAGRAPHS.

The single-sentence paragraph is, however, still a valuable emphasis tool. Readers can quickly read a single-sentence paragraph and can scan back easily to find such a paragraph. Of course, too many short paragraphs make a document choppy and hard to use.

So reserve single-sentence paragraphs for important ideas and don't overuse this technique.

10. Use typographical features and color to emphasize words and ideas.

CAPITALS, underlining, **boldface**, *italics*, color, and different type styles stand out when used within ordinary text. Don't overuse such techniques, but design your pages to draw on these tools when appropriate. See PAGE LAYOUT.

Color is also a valuable tool, especially if used in graphics. It is probably the most visually effective of the document design tools available to writers, but it is still a costly option and time consuming, given the need for multiple printing runs. As with typeface styles, don't overuse color or mix too many colors into a single page or graphic. See COLOR.

Ethics

Ethical dilemmas will confront every professional during his or her career.

As in the following cases, professionals must make hard choices about what to say and how best to say it. The line between right and wrong may be fairly clear, but what if jobs—especially your job—depend on what you choose to do?

- Your supervisor tells you that your business product plan is too negative in its financial projections. You feel that the new product will not break even for at least 18 months. Your supervisor argues that the break-even point could be as early as 6 months after product introduction.

- Your current project parallels previously published information. You wonder how closely you can follow the ideas and phrasing of this source. Do you need to write for permission?

- A technical colleague suggests that you soften your write-up of negative conclusions about some tests.

- Your boss tells you to write a proposal using the resume of an employee who retired long ago, and you know he'll never work on the project.

To help you confront such questions and make the hard choices, we present the following rules (or suggestions). Only you can make the necessary decisions, based on the realities of your own job and of your own professional code of ethics.

1. Use full, accurate, and honest information in everything you communicate.

This rule says that every reader and listener has the right to trust what

> ## Ethics
>
> 1. Use full, accurate, and honest information in everything you communicate.
>
> 2. Analyze who (including yourself) will be affected and how and when they will be affected by ethical or professional choices you make.
>
> 3. Assess your options, given your analysis of the situation (in rule 2), and then pick a course of action.
>
> 4. Prepare documents to support your decisions on ethical issues.

you tell them. Anything less would violate your own expectations about communication. So this rule becomes the golden rule: "Communicate with others as you expect them to communicate with you." See INTELLECTUAL PROPERTY.

This rule (or some version of it) appears in every code of sound professional practice or ethics. Under the Hippocratic oath, a doctor promises to deal ethically with patients—thus neither by word nor deed harming them. The Code of Ethics for the Society of Professional Journalists states: "Truth is our ultimate goal."

A person's word must be true and firm. That is, you must be able to depend on what someone tells you; otherwise, sound relationships, agreements, and decisions are impossible. Someone whose word is untrue and unreliable risks disclosure and sanctions, either personal or legal.

What are the legal sanctions from violations of this rule? Consider the case where you violate your professional code of practice (ethics) by not revealing a design flaw you've discovered.

From a legal perspective, you personally, as well as your company, could be liable for tens of thousands of dollars. Liability exists even if you

fail to test for obvious flaws. The law assumes that sound product engineering—that is, good professional ethics—would provide for tests to discover reasonably foreseeable problems. Failure to record tests is, therefore, no protection from legal sanctions.

2. Analyze who (including yourself) will be affected and how and when they will be affected by ethical or professional choices you make.

In ethical questions about past events, decisions of right or wrong are easy. George Washington chose not to tell a lie about cutting down the cherry tree. He was ethically right (according to rule 1).

Ethical questions become more ambiguous, however, when future events are involved. Will a proposed computer system pay for itself? How safe and effective is a new antibiotic? Is the new anti-lock braking system foolproof in ordinary driving?

Consider the following problem situation, where ethical or professional questions arise in relation to a business plan.

Problem: Your supervisor tells you that your business product plan is too negative in its financial projections. You feel that the new product will not break even for at least 18 months. Your supervisor argues that the break-even point could be as early as 6 months after product introduction.

Here is a brief analysis of what could happen if you go ahead with your financial projections of 18 months and if management decides to cancel or delay the introduction of the new product:

- **Who (including yourself) will be affected?**

  You, your supervisor, other employees, upper management, shareholders—maybe even customers.

- **How and when will they be affected?**

  You, as the source of negative news, risk your chances for advancement, future assignments, and, perhaps, even your job, if the new product group is disbanded.

  Your supervisor and other employees may also receive new assignments, or perhaps they might be laid off. Top management risks missing a business opportunity, and this decision may affect the company's dividends for several quarters or even several years. Shareholders will complain about the lost dividends, driving company stock prices down.

  Customers may be only indirectly affected. They may not have the option of buying the product. Or, if management rushes the product to market to meet financial goals, quality problems may occur.

3. Assess your options, given your analysis of the situation (in rule 2), and then pick a course of action.

In the simplest terms, you can either choose to revise your projections (the 18-month break-even point) or you can refuse to back down. Neither of these answers is clearly right or wrong because you are dealing with a forecast.

If you revise your projections, how much can you change them before they are dishonest? Can you in good conscience write a report stating that 6 months is a possible break-even point?

If your projections are open to negotiation, how hard do you want to fight for them? This question is usually the crucial one when an employee considers options dealing with ethical or professional questions.

Every organization answers such questions in different ways. Our suggestion is that you address these sorts of questions as honestly and as carefully as you can. And as the next rule states, prepare documents to support your decisions on ethical or professional issues.

4. Prepare documents to support your decisions on ethical issues.

Written documentation is essential when you have to confront ethical dilemmas that might have legal implications for you and for your organization.

What should you record? No quick or easy answer exists. With the high frequency, even likelihood, of litigation today, some might be tempted to record very little or even nothing that might reveal internal debates. This view is wrong. As noted above under rule 1, professional standards mandate good documentation.

For example, in the area of environmental law, the mandate of the National Environmental Policy Act (NEPA) is to disclose to the public and any other parties (including the courts) the pros and cons of a proposed government action. Honest and professional differences of opinion are encouraged, not prohibited.

We recommend that you carefully document your professional views. Remember, also, that from a legal perspective, documentation extends beyond formal documents to include, for example, your computer files, log books, day planners, and any team notes. Careful documentation means that you have analyzed and cataloged all the pertinent records.

Recall the old saying, "Honesty is the best policy." The saying reflects the reality that, if your honesty is called into question, nothing you say or do will be credible.

Exclamation Marks

Exclamation marks (!) follow words, phrases, or sentences that are surprising or unusual enough to merit the use of an exclamation mark.

Some style guides or grammars refer to *exclamation points* rather than to *exclamation marks*. The two terms mean the same thing.

1. Use an exclamation mark to end a sentence that expresses surprise or excitement:

We completed the proposal 2 weeks ahead of the deadline!

That error will cost them their jobs!

Excellent work! No one in the department could have done as well. (*Excellent work* is a sentence despite not having a verb.)

See SENTENCES.

NOTE: Use exclamation marks sparingly; they lose their power if overused, and they can make your language sound too informal, almost breathless.

2. Use an exclamation mark in direct quotations that are exclamations, with the mark itself usually coming inside the quotation mark:

"I sent you that check over 2 weeks ago!"

"No! You do not have permission to take the car tonight," responded Mother.

Bill exclaimed: "Ouch! That hurts!"

Optionally

"No, you do not have permission to take the car tonight!" exclaimed Mother.

Bill exclaimed, "Ouch, that hurts!"

See QUOTATION MARKS.

3. Place exclamation marks outside closing quotation marks if the quoted portion of an exclamatory sentence is itself not an exclamation:

I'm speechless that all you can say is, "We forgot"!

We were amazed to discover that "all earthquake damage is excluded"!

False subjects are words like *it* and *there* that have no concrete antecedents; that is, the words do not refer to anything real. They are abstractions.

False subjects often occur at the beginning of a sentence and displace the true subject:

> It is this phase that is important.

In this sentence, *it* seems to stand for *phase*, but replacing the pronoun with its apparent antecedent creates nonsense:

> This phase is this phase that is important.

The true subject of the sentence is *phase*. Beginning with the true subject creates a shorter, much crisper sentence:

> This phase is important.

False subjects can also appear within sentences:

> We decided that there were some costs that needed to be explained.

The false subject *there* weakens the middle of the sentence and adds unnecessary additional words. The sentence is far stronger without the false subject:

> We decided that some costs needed to be explained.
>
> *or*
>
> We decided to explain some costs.

1. Eliminate false subjects.

Whenever possible, eliminate constructions with *it* and *there* when those words have no clear antecedents. Getting rid of false subjects makes your writing more concise and often clearer.

False Subjects

1. Eliminate false subjects.

Sometimes, however, the false subject is necessary, as in the expression *it is raining*. The word *it* is an abstraction, but what could you say in its place? Ask yourself, what is raining? No other word or words will be as functional or as expedient as the false subject. In such limited circumstances as *it is raining* or *it is noon*, false subjects are acceptable. Otherwise, try to eliminate them.

Below are before and after examples of false subjects. Note how much simpler, more direct, and shorter the sentences are when we eliminate the false subjects along with certain accompanying words:

In designing a thermal protection system, it is possible to meet the 1,100-degree fire requirement yet not be reliable. (*20 words*)

Thermal protection system designs can meet the 1,100-degree fire requirement without being reliable. (*14 words*)

Within the family of hydrates, there are several solid metal oxides that both chemically combine with water (hydration) and mechanically retain water (capillary condensation). (*24 words*)

Within the family of hydrates, several solid metal oxides both chemically combine with water (hydration) and mechanically retain water (capillary condensation). (*21 words*)

It will also be possible, as the study proceeds, to identify and extract important performance degradations resulting from failure to improve a given technology. (*24 words*)

As the study proceeds, identifying and extracting important performance degradations resulting from failure to improve a given technology will also be possible. (*22 words*)

or

As the study proceeds, we can also identify and extract important performance degradations resulting from failure to improve a given technology. (*21 words*)

From table 5.3, it appears that the use of relatively compact heat-transfer surfaces in the 10- to 20-fins/in. range will provide the compactness necessary to achieve the Navy goal of reduced size and weight. (*34 words*)

As table 5.3 suggests, using relatively compact heat-transfer surfaces in the 10- to 20-fins/in. range will apparently provide the compactness necessary to achieve the Navy goal of reduced size and weight. (*31 words*)

There are five significant factors that influenced the assessment of disease severity. (*12 words*)

Five factors influenced the assessment of the disease severity. (*9 words*)

It will be the responsibility of the team manager to ensure that the total required time-phased quantity and skill mix can be supplied from the onsite pool. (*27 words*)

The team manager will ensure that the required time-phased quantity and skill mix can be supplied from the onsite pool. (*20 words*)

Faxes

Faxes (derived from the word *facsimiles*) are rapidly replacing standard letters as the primary communication tool between businesses and organizations.

In one sense, a good fax is no different from a well-written letter except that it is sent by telephone line instead of in an envelope. See LETTERS.

A letter in an envelope usually stays in the outgoing mail pile for a few hours or overnight, giving you time to reconsider what you've said and how you've said it. You may even decide to change or cancel a letter written in haste or anger.

Using a fax instead of a letter often allows no time for reconsideration. The customer receives your message within minutes of your sending it, and you can only regret an inappropriate or unreadable document.

Faxes can increase misunderstandings if they are not prepared carefully. The preparer of the fax may spend too little time gathering the information or making sure that pages to be sent are both appropriate and readable. The result is that the customer gets pages that frustrate or annoy rather than communicate.

Tasks done in haste are often poorly done. Faxes and electronic mail, when sent in haste, share many of the same problems. See ELECTRONIC MAIL and WRITING AND REVISING.

NOTE: Although we are using *fax* or *faxes* in this discussion, some writers choose to use all caps, similar to an acronym: *FAX* or *FAXs*. This use of capitals is especially common on cover sheets. Both versions of the word are acceptable.

Faxes

1. Check pages for appropriateness and usefulness before faxing them.

2. Send pages that are clean and likely to be readable after transmission.

3. Be sure to include a cover sheet both with your customer's name and phone numbers and with your own organization clearly identified.

4. List on the cover sheet the documents transmitted and, if appropriate, add a personal message.

---

1. Check pages for appropriateness and usefulness before faxing them.

Ask yourself: Would these pages be appropriate for and useful to the recipient or customer?

Often documents to be sent are prepared for other purposes and for other customers. At best, they may only indirectly address the current customer's questions. At the worst, they may mislead or annoy the current customer.

For example, a flyer describing a company's services or products often has features suitable only for a single type of customer. Other customers reading this same flyer might find benefits listed that are not relevant or appropriate.

A second example would be a document that is a rough working draft. Even if you stamp the document DRAFT and warn the customer that it is not final, you risk having the customer reject your substantive ideas because of a careless misspelling or a clumsy phrase. The best of readers is often distracted by a trivial proofreading error.

2. Send pages that are clean and likely to be readable after transmission.

The quality of a fax transmission copy is still a possible problem even though fax technology has improved greatly in the last several years. Today's copies are still more fuzzy and indistinct than those made on a good photocopy machine.

Often pages with a small typeface, handwritten comments, or shaded boxes will not be very readable when they are received. Handwritten comments often extend to the edge of the paper, thus risking being cut off during transmission, or the handwriting is so unclear as to be unreadable.

You and your organization owe it to yourselves to guarantee that documents sent are readable and professional looking. The documents you send, by whatever means, reflect your professional image and your organization's commitment to quality.

3. **Be sure to include a cover sheet both with your customer's name and phone numbers and with your own organization clearly identified.**

In haste, we are often tempted to send documents without a cover sheet. In many cases, you merely need to take a couple of minutes to fill in your organization's standard cover sheet. Often you'll have a template available on your personal computer. See the sample cover sheet below.

A "headless" transmission means that pages arrive at a fax machine without anyone knowing where they should be directed. Pages can stay in the fax machine overnight or even for days before someone troubles to find out who should receive the fax.

This delivery problem would be partially solved if you and the recipient agreed that you would receive a call either confirming the receipt of the pages or notifying you that the pages had not arrived as intended.

4. **List on the cover sheet the documents transmitted and, if appropriate, add a personal message.**

A list of documents transmitted is helpful if you have sent more than two or three separate documents. This list of titles is more helpful than the number of pages transmitted, although a page count is also a good idea.

This list of titles becomes an *ad hoc* table of contents for the fax and a helpful tracking tool beyond. As you list items, be sure to give their full title or an identifying phrase, such as their authors or the date prepared. See TABLES OF CONTENTS.

Finally, use the cover sheet to personalize your message. Make this message direct and specific:

Janice—

You'll find that the attached references can verify that we'll be able to deliver the widgets on time and within budget. We'd sure like to have your business!

This message can be typed, or a handwritten note is appropriate if you have a last-minute request or comment to make.

FAX COVER SHEET

Franklin Covey
Professional Services Group
2200 W. Parkway Boulevard, Third Floor
Salt Lake City, UT 84119

DATE: May 6, 1997   **TIME:** 2:45 p.m.

TO: Terri G. Langdon, Account Manager   **PHONE:** 303/757-1200, ext. 1257
COMPANY: Franklin Covey, Gaithersburg   **FAX #:** 303/757-4444

FROM: Alex J. Bowen, Finance   **PHONE:** 801/299-4700, ext. 4801
COMPANY: Franklin Covey, SLC   **FAX #:** 801/299-4701

SUBJECT: Information from Management Meeting, May 5

NUMBER OF PAGES INCLUDING COVER SHEET: 14

MESSAGE:

Terri,

Here is the information distributed during management meeting, including:

1. Financial statements for the Eastern Office (April Report)   6 p.
2. Travel expense reimbursement policy memo, May 4   2 p.
3. Announcement of Sales Training Retreat   1 p.
4. Company Credit Card: Policy changes, May 1   1 p.
5. Personnel changes/job openings   1 p.
6. Stock purchase application (new)   1 p.
7. Minutes of management meeting, May 5   1 p.

Call if you have any questions about these items. We look forward to seeing you at the Sales Training Retreat in June.

Alex

Footnotes

Footnotes are a common method of citing sources, especially in the humanities. As their name implies, footnotes originally appeared at the bottom of a page, but now they usually appear at the end of a chapter or article, making typing and page layout easier.

Some word processing software programs allow writers to insert footnotes on each page. Consider using this software feature, assuming you wish to use footnotes, because readers find footnotes at the bottom of the page easier to read while they are reading the text.

Instead of using footnotes, writers in the physical and biological sciences usually cite the author and the date of publication by enclosing them within parentheses in the text. These citations are developed fully in bibliographies that appear at the end of the text. See CITATIONS and BIBLIOGRAPHIES.

Choose parenthetical citations for most business and technical documents. Do not use footnotes unless you are writing for a publisher or a journal that reCoveys that you use footnotes.

1. Use superscript (raised) Arabic numerals immediately following a quotation or paraphrase to indicate that the quotation or paraphrase has a footnote:

Within your text you may have a quotation from a published book or article: "Writers should always use quotation marks for exact quotations."[1] Sometimes you may be paraphrasing someone's ideas.[2] In these cases, your footnote number should come as close to the idea as possible,[3] even if the particular sentence goes on to discuss a second source.[4] Naturally, in a normal document, you should avoid having footnotes after every sentence or phrase.

NOTE 1: The footnote number comes after all punctuation, except for a dash. Footnotes are numbered sequentially within a chapter of a book and within an article. See QUOTATIONS and QUOTATION MARKS.

NOTE 2: Footnotes in graphics sometimes use an asterisk (*) or a dagger (†) when an Arabic numeral might be confusing.

2. In the first footnote to a source, include the author or authors, the full title, complete publishing information, and the pages being referred to:

Book by one author

1. David G. Peters, *The Energetic West* (Los Angeles: The Peter Pauper Press, 1992), 90.

Book by two authors

2. Frank S. Sloan and Jane Seymour, *The Road West in the 1850's* (Salt Lake City: The Popular Press, 1976), 34–35.

Book by more than three authors; information from several pages

3. Ralph Davidson, et al., *The Western Fault System* (Omaha: University of Nebraska Press, 1968), 126–127, 175, and 189.

Journal article

4. Janice Wesley, "Metal Matrix Alignment in Fiber Production," *Massachusetts Institute of Technology Journal*, 16 (October 1991): 45–46.

Public document

5. U.S. Congress, Senate, Foreign Affairs Committee, *Report on Two Chinas in the Coming Decade*, 91st Cong., 2d sess., 1991 (Washington, D.C.: United States Government Printing Office, 1993), 187–188.

Dissertation or thesis

6. O. X. Jones, "The Influence of Congressional Resolutions on Trade with China: A Study of Inconsistencies" (PhD dissertation, University of Maryland, 1992), 87–88.

Personal letter

7. Senator Frank Church of Idaho to O. X. Jones, 23 November 1975. Personal files of O. X. Jones, Portland, Oregon.

Interview

8. Sidney Sung, interview during the annual meeting of the American Political Association, Seattle, Washington, November 1993.

NOTE 1: Footnotes are similar in form to paragraphs. The first line is indented, and all items are punctuated as if the information were the first sentence in the paragraph. The items are usually separated by commas.

NOTE 2: Titles of books, journals, and newspapers may be underlined rather than italicized if italics is not available. See TITLES.

NOTE 3: Writers can add a comment or additional facts to a typical footnote:

> 8. Sidney Sung, interview during the annual meeting of the American Political Association, Seattle, Washington, November 1993. Mr. Sung, the cultural attaché in San Francisco for the People's Republic of China, granted this interview with the understanding that all of his comments would be off the record until after the 1996 U.S. Presidential election.

NOTE 4: Superscripts are a common option for numbering footnotes presented either at the bottom of the page or at the end of the chapter or article:

> [9]Jason K. Bacon, *The Two-China Policy* (New York: Columbia University Press, 1976), 85.

NOTE 5: The eight examples in rule 2 illustrate only the most common types of footnotes. For other publications, check a source such as Kate L. Turabian, *A Manual for Writers of Term Papers, Theses, and Dissertations*, Sixth Edition Revised by John Grossman and Alice Bennett (Chicago: University of Chicago Press, 1996). Turabian devotes over 40 pages to detailed examples of footnotes.

3. In second and subsequent references, make footnotes brief. Generally, include only the author's last name and the page number of the material referred to:

> *Second or subsequent footnote for one author*
>
> 10. Bacon, 56–57.
>
> *Second or subsequent footnote for two authors*
>
> 11. Sloan and Seymour, 18–21.
>
> *Second or subsequent footnote in which two or more authors by the same last name have been mentioned in first footnotes*
>
> 12. Bacon, *Two-China Policy*, 76.

NOTE: Using the author's name and a short title for second and subsequent footnotes eliminates the need for such traditional Latin abbreviations as *ibid., op. cit.,* and *loc. cit.* These abbreviations make footnotes difficult to read.

Fractions

Fractions are mathematical expressions for the quotient (division) of two quantities: 1/2. In this fraction, the slash mark means *1* divided by *2*. Strictly speaking, decimals are also fractions. See DECIMALS.

Fractions

1. Spell out and hyphenate fractions appearing by themselves in ordinary text, especially if they are followed by *of a* or *of an*.

2. Use figures for fractions when they are combined with abbreviations or symbols.

---

1. Spell out and hyphenate fractions appearing by themselves in ordinary text, especially if they are followed by *of a* or *of an*:

two-thirds of an inch (*not* 2/3 of an inch)

decreased by one-third

one-half foot

one-fourth inch

one-tenth

one-hundreth of a mile

two one-thousandths

eighty-four one-thousandths (*better* 0.084)

NOTE 1: The longer a fractional expression becomes, especially if whole numbers are involved, the more desirable it is to express the fraction in figures (or a decimal):

56/64

98/100 (*or* 0.98)

21/2 times

63/4 (*or* 6.75)

291/3

NOTE 2: Measurements, especially in scientific and technical documents, require figures:

1/3-foot step

1/2-inch pipe

2/3-inch-diameter pipe

71/2 meters

81/2- by 11-inch paper

See NUMBERS and HYPHENS.

2. Use figures for fractions when they are combined with abbreviations or symbols:

341/3 km

81/2 hr

51/2" x 6 2/3"

Such fractions and abbreviations are most common in figures or in field reports. See NUMBERS.

Gobbledygook is not a recent problem. Some 200 years ago, opponents of Benjamin Franklin argued that to vote, a man had to own property. Franklin's supporters disagreed and stated their case as follows:

> It cannot be adhered to with any reasonable degree of intellectual or moral certainty that the inalienable right man possesses to exercise his political preferences by employing his vote in referendums is rooted in anything other than man's own nature, and is, therefore, properly called a natural right. To hold, for instance, that this natural right can be limited externally by making its exercise dependent on a prior condition of ownership of property, is to wrongly suppose that man's natural right to vote is somehow more inherent in and more dependent on the property of man than it is on the nature of man. It is obvious that such belief is unreasonable, for it reverses the order of rights intended by nature.

Franklin agreed with this argument but knew that people wouldn't be moved by such pompous oratory. So he explained his position as follows:

> To require property of voters leads us to this dilemma: I own a jackass; I can vote. The jackass dies; I cannot vote. Therefore the vote represents not me but the jackass.

Gobbledygook is language that is so pompous, long-winded, and abstract that it is unintelligible. Some dictionaries trace the term to the verb *gobble*, describing the sounds made by turkeys, and it is tempting to believe that writers of gobbledygook resemble this Thanksgiving favorite. Actually, such writers are usually well intentioned. They might even take pride in writing what they consider to be sophisticated and complex language.

Perhaps the best way to appreciate gobbledygook is to read a couple of more recent samples:

> This office's activities during the year were primarily continuing their primary functions of education of the people to acquaint them with their needs,

problems, and alternate problem solutions, in order that they can make wise decisions in planning and implementing a total program that will best meet the needs of the people, now and in the future.

> Because the heavy mistletoe infestation in the Cattle Creek drainage area has rendered the residual timber resources useless for timber production, the ultimate goal is to establish a healthy, viable new stand of Douglas fir.

The average reader has to read these passages several times before beginning to decipher such nonsense. Why are the passages so difficult?

—**Words and phrases are abstract.** What does *alternate problem solutions* mean? Similarly, are *residual timber resources* the same thing as *trees?* If so, the writer should say *trees.*

See WORDY PHRASES and REDUNDANT WORDS.

—**Words and phrases are pompous sounding.** Are the *office's activities* primarily their primary functions? Is a *healthy timber stand* different from a *viable timber stand?* If not, then the writer should stick with the simpler word: *healthy.*

—**Sentences are long and clumsy.** By themselves, the 57 words in the first paragraph would make reading difficult, but the clumsy phrasing makes the reading impossible. The 35 words in the second paragraph are closer to a reasonable number, but the

writer delays the major thought in the sentence with a massive introductory clause (beginning with *because*). As written, the sentence demands that readers remember a long opening condition while they try to absorb the main thought. The sentence would be clearer if the main and introductory clauses were reversed.

See SENTENCES, STRONG VERBS, ACTIVE/PASSIVE, and PARALLELISM.

How to Avoid Gobbledygook

1. Use concrete and specific words and phrases whenever possible:

this

To complete the recreational plan, we will need pictures of all tables, fireplaces, and other existing camping facilities in the state park.

not this

In order to bring the proposed recreational plan to completion; to evaluate existing recreation site appurtenances and facilities; and to include applicable facilities such as tables, fireplaces, etc., in the proposed new recreational plan, it will be necessary to receive photographs of all current appurtenances and facilities located within the state park area.

See WORDY PHRASES and REDUNDANT WORDS.

Gobbledygook

1. Use concrete and specific words and phrases whenever possible.

2. Avoid pompous words and phrases.

3. Make sentences short, direct, and clear.

Gobbledygook

2. Avoid pompous words and phrases.

The word *appurtenance* in the preceding example is an excellent example of a pompous word. Most readers will not understand *appurtenance*, and forcing them to look up the word in a dictionary might not clarify the passage. Two recent desk dictionaries define *appurtenance* quite differently: "something added to another, more important thing; accessory" (*The American Heritage Dictionary*) and "an incidental right (as a right-of-way) attached to a principal property right and passing in possession with it" (*Webster's New Collegiate Dictionary*). Which meaning should readers choose? More to the point, why make them choose?

If a word is not in common usage, avoid it or use it in such a way that the context provides a definition. In the example above, *appurtenance* surely fails the test. Here are some other pompous words and phrases with possible substitutes in parentheses:

Accordingly (so)
acquaint (inform or tell)
activate (start)
additional (more)
adhere (stick)
ameliorate (improve)
apprise (tell or inform)

Cognizant (aware)
commence (begin)
compensation (pay)
component (part)
concur (agree)
configuration (shape, design)
conflagration (fire)
curtail (slow, shorten)

Demonstrate (show)
descend (fall, climb down)
donate (give)

Encounter (meet)
evacuate (leave, empty, clear)
exhibit (show)

Fabricate (make)
factor (cause)
feasible (likely, possible)
fracture (break)
function (work, act)

Implicate (involve)
impotent (weak)
incinerate (burn)
increment (amount, gain)
indubitably (doubtless, undoubtedly)
inform (tell)
in isolation (alone, by itself)
initiate (begin)

Locality (place)
locate (find)

Major (chief, main)
manifest (show)
manipulate (operate)
manufacture (make)
modification (change)
moreover (besides)

Necessitate (compel)
necessity (need)

Paramount (main, chief)
perspective (view)
phenomenal (unusual)
philosophy (belief, idea)
potent (strong)
practically (nearly, most, all but)
proceed (go)
purchase (buy)

Ramification (result)
render (make)
request (ask)
reside (live)
residence (home)

Sophisticated (complex)
spotlight (stress)
state (say)
stimulate (excite)
succor (help)
sufficient (enough)

Thoroughfare (aisle, street)
terminate (end, fire)
transmit (send)

Utilization (use)
utilize (use)

Vacillate (waver)
veracious (true)
visualize (imagine, picture)

3. Make sentences short, direct, and clear.

Sentence length is only one sign of complexity. A 10-word sentence can be unclear because it is poorly structured and difficult to read:

these

Cost overruns continued throughout the second quarter. They continued even though we had audited all production and re-manufacturing processes.

We need to approve their financial proposal before the end of our fiscal year. If we don't, problems will arise.

not these

Despite a careful audit of all pertinent processes, cost overruns, especially those related to production and re-manufacturing, continued throughout the second quarter.

There are certain problems likely to develop if approval of their financial proposal is deferred until after the close of our fiscal year.

See SENTENCES, STRONG VERBS, ACTIVE/ PASSIVE, and PARALLELISM.

Gobbledygook and Jargon

Gobbledygook and jargon can both make reading difficult, but they are not the same.

Jargon includes terms used by a specific technical or professional group. Carpenters, for instance, have a number of jargon terms: *stud, joist, sill plate, header, cap plate, trip-L-grip*, etc. See JARGON.

Gobbledygook can include technical jargon, but gobbledygook also includes nontechnical words that are unfamiliar, unnecessary, or too long. Good writing can include some jargon, particularly if the words are defined or understandable within the context, but good writing never includes gobbledygook.

Graphics for Documents

Graphics are one of the best devices writers have to emphasize information. Because graphics are visual rather than verbal (as writing is), they are often much more emphatic than the text written around them. Readers will recall a graphic long after they have forgotten a thousand words of text.

Today's readers expect to see graphics in documents, even in routine office newsletters and business reports. Readers also expect these graphics to be professional looking. After all, sales brochures, news magazines, and even the daily newspaper now use high-quality, often full-color graphics. Readers now expect the same quality from everything they read.

Fortunately, computer technology has made high-quality, professional-looking graphics accessible to the ordinary writer. Graphics software programs allow writers to convert data into almost any kind of bar graph, pie graph, or numerical graph. These graphics are also available in color if the final document will be printed or copied in color.

Using a computer to create graphics is not, however, always as easy or simple as the software ads say. Sometimes a program can create a pretty graphic, but it isn't exactly what you wanted. Or, the graphic may be the wrong size or shape. Figure 1 contains some tips for creating graphics on computers. These tips apply to almost any type of graphic.

For the following discussion, graphics refers only to visual information used within documents. Many of the principles discussed, however, also apply to overhead transparencies, slides, visual aids, and other presentation graphics. See CHARTS, COLOR, GRAPHICS FOR PRESENTATIONS, GRAPHS, ILLUSTRATIONS, MAPS, PHOTOGRAPHS, and TABLES.

Graphics for Documents

1. Choose graphics to emphasize your primary purpose or major concepts.

2. Create your graphics before you write the text.

3. Select graphics that are appropriate for your topic and your audience.

4. Design or modify graphics so readers can easily interpret them.

5. Introduce graphics in the text before they appear.

6. Design graphics that are simple, uncluttered, focused, and easy to read.

7. Choose emphatic devices to stress important ideas graphically.

8. Number graphics in the order of appearance.

9. Use clear and interpretive captions.

1. Choose graphics to emphasize your primary purpose or major concepts.

Graphics should capture your key recommendation, a surprising trend, the unexpected financial problem, or the most convincing data. Choose graphics for the highlights of your message. Save the supporting details for your text (or better yet, for an attachment or appendix).

If your purpose is to recommend a new vendor to replace your new phone system, you might decide to present a series of bar graphs, each showing how the four competing phone systems compared on these criteria: (1) monthly lease fee and charges for a service contract; (2) installation charge; and (3) user satisfaction ratings for the last three years. Figure 2 shows the bar chart for the third criterion (user satisfaction ratings).

Control your readers' minds by using appropriate graphics to control their eyes. Don't use graphics for mere decoration.

By their very nature, graphics are highly emphatic, so reserve their use for important visual information that reinforces your message. If you waste graphics on unimportant or unnecessary information, you waste a valuable opportunity, and you might distract your readers from a key point.

A graphic and its caption should be clear and understandable without requiring readers to search for clarifying information in the text. See CAPTIONS.

2. Create your graphics before you write the text.

Graphics should never be an afterthought. Visualization drives the text. Create visuals first; write text last. Graphics are more emphatic than text and should therefore receive greater attention early in the writing process.

This rule complements the process you should use as you write and edit your entire document. Writing a document begins when you visually design the whole document. As recommended in WRITING AND

Graphics for Documents

Tips for Creating Computer Graphics

Computer graphics are increasingly available and adaptable for use in documents. Still, using a graphics software package to generate just what you want is not always easy. Use the following tips for working with graphics software. These tips are generic, not referring to any single software package or operating system.

- **Practice developing graphics of the sort you expect to need.** Are file formats compatible, and do your software packages allow easy transfers? Actually create or copy a graphic into a dummy document so you'll learn what the problems are.

- **Verify the size and format of the desired graphic.** Design and size your graphic for your intended use and audience, not for your own computer screen. What you see on the screen may **not** be what you get. Use the review function in your software (if available).

- **Check to see how the insertion or the enlargement of a graphic affects the surrounding text.** Does the text wrap (move) automatically or do you have to move it line by line or paragraph by paragraph?

- **Practice inserting a legend (key to symbols in a graphic), a caption, or explanatory notes to the graphic.** Some systems allow you to insert and correct these easily; others make it difficult.

- **Use existing graphics if possible, rather than starting from scratch.** Sources include computer files of clip art (which allow free use of professional graphics) or CD-ROM collections of photos and other graphics. Check other projects for art that you can use.

- **Choose a software package that others can help you with.** Never start with a Beta (test) version, no matter how attractive its features sound.

- **Don't be afraid to ask for help or even to call the software help number.** Everyone is still learning what computers will do, and new software comes out monthly, even weekly.

Figure 1. Tips for Creating Computer Graphics. *Remember to allow extra time for graphics preparation, especially if you are unfamiliar with the software.*

REVISING, document design begins with a prototype (or mock-up), which will include all projected graphics. See WRITING AND REVISING and PAGE LAYOUT.

Later, as you write the draft, return to your notes or the mock-up to assist you in refining or changing your graphics.

If you prepare your graphics early, you may discover that the graphics make some of your text unnecessary. If possible, you want to discover this duplication even before you have actually written the text in question. Cost effectiveness means that you shouldn't write text that is later discarded.

3. Select graphics that are appropriate for your topic and your audience.

Graphics come in many forms: charts, graphs, illustrations, maps, photographs, and tables. These forms—and all of the variations and combinations within them—give you many choices for organizing ideas and data into graphic visual representations. Use the matrix in figure 3 to help you determine which visual aids to use in a given document.

- Charts show relationships. Charts can display organizational relationships (organizational charts) and illustrate the flow and relationship of steps in a process (flow charts). See CHARTS.

- Graphs show the correlation of two or more variables and how they change. The most common graph is a simple line graph. Graphs also include bar graphs and pie graphs, both of which show comparisons and trends. See GRAPHS.

- Illustrations and diagrams help show abstract concepts as objects or assemblies and provide a perspective on existing objects or assemblies that unmodified photographs cannot capture.

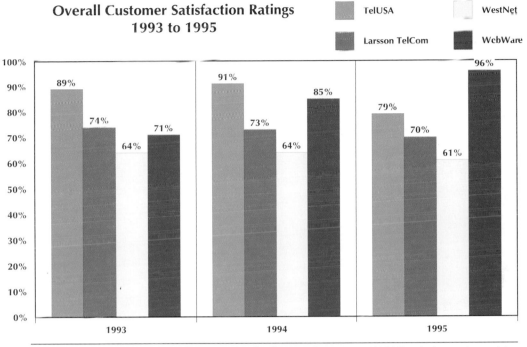

Overall Customer Satisfaction Ratings 1993 to 1995

Legend: TelUSA, WestNet, Larsson TelCom, WebWare

Figure 2. Overall Customer Satisfaction Rating for the Last Three Years. *WebWare is the most promising vendor, especially in light of its 1995 rating and its continuous improvement from 1993 to 1995.*

Type of Graphic	Document Purposes										
	Costs	Causes/ Effects	Trends	Organizational Relationships	Policies Procedures	Decisions Alternatives	Work Flow	Chronology	Design Parts Apparatus	Comparison Contrast	Advantages Disadvantages
Tables	X	X	X	X	X	X		X		X	X
Line Graphs	X		X					X		X	
Bar Graphs	X		X			X		X		X	X
Pie Graphs	X		X			X				X	X
Schematic Diagrams									X		
Flow Charts		X		X			X	X			
Maps/Site Plans			X			X					
Photographs		X								X	X	X
Tree Diagrams				X	X	X	X				
Illustrations									X		
Blueprints									X		
Combination	X	X	X	X	X	X	X	X	X	X	X

Figure 3. Graphics for Different Documents. *An X appears in a square to show when a specific type of visual aid would likely implement a particular document's purpose.*

Graphics for Documents

Illustrations can also show exploded views that focus attention on smaller parts of a larger object or assembly. See ILLUSTRATIONS.

- Maps show topographical relationships and indicate scale and distance. See MAPS.

- Photographs convey realism and authenticity. They purport to show readers exactly what something looks like. Retouched photos are illustrations. See PHOTOGRAPHS.

- Tables display data in rows and columns. They allow for quick comparisons of data with great precision. See TABLES.

The graphic you select depends on your readers, but also on what you are trying to achieve with it. The table in figure 3 shows how various information graphics can be used to accomplish a writer's purposes.

4. Design or modify graphics so readers can easily interpret them.

The graphics you choose should be consistent with the orientation, skill, and educational or technical level of your readers. For nontechnical readers, you would not use logarithmic graphs (they may not understand them); on the other hand, for highly technical readers you should not use simple bar graphs or pie graphs to present complex scientific data.

Remember, however, that your graphics (and your text) are indirectly controlled by the least technical of your readers. Keep these readers in mind as you generate your graphics and your text.

You may, at times, make a graphic or part of the text a little too difficult for such nontechnical readers, but if you do, you'll need to build in a nontechnical explanation elsewhere in the text.

The best technical writers and editors will intentionally vary the readability of their text and graphics; they assume that different readers will read and interpret different sections of a document. Technical readers may survey only the key table or the most technical graph. Less technical readers may read only the introduction and summary (or abstract) and then begin skipping or scanning the rest of the document for key points.

As a writer, you should carefully analyze your prospective readers—all of your readers. Once you know who your readers are and their technical levels, you can adapt your document and your graphics to these readers.

5. Introduce graphics in the text before they appear.

Always precede graphics with a clear introduction in the text. A graphic appearing suddenly, without an introduction or explanation, generally confuses the reader.

The introduction in the text should be informative and specific:

Informative and specific

As figure 3 shows, produced water from the 2nd Langley is much more acidic than produced water from the 1st Langley.

or

This project is estimated to cost $356,200. The cost breakdown in table 15 shows that hardware costs account for nearly 65 percent of the total costs, while labor costs constitute only 12 percent of the total.

Not informative

See Figure 3.

or

The total cost of this project is estimated to be $356,200. Table 15 provides a cost breakdown.

A good introduction indicates not only what the graphic is about but also explains how the reader should interpret it. The introduction in the text will repeat some of the ideas and even the language in the caption for the graphic. See CAPTIONS.

NOTE: Sometimes a graphic must appear in the text before you can introduce it. This may occur, for instance, when a small table or chart appears at the top of a new page and is followed by a column of text. Rather than break up the text, you might keep the graphic at the top of the page with the introduction following the graphic.

6. Design graphics that are simple, uncluttered, focused, and easy to read.

When you are designing a graphic, ask yourself key questions:

—What is the point?

—What is the most important idea that I am trying to convey visually?

—What is my central concept?

Keep things simple. Don't ask a graphic to do two or more things at the same time. When a graphic fails to communicate, it is often because the author tried to make it do too much (making it cluttered or too complex). Sometimes an author has not designed a graphic with a clear concept in mind (making the point of the graphic unfocused).

Graphics for Documents

Focus on your key purpose or concept and then build graphics around it. Like a good paragraph, a good graphic focuses on one idea and conveys it sharply and purposefully.

Make graphics uncluttered by eliminating all extraneous information. A preliminary coordinate graph or a full table of data readings contains a lot of valuable information, but either of these is likely to be more effective if you pare it down to the essentials.

If your readers cannot tell you what the point is in 5 or 10 seconds, the graphic is not effective.

Choose a simple typeface for lettering in graphics, and use capitals and lowercase letters for all headings and labels. (Lettering all in capitals is hard to read, especially if it extends beyond two or three words.)

Be sure that lettering is large enough so that if the graphic is reduced, the lettering will still be readable.

Make lines and lettering that indicate axes, scales, notes, and explanations lighter than the lines and lettering indicating data points, curves, areas, or bars.

7. Choose emphatic devices to stress important ideas graphically.

Create a document style sheet for graphics so that they will be consistent throughout each project. Choose the same emphatic device to stress the same kind of word or data. See PAGE LAYOUT.

Emphatic devices include:

- <u>Underlining</u>
- *Italics*
- **Boldface type**
- Larger type size
- Outline type
- Shadow type
- SMALL CAPS
- ~~Strikethrough~~
- Line patterns
- Dingbats ✳❖✖❟☆
- **Color**

See EMPHASIS and PAGE LAYOUT.

Color is particularly useful in helping readers understand graphics, locate key information, and distinguish between different parts, phases, or configurations. Use color to highlight a row, line, slice, area, column, circle, or data point to focus the reader's attention on that item.

Highlight special conditions in color: cautions are usually yellow and black; and warnings are often red and white. See COLOR.

As you select colors try to establish a color scheme that makes sense: green seems prosperous, yellow is transitional, red for failure. Or red and yellow are warm while blue is cool.

Use contrasting colors to show contrasting concepts or major changes; use shades of one color to show minor variations. Use the brightest colors to emphasize the most important ideas, the most muted shades to subdue the less important ideas.

Beware of too much color, making the graphic look kaleidoscopic. Finally, consider that, on average, 10 percent of your readers may be color blind. See COLOR, and GRAPHICS FOR PRESENTATIONS.

8. Number graphics in the order of appearance.

Figures include all graphics that are not tables, including graphs, charts, diagrams, illustrations, photographs, and maps

Traditionally, tables and figures were numbered separately. So, table 5 could appear in a document after figure 20. But, a current trend is to call all graphics figures, regardless of their type, and to number them consecutively.

In a short document or a document with few figures, number them sequentially through the entire text. In a document with chapters or numbered sections, give figures numbers with an en dash, such as figure 3–2. The first number is the chapter or section, and the second number denotes the number of the graphic (figure) within a chapter or section.

In longer documents, especially formal reports and publications (pamphlets, books, research studies, etc.), include a list of figures following the table of contents.

If the document has a large number of specialized figures, then create a separate list of each special type. A lengthy report with a number of maps might include a list of maps. Another report, in which photography plays an important role, might include a separate list of photographs. If the document does not warrant such special listings, however, don't create them.

Graphics for Documents

Lists of tables and figures appear immediately after the table of contents (usually on separate pages) and should themselves be listed in the table of contents. If you create both a list of tables and a list of figures, either may appear first. See TABLES OF CONTENTS.

9. Use clear and interpretive captions.

Interpretive captions usually require one or more sentences. But they should be informative without becoming too lengthy. See CAPTIONS.

A list of figures should provide, in sequence, each figure number, a title, and page number for each graphic.

Within text, captions for graphics should be informative and specific.

Captions that are only titles for a graphic are not very helpful, as these examples of weak captions show:

Figure 17. Pronghorn Population Trends in Nevada

Table 2. Particulates in Sonoma Valley, California

Interpretive captions give specific information. They not only name the graphic but they also tell readers what the point or importance of the graphic is. Notice how the following examples improve on the captions above:

Figure 17. Pronghorn Population Trends in Nevada. *The pronghorn antelope population has declined steadily since 1971.*

Table 2. Particulates in Sonoma Valley, California. *From May to October 1994, particulates in Sonoma Valley, California, remained well below EPA emission standards.*

See CAPTIONS for further examples.

Graphics for Presentations

Graphics for presentations refer to graphics used in oral presentations (either recorded or live) and created with any media or technology. The following suggestions apply to any of the possible media: overhead transparencies, slides, computer visuals, or videos. For graphics used within documents, see GRAPHICS FOR DOCUMENTS.

The role of graphics (visuals) in communication is increasing. A century ago, most communication relied on speech and listening skills, whether in live stage productions or around the family dinner table. Even a generation ago, a visual aid in education often meant only a single photograph passed from person to person or a sketch on the chalkboard.

Nowadays, graphics either replace or reinforce the oral message. And today's graphics appear everywhere and in such brief flashes that viewers may be hardly aware of some of them. Consider, for example, that images in a fast-cut video segment may last a fraction of a second; a 3-minute segment may contain several hundred images. This sort of visual sequencing (cutting) is often used, for example, at year's end to review a year's events for television viewers.

Despite changing technology, many presentations still rely on flip charts, overhead transparencies, and 35mm slides. Traditional whiteboards and still photographs are useful, even if not as trendy as a virtual reality scene created on a computer.

Multimedia used to mean a canned slide-tape program. Canned programs were used to present programs that didn't change, so they were not very flexible. The new multimedia is a dynamic

---

Graphics for Presentations

1. Choose and design graphics to emphasize important ideas and a major theme and to match your audience's needs.

2. Limit your graphics to no more than you can easily show in the time allotted for your presentation.

3. Design graphics so they are clear and easy for all members of the audience to read.

4. Create eye-catching presentation graphics.

5. Use color to focus attention, but don't overuse it.

6. Plan enough time to complete and revise the graphics.

7. Use graphics to signal transitions at natural breaks in the program.

8. Use graphs, charts, tables, and illustrations instead of text if they are easier to understand.

9. Make handouts of your primary presentation graphic.

10. Save versions of graphics files for future use.

---

combination of text, graphics, digital images, sound, and animation. In a current multimedia presentation, the graphics will usually be generated by a computer.

Graphics—whether traditional or computer-generated—show data in a concise and effective manner (in tables); they show changing data relationships (in graphs); and they show configurations that would be difficult, if not impossible, to describe (in charts and illustrations). See CHARTS, GRAPHICS FOR DOCUMENTS, GRAPHS, ILLUSTRATIONS, MAPS, PHOTOGRAPHS, and TABLES.

---

1. Choose and design graphics to emphasize important ideas and a major theme and to match your audience's needs.

Graphics for presentations should capture the key recommendation, the surprising trend, the unexpected financial problem, or the most convincing data. Use graphics that will have an impact on and be memorable to your audience.

Always profile your potential audience and their needs. In a single presentation you may face senior executives, corporate accountants, sales representatives, geologists, and engineers, each with only partial knowledge of the issues you are presenting.

Remember, also, that some of your audience may not be fluent in your language, nor share your cultural assumptions. In such cases, analyze the audience to assess whether your message is missing part of your audience. If your message does need emphasis, expansion, or even condensing, consider using a graphic.

Begin planning your presentation by designing a primary graphic or several graphics showing the key points or the major theme you want to get across to your audience.

Figure 1. Three Sources of Products Returned. *This graphic is an illustration designed to show the three sources, not just list them. This graphic would be more memorable than an ordinary bulleted (or numbered) list of sources.*

Figure 1 is an example of a graphic designed for a specific presentation. The graphic is an illustration designed to show the three sources of products returned to a training company. This illustration would be more memorable and effective than an ordinary bulleted list of the three sources.

A bulleted list of the three sources, however, would be much easier to prepare than the illustration in figure 1. Most people would not have the computer skills necessary to prepare the illustration.

Use a primary graphic, such as figure 1, at the beginning of your presentation, particularly if top managers are in the audience (they tend to be time conscious and may not stay for the whole presentation). You might also use the graphic at the end as a summary.

See GRAPHICS FOR DOCUMENTS for a discussion of how to select charts, diagrams, graphs, illustrations, maps, photographs, and tables. Any one of these different graphics will work equally well in a presentation, assuming that the format and type size allow an audience to read or view the content easily.

Figure 1, for example, is one part of a more detailed illustration presented in ILLUSTRATIONS. Figure 1 contains only a part of the original illustration because the full illustration would not be visible to the entire audience in a large room.

As you are planning your presentation, list possible graphics before or concurrently with your actual words. If you provide graphics after you have the words, the graphics will be an afterthought. They will not be an integral part of your presentation.

2. Limit your graphics to no more than you can easily show in the time allotted for your presentation.

A good rule of thumb for presentations is that you should have no more than two or three graphics per minute. And this number is excessive if you plan on taking time to explain to your audience what they are seeing and what the implications of the graphics are. Even in a series of photos (slides) that are self-explanatory, you will find that you have to give viewers 10 or 15 seconds to analyze and absorb the images in a single slide.

The preceding time estimates assume a presentation framework where your goal is to share cognitive information. If, as in a fast-cut video, you want to convey only images and a mood or feeling, then the images can and should last for only a fraction of a second. Similarly, if you are preparing an informational video, you may find that some segments may require 15 or 20 seconds of screen time, while other segments can use the fast-cut sequence of images.

In some technical presentations, presenters make the mistake of using too many slides or overhead transparencies. A good strategy is to choose the key 12 slides for viewing and some discussion. If another 12 or 20 remain important as background, consider including copies of such of graphics in your handouts (see rule 9). The audience can then review background graphics after you finish your presentation.

3. Design graphics so they are clear and easy for all members of the audience to read.

The ideal graphic for a presentation is designed so that the message can be perceived in less than 5 seconds. **Don't try to squeeze in too much on each graphic.** Figure 2, for example, would be fine as a page in a document, but as an overhead, it would not be visible much beyond the second row in a small room. Often presenters settle for an overhead version of a page such as in figure 2. They fail to plan far enough ahead to have graphics prepared especially for their presentation.

Figure 3 is an adaptation of one part of the page shown in figure 2. An adaptation is necessary so that the size of type used will be readable.

Type size and type design are major concerns when you are designing graphics. Figure 4 is a page of sample type sizes. You may want to make a test transparency using figure 4; then try it with your own equipment to see how legible text is at different sizes. Remember to stand as far back from the screen as the most distant viewer in your audience. Which line can you read clearly from there?

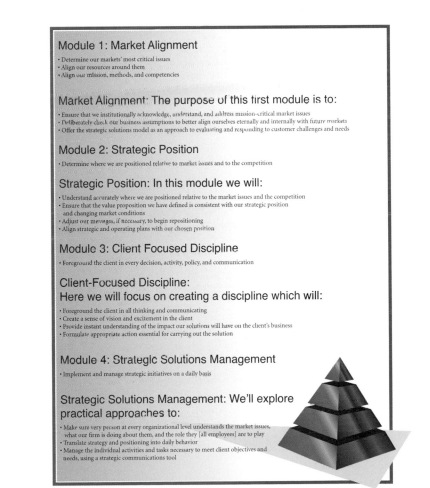

Figure 2. Four Modules on Strategic Selling. *This figure would be unreadable as an overhead. It could be the basis for four or five overheads if a presenter wanted to present this information graphically.*

Client-Focused Discipline

- **Foreground client in thinking and communicating**

- **Create vision and excitement in client**

- **Provide instant understanding of impact our solutions will have on client's business**

- **Formulate action for carrying out the solution**

Figure 3. Client Focus in Strategic Selling (Module 3). *This overhead presents only a summary of one of the four modules in figure 2. This focus on essential words and phrases allows for large type, making the figure more suitable for an overhead.*

For titles on an overhead, a sans serif typeface is clear and easy for most people to read. See PAGE LAYOUT for a discussion and examples of both serif and sans serif typefaces. Avoid all-caps for titles because they are harder to read; instead, use caps and lower case.

Text within documents is often set in a typeface with serifs, like the sentence you are reading, which is in 10.5 point *Minion*. Type this small is impossible for most viewers to read on overheads or slides.

When (or if) you use a fancy typeface, such as cursive script, use it sparingly and only for emphasis.

For greater visual emphasis in your graphics, **bold your main points or major headings.**

4. Create eye-catching presentation graphics.

Today, presentation graphics are usually produced with a computer and printed on a color printer. Almost daily, more sophisticated programs are appearing and capabilities are added to existing programs.

Sound, animation, and digital video can be added using computers. These new high-tech features should be used to emphasize important points. Beware of using too much of a good thing; your message may be lost.

Specialized presentation software programs offer proactive guidance through the design process. The powerful capabilities at your disposal make it tempting to use technology for technology's sake. Be cautious because many flashy elements will make your graphics cluttered.

Multimedia presentations require more sophisticated software programs to take full advantage of new capabilities. You probably will need a powerful computer and special add-in boards containing decoding chips to show digital movies and to reproduce high-quality sound.

5. Use color to focus attention, but don't overuse it.

For overhead transparencies, normally, use a light background and dark letters. The high contrast of a dark background and light letters can be powerful if used only occasionally. Some colors just don't work well together; figure 5 is an example of poorly chosen colors.

For computer projections, use a dark background and light letters. White or yellow lettering will stand out against a dark blue or gray background.

Don't rely exclusively on color because red-green color blindness affects one of every ten males and a small number of females. Usually, you can combine colors with designs or textures that even a color-blind person can distinguish. Figures 6 and 7 illustrate two uses of color in graphics. A color-blind person would not have trouble interpreting either figure 6 or figure 7.

Use color, but don't overuse color. Color heightens interest, provides emphasis. Too much color may cause a loss of focus on the topic. The focus becomes the color, and your graphics merely look busy and cluttered. See COLOR.

Figure 4. Readability Test Sheet. *Make an overhead of this page and then use this test overhead to determine which type size is best suited to the size of room where you will be making a presentation.*

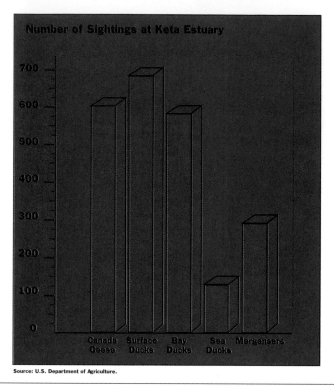

Source: U.S. Department of Agriculture.

Figure 5. A Dreadful Graphic. *Highly contrastive colors can often be too bright, even glaring. Stay with softer hues and tints. See* Color. *The three-dimensional bars are also misleading; for example, do the Canada geese number 600 or 625?*

Figure 6. Single-Family Houses Sold and Their Sales Price. *Putting both graphs on the same overhead allows for easy comparison and interpretation of the data. In a large room, however, the type used within the graphs would be too small. Two overheads would be the better choice.*

Number of Sightings at Keta Estuary

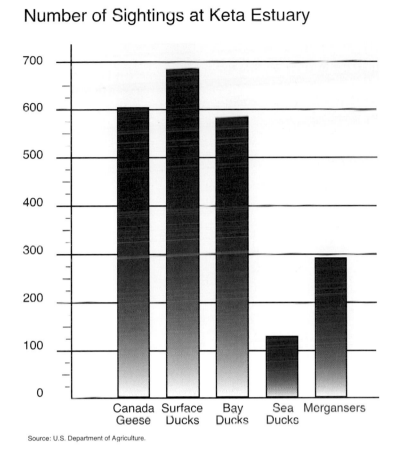

Source: U.S. Department of Agriculture.

Figure 7. Waterfowl Sightings at Keta Estuary in 1982. *The 1982 annual waterfowl count at the Keta Estuary (Alaska) showed heavy use by some waterfowl, but sea ducks were relatively scarce. Note that this figure and its interpretation would likely require one or more other graphics with data from a baseline year (perhaps 1972) or even earlier (1962). The presenter would need to decide what trend, what conclusion, or what interpretation was most important.*

6. Plan enough time to complete and revise the graphics.

Discuss your needs in detail with your graphics preparer. Say plainly what is flexible and what must be done exactly. Give your graphics preparer leeway where you can, but clearly identify what cannot be changed.

Even if you are preparing your own graphics, allow extra time for trial and error adjustments. Also, if you are not familiar with the software, you will experience many delays while producing graphics. See GRAPHICS FOR DOCUMENTS for suggestions about using computer software to prepare graphics.

Schedule time to review all of your presentation graphics. This is also a good time to do a dry run of your presentation.

Remember, also, if color slides or overheads are to be produced commercially, you need extra time and then even more time for any revisions. If you have planned enough time to complete and revise the graphics, you should still have time to add one or two graphics, if necessary.

7. Use graphics to signal transitions at natural breaks in the program.

Transitions are changes that occur in all presentations. A smooth transition helps the audience understand your message. Introduce the transition by briefly summarizing the point you have just made.

This is where you recapture the attention of the audience because their attention may start to wander after about 7 minutes.

Signal a transition at a natural point with a change of color or of the kind of graphic; for example, text to picture, or photo to chart.

Identify groups of presentation graphics that go together so the computer artist or you can make them look similar.

Number the graphics in the draft copy or in your computer file. Avoid changing numbers of the graphics during preparation. Number changes often cause confusion. If you insert a visual between 1 and 2, make it 1a. Renumber graphics after everything is done.

8. Use graphs, charts, tables, and illustrations instead of text if they are easier to understand.

It's better to show an effective graphic (with highlights) and talk about it than show detailed text and read it. Graphics should be digestible in less than 5 seconds (see rule 3). Simplify, simplify! Leave out data if its loss doesn't detract from the message.

Graphics for Presentations

Captions used on presentation graphics usually appear at the top, as in figures 1, 3, 5, 6, and 7. These same graphics in text would often have their captions at the bottom. See CAPTIONS.

Text captions on overheads must use larger type if on-screen legibility is a concern.

9. Make handouts of your primary presentation graphic.

Always make handouts of your primary graphic showing the main points you want to get across to your audience (See rule 1). Use a primary graphic at the beginning of your presentation to convey your message to people who may not stay for the entire presentation. Then use it later for transitions or to review points. Finally, use it at the end as a summary.

A good practice is to have handouts for **all** graphics, both primary and supporting, that you display during a presentation. If you don't provide handouts, some members of the audience will be frantically trying to take notes or to copy graphics. They will often not be following what you are saying.

As computer-driven presentations become more common, handouts will be more important because the audience will have less time to take notes. As an option and as a way to save paper, you might make copies of your graphics available on the Internet or on your company intranet.

10. Save versions of graphics files for future use.

Save in-progress versions of graphics files off-line or on a floppy disk and keep the disk in your file. You may need these ideas again to prepare for a follow-up presentation.

Graphs depict numerical data and are useful for showing trends, cycles, cumulative changes, relationships between variables, and distributions. They are not as effective as tables in providing precise data, but readers should be able to extract relatively accurate numerical data from the lines plotted or from the size of the bar or pie segments in bar graphs and pie graphs. Graphs are better than tables if you want to help your readers understand the meaning of your data. See TABLES.

Graphs include **line (or coordinate) graphs**, **bar graphs**, and **pie (or circle) graphs**. As explained in CHARTS, bar graphs and pie graphs are often called bar charts and pie charts. Don't be bothered by the confusion between terms; the more important issue is to ensure that your graphs (or charts) are well conceived and professional looking.

Line (or coordinate) graphs and bar graphs are normally plotted using grid lines, with a horizontal axis (x-axis/abscissa) and a vertical axis (y-axis/ordinate). Grid lines are usually equally spaced in horizontal and vertical directions and reflect the numerical scales along each axis. Figure 1 includes two simple line graphs with equally spaced grids, one showing the number of single-family houses sold over the last 25 years and the other showing their median sales prices.

For general information on graphics, see GRAPHICS FOR DOCUMENTS and GRAPHICS FOR PRESENTATIONS. See also COLOR, ILLUSTRATIONS, MAPS, PHOTOGRAPHS, and TABLES.

The most common graphs are **line (or coordinate) graphs**, **bar graphs**, and **pie (or circle) graphs**. Other types of graphs exist, however, such as graphs using logarithmic scales or

Graphs

1. Use a line graph, a bar graph, or a pie graph to help readers visualize quickly and easily the major points in a document.

2. Ensure that the visual characteristics of the graph reflect the magnitude and importance of the data being represented.

3. Number each graph sequentially, provide a title, and then add an informative caption to identify the purpose of the graph.

4. Place footnotes and source information below graphs.

5. Use grid lines or tick marks to help readers interpolate data.

6. Orient all labels, numbers, and letters so that they are parallel with the horizontal axis.

Line or Coordinate Graphs

7. Choose and label scales to indicate the quantity, magnitude, and range of each axis.

8. Make your key data lines heavier than axis and grid lines and less important data lines.

9. Use multiple lines, if necessary, to show the relationships between three or more variables, and use different line patterns to depict different variables.

10. Do not smooth out data lines.

11. Label important values on a data line.

12. If labels or numbers appear within the grid, blank out the grid area beneath the labels or numbers.

Bar Graphs

13. Clearly label each bar.

14. Make the bars wider than the spaces between them.

15. Use different bar patterns to indicate differences in types of data and label these patterns clearly.

16. Use segmented bars to depict multiple variables or component parts of a whole.

Pie Graphs

17. Identify each sector of the pie and, if appropriate, the percentage it represents.

18. Differentiate adjacent pie sectors by using alternating fill shades or patterns.

19. Group small percentage items under a general label, such as "Other."

20. Use pie-bar combination graphs to show the composition of an important sector of the pie.

21. Use a series of pie graphs to add time as a variable.

Graphs

Single-Family Houses Sold and Median Sales Prices: 1970 to 1992

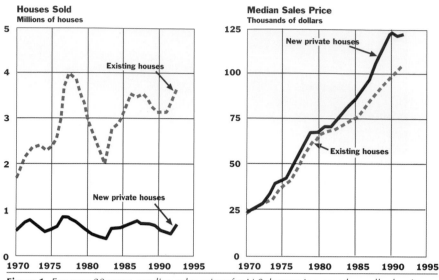

Figure 1. *For over 20 years, median sales prices for U.S. homes increased anually despite a major decline in the number of existing (previously constructed) houses sold during the early to mid-1980s.* (Statistical Abstract of the United States 1995, p. 710)

polar coordinates; these other types of graphs are beyond the scope of the following discussion, which deals with line or coordinate graphs, bar graphs, and pie graphs.

1. Use a line graph, a bar graph, or a pie graph to help readers visualize quickly and easily the major points in a document.

The most technically complex and even elegant graph fails if it is not simple and easy to read. Keep your graphics simple, even obvious.

Ensure that each graph has a single important point to make or a single relationship to show. Then tell your readers what the relationship is, both in the text and in a caption. See CAPTIONS. Be careful not to confuse readers by assuming that they understand the relationship between variables; for instance, do not use *versus* without an explanation of the relationship between the variables.

Don't try to do too much with each graph. Figure 2, which is a simple bar graph, shows how the communication media have

changed in U.S. households over the last 12 years. This bar graph has a simple message because it displays only two sets of data, one for 1980 and the second for 1992. In contrast, the original data for this graph comes from Table 900 in the *Statistical Abstract of the United States 1993*; in this table, data cover the years 1970, 1980, and each year

from 1985 through 1992. Also, the media in that table have several categories not presented in figure 2. Figure 2 is designed to focus on only its simplified message, not all the complex year-by-year details.

Complicated graphs are often confusing, even to technically competent readers. Simplify graphs by eliminating everything that does not contribute to the central message of the graph. Do not use more labels, numbers, tick marks, or grid lines than necessary to do the job. Too much clutter makes graphs difficult to read.

2. Ensure that the visual characteristics of the graph reflect the magnitude and importance of the data being represented.

The value of graphs is their visual impact. Consequently, writers can mislead readers by producing graphs that give more or less prominence to an idea or piece of data the writer wishes to emphasize or deemphasize. See ETHICS.

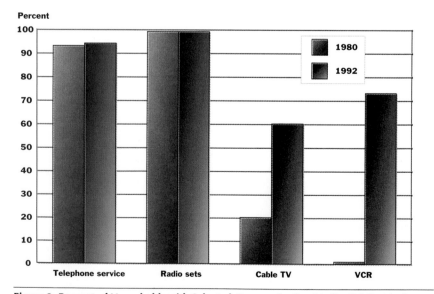

Figure 2. Percent of Households with Selected Communication Media. *While telephones and radios were almost universally available in 1980, other media, such as cable television and VCR's, were just beginning to become accessible to most households.* (Based on Table 900, p. 561, in the Statistical Abstract of the United States 1993.)

© 1985–1999 FranklinCovey Co.

Distorting coordinate scales, bar lengths, or pie slice areas can mislead readers into thinking that something is larger or smaller than it really is. Similarly, using bright colors for insignificant data and dull colors for significant data can confuse readers and lead some to think that the insignificant is really significant. To ensure that you have presented a truthful and accurate picture of the situation being depicted, strive to make the visual impression created by the graph consistent with reality. See GRAPHICS FOR DOCUMENTS.

3. Number each graph sequentially, provide a title, and then add an informative caption to identify the purpose of the graph.

Graphs and all other graphics are usually labeled as figures, so the numbering would be *Figure 1*, *Figure 2*, etc. Or, if the document has chapters, *Figure 1–1*, *Figure 1–2*, *Figure 1–3*, where the first number is the chapter number.

Following *Figure* and the number comes the title of the graph:

Figure 3–1. Absorption (Percentage) of Drug A over Time (Minutes).

Sometimes, however, the title appears above a figure, functioning more like a headline. See figures 1, 3, 4, 6, 7, 8, 11, and 12 for examples of headlines used above figures. Then, provide an informative or interpretive caption to guide readers to see the point of the graph:

Figure 3–1. Absorption (Percentage) of Drug A vs. Time (Minutes). *Drug A is very slowly absorbed until it has been in the patient for at least 30 minutes; then absorption is rapid.*

For the graphs used as examples in this discussion, we have varied the presentation to show the different placements of titles and captions. In an actual report or formal document, you would want to

choose one placement pattern and use it for all figures. See CAPTIONS and GRAPHICS FOR DOCUMENTS.

4. Place footnotes and source information below graphs.

Footnotes typically explain or clarify the information appearing in the entire graph or in one small part of it. Often, footnotes tell what the data apply to, where they came from, or how accurate they are:

[1]All data are in constant 1990 dollars.

[2]For companies with no foreign assembly plants.

[3]According to the National Stockmen's Council. The data come from each state's database, so some variations will appear because each state has slightly different reporting standards.

The footnotes for each graph are numbered independently from footnotes in the text and from footnotes in other graphics. Begin with footnote 1 and proceed sequentially for that single graph; for the next graph start the numbering again. Within the body of the graph, use superscripted footnote numbers. Place the footnote explanations (in numerical order) immediately below the graph and flush with the left margin. Repeat the superscripted footnote number and then provide the appropriate explanation, followed by a period.

If the graph covers more than one page, place the appropriate footnotes with each page. If caption and footnotes appear below a graph, place the footnotes above the caption. If the caption is above the graph, place the footnotes below the graph but ahead of the text.

If footnote numbers would be confusing in the body of the graph, use letters ([a], [b], [c], [d], etc.), asterisks (*, **, ***), or other symbols.

Source information may appear in footnotes if the referenced source provided only that data indicated by the footnote and not the data for the rest of the graph:

[4]From *Journal of Experimental Biology*, Volume 8 (March 1996).

[5]Source: U.S. Department of the Interior, Bureau of Land Management.

Source information may also appear within parentheses in the caption (regardless of where the caption appears) or within brackets under the caption if the caption appears ahead of the graph:

Figure 1. U.S. Aerospace Mergers and Acquisitions, 1960–1995 (U.S. Department of Commerce)

Figure 1. U.S. Aerospace Mergers and Acquisitions, 1960–1995
[U.S. Department of Commerce]

See FOOTNOTES, CITATIONS, and INTELLECTUAL PROPERTY.

5. Use grid lines or tick marks to help readers interpolate data.

Including grid lines on graphs was the status quo for many years. Nowadays, many graphs appear without grid lines, principally because graphs are now produced by computer (see figure 3). Omitting grid lines is acceptable. However, if you expect readers to extract precise data from graphs, you should not omit grid lines unless you combine the graph with a table (see figure 6 for an example of a combined graphic).

If you decide to omit grid lines, retain tick marks to help readers interpret data. Tick marks are short lines on and perpendicular to an axis that indicate the intervals along a scale. Use longer tick marks beside interval labels; use shorter tick marks between labels. Generally, try to use twice as many tick marks as labels (so that you have tick marks

Graphs

Single-Family Houses Sold and Median Sales Prices: 1970 to 1992

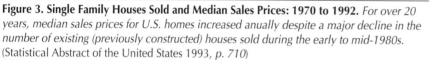

Figure 3. Single Family Houses Sold and Median Sales Prices: 1970 to 1992. *For over 20 years, median sales prices for U.S. homes increased anually despite a major decline in the number of existing (previously constructed) houses sold during the early to mid-1980s.* (Statistical Abstract of the United States 1993, p. 710)

at the midpoints between labels). Figure 3 shows the same graphs as in figure 1, but in this instance, the grid lines are removed, leaving only tick marks.

Do not use too many tick marks. The more tick marks you use, the more crowded the scale becomes. Do not create finer distinctions than necessary for the data being shown.

---

6. Orient all labels, numbers, and letters so that they are parallel with the horizontal axis.

Placing all lettering horizontally on the page makes graphs easier to read. The labels in figures 1, 2, 3, and 4 illustrate horizontal lettering. However, some federal agencies require that the labeling of the ordinate axis be vertical.

Overly long vertical labels are an exception to this rule. If your ordinate axis label is too long to write horizontally, then write it vertically with the base of the letters parallel and adjacent to the ordinate axis. Readers should be able to read long vertical labels by turning the page clockwise.

Line or Coordinate Graphs

Line (or coordinate) graphs are normally plotted using grid lines or tick marks, with a horizontal axis (x-axis/abscissa) and a vertical axis (y-axis/ordinate). Grid lines are usually equally spaced in horizontal and vertical directions and reflect the numerical scales along each axis. An exception would be logarithmic graphs or polar coordinates, where the scales are not equally spaced, but these are beyond the scope of the present discussion.

Figure 4 is a typical line graph, with data on the Federal budget from 1970 to 1995. As in most line graphs, figure 4 plots the time (in years) on the horizontal axis and the dollars (in billions) on the vertical axis.

---

7. Choose and label scales to indicate the quantity, magnitude, and range of each axis.

If the horizontal (x) axis or the vertical (y) axis indicates quantities, magnitudes, and ranges, use scales and grids or tick marks that show the axis minimum and maximum, as well as the numeric intervals. (See the vertical and horizontal scales on figures 1, 2, and 3.)

Label the minimums and maximums. Sometimes these are both positive values; in other cases, as in figure 4, negative values are also presented.

Also label a sequence of intervals along the scale. If the minimum is 0 and the maximum is 1,000, for instance, you might label the scale in steps of 100. These interval labels indicate the scale and allow readers to interpolate data. Do not use so many labels that the scale becomes crowded; however, do not use so few that readers cannot easily interpolate data. Generally, try to leave one or two spaces between interval labels. These labels will correspond to either grid lines or tick marks (see rule 6).

Use axis labels to identify each axis. Placement of these axis labels varies. Sometimes they come under the units on the horizontal axis and to the left of the vertical axis. But as in figures 1, 2, 3, and 4, the label for the vertical axis appears at the top of the graph. Indicate the units of measurement in the axis label or place the units of measurement within parentheses after or below the axis label:

Wheat Shipments, in Metric Tons

Wheat Shipments (Metric Tons)

Wheat Shipments
(Metric Tons)

If time is one variable, plot it on the abscissa. See figures 1, 3 and 4.

Scales must increase from bottom to top along the ordinate axis and left

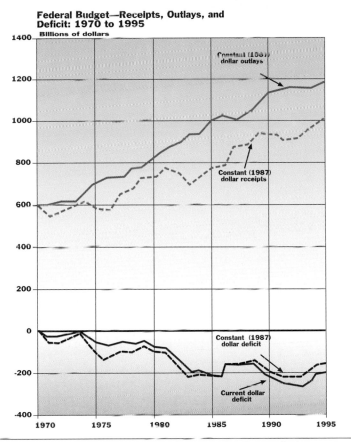

Federal Budget—Receipts, Outlays, and Deficit: 1970 to 1995

Figure 4. The Federal budget has continued to grow sharply over the last 25 years, both in actual dollars and in constant (1987) dollars. Outlays have exceeded receipts (income) in every year since 1970, producing an increasing Federal deficit. (Statistical Abstract of the United States 1995, p. 332)

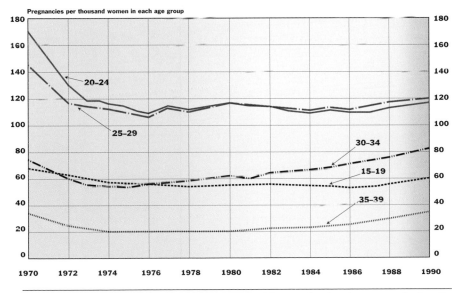

Figure 5. Age-Specific Fertility Rates: 1970–1990. *After a major drop in pregnancies for all age groups in the early 1970s, fertility rates stabilized for all age groups under 30. For females over 30, fertility rates increased substantially during the 1980s, probably reflecting the growing trend for women to have children later in life than was common in earlier decades. (Statistical Abstract of the United States 1993, p. 70)*

to right along the abscissa. Scale maximums and minimums must appear on the farthest grid lines along each axis. Scale labels must appear at appropriate intervals to facilitate data interpretation (see rule 8).

Do not use scales that exaggerate or distort the numerical relationships that actually exist. You can make small and insignificant differences look important by using a minute scale, and you can hide critical differences by using an overly large scale.

Your graphs should reflect the reality of the data being plotted. Therefore, your choice of scale is critically important.

Generally, scales are indicated along the left and bottom axes; however, if you enclose the graph in a box and the graph is unusually wide, you may label the ordinate scales on both left and right axes. See figure 5, which plots age-specific fertility rates over time. The repetition of the axis scale on the right-hand side of the graph is optional.

8. Make your key data lines heavier than axis and grid lines and less important data lines.

Axis and grid lines are less important than data lines and must therefore be thinner and lighter. The visual emphasis in the graph must be on the plotted (data) lines, not on the grid lines or axes. Equally, your important data lines must be more emphatic than less important data lines.

Note that in figures 1, 2, 3, and 4, the plotted data lines are darker than the axis or grid lines (if used).

Graphs

9. Use multiple lines, if necessary, to show the relationships between three or more variables, and use different line patterns to depict different variables.

Lines of different patterns are useful for plotting more than two variables. In figure 5, for example, the graph presents three variables: the year (x-axis), the fertility rate (y-axis), and the women's age groups (plotted lines). Because the graph shows five age groups, the five plotted lines have to have some distinguishing patterns.

Line patterns include solid, thin solid, wide solid, thin dashes, wide dashes, small dots, large dots, hollow (two thin lines together), and mixed dots and dashes of varying sizes. If you use different line patterns, label the lines, as in figure 5. Optionally, you can omit the labels within the grid pattern and use an explanatory key to the right or below the graph. The key for figure 5 would be as follows:

10. Do not smooth out data lines.

Make graphs as realistic as possible, even if the data lines are "jerky" and erratic. The small but unsightly dips that make lines look ragged also make them look real. Data lines that are too smooth and polished look unreal.

11. Label important values on a data line.

If you wish to highlight or discuss certain important values on data lines, label them within the grid system. Readers will pay more attention to labeled data values and will not be forced to interpret data values.

In figure 6, for example, the final values of the three transaction balances in 1992 (the end of the plotted values) are of special interest, so that final values are inserted in the graph. Similarly, other values could be inserted for special years, perhaps for 1990 or 1980.

Sometimes, for a graph with important data, you may decide to present the table from which the graph came along with the graph. Figure 6 includes the background table for the graph. Note the additional categories (in columns) and the additional values (by year). The graph in figure 6 has the advantage of telling its story in a glance, but the table is also powerful, especially with the heavy clustering of negative values in more recent years.

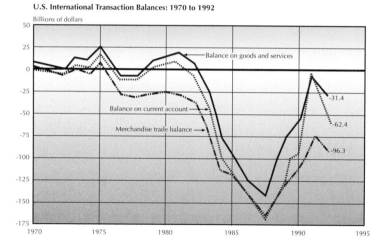

U.S. International Transactions—Summary: 1960 to 1992

In billions of dollars. Reserve assets are for end of period. [Minus sign (-) indicates debits]

YEAR	Merchan- dise trade balance	Net investment income	Net military transac- tions	Net travel and trans- portation receipts	Other services, net	Balance on goods, services, and income	Unilateral transfers	Balance on current account	Net foreign assets in U.S.	Net U.S. assets abroad	Net U.S. official reserve assets
1960	4.9	3.4	-1.1	-1.0	0.6	6.9	-4.1	2.8	2.3	-4.1	19.4
1965	5.0	5.4	-0.5	-1.3	1.5	10.0	-4.6	5.4	0.7	-5.7	15.5
1966	3.8	5.0	-1.0	-1.3	1.5	8.0	-5.0	3.0	3.7	-7.3	14.9
1967	3.8	5.3	-1.2	-1.8	1.7	7.9	-5.3	2.6	7.4	-9.8	14.8
1968	0.6	6.0	-0.6	-1.5	1.8	6.2	-5.6	0.6	9.9	-11.0	15.7
1969	0.6	6.0	-0.7	-1.8	2.0	6.1	-5.7	0.4	12.7	-11.6	17.0
1970	2.6	6.2	-0.6	-2.0	2.3	8.5	-6.2	2.3	6.4	-9.3	14.5
1971	-2.3	7.3	0.7	-2.3	2.6	6.0	-7.4	-1.4	23.0	-12.5	12.2
1972	-6.4	8.2	1.1	-3.1	3.0	2.7	-8.5	-5.8	21.5	-14.5	13.2
1973	0.9	12.2	0.7	-3.2	3.4	14.1	-6.9	7.1	18.4	-22.9	14.4
1974	-5.5	15.5	0.2	-3.2	4.2	11.2	-9.2	2.0	34.2	-34.7	15.9
1975	8.9	12.8	1.5	-2.8	4.9	25.2	-7.1	18.1	15.7	-39.7	16.2
1976	-9.5	16.1	0.9	-2.6	5.0	10.0	-5.7	4.3	36.5	-51.3	18.7
1977	-31.1	18.1	1.7	-3.6	5.7	-9.1	-5.2	-14.3	51.3	-34.8	19.3
1978	-33.9	20.4	0.9	-3.6	6.9	-9.4	-5.8	15.1	64.0	-61.1	18.7
1979	-27.6	30.9	-1.3	-2.9	7.3	6.3	-6.6	-0.3	38.8	-66.1	19.0
1980	-25.5	30.1	-1.8	-1.0	8.9	10.7	-8.3	2.3	58.1	-87.0	26.8
1981	-28.0	32.9	-0.8	0.1	12.6	16.7	-11.7	5.0	83.0	-114.1	30.1
1982	36.5	29.8	0.1	-1.0	13.2	5.6	-17.1	-11.4	92.4	-122.3	34.0
1983	67.1	31.9	-0.6	-4.2	14.1	-25.9	-17.7	-43.6	83.4	-58.9	33.7
1984	-112.5	30.8	-2.5	-8.3	14.3	-78.2	-20.6	-98.8	102.0	-29.2	34.9
1985	-122.2	23.2	-4.4	-9.7	14.3	-98.8	-23.0	-121.7	131.0	-34.1	43.2
1986	-145.1	15.4	-5.2	-7.3	18.9	-123.4	-24.2	-147.5	223.2	-91.1	48.5
1987	-159.6	10.9	-3.8	-6.4	18.4	-140.4	-23.1	-163.5	230.0	-62.4	45.8
1988	-127.0	12.5	-6.4	-1.4	20.4	-101.8	-24.9	-126.7	219.5	-92.7	47.8
1989	-115.7	14.4	-6.8	5.9	26.8	-75.5	-25.6	-101.1	213.7	-114.9	74.6
1990	-108.9	19.3	-7.8	10.1	29.7	-57.5	-32.9	-90.4	99.4	-56.3	83.3
1991	-73.4	16.4	-5.5	17.1	33.7	-11.7	8.0	-3.7	67.0	-62.2	77.7
1992, prel.	-96.3	10.1	-2.5	17.5	40.1	-31.1	-31.4	-62.4	120.4	-44.9	71.3

Figure 6. U.S. International Transaction Balances 1970 to 1992. *The U.S. foreign trade balance (including merchandise, goods and services, and current financial accounts) turned increasingly negative during the middle 1980s. Despite a major recovery from about 1988 to 1991, the transactional balances remain negative, and the trend appears to be turning down again.* (Statistical Abstract of the United States 1993, *pp. 790 and 796*)

12. If labels or numbers appear within the grid, blank out the grid area beneath the labels or numbers.

Grid lines can "mask" letters and numbers. So if your labels or numbers appear within the grid, blank out the grid lines beneath the labels or numbers by creating a white rectangular area (see figure 6). Make these blank areas no larger than necessary and try to minimize your use of them within the same graph. Too many blank areas make the graph look choppy and erratic.

Bar Graphs

Bar graphs depict the relationship between two or more variables, one of which is usually time. These graphs typically show how one or more variables change over time. Consequently, bar graphs are useful for depicting trends (see figure 8). Because bar graphs can show multiple variables, they can also depict how several variables change relative to one another over time (see figure 7).

Bar graphs are **not** useful if the quantities depicted do not differ significantly. And if you expand or distort the axis scales to dramatize slight differences, the bar graphs will look suspicious to alert readers and might damage your credibility.

Bar graphs may be horizontal or vertical. In vertical bar graphs, time is usually plotted along the horizontal x-axis (see figure 7). In horizontal bar graphs, time is usually plotted along the vertical y-axis.

Some writers and illustrators argue that vertical bar graphs are better for showing trends and that horizontal bar graphs are better for comparisons and for showing magnitude changes. Certainly, readers are more used to seeing trends shown along a horizon-

tal axis. However, comparisons and magnitude changes are usually clear in either orientation. Use your judgment.

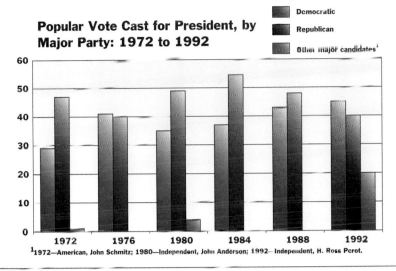

Figure 7. *In the record 1992 voter turnout, a third-party candidate (H. Ross Perot) won enough of the popular vote potentially to reverse the voters' choice as to which major-party candidate would win. In both 1972 and 1980, third-party candidates received so few votes that the final election results were not affected. (Statistical Abstract of the United States 1993, p. 262)*

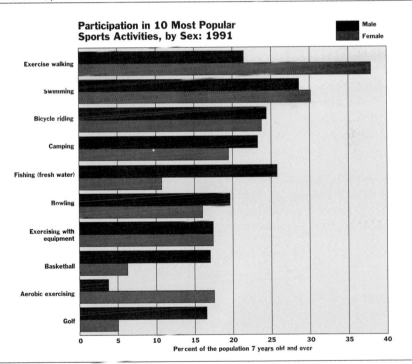

Figure 8. *In 1991, the most popular female sports activities were walking, swimming, and aerobic exercising. For males, the most popular activities were camping, fishing, bowling, basketball, and golf. In some sports, such as swimming, bicycle riding, and exercising with equipment, males and females had similar preferences. (Statistical Abstract of the United States 1993, p. 242)*

Bar graphs may be used with other visual forms, such as line or coordinate graphs, maps (see MAPS), or pie graphs (see figure 12).

Graphs

13. Clearly label each bar.

Ensure that readers understand what each bar represents. See figures 7 and 8 for examples of two different bar graphs with appropriate labels.

As an example, figure 7 is a vertical bar graph, with time (years) on the x-axis and with the number of votes cast for U.S. president on the y-axis. The bars (labeled in the explanatory key) show how each party voted in each of the election years. Figure 8 is a horizontal bar graph, showing labeled sports activities on the y-axis, with the percent of population participating on the x-axis. Notice that figure 8 does not use variations in time because the data is for a single year (1991).

14. Make the bars wider than the spaces between them.

See figure 7. A bar graph with the spaces wider than the bars would seem "airy." The dominant visual effect in a bar graph should be the bars.

15. Use different bar patterns to indicate differences in types of data and label these patterns clearly.

Bar patterns allow you to distinguish areas, regions, groups, and parts. Patterns also allow you to focus readers' attention on areas of the graph you consider most important. Bar patterns include diagonal lines, cross-hatching, or even colors. Remember, however, that colors are a problem if you are using black and white photocopies. Whatever pattern of bars you choose, be sure that the pattern is clearly labeled.

16. Use segmented bars to depict multiple variables or component parts of a whole.

Segmented bars allow you to show segments of a total figure. Figure 9 contrasts household assets with the liabilities for 1992. The shaded segments divide assets and liabilities into their components, which are labeled. In figure 10, the waterfowl sightings for a single year (1982) are presented for three different areas. The different segments in the bar refer to the different areas.

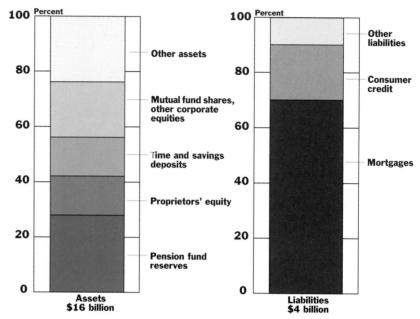

Figure 9. Household Funds as Percentage of Assets and Liabilities: 1992. *Mortgage obligations represent the overwhelming financial liability of U.S. families. Assets, on the other hand, include a variety of financial fund instruments. Assets recorded here do not include equity positions in property.* (Statistical Abstract of the United States 1993, p. 500)

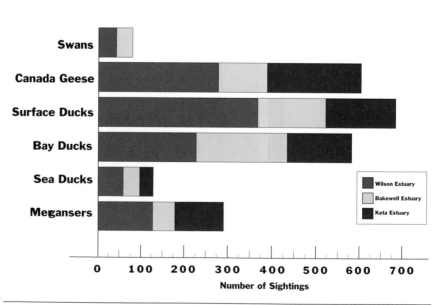

Figure 10. Waterfowl Sightings in 1982 at Three Alaskan Estuaries. *Of the three surveyed estuaries, the Wilson Estuary has the largest and most productive waterfowl population. (Source: U.S. Department of Agriculture.)*

Pie Graphs

Pie graphs are circles (pies) divided into sectors (slices) to show the relationship of parts to a whole. The sectors must add up to 100 percent.

Pie graphs are useful for general comparisons of relative size. However, they are not useful if accuracy is important. Further, pie graphs are not useful for showing a large number of items.

The eye can measure linear distances far more easily than radial distances or areas. Therefore, visual comparisons of bars on a bar graph are much easier than visual comparisons of sectors in a pie graph. Moreover, readers can usually make more accurate judgments about data relationships expressed in a linear fashion.

So if you need accuracy, use a bar graph or a line graph. If you need to show how parts relate to one another and to a whole—and if precise numbers are not important—use a pie graph.

17. Identify each sector of the pie and, if appropriate, the percentage it represents.

Pie graphs do not have axes and therefore cannot be very precise, so if percentages are important, identify them. As in figure 11, the percentage is more important than the actual numbers, but if a reader wanted to, a simple calculation with the percentages, based on the total $74 billion, would reveal the actual component numbers.

Criminal Justice System Expenditures of $74 Billion in 1990 for Public Service

$74 Billion

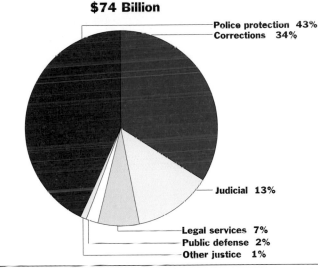

- Police protection 43%
- Corrections 34%
- Judicial 13%
- Legal services 7%
- Public defense 2%
- Other justice 1%

Figure 11. Criminal Justice System Expenditures. *Despite some reports in the public press, expenditures for public defense, which include legal aid services and public defenders, constitute only 2 percent of the money spent nationally on the criminal justice system.* (Statistical Abstract of the United States 1993, p. 219)

Always identify each sector of the pie. You can do this by using labels (figures 11 and 12) or fill patterns and an explanation block. For further information on fill patterns, see the preceding discussion of bar graphs.

18. Differentiate adjacent pie sectors by using alternating fill shades or patterns.

To help readers distinguish the sectors, use alternating fill shades or patterns. In figure 11, for example, the various patterns for each slice or segment help distinguish between the segments. These patterns are somewhat redundant (intentionally) with the labels which report the different revenue sources. Reserve the solid (or black) fill pattern for the prominent sectors, the ones you wish to emphasize. Never use the same fill pattern for adjacent sectors.

19. Group small percentage items under a general label, such as "Other."

Pie graphs should have no more than 8 to 10 sectors, depending on the size of the pie. The larger the pie, the more sectors you can safely divide it into. However, beyond some reasonable number of sectors (10), a pie graph becomes too busy and therefore difficult to read.

If you have a number of small percentage items, you should group them and give them a common label, such as "Other Parts," "Other Exports," or simply "Other" if the context of the graph and the names of the other labels indicate what "Other" refers to.

Sometimes for the "Other" category or another segment of the pie graph, you will want to break out the different components (see rule 20).

Graphs

20. Use pie-bar combination graphs to show the composition of an important sector of the pie.

Figure 12 shows a combination pie-bar graph, where the largest segment "Sales and gross receipts" would not be very clear to readers who did not know what items went into this category. For such readers, in figure 12, this category is broken

down into the adjacent bar graphs, which show the various percentages for the two years.

Each sector of a pie can potentially be expanded into a segmented bar. In this way, you are adding one more variable to the pie graph.

21. Use a series of pie graphs to add time as a variable.

The two pie graphs in figure 12 are only two of the possible series of pie graphs for tax collections. Depending on the purpose for a document, a writer might choose to present pie graphs for the years 1970, 1980, 1990, 1995, and 2000 (estimated). This series would undoubtedly portray the interesting economic adjustments made by state governments over the last 30 years.

State Government Tax Collections, by Type: 1970 and 1991

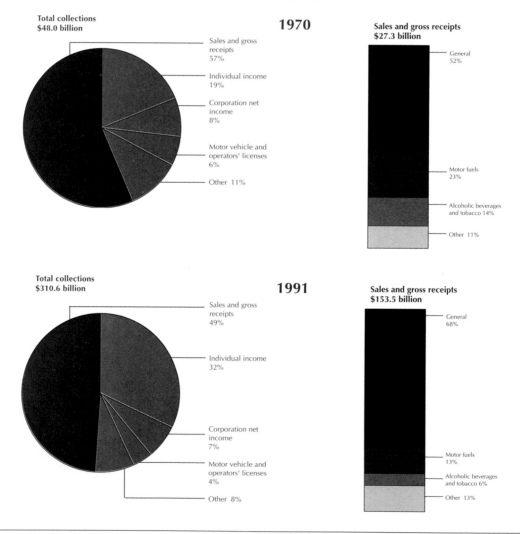

Figure 12. *Sales taxes and general consumption taxes (motor fuels, alcohol, and tobacco) still constitute in 1991 the major source of state funds. Taxes on individual income, as a percentage of the total, have increased from 19 percent in 1970 to 32 percent in 1991. (Statistical Abstract of the United States 1993, p. 291)*

Headings are essential features of any business or technical document. Without headings, documents become a jumble of paragraphs for readers to interpret. Even well-written paragraphs are not easy to read unless they are paired with good headings. See EMPHASIS and PARAGRAPHS.

Well-written headings allow readers to skim and scan a document. Most readers of business documents read to find key information or a missing fact. They do not read a document line by line because their prior knowledge of the subject makes careful reading unnecessary.

Headings include any headline information within a document. The most basic headings appear as labels or signposts before blocks of text. However, headings also include subject lines that introduce a letter or memo and titles of articles or chapters.

Headings

1. Use informative, specific, and inclusive headings in any business or technical document, even those as short as a single page.

2. Design documents by planning and drafting your headings even before you have finished writing the text.

3. Choose different levels of headings to indicate logical divisions and groupings in the text. Avoid using too many levels.

4. To show the level of the heading, use the three types of typographical variations: the *placement* of the heading on the page, the *size* of the type, and the *appearance* of the type.

5. Use a numbering system with your headings if you have more than four levels of headings or if your document is lengthy and you or your readers will need to refer to sections of it by number.

6. Make headings parallel in structure and use the same type of headings at each heading level.

7. Capitalize headings using the same conventions as for titles of books, articles, or other documents.

---

1. Use informative, specific, and inclusive headings in any business or technical document, even those as short as a single page.

Informative, specific headings allow readers to determine immediately the contents of a section. Unfortunately, many standard headings are neither specific nor informative:

> Introduction
>
> Discussion
>
> Results

Better versions of these would be:

> Purpose of the Drilling Proposal
>
> Implications of Three Proposed Tests
>
> Valid Data from the Third Test

Informative headings are similar to the captions for graphics. As with headings, good captions are visual signposts for readers who do not want or need to read dense sections of text. See CAPTIONS.

Inclusive headings signal that only material mentioned in the heading will actually be covered in the section. If the heading is *Valid Data from the Third Test*, then no data from the second or first test should appear following the heading.

The subject heading (subject line or title in a letter or memo) is perhaps your best opportunity for communicating your purpose and main point. Again, many subject headings are uninformative:

> Town Center Building
>
> Information Management Project
>
> Customer Satisfaction Survey

Better versions tell readers what is important in the document and what you're asking them to do:

> Proposal to rehabilitate the Town Center Building at cost
>
> Recommendation to approve information management project
>
> Invitation to participate in a survey to help us serve you better

Informative subject headings contain key words to signal the purpose of the document:

> Proposal to . . .
> Recommendation to . . .
> Request for . . .
> Invitation to . . .
> Warning about . . .
> Report of . . .
> Agenda for . . .
> Information about . . .
> Notice of . . .
> Procedure for . . .

As noted, subject headings should also summarize your main point:

> Recommendation to adopt new scrubbers to meet EPA requirements
>
> Proposal to reorganize our division for greater customer focus

Headings

2. Design documents by planning and drafting your headings even before you have finished writing the text.

Headings should come early in your writing process so you can write text to fit the heading structure.

For example, when you and colleagues use a prototype or a mock-up to plan a document, that mock-up should include all headings, even if they are provisional. See WRITING AND REVISING.

Writers can see the headings on a blank page and begin to visualize the text that will follow the heading. Writers will be writing to the headings and to the overall structure of the document, as reflected in the headings. This document design approach will help you avoid costly rewriting and time-consuming editing.

3. Choose different levels of headings to indicate logical divisions and groupings in the text. Avoid using too many levels.

A chapter title, for instance, may be a major (or first-level) heading. Section titles in the chapter may be minor (or second-level) headings. Subsection titles could then be subheadings (third-level headings), and so on.

The level of the heading indicates its logical relation to other headings as well as to the whole. The levels are most apparent in an outline:

3.4　Component Descriptions
　　3.4.1　Gearbox Assembly
　　3.4.2　Brakes
　　3.4.3　Hydraulic Motors
　　3.4.4　AIU Interfaces
　　　　3.4.4.1　Controller
　　　　3.4.4.2　Encoder
　　　　3.4.4.3　Tachometer
　　3.4.5　Servo Valves

In both text and outlines (such as a table of contents), the levels may be indicated by a numbering system (like the one above) or by the placement, size, or appearance of the heading. See OUTLINES and TABLES OF CONTENTS.

How many levels should you use? Dozens are possible, but readers could not comprehend that many levels of subordination. Practically speaking, you should use no more than four or five levels, depending on your readers.

The less technical or less educated your readers, the fewer levels you should use. Experienced and well-educated scientific readers are more accustomed to reading text with multiple levels of subordination. If you suspect that your readers will have trouble remembering the heading levels, use fewer levels.

4. To show the level of the heading, use the three types of typographical variations: the *placement* of the heading on the page, the *size* of the type, and the *appearance* of the type.

Placement variations include centering, placing the heading flush left, indenting, and using a run-in heading (placing the heading on the same line as the text following it):

A Centered Heading

A Flush-Left Heading

  An Indented Heading

  A Run-in Heading. The text begins following the period (or colon) and one or two spaces.

See PERIODS.

Sometimes a run-in heading has only three spaces between it and the succeeding text and no punctuation:

A Run-In Heading　When you do not use punctuation (as in this case), you should make the heading visually distinct from the text in the rest of the paragraph. You might use boldface type or a larger typeface.

Size variations are possible when you can vary the point size of the lettering in the heading. The larger the point size, the greater the level of the heading. A 24-pt heading is on a higher level than a 12-pt heading, etc.:

A 24-pt Head

An 18-pt Headi

A 14-pt Heading

A 12-pt Heading

Appearance variations include ALL CAPITAL LETTERS, underlining, **boldface type**, different typefaces, color, and *italics*. See PAGE LAYOUT and EMPHASIS.

Use the following placement and appearance lists to create different levels of headings. The variables are listed in decreasing order of importance:

Placement

1. Centered
2. Flush left
3. Indented
4. Run-in (on the same line as text)

As the preceding list shows, a centered heading is on a higher level than a flush-left heading. A flush-left heading, on the other hand, is on a higher level than an indented heading.

Appearance

1. ALL CAPITALS
2. Underlining
3. **Boldface**
4. *Italics*

The appearance variations may be added singly or in combination. Thus, a heading may be in all capital letters, or it may be underlined, or both. Appearance variations used in combination create higher-level headings than headings with a single appearance feature. So, an underlined, all-capital letter heading is on a higher level than a heading featuring only all capital letters.

Appearance, size, and placement variations used together allow writers many heading types—and consequently many heading levels. See PAGE LAYOUT and WORD PROCESSING.

5. Use a numbering system with your headings if you have more than four levels of headings or if your document is lengthy and you or your readers will need to refer to sections of it by number.

Report writers normally construct their tables of contents by listing the headings and subheadings in their reports. If you use a numbering system with your headings, include the numbers in the table of contents. See NUMBERING SYSTEMS, TABLES OF CONTENTS, and OUTLINES.

6. Make headings parallel in structure and use the same type of headings at each heading level.

Parallel structure means that all headings at the same level have the same basic grammatical structure. So if one heading opens with an *–ing* word, the other headings will also:

this

Developing the Appropriate Tests

Sending Out for Bids

Selecting the Winner

Agreeing on Preliminary Contract Talks

not this

Developing Appropriate Tests

Sending Out for Bids

Selection of the Winner

Preliminary Contract Talks

See PARALLELISM.

Most headings are declarative. They state or announce a topic:

Facilities in the Local Impact Area

Summerhill Treatment Plant to Close

Complex Traps in Gulf Coast Fields

The Geomorphology of Exploration

An alternative heading form is the question heading:

How Great Is the Avalanche Danger?

Will Surface Water Quality Be Degraded?

What Are the Alternatives?

Should Exxon Proceed with the Project?

Will the Public Accept Our Position?

How Likely Is a Major Bank Default?

As long as you don't overdo them, question headings offer interesting possibilities and can be very effective. question headings not only announce the topic but also stimulate interest because they pose questions that curious readers will want to see answered.

Question headings are generally more engaging than declarative headings because they seem to speak directly to the reader. However, be careful not to pose obvious or condescending questions:

Doesn't Everyone Know about Anticlines?

Be consistent. If you decide to use question headings, use them for all headings at that heading level. Mixing question and declarative headings at the same level is confusing. However, you can use question headings at a major level and then use declarative headings at subordinate levels, or vice versa.

7. Capitalize headings using the same conventions as for titles of books, articles, other documents:

Three Recommendations for Staff Improvement

A Closing Plea for Sanity

Conclusions about Your Marketing Plan

See CAPITALS.

NOTE 1: A few publications, especially ones with an advertising purpose, are beginning to use headings with only the initial word capitalized:

Three recommendations for staff improvement.

NOTE 2: Subject lines for letters or memos (a type of heading) are increasingly using a capital only on the initial word:

Subject: A closing plea for sanity

This pattern is acceptable, but be consistent within a single document or set of letters.

Hyphenation is one of the trickier aspects of English. There are many rules of hyphenation—including some that apply only in limited circumstances—and all of the rules have exceptions. Below are the most common conventions of hyphen usage. For further discussions of hyphenation, refer to *The Chicago Manual of Style, The Gregg Reference Manual,* or the *United States Government Printing Office Style Manual.* See REFERENCES.

Fundamentally, hyphens show a connection. Typically, the connection is between two words or occasionally between a prefix and a word. The connected words (known as compounds) can function as nouns, verbs, or adjectives:

Connected words as nouns

brother-in-law
ex-mayor
follow-up
foot-pound
know-how
run-through
self-consciousness
two-thirds

Connected words as verbs

to blue-pencil
to double-space
to spot-check
to tape-record

Connected words as adjectives

all-around person
black-and-white print
coarse-grained wood
decision-making authority
high-grade ore
high-pressure lines
interest-bearing notes
little-known program
long-range plans
low-lying plains
matter-of-fact approach
off-the-record comment
old-fashioned system
part-time employees
30-fold increase
three-fourths majority
twenty-odd inspections
up-to-date methods
well-known researcher
high-level edit

Hyphens

1. Hyphenate two or more words that act together to create a new meaning.

2. Hyphenate two or more words that act together to modify another word.

3. Do **not** hyphenate connected words that function as adjectives if they occur **after** the word they modify.

4. Hyphenate compound numbers from twenty-one to ninety-nine and compound adjectives with a numerical first part.

5. Do **not** hyphenate connected words that act as adjectives if the first word ends in *-ly.*

6. Avoid using hyphens with most prefixes.

7. Hyphenate words that must be divided at the end of a line.

Unfortunately, not all connected (or compound) nouns, verbs, and adjectives require hyphens. Here are a few of the exceptions:

Connected but unhyphenated nouns

ball of fire
breakdown
fellow employee
goodwill
problem solving
quasi contract
takeoff
trademark
trade name

Connected but unhyphenated verbs

to downgrade
to handpick
to highlight
to proofread
to waterproof

Connected but unhyphenated adjectives

barely known researcher
bright red building
crossbred plants
halfhearted attempts
highly complex task
10 percent increase
twofold increase
unselfconscious person
worldwide problem

As the above examples illustrate, connected words have three possible forms. They can appear as two separate words *(highly motivated),* as one word formed by connecting the two original words with a hyphen *(high-pressure),* and as one word formed by joining the original two words *(highbrow).* See COMPOUND WORDS.

---

1. Hyphenate two or more words that act together to create a new meaning:

a counterflow plate-fin
the V-space between units
the Grumman F-14A airplane
one-half of the annular ring
to double-check the tests

This rule indicates a potential use of the hyphen, not a mandatory one. In some instances the two words become a single word, without a hyphen: *highlight, bumblebee, barrelhead.* In other instances, the two words remain separate: *base line, any one* (one item from a group), *amino acid.* The words sometimes remain separate because combining them would produce strange-looking forms: *aminoacid, beautyshop, breakfastroom.* Because the presence or absence of a hyphen is often a matter of convention, check a current dictionary if you are not sure how the compound word should be written. See CAPITALS for the proper capitalization of hyphenated words in titles.

2. Hyphenate two or more words that act together to modify another word:

brazed-and-welded construction
cross-counterflow unit
engine-to-recuperator mountings
full-scale testing
no-flow heat exchanger
pressure-drop decrease
3-year, multimillion-dollar program
12-foot-wide embayment
up-to-scale modeling
U tube arrangement
well-documented success

This rule applies only when the connected or compound modifier occurs **before** the word it modifies. See rule 3 below.

3. Do *not* hyphenate connected words that function as adjectives if they occur *after* the word they modify:

The boiler was brazed and welded.
The compartment is 32 feet wide.
The program is well documented.

but

The brazed-and-welded boiler
The 32-foot-wide compartment
The well-documented program

NOTE: An exception to this rule is the use of a hyphen after a verb when the connected words have an inverted order:

They were sun-bathing. (*or* a bathe in the sun)
That transaction was tax-exempt. (*or* exempt from tax)
They were on a fire-watch. (*or* a watch for fire)

4. Hyphenate compound numbers from twenty-one to ninety-nine and compound adjectives with a numerical first part:

thirty-four
eighty-one
five-volume proposal
13-phase plan
24-inch tape
500-amp circuit
4- or 5-year audit cycle

but

22 percent fee

See COMPOUND WORDS and NUMBERS.

5. Do *not* hyphenate connected words that act as adjectives if the first word ends in *–ly:*

highly motivated engineer
poorly conceived design
vastly different approach
completely revised program

NOTE: The words ending in *–ly* are actually adverbs. The *–ly* form indicates the structure of the modifying phrase, so a hyphen is unnecessary.

6. Avoid using hyphens with most prefixes:

counterblow
midpoint
nonperson
progovernment
supercar
undersea

NOTE 1: Hyphens do appear when the prefix precedes a capitalized word:

un-American
mid-August

NOTE 2: Hyphens are sometimes necessary to prevent confusion: *re-treat* (to treat again) versus *retreat* or *un-ionized* versus *unionized*. If you are not sure whether a prefix requires a hyphen, refer to a current dictionary. See COMPOUND WORDS and REFERENCES.

7. Hyphenate words that must be divided at the end of a line.

Words are always divided between syllables, and hyphens should appear at the end of the line where the word division has occurred. Try not to end more than two consecutive lines with hyphens. Try not to divide at the end of the first line or at the end of the last full line in a paragraph. Do not divide the last word on a page.

Hyphens and Technical Terminology

The use of hyphens in technical expressions varies considerably. Technical writers often violate the rules of hyphenation when they believe that the technical expression will be clear:

We will need a high pressure hose.

In this sentence, *high* modifies *pressure*. The sentence refers to a hose that is capable of withstanding high pressures. It is not a pressure hose that happens to be high (off the ground). Yet if we followed the rules of hyphenation strictly, the sentence should be:

We will need a high-pressure hose.

Hyphens are often omitted in technical expressions because the context clarifies the expression. In many cases, however, missing hyphens can cause confusion or a complete lack of comprehension, as in this sentence from an aircraft maintenance manual:

Before removing the retaining pin, refer to the wing gear truck positioning actuator assembly schematic.

Nontechnical (or technical but unknowledgeable) readers can only guess which words are associated with which other words. Does *truck* link with *wing gear,* or does *truck* modify *positioning?* Hyphens would help clarify the modifier relationships:

wing-gear truck-positioning actuator assembly

Proper use of hyphens will not baffle knowledgeable technical readers, and it will help those readers who are not familiar with a technical expression. See ADJECTIVES.

Illustrations, diagrams, and drawings include a wide range of graphics whose purpose is to depict parts, functions, relationships, activities, and processes that would be difficult or impossible to describe in text.

Illustrations can help you visualize or conceptualize an idea or a discovery. Rather than merely talk about an idea, try sketching it. A sketch, no matter how rough, can be a valuable tool for you and for others who may be trying to visualize what you are thinking.

The many sketches in Leonardo da Vinci's notebooks are outstanding examples of how illustrations can help in the visualization of concepts. In his notebooks, da Vinci (1452–1519) sketched many images from nature, such as the components of a bird's wing or the muscles in a human arm. Then he used these images to visualize (conceptualize) machines and tools that used the same natural or physical principles.

Figure 1 is an example of a da Vinci sketch. In this instance, da Vinci conceived of a tank-like machine, whose base (in the left image) contained the wheels and gears for providing motion. The right image shows the base covered with a shielded top that would hold men and weapons. The combination of engineering details with the dust clouds suggests rapid movement.

Illustrations

1. Use illustrations, diagrams, and drawings to visualize a system, process, or piece of equipment that would be difficult to describe in text.

2. Use symbols, icons, or other recognizable illustrations to convey messages to readers.

3. Use color to enhance your illustrations, symbols, icons, and logos.

4. Keep illustrations simple, and give each one a perspective that enables readers to understand it.

5. Label each illustration clearly and, if necessary, label the parts of the object shown.

6. In a series of illustrations, make the viewing angle consistent.

7. Ensure that all letters, numbers, and labels are horizontally oriented on the drawing or illustration.

8. If necessary for clarity, remove surrounding detail from illustrations.

9. Use line patterns in an illustration to show how different subsystems interact within a system.

10. If your drawing shows a process, structure the process from top to bottom and left to right.

11. Use special-purpose illustrations when necessary.

Producing good illustrations almost always requires a professional graphic artist. The following discussion does not address the art or mechanics of creating effective illustrations, diagrams, and drawings. Instead, it focuses on how writers should conceive of and use illustrations and what writers can do to assist graphic artists.

For further information on illustrations and graphics, see GRAPHICS FOR DOCUMENTS and GRAPHICS FOR PRESENTATIONS. See also CHARTS, COLOR, GRAPHS, MAPS, PHOTOGRAPHS, and TABLES. For information on captions, see CAPTIONS.

Figure 1. Leonardo da Vinci's Sketch of a Tank (Right Image) and Its Working Mechanisms (Left Image). *Although he lived in the fifteenth century, da Vinci's sketches foreshadowed mechanical or engineering discoveries that only appeared centuries later.*

1. Use illustrations, diagrams, and drawings to visualize a system, process, or piece of equipment that would be difficult to describe in text.

Illustrations are very effective at showing views of objects or systems that do not exist (a drawing of a proposed tool), that are abstractions (organizational or functional systems), or that would be impossible to show otherwise (exploded views or cutaways).

Illustrations allow readers to see inside something that is sealed; to see opposite and hidden sides of an object simultaneously; and to see, in close-up, the details of a small assembly that would otherwise not be visible while looking at the larger object that contains the small assembly (see figure 2).

Exploded views allow you to exaggerate (magnify) certain parts of an object to show the details of the exaggerated part while keeping the rest of the object in its correct perspective. Figure 3 uses an exploded view (enlargement) to show the components in the lining of the eye. Although drawn to reflect the actual structure of an eye, the illustration uses nonrealistic, contrasting colors.

Cutaways are like an orange sliced in half: They show the internal structure (assembly) of an object that is normally sealed (see figure 4).

2. Use symbols, icons, or other recognizable illustrations to convey messages to readers.

Symbols and icons are increasingly valuable communication tools, especially within the international business and technical communities.

Figure 2. Spring-Actuated Diaphragm. *Remove the bonnet slowly to prevent losing small parts that are under spring compression.*

Figure 5 is an illustration of two of the many symbols that have become international through use if not through governmental agreements. Such symbols usually have an associated color.

This rule contrasts with the suggestion in rule 1 that you use illustrations to conceptualize or visualize your ideas. Actually, as you conceptualize your document or your presentation, you may want to explore your options for using possible symbols or icons. Notice, for example, the icons used next to the subsection titles in this *Style Guide*.

Figure 3. A Cross-Section View of the Inner Lining of the Eye. *The optic nerve fibers enter the eye through the optic disc (blind spot). The nerve fibers then spread out across the lining of the eye, connecting the rods, cones, and other visual receptors.*

Illustrations

FULL-FLOATING AXLE

1 Outer Bearing
2 Inner Bearing
3 Grease Seal
4 Axle Housing and Spindle
5 Hub
6 Gasket
7 Lock Washer
8 Cap Screw
9 Driving Axle

Figure 4. Full-Floating Axle. *Radial and axial thrust loads are carried by the spindle, leaving the driving axle free of all but torque loads.*

Icons, especially those registered as corporate trademarks or corporate logos, are more and more sophisticated, often with colors that match the corporate mission. See the model documents at the end of the *Style Guide* for examples of various corporate logos. See INTELLECTUAL PROPERTY.

Wheelchair Access Sign

Warning Sign for ☐ Radioactivity

Figure 5. Standard Symbols. *Symbols such as the two shown are increasingly used in international communication.*

3. Use color to enhance your illustrations, symbols, icons, and logos.

Color is increasingly important as a tool in business and technical documents. Most readers of documents and most attendees at presentations expect to see color illustrations. They are accustomed to sophisticated graphics, and they often respond negatively when shown materials that look outdated

or primitive. See COLOR, GRAPHICS FOR DOCUMENTS, and GRAPHICS FOR PRESENTATIONS.

Figures 1–3, 5, 6, 9, and 11 illustrate various ways to use color in illustrations.

Sometimes, you may find that full color is not feasible, based on production costs. An option is to work with two colors. Figure 6 is an example of an illustration using only shades of a single color to represent the different modular furniture. This illustration would be an attractive addition to a document that uses only black text. Of course, the blue-gray color could appear elsewhere in the text beyond this single graphic, most probably in the headings and subheadings or in marginal callouts.

If you decide not to use color, be sure to prepare your illustrations and to design your document so that your message will still be clear and appear professional. In illustrations, for example, you may need to use shading or design patterns instead of color to distinguish between different steps or components of machines.

Figure 6. Two Layouts within a Cubicle Arrangement. *The arrangements shown here, as seen from above, present only two of the many options available.*

Always preview sample pages (for documents) or sample transparencies (for presentations) to determine if your message is clear and appears professional.

4. Keep illustrations simple, and give each one a perspective that enables readers to understand it.

Illustrations and drawings should be focused. That is, they should present a single concept. They should be clean and uncluttered. Everything not pertaining to the single concept should be eliminated. No detail should be present that does not contribute to the presentation of that single concept.

As well as being simple, a good illustration has a clear perspective. Illustrations allow you to distort reality, so you must ensure that readers understand the perspective from which the illustration presents its subject. Illustrations almost always show their subjects out of context. Therefore, you might need to establish what the reader is viewing and how that thing relates to other things in its real environment.

Size scales might be necessary if the size and relationship of the object depicted to other things in its environment are not clear. You can also use labels to indicate size, direction, orientation, and nomenclature. If you do not indicate size and distance relationships, readers might not be able to determine the correct proportions of the object shown or its correct orientation in the world outside the illustration or drawing.

5. Label each illustration clearly and, if necessary, label the parts of the object shown.

Figure 2 shows a typical nomenclature illustration. The valve body is shown as one unit because it is not the focus of the illustration. The diaphragm, spring, and bonnet are the reason this illustration exists, so each is labeled separately. Center lines drawn through the axis of each part show how the parts fit together.

Labeling of the significant parts of a drawing is crucial for reader comprehension. You may use word labels, lines, and arrows (figures 2 and 3), or you may use numbers, letters, or symbols in the drawing itself (figure 4) with an explanation block.

6. In a series of illustrations, make the viewing angle consistent.

If you are showing the same object in a series of illustrations, and the point of the series is to show assembly/disassembly steps or operational phases, ensure that readers see the object from the same perspective in each illustration. Changing the perspective is very confusing.

7. Ensure that all letters, numbers, and labels are horizontally oriented on the drawing or illustration.

The text appearing on any part of a drawing or illustration should never be vertically oriented unless the bases of the individual letters or numbers are horizontal, as in this example:

The lettering and numbering on an illustration should be oriented so that readers can read it without reorienting the illustration. If you run out of space, use arrows and move the labels away from the busy area of the illustration. If necessary, omit the labels and use letters, numbers, or symbols and an explanation block (see rule 5 above).

8. If necessary for clarity, remove surrounding detail from illustrations.

Figure 7 shows a schematic drawing or illustration in which surrounding but irrelevant detail has been removed. You often see this sort of illustration in subsystem pictorials.

Figure 7. Pneumatic Operating and Control System. *By eliminating electrical controls, potential spark hazards are avoided, allowing operation in hazardous environments.*

Illustrations

Removing the surrounding detail allows readers to focus on the system being shown. The drawing isolates its subject and therefore provides an excellent focus.

9. Use line patterns in an illustration to show how different subsystems interact within a system.

If you are showing how different subsystems fit together and function, you might need to use different line patterns, as in figure 8. The line patterns allow readers to isolate subsystems while viewing the whole system. For additional examples of line patterns, see GRAPHS.

If you use line patterns, provide an explanation of what the different patterns represent. For example, in figure 8 the diesel fuel lines and the coolant line use different line patterns.

10. If your drawing shows a process, structure the process from top to bottom and left to right.

Figure 9 is a schematic flow chart. It shows a process and the equipment used in that process. This type of drawing should be oriented from top to bottom and left to right so that readers "read" it as they would read text. In all process drawings, readers will expect the process to start at the left and end at the right. Don't disappoint them. See CHARTS.

11. Use special-purpose illustrations when necessary.

Work closely with graphics personnel when you need special illustrations. The following three examples are only a sample of what illustrations can bring to documents.

Figure 8. Diesel-Fuel Preheating System. *The burning of the fuel is approximately 10 percent more effective with the fuel preheating system.*

Figure 9. The Returns Process in a Manufacturing Setting. *Products or parts returned fall into one of these categories: good, questionable, or bad. Depending on its category, a part is returned to stock, reworked, or recycled.*

124

Example 1. You might need a realistic rendering of a proposed product for use in promotional literature or in a proposal.

Figure 10 is an example of a realistic illustration produced on a computer. The initial step was to create the line drawing; although the line drawing in figure 10 was done on a computer, it could have been done using traditional projection and hand drawing. Next, realistic details are added, either with computer or with an airbrush.

Figure 10. Power Take-Off Housing. *This housing is made of ductile iron using standard sand casting and cores.*

Example 2. Illustrations often combine realistic details into a montage designed to capture a theme or an atmosphere. In figure 11, the rich range of modern communication options are the main theme. The small figure sitting in front of the television screen sees only the surface images on the TV screen. The person viewing the montage is shown how computers, satellites, and transmission towers all combine to produce the images on the TV screen.

Montages such as this one were and still are common in advertisements and other marketing publications. Today, they are often replaced by a montage of actual photographs. See PHOTOGRAPHS.

Figure 11. The Transmission World Behind the TV Screen. *The seated figure can only imagine the transmission tools required to produce images on the screen.*

Example 3. Illustrations often become part of or combine with other graphics. Figure 12 is a combination between an illustration (the cross section of the dam) and a graph (informal) of the different sediment depths. As a combination graphic, the image does not attempt to be a realistic illustration. Instead, the detailed features about the dam and its operations are ignored (not even labeled). Instead, the labels on the illustration focus on the different elevations for the sediment at selected dates in the future.

A simple bar graph could easily replace this illustration. The bars on the graph could record just how high the sediment would become at a certain date.

Figure 12. Sediment Buildup Behind Glen Canyon Dam. *Sediment will collect behind Glen Canyon Dam, finally filling in the reservoir (Lake Powell) about 2700 A.D.*

Indexes

Indexes are alphabetical lists of the subjects within a published (printed) document. For each subject, the index gives a page number (or sometimes a section number) so that readers can easily find where a specific subject is discussed.

Online documents sometimes include an index, especially if the online information is complex and lengthy. See ONLINE DOCUMENTS.

Published documents usually have indexes unless the document is so short that an index is unnecessary—as, for example, in a brochure or in a marketing summary.

The longer a document, whether published or not, the more helpful an index becomes.

The following rules present the basics of indexing a published (printed) document, but the subject is complex enough that if you want to prepare a detailed index, consult *The Chicago Manual of Style,* 14th edition. See REFERENCES.

---

1. Provide an index for any document longer than 50 pages and for any document that will have many and frequent readers.

The 50-page threshold is only a suggestion. Whether you decide to provide an index also depends on how many readers will be using your document. For example, if you are preparing an internal policy manual that will have only 30 or 40 pages, even a manual this short can be confusing when many employees want to look up specific answers to their questions. In such a manual, both a good table of contents and a simple index would be helpful. See TABLES OF CONTENTS.

Indexes

1. Provide an index for any document longer than 50 pages and for any document that will have many and frequent readers.

2. Adjust the scope of your index to the needs of your readers.

3. Begin to prepare an index by identifying key words and concepts that readers would likely be interested in locating, given the purpose of the document.

4. Use either a computer program or traditional hand-sorted cards to prepare the actual index.

5. In a detailed index, use subheadings and cross-references.

6. Don't forget basic proofreading and cross-checking.

For documents with few readers, no index is necessary even if the document exceeds 50 pages.

---

2. Adjust the scope of your index to the needs of your readers.

Indexes can be fairly simple or very detailed, and they can cover special areas of interest.

A simple index primarily includes key words from the document. Such words are usually those that appear in the title, chapter headings, and subheadings. Such an index might list only two or three topics from each page of a document.

A detailed, professional index can be quite exhaustive, often listing 10, 15, or more topics from each page in a text. Because such indexes are very time consuming and expensive, you may choose not to prepare them for most unpublished documents. Even published documents sometimes might not need such a detailed index. See the index for this *Style Guide* for an example of a detailed index.

Detailed indexes can also be prepared for special areas of interest. For example, a separate index might list all the people's names in a historical document. Separate indexes sometimes exist for geographical names or for works of art (as in a list of musical titles). Such special indexes usually supplement, not replace, the traditional subject index.

---

3. Begin to prepare an index by identifying key words and concepts that readers would likely be interested in locating, given the purpose of the document.

Indexing is not a mechanical task. Anyone preparing an index has to have a good grasp of the content and of the purpose of the document. For this reason, the author of a document is often the best person to prepare the initial or draft index.

Not every fact nor every reference automatically appears in an index. For example, if a text mentions the *Mississippi River,* should the index list this reference under *River* or under *Mississippi?* Should the index even list either reference at all?

Answers depend on the purpose of the document. A document discussing all sorts of geographical features might have major index entries on national parks, lakes, rivers, bayous, etc. If the Mississippi itself was merely mentioned in passing as one of a list of well-known U.S. rivers, then it might not appear in the index, and it would surely not be a major (separate) entry in the index.

A document discussing major U.S. rivers, their length, their flow, their flood stages, their pollution, etc., would likely list the Mississippi, the Ohio, and every other river discussed in the document. These individual names would be major entries in the index. Then under each river would appear subheadings:

Mississippi River, 8, 12, 15–18; flood control, 8; pollution on and near, 65, 68–70; source of, 14; tourism on, 48–49

4. Use either a computer program or traditional hand-sorted cards to prepare the actual index.

Most word processing programs have an indexing feature. With this feature, writers can identify key words and phrases either while they are writing the draft or after they have finished the draft. Usually, they code these words and phrases with a computer code that will not appear in the printed copy. The word processing program can, however, identify the code and will alphabetize the identified words and phrases into major entries and will attach the proper page numbers to them.

Such mechanical indexes can be helpful, but they do not replace the many judgments necessary when a full, detailed index is needed. Only a human indexer (or the author of the document) can make such judgments.

The traditional indexing system uses individual cards (preferably with typed citations) as the basis for the index. The indexer goes through the entire text (in its final desktop or typeset form) preparing separate cards for each potential entry and for subheadings within entries. Next, the cards are alphabetized and subheadings properly arranged. Finally, the total index is entered into a computer.

NOTE: A word processing index might not contain the correct page numbers if the final copy is to be inserted into a desktop publishing system. See PAGE LAYOUT.

5. In a detailed index, use subheadings and cross-references.

Subheadings are important because they reveal how various topics relate to each other. In most cases, subheadings have a grammatical or syntactic relation to the main heading and are presented alphabetically:

Automobiles, 18–20; design of, 43, 48–49; maintenance costs of, 123, 126; maintenance guidelines for, 115–118; optional equipment for, 84–85; resale values of, for retailers, 79; resale values of, for wholesalers, 78

In other instances, the subheadings are merely a list of items:

Fortune 500 companies: Amoco, 45; Exxon, 53; Ford, 17–19; General Dynamics, 115–119; General Motors, 10–11; Texaco, 58, 62–64

As in the preceding examples, the main heading is usually flush with the margin while the succeeding lines are indented. Traditionally, commas separate headings or subheadings from page numbers, and semicolons separate the different subheadings. Subheadings are alphabetized by main words, not propositions or conjunctions. No final punctuation follows the entry, including all its subheadings.

Inclusion of *See* and *Also see* (or *See also*) references is important when readers are likely to look up a variety of topics.

See references are useful when the indexer has had to choose between several different main headings:

Businesses. *See* Fortune 500 companies

Corporations. *See* Fortune 500 companies

Also see references are usually restricted to added information:

Texaco, 58, 62–64. *Also see* Fortune 500 companies

6. Don't forget basic proofreading and cross-checking.

Nothing destroys reader faith and your credibility more than errors in the index. Users rightly expect to find what you tell them is on a specific page.

Plan, therefore, to allow time for careful proofreading and even cross-checking of items. If possible, go through the entire index verifying that the cited information is indeed on the pages noted. For published indexes, the publisher is usually responsible for this final cross-check of an index for accuracy.

Intellectual Property

Intellectual property includes both ideas and the expression of these ideas. A person's or an organization's intellectual property is potentially protected by the registration of a patent, a trademark, a service mark, or a copyright.

The following discussion summarizes the highlights of current copyright rules. It also includes a brief mention of service marks and trademarks. It does not cover patents, which have special and very detailed legal requirements.

If you have questions about copyrights, service marks, trademarks, or patents, you should obtain legal advice from an attorney who specializes in intellectual property.

1. Accurately quote and credit the sources for any information you use in your own writing or speaking.

Abiding by this rule is both ethically and legally important.

Personal ethics require that you give others credit for their ideas, contributions, and originality. You expect no less when someone uses your ideas or words. See ETHICS.

Legally, you must carefully quote and cite the source for any published information you choose to use. If you don't, you will violate U.S. copyright laws. You may also be violating non-U.S. copyright laws. Major violations can be costly, both for you and your company. See QUOTATIONS and CITATIONS.

Copyrights. Anyone's original work is protected by a copyright, even if the person who creates a work has not chosen to apply formally for

---

Intellectual Property

1. Accurately quote and credit the sources for any information you use in your own writing or speaking.

2. Include in anything you produce a written notice of its copyright status and register any commercially valuable work with the U.S. Copyright Office.

3. Identify the source for any photographs or other graphics. Also, do not modify visual creations without considering the rights of the original creator of the visuals.

---

copyright (see rule 2). The copyright exists when the writer makes the first original version, even a mere handwritten copy.

Copyright covers the expression of an idea, not the idea itself. You must always credit actual words and phrases that you borrow. Ideas may not be legally copyrightable, but ethically you should still credit other people's ideas if they are distinctively theirs, not yours. See QUOTATIONS.

Copyright protection initially applied only to "writings," but protection now covers videos, paintings, photographs, cartoons, recordings, songs, sculptures, computer software, or any other creative product when it is physically recorded. Thus, the manuscript for a song can be copyrighted and the physical recording can be copyrighted, but the actual live performance is not copyrighted unless it is recorded.

Under copyright law, you must obtain permission from the author(s) (or the holder of the copyright, if an author has signed over her rights to someone else—for instance, her publisher). Often, you will pay a fee if you choose to use copyrighted material in something you wish to publish for profit.

If you obtain permission, you should retain the written permission (usually a brief form letter). In your own work, you should identify the author and the holder of copyright (usually a full bibliographic citation) and include a note like the following:

Reprinted by permission of (the name of the author or the publisher).

or

Reproduced courtesy of the photographer's heirs. (List the heirs.)

Fair Use. In some instances, especially in academic studies or in critical reviews, you may reproduce without permission excerpts (written or visual) from a copyrighted work. In such cases, you need not obtain written permission before you publish. You must still identify the source for any quotations or excerpts you use.

Fair use applies if you are not using enough of the original to affect its value. The number of words is not the measure of fair use. A quotation of several hundred words from a book might fall under fair use, but a few key words from a short poem might violate fair use. A detail from a single painting might be fair use; the whole painting would likely not be.

Don't rely on the fair use exemption if you are in doubt about the fair use status or if you are going to commercially profit from quoting someone else's copyrighted material. In these cases, write for permission and pay any necessary fees.

Public Domain Works. Works produced by the U.S. government are in the public domain. These works include works produced by individuals working under U.S. government contracts.

Some works also are in the public domain because their copyright has expired. The time limits for a copyright vary, based on different copyright laws. Under the 1976 law, which took effect on January 1, 1978, the general rule is that copyright lasts for the life of the author, plus 50 years. In cases of joint authorship, the copyright lasts 50 years after the death of the last surviving author.

You can freely quote, without permission, from public domain works, but you should still include full citations for any materials you are borrowing. Your readers need to know which are your words (and ideas) and which words you are borrowing. See QUOTATIONS and CITATIONS.

Trademarks. Trademarks are names or symbols used by a company to identify a particular product or service. Examples are *Coca-Cola*®, *Mustang*®, and *Chloraseptic*®. In some instances, a trademark can be a graphic symbol and will be called a service mark.

Trademarks are registered with the U.S. government, and their use is prohibited without the approval of the trademark's owner. Trademarks are usually capitalized. See CAPITALS.

As in the preceding examples, trademarks usually have the symbol ® immediately following

them. In text, the ® need only appear on the first use. Later references to Coca-Cola would be capitalized, but with no ®.

Before registration, a trademark will have had an attached ™ or ˢᴹ, to signify the name or symbol as either a trademark or service mark. After registration, the ® replaces the ™. In some instances, both the ® and the ™ will appear next to a trademark.

Other common examples of trademarks include *Kleenex*®, *Jell-O*®, and *Xerox*®. For these three examples, the generic terms would be *facial tissue*, *gelatin*, and *photocopy*. Writers should use the generic terms unless they actually mean, for example, the brand of tissue known as Kleenex®; then the name will be capitalized and followed by the ®.

---

2. Include in anything you produce a written notice of its copyright status and register any commercially valuable work with the U.S. Copyright Office.

Using a written notice applies equally to a few pages as to a full volume. The written notice includes (1) the symbol © or the word *copyright*, (2) the year it originated or was published, and (3) the name of the author (or copyright holder, if they are different people). This notice protects writing or other original works even if they have not been formally registered.

Consider registering any works of particular importance, especially any with commercial value. Registration includes submission of a form to the U.S. Copyright Office, the payment of a $20 fee, and the sending of two printed copies along with the form. The current phone

number for forms and instructions is 202/707-3000, or you may write the following address:

U.S. Copyright Office
Library of Congress
Washington DC 20559

Your copyright exists even without registration, but registration does fix, for legal purposes, the nature of your work and the date of its publication. Registration is necessary if you have to file suit for copyright infringement, unless your work was published outside the U.S. and its territories.

Fixing the copyright date also starts the legal timing, which under the 1976 copyright law extends copyright protection for the life of the author, plus 50 years. Note that the timing for a copyright is different for works published or copyrighted before 1978, which is when the 1976 law took effect.

Works for Hire. If you are an employee or a paid independent contractor, you will usually be unable to apply for or to claim a personal copyright on your work, if it is produced for your employer. Whatever you write or produce will be called work for hire. Your employer can and usually will register such work.

---

3. Identify the source for any photographs or other graphics. Also, do not modify visual creations without considering the rights of the original creator of the visuals.

Photos and computer graphics have copyright protection, just as any other publications do. Sometimes writers borrow a photograph or computer graphic without remembering that a tangible, reproducible image merits the same copyright protection as words.

Intellectual Property

This same guidance applies, for example, to your favorite newspaper cartoon. A one-time use of the cartoon for educational purposes would probably fall under fair use, but ongoing use would not. And even one-time commercial use would not be fair use. As with any copyrighted material, using a cartoon requires you to contact the cartoonist or a publisher (often a newspaper syndicate) for permission, which is usually granted after payment of a one-time fee or a royalty fee for each copy made.

Modifying a graphic does not make it yours! As with the cartoon example, some people provide their own captions or write in new balloon comments. Use of this modified cartoon is still a violation of the cartoonist's copyright.

Similarly, you are not free to modify or adjust a copyrighted photograph or an illustration to suit your own purposes. Even if your have obtained permission, for example, to use a photograph, this permission can include requirements as to how and when you will reproduce the photograph. For example, printing a small black-and-white version of a large color photograph might damage the original intent or artistic value. Sometimes the photographer might even refuse permission based on what you intend to say about the photograph.

With computers linked nationally and internationally, be careful not to "borrow" images or text that may be copyrighted. Unfortunately, your source may not mark an image with a copyright symbol. Your ignorance of the copyright status does not remove your legal liability.

When you have questions about intellectual property of any kind, consider obtaining legal advice from an attorney who specializes in copyrights, service marks, trademarks, and patents.

International Business English is the most common medium for conducting business worldwide. For historical, political, and economic reasons, English is often the only common language among individuals of diverse nationalities and tongues.

Users of English should not assume, however, that they are automatically understood by English speakers from other cultures. The pace, formality, and social context of communication differ among cultures.

Because of the inherent difficulty of cross-cultural communication, even in a common language, business and technical professionals should take pains to use English that is easily understood and discourages misinterpretation.

Following these rules will lead to clarity and a minimum of misunderstanding across cultures.

International Business English

1. Use simple sentences, but do not omit necessary words.

2. Use simple, understandable words, and avoid idiomatic expressions.

3. Be sensitive to the cultural pace of communication.

4. Account for varying levels of formality and personal distance across cultures.

5. Be particularly sensitive to social hierarchies across cultures.

1. Use simple sentences, but do not omit necessary words.

Keep sentences short. Limit yourself to one idea per sentence, and avoid dependent clauses. See SENTENCES.

Often native speakers omit words for the sake of economy, but this practice can confuse non-native readers:

not this

Send fax this a.m. care of CFO assistant.

this

Please send the fax this morning in care of the assistant to the Chief Financial Officer.

2. Use simple, understandable words, and avoid idiomatic expressions.

Consciously choose words that readers will readily understand. Avoid grammatical complications like verb forms with *-ing* endings. Break up noun strings that contain more than three nouns. See NOUNS.

Avoid using idioms, which are peculiar or specialized expressions you might use every day but which may be unfamiliar to members of the culture you are addressing.

Even common idioms can be a source of confusion. When possible, use synonyms that cannot be misunderstood.

Idioms	Synonyms
get ahead	advance/move forward
get someone's goat	annoy/anger someone
get around a place	walk/drive
get at someone	criticize/nag
get away with something	cheat/steal
get up (verb)	stand/rise
get-up (noun)	costume
get-together	meeting/gathering
get-up-and-go	energy
in the right mind	sane
be of one mind	agree
bear in mind	remember
come to mind	remember
slip one's mind	forget
meeting of minds	agreement
prey on one's mind	worry

put up with	tolerate
put down	insult
put over	trick/cheat
put out	offend
put through	connect/get approval
input	enter (into a computer)

English (as do all languages) has thousands and thousands of idioms like the preceding examples. For help interpreting idioms (especially if English is not your native language), refer to A. S. Hornby's *Oxford Advanced Learner's Dictionary of Current English*, 4th Edition (Oxford, England: Oxford University Press, 1989). See REFERENCES.

Idioms included in ordinary text are especially hard to spot. In the following example, the words *shutdown, thoroughgoing, clean-up,* and *re-siting* are all fairly common idioms, but because of these idioms, the original sentence would be hard for a non-English speaker to interpret. Even a native speaker of English would likely prefer to read the revised version. See GOBBLEDYGOOK.

not this

Determining on a site shutdown, we forwarded recommendations for thoroughgoing site clean-up and re-siting of contaminate.

this

We decided to close the site. We also recommended ways to clean the site completely and remove the contaminated soil.

International Business English

Non-native speakers should be particularly careful about attempts at using English idioms, as in this sign in a Copenhagen ticket office:

We take your bags and send them in all directions.

Or, consider the following example from a manual prepared by a car rental firm:

When passenger of foot heave in sight tootle the horn. Trumpet him melodiously at first, but if he still obstacles your passage then tootle him with vigor.

International Business Style

Even when communicating in English, business professionals traveling abroad should be aware of the local "communication culture." Although they need not radically change their communicative style, they should be prepared to adapt to differences in three areas: the pace, territoriality, and social hierarchy of the communication culture in which they find themselves.

3. Be sensitive to the cultural pace of communication.

Diverse cultures communicate at different paces. For example, southern Europeans and Asians tend to be more concerned initially with establishing personal relations than with "getting to business." On the other hand, Americans and northern Europeans are more likely to want to go straight to the point and to move quickly through issues.

4. Account for varying levels of formality and personal distance across cultures.

The need for "personal space" or territoriality differs across cultures. The northern European and Asian cultures require a certain formality and distance in language as well as space, whereas Americans and southern Europeans tend to be informal.

North Americans often need more personal space than Latin Americans or southern Europeans do. So, a North American can become uncomfortable when a Latin American speaker moves too close, thus violating the North American's space.

5. Be particularly sensitive to social hierarchies across cultures.

Business professionals should be acutely aware of social hierarchy when communicating with members of other cultures. Asians will offer business cards to begin a meeting and expect to see yours so they can gauge your social and professional standing relative to theirs. They are very conscious of rank, and it pays to be deferential and avoid too much familiarity.

Asians and northern Europeans often think of themselves as representatives of their organizations rather than as individuals engaging in business. Southern Europeans and Latin Americans are less concerned with rank or organizational protocol.

Although business professionals abroad need not mirror their hosts' behavior, it makes good sense to be patient, observant, and adaptive to the pace and temperament of the local communication culture.

See BRITISH ENGLISH and LETTERS for information on dealing with specific cultural differences in documents.

Introductions introduce—as the name suggests. An introduction conducts the reader into a document, usually by establishing the reason for the document's existence; its relation to other documents or projects; and any special circumstances, facts, conditions, or decisions that help the reader understand the body of a document.

The body of a document is more project or product oriented—it focuses on the situation or thing being described or analyzed.

The introduction (as well as the conclusion) is more reader oriented—it orients the reader by providing a context for the reading. In short, the introduction prepares the reader for what will follow.

1. Adjust the length and scope of your introduction to meet your readers' expectations and needs.

Ask yourself if your primary readers absolutely must know certain facts or other data before they can understand your document. If they must know such facts, then include them in your introduction. And then adjust the introduction, as discussed below in rules 2, 3, and 4. Otherwise, get right to your major points (usually the *to do* in the document). See LETTERS and MEMOS.

Many short business documents, especially internal ones, may not even require an introduction. Instead, these documents will begin with the writer's proposal or a statement of fact, usually in the subject line. Any background (or setup) information is covered several lines or paragraphs later. See ORGANIZATION.

Introductions

1. Adjust the length and scope of your introduction to meet your readers' expectations and needs.

2. Replace the introduction with an executive summary, especially in business documents.

3. If appropriate, as in a technical or scientific report for publication, prepare a full introduction, using the traditional content.

4. Use a brief introduction in a letter or memo to set the tone, not to delay the main points.

2. Replace the introduction with an executive summary, especially in business documents.

Introductions are increasingly unnecessary in many business documents. Too often in the past, the introduction was so general that it really didn't help readers.

In contrast, an executive summary contains the essential facts, findings, and interpretations from the later pages in the report. If well done, an executive summary (perhaps only a page or two) will be all that most readers need. Subsequent pages in your document become attachments or file information. See SUMMARIES.

Readers of business reports are often busy managers or supervisors. They are usually aware of the general details of an investigation or project but trust subordinates to evaluate the problem properly and to solve it efficiently. Such readers will become impatient with lengthy digressions and unnecessary explanations, support, and justification. Consequently, they typically want a succinct executive summary. Only if questions arise will they go beyond the summary and read the background information and analysis.

The key feature of a combined introduction and executive summary is a statement of major conclusions and recommendations. A full list of conclusions and recommendations often appears later in the report, but you should never force managers or supervisors to search for them. See REPORTS and SUMMARIES.

3. If appropriate, as in a technical or scientific report for publication, prepare a full introduction, using the traditional content.

Formal reports are likely to have the most developed and structured introductions. SEE REPORTS. No two introductions are alike, but most include some of the following information:

—The **problem** or **opportunity** prompting the project or investigation

—The **goals** or **purposes** of the project or investigation

—The likely **audience** for the project or investigation

—The **scope** of the project or investigation

Introductions

—The **sources** of relevant information

—The **methods** used in the project or investigation

—This project's or investigation's **relation** to previous or concurrent projects or investigations

—Any useful working **definitions**

The **problem or opportunity** that the document addresses arises from the historical background. What work was done that stimulated this project? What other work has been done in this or related fields? Often, this section will survey relevant literature. See CITATIONS.

If this project is part of a larger or related project, state the relationship briefly. Brevity is important because readers rarely want or need to learn the point-by-point history of a project or related project.

The **purpose** of the project explains why the project was undertaken and what it is expected to achieve. The key objectives might read as follows:

1. To evaluate the groundwater resources of the alluvial aquifer of the Carmel Valley, California, groundwater basin

2. To develop a two-dimensional, digital, groundwater flow model of the aquifer that will aid in the understanding of the geohydrology of the aquifer

3. To identify data inadequacies that might be needed for future studies of this aquifer

The **scope** refers to the limits of the project and the document itself. Provide the scope by stating what the document will cover and what it will not cover.

The **methods** explain how a project was conducted: how the investigator developed the experimental design, constructed or designed the apparatus, collected the data, analyzed the results, and developed the conclusions. If the methods were routine, provide no more than a brief summary. If the methods were unusual or original, explain them thoroughly in the introduction or consider discussing methods in a separate section or subsection of the document.

---

4. Use a brief introduction in a letter or memo to set the tone, not to delay the main points.

Introductions to letters and memos establish the writer's tone and approach as well as set the stage for the ideas and supporting details that follow. See LETTERS and MEMOS.

Establishing a Tone

Letters and memorandums are intended to be more personal and less formal than reports. To convey this more human dimension, some writers choose to use personal pronouns: *I*, *you*, and *we*. Others open with personal remarks or social greetings, much as we often do in personal conversations. Even writers whose purpose is avowedly serious might "break the ice" by calling the reader by name:

> Please let us know, Jim, if our proposal for the replacement pumps begins to answer your needs.

See TONE.

Setting the Stage

Setting the stage might mean no more than a brief phrase: *As we discussed yesterday . . .* or *According to our records . . . .*

In other instances, writers might decide to provide the background for the document before stating the point. This background or setup is quite common in letters conveying bad news, such as enforcement of a financial penalty or a personnel reprimand. See LETTERS.

However, be cautious about spending too much time setting the stage. Almost always, the best strategy is to get to the point quickly. See ORGANIZATION.

Italics (a slanted typeface) is available only in printed material or on word processing systems capable of printing italics. In handwritten or typed material, underlining replaces italics. See UNDERLINING.

Some conventions about italics concern only printers. For example, in printed mathematical expressions, letters are italicized and numerals are set in normal type. This distinction is not normally made in handwritten or typed material. The following standard rules apply in most technical and business documents.

> **Italics**
>
> 1. Use italics for words or phrases used as examples of language.
>
> 2. Use italics for foreign words and phrases that have not yet been absorbed into English.
>
> 3. Use italics for titles of books, magazines, newspapers, movies, plays, and other works individually produced or published.
>
> 4. Use italics for the names of aircraft, vessels, and spacecraft.
>
> 5. Use italics for names of genera, subgenera, species, and subspecies. Names of higher groups (phyla, classes, orders, families, tribes) are not italicized.

---

1. Use italics for words or phrases used as examples of language.

Words used as examples occur when a writer discusses specific words or phrases as examples of language:

> In all offshore contracts, *consolidation* does not mean what it normally means.

> The Anaguae reservoir study was confusing because the author kept referring to the anomalous formations as *anonymous* formations.

NOTE 1: Use italics to emphasize words, phrases, and even letters when discussing them as examples of language. This use of italics (or underlining) sets the words or phrases apart from the other words in the sentence:

> Traditionally, the symbol *M* has been used to mean million. In some disciplines, *M* means thousand, so one indicates million with the symbol *MM*.

> One should avoid opening letters with the phrase *In reference to*. Similarly, according to our corporate guidelines, one should never end a letter by saying *Very truly yours*. Both phrases are too wordy.

NOTE 2: Quotation marks sometimes replace italics (underlining) as a way of highlighting words and phrases, especially in handwritten texts:

> In all offshore contracts, "consolidation" does not mean what it normally means.

---

2. Use italics for foreign words and phrases that have not yet been absorbed into English:

> The initial concept of the United Nations captured a certain *Weltanschauung*.

> The *couturier* insisted on keeping the new dress designs secret.

> The staple crop in South Africa is *kaffir*, which is a form of sorghum raised for cattle fodder.

NOTE: Some foreign words and phrases have become so common in English that they are not italicized:

> ad hoc
> habeas corpus
> per annum
> rendezvous
> vice versa

Some recent dictionaries indicate if words are still considered foreign, but other dictionaries do not. If your dictionary does not, use your judgment to determine if a word is sufficiently foreign to be italicized. Foreign words usually retain their foreign spellings, pronunciations, and meanings.

---

3. Use italics for titles of books, magazines, newspapers, movies, plays, and other works individually produced or published:

> To remain current on advances in space technology, we subscribed to *Design Digest*.

> The documentary *Before Their Time* showed what is possible when companies wisely invest IR&D funds.

See TITLES.

NOTE 1: Quotation marks sometimes replace italics for titles. For example, newspapers have traditionally preferred quotation marks:

> After some discussion, we decided to order "A Dictionary of Mining, Minerals, and Related Terms" and the "Society of Petroleum Engineers Publication Style Guide." The two volumes should help us prepare articles for the "Journal of Petroleum Technology" and "Petroleum Transactions."

NOTE 2: Sections of these published works are not italicized. So chapters, magazine articles, acts within a play, and editorials in a newspaper require quotation marks, not italics:

> Last week's *Time* had an article entitled "The Roots of International Terrorism."

> The final chapter of the annual report is entitled "Prospects for Growth in the 1990s."

See QUOTATION MARKS.

Italics

NOTE 3: In some typed documents, especially in the publishing business, the titles of books, magazines, and newspapers are in all capital letters and are not underlined:

DELTAIC OSCILLATION
FORBES
GEOTIMES
THE WALL STREET JOURNAL

4. Use italics for the names of aircraft, vessels, and spacecraft:

Discovery
Friendship 6
H.M.S. *Intrepid*
NS *Savannah*
U.S.S. *Iowa*
U.S.S. *Nautilus*

NOTE: In these examples only the names are italicized, not the abbreviations or numerals associated with the names.

5. Use italics for names of genera, subgenera, species, and subspecies. Names of higher groups (phyla, classes, orders, families, tribes) are not italicized:

the genera *Quercus* and *Liriodendron*
the family Leguminosae

See the *Council of Biology Editors Style Manual* for additional information and examples. See REFERENCES.

Jargon has two meanings. First, it means using familiar words in unfamiliar ways (using *hot* to mean *crucial* or *exciting*) or using an excessive "shorthand" to describe something that would normally require more words (a police officer saying, "That guy was really a ninety-nine," which is police jargon for code 99, the radio code indicating an unbalanced person).

Second, *jargon* means technical or specialized language unfamiliar to a particular reader or listener. Thus, one person's technical or specialized vocabulary becomes another person's jargon. The following discussion focuses on this second, more common meaning of the word *jargon*.

Every technical discipline needs and has its own vocabulary.

Medical doctors have innumerable special terms, often derived from Latin: *amebic dysentery, uvula, gastric hernia.*

Lawyers also use a number of common terms that have developed special meanings: *property, liability, consideration, conveyance. Consideration*, for instance, means a payment of some kind as a sign of agreement on a contract. This special legal meaning is not obvious to the uninitiated, who might not even know the word has a special meaning. In some contexts, readers might not know whether the ordinary meaning or the technical legal meaning is intended.

The cooks and waitresses in restaurants might develop special slang terms and abbreviations, so when a patron picks up a check, the items written on it are not immediately clear. This is a form of jargon, one very local and limited, yet still very useful.

Jargon

1. Do not use jargon unless your readers will understand it. If they will not understand—and you must use a term—then define it.

Carpenters and architects also have their own language: *joist, rafter, gambrel roof, header, sole plate, cross bridging.* These jargon words have special meanings and are useful terms, but someone not familiar with carpentry is not likely to understand them. See Style, Scientific/Technical Style, and Tone.

---

1. Do not use jargon unless your readers will understand it. If they will not understand—and you must use a term—then define it.

The doctor who gives a diagnosis only in medical terminology has failed to communicate with most patients. Similarly, the engineer who speaks only through coordinate graphs and equations will baffle, and perhaps alienate, the general reader who wants an overall sense of the proposed engineering project.

Here are two technical examples, both of which may use jargon unfamiliar to nontechnical readers:

> Wastewater treatment that employs fixed-film biological BOD removals has been shown to be more efficient than was predicted in our pilot studies. This result may be due to product mix, concentration, primary treatment, media type, wall effects, etc.

> Dry rubble stones shall consist of trap rock; granite; gneiss; or other approved hard, durable, tough rock. They should be sound, free from weathered or decomposed pieces, shattered ends, and structural defects, and shall be approved by the Contracting Officer.

In both of these examples, a general or nontechnical reader would encounter unfamiliar terms and abbreviations: *BOD, primary treatment, media type, trap rock, gneiss, shattered ends, structural defects*, etc. To the right reader, these terms have perfectly legitimate meanings, but to the uninitiated reader, the words might be confusing or nonsensical.

Jargon and the Social Sciences

Writers in the social sciences— especially in psychology and sociology—have often been accused of using excessive jargon. Writers in both fields use many common English words with special meanings: *response, learning, training, feeling, concept*, etc.

A psychologist discussing a *tertiary mediated response* is referring to a response coming through an intermediate person and delivered thirdhand. The concept and its expression are valuable in a limited context and to a limited audience. Otherwise, they are meaningless.

Jargon and Gobbledygook

Jargon and gobbledygook are not the same. Gobbledygook is the use of abstract or pompous words and long, convoluted sentences. It is clearly bad writing. Jargon, by contrast, is a specialized vocabulary for a particular technical field and is an often useful shorthand.
See Gobbledygook.

Key words are like flags—they rise above the rest of the text and signify what is most important. In a paragraph, section, or subsection, the key words are those that give the text meaning. Key words impart the central message.

You can deliberately repeat key words and phrases to reinforce your message. Key words ensure that readers who are not reading carefully will still get the point of what you are saying and remember the most important ideas. See REPETITION.

---

1. Use key words to mark key concepts; then repeat key words to reinforce your message.

The example below is from a short section on condenser operation. Note how the writer drives home the message by using repeated key words as variations on an important theme:

> This highly effective water-separation process is possible because the condenser design positively prevents two potential **icing** problems: (1) blockage of the low-pressure side by **snow-laden cold** air and (2) **freezing** of condensate on the **cold** metal surfaces. The entering **cold-side** air is below the **freezing** point of water and, although the condenser **heats** it, the outlet **temperature** is still **below 32 degrees F**. Consequently, much of the entrained **snow** is not evaporated and must pass completely through the condenser without blocking the flow passages. Because **cold-side** air **temperatures** are consistently below the **freezing** point, the condenser must be carefully designed so that the metal surface **temperatures** remain above the **freezing** point.

Key Words

1. Use key words to mark key concepts; then repeat key words to reinforce your message.

The key words concerning temperature represent one important line of thought in this paragraph. An equally important line of thought concerns the design, mechanics, and operation of the condenser:

> This highly effective water-separation process is possible because the **condenser design** positively prevents two potential icing problems: (1) **blockage** of the low-pressure side by snow-laden cold air and (2) freezing of **condensate** on the cold **metal surfaces**. The **entering** cold-side air is below the freezing point of water and, although the **condenser** heats it, the **outlet** temperature is still below 32 degrees F. Consequently, much of the entrained snow is **not evaporated** and must **pass** completely through the **condenser** without **blocking** the **flow passages**. Because cold-side air temperatures are consistently below the freezing point, the **condenser** must be carefully **designed** so that the **metal surface** temperatures remain above the freezing point.

Note how the two sets of key words work together to create the overall effect and to establish both a primary problem (icing) and a primary need (a condenser design that will prevent it). See PARAGRAPHS and TRANSITIONS.

The key words in the next paragraph provide both a solution and a sharp contrast:

> Figure 2–1 shows how the **condenser design prevents** these **icing** problems. A special **hot** section on the **cold-side** face **prevents ice blockage**. A small **flow** of **hot** air from the compressor outlet **passes** through the **hot** section tubes, **raising** the metal **temperatures above freezing** and allowing the **snow or ice** to be **evaporated** in the main core. The **hot** air then reenters the high-pressure **air-flow** at the turbine inlet.

Headings and Captions

Headings and captions should contain the most important of the text's key words. For example, a heading for the previous paragraphs on condenser design would contain key words:

Condenser Design Prevents Icing

See HEADINGS, CAPTIONS, REPETITION, and EMPHASIS.

Letters remain a key communication tool despite an increased preference by business and technical professionals for electronic mail and voice mail. But if you are writing a traditional letter, remember that computers have changed the format and appearance of letters.

Traditional hard-copy letters are now reserved for key, fairly formal communication about agreements or other organizational decisions. The informal and chatty personal letter is an antique, and the traditional written thank-you note is now usually no more than a quick phone call. Many messages conveyed in traditional letters are now recorded in speed memos or handwritten notes on the cover sheet for a fax. See FAXES.

Today's letters, when written, are less lengthy and rambling than ones written in earlier times because readers want letters that visually emphasize key ideas and that include no irrelevant information.

Letters with business or technical content must be visually effective because readers need to find or retrieve the main points at a glance. Good letters are 100 percent unambiguous. See WRITING AND REVISING and EMPHASIS.

Most readers of today's letters are skim-and-scan readers. They are not interested in a long rambling journey as the writer explores issues and implications. Such confusing and time-consuming journeys are unfortunately still present in much electronic mail. See ELECTRONIC MAIL.

Letters

1. Open letters with an informative and interpretive subject line.

2. Include your main point(s) in the first lines of your text.

3. Design and organize your letters so that key points are immediately visible.

4. Make your letters personal and convincing.

5. Choose direct and simple letter closings.

The following discussion of letters opens with five content rules for effective letter writing, as summarized in the checklist above. Following these rules is a description of letter formats, including the block, modified block, semiblock, and simplified styles.

The final two pages in this discussion explain how to address an envelope.

Effective Letter Writing

The following rules rely on two principles. As explained above, the first and most important is that the message in any letter be 100 percent unambiguous. The second is that a letter be personal and convincing, despite the limitations of written language, versus a dynamic one-on-one oral exchange of information. See TONE and PERSUASION.

---

1. Open letters with an informative and interpretive subject line.

We recommend that all business and technical letters have a subject line. The only exception would be informal (preferably handwritten) letters, such as a thank-you note or a note of condolence.

Test any letter by covering up all but the subject line. Does the subject line capture the major point(s)? Can you predict exactly what ideas will follow the subject line? If readers can't make an accurate prediction, your letter invites misreading and misunderstanding.

A subject line should be informative and interpretive, giving both the purpose and the key facts related to that purpose. An effective subject will often require six, eight, ten, or more words and will use two or more lines of type. A brief or telegraphic subject line hinders communication.

these

Subject: Authorization to Advertise for an Additional Analyst for Our Marketing Team

Request for Invoicing Turnaround Every 10 Working Days, Not Monthly

not these

Subject: Hiring of an Analyst

NEW INVOICING

As in the preceding examples, subject lines should use boldface, underlining, or other emphasis techniques. See HEADINGS and EMPHASIS. Also, sometimes the lead-in word *Subject* or old fashioned *Re:* is omitted.

Letters

2. Include your main point(s) in the first lines of your text.

If you open your text with main points, your letter will be leading from these main points, not up to main points later in the letter. Readers will see the main points immediately.

The opening lines of text will usually repeat words and phrases from the subject line. This repetition is desirable. See REPETITION.

If your opening lines are not informative, your readers are likely to begin to skim and scan for a main point or supporting ideas. If they don't find anything of importance within 15 or 20 seconds, your letter will go on the bottom of their to-do stack.

this

Subject: Authorization to Advertise for an Additional Analyst for Our Marketing Team

Dear Susan:

Please advertise immediately for an additional analyst for the Marketing team. As you noted, our current analyst is unable to provide the information we need in a timely fashion. If possible, let's have the new person hired and trained by June 15.

not this

NEW INVOICING

Dear Frank:

As you are aware, we are in an ongoing effort to streamline our organization and cut costs. Please find the enclosed memo documenting this cost-cutting initiative. One of the ways that we project might save costs would be to increase our invoicing cycle so that vendors have less slack time from the time they deliver services to us until they receive a full invoice for these services. We have analyzed the billing cycle and according to this analysis, a two-week interval . . .

NOTE: As in the preceding example of poor content, don't let incidental background information replace a powerful and direct subject line and the crucial opening lines.

Never open a letter with the following common delaying techniques:

—Obvious references that delay or confuse the main point:

This is in reference to your letter of February 14.

This confirms Mary Evans' telephone conversation with you on June 15 regarding our June 3 meeting with Bilko's attorneys to discuss the acquisition of the Skews property. This is going to be a problem for us if . . .

—Unnecessary and phony social statements:

Here's hoping that the weather in Tampa is fine and that your family is doing well in the new year.

I hope this letter finds you hale and hearty and that everyone in your family is fine.

—Mechanical enclosure indications:

Enclosed is . . .

Attached is . . .

Attached herewith . . .

Enclosed please find . . .

—Statements that hint about your topic but not your position on the topic:

Delaying the division reorganization is an idea of some merit and worth considering. Let's explore some of these notions as we . . .

—Nonessential background information that supports, explains, or illustrates your major points (unless this information legitimately sets up your major points):

Delaying platform renovation until the 4th Quarter would mean rebudgeting funds that have already been allocated during the 2nd Quarter. I have decided that rebudgeting is not a desirable option at this time.

As in this example, the better version would have led off with sentence 2, which has the actual decision, not the delaying setup information.

NOTE: A document setup is desirable less than 10 percent of the time. Instead, give readers a direct statement in your opening sentence. Then follow up with any necessary background explanations.

Even when you have bad news to convey, you gain little by delaying the message for purpose of softening the impact. And if you delay too long, you risk annoying the reader, as in the following evasive example:

Dear Mr. Vikor:

As you can imagine, we received over 100 applications for the position we advertised in the Sunday *Globe*. These responses were from well-qualified people, so our task was doubly hard. We looked for people with a solid work experience and outstanding references. We also wanted someone with demonstrated excellence on the Macintosh computer, which happens to be used throughout our company. Your qualifications, while excellent, did not quite fit all of these requirements.

To conclude, thank you for taking the time to submit an application for employment.

Better

Dear Mr. Vikor:

I regret that we can't offer you a job as our corporate accounts receivable clerk. As with many of our applicants, your qualifications were excellent. After a careful review, however, we decided that another applicant's skills more closely matched our company's current needs.

We will keep your resume in our active file of qualified applicants and will call you if we have another opening that could draw on your training and experience in accounting.

3. Design and organize your letters so that key points are immediately visible.

The design of your whole letter should naturally grow out of your strong opening (rules 1 and 2 above). A solid, informative opening often even outlines the supporting points that follow. See ORGANIZATION.

An effective visual design includes headings, lists, graphics, and other emphasis techniques. See EMPHASIS.

Visually design your letters by answering these key questions:

—What are the key points you want to make?

—Which points must the reader remember? Are these the same as your own key points?

—What subheadings and lists should you use?

—Which points come first? Which come next? Should any be moved into attachments?

—How much repetition is useful?

—What tables and other graphics should you include?

—Which letter format is most suitable—block? semiblock? simplified?

—Does the page layout reinforce the message?

A writer's goal is to design and to organize a letter so that every reader carries away a 100 percent unambiguous message. Research has shown that the more visual the message or image, the more readable and memorable.

Some years ago, a major corporation surveyed its writers and customers as to the adequacy of the corporation's letters. The survey revealed that nearly two-thirds of the letters required a follow-up call or a revised letter. Messages in the original letters were occasionally missing, often ambiguous, or even deliberately buried.

Answers to the above document design questions will guide you in choosing subheadings, lists, tables, and other graphics. See EMPHASIS. These and other emphasis techniques are the best way to guarantee that the readers' eyes see exactly what you want the them to see.

For important or lengthy letters, use an early prototype or mock-up to help you visualize your design before spending time writing down everything you want to say. See the discussion of prototypes in WRITING AND REVISING.

4. Make your letters personal and convincing.

A letter, as in earlier handwritten manuscripts, was originally a written record of what would have been one side of a conversation. Oral communication was primary, writing secondary. Writers and scribes even routinely spoke the words as they wrote them.

Writers in these earliest letters assumed they were talking to readers, so oral conventions of presenting information were common. For instance, the closing (or surprise ending) was important, and skillfully building up to major points was the goal. These traits of the oral storyteller worked well around fires in caves, but they do little to help today's business communication.

Today's letters are also less conversational because they rely more on document design, as discussed under rule 3. Document design relies on the readers' visual memories to reinforce the message conveyed by individual words and sentences.

Still, your voice speaks through the words and phrases you choose, even if softly. You must, therefore, choose language that is personal and as convincing as possible. The following techniques will help you make such choices. They will make your letters more credible and effective.

—Use pronouns throughout, especially *you*. Assess your readers' interests and needs, and then address these interests by speaking directly to the reader(s):

One of your priorities included an adjustment of the due date for contract renewal. Your estimate of dates also included associated cost savings. We agree with you.

—Use contractions when they would normally occur in speech. See CONTRACTIONS.

Once your program has been approved, we'll move ahead to hire the necessary professionals. We're doing this with existing funds because next year's budget has yet to be approved.

—Avoid jargon and gobbledygook, as used in the following bad example. See JARGON and GOBBLEDYGOOK.

According to the aforementioned agreement, the elements of the items to be discussed are likely of some interest, yet they may well not be greatly and completely significant. These are of some concern because the agenda considered is primarily based on prior assumptions generated and discussed by our committee of professionals.

As in this example of poor and

insulting writing, writers of jargon and gobbledygook use language recklessly, without regard for the basic meanings beneath the language. The writer of this example takes 51 words to say nothing. Every phrase is weakened by an empty modifier. Every reader would take away a different, muddled message.

—Prefer the simple, direct sentence and phrasing. See STYLE and SENTENCES.

> The committee met and made its recommendation Monday. They urged a new stock issue by January 1995. This issue would finance an expansion of the Hong Kong plant, which now runs three shifts (about 110 percent of its capacity).

As in this simple and direct example, average sentence length should be low—13 in this instance. Prefer the common word or phrase—for example, *met* instead of *convened* and *plant* instead of *manufacturing facility*.

If you make your writing personal, as discussed in the preceding rules, you will also be convincing. A convincing style arises more from your tone or your implied credibility than from facts and figures. If you keep your language simple and direct, you will gain your readers' respect. See PERSUASION and STYLE.

5. Choose direct and simple letter closings.

Make your closing as simple and direct as you made your opening lines. Don't settle for old-fashioned cliches from traditional letters.

One option is to close your letter with a restatement of your main point:

> I hope you'll make room in your busy schedule for the coordination meeting on June 15 at 2:30 in the Human Resources conference room.

> All of your tests, as outlined above, indicate that we should identify a new vendor for our factory-installed CD player. We hope that you concur and that you'll authorize initial funding by September 22.

> Please call me (Ext. 4455) if you're unable to meet with the Senior VP from King Enterprises. He'll be available in Room 439 all morning April 15. I can set an appointment time, or you can just stop by for a brief introduction.

Another option is the standard reference to questions or problems. If you choose this option, keep it short and be sure to give your phone number:

> If our proposal leaves any questions unanswered, please call either Jane Evans (Ext. 9922) or me (Ext. 8933).

> Please call or write Jack Owens (412-333-2245) if you have any questions about our proposed investment schedule. As our financial advisor, Jack can tell you how we generated the figures in our proposal.

NOTE: Avoid the old-fashioned cliched closing lines:

> Thanking you in advance, I remain,
>
> Yours very truly,

> Should you have any questions, don't hesitate to call.

> Feel free to contact us if you have questions.

Also, as noted below under the discussion of letter formats, avoid the old-fashioned and overdone complimentary closings:

> Very truly yours,
>
> Deepest regards,
>
> Thanking you for everything,
>
> In sincerest and deepest appreciation,

Letter Formats and Styles

Each company or each division within a company should decide which letter format and style is the best for its purposes. Such format and style decisions include how the letter is spaced on the page, the type of letterhead and paper chosen, the typeface used in the text, and even which words and phrases to use or avoid.

Decisions about format and style convey the company's image.

After managers have made such decisions, writers can start with a given format (style sheet), so the writer's options properly focus on content questions. See PAGE LAYOUT for a sample style sheet.

Letter Formats

Two major types of letter formats are possible: the traditional ones and the simplified one.

Traditional formats include the block, modified block, and semiblock. See the illustrations in figures 1, 2, and 3 for the way these traditional formats would appear on a page. Traditional formats remain popular in most business contexts because they are what many readers expect to see. Traditional formats rarely draw on all the potential format options available in today's software programs.

The simplified format is less

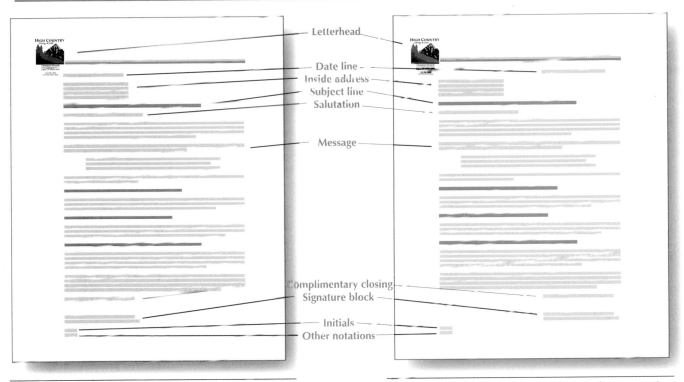

Figure 1. Block Style. *All parts of a block letter are flush left.*

Figure 2. Modified Block Style. *This letter is the same as the block style except that the date line and the complimentary closing are positioned to the right of the center line.*

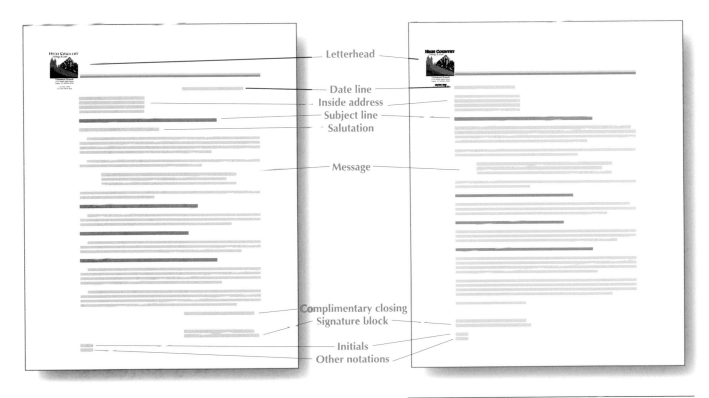

Figure 3. Semiblock Style. *The semiblock and the modified block are the same except that the semiblock has indented first lines of paragraphs.*

Figure 4. Simplified Style. *This style omits both the salutation and the complimentary closing. The rest of the letter is flush left like the block style.*

Letters

popular, but still very useful. As figure 4 shows, the simplified letter omits the traditional salutation (e.g., *Dear Ellen*) and the complimentary closing (e.g., *Sincerely,*). A simplified letter looks almost like an internal memo except that it still appears on the company's letterhead.

Simplified letters eliminate most of stock phrases typical of traditional letters, such as *Dear _____*, or *Yours sincerely*. Although outdated, such phrases are reassuring to readers, so many companies choose not to use the simplified format. They want to maintain a more formal, traditional image.

Punctuation Styles for Letters

In the open style, the writer omits all nonessential punctuation, including the colon after the salutation and a comma after the complimentary closing. See PUNCTUATION. The simplified letter reflects the open style because it omits both the salutation and the complimentary closing.

In the standard style, the writer uses minimal punctuation in the letter but does include a colon (or a comma) after the salutation and a comma after the complimentary closing. The standard style is almost always used with the traditional formats.

The closed (or close) style has all but vanished from business letters written in the United States, although some European firms still use it. In the closed style, writers retain all of the punctuation marks used in standard punctuation and add others:

—A period after the date

—Commas after each line of the address, with a period after the final line:

Mr. Edwin Jones,
Acme Office Supplies,
2211 Elm Street,
Dayton, Ohio 65432.

—Commas after each line in the signature block, with a period after the last line:

Elaine P. Hardesty

Elaine P. Hardesty,
Senior Financial Analyst,
Investments Department.

Margins and Spacing

The left and right margins should be roughly equal but the exact spacing depends on the length of the letter. In long letters, the margins are usually at least an inch and a quarter wide. In short letters, the margins can be wider; in extremely short letters, wide margins combine with double or triple spacing of the text.

Your goal should be to center the letter, so you might have to reset the standard margins in your word processing software.

Features (Parts) of Letters

Traditional formats retain the bolded items in the following list of letter features. The non-bolded items are optional for either traditional or simplified letters. As noted above, the simplified format omits both the salutation and the complimentary closing.

Letterhead/return address

Date line

Reference line

Special notations

Inside address

Attention line

Salutation (Optional for simplified letter)

Subject line (Recommended for all business letters, but optional for informal notes)

Text

Headings for continuation pages

Complimentary closing (Optional for simplified letter)

Signature block

Reference initials

Enclosure initials

Copies and blind copy notations

Postscript

The following pages survey each of these features of typical business letters. The survey presents information in a three-column table.

• Column one identifies and defines the feature.

• Column two presents actual examples.

• Column three adds notes and warnings about the use and abuse of each feature.

Explanation	Examples	Notes
Letterhead/Return Address All business letters should have a letterhead or a return address with the same information as in a letterhead: —Logo (optional) —Full legal name of organization or person —Full address—including post office box, suite number, street, city, state, and full ZIP code —Area code and telephone number(s) —Fax or modem instructions —Electronic mail or World Wide Web address For a letterhead, the above items are variously arranged. Sometimes, they all appear at the top of printed letterhead paper. Letterhead paper often has an address or other details as a footer, with the logo and company title reserved for the header. See PAGE LAYOUT.	**HIGH COUNTRY** Savings & Loan ***Viewmont Branch*** 1234 South Main Street Logan, CO 80000-0000 123/456-7890 123/456-9876 (fax)	NOTE 1: Your letterhead is one of the first things a customer sees produced by you. Make it a quality product by hiring a professional artist to help design the page. Then have the letterhead paper printed on high-quality letter bond paper. NOTE 2: Occasionally, departments, branch offices, or even company officers will have their own letterhead, which can include names and titles of managers, building numbers, and other identifiers. NOTE 3: In handwritten or typed personal letters, replace the letterhead with the writer's legal address. By tradition, the writer's name is not at the top of the page, only the address is.
Date Line The date line is either flush left (as in the block letter and in the simplified letter) or positioned several spaces to the right of the center line (as in the modified block and semiblock letters). See figures 1, 2, 3, and 4 for an illustration of these placements. The date line should never extend into the right or left margins. The date line usually appears two or three lines below the letterhead, but you can leave more spaces if your letter is very short. If you do not have letterhead stationary, then the date will come below the return address, as in the second example.	March 15, 1994 *or* 15 March 1994 ——— In letters written without a printed letterhead: 1729 Jackson Avenue Sparta, AL 12345-6789 March 15, 1994	NOTE 1: The optional format (15 March 1994) is common in letters written in the U.S. military services. This optional format requires no commas. See COMMAS. NOTE 2: Write March 15, 1994, not March 15th, 1994. Even though numbers in dates, when read, have the suffix indicating that they are ordinals, the standard U.S. practice is not to use this suffix in writing. British practice uses the suffix: June 7th 1994. Note the omission of the comma in the British version. NOTE 3: Do not use abbreviations for the month in general business letters. But U.S. military services often do use abbreviations in their correspondence—for example, 15 MAR 94. NOTE 4: Do not use the shortened version with numbers and slash marks: 5/6/94. These shortened versions are often ambiguous—for example, this abbreviation could mean either May 6, 1994 (U.S. style), or 5 June 1994 (British or European style). See NUMBERS.

Letters

Explanation	Examples	Notes
Reference Line or Block Reference lines appear beneath the date line, usually two lines down. Reference lines are typically aligned with the date, either flush left or several spaces right of the center line, depending on the chosen format for the letter. Reference lines are optional, but use them whenever you are responding to prior contacts. Mentioning documents or information in the reference lines will eliminate the need for you to include such references in the opening lines of the text of the letter. As an option, writers sometimes include the reference lines below the inside address, either flush left or centered. These reference blocks often begin with *RE:* and may run several lines. In the style used in the Department of Defense, the references are listed by number or letter so that the letter can easily cite the references as they are discussed. When letters run several pages long, the reference lines (if short) often appear on all continued pages as part of the continuation headings on these pages.	March 15, 1994 Invoice SX-4567A *or* 15 March 1994 Phone conversation ――――― 15 March 1994 **References** A. DoD Directive 5202.43-1 B. SECNAVINST 452.1 C. COMCINCPAC Ltr 85-00064-5, dtd 23 April 1993 D. DoD Manual 34.3 ――――― Reference E suggests that formulation of a new European policy is imminent. However, reference F cites an EEC memo stating that economic goals set last year would not be changed until 1995. Header for continuation pages: Page 4 Lynn J. Flaherty March 15,1994 Invoice SX-4567A	NOTE: Reference lines include both written or published material and informal contacts, such as phone calls or meetings. These lines can serve, therefore, to record what went on earlier during these informal contacts. You might even want to include in your reference line the names of the attendees at the meeting. Directors' Meeting, 5 November 1994. Attendees: S. Lynne, J. Swan, and F. Trenner.
Special Notations Special notations appear between the date (and the optional reference lines) and the inside address. These notations usually appear two lines above the inside address and are usually typed in all capitals. If two or more notations apply to a letter, the additional one(s) appear directly below the first one, with no lines between the notations. Such notations should also appear on the envelope, above and between the address and the stamps. Do not place them below the address block on the envelope because they will interfere with the Postal Service's optical scanner.	SPECIAL DELIVERY REGISTERED MAIL CERTIFIED MAIL CONFIDENTIAL PERSONAL	

Explanation	Examples	Notes

Inside Address

The inside address includes the following:

—The addressee's courtesy title (Mr., Mrs., Ms., Miss, or Dr.)—Optional
- The addressee's name
—The addressee's title—Optional if the name is sufficient
— The name of the organization
— The street address and the post office box number
—The city and state
- The ZIP code (+4 if known)

The inside address usually appears three or four lines below the date, but the spacing will vary depending upon the length of the letter. For very short letters, the inside address can be six or eight lines below the date.

The format and content in the inside address should match as closely as possible the information in the receiver's own correspondence (assuming that you have copies of it). You should spell the company's name as they do; you should use their exact spelling for the address; and you should use the person's courtesy and business titles if they appear on the person's correspondence.

Courtesy titles are a complex issue. Sometimes even the sex of the person you are writing to is unknown—for example, letters written to you from C. L. Saxon. And if you do happen to know that C. L. Saxon is a woman, you may not have any information about whether she prefers Mrs. or Ms. See BIAS-FREE LANGUAGE.

When in doubt, use merely the person's name as you received it—C. L. Saxon, as in the preceding example, or Carolyn L. Saxon, if you know the person's given name. As an option, call C. L. Saxon's office and ask for information about titles and, if appropriate, the correct address.

Courtesy titles for national political figures, religious dignitaries, royalty, or foreign heads of state are all different and unpredictable. If you are writing to one

---

Ms. Louise H. Johnson
Director of Human Resources
The Locklear Company, Inc.
First National Building
456 SECOND STREET SUITE 408
HOUSTON TX 12345-6789

Dr. Edwin B. Roberts
Chief, Psychiatric Services
Saint Benedict's Hospital
PO BOX 67
NORTH MEDFORD OR 76543-4321

C. L. Saxon
District Engineer
U.S. Corps of Engineers
879 RIVER STREET
COLUMBUS OH 99876-5432

Attention C. L. Saxon
District Engineer's Office
U. S. Corps of Engineers
879 RIVER STREET
COLUMBUS OH 99076

NOTE 1: The last two lines of the inside address are the most important, especially if you print the address on the envelope from the same computer file as the letter. The U.S. Postal Service asks that the last two lines be printed in capitals and with no punctuation. We recommend using the same choices in the inside address.

NOTE 2: To assist the optical scanning process, use clear sharp letters, preferably all capitals. Do not use italic or slanted script or other unusual fonts. Sans serif fonts are best. See PAGE LAYOUT. Also, use dark high-contrast print because the scanner will have trouble with light colored text or text from a poor-quality dot matrix printer. Do not use any punctuation in the last line.

No special notations or corporate logos should appear in the address box or below it. These will confuse the scanner.

NOTE 3: Formats for Canadian and other foreign addresses are different from U.S. addresses. The U.S. Postal Service recommends that only the country name in capitals appear at the bottom of the address block. Also, include any foreign delivery zone information if known.

Letters

Explanation	Examples	Notes
Inside Address, continued of these categories, check a standard secretarial reference, such as Mary A. De Vries' *Complete Secretary's Handbook*, 7th edition (1993) or Susan Jaderstrom, et al., *Complete Office Handbook* (1992). The two most critical lines in the inside address are the last two: the street address and the city, state, and ZIP Code + 4. The U.S. Postal Service uses these in its optical scanning system. So these lines in the inside address should match those in the address on the envelope. If you intend to print both the inside address and the envelope address from the same computer file, the format of the envelope address should take precedence. For example, the Postal Service prefers capitals, especially for the critical last two lines. See the example of V. H. Crenshaw's address.	V. H. Crenshaw Bolter Machine Tools, Inc. 4571 CHESTNUT DRIVE IDAHO FALLS ID 99543-2278 *or* V. H. CRENSHAW BOLTER MACHINE TOOLS, INC 4571 CHESTNUT DRIVE IDAHO FALLS ID 99543-2278 ——— MR. THOMAS CLARK 117 RUSSELL PLACE LONDON W1P6HQ ENGLAND ——— Josephine Andrews First Option Software Corp, Ltd. 129 Western Province Boulevard Edmonton, Alberta T5J2H7 CANADA	NOTE 4: Use the approved U.S. Postal Service abbreviations. We give only those for states and territories. These two-character abbreviations are mandatory for envelopes. For consistency, more and more organizations are also using these same abbreviations for inside addresses. We recommend their use in inside addresses. Within the text of letters, however, you would use *Alabama* instead of *AL*. NOTE 5: Omit the comma between city and state in the last line of addresses prepared to match U.S. Post Office envelope standards.

Approved U.S. Postal Service Abbreviations:

Alabama	AL	Montana	MT
Alaska	AK	Nebraska	NE
Arizona	AZ	Nevada	NV
Arkansas	AR	New Hampshire	NH
California	CA	New Jersey	NJ
Colorado	CO	New Mexico	NM
Connecticut	CT	New York	NY
Delaware	DE	North Carolina	NC
District of Columbia	DC	North Dakota	ND
Florida	FL	Ohio	OH
Georgia	GA	Oklahoma	OK
Guam	GU	Oregon	OR
Hawaii	HI	Pennsylvania	PA
Idaho	ID	Puerto Rico	PR
Illinois	IL	Rhode Island	RI
Indiana	IN	South Carolina	SC
Iowa	IA	South Dakota	SD
Kansas	KS	Tennessee	TN
Kentucky	KY	Texas	TX
Louisiana	LA	Utah	UT
Maine	ME	Vermont	VT
Maryland	MD	Virgin Islands	VI
Massachusetts	MA	Virginia	VA
Michigan	MI	Washington	WA
Minnesota	MN	West Virginia	WV
Mississippi	MS	Wisconsin	WI
Missouri	MO	Wyoming	WY

Explanation	Examples	Notes
Attention Line An attention line was formerly used when the inside address did not contain either the name of an individual or a department. The attention line allowed writers to identify a person or department that would review the letter as soon as it arrived. In traditional letters, the attention line came between the inside address and the salutation. Instead of this traditional placement, the U.S. Postal Service prefers the attention line, if included on envelopes, to be above the street address and the city and state. This preference means that the traditional attention line, which in letters appeared under the inside address, may be still used, but you need to remember to move it up above the address when you print the envelope.	In letters: H. Allen and Associates, Inc Valley Bank Building, Suite 3409 408 Pico Boulevard LONG BEACH CA 55387-2298 Attention Georgia Banks ——————— Denver Regional Office Midland Oil and Gas Company 4509 Western Avenue DENVER CO 96499-2235 Attention EXPLORATION DEPARTMENT On the envelope to these letters: Attention Georgia Banks H. Allen and Associates, Inc. Valley Bank Building, Suite 3409 408 Pico Boulevard LONG BEACH CA 55387-2298 ——————— Attention EXPLORATION DEPARTMENT Denver Regional Office Midland Oil and Gas Company 4509 Western Avenue DENVER CO 96499-2235	
Salutation The salutation has traditionally begun with the greeting *Dear* followed by the courtesy title and name of the addressee. See the discussion of courtesy titles under the discussion on inside address. When you know the person's preferred title, then use it along with their family name. If you don't know the addressee's gender or their preference as to a title, the safest choice is to use no title, merely their name: Dear A. L. Jones: Dear Abigail L. Jones: In many cases the use of no title is the best choice even when gender is not an issue: Dear Clarence Johns:	When the title is known: Dear Mr. Neal: Dear Frank: (*or* Dear Frank,) Dear Mrs. Skoal: Dear Miss Anderson: Dear Ms. Branck: Dear Cheryl: (*or* Dear Cheryl,) Dear Professor Maloney: Dear President Crouch: Dear Ms. Dearden and Mr Wong: Dear Mrs. Anderson and Ms. Blaine:	NOTE 1: Some formal notes in the past used a formal salutation: My dear Mr. Devon: My dear Susan: These salutations sound too stiff to be acceptable today. Avoid them. You should also avoid the previously acceptable salutations using French titles: Dear Messrs. Franks and Harris (*for two men*) Dear Mesdames Long and Minor (*for two women*) Even very educated readers in the U.S. would have difficulty pronouncing these French forms and would likely consider the writer odd.

Letters

Explanation	Examples	Notes
Salutation, continued In cases where you don't know who the addressee is or whether the addressee is a company or department, the choice of salutation is a problem. Do not choose the traditional *Gentlemen*, which ignores the women who may receive the letter. The option of *Ladies and Gentlemen* is almost as poor. Some people now object to the word *Ladies* as suggesting an out-of-date image of women. What is politically or socially acceptable is increasingly unclear! See BIAS-FREE LANGUAGE. We recommend omitting the salutation from a letter if you have any doubts about the correct salutation. If you follow this recommendation, you will be following the basic format and arrangement of the simplified letter. In a simplified letter you'll have the inside address, a subject line, and then the text begins. The salutation is unnecessary. In the open punctuation style, no punctuation follows the salutation. In standard punctuation, use a colon (for formal letters) or a comma (for informal letters) after the salutation.	When a title is uncertain or unknown: Dear G. B. Harrison: Dear Sydney Carton: Dear Georgie Cohan: When the identity of the reader(s) is unknown: Omit the salutation, as in the simplified letter format.	
Subject Line We recommend using subject lines in all business and technical letters. The only exception would be informal letters and notes, often handwritten. The subject line (or lines, in many instances) should be informative and interpretive. As noted at the beginning of this entry (rule 1), test your letter by covering up the text and reading only the subject line. If you can't predict the message and content of the letter, you've failed to capitalize on the potential of the subject line. Traditionally, subject lines, if used, appeared two lines below the salutation and two lines above the first line of text.	*these* Recommend That We Replace All Macintosh Pluses with Quadra 900 Models Three Phases in Merger of Personnel and Functions with Compunet, Inc. Approval Requested for New Marketing Task Teams Organized around Market Niches instead of Regional Areas *not these* Replacement Computers Our Merger Plans Marketing Teams	NOTE 1: Many subject lines, if adequate, will run six, eight, or ten words and will require two or three lines of text. This length is often surprising to traditional writers, who occasionally assumed that a subject line was brief, even telegraphic. NOTE 2: Most subject lines should be capitalized like titles of books. See CAPITALS. This practice occasionally changes, especially when the writer makes the subject line a full sentence. In this case, only the first word and any proper nouns are capitalized: We recommend that Acme Industries take a one-time loss of $5.5 million to cover back payments to the employee pension plan.

Explanation	Examples	Notes

Subject Line, continued

In a few instances, writers prefer placing the subject line before the salutation. Either practice is acceptable, but just be consistent.

Highlight the subject line by using boldface, all capitals, or underlining. Also, you need not use the word *Subject* and a colon; the role of the subject line is clear without this lead-in word.

Text

The text (or body) begins two lines below the subject line, or if there is no subject line, below the salutation. In the simplified style, the text begins three lines below the subject line, and no salutation is used.

The text of most letters is single spaced, with double spaces between paragraphs. If a letter is very short, it may be printed with double spacing instead of single spacing.

Use a full range of emphasis techniques to highlight key information in the text. These include boldface, lists, headings, single-sentence paragraphs, and graphics. See EMPHASIS. Also see rule 3 above at the beginning of this entry on letters.

Indentation of paragraphs is optional. In the block, modified, and simplified styles, do not indent paragraphs. In the semiblock style, indent paragraphs, usually five spaces. Some organizations prefer up to ten spaces.

Reversed indentation (sometimes called "hanging indentation") is a format option, especially in letters with lists. Use this reversed indentation with any of the letter styles.

A hanging-indented paragraph begins flush with the left margin, but subsequent lines in the paragraph are indented, usually three to five spaces.

not this

this

Letters

Explanation	Examples	Notes
Headings for Continuation Pages Continuation pages are necessary if you have more than three lines of text left over from the preceding page. With fewer than three lines left over, adjust the spacing on the first page to accommodate the additional lines. The continuation page opens with a header that contains the name of the person receiving the letter, a page number, and (optionally) the date.	Page 2 R. E. Blessing May 15, 1994 R. E. Blessing Page 2 May 15, 1994	NOTE: Most word processing programs now allow for easy creation of a header, so the items in the continuation page can be and often are spaced across the top of the page, not lined up flush with the left margin. Either design of the continuation page is acceptable. See PAGE LAYOUT.
Complimentary Closing Traditional letters require a complimentary closing followed by the writer's name and signature. Simplified letters omit the closing, while retaining the writer's name and signature. Alignment of the complimentary closing varies. In the block style, the complimentary closing is flush with the left margin. In modified and semiblock styles, the complimentary closing appears right of center. Choice of a closing signals how formal you intend your letter to be. In most business letters, you can use the simple closings of *Sincerely* or *Sincerely yours*. Another less common option would be *Thank you*, which moves away from the more traditional ones with *Sincerely*.	Use these in most business letters: Sincerely, Sincerely yours, Or in less formal letters: Thank you, Best wishes, Regards, Cordially, Best regards, Or in highly formal letters (to dignitaries or governmental officials): Respectfully yours, Respectfully, Yours sincerely,	NOTE 1: As in all of the examples, the first letter of the first word in the closing is capitalized. Later words in the closing are lowercase. NOTE 2: A comma follows the closing if you are using standard punctuation. If you choose open punctuation, no punctuation is needed.

Explanation	Examples	Notes
Signature Block The signature block follows the complimentary closing. In the simplified style, the signature block appears four or five lines below the last line of the text. Alignment of the signature block varies with letter formats. In the block and simplified styles, the signature block is flush with the left margin. In the modified and semiblock style, the signature block is right of center. The contents of the signature block are as follows: • Company name (optional) • Handwritten signature, either full name or only the given name • Full typed name of writer • Title of the writer (optional)	Yours sincerely, D&L Drilling Equipment *Dwight G. Edwards* Dwight G. Edwards Sales Manager Sincerely, *Jane G. Nostromo* Jane G. Nostromo Chief District Engineer Best wishes, *Howard* Howard G. Balaock, PhD Personnel Manager Engineering Division Sincerely, *Elaine Raddison* Elaine Raddison Treasurer *or* (Mrs.) Elaine Raddison Or rarely today Sincerely yours, *Elaine Raddison* Mrs. Thomas Raddison Treasurer ——————————— Grace Babbitt, M.D. *not* Dr. Grace Babbitt, M.D.	NOTE 1: The company name appears in the signature block only when the letter represents a company policy, position, or decision, especially in legal matters. Even with the company name, the signature block also contains the name and title of the person signing for the company. NOTE 2: Sign formal and official letters with your full legal name. In informal letters, you need to sign only your first name. NOTE 3: Do not include courtesy titles such as *Mr., Mrs., Miss, Ms.,* or *Dr.* in a signature block, either in the typed name or in the handwritten signature. But see note 4 below for an exception. NOTE 4: Women's signatures generally include only the woman's given and family names, with no courtesy titles. These titles, if the woman chooses to include them, would appear with the typed name, either with or without parentheses. Most women today do not choose to note their marital status. After all, men never have indicated their marital status when signing letters. NOTE 5: Academic titles or professional degrees are not part of the handwritten signature. If you use them, they are typed with the name and usually come after the name. NOTE 6: If you are signing for a colleague or your manager, you have a choice. One way is to sign their name and add your initials to the handwritten signature. The other way is to sign your own name and then include the word *for* in the typed title. Sincerely, *James Westwood* For Frank Proctor, P.E. District Engineer

Letters

Explanation	Examples	Notes
Reference Initials The reference initials appear two lines below the last line of the signature block and are always flush with the left margin. These initials consist of the secretary's or clerk's initials, along with (optionally) the writer's initials.	The secretary's initials alone: goj Writer's plus the secretary's: HFG:goj *or* HFG/goj Initials of the person signing, plus the writer's, plus the secretary's: KR/HFG/goj *or* KR:HFG:goj	
Enclosure Notation Enclosure notations remind readers that one or more documents were enclosed with the letter. Such notations usually come directly under the reference initials. Enclosure notations differ greatly in their forms, as the examples show. We recommend that you list the actual enclosures under the word *Enclosure* (whichever form you choose). A list of items, unless so long as to be unwieldy, helps readers check to see what should be attached. Sometimes, separate items are listed as being sent separately. This listing helps readers check to see what they should be receiving, either with the letter or in a separate mailing.	Enclosure Enclosures (4) 4 Enclosures Enclosures 4 Enc. With content information: Enclosures 1. Invoice 547/33 2. File 54A-R33 3. Map 54M With separate mailings: Enclosures 1. Invoice 547/33 2. File 54A-R33 Sent separately 3. Map 54M	

Explanation	Examples	Notes

Copy Notations
 	
Copy notations show the distribution of the letter. Originally copy notations were abbreviated *cc*, which stood for carbon copies. With the decline of carbon paper use, *cc* became associated with "courtesy copy."
 	
The recent trend is to use merely a single *c*, and, as in metric abbreviations, the single *c* stands for both singular and plural forms of copy.
 	
Whichever abbreviation you choose to use (*c* or *cc*), either with or without a colon, you should list the people who are receiving copies. This distribution list is usually important for organizational reasons.
 	
In some cases, you may not want to list the distribution on the original copy, but merely on the copies to be distributed. In this instance, writers use the abbreviation *bc* for blind copies. As with *c*, a list of names follows the *bc*.
	c T. E. Damer
	     Alicia Johnstone
	
	or
	
	c: Mel Barnes
	     L. H. Strachan
	     V. Sacloft
	
	or
	
	Copy to Claudie Mannes
	
	———
	
	Copies to George Siebert
	            A. S. Viceroy
	            Uhlan Yost
	
	———
	
	bc L. H. Strachan
	     V. Sacloft
	
	or
	
	bc: L. H. Strachan
	     V. Sacloft	

Postscript Postscripts are additions to a letter after it has been printed. These were handy format options in earlier times when retyping the whole letter was time consuming and an annoyance. With today's computer files, postscripts are almost never necessary because insertions and corrections can be made to the letter file and a new copy printed in a few seconds. If you use a postscript, start it flush with the left margin and use the abbreviation *PS* without any punctuation. We recommend avoiding postscripts unless you have a last-minute handwritten reminder you wish to add to your letter.		

Letters

Envelopes

"Addressing for Success," a pamphlet published by the U.S. Postal Service in 1988, provides the best guidance on how to address letters so they will move smoothly through the postal system.

Addressee's Name and Address

Figure 5 comes from this U.S. Postal Service pamphlet. As the figure shows, you should put all necessary information in the address block and use capital letters so that the address can be optically scanned.

The processing of letters begins with the optical scanning of the address. Next, a machine prints a bar code on each letter specifying exactly where a letter is to go. This bar code then controls where the letter is sent.

Poor-quality printing, inaccurate information, or other problems can prevent optical scanning, thus delaying your letter.

As noted above in the discussion of the inside address for letters, the format requirements of the envelope are making changes in how we expect the information to appear inside the letter.

For instance, we recommend using the same format for the city, state, and ZIP code in both the inside address and on the envelope. Using the same format will help prevent problems, especially if you are printing mailing labels from the same file where you have the inside address.

So the city, state, and ZIP code always will appear like this in letters and on envelopes:

BOUNTIFUL UT 84010

As in figure 5, the other lines on the envelope should be in capitals. Whether you choose to use all capitals for all lines in your inside address is a matter of personal preference—the choice is yours.

Sender's Return Address

Place the sender's name and correct address, including the ZIP code, in the upper left corner of the envelope two or three lines from the top and five spaces from the left edge.

Be careful to print the return address so the lines in it do not enter the block reserved for the addressee's name and address.

Special Notations

Special mailing notations (*Special Delivery, Certified Mail, Registered Mail*) come beneath the stamp in the upper right corner. These should not extend into the area reserved for the name and address of the addressee.

Similarly, position miscellaneous notations (*Personal, Confidential, Please Forward,* and *Hold for Arrival*) above the name and address of the addressee. These should not extend into the area reserved for the name and address.

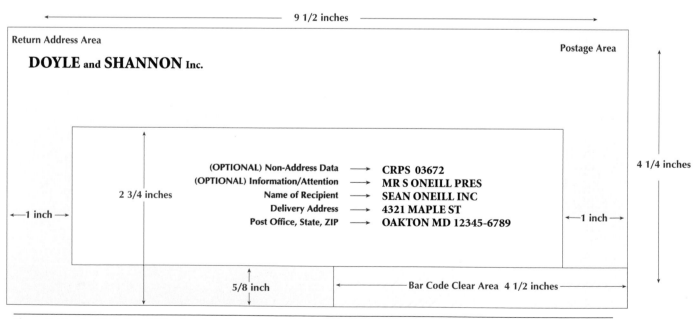

Figure 5. Standard U.S. Post Office Envelope Format. *Use this format for all envelopes. Note the use of capitals, especially in the last line.*

NOTE 1: Use only U.S. Postal Service abbreviations. Earlier in this discussion of the inside address we provided the approved U.S. Postal service list of abbreviations for states and territories. In addition, the U.S. Postal Service can provide an extensive list of other abbreviations, including shortened forms of cities with longer names as well as abbreviations for common terms like *road* or *university*.

NOTE 2: Carefully fold letters before inserting them into envelopes. The two common methods of folding letters are as follows:

Folds for Long Business Envelopes (No. 10)

—Fold the bottom third of the letter up and crease. Next fold the top third of the letter down and crease. (Caution: The top fold should not come far enough down to bend or crease the third of the paper folded up from the bottom.) See figure 6.

Folds for Regular Business Letters (No. 6 3/4)

—Fold horizontally almost in half, with about one-half inch of the top of the paper visible above the folded portion.

—Then fold the paper in the vertical direction. This time, fold the paper into thirds: the right third over the middle third, and the left third over the other thirds. (If folded properly, the upper left corner of the letter is on the top of all of the folds.) See figure 7.

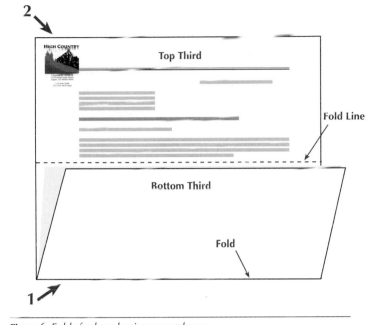

Figure 6. *Folds for long business envelopes.*

Figure 7. *Folds for regular business envelopes.*

Lists

Lists are increasingly important as a major aid for readers in interpreting and remembering information.

Lists, headings, graphics, and other emphasis tools are now essential in business and technical writing. These tools have now replaced the long, academic paragraphs of earlier times. See EMPHASIS and PARAGRAPHS.

Lists help readers in two ways. First, a reader can easily scan a list to survey the points mentioned. Careful reading of every word and phrase is often unnecessary. Second, a reader can remember more information longer if it appears in a list. The reason is that the visual image of a page reinforces the verbal message.

The most effective lists are **displayed lists**, where items are listed vertically.

1. Listed item a
2. Listed item b
3. Listed item c

Paragraph lists, where items are embedded within a paragraph, are less visually obvious to readers and less memorable.

Displayed Lists

Displayed lists are now an essential tool in business and technical writing. A well-written displayed list can and often should replace a traditional paragraph. See PARAGRAPHS.

Use displayed lists for the following information, especially in longer documents:

- Preview of topics
- Summary of reasons
- Assumptions
- Steps in a procedure
- Findings
- Recommendations
- Conclusions
- Methods surveyed
- Sources of information

Often the items in a displayed list will repeat points made elsewhere in a document. For example, all of the preceding types of information can be briefly listed, but then, they will usually require more detailed explanations. See REPETITION.

Lists

Displayed Lists

1. Use a displayed list for a long series of items and for any series you wish to emphasize.

2. Use numbers, letters, bullets, or dashes to identify each item in a displayed list.

3. Capitalize the first word of each item in a displayed list.

4. Use bullets or dashes to identify each item in a displayed list when the list contains items of equal importance and those items will not have to be referred to by number or letter.

5. Use a colon to introduce a list when the sentence preceding the list contains such anticipatory words or phrases as *the following, as follows, thus,* and *these.*

6. Do **not** end the introductory sentence with a colon if the sentence is lengthy and the anticipatory word or phrase occurs very early in the sentence or if another sentence comes between the introductory sentence and the list.

7. End items in a displayed list with periods if one or more of the items is a complete sentence.

Paragraph Lists

8. Use a list within a paragraph whenever the list is short (fewer than six items) and you do not wish to emphasize the list.

9. Use numbers or letters to identify each item in a paragraph series. Enclose the number or letter within parentheses.

10. Capitalize the first word of each item in a paragraph list only if each item is a complete sentence or if an item begins with a proper noun.

11. In paragraph lists, do not precede the list with a colon if the list follows a preposition or a verb.

Lists within Lists

12. Whenever one list occurs inside another list, use numbers for the outer list and letters for the inner list.

Lists and Parallelism

13. Ensure that items in lists are parallel in structure. Begin each item with the same type of word (noun, verb, adjective, etc.).

1. Use a displayed list for a long series of items and for any series you wish to emphasize:

Five collective protection countermeasures were identified:

1. Simple activated-carbon absorption filters
2. Regenerative filters
3. Closed-loop or recirculation environmental control systems
4. Pyrolytic destruction of agents
5. Corona discharge and other molecular disruption techniques

2. Use numbers, letters, bullets, or dashes to identify each item in a displayed list.

Use numbers or letters whenever the list is lengthy, whenever the text must refer to items in the list, or whenever the items are listed in decreasing order of importance. The numbers or letters should not be enclosed by parentheses, but they should be followed by a period:

a. Definition of systems and subsystems

b. Progressive apportionment of figure-of-merit requirements to subsystems

c. Progressive definition of functional requirements for subsystems to meet mission requirements

d. Definition of subsystem design and interface constraints as dictated by the chosen deployment strategy

See NUMBERING SYSTEMS.

3. Capitalize the first word of each item in a displayed list:

- Item a
- Item b
- Item c

NOTE: The exception to this rule occurs whenever the listed items complete the thought begun in the introductory sentence (see rule 7, note 2).

4. Use bullets or dashes to identify each item in a displayed list when the list contains items of equal importance and those items will not have to be referred to by number or letter:

We selected these means of accomplishing the scope of work for the following reasons:

- They respond to the program needs as defined in the RFP.

- They reflect the approach to project definition steps that experience indicates is effective in other isotope separation projects.

- They reflect our experience in assisting R&D personnel in transferring the requisite technology to documentation rapidly enough to support tight project schedules.

5. Use a colon to introduce a list when the sentence preceding the list contains such anticipatory words or phrases as *the following, as follows, thus,* and *these:*

The 1553 interface will be programmed to respond to the following mode commands:

a. Synchronize (without data word).
b. Synchronize (with data word).
c. Transmit status word.
d. Reset terminal.

NOTE: A recent trend is to omit anticipatory words and even break the syntax of the lead-in sentence:

As written, the 1553 interface will allow users to:

a. Synchronize
b. . . .

Some editors would object to this use of the colon to break the syntax. For consistency in this *Style Guide*, we have avoided such uses of the colon. See rule 11.

6. Do *not* end the introductory sentence with a colon if the sentence is lengthy and the anticipatory word or phrase occurs very early in the sentence or if another sentence comes between the introductory sentence and the list:

The following steps are required to process the message received by the bit processor. Note that the sequence parallels both subsystem interface architectures.

1. Recognize a valid RT enable flag.
2. Read the 16-bit word from the bit processor.
3. Check the T/R bit.
4. Decode the subaddress field where incoming data will be stored.

7. End items in a displayed list with periods if one or more of the items is a complete sentence:

Western Aeronautics has a wide range of related experience:

- We built and tested crash-proof recorders for the T41 and T7G engine data analyzers.

- We designed, developed, tested, and manufactured the Central Air Flight Data Computer (CAFDC) systems for the Air Force.

- We produced the full range of flight data computers with 18 different designs flown on 35 different aircraft.

NOTE 1: The above listed items are clearly sentences, so periods are necessary. Sometimes, however, items may not be clearly sentences:

—Convene.
—Caucus.
—Vote.
—Adjourn.

Each of these words is an imperative sentence and should require a period (see SENTENCES), but their shortness has led some editors to prefer no periods. Items without periods also reflect a trend in advertising and in media documents to use lists without final punctuation.

Lists

NOTE 2: Sometimes a displayed list completes the sentence begun with the introductory statement. In this instance, even though the listed items are not sentences, the final one will require a period. Also, note that such lists usually do not follow a colon and that they use commas or semicolons after all but the last item:

> You may gain access to the Human Resources Department database by
>
> 1. clicking on the HRD logo on your screen,
> 2. logging on by entering your name and department code, and
> 3. entering your password and the last four digits of your phone number.

Lists with continued punctuation (as in this example) are now rare, probably because writers, influenced by advertising, are using colons, capitals and spacing to make lists more visually emphatic.

Paragraph Lists

8. Use a list within a paragraph whenever the list is short (fewer than six items) and you do not wish to emphasize the list:

> Five collective protection countermeasures were identified: (1) simple activated-carbon absorption filters, (2) regenerative filters, (3) closed-loop or recirculation environmental control systems, (4) pyrolytic destruction of agents, and (5) corona discharge and other molecular disruption techniques.

9. Use numbers or letters to identify each item in a paragraph series. Enclose the number or letter within parentheses:

> The HCF memory is in three sections: (1) program, (2) nonvolatile RAM, and (3) scratch-pad RAM.

or

> The HCF memory is in three sections: (a) program, (b) nonvolatile RAM, and (c) scratch-pad RAM.

10. Capitalize the first word of each item in a paragraph list only if each item is a complete sentence or if an item begins with a proper noun:

> We propose that the qualification program include (1) documentation of tests conducted on similar equipment, (2) service history of similar equipment, and (3) Bell Laboratories' testing of the equipment.

11. In paragraph lists, do not precede the list with a colon if the list follows a preposition or a verb:

> The 1553 interface will be programmed to respond to (a) synchronize (without data word), (b) synchronize (with data word), (c) transmit status word, and (d) reset terminal.

NOTE 1: If this list becomes a displayed list, however, use the colon even though the list follows a verb:

> The 1553 interface commands are:
>
> a. Synchronize (without data word).
> b. Synchronize (with data word).
> c. Transmit status word.
> d. Reset terminal.

NOTE 2: This example (where a colon follows a verb introducing a list) is more and more widely accepted. However, some editors would still revise the lead-in sentence to read as follows:

> The 1553 interface has these commands:

In this *Style Guide*, for instance, we have avoided introducing displayed lists with sentences that end with a verb or preposition. See rule 5.

Lists within Lists

12. Whenever one list occurs inside another list, use numbers for the outer list and letters for the inner list:

> 1. The physical characteristics of the regenerator include (a) ferritic stainless steel construction, compatible with a moist, coastal salt-air environment; (b) an internally insulated turbine exhaust duct; (c) a horizontal configuration; and (d) high-performance rectangular fins.
>
> 2. The performance data include (a) 88 percent thermal effectiveness, (b) over 4,600 hours of operating time, and (c) no evidence of corrosion or fouling.

NOTE: For a third level of nested lists, use lowercase Roman numerals (*i, ii, iii*, etc.). Also use caution. Lists within lists within lists become confusing and irritating.

Lists and Parallelism

13. Ensure that items in lists are parallel in structure. Begin each item with the same type of word (noun, verb, adjective, etc.):

> This programming language interface allows the simulation model programs to access the database in the following ways:
>
> 1. Retrieve records with specific key values.
> 2. Retrieve records in database sequences.
> 3. Insert records into the database.
> 4. Delete records from the database.
> 5. Modify and replace records in the database.

Each item begins not only with a verb, but also with the same kind of verb. The list would **not** be parallel if the verb or sentence forms were changed:

> This programming language interface will allow the simulation model programs to access the database in the following ways:
>
> 1. Retrieve records with specific key values.
> 2. Records in data base sequences can also be retrieved.
> 3. Insertion of records into the database.
> 4. Deleting records from the database.
> 5. Modification and replacement of records in the database.

Lists, whether in paragraph or display form, must always be parallel. The items listed must be consistent in form and structure. See PARALLELISM.

Managing information requires, first of all, that you have strategies for discovering and analyzing key information. Next, you must be able to retrieve easily and rapidly such information.

In the following discussion, *information* means interpreted and analyzed facts and ideas. By this definition, information arises from a person's intellect or intelligence. In contrast, voluminous computer data files do not become information until someone analyzes or interprets them.

For too long the management of information has meant computer hardware, software, and the architecture of networks. Typically, the MIS (managed information systems) person is a computer technician who has little or no interest in the content of the computer files.

Intellectual productivity today depends, as it always has, on the insights from a single human brain. The computer can assist in the collection and recording of data, but it cannot replace the human brain.

Discovering and analyzing key information is the crucial phase of any business or technical task. Analysis requires you to search for patterns, linkages, and relationships within available facts and ideas. Through analysis, discrete and unconnected facts become useful information.

Retrieving information is also crucial because the best ideas are worthless unless you can retrieve them and use them whenever you want.

In today's technological society, discovering and analyzing information cannot be a solitary activity. Today's technical and business professionals must constantly collaborate and exchange ideas. These professionals must be proficient communicators—within a business team, a research group, or even an ad hoc interest group on the Internet.

As a professional communicator, you likely spend three-fourths of your time communicating with others—writing documents, sending voice- or E-mail messages, participating in (and recording) meetings, or merely talking on the telephone.

The following rules suggest ways for you personally to manage information, as defined above. The rules only incidentally refer to high-tech computer tools for filing and retrieving data.

Managing Information

1. Identify a purpose, strategy, or goal to guide you as you strive to discover and analyze the increasingly complex flow of information.

2. Use an organizing tool to discover information and to record your communication tasks.

3. Record and prioritize key information and communication tasks.

4. Initiate a written dialogue with your recorded and prioritized information.

5. Provide for easy and rapid retrieval of all information.

6. Implement a document retention (and destruction) policy.

7. Decide how you want to share information you have discovered.

1. Identify a purpose, strategy, or goal to guide you as you strive to discover and analyze the increasingly complex flow of information.

Not all information is inherently important. So from the start, you need to establish priorities. You have to decide what's most important to you professionally and personally.

Is a strategic business goal your primary interest? Do you want to expand your grasp of a technical or scientific process? Perhaps an environmental issue has become an important concern.

As you answer these and other similar questions, you will be setting goals and establishing priorities. Without established priorities, you will be overwhelmed by the flood of information (often only data and facts) available today.

2. Use an organizing tool to discover information and to record your communication tasks.

The Franklin Planner® is an excellent example of one such tool. Also available is the computer version of the Franklin Planner—called *Franklin Planner ™Software*.

Whether you choose the loose-leaf version of the Planner or the computer version, you will be creating an intellectual record or

Managing Information

diary. This record or diary parallels the data books often used by research scientists to record both facts and interpretations.

Some people view the Planner as purely a scheduling book. They fail to see and to capitalize on the Planner as a powerful intellectual tool.

As an intellectual tool, either version of the Planner is valuable for these reasons:

- It encourages you to write down or record ideas when they occur to you.

- It makes key information visible now and available for later consideration.

- It provides tools for planning meetings, monitoring projects, designing documents, and scheduling events.

- It provides an organizational memory or history of events (meetings, telephone calls, etc.).

- It permits you to cross-reference and index information for efficient retrieval.

An increasing number of special supplements are available for use with your planner. These supplements include pages designed to help you write a document, prepare a speech, work through environmental issues, develop a public involvement plan, plan a meeting, or develop strategies for a winning proposal.

Add supplemental pages to your planner whenever appropriate. As you use them, you will be managing information in an increasingly systematic manner.

3. Record and prioritize key information and communication tasks.

Use the organizing tool (rule 2) to record and prioritize key information and communication tasks. This suggestion makes the organizing tool an intellectual tool, not merely a scheduling book for future appointments.

Information overload is a primary intellectual barrier. Scientific and technical information is now doubling every three or four years. Key articles and books on a single specialized topic now number in the dozens or even hundreds. The recorded and archived data and facts are overwhelming.

To deal with information overload, regularly practice recording and prioritizing information that is or might be useful to you by using the following strategies:

—**Record facts, ideas, and key words or phrases.** Any and all information is appropriate, whether it comes from a written document, from E-mail, or from a telephone call. And remember that even an off-the-wall idea today may be valuable at a later date and in a different context. So don't ignore facts or ideas that don't have immediate applications.

—**Record enough information so you (or even someone else) can understand the meaning of what you record.** Cryptic, telegraphic sentences are a problem, even for yourself. So provide enough words and phrases to make the meaning or message clear.

—**Credit carefully the source for any ideas, words, and phrases.** A record of a business meeting, for instance, will be inadequate if different persons' ideas are not clearly labeled. See CITATIONS and INTELLECTUAL PROPERTY.

—**Review and, when appropriate, summarize information.** A summary is one of the best ways to prioritize key information. See SUMMARIES.

—**Use symbols, lines, and other visual signals to link and prioritize key information.** Any alphanumeric system would work. Or you might decide to use your own system of stars or arrows in the margins. You might even want to record information using clustering or some other visualization pattern. Your goal should be to visually emphasize information so you can more easily remember it.

The recorded notes in figure 1 illustrate some of the preceding strategies. Plan, however, to develop your own strategies so you make your planner an efficient intellectual tool for you. See THINKING STRATEGIES.

Figure 2 indexes the topics recorded in figure 1. A complete and well-designed index is important when you want to retrieve key information.

4. Initiate a written dialogue with your recorded and prioritized information.

Recording only facts and other people's ideas is just a beginning. Your analysis or interpretations of these facts and ideas are more valuable than the facts and ideas themselves.

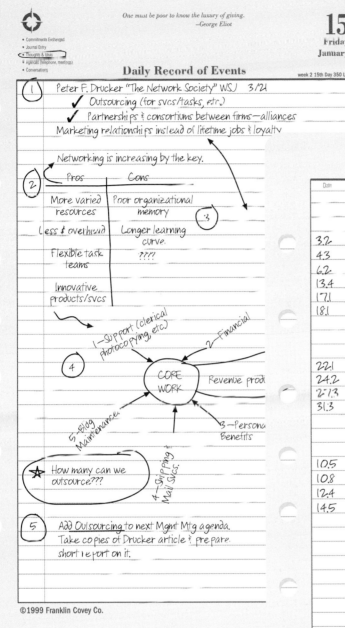

Figure 1. Sample of Recorded and Analyzed Information.
Based on ideas from Drucker's Wall Street Journal *article, the writer of this page records key points (item 1); analyzes the information (items 2 and 4); and develops a plan for action (item 5). Item 3 records a related quotation with its source.*

January Index

Date	Index important information and events recorded on this month's pages.
	Travel Reimbursment Policy
3.2	Mgmt Mtg—task to access policy
4.3	Discover Card Mtg
6.2	AMEX Mtg
13.4	Bank One Visa/Mastercard
17.1	Task team minutes
18.1	Report to Mgmt. Recommend AMEX
	Outsourcing
22.1	Drucker's article (WSJ) on networking
24.2	Mgmt Mtg notes: assignments
27.3	Finance Dept.—outsourcing options
31.3	Report to Mgmt on Financial outsourcing options
	QA Problem
10.5	Attended monthly production review: key problem of QA
10.8	Toured XYZ Copy's production line
12.4	Prepared QA assessment report
14.5	Met with CEO on possible initiations

© 1999 Franklin Covey Co.   Original-Classic

Figure 2. Sample Monthly Index. *Make the index a thoughtful summary of intellectual activities. Organize indexed items by topic or subject. The numbers in the date column record the date and the item number on that date. So 3.2 means that on March 3 item 2 recorded the Management Meeting.*

Managing Information

Recall that *information* means the interpretation and analysis of data (facts, opinions, ideas). In this sense information is an intellectual product. Unanalyzed data is not an intellectual product.

Begin by questioning the data. What details are missing? Where would you find answers to questions? Who can help you? Record these and other thoughts!

More specifically, use the following discovery questions to initiate a dialogue with information. Again, be sure to record both the questions you ask and any answers you discover.

—What caused the existing situation?

—What effects will occur from the situation?

—What category would the event or situation fit into?

—What are the constituent parts or steps in the event or the product?

—Who will be affected and how important are those effects?

—What steps or options would permit an event to occur?

—How technically and economically feasible are these options?

—What events or situations are analogous to the existing situation? How do these other events or situations compare (or contrast)?

—What objections exist to the situation or to assumptions you are making?

These questions are, of course, generic ways of analyzing or thinking about information. If used carefully and consistently, these questions will become a valuable tool whenever you confront unanalyzed data.

As appropriate, ask other questions more specific to the information you are working with. For example, if your recorded information is about a business plan, you might ask questions dealing with discount rates, finance agreements, or marketing surveys. See Thinking Strategies.

---

5. Provide for easy and rapid retrieval of all information.

Retrieval is important both for you and, often, for your organization. For you, finding and connecting remembered information is important. For your organization, good retrieval often means that a paper trail exists that shows how and why the organization made certain decisions. See Ethics.

Fewer and fewer organizations are maintaining a paper trail. Electronic files in the computer now often replace the paper trail. Still, from a legal and operational point of view, a paper trail may be desirable, so, when appropriate, prepare and file hard copies.

Retrieval techniques often rely on things you may have done while discovering and recording information.

Did you, for instance, highlight or underline key words and phrases? Did you, as you summarized and interpreted information (rule 3), cross-reference related ideas? If you are using a Franklin Planner®, for example, have you prepared the monthly index of key contents? Have you also recopied major points for ongoing use?

If you are working on a computer, have you marked major words and phrases for inclusion in an electronic index? Are you naming your files efficiently?

Often, computer files have whimsical or unrelated names. Consider how difficult it might be for someone else to locate a specific document if they have to rely on your names for files.

Some software does allow for global word searches, but if a document is lengthy, such word searches may be time consuming and inefficient.

---

6. Implement a document retention (and destruction) policy.

Both individually and within your organization, implement a document retention (and destruction) policy.

At the organizational level, a written retention policy is a good legal defense if you or your organization faces a legal challenge.

Many records now are legally important and even legally required. Corporate business records will answer questions about taxes. Product design reports and memos will resolve questions about product liability. Management memos will show why personnel decisions were made. Environmental record-keeping will defend you against accusations about the release of hazardous substances.

In your personal record-keeping, remember that if the courts subpoena your records, they will collect all your hard (printed) documents, your computer files, and your planner notes.

As you record information, do so carefully and deliberately. For example, if you prepare a spreadsheet using a hypothetical discount rate, identify such an assumption on the spread sheet. Your goal is to prevent any users from drawing the wrong implications from your information.

Record retention necessarily implies decisions about when to destroy documents or to erase files. If your organization has a written retention policy, you will be protected from questions about why you chose to destroy a document if you followed the written policy.

Failure to record or to retain documents does not lessen your legal responsibilities under many current legal statutes. For example, in product liability cases, the courts assume that engineering professionals will have analyzed potential risks, whether such analyses were recorded or not. See ETHICS.

RULE 2: Use an Organizational Tool

Figure 3. The Cycle of Information Management. *Information becomes an intellectual product through recording (rule 3), analyzing (rule 4), retrieving (rule 5), and publishing (rule 7). Then the cycle repeats itself as new information is recorded. Note that rule 1 precedes the steps in this cycle, and is not included as part of this figure. Similarly, rule 6 is not a part of this cycle.*

7. Decide how you want to share information you have discovered.

Sharing or publishing information is important because you need to validate your findings and conclusions through colleague or peer review.

Then when colleagues respond, you will be receiving facts and ideas that you need to record (rule 3). So the management cycle for information properly ends with sharing, but then returns to the beginning. See figure 3 for a schematic that shows how the cycle of information management repeats itself.

The Franklin Planner® (either the binder or the computer version) is a tool for planning and scheduling ways to share. For instance, you might plan a meeting, or you could write a reminder to call someone on a given day and time. Or, you might decide to prepare a written report or send an E-mail message.

Sharing can be either oral or written.

Once you decide how you want to share your information, you must design and structure your information so that all people receiving your information can easily and rapidly identify your key points.

For tips on the planning and design of written communication, see the rules and suggestions in EMPHASIS, ORGANIZATION, WRITING AND REVISING, and GRAPHICS FOR DOCUMENTS.

For tips on the planning and design of oral communication, see GRAPHICS FOR PRESENTATIONS, EMPHASIS, and ORGANIZATION.

Maps

Maps show the basic geographic features of an area and indicate spatial relationships, locations, and distances. Geographic maps can also show geologic features, mineral occurrences, watersheds, housing developments, manufacturing sites, wells, crops, and how to get to grandmother's house.

Not all maps are geographic—that is, land-based creations. Maps exist of the Milky Way and of distant galaxies. Medical researchers speak of mapping the areas within the brain or of mapping the genes within a chromosome. Metallurgists prepare maps of the atomic structure of a crystal. These and other non-geographic maps are beyond the scope of the following discussion.

The principles discussed below and the sample maps all focus on geographic maps. By analogy, however, these principles might apply to non-geographic maps, especially those included in technical or business documents.

Geographic maps today rely on increasingly sophisticated GIS (geographic information system) technologies. GIS is a computer application that generates maps using information from a database. GIS starts with an actual map or plot of a geographic area or site. Next, database information is combined with the map features. A database can include information about all sorts of site characteristics or features:

—Rivers, brooks, lakes, and ponds

—Roads, trails, and cow paths

—Water, gas, and electrical lines

—Legal, political, or zoning boundaries

—Distributions of plants and animals

—Elevations above or below sea level

—Buildings, monuments, and cultural sites

—Census data by age, employment, sex, race, etc.

—Any set of data tied to land locations

For general information on graphics, including maps, see GRAPHICS FOR DOCUMENTS and GRAPHICS FOR PRESENTATIONS. For information on captions for maps, see CAPTIONS. For listing a number of maps in a document, see TABLES OF CONTENTS.

---

1. Prepare or obtain a baseline map of the area you are studying.

In the past, people often began a project using an existing map, perhaps from an atlas, from a state highway department, or from a store that sold U.S. Geological Survey maps. These sources were inexpensive and accessible, but the maps were often either the wrong scale or too cluttered with unnecessary information. Creating a project-specific map often had to wait on time-consuming land surveys and days spent at the drafting table.

Nowadays, having a project-specific map prepared is increasingly possible, even necessary. Aerial mapping and digitizing techniques can now provide relatively inexpensive baseline maps of an area. Figure 1 is a sample of a baseline map prepared from aerial photographs. Such a baseline map would usually be the minimal map required, for instance, if a land developer wanted to make a proposal to a city or county planning department.

Maps

1. Prepare or obtain a baseline map of the area you are studying.

2. Ensure that maps are designed and sized to complement the format and purpose of your document. As necessary, remove unnecessary clutter to allow readers to focus on your main purpose.

3. Use GIS capabilities creatively to generate ideas, synthesize concepts, and discover information.

4. If you don't have adequate GIS data, look to an outside source because someone may have the data you need.

5. Label and number each map, explaining its features and including an informative caption.

6. Use inset location maps to orient readers to the location of the site recorded on a map.

7. Include a north arrow or include latitude and longitude references, and always orient north toward the top of the page.

8. Combine maps with other graphics when you want to connect outputs, physical characteristics, or other data with geographical distributions.

Figure 1. Segment of a Topographic Map of White City, Utah. *Maps of this detail are the routine baseline maps for engineering design and for planning decisions. This map was prepared from aerial photographs and from on-the-ground readings from a GPS (global positioning system). Because it is only a small segment of the full map, we have not included a location map even though we retained the legend so that readers could interpret the map and its symbols.*

Maps

With a project-specific baseline map, you can specify your scale and the level of detail to support your analysis goals. In figure 1, the detailed scale allows for a close look at the buildings and other developed features in the roughly three square blocks covered by the map.

Figure 1 was prepared using both aerial photographs and information from GPS (global positioning system) technology. GPS uses hand-held or land-based monitors to receive signals from three or more space satellites. Based on these signals the monitors can instantly record latitude and longitude and the elevation of any point. In figure 1 the GPS elevation readings for certain points appear in blue on the map, especially at regular intervals in the streets. These readings, when combined with information from aerial photographs, permit highly accurate site maps.

Figure 1 presents the current conditions at the site. It does not reflect complex interpretations or other analytic techniques that might be important if someone wanted to analyze site features or project future design options. These additional techniques become available when data for baseline maps are transferred over into a GIS system, as illustrated in figures 3, 4, 5, 6, and 7.

2. Ensure that maps are designed and sized to complement the format and purpose of your document. As necessary, remove unnecessary clutter to allow readers to focus on your main purpose.

Choosing the proper scale and deciding on the amount of detailed information to include are both

Figure 2. A Smaller and More Detailed Version of the Map in Figure 1. *Both its small size and its increased detail make this map seem cluttered and hard to read. The reduction also means that the scale is not accurate; an inch represents more than 100 feet.*

important considerations. The wrong scale can make map features too large or too small to be useful to readers of your document. Similarly, too many extraneous features on a map become mere clutter.

Figure 2 is another version of figure 1. Figure 2 illustrates two common problems with maps that are improperly sized or unplanned.

The reduced size of figure 2 means that the scale is now inaccurate, so always be careful about using photo reductions within documents. You should usually have the map prepared to match the exact scale (size) of the

map you intend to reproduce. The reduced size of the map also makes the map difficult to read.

Without careful planning, the details recorded on a map may be excessive. In figure 2, for instance, the added vegetation in the project area makes the map appear cluttered. If vegetation data are important, then you might prepare a version of the map with only vegetation plotted and with buildings omitted.

The increased scale in figure 3 and its use of limited details make it a useful overview or summary map.

Figure 3. Map of Washington City, Utah. *Because of its scale and the smallness of the map itself, the details are little more than suggestive of the geographic features. A more useful and realistic map would probably be a folded version two feet or more on a side. Note that the scale is expressed as a ratio (1 inch to 1,900 meters); an option would be a line with notched marks showing meters.*

Maps

Figure 4. Zoning Areas within Washington City. *This map is primarily an illustration of GIS techniques. Its small size would prevent its being used in actual planning contexts. It might, however, be useful in a publication discussing zoning trends, so the size of the map necessarily changes when the purpose of the map changes.*

For land management purposes, a general map at 1:250,000 (1 inch to 250,000 feet) might be suitable for showing the main features of an area including thousands of acres, but a more detailed map with contour lines at 1:24,000 scale might better show nitrate contamination of ground water in a municipal area or how steep the road is to grandmother's house. Even more detailed maps, using a smaller scale, might be necessary to show the details of a small area (as in figures 5, 6, and 7).

With GIS, you can test legibility and usability at various scales, then leave out or include data sets to improve legibility. See rule 3.

Design maps so that they will have good readability at the scale you select. Remember that changing the scale by reducing the size on a photocopier can produce maps that are unreadable. For example, the letter "o" usually becomes a dot when the map is reduced by a factor of two or more. Remember, also, that maps photocopied several times lose much of their contrast and clarity.

Choosing the proper scale is difficult if you are limited by your publication medium, by your budget, and by the size of the printing press at your local printer. If you can afford to create

and print a large, fold-out color map, you can do many things that you cannot do if your budget allows only a black-and-white, page-sized map.

Plan the type, scale, and size of your maps in the earliest phases of project and document planning, not when you are preparing the final draft of your document. Include map specifications and standard GIS parameters in the document style sheet. The earlier you plan your maps, the better their quality will be. See PAGE LAYOUT.

Figure 5. Sewer Lines within Washington City. *As a further illustration of GIS techniques, this map shows, by size and composition, the sewer lines within a six-block area. Sewer line data would need to come from sources such as city engineering files or other planning documents because sewer lines would not appear in aerial photographs.*

3. Use GIS capabilities creatively to generate ideas, synthesize concepts, and discover information.

Maps have always been essential, beginning when hunter-gatherers drew in the mud to indicate where a herd of bison was feeding. Until GIS, maps primarily captured a static view of a geographic site and its geographic features. Figure 3 is a basic site map for Washington City, Utah. Figure 3 would be based on the detailed data shown in a map such as illustrated in figure 1. Figure 3 shows what is currently present within Washington City. Such a map would

be the baseline map for any number of follow-on GIS maps that focus on real or projected (hypothetical) site features of Washington City.

With GIS maps, users can see details not visible from aerial photographs (such as buried utility lines or zoning boundaries). Users can even project future conditions and design options by asking "What if?" about the existing baseline data.

Figure 4 shows the zoning designations for Washington City. As in most GIS applications, different colors reflect different zoning features. These zoning designations constitute an overlay for the base map in figure 3. See COLOR.

Figure 5 is a detailed survey of six blocks within Washington City. The unseen features in this map are the sewer lines, which are shown by type and by their position within these blocks. Such features would be of interest to, for instance, the Washington City Sewer District.

Figure 6 shows the same six blocks as in figure 5, but in this case all utility lines are displayed. Again, only a few of these utilities would be visible to an aerial photographer or to a person surveying the area on foot. Data used to prepare figures 5 and 6 came from Washington City engineering records and records from utility companies.

**WASHINGTON CITY, UTAH
UTILITY LOCATIONS**

⋀ Building Footpads   ⋀ Gas Lines

⋀ Hydrology   ⋀ Water Lines

⋀ Fence   ⋀ Sewer Lines

    ⋀ Road Features

Washington City

Inset

MAP SCALE

1 inch = 100 meters

SUNRISE ENGINEERING INC.

DRAPER, UT

Figure 6. Utility Lines within Washington City. *GIS would allow this expansion of the information in figure 4. While still including the sewer lines (in green), the map also shows all other utility locations within the six blocks.*

Finally, GIS can map different future scenarios so that their effects can be assessed. Figure 7 shows a section of Washington City surrounding a certain building (perhaps a church or school).

What if the Washington City Council passed a zoning restriction stating that no liquor stores would be allowed within 150 meters of any church or school? This 150-meter boundary appears in figure 7, so council members could use this map to decide if 150 meters is a reasonable boundary. Perhaps, based on the map, they would decide that 150 meters is not restrictive enough. They could then request a GIS version showing

the boundary at 200 meters or even one at 300 meters.

In cases such as this zoning example, GIS maps can be a powerful tool for conceptualizing and analyzing options. Land management agencies have been using GIS for years to analyze vegetation, recreation levels, and other sorts of data. These agencies can prepare detailed maps showing different levels of potential activities and the effects of these activities on the soil, water, vegetation, and animals in an area.

NOTE: With GIS, bad data are like the proverbial rotten apple. One error in the database can ruin all the

dependent analyses. Each extrapolation from the data will magnify the errors.

4. If you don't have adequate GIS data, look to an outside source because someone may have the data you need.

Most major cities now have engineering firms with GIS capabilities. So if you need a GIS map prepared for a project, survey local firms for the necessary expertise. Such firms can also assist you if you need to have a project-specific map prepared using aerial photographs.

**WASHINGTON CITY, UTAH
PLANIMETRIC FEATURES**

Legend:
- Buildings
- Buffered Building
- Vegetation
- Paved Roads
- Sidewalks
- Alley
- Fence
- Contours
- Buffer/Safety Zone

Washington City Inset

MAP SCALE
1 inch = 100 meters

SUNRISE ENGINEERING INC.
DRAPER, UT

Figure 7. Planimetric Features. *A planimetric map includes enough details, such as buildings, vegetation, and roads, to be useful in general planning discussions. Such discussions would necessarily include how to buffer (or restrict) development within a specified radius from the midpoint of the buffered building (for instance, a school or a church). In this case, the radius shown by the green line is 150 meters from the midpoint of the buffered building.*

Sometimes neither you nor local engineering firms have all the necessary GIS data for a proposed project. If limited data is a problem, you might find that your city or your county government has useful data. Many local governments and most federal agencies use and maintain extensive and sophisticated GIS programs, such as:

—Your state Geological Survey or Highway Department

—Your county or city Planning or Engineering Department

—U.S. Forest Service

—U.S. Natural Resources Conservation Service (formerly the Soil Conservation Service)

—U.S. Commerce Department, Bureau of the Census

—U.S. Geological Service

—Bureau of Land Management

—National Park Service

—Department of Defense

Be sure to include complete citations to any sources of data you are using. See CITATIONS and rule 5.

5. Label and number each map, explaining its features and including an informative caption.

Because maps are a type of figure, label and number your maps *Figure 1, Figure 2*, etc. If you are using many maps in your document, you might label them as maps, not figures. In this case, you would also have a separate list of maps as well as a list of figures following the table of contents. See TABLES OF CONTENTS.

The name of the map should indicate the principal feature(s) of the map (see figures 1 through 8). A

Maps

Figure 8. Disposition of Forces at Dien Bien Phu. *The satellite outposts around Dien Bien Phu were intended to cover the central position and to break up mass attacks against it. They were isolated and eliminated one by one in the early spring, 1954.* (Map courtesy of Fred Boyd)

map name should be brief but accurate. Accuracy is more important than brevity.

Leave out "Map of" as part of the name on the map. But in a list of figures add *Map of* or use *Map* in parentheses to help readers tell which figures are maps.

Include an explanation block (legend, key) to ensure that readers understand all of the symbols, numbers, letters, patterns, and colors on your maps (see figures 1 through 8).

Orient the letters, numbers, and labels in your legend horizontally on the page. Place the explanation where it does not interfere with items on the map. Keep the

explanation block small enough that it does not dominate the map.

Include the scale in the explanation block. Metric units are increasingly the primary units in a map scale. If you also want to provide a scale using miles, retain the metric system as primary with the non-metric units as secondary. Users can then easily convert the scale from one system to the other. See METRICS and UNITS OF MEASUREMENTS.

Include an informative caption (following the name of the map) that states the key message that you want the reader to learn from studying the map (see the informative captions on figures 1 through 8). See CAPTIONS. The

caption and the accompanying text will usually repeat each other so that the map (or figure) can stand alone.

Be sure to include the source for any of your maps. Usually the source follows the caption. See CITATIONS and BIBLIOGRAPHIES.

6. Use inset location maps to orient readers to the location of the site recorded on a map.

Use inset maps either to establish the geographical location and perspective or to provide greater detail for some site or feature. Inset maps are essential when users of the map might not know where a country, state, or other geographical feature is located. Figure 8 shows the two kinds of inset location maps. Vietnam's general location in Southeast Asia is indicated by the inset map to the right of the figure.

Figure 8 also illustrates the second type of inset map: a map giving greater detail on one feature or site. The inset map to the left of the figure enlarges the Dien Bien Phu area to show the distribution of French-held outposts. Either kind of inset map should be as uncluttered and simple as possible, but consider retaining the names of major cities, major highways, or other key landmarks.

See figures 3 through 7 for other examples of inset maps. In figures 3 and 4, the inset map shows where Washington City is located within Utah. The location is important because most users of the maps would not be familiar with the location of a small Utah city. Figures 5, 6, and 7 provide a different location map. Users of these three figures, which present a detailed view of only six square blocks, would likely be more interested in the location of the blocks within Washington City, so the location map shows an outline of Washington City, with the six blocks identified. Deciding which kind of inset map necessarily depends upon how readers will be using the map.

In the past, writers often did not include inset maps, especially when they were using photocopies of maps prepared for other purposes. Also, figures 1 and 2 do not include inset maps. In these two figures, the aerial mapping specialist noted that a location map would take up too much space in the map, which is already very small scaled because it is only a small piece of a large site map.

7. Include a north arrow or include latitude and longitude references, and always orient north toward the top of the page.

Unless you are using a map of Antarctica, you should orient the map so that north is toward the top of the page and south is toward the bottom. In any case, include a north arrow unless the orientation is obvious.

A map of Antarctica (yes, we were serious) should be oriented with the South Pole toward the top of the page. Everything in Antarctica is upside down. Even in maps of Antarctica, an exception is often made if a map includes any part of another continent. Then, north is usually at the top.

On a very large-scale map, a latitude and longitude reference is better than a north arrow because the north arrow is accurate for only a small portion of the map. GPS technology can instantly provide latitude and longitude for any point on land or sea. See rule 1 for a discussion of GPS.

8. Combine maps with other graphics when you want to connect outputs, physical characteristics, or other data with geographical distributions.

Data often can be interpreted or divided along geographical divisions. Census analysts compile data into totals for each state or for major metropolitan areas. Climatologists speak of states or regions when they profile data on rainfall, windchill factors, or soil moisture. Criminologists survey their statistics by summing up trends across a region, within a state, or even within a neighborhood.

Figure 9 is an example of data presented from a geographical perspective. Figure 9 presents the results of a survey of residents in each state. As part of the 1990 U.S. census, sample groups of residents identified their primary ancestry according to their parents' or grandparents' original country or ethnic group. Figure 9 then records, by color, the largest ancestry group identified for each state.

Figure 9 is, however, a poorly designed graphic, despite being created in color with excellent graphics software. The first problem with the figure is its reliance on colors to identify the primary ancestry groups. Color-blind readers would have difficulty interpreting the figure, and a black-and-white copy would fail to separate accurately the ancestry categories. The second problem with the figure is its failure to include the names (or abbreviations) for the states. Many users would be unable to identify states other than their own. Even with excellent software, you have to plan carefully what you want to convey to readers.

Figure 10 avoids many of the problems with figure 9. Figure 10 reflects data on population growth, and while colors are used, the graphic does not rely solely on color. A black-and-white copy of the figure would communicate its message because the colors are combined with some added screens (shading). See COLOR. Figure 10 also includes the abbreviations for each state so that readers cannot mistake which state has which growth rate.

Maps

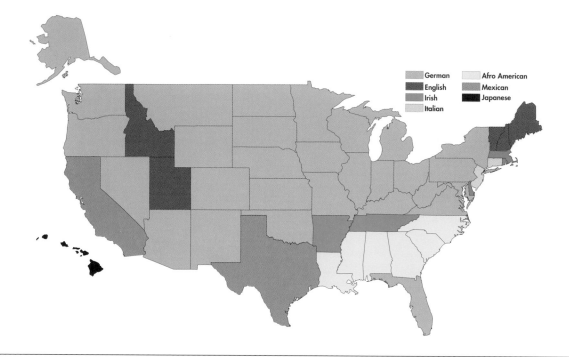

Figure 9. Primary Ancestry of State Residents by Country or Ethnic Group. *While the data are interesting, this figure is poorly designed. The reliance on colors alone might make interpretations of this figure difficult for a reader who was color blind. Also, many readers would likely confuse the data because they would fail to identify the states correctly. This figure should also include the names of the states (or their abbreviations). (Data drawn from Table 58 in the* Statistical Abstract of the United States, 1993–1994, Washington, D.C.: U.S. Bureau of the Census, 1994.)

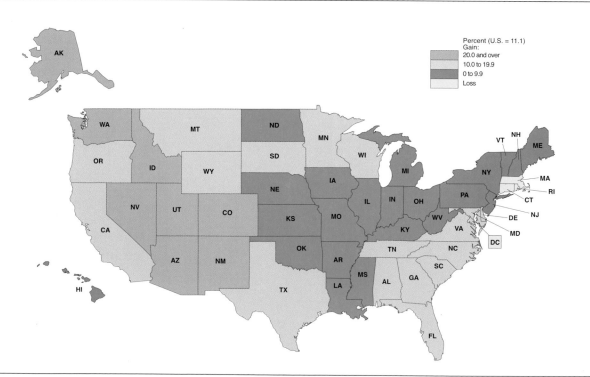

Figure 10. Projected Percent Change in State Populations from 1990 to 2000. *Using the 1990 U.S. Census data, this figure records the projected changes that will occur by 2000. While colors are a primary signal to readers of the various categories of change, the figure also has included shading so that the different states will be distinguishable to readers (even if they are looking at a black-and-white photocopy). Notice also that the figure includes abbreviations for each state so that readers will not have to guess which state is which. (This figure is adapted from Figure 1–1 [p. 7] in the* Statistical Abstract of the United States, 1995–1996, Washington, D.C.: U.S. Bureau of the Census, 1996.)

Mathematical Notations

Mathematical notations vary from one journal to another and from one publisher to another. So, before preparing manuscripts for professional submission, determine which style the editor or publisher prefers. Adhering to the preferred style is especially important if the manuscript will be typeset because setting mathematical symbols is often the most costly phase of typesetting.

The following principles of mathematical notations apply to most publications.

1. Be consistent in writing mathematical signs, symbols, and units.

Because the conventions for writing mathematical signs, symbols, and units vary, you must establish a consistent methodology and adhere to it. If you are writing the Greek letter *sigma* (Σ) for instance, you can use either σ or ς for lowercase sigma. Either form is acceptable, but be consistent in the one you choose.

A related principle is to be consistent in your choice of units from one equation to the next. If in one equation a figure is expressed in meters, then related equations should express equivalent figures in meters, not yards. See SIGNS AND SYMBOLS.

NOTE 1: Consider keeping a list of the conventions you prefer for writing signs, symbols, and units. Referring to the list as necessary will help you maintain consistency throughout your text. See EDITING AND PROOFREADING.

NOTE 2: Style guides and editors are not consistent as to how to space mathematical symbols within equations or expressions. The *GPO Style Manual*, published over 10 years ago, specifies no space between the common operations and numerals:

2+4

b-c

6÷3

axb

Other, more recent authorities would use narrow spaces around these operations as well as the equals sign (=), greater than (>), less than (<), and other operational signs:

2 + 4

b - c

6 ÷ 3

a x b

2 + 4 = 6

9 > 3

3 < 9

Software programs designed to present mathematical expressions will often provide automatic spacing. If so, follow that pattern used in your software unless you have reasons to change the spacing. The key is to decide on your spacing pattern and then be consistent throughout your text.

2. Use displayed (separate-line) expressions for lengthy equations or for special equations.

Displayed expressions are separated from the text and are usually centered on the page with two or more spaces above and below the equation. Major equations and those equations too lengthy or too complicated to place within the text should be displayed. You can also display equations you wish to emphasize:

The initial form of the equation was

$$\int_a^b f(x)\,dx = \frac{b-a}{6}\left[f(a) + 4f\left(\frac{a+b}{2}\right) + f(b)\right]$$

Meetings Management

the group). The basic questions are these:

What do I want the participants—

    TO DO?

    TO KNOW?

    TO FEEL?

A helpful exercise in planning a meeting is to ask these questions both before going into a meeting and before leaving it. For example, "What do I want the participants TO DO in the meeting itself?" Then, "What do I want them TO DO as a result of the decisions made in the meeting?"

Also ask, "What do I want the participants TO KNOW going into the meeting?" This might require some additional effort in preparing and distributing information before the meeting so participants will come prepared to discuss items intelligently.

Whatever your purpose(s), they should be made clear at (or before) the very outset of the meeting. They provide the focus for truly productive meetings.

4. Invite only those people who need to be there and who have something to contribute.

How often have you sat in a meeting and wondered, "Why have I been asked to attend?" Inviting people who have nothing to contribute or who have no business being at the meeting is one of the greatest "hidden" business expenses.

By inviting people unnecessarily, you not only incur additional expense, but you increase the level of inefficiency and frustration.

The Franklin Meeting Planner refers to the people invited to meetings as "participants," not as "attendees." An attendee is simply one who warms a seat. A participant has a specific role to play.

The role of any participant depends on the purpose of the meeting. If someone has certain information, knowledge, skill, or the power to make decisions regarding the purpose of the meeting, he or she should be invited to attend. If people have nothing to contribute toward achieving the purpose, why invite them?

Once you determine that someone has a contribution to make to the meeting, contact that person and make sure that you agree on what that contribution should be, and how much time will be scheduled for that contribution. The "Contribution" column on the Meeting Planner is for that information.

5. Start and end your meetings on time.

If you begin on time, even though not everyone has arrived—and if you continue that pattern—your chances for prompt arrivals in the future will be greatly improved.

Waiting for latecomers to arrive before starting meetings is one of the greatest hindrances to productive meetings. It is also very costly.

Why penalize those who are on time by having them wait for those who come late? Build a reputation in your organization as one who starts (and ends) meetings on time.

6. Fulfill your responsibility (either as a meeting leader or participant) to keep the meeting on track, moving toward the achievement of the purpose.

As a leader or as a participant, you have a responsibility to assist the group to achieve its purpose. Everyone in the meeting should be there because they have important contributions to make.

Diverting the attention of the group to irrelevant topics, monopolizing the time, and wasting time on unnecessary details or explanations are expensive ways of ruining a meeting.

7. Conduct your meeting with appropriate "people skills."

People skills are simply common acts of courtesy, kindness, and tact.

Keep in mind that one of the questions you should ask yourself as you determine the purpose of your meeting is, "What do I want the participants TO FEEL?"

Seldom do you achieve your purpose if you instill negative feelings among the participants. Therefore, treating every participant with respect and kindness can go a long way in helping you reach your desired purpose.

Other people skills refer to handling problems caused by those who are sometimes called "meeting wreckers" or "meeting robbers." Dealing tactfully and calmly with such individuals can sometimes be a challenge.

The first deterrent is the Meeting Planner itself. If you as a meeting leader have spoken with each participant beforehand and have defined his or her role and determined just how much time that person will have in the meeting, chances are that those people will be less apt to cause problems than if their role in the meeting has not been clearly defined.

The second deterrent is to tactfully, yet firmly, refer to the purpose of the meeting. A gentle (or sometimes more forceful) reminder about the purpose of the meeting also tends to keep annoying interruptions from becoming major hurdles.

8. Identify and follow up on action items.

Without follow-up, a meeting may be just a waste of time.

You hold a meeting to achieve a certain purpose. Often that purpose is something that can only be achieved through the implementation of the decisions made during the meeting. Unless someone implements those steps, the purpose of the meeting may never be accomplished.

The reverse side of the Franklin Meeting Planner includes an Action Plan, a place to note not only the tasks assigned, but the persons responsible for their completion, and a target date as well. See figure 2.

Proper follow-up, using this tool or one similar to it, can make holding your meeting worthwhile.

You will also want to establish some method for letting the meeting participants know about the progress and completion of the assigned tasks.

Figure 1. The Franklin Meeting Planner (front page). *Use the Planner instead of an ordinary agenda so you can prepare thoroughly for your meeting.*

Figure 2. Notes & Action Plan (back page). *Taking accurate notes and recording an action plan will help you follow up on those items that make meetings successful. This page provides well-organized minutes.*

Meetings Management

9. Evaluate the effectiveness of your meetings.

From time to time in a meeting, evaluate its effectiveness and productivity.

Such an evaluation might logically include such topics as you see listed on the Franklin Meeting Review form. See figure 3.

You may choose to have the meeting participants rate the meeting and your performance as meeting leader. Or you may elect to conduct such a review as a group activity— evaluating the participation of the group as a whole.

Another alternative is to use the Review form to assist those who report to you, in training them to hold more productive meetings.

Using such an evaluation tool tactfully, yet candidly, can be very helpful in improving meeting quality.

Meeting _____ Date _____ Leader _____ Reviewer _____

Meeting Review

Please rate the meeting leader's performance against the criteria below in the comment box, give the reason for your rating specifying what you like about the meeting as well as suggestions for improvement.

Rating Criteria
1=Strongly Disagree
2=Disagree
3=Neither Agree nor Disagree
4=Agree
5=Strongly Agree

MEETING STANDARDS	1	2	3	4	5	REVIEWER COMMENTS
PREPARE						
1. Uses Meeting Planner Form						
2. Clarifies purpose(s) of meeting						
3. Invites only necessary people						
4. Clarifies a code of conduct						
5. Considers setting and location						
6. Links methods to purpose						
Total						
PARTICIPATE						
1. Has equipment/materials ready						
2. Begins on time						
3. Appoints Record/Time keeper						
4. Exhibits Knowledge of roles						
5. Involves everyone meaningfully						

©1994, 1999 Franklin Covey Co. Printed in the U.S.A.

MEETING STANDARDS	1	2	3	4	5	REVIEWER COMMENTS
PARTICIPATE (continued)						
6. Practices proper meeting behavior						
7. Applies methods effectively						
8. Maintains focus and direction						
9. Bases decisions on methods						
Total						
FOLLOW THROUGH						
1. Clarifies tasks						
2. Gets commitments for tasks						
3. Follows up on assignments						
4. Puts action items in planner						
5. Ends on time						
Total						
Total from PREPARE						
Total from PARTICIPATE						
Total from FOLLOW THROUGH						
OVERALL RATING						Add the points for an overall rating _____

©1994, 1999 Franklin Covey Co. Printed in the U.S.A.   72913

Figure 3. The Franklin Meeting Review Form. *A candid, periodic evaluation of your meetings contributes to their continued improvement and productivity.*

Memos are essentially letters written to persons within a writer's organization. Hence, they are often called "interoffice correspondence." As noted below, the principles of good letter writing apply equally well to memos. See Letters.

Memos is a shortened version of *memoranda* or *memorandums*. Most writers now prefer the short form, but either of the long forms is correct.

Electronic mail (E-mail) is increasingly replacing printed memos. E-mail is much faster and more immediate in its impact. However, a drawback of electronic mail is that it does not automatically provide a hard copy record of important information (unless the writer or the recipient of the E-mail message prints a hard copy). Organizations should have a clear policy on what information to retain in printed form versus information merely in electronic files. See Electronic Mail, Managing Information, and Ethics.

Memos can include any type of organizational information—from brief notices of meetings to full analyses of data. In some companies, for example, memos record internal technical or scientific reports. So, no clear distinction exists between memos and reports, except perhaps in their format. A memo uses a memo heading (*To, From,* etc.) while an external report will often have a title and an abstract on the cover page. See Reports.

Effective Memo Writing

Because memos are essentially letters that stay within an organization, the principles of good letter writing apply equally to memos:

Memos

1. Open memos with an informative and interpretive subject line.

2. Include your main point(s) in the first lines of your text.

3. Design and organize your memos so key points are immediately visible.

4. Make your memos personal and convincing.

5. Choose a direct and simple memo closing.

1. Open memos with an informative and interpretive subject line.

See Letters.

2. Include your main point(s) in the first lines of your text.

3. Design and organize your memos so key points are immediately visible.

4. Make your memos personal and convincing.

5. Choose a direct and simple memo closing.

For a thorough discussion of these five principles, see Letters. See also Organization, Emphasis, Repetition, Key Words, and Paragraphs.

Memo Format

Memo format varies considerably from organization to organization. However, memos often have these components: **heading, body, signature line, reference initials, attachment notation,** and **courtesy copy notation.** See figure 1 for an illustration of these components.

Heading

Memo headings, whether printed or typed, usually contain these elements:

To:
From:
Subject:
Date:

The order of these elements, their spacing and punctuation, and their placement on the page vary considerably. In printed memo forms, the heading elements often do not have colons. Typed headings usually have colons. See figure 2 for two examples of memo headings.

Some memos open with *To* and then give the subject line. Others place the date after the *To* line. Still others arrange the items in two parallel lists:

To	From
Department	Department
Subject	Date

Some memos omit the *From* line, opting instead for a typed name and signature at the end of the memo.

Two optional elements of the heading are a distribution list and a reference line or block.

The distribution list can appear in a box that follows or includes *To.* If used in the heading, the distribution list replaces the *cc* (courtesy copy) list at the end of the memo.

Memos

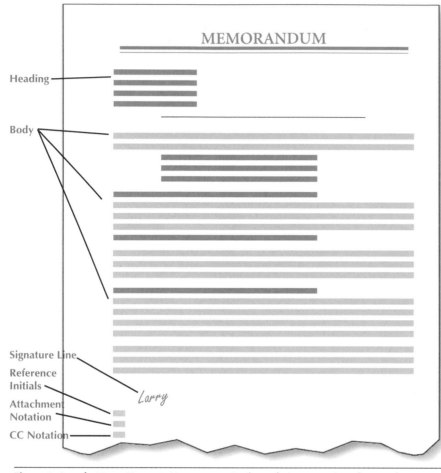

Heading

Body

Signature Line

Reference Initials

Attachment Notation

CC Notation

MEMORANDUM

Larry

Figure 1. Sample Memo Format. *Most companies have their own unique formats for memos.*

Body

Paragraphs in the body of the memo are usually single-spaced with a double space between them. These paragraphs may or may not be indented (5 to 10 spaces). Both the indented and block forms are correct and usually acceptable; however, your company may have a preferred style.

Headings and lists are important devices, especially when a memo is more than a page or two long. See HEADINGS and LISTS.

Continuation Pages

Use a heading on pages beyond the initial page (with its memo format). Usually, continuation pages have the name of the receiver(s), the date, and a page number. The most common arrangement is to have the name of the receiver and the date flush left, with the page number centered.

Signature Line

Traditional memos had no signature line because the author's name appeared after *From* in the heading.

Recently, however, many writers have begun signing their initials or their whole name two lines below the final line of the text. The name or initials may be typed, but they may also be handwritten.

Rarely do such signature lines contain titles, probably because the people within a company already know job titles or can easily look them up in a directory.

Short reference lines or blocks can appear two lines below the date if the date appears by itself just right of the center of the page. Extensive references need to have their own lines, usually before or after the *Subject* line:

1. F. H. Howell, "Testing of the Wing Plate Assembly," May 18, 1990.

2. J. K. Jameson, "Design Options in the Wing Plate Assembly," March 22, 1990.

Numbering references helps writers refer to the references later in the text:

Reference 1 notes that all wing plate assemblies have passed inspection this year. However, reference 2 indicates that design modifications must be undertaken to improve reliability.

The names of both the sender and the receiver do not require courtesy titles (*Mr., Mrs., Ms.,* or *Miss*), but

Dr. is sometimes used. Names should be as complete as possible even if the sender and receiver are close friends. Long after the memo has been filed, future readers will probably not know whom Hank or Sue refers to, and the names could be important.

The subject line should be as specific as possible (see HEADINGS):

this

Subject: Recommendation to Test Two Methods of Lowering Salt Content

not this

Subject: Salt Content Tests

this

Subject: The Sales Decline in the Northern Region

not this

Subject: Northern Region Sales

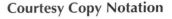

Reference Initials

Reference initials in memos usually contain only the typist's initials. These initials appear either two lines below the signature line or two lines below the final line of text (if the memo has no signature line). The initials are usually in lowercase letters:

> jtk

If the reference initials also contain the author's initials, then they would precede those of the typist and would follow one of these forms:

> GLK/jtk   GLK:jtk   glk:jtk

When someone other than the sender writes the memo, the sender's initials come first, then the writer's initials, and then the typist's initials:

> GLK/TER/jtk   GLK:TER:jtk

NOTE: Reference initials are unnecessary if the writer prepares and then prints the memo with no help from anyone else.

Attachment Notation

Attachment notations are not very common in memos. If used, they appear on the line immediately below the reference initials:

> GLK/jtk
> Attachments (3)

In some very technical memos with a number of attachments (such as maps or charts), the attachments may be listed at the bottom of the memo following the attachment notation.

Courtesy Copy Notation

If used, *cc* or *c* (courtesy copy or carbon copy) notations appear two lines below the reference or attachment notations. Increasingly, the single *c* is used rather than *cc*—much as symbols in the metric system. The form varies:

> c
> c:
> cc:
> Copy to
> Copies to

Memos sent to a large number of readers often have a distribution list instead of a courtesy copy list. The word *Distribution* appears in the heading following *To*. *Distribution* also appears instead of *c* or *cc* in the courtesy copy notation, and following *Distribution* is a list of the names and (if appropriate) departments of those people who should receive copies of the memo.

Only occasionally do *bcc* (blind courtesy copy) lists appear on memos. Blind courtesy copy lists appear only on the copies and not on the original memo.

If used, the *bcc* list appears two lines below the *cc* list. See SPACING.

MEMORANDUM

Date:

Subject:

To:

From:

MEMO

Date:

Subject:

To:

From:

Figure 2. Two Possible Memo Headings. *While the content of a heading is usually standard, the items can be arranged in many different ways. Check to see if your company has a standard arrangement for memo headings.*

Metrics

Metric units of measurement are now used worldwide by scientists in the physical and biological sciences. The most precise version of the metric system is the International System of Units or SI (from *Système international d'unités*).

Despite its widespread acceptance, SI has not been adopted by all U.S. firms and government agencies. Retooling to metric standards has been a slow and costly process, and redrafting existing maps and design layouts has been unfeasible.

Nevertheless, SI is accepted internationally and uses unambiguous symbols. It is, therefore, the preferred system of measurement for all sciences and many areas of engineering.

Metrics

1. Use base units with their SI symbols.

2. Do not capitalize or italicize SI symbols, except those derived from proper names (e.g., A and K) and except for L for liter. The symbols do not change in the plural and are never followed by a period.

3. Use a point (period) as the decimal marker, and use spaces to separate long numbers into easily readable groups of three.

4. Some SI-derived units have special names.

5. Some SI-derived units have no special names.

6. Use the table of prefixes to form the names and symbols of multiples and submultiples of SI units.

7. Some non-SI units are still permissible within SI.

8. Avoid certain metric units that have been replaced by SI units.

9. Use table 6 to convert SI units into the common units of measure still widely used in the United States.

1. Use the following base units and their SI symbols:

> length .... meter (m)
> mass .... kilogram (kg)
> time .... second (s)
> current .... ampere (A)
> thermodynamic
>   temperature .... kelvin (K)
> amount of substance .... mole (mol)
> luminous intensity .... candela (cd)

NOTE: Volume (liter) is not considered an SI base unit because it can be derived from length (dm^3). See table 4 for the listing for volume.

2. Do not capitalize or italicize SI symbols, except those derived from proper names (e.g., A and K) and except for L for liter. The symbols do not change in the plural and are never followed by a period:

> 46 m (*not* 46m)   6 K
> 1 kg   6 kg
> 15 s   22.5 cd

NOTE 1: Use the metric abbreviations only when the metric unit follows a number. If the metric unit appears without a number, spell it out:

> We measured 2 kg of salt.
>
> *but*
>
> We had several kilograms of salt.

NOTE 2: Wherever possible, choose SI units so that the numerical values will be between 0.1 and 1000:

> 54 m (*not* 54 000 mm)
> 3.6 mm (*not* 0.0036 m)

3. Use a point (period) as the decimal marker, and use spaces to separate long numbers into easily readable groups of three:

> 45 671.378 34
> 0.634 701

NOTE 1: When only four numbers appear on one side of the decimal, the space is optional but not preferred:

> 5.7634 *or* 5.763 4
> 8764 *or* 8 764

NOTE 2: In some countries outside the United States, writers use a comma as the decimal marker. If you are writing for a non-U.S. journal or publisher, you may need to use a comma as the decimal marker:

> 5,763
> 0,634
> 3,1415

See DECIMALS and PERIODS.

4. Some SI-derived units have special names.

See table 1 on the next page.

Table 1. SI-Derived Units with Special Names

Quantity	Name	Symbol	Derived From
absorbed dose of ionizing radiation	gray	Gy	J/kg
activity of radionuclides	becquerel	Bq	s^{-1}
electric capacitance	farad	F	C/V
electric charge	coulomb	C	A·s
electric conductance	siemens	S	A/V
electric potential, potential difference, electromotive force	volt	V	W/A
electric resistance	ohm		V/A
energy, work, quantity of heat	joule	J	N·m
force	newton	N	$m \cdot kg/s^2$
frequency	hertz	Hz	s^{-1}
illuminance	lux	lx	lm/m^2
inductance	henry	H	Wb/A
luminous flux	lumen	lm	cd·sr
magnetic flux	weber	Wb	V·s
magnetic flux density	tesla	T	Wb/m^2
plane angle	radian	rad	m/m
power, radiant flux	watt	W	J/s
pressure, stress	pascal	Pa	N/m^2
solid angle	steradian	sr	m^2/m^2

5. Some SI-derived units have no special names.

See table 2.

6. Use the table of prefixes to form the names and symbols of multiples and submultiples of SI units.

See table 3.

NOTE 1: Without using a space or a hyphen, attach the prefixes directly to the SI base unit: kilogram, millisecond, gigameter, etc. Similarly, the abbreviations for the prefixes attach directly to the abbreviation for the SI units: cm, Mg, mK, etc.

NOTE 2: Do not use two or more of the prefixes to make compounds of the SI units. Write ns (nanosecond), not mμs (millimicrosecond).

NOTE 3: Although kilogram is the base unit for mass, the prefixes are added to gram (g), not kilogram (kg).

7. Some non-SI units are still permissible within SI.

See table 4.

8. Avoid certain metric units that have been replaced by SI units.

See table 5.

9. Use table 6 to convert SI units into the common units of measure still widely used in the United States.

For an excellent recent reference, see Theodore Wildi, *Metric Units and Conversion Charts*, Second Edition (New York: IEEE Press, 1995).

Metrics

Table 2. SI-Derived Units with No Special Names

Quantity	Description	Expressed in SI Units
acceleration		
—linear	meter per second squared	m/s^2
—angular	radian per second squared	rad/s^2
area	square meter	m^2
concentration (of amount of substance)	mole per cubic meter	mol/m^3
current density	ampere per square meter	A/m^2
density, mass density	kilogram per cubic meter	kg/m^3
dynamic viscosity	pascal second	$Pa·s$
electric charge density	coulomb per cubic meter	C/m^3
electric field strength	volt per meter	V/m
energy density	joule per cubic meter	J/m^3
heat capacity, entropy	joule per kelvin	J/K
heat flux density, irradiance	watt per square meter	W/m^2
luminance	candela per square meter	cd/m^2
magnetic field strength	ampere per meter	A/m
molar energy	joule per mole	J/mol
molar entropy, molar heat capacity	joule per mole kelvin	$J/(mol·K)$
moment of force	newton meter	$N·m$
permeability	henry per meter	H/m
permittivity	farad per meter	F/m
specific energy	joule per kilogram	J/kg
specific heat capacity, specific entropy	joule per kilogram kelvin	$J/(kg·K)$
specific volume	cubic meter per kilogram	m^3/kg
speed —linear	meter per second	m/s
—angular	radian per second	rad/s
surface density of charge, flux density	coulomb per square meter	C/m^2
surface tension	newton per meter	N/m
thermal conductivity	watt per meter kelvin	$W/(m·K)$
volume	cubic meter	m^3
wave number	1 per meter	m^{-1}

Table 3. Prefixes and Their Symbols for SI Units

Multiplying Factor			Prefix	Symbol
1 000 000 000 000 000 000	=	10^{18}	exa	E
1 000 000 000 000 000	=	10^{15}	peta	P
1 000 000 000 000	=	10^{12}	tera	T
1 000 000 000	=	10^{9}	giga	G
1 000 000	=	10^{6}	mega	M
1 000	=	10^{3}	kilo	k
100	=	10^{2}	hecto	h
10	=	10^{1}	deca (deka)	da
0.1	=	10^{-1}	deci	d
0.01	=	10^{-2}	centi	c
0.001	=	10^{-3}	milli	m
0.000 001	=	10^{-6}	micro	μ
0.000 000 001	=	10^{-9}	nano	n
0.000 000 000 001	=	10^{-12}	pico	p
0.000 000 000 000 001	=	10^{-15}	femto	f
0.000 000 000 000 000 001	=	10^{-18}	atto	a

Table 4. Non-SI Units Permissible within SI

Quantity	Name	Symbol	Definition
area	hectare	ha	$1 \text{ ha} = 1 \text{ hm}^2 = 10\ 000 \text{ m}^2$
mass	ton, tonne	t	$1 \text{ t} = 1000 \text{ kg} = 1 \text{ Mg}$
plane angle	degree	°	$1° = (\ /180) \text{ rad}$
	minute	′	$1′ = (\ /10\ 800) \text{ rad}$
	second	″	$1″ = (\ /648\ 000) \text{ rad}$
temperature	degree Celsius	°C	$0°C = 273.15 \text{ K}$ However, for temperature intervals $1°C = 1 \text{ K}$
time	minute	min	$1 \text{ min} = 60 \text{ s}$
	hour	h	$1 \text{ h} = 3600 \text{ s}$
	day	d	$1 \text{ d} = 86\ 400 \text{ s}$
	year	a	
volume	liter	l or L	$1 \text{ l} = 1 \text{ dm}^3$

Metrics

Table 5. Metric Units Replaced by SI Units

Quantity	Metric Unit	Symbol	Definition
absorbed dose of ionizing radiation	rad	rad	1 rad = 10 mGy = 10 mJ/kg
activity	curie	Ci	1 Ci = 37 GBq = 37 ns^{-1}
area	are	a	1 a = 100 m^2
	barn	b	1 b = 100 fm^2
conductance	mho	mho	1 mho = 1 S
energy	calorie	cal	1 cal = 4.1868 J
	erg	erg	1 erg = 0.1 µj
force	kilogram-force	kgf	1 kgf = 9.806 65 N
	kilopound	kp	1 kp = 9.806 65 N
	dyne	dyn	1 dyn = 10 µN
illuminance	phot	ph	1 ph = 10 klx
length	angstrom	Å	1 Å = 0.1 nm
	micron	µ	1 µ = 1 µm
	fermi	fm	1 fermi = 1 femtometer = 1 fm
	X unit	—	1 X unit = 100.2 fm
luminance	stilb	sb	1 sb = 1 cd/cm^2
magnetic field strength	oersted	Oe	1 Oe corresponds to $\frac{1000}{4\pi}$ A/m
magnetic flux	maxwell	Mx	1 Mx corresponds to 0.01 µWb
magnetic flux density	gauss	Gs, G	1 Gs corresponds to 0.1 mT
magnetic induction	gamma	γ	1 γ = 1 nT
mass	metric carat	—	1 metric carat = 200 mg
	gamma	γ	1 γ = 1 µg
pressure	torr	torr, Torr	1 torr = 1.333 22 x 10^2 Pa
viscosity			
—dynamic	poise	P	1 P = 1 dyn·s/cm^2 = 0.1 Pa·s
—kinematic	stokes	St	1 St = 1 cm^2/s
volume	stere	st	1 st = 1 m^3
	lambda	λ	1 λ = 1 µl = 1 mm^3

Table 6. Metric Values and Their Equivalents

Length

Myriameter (obs.)	10,000 meters	6.2137 miles
Kilometer	1,000 meters	0.62137 mile
Hectometer	100 meters	328 feet 1 inch
Dekameter	10 meters	393.7 inches

Meter	1 meter	39.37 inches
Decimeter	0.1 meter	3.937 inches
Centimeter	0.01 meter	0.3937 inch
Millimeter	0.001 meter	0.0394 inch

Area

Hectare	10,000 square meters	2.471 acres
Are	100 square meters	119.6 square yards
Centiare	1 square meter	1,550 square inches

Weight

	Number of Grams	Volume of Water Corresponding to Weight	Avoirdupois Weight of Water
Metric ton, millier, or tonneau	1,000,000	1 cubic meter	2,204.6 pounds
Kilogram or kilo	1,000	1 liter	2.2046 pounds
Hectogram	100	1 deciliter	3.5274 ounces
Dekagram	10	10 cubic centimeters	0.3527 ounce
Gram	1	1 cubic centimeter	15.432 grains
Decigram	.1	0.1 cubic centimeter	1.5432 grains
Centigram	.01	10 cubic millimeters	0.1543 grain
Milligram	.001	1 cubic millimeter	0.0154 grain

Capacity

Name	Number of Liters	Metric Cubic Measure	United States Measure	British Measure
Kiloliter or stere	1,000	1 cubic meter	1.308 cubic yards	1.308 cubic yards
Hectoliter	100	0.1 cubic meter	2.838 bushels	2.75 bushels
			26.417 gallons	22.00 gallons
Dekaliter	10	10 cubic decimeters	1.135 pecks	8.80 quarts
			2.6417 gallons	2.200 gallons
Liter	1	1 cubic decimeter	0.908 dry quart	0.880 quart
			1.0567 liquid quarts	
Deciliter	.1	0.1 cubic decimeter	6.1023 cubic inches	0.704 gill
			0.845 gill	
Centiliter	.01	10 cubic centimeters	0.6102 cubic inch	0.352 fluid ounce
			0.338 fluid ounce	
Milliliter	.001	1 cubic centimeter	0.061 cubic inch	0.284 fluid dram
			0.271 fluid dram	

Common Measures and Their Metric Equivalents

Common Measure	Equivalent
Inch	2.54 centimeters
Foot	0.3048 meter
Yard	0.9144 meter
Rod	5.029 meters
Mile	1.6093 kilometers
Square inch	6.452 square centimeters
Square foot	0.0929 square meter
Square yard	0.836 square meter
Square rod	25.29 square meters
Acre	0.4047 hectare
Square mile	259 hectares
Cubic inch	16.39 cubic centimeters
Cubic foot	0.0283 cubic meter
Cubic yard	0.7646 cubic meter
Cord	3.625 steres
Liquid quart, United States	0.9463 liter

Common Measure	Equivalent
Dry quart, United States	1.101 liters
Quart, imperial	1.136 liters
Gallon, United States	3.785 liters
Gallon, imperial	4.546 liters
Peck, United States	8.810 liters
Peck, imperial	9.092 liters
Bushel, United States	35.24 liters
Bushel, imperial	36.37 liters
Ounce, avoirdupois	28.35 grams
Pound, avoirdupois	0.4536 kilogram
Ton, long	1.0160 metric tons
Ton, short	0.9072 metric ton
Grain	0.0648 gram
Ounce, troy	31.103 grams
Pound, troy	0.3732 kilogram

Modifiers are words or groups of words that describe or limit other words. Modifiers include adjectives, adverbs, prepositional phrases, nouns used as adjectives, and clauses that function as adjectives or adverbs:

> The **entire** proposal had **excellent** graphics. (*adjectives*)

> The manager **eventually** explained the reasons for his disapproval. (*adverb*)

> The pump **next to the intake line** was serviced last month. (*prepositional phrase*)

> The Sky Aviation proposal, **which scored second in technical merit**, had some interesting innovations. (*adjectival clause*)

> The ventilation fan was replaced **because its peak circulation volume fell short of our needs**. (*adverbial clause*)

See ADJECTIVES, ADVERBS, NOUNS, PREPOSITIONS, and CONJUNCTIONS.

Writers and editors usually depend on their ears to tell them where a modifier should appear in a sentence. Essentially, however, modifiers should be as close as possible to the words they modify. If they aren't, readers might misinterpret the sentence. The most common sentence problems associated with modifiers result from dangling or misplaced modifiers.

Dangling Modifiers

Modifiers dangle if they do not seem to be related to anything in the sentence or if they are not placed near enough to the words they modify to seem attached to those words. Modifiers dangle when they float, unattached, in a sentence.

Dangling modifiers can be adjectives, adverbs, prepositional phrases, infinitive verbs, appositives, or clauses. Quite often, dangling

---

---

modifiers are participial phrases, usually beginning with a present participle (such as *knowing*):

> Knowing that standard 3/4-inch pipe was too small, the specifications included provisions for larger pipe.

The phrase beginning with *knowing* seems to modify the noun *specifications*, but, clearly, specifications cannot know anything. The phrase must modify a human being to make logical sense, but no humans are mentioned in the sentence, so the modifier dangles.

Whenever you open a sentence with an action stated with an *–ing* verb (present participle) or *–ed* verb (past participle) and do not follow it with the name of the person doing the action, you will have a dangling modifier (sometimes called a dangling participle):

> *this*
> After discussing interest rate trends, we decided to refinance our present loan.

> *not this dangling modifier*
> After discussing interest rate trends, the decision was made to refinance our present loan.

> *this*
> Having analyzed the technical problems, she recommended routing the feed-forward signal through a broadband transmitter.

> *or this*

An analysis of the technical problems led researchers to suggest routing the feed-forward signal through a broadband transmitter.

> *not this dangling modifier*

Having analyzed the technical problems, the recommendation was to route the feed-forward signal through a broadband transmitter.

---

1. Ensure that modifiers, particularly those expressing action, have a clear noun to modify:

> *this*
> Having missed our connecting flight, we discovered that no later flights were going to Albuquerque.

> *not this dangling modifier*
> Having missed our connecting flight, no flights later that day were going to Albuquerque. (*Who missed the flight?*)

> *this*
> While reviewing the figures, we discovered many errors.

> *not this dangling modifier*
> While reviewing the figures, many errors became apparent. (*Who reviewed the figures?*)

> *nor this dangling modifier*
> Many errors became apparent while reviewing the figures.

NOTE 1: Dangling modifiers do not

necessarily introduce the sentence; they can appear anywhere:

> The report was inaccurate, comparing it with the prior ones. (*Who compared it?*)

NOTE 2: Some introductory participles (usually ending in *–ing*) have become so common that they do not require clear words to modify:

> Considering your reluctance, you should not represent us before the Texas Railway Commission.

> Judging from the revised figures, the report will never be approved.

Misplaced Modifiers

Modifiers are misplaced when they do not appear in their customary place in a sentence. Readers often misread sentences in which the modifiers are misplaced:

> *this*
>
> The personnel manager told Hughes that the company no longer needed him.
>
> *not this misplaced modifier*
>
> Hughes was told that he was no longer needed by the personnel manager.

> *this*
>
> The factory reopened on March 1 after a 3-month lockout of employees.
>
> *not this*
>
> The factory reopened after a 3-month lockout of employees on March 1.

In both of these examples, the writer might not have intended what the "better" versions say, but the "better" versions are much clearer. Your goal as a writer should be to write so that you cannot be misunderstood. One way to achieve this goal is to ensure that modifiers appear where they should.

2. Ensure that modifiers appear either next to or as close as possible to the word or words modified:

> *this*
>
> The manager was interested only in production data.
>
> *not this misplaced modifier*
>
> The manager only was interested in production data. (*Does* only *modify* manager *or* data?)

See ADVERBS.

> The book on the shelf with all the samples is our only copy. (*Does the book or the shelf contain the samples?*)

> The report on osteoarthritic outpatients that our team studied was as up to date as possible. (*Did the team study the report or the outpatients? The clause* that our team studied *should appear immediately after* report *or immediately after* outpatients.)

> *this*
>
> A computer program for estimating gradients has been written for the mainframe IBM in the Production Department.
>
> *not this*
>
> A computer program has been written for calculating estimates of the gradients on the mainframe IBM in the Production Department.

> *this*
>
> We are separately shipping the faulty circuit board.
>
> *or this*
>
> The circuit board that failed is being shipped separately.
>
> *not this*
>
> We are shipping the circuit board that failed separately. (*Was it okay until you shipped it separately?*)

NOTE 1: If a modifier refers to two nouns, it should appear with the first noun mentioned:

> *this*
>
> The land is rocky on the west side of the allotment and somewhat less rocky on the east side.
>
> *not this*
>
> The land is rocky on the west side and somewhat less rocky on the east side of the allotment.

NOTE 2: Unmodified nouns might need an article (*a, an,* or *the*) or an adjective to clarify their meaning:

> *this*
>
> The secretary and the treasurer attended our meeting.
>
> *not this*
>
> The secretary and treasurer attended our meeting. (*Is the secretary and treasurer one person or are they two people?*)

Nouns signify persons, places, things, and ideas. Even more important, nouns are the main words in a variety of noun phrases:

a **bottle**
the comprehensive **report**
a slowly changing **pattern**
some **tomatoes** for lunch
the young **engineer** who works next door

Noun phrases, in turn, become key building blocks in the English sentence. Within a sentence, a noun phrase can be a subject, an object, or a complement:

The proposed electrical changes will be expensive. *(subject)*

The engineer designed **two holding ponds**. *(object)*

The applicant was **the person who was busily filling out forms**. *(complement)*

Noun phrases can also complete a prepositional phrase by becoming the object of the preposition:

near **the fuel storage tank**
beyond **the property line**
at **the amount we requested**

---

1. Distinguish between count and non-count nouns.

Count nouns can be counted individually—*people, posts, ducks, pencils.* Non-count nouns cannot be counted individually—*honey, gasoline, air, hospitality.* See ARTICLES.

Count nouns can be either singular or plural:

a bottle/two bottles
every desk/six desks
neither proposal/three proposals
each pump/30 pumps
either ox/five oxen

Nouns

1. Distinguish between count and non-count nouns.

2. Use collective nouns and the names of companies as either singular or plural.

3. Distinguish between common and proper nouns.

Non-count nouns are collective in meaning, not singular or plural:

furniture/some furniture
meat/most meat
wheat/less wheat
hospitality/more hospitality
warmth/some warmth

See PLURALS and AGREEMENT.

Count and non-count nouns accept different modifying words:

count nouns

fewer animals (*not* less animals)
three fewer pumps (*not* less pumps)
fewer gallons of gasoline (*not* less gallons)

non-count nouns

greater warmth (*not* seven warmths)
less gasoline (*not* fewer gasolines)
more hospitality (*not* three hospitalities)

Native speakers of English usually choose the proper modifying words unconsciously. Only occasionally do they make mistakes: *The zoo had less animals than we expected.* Because *animals* can be counted, the proper modifier is *fewer*: *The zoo had fewer animals than we expected.*

Many nouns can belong to either type, but their meanings change:

She's had many odd experiences. *(count)*
This job requires experience. *(non-count)*
The talks will take place in Cairo. *(count)*
He dislikes idle talk. *(non-count)*

---

2. Use collective nouns and the names of companies as either singular or plural.

Collective nouns are nouns that signify groups of people or things: *staff, team, family, committee, majority, crew, squad,* etc.:

The committee has met, and it has rejected the amendment. *(singular)*

The committee have met, and they have rejected the amendment. *(plural)*

The majority has made its viewpoint clear to the candidate. *(singular)*

The majority have made their viewpoint clear to the candidate. *(plural)*

Company names are similar to collective nouns because both can be either singular or plural:

Sky Aviation has submitted its proposal. *(singular)*

Sky Aviation had their annual report sent to all stockholders. *(plural)*

See AGREEMENT and ARTICLES.

---

3. Distinguish between common and proper nouns:

common nouns

a company	the professor
three lines	the avenue
some paper	a river
an idea	our dentist

proper nouns

Acme Glass Company
Professor Thomas Miles
Second Avenue
the Mississippi River
Dr. John Wray

NOTE: Proper nouns are capitalized, and common nouns are not. For more information, see CAPITALS, TITLES, and ADJECTIVES.

Numbering systems are used with outlines, tables of contents, and headings to display a document's organization and allow readers easy access to parts of the document. The two basic numbering systems are the traditional outline system and the decimal system. See OUTLINES and TABLES OF CONTENTS.

Numbering Systems

1. Use the decimal system for most outlines, especially if your outline will be the basis for headings in a longer document.

2. Use no more than four or five numbered subheadings in documents.

Traditional System

Traditional outlines use the following numbering and lettering conventions:

```
I.
    A.
        1.
            a.
                (1)
                    (a)
                        1)
                            a)
```

Decimal System

In the decimal system, successive dots or periods indicate levels of subordination:

```
1.
    1.1
        1.1.1
        1.1.2
        1.1.3
            1.1.3.1
            1.1.3.2
2.
    2.1
    2.2
        2.2.1
        2.2.2
```

Note: The title "Decimal System" is a handy label, but it is not quite accurate. This numbering system does not use mathematical decimals.

To prevent confusion with traditional decimals, some publications use a raised dot: 1·1·1 or 2·2

---

1. Use the decimal system for most outlines, especially if your outline will be the basis for headings in a longer document.

The decimal system is preferable in lengthy documents with a multitude of numbered subsections. For example, a reader seeing heading number 6.3.5 knows that the heading is in chapter 6, subsection 3, and additional subsection 5. Traditional outlines would only have a 5, which is not a clear indicator of chapter or subsection.

---

2. Use no more than four or five numbered subheadings in documents.

Even four or five levels is often confusing. Additional subheadings can be unnumbered and with format options:

Soil Types. In the Lornack Allotment, most soils are . . .

Numbering Systems and Punctuation

In the traditional system, a period or a single right parentheses always follows the outline number or letter:

```
1. First-order heading
    A. Second-order heading
        1. Third-order heading
            a. Fourth-order heading
                (1) Fifth-order heading
                    (a) Sixth-order heading
                        1) Seventh-order
                           heading
                            a) Eighth-order
                               heading
```

In the decimal system, two or more spaces follow the number. No punctuation is used after the number:

```
1.  First-order heading
    1.1 Second-order heading
    1.1.1 Third-order heading
    1.1.2.1 Fourth-order heading
    1.1.2.1.1 Fifth-order heading
    1.1.2.1.1.1 Sixth-order heading
```

or

```
1.  First-order heading
    1.1 Second-order heading
        1.1.1 Third-order heading
            1.1.2.1 Fourth-order heading
                1.1.2.1.1 Fifth-order heading
                    1.1.2.1.1.1 Sixth-order heading
```

See HEADINGS and LISTS.

Numbers

Numbers

1. Use numerical figures for any number expressing time, measurement, or money.

2. Write out numbers if they are below 10. If they are 10 or above, use figures.

3. Write out numbers that begin a sentence.

4. Rewrite sentences beginning with a very large number.

5. Use figures to express approximations that are based on experience, evidence, or both.

6. Write out approximations that are obvious exaggerations for effect.

7. Use a combination of letters and figures for very large round numbers (1 million or greater).

8. Be consistent.

9. Use figures for quantities containing both whole numbers and fractions.

10. Always use figures for percentages and decimal fractions.

11. Always use figures for dates.

12. Form the plural of a number expressed as a figure by adding a lowercase *–s*.

13. Use a comma to separate groups of three digits.

Numbers can be written out or can appear as figures, depending on the size of the number, what it stands for, and how exact it is. The stylistic conventions for number usage vary, so you will find conflicting suggestions from one dictionary or style guide to the next. The recommendations that follow are based on the current standard practice for technical and scientific writing.

1. Use numerical figures for any number expressing time, measurement, or money:

> 3 a.m.
> $15
> 45 ft
> 1 in.
> 8 cm
> 34.17 m

Measurement includes length, weight, volume, velocity, and other units of measurement.

Figures are easier to read and are remembered more accurately and longer than their spelled-out versions. Rules 2 through 12, which follow, present instances where rule 1 may not apply, however.

2. Write out numbers if they are below 10. If they are 10 or above, use figures:

> five systems
> 15 systems
> three mission capabilities
> 14 mission capabilities
> two technicians
> 22 technicians

NOTE 1: Regardless of the number's size, use figures if they are followed by a unit of measurement (see rule 1):

> 5 pounds
> 2 yards
> 1 kilometer

NOTE 2: In nontechnical writing, writers often write out numbers less than 100—for example, *thirty-five,*

seventy-one, eighty-nine. Note the hyphens in these written-out forms. See HYPHENS. Writing out numbers less than 100 avoids over-emphasizing double-digit numbers in nontechnical documents, which typically contain few numbers.

3. Write out numbers that begin a sentence:

> Thirty-three patients were involved in the double-blind tests.

> Twelve inches from the centerline are two slots for plate fins.

> Four years ago, we initiated an IR&D study of argon-atmosphere braze furnaces.

The last two examples do not use figures even though they are followed by units of measurement. Rule 3 overrules rule 1.

4. Rewrite sentences beginning with a very large number:

> *not this*

> 363 times a second the oscillator receives a signal from the bit generator.

> *nor this*

> Three hundred sixty-three times a second the oscillator receives a signal from the bit generator.

> *this*

> Every second, the oscillator receives 363 signals from the bit generator.

5. Use figures to express approximations that are based on experience, evidence, or both:

> about 3,000 samples
> approximately 60 applicants
> roughly 2 cubic feet per second
> over 3 million orders this quarter

NOTE: While some editors would retain the written out forms in the above examples, others (notably the *U.S. Government Printing Office Style Manual*) prefer numerals with such words as *nearly, about, around,* and *approximately.* Use your judgment. Figures convey a greater sense of precision than words. Thus figures may seem to contradict the idea of approximating.

6. Write out approximations that are obvious exaggerations for effect:

That computer is not worth two cents.

The boss received a thousand telephone calls today.

His mother told him a million times to clean up that mess.

7. Use a combination of letters and figures for very large round numbers (1 million or greater):

We have invested over $45 million on laser research in the last 5 years.

Our annual IR&D budget exceeds $16 million.

8. Be consistent.

Treat numbers of the same type equally within a sentence, paragraph, or section. However, **never** begin a sentence with a figure:

this

Unit A will require 5 outlets; Unit B, 17 outlets; Unit C, 9 outlets; and Unit D, 14 outlets.

not this

Unit A will require five outlets; Unit B, 17 outlets; Unit C, nine outlets; and Unit D, 14 outlets.

this

Seven of the stations carry 39 spare controllers. The other 14 stations carry only 8 spares.

not this

7 of the stations carry 39 spare controllers. The other 14 stations carry only eight spares.

nor this

Seven of the stations carry thirty-nine spare controllers. The other fourteen stations carry only eight spares.

nor this

Seven of the stations carry 39 spare controllers. The other fourteen stations carry only 8 spares.

The sentence cannot begin with a figure, so *seven* must be written out. The *14 stations* uses figures because 14 is greater than 9; so the two references to *stations* cannot be consistent. The number *39* is too large to write out, so both of the numbers referring to spare controllers are written as figures, although *8* is less than *10*.

9. Use figures for quantities containing both whole numbers and fractions:

The proposal calls for 8½- by 11-inch paper.

See FRACTIONS.

10. Always use figures for percentages and decimal fractions:

The rectangular fins are 0.07 in. high.

The maximum core diameter is 2.54 mm.

The tests require an 8 percent solution.

NOTE: In the last example, *8%* would also be acceptable, although many style guides prefer that writers use the percent sign only in tables and visual aids. In accounting and other financial documents, the percent sign is common in text. See DECIMALS and SIGNS AND SYMBOLS.

11. Always use figures for dates:

June 14, 1996
14 June 1996
the 14th of June 1996
June 1996

NOTE: If you use the preferred U.S. style (month-day-year, as shown in the first example above), always separate the day and year with a comma. The second example shows the alternate style: day-month-year, with no punctuation.

The third example is wordy but still acceptable in some contexts, such as in legal documents.

If you write only month and year (as in the last example above), use no punctuation. Separating the month and the year is unnecessary. See COMMAS PUNCTUATION, and LETTERS.

12. Form the plural of a number expressed as a figure by adding a lowercase *-s:*

before the 1970s
temperatures well into the 100s
the 5s represent actual strikes

NOTE: Plurals of numbers written out are formed like the plurals of other words:

in the twenties
groups of threes or fours

See PLURALS.

13. Use a comma to separate groups of three digits:

55,344,500
10,001
9,999
678

NOTE 1: In some technical fields, the preferred style is to omit the comma separating digits in numbers only four digits long:

5600
9999

NOTE 2: A practice outside the United States is to use a space instead of a comma to separate groups of three digits:

7 143
98 072.1
1 742 600 503

See METRICS.

Online Documentation

Online documentation includes any information designed to appear on a computer screen. Designing how each screen will appear and deciding how multiple screens will link with each other are key design issues.

Designing for the computer screen is a visual problem. Elsewhere in this *Style Guide*, we emphasize that document design (visualization) is a key step in the writing process. Design is even more important when information is to appear on a computer screen. Screen designers have to choose icons, typefaces, margins, borders, colors, and other visual tools. Many of these tools are similar to those used in the design of a page of printed text. See PAGE LAYOUT.

Computer screens are not the same as sheets of paper or a printed document. Screens are smaller and a block of text on a screen is often more difficult to read than the same text printed on a page.

Research studies and handbooks dealing with online documentation are increasingly available. Perhaps the most comprehensive current reference is William Horton's *Designing and Writing Online Documentation: Hypermedia for Self-Supporting Products,* 2nd Edition (New York: John Wiley and Sons, Inc., 1994). Horton surveys the entire field of online documentation and provides hundreds of practical suggestions and detailed examples.

The following rules are only general suggestions. If you need more detailed guidance, then you should obtain Horton's book.

Online Documentation

1. Decide if the information in a document and if the estimated time and money of going online make online documentation desirable.

2. Survey or profile potential online users as to how they will likely use the online documentation.

3. Give online users a visual image (or map) of your entire document and its major sections.

4. Design your basic online screen so that its content items are clear, consistent, and predictable.

5. Break your text (content) into manageable and readable chunks.

6. Use graphics, but don't overdo them.

7. Prepare an online index for documents that are complex and lengthy.

---

1. Decide if the information in a document and if the estimated time and money of going online make online documentation desirable.

Online documents are valuable for conveying these types of information:

- Urgent messages that cannot wait for paper distribution

- Brief general announcements or quick informal messages

- Documents that change frequently (such as parts lists, catalogues, specifications, procedures, bibliographies, or indexes)

- Online training programs, many of which would be interactive

- Information pages for the World Wide Web

In contrast, printed (paper) documents are especially valuable for these types of information:

- Documents that don't change or don't need frequent updating (such as novels, histories, or other works of fiction and nonfiction with content that is set once the book is published)

- Documents with a primary legal purpose (such as contracts, wills, and internal company records)

- Documents with a limited circulation (such as specialized research studies, proposals, business reports, and financial plans)

Going online is not always less expensive than printed documents. Existing documents must be rewritten and reformatted to make them fit a screen format. Such rewrites can be time consuming, and you may have to hire outside experts to help you set up your software and design custom tools, such as help menus or other features.

These initial preparation costs will only increase if you are writing a text from scratch and going online at the same time.

Also, for both printed documents and for online versions, don't forget to add in production costs (desktop publishing, printing, preparing software disks, etc.). You should estimate how many copies you will need in both the online version and in the printed version. Then check with your documentation department for typical costs for all estimated copies.

Will running an online version save time and money? In many cases, but in other instances, you may decide that a limited print run will be the most cost-effective option. Or, your estimated costs may show that the online version will save you money after initial setup costs.

2. Survey or profile potential online users as to how they will likely use the online documentation.

A survey means that you go directly to users and ask them questions such as those listed below. A profile, in contrast, means that you use existing information to compile probable answers to the same list of questions.

Whether you use an actual survey or existing information, you should have answers to the following questions before you begin to design online documentation.

—Who are the users? Their job titles? Their experience? Their knowledge?

—What hardware and software will be available for each user?

Figure 1. The Opening Screen for the Online *Style Guide.* *The icons on this screen would be the initial "map" for users to survey and then to click on to access the Style Guide.*

—When and how often are users likely to want to access the online documentation?

—What information are they most interested in finding?

—What biases or assumptions will they bring to the task of finding information?

—What provisions are there for updating the online information

—Will a printed version of the online information be available? Is this redundancy desirable?

3. Give online users a visual image (or map) of your entire document and its major sections.

Developing this visual image (or map) should be one of your earliest tasks (following your survey of users, as described in rule 2).

Visualization is important because online users (and even readers of printed documents) have well-developed spatial memories. In an online format, they will remember

the sequence of steps they used to arrive at a certain piece of information. Usually the sequence begins with the primary menu of options, often captured in a set of initial icons or subheadings.

The design of an online version of this *Style Guide* is one example of an initial visual image in an online document. Users of the online *Style Guide* will see the screen shown in figure 1. This screen uses the frame image of an open briefcase containing several icons. A user who wants to search for a specific topic in the *Style Guide* would click on the magnifying glass icon. A user who wants to find a certain model document would click on the folder.

Display for users (and readers) the menu showing how you have organized information in the document. Figure 2 shows the menu of items a user would find in the index under the category that includes all the grammatical parts of speech.

Figure 2. The *Style Guide* Menu for Parts of Speech. *This menu is only one of the nine menus used in the Reference Glossary section of the* Style Guide.

As a second example of this visualization process, assume that you are preparing a maintenance/parts manual for a complex piece of equipment. You initially identify the following options for organizing the online manual:

- Parts or constituents by their function within the machine (process step A, process step B, etc.)

- Components separated according to their operations (electrical, mechanical, hydraulic, etc.)

- Parts/processes by part number (parts numbered from 1 to 99, 100 to 199, etc.)

- Subsystems according to the most common failure events (failure of conveyor; failure of control computer; failure of mechanical packaging unit, etc.)

Which of these options would be the best one for the online manual? No single answer is correct, and different users would likely prefer different organizations.

Visually display your chosen option. This visual display becomes a map to your entire online program. It would also be a handy map showing how you have organized a printed document (assuming that you have decided that an online version is unnecessary).

4. Design your basic online screen so that its content items are clear, consistent, and predictable.

Clarity arises from making sure that you don't overload a screen with too much information and too much text. Beyond a certain point, users will be overwhelmed if you try to pack too much information into a single screen.

Type size should be no smaller than 9 or 10 points, and be sure to choose a proportionally spaced typeface (and one that is not too ornate so as to be difficult to read). Be sure to leave an extra line between paragraphs and to provide generous margins so that text doesn't crowd the edges of your screen. See PAGE LAYOUT.

Once you have arrived at a screen design, show it to colleagues or your manager. Ask them if they find it readable and accessible. If they don't, make adjustments. This survey, actually a mini usability test, should be part of any documentation process (either online or printed).

Consistency means that each screen has the same items in the same place and in the same order. Perhaps you have developed a standard set of icons. These should appear throughout in the same format and in the some spatial position on the screen.

Or, assume that you want to provide automatic safety warnings within an online maintenance manual. These warnings should always appear in the same place on the screen and with the same format (type size, typeface, shading, margins, etc.).

If you are clear and consistent, you will be predictable. The more predictable your online version, the more usable (readable) it becomes.

Predictability also means that your users will not get lost in online hyperspace. Users should be able to tell from each screen exactly where in the program they are. A well-designed, predictable screen design will have enough road signs (icons, headings, cross references) so that users are comfortable navigating through the program.

5. Break your text (content) into manageable and readable chunks.

Make your text as schematic and as visually accessible as possible. This rule applies whether you are rewriting existing text or you are writing an online document from scratch.

Employees who are on travel assignments should be classified for reporting in the following ways. Those who are on assignments for at least one month but not more than six months are classified as Extended Travel. Temporary Change of Station applies to those offsite for six months but for less than one year, while those gone for between one and two years should be categorized as on Indefinite Assignment.

Classify employees on travel assignments in these ways:

Classification	For Employees on Assignment
1. Extended Travel	At least one month but not more than six months
2. Temporary Change of Station	Six months but less than one year
3. Indefinite Assignment	At least one year but not more than two years

Figure 3. Contrast Between Two Screens. *The original (top) screen comes directly from the paper copy with no editing. The revision (bottom) is more readable, whether on paper or on a screen.*

Traditional text was and still is too dense and difficult to read. It has long paragraphs and too few headings, lists, and tables. See figure 3 for an example of how original text (the traditional model) can be revised to become more manageable and readable. See PARAGRAPHS and TABLES.

Textual chunks should be designed to fit within the screen format you have developed (see rule 3). The format of the online document should govern how you decide to chunk or format text. The most efficient way to create new text is to write to fit the format, not to write text and then have to rewrite it to fit the format. See EMPHASIS for a list of techniques for emphasizing information within business and technical documents. Most of the techniques mentioned apply equally well to online documents as to printed documents.

6. Use graphics, but don't overdo them.

Graphics aid users (readers) to interpret and to remember key information. So, plan to use graphics creatively to capture key information and to highlight major conclusions.

You already will be using graphics when you show users your menu of key information (see rule 3 above). This opening menu might be a set of basic icons, or it might be a schematic illustration with subheadings that link to subsequent screens. Whatever graphic approach you choose, you will be giving users a map (visualization) of how you have organized your online document.

Remember, however, that graphics will not save a document that is not otherwise solidly conceived and well prepared. Also, graphics are time consuming in two ways. They take time to create, and they often use more memory, so they slow down the online program.

Graphics for an online document can be even more rich and varied than graphics for printed documents. Your online program may be able to include colored graphics (assuming that your users' software and monitors are geared to color).

Online documents can include any of the common graphics: charts, graphs, illustrations, maps, photographs, and tables. See the separate discussions of these graphics in CHARTS, GRAPHS, ILLUSTRATIONS, MAPS, PHOTOGRAPHS, and TABLES. As with graphics for documents and for presentations, graphics for an online document need to be well designed and appropriate. See GRAPHICS FOR DOCUMENTS and GRAPHICS FOR PRESENTATIONS.

Color is one feature of graphics to use sparingly in an online version. Too many colors can be a distraction. Also, some users may be color blind. If you do use color, add a redundant feature that does not depend on color alone. For example, if you decide to use a red message box, you might add a separate icon or a distinctive border that does not depend on color to convey its message.

Online Documentation

7. Prepare an online index for documents that are complex and lengthy.

The terms "complex" and "lengthy" are necessarily subjective, but you should consider preparing an online index if you know that users of your online documentation will often need to search for information. Also, your survey or profile of users (as discussed in rule 2) should indicate that they are not fully knowledgeable about your topic, so they will need assistance searching for key concepts or distinctions.

The design features of online indexes are still developing and evolving, but two general observations are important starting points if you intend to prepare an online index.

First, an online index is not just a screen copy of the index for the printed document. In a document, the index topics are usually keyed to pages, but pages don't exist in the online version and individual screens are not numbered in a traditional fashion. Also, the hierarchical arrangement within the traditional index will not match the sequence of screens in an online document.

Second, a traditional SEARCH tool for the whole document does not replace a separately designed online index. In a typical search function, the user types a word or a phrase and then sees all uses of the phrase in the text. For example, a user of the online version of this *Style Guide* might search for the term *organization*. The search function would likely show the user 200 different contexts using the word *organization*. Such a lengthy list is not very helpful and is time consuming to scan.

An online index is a separate subsection of your online document. Users, having accessed the index, can then either visually scroll through the index or, more efficiently, use the search tool on only the index to discover related information, synonyms, or other helpful links between sections of the document.

As an example of how the online index might work, a document on environmental issues might contain numerous uses of the following related terms (actually partial synonyms):

> impacts
> effects
> consequences
> irreversible/irretrievable commitments of
>   resources
> short-term uses vs. long-term productivity

In the online index, these terms would be linked so that users unfamiliar with one or more of these would be alerted to search the text for these other phrases, each of which is partially related to the simple terms *impacts* or *effects*. These linkages parallel, of course, the *See* and *Also See* functions of a traditional index, but what is different here is that the software associated with the index would show the linkages and would help users to navigate from the index back into the online document itself. See INDEXES.

Organization is the key writing principle. If you organize your documents well, you almost surely will have successful documents—even if you violate other writing principles. But if your documents are poorly organized, nothing can save them.

The ideas presented in a document should be structured in a natural but emphatic sequence that conveys the most important information to readers at the most critical times.

The principles of organization differ slightly from document to document, depending on the type of document, the readers, the content, and the writer's purpose. Nevertheless, logic and common sense dictate that a well-organized document must have certain features:

- The document should announce its organizational scheme and then stick to it.

- The ideas in the document must be clear and sensible, and comprehensible, given the readers.

- The document should conform to the readers' sense of what the most important points are and of how those points are arranged.

Letters, memos, and reports differ somewhat in their organizational patterns, mostly because their readers differ. See LETTERS, MEMOS, and REPORTS.

Readers of letters are typically outside the company or agency sending the letter. Their relationship to the writer is therefore more distant, and consequently more formal, than the relationship between the writer and others within the writer's company. See LETTERS.

Organization

1. Organize information according to your readers' needs.

2. Group similar ideas.

3. Place your most important ideas first.

4. Keep your setups short.

5. List items in descending order of importance.

6. In most business or technical documents, preview your most important ideas and your major content areas, and review (summarize) major points at the end of sections.

7. Discuss items in the same order in which you introduce them.

8. Use headings, transitions, key words, and paragraph openings to provide cues to the document's organization.

9. Use the Document Planner for Documents™ when you need to design a document quickly and efficiently.

Readers of memos, on the other hand, are typically from within the writer's company or agency and share various assumptions, experiences, and knowledge—all of which tend to make memos less formal than letters. See MEMOS.

The distance and formality between writer and reader affect organization in several ways. The greater the distance, the more the need to set up (introduce and perhaps explain) the ideas in the document. The greater the distance, the greater the need to substantiate information that might be subject to differing interpretations. The more formal the document, the more the writer must consider format traditions and reader expectations in organizing material.

Reports, technical or otherwise, often have prescribed organizations. Scientific report organization is based on a long tradition in the sciences. The organization of such reports is strictly prescribed, and

writers have very few options in varying that organization. Technical (but nonscientific) reports offer somewhat more latitude, but some companies still have strict guidelines on organizing technical reports.

Within the limitations imposed by tradition, logic, and audience, writers must carefully consider how to arrange their ideas and supporting data so a document serves its purpose and satisfies the readers' needs.

The first eight rules listed below suggest how you can accomplish these tasks. Rule nine introduces the Franklin Document Planner™, which shows how the preceding eight rules would apply to the design of documents. See LETTERS, MEMOS, REPORTS, and ELECTRONIC MAIL.

Organization

1. Organize information according to your readers' needs.

How you organize information depends on your readers. You might organize the same information differently for different readers, depending on their needs and your purpose in writing to them. Here, for instance, is the text of a short letter written to the test director of a laboratory:

> We request the following tests on the dry field cement samples that we shipped on July 20 to Mr. J. F. Springer of your laboratory:
>
> - Thickening time
> - Rheology
> - High temperature/high pressure fluid loss
> - 12- and 24-hr compressive strength
>
> Davidson-Warner, a cementing company, has been using this cement in our Mt. Hogan Field. On July 17, they experienced a cementing failure while setting a string of 3½-in. casing at 11,323 ft in our Hogan BB-62 well. They pumped 688 barrels of cement and 78 barrels of displacement fluid before halting displacement when the pressure increased to 5,000 psi.
>
> To facilitate your testing, we have attached pertinent well logs, cement data, and a copy of Davidson-Warner's laboratory blend test results. Please submit your findings to me at your earliest convenience.

This letter begins, appropriately enough, with a request. The writer wants something of the reader. Establishing what the writer wants makes sense as an opening statement. The specific details concerning the cementing failure do not appear until the middle paragraph because this particular reader will not need to know this information except as background for conducting the tests. The details of the cementing failure are less important than a list of the tests the writer is requesting.

However, if the document had been written to the production engineer who will now be responsible for this well, it might have begun like this:

> The Hogan BB-62 is currently shut in because of a cementing failure that occurred on July 17. The regional office would like us to return this well to production by July 28.
>
> On July 15, this well was shut in to allow Davidson-Warner to set a new string of 3½-in. casing from 10,500 ft to 11,890 ft. While setting the string at 11,332 ft, they halted displacement when the pressure increased to 5,000 psi. Before stopping, they had pumped 688 barrels of cement and 78 barrels of displacement fluid. They left approximately 35 barrels of cement in the casing (with a cement top at 8,992 ft).
>
> Wiley Laboratories has been asked to test dry field samples of the cement. In the meantime, AGF Cement has been contracted to finish setting the string. They will be onsite no later than July 25. You should plan to be present.
>
> Mt. Hogan Field production figures are down 4.3 percent in July, primarily due to this cementing failure. The regional production manager has asked that we resume full production by July 28. If you need assistance, call me at 555-6666.

This memo is written from supervisor to subordinate. Its tone is obviously different (more forceful, more directive) than the letter written to the laboratory. The organization of ideas is also very different.

The memo to the engineer begins with a statement of fact (a setup), followed by a deadline. As in the first letter, the details of the cementing failure appear in the middle, but in this second example, the details lead to an amplification of the implied directive that appears in the opening paragraph. The memo closes with a compelling reason for action (production figures down) and a reminder of the deadline.

As you organize a document, always consider what information your readers need from you. In the examples above, the test director at Wiley Laboratories will not care that Davidson-Warner left 35 barrels of cement in the casing. The engineer will not care that the dry field samples were shipped to Mr. Springer. Each document above reflects those concerns that its readers will care most about.

2. Group similar ideas.

Separating similar ideas creates chaos. In the examples above, the details concerning the cementing failure appear in the same place. If they had been scattered, the effect could have been devastating for readers:

> The Hogan BB-62 is currently shut in because of a cementing failure that occurred on July 17. Wiley Laboratories has been asked to test dry field samples of the cement.
>
> On July 15, this well was shut in to allow Davidson-Warner to set a new string of 3½-in. casing from 10,500 ft to 11,890 ft. Please try to return this well to production by July 28. AGF Cement has been contracted to finish setting the string. Before stopping, Davidson-Warner had pumped 688 barrels of cement and 78 barrels of displacement fluid. AGF Cement will be onsite no later than July 25.

3. Place your most important ideas first.

A frequent problem with business and technical writing is the tendency to lead **to**, rather than **from**, major ideas. Many writers believe that they have to build their case, that skeptical readers will not agree with their conclusions unless they first demonstrate how they arrived at those conclusions. This tendency results in documents that are unemphatic, difficult to follow, and filled with unnecessary detail.

The strongest part of a document is its beginning. Readers typically pay more attention at the beginning because they are discovering what the document is about. The beginning, then, is the most emphatic part of the document by virtue of its position. Because the beginning is so strong, you should begin with the most important ideas in the document—and then support those ideas by presenting your evidence afterward.

The Scientific Format. Many of those writers who tend to lead down to their major ideas have been schooled in the scientific method. According to the scientific method, one presents the facts, observations, and data that lead to and support a conclusion. The strength of this method is that it presents a series of steps that culminates in an **inevitable** conclusion. Therefore, the steps are as important as the conclusion.

In some scientific reports (notably those written from one scientist to another), an organizational scheme based on the scientific method is desirable:

Abstract
Summary
Introduction
Materials and Methods
Results and Discussion
    Fact 1
    Fact 2
    Fact 3
    Fact 4
    (therefore)
Conclusions
Recommendations (optional)
Summary (optional)

This format is acceptable only if readers will be as interested in the process of arriving at the conclusions as they are in the conclusions themselves. When readers are more interested in the conclusions, follow the managerial format.

The Managerial Format. You should follow the managerial format in all documents except scientific documents written for scientific peers.

The managerial format is the reverse of the scientific format. Managers (and most other nonscientific readers) are far more interested in the conclusions than they are in the steps leading to them. This is not to say that these readers will not want to see the conclusions supported— only that they will want the conclusions before the results and discussion:

Summary/Executive Summary
Introduction
Conclusions (and Recommendations)
(because of)
    Fact 1
    Fact 2
    Fact 3
    Fact 4
Results and Discussion

Having the conclusions early in the report facilitates reading because the reader is given a perspective from which to understand the facts and data being presented. Furthermore, busy managers often know the background and tests that have led to the conclusions. See REPORTS.

NOTE 1: The principle of emphasis through placement extends to all documents and all sections of documents. Your most important ideas should appear at the beginning of your documents and of individual sections. The most important idea in most paragraphs should appear in the opening sentence. The most important words in a sentence typically come at the beginning of the sentence. See PARAGRAPHS and SENTENCES.

NOTE 2: A corollary to note 1 is that you should always subordinate detail. Place it in the middle of sentences, paragraphs, sections, and documents. Detail includes data, explanation, elaboration, description, analyses, results, etc.

NOTE 3: In lengthy documents, begin **and** end with important ideas.

The longer a document becomes, the more crucial this rule is. Readers of long passages need to be introduced to the subject, learn the most important points early, receive the supporting detail and explanation, and then have it all wrapped up in a tidy closing statement that reiterates the important points.

An adage regarding oral presentations (but applicable to writing) is that you should tell 'em what you're gonna tell 'em, tell 'em, and then tell 'em what you told 'em. See REPETITION, REPORTS, and EMPHASIS.

4. Keep your setups short.

Sometimes you cannot begin by stating your most important idea because the reader either will not understand it or will not accept it. If such is the case, you need to set up the most important idea by providing introductory information meant either to inform readers or to persuade them.

A fundamental of organization in business and technical writing is to keep your setups short. Do not delay your major ideas any longer than necessary.

When you give people positive

information, you should give them the positive information right away. They want to hear it, and hearing it will make them more receptive toward you and the rest of the information you provide.

However, when you give readers negative information, giving them the negative information first will put them off, and they will not be receptive to what follows. Moreover, they might become antagonistic toward you.

Therefore, you should say "no" to readers only after you have set them up for it. Be careful, however, not to delay the "no" too long. Keep your setups short, as in the following example:

> I have been asked to reply to your request for additional compensation following approval of your Engineering Change Order dated March 3.
>
> As you know, a Health Department inspector ordered the design changes, and our contract states that all design changes required for safety reasons are warranted under the contractor's bond. Therefore, additional compensation would be inappropriate at this time.

The first sentence sets the stage. The second provides brief rationale for the decision. The third states the decision. The two-sentence setup in this example makes the decision more palatable than if the writer had begun by saying: *"We will not be providing the additional compensation you requested."* See INTRODUCTIONS.

5. List items in descending order of importance.

Readers typically assume that information in lists appears in descending order of importance: most important listed item first,

least important item last.

Numbering and lettering systems reinforce this assumption. We all know that being number 1 is better than being number 6. We know from school that an A is better than an F. Rightly or wrongly, we assume a natural ranking of items. Therefore, writers should list items in descending order of importance.

If you wish to create a list in which items are equally important, use bullets or dashes instead of numbers or letters, and state that the listed items are equal. See LISTS.

6. In most business or technical documents, preview your most important ideas and your major content areas, and review (summarize) major points at the end of sections.

In most business and technical documents, you must establish the structural framework of the documents. Opening previews and concluding reviews are essential if you want readers to grasp your major points. See INTRODUCTIONS, SUMMARIES, REPORTS, and REPETITION.

Even mechanical or routine features of a document can help readers understand its content. For example, a detailed, quite specific table of contents can almost be a summary of the document. In some special types of documents, the table of contents is supplemented by a matrix outlining where in the document each requirement or issue is addressed. Such a matrix is especially helpful in proposals, where the writer must respond to every one of the client's requirements. See TABLES OF CONTENTS.

Summaries and introductions are

ideal devices for previewing content, but you can also preview content in opening paragraphs. Generally, however, when the preview refers to itself as a preview, it is obtrusive. Your preview should sound natural and should be unobtrusive:

> *this*
>
> The Hamerling Study (March-October 1979) found that predators have played only a minor role in the recent population decline of the cutthroat trout. Far more serious impacts on this species are (1) a degraded watershed, (2) temperature increases, and (3) deforestation.
>
> Together, these environmental changes have reshaped the cutthroat trout's habitat, perhaps beyond the species' ability to adapt.
>
> *not this*
>
> This report discusses the results of the Hamerling Study (March-October 1979), which found that predators have played only a minor role in the recent population decline of the cutthroat trout. The first section concerns the quality of the watershed, which has declined significantly since 1965.
>
> Following that section is a discussion of the role of climate changes, particularly a 2-degree increase in temperature throughout the study area. In section 3, the report notes the effect of deforestation in one part of the study area. In its concluding section, the report discusses the combined impact of watershed degradation, climate changes, and deforestation. As the report notes, these changes have reshaped the cutthroat trout's habitat, perhaps beyond the species' ability to adapt.

The first (preferred) version amounts to a summary of the report. It could actually appear in the summary, become part of an abstract, or open the introduction. It could even appear in all three places.

7. Discuss items in the same order in which you introduce them.

When you introduce items, you should discuss them in the same order later. Saying that you are going to talk about A, B, and C, but then beginning with B violates the readers' sense of order. Follow these examples:

> The three greatest influences on cutthroat trout population are *a degraded watershed, temperature changes,* and *deforestation.*
>
> *The watershed* has been declining in quality since 1965 when . . .
>
> *Temperature changes* over the last 5 years have resulted in a 2-degree . . .
>
> *Deforestation* through the study area has also affected . . .

> *this*
>
> The acquisition improved our *cash flow* while providing significant tax advantages and allowing us to capitalize expenses. Prior to the takeover, we had negative *cash flow* on several . . .
>
> *not this*
>
> The acquisition improved our *cash flow* while providing significant tax advantages and allowing us to capitalize expenses. Prior to the takeover, our *expenses* were not capitalized . . .

This second example demonstrates a subtle but important use of organization. The writer introduces three ideas: cash flow, taxes, and expenses. To be consistent with the order in which these ideas were introduced, the writer must follow the introductory statement with *cash flow*, not *expenses*, as occurs in the final version.

---

8. Use headings, transitions, key words, and paragraph openings to provide cues to the document's organization.

Throughout documents, you should signal organizational shifts or changes in direction by using headings, transitions, repeated key words, and opening or closing statements in paragraphs.

Headings are especially useful when you need to signal abrupt changes in direction, such as the transition from one topic to another (unrelated) topic. If the shifts are too radical, you cannot easily indicate them in text.

Transitions and repeated key words provide for smoother changes in direction and are useful between sentences and paragraphs, as in the example below. Note how the bolded words indicate organizational patterns and shifts in direction:

> The coal seam trends northwesterly for approximately 9,500 meters before pinching out on a fault line. **However**, seismic evidence suggests that **another** seam of coal extends from a point 75 meters downdip of the pinchout. This **second** seam appears to trend northerly for another 5,000 meters. **Together**, these seams represent a sizeable reserve of recoverable coal, **but** initiating mining operations will still be extremely **difficult**.
>
> The biggest **difficulty** is landowner resistance to strip mining. . . .

See HEADINGS, KEY WORDS, PARAGRAPHS, and TRANSITIONS.

---

9. Use the Document Planner™ when you need to design a document quickly and efficiently.

Use the Document Planner, as shown on the next page, to organize and design documents of all types and lengths. The Document Planner can help you plan letters, memos, and short reports (up to 8 to 10 pages long). For these shorter documents, you would fill out only a single Document Planner.

For longer documents—business plans, economic studies, technical reports, audit reports, etc.—you could potentially use the Document Planner more than once. First, use the Planner to plan the whole document. Next, use a second Planner to design each major

chapter or subsection. So, if the whole document has four chapters, you would fill out four additional Document Planners, one for each of the four chapters.

The following paragraphs explain what you should record on a Document Planner.

1-Purpose. State the main point for the document. This written statement should focus on what you want readers to do and to know.

The to-do statement is especially important, and most effective letters or memos should have a clearly identified action (a to-do statement):

> **To-Do Statements**
>
> I want the Financial VP to approve the funding request for the Oatmark Building.
>
> Jaclyn (my boss) should authorize the hiring of two new sales representatives.
>
> Contemporary Architects, Inc., should design a new entry atrium for our headquarters.
>
> Financial Analysts, Inc., should prepare a new staffing plan to reflect changes in our global market.

Occasionally, however, a letter or memo will not identify an action; instead, it will present information that readers should know. Such a document should begin with a to-know statement:

> **To-Know Statements**
>
> Our Executive Board wants to know why the Plum Creek Assembly Plant is less efficient than the Albany Plant.
>
> Our CEO needs to know the steps for acquiring a controlling interest in Balkan Corporation, Inc. (He has already decided to acquire Balkan.)
>
> The manager of marketing wants an explanation of the minimum marketing requirements for HiGro (a new liquid for growing hair).

Title/Subject Line. Write a subject line to reflect your initial to-do or

Page Layout

However, if you expect to use many charts and graphs or if you may later use the material on a video monitor, you may want to choose a horizontal or landscape format. In a horizontal format, pages are wider than they are long.

Another option is a square format. A square format is unusual looking and attractive, but it is more expensive and difficult to prepare because standard paper for printing or photocopying is rectangular.

After you choose a page shape, you need to choose the design features you will use on that page. Design features for a page include the following options:

- Margins
- Borders and divider lines
- White space
- Headers and footers
- Columns
- Typefaces
- Headings
- Graphics

Figure 1 illustrates each of these design options, as presented in a portrait format. Each of these options is addressed in separate rules.

Figure 2 shows these same design options, but in a landscape format.

3. Set your margins and borders so that you have enough white space to make the page attractive and readable.

Each page and each section of a page has margins—that is, the white space separating pieces of text from each other or from the sides of the paper. Your computer may have default (standard) margins, but these are often too narrow or too wide. So try different margins to see how the page will look with these margins.

Setting margins for letters can be a problem, especially if the text is very brief. The overall rule is to center a letter on the page so that the page looks balanced. The left and right

First-Level Headings, 18-pt. Helvetica Bold (centered)

Second-Level Headings, 14-pt. Helvetica Bold (flush left)

The text will be formatted on pages with a 1/3- to 2/3-column layout. The 1/3 column is 2 inches wide. Space between columns is 0.167 inch. A 0.5-pt. divider line will separate the two columns.

The footer of each page will contain the company logo with a 1-pt. line placed 0.875 inches from the bottom of the page and extended to the right margin. The left side of the logo will line up with the left margin. Inside margin (gutter) will be set at 1.00 inch, top margin at 1.25 inch, outside margin at 0.85 inch, and the bottom margin at 1.5 inch.

Employee questions will be listed in the left 1/3 column in Helvetica 10-pt. bold italic.

1

Figure 2. Sample Style Sheet for a Horizontal or Landscape Format. *This sample is the opening section of same style sheet from the previous pages, presented in a horizontal or landscape format.*

Figure 3. Sample Rules. *Divider lines or rules, of differing widths, are labeled with their point size.*

margins will be roughly equal, and if the letter is very short, the text should be dropped down so that white space at the top roughly equals the white space at the bottom. See LETTERS.

Borders and divider lines can help frame your text and can be as simple as a line around the entire text on a page. They can also be complex—for example, a line of asterisks or even a curving design. Divider lines are lines used to divide or set off a column or a section of text.

Printers call these lines rules. Rules can be very fine (called hairlines and 1 point wide) or quite heavy (perhaps 12 point, the height of the type you are reading). See figure 3 for a sample of several common divider lines, with their point size indicated.

Remember that you want your page to look simple. Plenty of white space can contribute to the simplicity of your page. Remember, also, that too many borders and divider lines can ruin an effective page.

4. Add headers and footers that will help your readers know exactly where they are as they are reading your document.

Headers and footers are like road signs. They tell readers which section, subsection, and page they are reading. Most published books have headers and footers. Notice the header and footer on this page.

Everyday documents in the past did not use headers and footers, except for a page number. But computers have made headers and footers a common feature on brief reports, informal memos, and other common business documents.

Headers usually have a page number and the number and title of a chapter or subsection in a lengthy chapter. Footers often have the name of the company or organization publishing a document, as well as an organizational logo or some other symbol, such as a trademark. See INTELLECTUAL PROPERTY.

5. Use more than one column if you have this option available to you.

Two or even three columns on a normal page will make your text seem to be more professional and attractive than a single column. Multiple columns have shorter lines of text, which make them more readable than text that moves all the way across a page. The eye can read a narrow column about 50 characters wide (six or seven words) faster than lines as wide as a full page (about 75 characters).

Two or three columns are basic to most desktop publishing situations, but four or even five columns can be useful on occasion. A lengthy list of rivers, cities, or foods would go very nicely in four or even five columns. Four or five columns on regular 8 ½ by 11-inch pages would rarely be used for normal text, but might be used in a document printed in horizontal (landscape) format.

6. Choose a type size and style to complement your page layout decisions in the preceding rules.

A typeface includes both the size and style of letters, numbers, and symbols. Typefaces are also called fonts.

Use a plain typeface when quick comprehension is needed. A fancy or display face should only be used when fast comprehension is not important or to make a point—STOP—for example. The examples in the following discussion will suggest some of the options you have for either plain or fancy typefaces.

Choose a type size and typeface and then stick to your choices. Too many options or choices on the same page become busy-looking or cluttered.

Desktop publishing, word processing, and computer authoring programs provide a wide selection of typefaces and styles. Usually, these typefaces also allow a wide selection of sizes.

Proportional typefaces are available on many computer programs. That means that the space used by a letter is variable depending on the appearance of the letter. That is, *i*'s are narrower than *n*'s while *m*'s are wider still. Capital letters also have different widths—for example, a *W* is wider than an *I*.

To make the letters of different widths flow together in a pleasing manner, programs use proportional spacing to make the letters seem to be equally spaced even though the actual spacing is variable depending on which letters are next to each other.

Proportionally spaced typefaces are called laser fonts, postscript fonts, True Type fonts, or other similar names. Several of the currently popular proportional fonts are Bookman, Century, Times, and Helvetica. These names come from old printing fonts, which had to be set up character by character in the days before typesetting machines and computers. See figure 4 for examples of these and other common proportional typefaces.

Avant Garde
Bookman
Century School Book
Futura
Garamond
Helvetica
Helvetica Condensed
Optima
Minion
Palatino
Souvenir
Times

Figure 4. Typical Type Fonts. *Many popular proportionally spaced typeface fonts are based on old printing font families. Although these faces are all shown in 12-pt. size, some look smaller because the descenders on j, p, q, and y are part of the height of a typeface.*

Sometimes two typefaces look almost alike but have different names. There are differences in some characters; look particularly at *a, e, f, g,* and *q.* These differences are important because artists design typefaces, and these designs are often copyrighted. See INTELLECTUAL PROPERTY.

Mono-spaced typefaces is the term for non-proportional-spaced type. They use the same width for all letters.

Typewriters, except some special machines, had mono-spaced type. Courier typeface is a reproduction of a traditional typewriter font. See figure 5.

We recommend that you avoid using mono-spaced fonts if you have proportional fonts available on your computer or word processor. Mono-spaced typefaces look old-fashioned and stiff today.

Courier
Geneva
Chicago
Letter Gothic
Prestige Elite

Figure 5. Typical Mono-Spaced Type Fonts. *Non-proportionally-spaced typefaces are mono-spaced, meaning all letters are about the same width.*

Serif and **sans serif** differ in their shape or design.

A **serif** typeface has extra lines or hooks on letters which make them more stylistic. In a serif typeface the letters have extra finishing lines—for example in figure 4, the Garamond typeface is a serif font, as illustrated in the lines at the base of the *a* or the *d* and the hooks on the *G.*

A **sans-serif** typeface does not have the finishing lines of the serif typefaces. For example, in figure 4, the Avant Garde typeface is a sans-serif typeface. Note that the both *A* and *a* are plain in appearance and have no finishing feet or hooks.

In figures 4 and 5, the serif typefaces are Bookman, Courier, Century School Book, Garamond, Minion, Palatino, Prestige Elite, Souvenir, and Times. The sans-serif typefaces are Avant Garde, Chicago, Futura, Geneva, Helvetica, Helvetica Condensed, Letter Gothic, and Optima.

Different styles of letters exist for both serif and sans-serif typefaces. The common optional styles include bold, extra bold, condensed or narrow, italic, and outline. See figure 6.

Times
Times Italic
Times Bold
Times Bold Italic
TIMES SMALL CAPS
Times Outline
Times Shadow

Figure 6. Times Roman Typeface Shown in Several Forms. *Italic and bold forms of any typeface can be produced by word processing programs, However, more attractive and well designed special faces give a more pleasing result.*

Type size is also an option on most computers. The size is measured in points—that is, from the tallest ascender (on *b, d, l,* or *h*) to the deepest descender (on *g, p, q,* or *y*). One inch is 72 points. See figure 7 for examples of different type sizes.

36 pt. Ti
24 pt. Times
18 pt. Times
14 pt. Times
12 pt. Times
10 pt. Times
9 pt. Times
6 pt. Times

Figure 7. Times Typeface Shown in 6 pt. through 36 pt. *Most programs permit type size changes in fractions of a single point size.*

7. Establish a consistent system of headings and lists and stick with it throughout your document.

Design a system of headings and lists that allows you to divide the text frequently and to highlight key ideas. A consistent, well-designed set of headlines is helpful to readers. Headings are also valuable in business letters and memos, especially if a letter or memo is longer than a single page.

A system of headings means that you have decided on headings that signal the different sections of your text. See figure 4 for a simple list of possible headings. Also see HEADINGS and LISTS.

As in figure 8, your decisions about headings will include the typefaces to use, their size, and any other distinguishing features.

A very common pattern is to use sans-serif typefaces for headings and a serif typeface for the text. See rule 6 for a definition of *serif* and *sans-serif*. This is the practice followed in this *Style Guide*.

FIRST-LEVEL HEADINGS

Second-Level Headings

Third-Level Headings

Fourth-Level Headings. Text . . .

Figure 8. *Typical headings use various typeface options—for example all capitals, different sizes, boldface, and even italics.*

An optional feature is to number headings—for example, 2., 2.1, 2.1.1, etc.

Lists also allow for a number of options. At the simplest, decide whether you will number lists, use bullets, or use dashes. Also, you need to decide how you intend to indent or frame lists using white space. See figure 1 and LISTS.

8. Choose and place graphics for maximum impact and increased readability.

A well-chosen, high-quality graphic is worth a thousand words. And it is ten times more memorable than mere text. So plan for and prepare high-quality graphics.

Your style sheet (see rule 1) should plan for graphics and the placement of captions as a part of graphics. See GRAPHICS FOR DOCUMENTS, GRAPHICS FOR PRESENTATIONS, and CAPTIONS.

Decide what your main point is before you decide what graphics you want to include. If your goal is to present a trend or a contrast between two different methods, you might want to use a bar graph or even a graph with a plot of two trends.

In other cases, if you want to describe a piece of unfamiliar equipment, you should consider either a photograph or an illustration (maybe a schematic or outline version of the equipment).

Finally, you might want to use a flow chart or other tree diagram to show the steps in a process or to present who is serving on different committees.

Your goal is to make your graphics fit your main point or document purpose.

Placing graphics is often a subjective skill, but the following suggestions are generally true:

- Mention a graphic in the text before it appears.

- Make a graphic and its caption largely independent from the text.

- Make a graphic large enough to be readable and don't expect readers to turn the page to read the caption or notes.

- If a graphic is too complex or cluttered, break it into two graphics or consider making it an attachment to your document.

9. Avoid overloading pages with too much text and too many layout features.

Writers often cram too much writing onto a page, trying to stay within page limits or adhering to custom, an arbitrary format, or just plain myth about how pages ought to look.

Writers may even ignore the appearance of the document because they believe that page layout is someone else's concern. They think an editor or publisher should take care of the layout.

Later they (or an editor many weeks later) have to go through the text shortening a discussion, changing an introduction, and adjusting all the graphics. Time and money are wasted because much of the text must be rewritten to match the page layout (or style sheet).

10. Don't forget the basics just because you have a fancy design.

Final proofreading and checking are essential. Errors creep into the best of documents. For instance, changing the subheading text in the middle of a chapter, may also require changes in many other places: the introduction to the chapter, the table of contents for the document, the index, the summary of key points in the chapter, and others.

Most word processing programs permit tagging of text (attaching invisible programming characters). A special subprogram copies tagged text, later aggregating it into indexes or tables of contents. See INDEXES and TABLES OF CONTENTS.

However, some other changes may not occur automatically. With word processing programs, the ease of changing something can cause some problems. Moving text often results in leftover letters, punctuation, or spaces.

Paragraphs were the mainstay of writing a generation ago. Many excellent documents broke their content into logical sections by using only paragraphs. Headings and lists were unknown or infrequent.

The traditional paragraph, especially in its more lengthy versions, is becoming less common in today's business or technical writing. Interestingly, academic writing still relies on and composition teachers still teach the structure and form of the long paragraph.

The first eight rules in the box to the right apply to situations where you want to write your paragraphs with a traditional logical structure. Rule 9 suggests an option to the traditional paragraph.

In many types of documents, however, you will find that headings, lists, graphics, and other emphasis techniques can and should replace traditional paragraphs. See figure 1 for an example of how emphasis techniques can easily replace a traditional paragraph. See EMPHASIS, HEADINGS, and LISTS.

Paragraphs

1. Limit paragraphs to a single topic or major idea.

2. Do not allow paragraphs to become too long.

3. Vary the length of your paragraphs.

4. Ensure that the opening sentence of every primary paragraph accurately reflects the content of that paragraph and any following secondary paragraphs.

5. Organize paragraphs logically.

6. Use key words and other devices to ensure that paragraphs are coherent.

7. Emphasize the important ideas within a paragraph.

8. Provide transitions between paragraphs.

9. If appropriate, break up or replace paragraphs with lists.

As figure 1 illustrates, a traditional paragraph is often difficult to read. The typical reader cannot easily scan a traditional paragraph because an assumption behind the traditional paragraph is that a reader must read it line by line and word by word.

In contrast, the schematic or emphatic paragraph in figure 1 assists readers by visually segmenting the points into chunks. Scanning schematic paragraphs is easy.

1. Limit paragraphs to a single topic or major idea.

Ensure that your paragraphs focus on a single topic or idea. When you go to a new topic, start a new paragraph. If your paragraph on a single topic becomes too long, start a new paragraph at a logical point and have two (or more) paragraphs dealing with the same topic. When such is the case, you normally focus each paragraph on a subtopic related to the overall topic.

Traditional Paragraph	Schematic or Emphatic Paragraph
The engineering design team needs a full-time graphics specialist assigned to be in the team's work area. Current graphics support does provide high-quality graphics, but their delivery times are not as rapid as we would like. In some cases a requested graphic takes over a week before coming back to the design team for review and revision. Some graphics require several review loops, so some graphics may require as much as a month before they are ready for publication in the design team's documentation procedures. Having a full-time graphics person would lessen the delays and would allow the team members easily to share their design concepts with a graphics specialist.	**Recommendation: Full-Time Graphics Support for the Team** Having a full-time graphics specialist at the team site would provide these advantages: • **Shorten turnaround time** for routine graphics. Current times average nearly a week for requested graphics. • **Decrease review loops** by working with team members during the conceptual phase. Current review loops often require as much as a month. • **Allow immediate corrections and adjustments** while the graphic specialist is creating a graphic. This collaboration would also enhance conceptualization.

Figure 1. Two Contrastive Versions of the Same Content. *The traditional paragraph is 112 words long and follows the traditional pattern of a topic sentence, supporting details, and a concluding sentence. The schematic or emphatic version (78 words) covers many of the same ideas, but it is much more readable.*

2. Do not allow paragraphs to become too long.

Quantifying paragraph length is difficult, but in business and technical writing, paragraphs exceeding 100 to 125 words should be rare. Most paragraphs will consist of three to six sentences. If a single-spaced paragraph goes beyond one-third of a page, it is probably too long. A double-spaced paragraph should not exceed half a page in length.

The document's format should influence paragraph length. If a document has narrow columns (two or three to the page), then paragraphs should be shorter, perhaps on the average of no more than 50 words. If a document uses a full-page format (one column), then average paragraph length can reach 125 words.

Length is therefore a function of appearance and visual relief. Almost all readers have difficulty with dense pages of print, no matter how well written and logically organized the text may be. Remember that paragraphs are visual devices meant to make reading easier, so keep them shorter rather than longer.

3. Vary the length of your paragraphs.

A document containing paragraphs of uniform length would be dull and difficult to read. For the sake of variety and to stimulate reader interest, you should vary the length of your paragraphs, especially in documents longer than one page.

The length of successive paragraphs will of course depend on content. The logic of the material will dictate, at least to some extent, where paragraphs can logically begin and end, but you still have a great deal of latitude.

A particularly involved point may require lengthy explanation and two or three examples. If so, you might state the point, explain it in one or two paragraphs, and then make each example a separate paragraph. Dividing the topic in this fashion is necessary in a double- or triple-column page format.

Your paragraph stating the main point could be relatively short. Short paragraphs usually draw attention to themselves, so they are useful for stating major ideas. The explanatory paragraph should be much longer. The paragraphs providing the examples should vary in length, with the most important example appearing in the longest paragraph.

Are single-sentence paragraphs acceptable?

Yes. A common misconception about paragraphing is that single-sentence paragraphs somehow violate a principle of writing. In fact, single-sentence paragraphs are very emphatic, especially if they are surrounded by longer paragraphs. You should take care not to use single-sentence paragraphs too often, however. See EMPHASIS.

4. Ensure that the opening sentence of every primary paragraph accurately reflects the content of that paragraph and any following secondary paragraphs.

Primary paragraphs introduce an idea. Secondary paragraphs develop and support that idea. All primary paragraphs should have an opening sentence that introduces the content of the primary and any following secondary paragraphs. The opening sentence is called a topic sentence.

The opening sentence should establish a key word or phrase that indicates the paragraph's topic. If your paragraph will focus on health problems, then the opening sentence should contain at least two key words: *health* and *problems*. These key words help establish the paragraph's viewpoint, which is often called its thesis. The three examples below each have a topic sentence that announces the thesis of the paragraph:

> Software sales in the Eastern Region have substantially increased. From 1992 to 1993, the Sales Division conducted four sales campaigns that . . .

> MOGO's reservoir study of May 1994 indicates that remaining recoverable reserves exceed previous estimates by over 66 percent. Seismic data gathered in conjunction with the study . . .

> The Packaging Department examined the problem and recommends replacing our standard cardboard containers with molded plastic wrap. The plastic is applied from a hot roller after the cases . . .

Secondary paragraphs do not begin with topic sentences. In a technical report discussing a series of tests, for instance, the results section of the report might have several paragraphs opening as follows:

> Test 1, series 1, involved decreasing eluants by 0.4 cm^3/hr and noting pH changes occurring as the solution was heated to 250 degrees F . . .

> During test 1, series 2, eluants were removed altogether, and the solution was subjected to pressure variations during heating . . .

These paragraphs develop and support the thesis that was established within a topic sentence in a previous primary paragraph.

Paragraphs

As readers, we should expect the first secondary paragraph to focus entirely on test 1, series 1. Any information in that paragraph that is not related to test 1, series 1, does not belong there. Similarly, the second secondary paragraph should focus on test 1, series 2.

Open every primary paragraph with a topic sentence that states the thesis of that paragraph and any following secondary paragraphs. See ORGANIZATION.

---

5. Organize paragraphs logically.

The structure of the ideas within a paragraph should be logical. Furthermore, the paragraph structure should be obvious to readers.

Sometimes this structure follows a classic organizational pattern: chronological, whole to parts, problem to solution, cause to effect, most important to least important, general to specific, and so on. Sometimes the structure follows some logic that is inherent to the subject. A paragraph on drilling-rig problems, for instance, might be organized according to a series of problems that relate to each other in some way that uninformed readers would not perceive.

The following paragraph is paraphrased from Charles Darwin's *Origin of Species*. It demonstrates a classic organizational pattern: general to specific. Note that the opening sentence is a topic sentence and that the three succeeding sentences substantiate Darwin's thesis. The boldfaced key words indicate one of the most common methods of achieving coherence: repeating key words. The key words in the Darwin paragraph form a clear link between sentences.

Without exception, every species naturally **reproduces** at so high a **rate** that, if not destroyed, the earth would soon be covered by the progeny of a single pair. Even **slow-breeding** man has **doubled** in 25 years, and at this **rate**, in less than 1,000 years, there would literally not be standing room for his progeny. Linneaus has calculated that if an annual plant **produced** only two seeds—and no plant is so **unproductive**—and their seedlings next year **produced** two, and so on, then in 20 years there should be 1,000,000 plants. The elephant is reckoned the slowest **breeder** of all animals, and I have taken some pains to estimate its minimum **reproductive rate**; it will be safest to assume that it begins **breeding** when 30 years old, and goes on **breeding** till 90 years old, bringing forth six young in the interval, and surviving till 100 years old; if this be so, after 750 years there would be nearly 19,000,000 elephants alive, descended from the first pair.

---

6. Use key words and other devices to ensure that paragraphs are coherent.

Coherence refers to the cohesiveness of a paragraph's sentences. In a coherent paragraph, the sentences seem to "stick together"—they all clearly belong in the paragraph and are logically connected to one another.

As you read the paragraph below, note the lack of coherence:

A great number of apparatus are available today for field work in the broad sense, including gas-chromatographs, as well as infrared, electrochemical, and other analyzers. In connection with the early prediction of possible pollutants and the assessment of natural discharge prior to the development of geothermal resources, however, hydrogen sulfide and volatiles such as ammonia, mercury, and arsenic are the major concern. Under the conditions prevailing before industrial development, preliminary evaluation and prediction of the discharge of such chemicals depends to a sizeable extent on water analyses. Surveying mercury content in air might deserve consideration; however, it is not discussed here, as mercury determination in soil is likely to be a valid substitute for it.

The opening sentence to this paragraph suggests that the paragraph will discuss the apparatus available for field work, particularly those apparatus listed. However, this equipment is never again discussed. The second, third, and fourth sentences seem loosely connected, but the paragraph never "gels"; it never seems to be focused on a single topic. In short, the paragraph is incoherent. See PARAGRAPHS.

You can achieve coherence by opening with a topic sentence, by using a clear organizational scheme, by repeating key words, by using transitional words (such as *however, furthermore, consequently, next, then, additionally,* etc.), and by using pronouns to link sentences to the major idea or theme of the paragraph. See ORGANIZATION, KEY WORDS, TRANSITIONS, and PRONOUNS.

---

7. Emphasize the important ideas within a paragraph.

As figure 1 illustrated, one way to emphasize important ideas is to use a schematic or emphatic approach to the content. Lists, headings, and graphics are all common tools for emphasizing important ideas. See EMPHASIS.

In one sense, extensive use of such emphasis techniques makes many of the traditional rules for writing paragraphs unnecessary.

In traditional paragraphs, however, important ideas are emphasized by being placed in the initial or topic sentence. The initial sentence is visually and logically the most important sentence in a paragraph, so use it to capture the most important ideas.

Traditionally, the final sentence in a paragraph was the second most emphatic position. This viewpoint assumed that readers would take time to read the final sentence. In most technical or business writing, however, the final sentence either drops out (because it is repetitive) or it moves up to become part of the initial sentence.

8. Provide transitions between paragraphs.

In most well-written documents, the information flows from paragraph to paragraph. To achieve this effect, you must provide smooth transitions between paragraphs.

Writers can set up transitions by previewing content. If you announce, for instance, that you will be discussing five topics and then list those topics, you have set up a progression that the reader will expect. As you move from topic to topic, the transitions will be automatic:

> The first topic concerns . . .
>
> Likewise, the second topic . . .
>
> The third topic . . .
>
> However, the fourth topic . . .
>
> Finally, the fifth topic . . .

As you can see, these paragraph openings also use some transitional words to make the transition, but merely moving to and announcing the next topic is sufficient.

Sometimes you can create the transition between paragraphs by using key words to connect the closing sentence of one paragraph and the opening sentence of the next:

> . . . because deep **salt domes** usually occur as a result of normal **faulting.**
>
> Thrust (reverse) **faults**, on the other hand, are normally responsible for piercement **salt domes** . . .

In this excerpt, the first paragraph closes with a key word (*faulting*), a variation of which is repeated in the opening sentence of the next paragraph. The first paragraph concerns deep salt domes; the second concerns piercement salt domes. Repeating a variation of *faulting* helps make the transition.

In this example, the opening sentence of the succeeding paragraph makes the transition. However, the transition could also be made by the closing sentence of the preceding paragraph:

> . . . because deep **salt domes** usually occur as a result of normal **faulting**. Thrust (reverse) **faults**, on the other hand, are normally responsible for **piercement salt domes.**
>
> **Piercement domes**, which are common along the Texas and Louisiana Gulf Coast, are produced from traps caused when complex **faulting** forces a salt core upward through overlying sediments . . . .

In some documents, the information cannot easily flow from paragraph to paragraph because the paragraph topics are too disjointed. When such is the case, use headings, lists, and numbering systems to indicate the transition from one topic to another:

> . . . Reef-producing areas might or might not be obvious from overlying sediments.
>
> **Piercement Domes**
>
> Piercement domes, which are common along the Texas and Louisiana Gulf Coast, produce from traps caused when complex faulting forces a salt core upward through overlying sediments . . . .

See HEADINGS, LISTS, NUMBERING SYSTEMS, and TRANSITIONS.

9. If appropriate, break up or replace paragraphs with lists.

If a paragraph contains or consists of a long series of items, consider replacing the paragraph with a displayed list. Lists are more emphatic than paragraphs, so if you want to emphasize the series of items, display it. See LISTS.

A Final Case Study in Paragraphing

Some writers dump everything they can think of about a topic into a single paragraph. Then when a paragraph becomes long enough (by whatever standard), these writers pause, indent, and start another paragraph. This sort of paragraphing is neither logical nor effective, as the following example illustrates:

> Oxides of nitrogen include nitrogen dioxide (NO_2) and nitric oxide (NO). NO_2 is a pungent gas that causes nose and eye irritation and pulmonary discomfort. NO is converted to NO_2 by atmospheric chemical reaction. Both NO and NO_2 participate in photochemical reactions leading to smog. Sulfur dioxide (SO_2) is a colorless and pungent gas that causes irritation to the respiratory tract and eyes and causes bronchoconstriction at high concentrations. Hydrocarbons react with NO or NO_2 and sunlight to form photochemical oxidants or smog. Health effects include irritation of the eye, nose, and throat. Extended periods of high levels of oxidants produce headaches and cause difficulty in breathing in patients suffering from emphysema.

What did the writer of this paragraph want to accomplish? Is the first sentence on NO and NO_2 an accurate reflection of the rest of the content? How do the other facts and points in the paragraph fit together? Can readers see a definite pattern or structure to the facts?

Paragraphs

A Traditional Rewrite

You could rewrite the paragraph using these traditional remedies:

- Shorten the paragraph and focus on only one topic.

- State the topic in the opening sentence.

- Supply organizational cues in the opening sentence and, as appropriate, in later sentences.

By applying these remedies, we can improve the paragraph as follows:

> Nitrogen oxides, hydrocarbons, and sulfur dioxide—these constituents of smog can cause health problems. Nitrogen dioxide (NO_2) is a pungent gas that causes nose and eye irritation and pulmonary discomfort. Hydrocarbons that react with NO_2 or with nitric oxide (NO) and sunlight form photochemical oxidants that can irritate the eyes, nose, and throat. Extended exposure to high levels of oxidants can produce headaches and cause persons with emphysema to have trouble breathing. Sulfur dioxide (SO_2) is a colorless and pungent gas that irritates the eyes and respiratory tract and, at high concentrations, can cause bronchoconstriction.

A Nontraditional Rewrite

You might decide to transform the paragraph into a graphic, especially if you decide that the information merits high emphasis. Figure 2 is a possible version of such a nontraditional rewrite. See ORGANIZATION and GRAPHICS FOR DOCUMENTS.

Components of Smog	Health Effects
Nitrogen dioxide (NO_2)	Eye irritation and pulmonary discomfort
Photochemical oxidants (Hydrocarbons + NO_2 or NO)	Eye, nose, and throat irritation
Sulfur dioxide (SO_2)	Eye and respiratory irritation (especially bronchoconstriction)

Figure 2. Major Components of Smog and Their Health Effects. *All three components are colorless, yet pungent and irritating, especially in high concentrations.*

Parallelism is essentially a convention of sentence construction. The principle behind it is that similar ideas should be expressed in a similar fashion, thereby demonstrating their similarity and making reading easier. The following sentence is not parallel:

> The analysis will include organizing, dividing, and assessment of turnaround functions.

The sentence verb *include* is followed by three key words: *organizING, dividING, and assessMENT.* These three words appear in series. They are equal in purpose and use in the sentence. Therefore, they should have the same grammatical form:

> The analysis will include organizing, dividing, and assessing turnaround functions.

1. Ensure that two or more parts of speech behaving similarly in a sentence, or coordinated (connected) in some way, are parallel in construction.

Parallelism applies not only to verbs, but also to nouns, adjectives, phrases, and every other part of a sentence:

> The Interface Team will be responsible **for integrating** the functional units developed by the QA Team and **for executing** the model test matrix.

> Applying **abstraction, partition,** and **projection** to the system development process results in the traditional top-down view of the software engineering process.

> Figure 2.2–1 shows the documentation relationships: **where things happen, why things happen, and how things can be changed.**

> Multilevel training was necessary to meet the needs of **managers, designers,** and **programmers.**

> A final report was prepared **describing** the case study process and **referencing** the documents containing the code.

NOTE: Often a repeated *who, which,* or *that* will signal a sentence with parallelism:

> The departmental white paper specified **who** would head the new project team and **who** would be the team members.

not

> The departmental white paper specified the head of the new project team and who would be team members.

2. Make items in lists parallel.

Parallelism is especially important in lists. A list, whether displayed vertically on the page or embedded within a paragraph, is a series. To make it parallel, each item should be constructed similarly and should begin with the same kind of word (noun, verb, etc.):

> This file will include the following items:
>
> 1. Problem headings
> 2. Database specifications
> 3. Reporting intervals
> 4. Restart options
> 5. Report macros

The following list is also parallel (each item completes the sentence started by the introductory statement). Note that each item begins with the same kind of verb:

> The study concluded that the ATAC fighter must:
>
> 1. Have a long-range, high-payload capability.
> 2. Be flexible in mission and payload design.
> 3. Be survivable against A-A and S-A threats.
> 4. Be maneuverable in the F-15/F-16 class.

NOTE: This example has several variations. Many editors, including the authors of this *Style Guide,* would prefer a different lead-in sentence (one with a complete grammatical structure):

> A study concluded that the ATAC fighter must have these features:

See COLONS, CONJUNCTIONS, and LISTS.

Parentheses are used to insert material into a sentence. Dashes—which are more emphatic than parentheses—are also used to insert material. Commas, which are also used to insert material, are less emphatic than either dashes or parentheses.

Using parentheses appropriately and effectively is an art. The following rules will help you develop this art.

> ## Parentheses
>
> 1. Parentheses enclose explanatory sentences within a paragraph.
> 2. Parentheses enclose references, examples, ideas, and citations that are not part of the main thought of a sentence.
> 3. Parentheses enclose numbers in a paragraph list.
> 4. Parentheses enclose acronyms, abbreviations, definitions, and figures that have been written out.

---

1. Parentheses enclose explanatory sentences within a paragraph:

Only the total systems approach can deal with the trade-off in performance between the weapon and the aircraft platform. Existing beyond-visual-range air-to-air missiles are inhibited, for instance, by the lack of an effective IFF system. The total systems approach, with its full range of analysis tools, may be the only acceptable means of evaluating trade-offs prior to the detail design phase. (The discussion of IFF design under Targeting Systems on p. 89 reveals how we solved the problem cited above.)

2. Parentheses enclose references, examples, ideas, and citations that are not part of the main thought of a sentence:

Our Level 6 analysis (see figure 9.4) illustrates how a single multi-mission destroyer can contribute to task force operations.

Our design accounts for all environmental factors that may affect sensitivity (smoke, terrain, weather, and physical damage).

Affordability (cited in the RFP as a primary concern) was the guiding principle behind our application of new technologies.

Our previous state-of-the-art survey (conducted over a 3-month period in 1987) suggested that RDF SOPs were not current.

The most recent research (Smithson 1988) revealed pollution problems from nearby gasoline storage tanks.

See Citations.

Parentheses, Commas, and Dashes

Commas and dashes also enclose explanatory ideas. Commas are less emphatic than parentheses; dashes are more emphatic. Note how emphasis progressively increases in the following examples:

Cost analyses using both parametric and detail O&S cost methodologies helped us determine the right support systems.

Cost analyses, using both parametric and detail O&S cost methodologies, helped us determine the right support systems.

Cost analyses (using both parametric and detail O&S cost methodologies) helped us determine the right support systems.

Cost analyses—using both parametric and detail O&S cost methodologies—helped us determine the right support systems.

See Commas and Dashes.

3. Parentheses enclose numbers in a paragraph list:

The operational characteristics we will discuss below are (1) manning, (2) training, and (3) providing required support.

See Lists.

4. Parentheses enclose acronyms, abbreviations, definitions, and figures that have been written out:

The CARP (Capital Area Renovation Project) is adequately funded as long as the contractor trims costs by using off-the-shelf materials wherever possible.

United's South Fork Mine can deliver over 20,000 dwt (deadweight tons) of ore every month.

Artesian water (water naturally confined in the ground under pressure) is the primary source for the city's culinary use.

By the project deadline date, Northrop will deliver fifty (50) centrifugal pump assemblies to the San Diego facility.

See Abbreviations and Acronyms.

Note 1: As in the first example above, we recommend using the acronym followed by its explanation in parentheses. Some editors prefer the reverse:

The Capital Area Renovation Project (CARP) is adequately funded as long as the contractor trims costs by using off-the-shelf materials wherever possible.

Note 2: The practice of writing out numbers and enclosing the figure in parentheses is not necessary except in legal, contractual, or requisition documents. Do it only when you need to protect against unauthorized alteration of numbers in a document. See Numbers.

Parentheses and Brackets

Brackets are, in effect, parentheses. They enclose incidental or explanatory words and phrases within parentheses or within quoted material:

> The environment and activities of opposing forces may change the capabilities of a particular sensor (see appendix 4, Battlefield Adaptability Requirements, for a fuller discussion of RGS [Remote Ground Sensing] and ground-based sensor limitations).

> Your original letter stated: "Our onsite project coordinator [Walt Petersen] will be responsible for maintaining the Schedule of Deliverables."

See BRACKETS.

Parentheses and Periods

If the entire sentence is enclosed by parentheses, the period at the end of the sentence goes inside the closing parentheses:

> (See appendix 2 for the complete test results.)

If only part of a sentence is enclosed by parentheses and the closing parenthesis occurs at the end of the sentence, the period goes outside the closing parenthesis:

> Hydrostatic and thermostatic monitors ensure system equilibrium (see figure 5–15 for monitor locations).

See PERIODS.

Parentheses and Question Marks

Question marks come inside parentheses when they are part of the parenthetical (added) information:

> *this*

> The project deadline (April 1?) is never stated in the Statement of Work.

> *not this*

> The project deadline (April 1)? is never stated in the Statement of Work.

See QUESTION MARKS.

Periods

Periods primarily indicate a break or a full stop in text. At the end of a spoken sentence (signaled by a period), the voice drops and the speaker takes a breath.

Periods

1. Use periods following statements, commands, indirect questions, and questions intended as suggestions.

2. Use periods following numerals or letters marking a list, but periods need not follow the items listed unless they are full sentences.

3. Use periods (decimal points) to separate integers from decimals.

4. Use a period with run-in headings, but not with displayed headings.

5. Use periods following some abbreviations.

1. Use periods following statements, commands, indirect questions, and questions intended as suggestions:

Statements

The workover plan was finished.

Tomorrow we will visit the mine site.

Mr. Smythe owes OP&L $75.

Commands

Stop working on the project now.

Please help us tomorrow.

Redesign the pump housing to accommodate the larger intake pipe.

Indirect questions

I wonder how he managed the project.

Jane Greer asked whether we would approve the budget.

Questions intended as suggestions

Will you please return the forms by a week from Monday.

Would you let me know if you have any questions.

2. Use periods following numerals or letters marking a list, but periods need not follow the items listed unless they are full sentences (see rule 1 above):

a. A larger pump
b. An extra ventilation fan
c. A heavy duty circuit breaker

1. The cost is 50 percent greater than was budgeted.
2. Materials were not equal to those specified.
3. Installation procedures were violated.

NOTE: You may need a period to end a list that continues the syntax established in its lead-in sentence:

We tested the procedure by
1. increasing the flow,
2. decreasing the temperature, and
3. contaminating the water.

This pattern of continued syntax and punctuation is much rarer than it used to be. See LISTS.

3. Use periods (decimal points) to separate integers from decimals:

4.567
327.5
1,456.25

NOTE 1: In tables, the decimal points (periods) are aligned:

4.567
327.5
1,456.25

NOTE 2: In some foreign countries, a comma separates integers from decimals, and spaces separate groups of three numerals in longer numerals:

4,567
56 764,534 45

See METRICS and NUMBERS.

4. Use a period with run-in headings, but not with displayed headings:

Two Options. The first option is to discontinue the testing until safety procedures are developed. The second option . . .

This same heading would not be followed by a period if it appeared on its own line:

Two Options

The first option is to discontinue the testing until safety procedures are developed. The second option . . .

NOTE: You can also use run-in headings with dashes, colons, or no punctuation. But be consistent. Once you've established a pattern, use it throughout a document. See HEADINGS.

5. Use periods following some abbreviations:

10 a.m.	6 p.m.
A.D. 1910	225 B.C.
U.S.A.	Mr./Mrs./Ms.
e.g.	S. Pugh
Dr. Will Lange	U.K.
i.e.	

NOTE: Many abbreviations and most acronyms no longer require periods, especially names of fraternal organizations, government agencies, corporations, and colleges and universities:

BPOE	BLM
DOE	GM
UCLA	LSU
HUD	FERC
NASA	

See ABBREVIATIONS, ACRONYMS, and PARENTHESES.

Persuasion relies on any techniques used by a writer or speaker to gain agreement or to support an idea. The most obvious persuasive technique is an appeal based on a logical rationale and on solid reasons, but the most effective technique is really the one that also enlists the reader's or listener's emotional support.

Successful persuasion is 50 percent emotion and only 50 percent logic and facts. Without the emotion and the subjectivity, logic and facts just don't convince.

The following rules use examples primarily from written documents. The rules, however, would apply equally well to oral presentations.

The following rules also refer to customers rather than readers. A customer is someone involved in a process or activity and someone to negotiate with. World-of-work documents presume that readers are like customers— that is, these readers have something they need to learn, and your task is to service their needs.

Some documents are all persuasion—for example, a sales letter or a proposal to hire more employees. Other documents may not be obviously persuasive, yet they usually have a persuasive intent. A scientific study or a financial audit report may be primarily factual, but their writers still intend that readers understand and act upon the value and reliability of the information presented. Therefore, the scientific study and the audit report are persuasive documents, whatever their other purposes might be.

1. Assess your customers' needs and objectives.

The customers' needs and objectives are important starting points because

---

Persuasion

1. Assess your customers' needs and objectives.

2. Define your own role and objectives in relation to those of your customers.

3. Collaborate with customers to generate persuasive solutions and benefits.

4. Design a message that speaks clearly, effectively, and persuasively to your customers.

5. Maintain a credible position so customers have reasons for agreeing with you and your ideas.

---

persuasion must be a two-way process. The old model of the salesperson with a pitch is gone. Today's persuasive writing is based on problem solving and consultation, not pitching a canned presentation to skeptical customers.

Initially, list your customers, both internal and external. Next, profile each of them by asking the following questions:

—What are their jobs and professional responsibilities?

—What level and type of decisions can they make?

—Whom do they work for and whom do they supervise?

—What problems or questions are they working on now?

—What do they already know about your services or your ideas?

—How likely are they to use the information you can provide?

Your primary goal in asking these questions is to determine what your customers' needs are.

Example 1—Recommendation Document. Your customer needs to obtain a more reliable source for computer network service. Your questions reveal just how important this need is to the customer, and you discover that the customer values a solution enough to spend money hiring a new employee or a new vendor. You have to decide what to recommend to the customer.

Example 2—Research Report. Your customers are readers of your report on a new surgical procedure. As you profile these customers, you determine how they intend to use your report and how likely they are to agree with your views. Based on what you determine about their needs, you can either adjust your existing report or, perhaps, add to it.

As in both of these examples, you must identify your customers' needs before you can begin to design persuasive documents.

---

2. Define your own role and objectives in relation to those of your customers.

As two-way communication, effective persuasive writing requires you to know your own role and objectives.

The following examples expand on the two examples introduced under rule 1 above.

Example 1—Recommendation Document. You decide that you would propose that the customer hire a new network computer specialist rather than obtain a new vendor. You might have a choice of roles, however. If your role is as an advisor, then your approach is more factual and neutral than it would be if you would profit from the decisions being made. Your second role might be as an advocate for a friend or family member. With this role, you move from neutrality to a more aggressive presentation of your points. Your changing roles control the slant of your persuasive documents.

Persuasion

Example 2—Research Report. If you discover that readers of your report are likely to be very skeptical about your new surgical procedure, you can adjust your research report to make it more convincing. Perhaps you add more detailed explanations of the prior literature related to your procedure.

At times, your role in relation to customers may lead you to ask questions where your honesty will be tested. For instance, do you need to admit to the customer that you made a mistake or that your equipment won't meet the written specifications? Such questions and problems are essentially ethical issues. See ETHICS.

Hesitation over an ethical question is perhaps the surest way to lose your persuasive credibility. See rule 5 below.

Unless you establish your own role, your objectives, and, if appropriate, your ethical stance, you cannot prepare persuasive documentation.

3. Collaborate with customers to generate persuasive solutions and benefits.

This rule means that you continue to work with your customers, validating your initial perceptions and checking up on your progress. You never want your customers to feel neglected.

The following two examples build on details already introduced in the prior rules.

Example 1—Recommendation Document. As you work to list the pros and cons of the hiring of a new computer network specialist, you discover that you still have some unresolved questions about the problem. How frequent and severe are the network problems? Who is currently handling them and what does this service now cost? You need the data before you can complete your recommendations.

Your goal with these or similar questions is to refine your ideas so you can specify the benefits related to your proposal.

Example 2—Research Report. You transmit a working copy of your research report to a colleague who will be a sharp critical reviewer. Your intent is to find out if your approach and the details in your draft are on target. This review—essentially a usability test—is a crucial step if you want to guarantee that your report has the most persuasive impact possible. This review would parallel the peer review often required prior to publication in the scientific arena.

See the reviewing section of WRITING AND REVISING.

4. Design a message that speaks clearly, effectively, and persuasively to your customers.

Make your message customer centered. An effective and persuasive message will have the customer in the foreground. You and your interests remain in the background.

Test yourself by looking at a recent persuasive letter or sales document: The *you's* in your message should outnumber two to one the *I's* and *we's*.

The two letters in figure 1 illustrate what we mean by customer-centered writing. The "Before" letter is typical of many sales letters. Its persuasive power is lost because the writer can't stop talking about her own product and her own interests.

The "After" letter moves the customer to center stage. It also illustrates the following three writing principles:

1. **Be as clear as possible.**

2. **Organize your information with your customers' needs in mind.**

3. **Choose effective and forceful examples.**

1. **Be as clear as possible.** An undefined term or an unclear explanation allows customers to dismiss your ideas on the trivial grounds of their not being able to understand you. So do everything you can (or need to) to make sure that you have been clear. Be especially careful to define all technical terms and technical assumptions. Use page layout, boldface, headings, lists, and other format options to make your message as unambiguous and as effective as possible. See EMPHASIS.

2. **Organize your information with your customers' needs in mind.** Organization means that you have considered both the logic of your points and the arrangement of these points for the maximum effectiveness on your customers. See ORGANIZATION.

    Example 1—Recommendation Document. You have two options. One is to open with your recommendation and state it both in the subject line and in your opening lines of the document. This option is the strongest and clearest way to begin your document.

    A second option would be to lead up to your recommendation by giving some background—perhaps the scope of your investigation or some details about similar problems you've analyzed. This option delays your recommendation for a few lines or a paragraph or two. You would use this option only if you felt that your customers needed to be prepared for your recommendation. This opening is not as forceful as the opening in option one, and it will likely not be as clear.

    Example 2—Research Report. Often you have no discretion as to how to organize the body of your report. The major headings are standard as they are in many scientific reports: Introduction, Methods, Materials, Results, Conclusions, and Recommendations. Still, you have some choices to make. For example, you may precede the report with a summary, an abstract, or a transmittal letter. If so, you need to decide how direct and specific you want or need to be. This decision will rely on your view of the customers' point of view about your proposed surgical procedure.

3. **Choose effective and forceful examples.** Persuasive writing requires an interplay between general principles and good examples. Choose examples that match the backgrounds of your customers. If your customers have a limited technical background, choose non-technical examples.

BEFORE

Ann Devi
Manager, Information Systems
TuffMax, Inc.

Subject: WebWare

Dear Ann:

This letter is a follow-up to a conversation we had some time ago about switching your networks to WebWare. As you may not be aware, WW has been selling network products since 1985 through our direct dealers. Our WebWare product is a second-generation product tested in direct dealerships for the last two years.

WebWare is actually a family of products which allow computers to be connected to most kinds of phone lines, even to dedicated phone lines already being used for phones. It offers many of the features on cardcage products, including built-in support of multiple modem types and network management with secure multi-user and remote control.

I think we have a great product and I could go on and on, but I really wanted to remind you that WW has just opened a direct channel office in your area. I would really like you to consider visiting our office and talking with some of our representatives about our full-featured networking product. I have enclosed a customer survey I would like you to fill out.

I hope all is going well with you. If you have any questions, please do not hesitate to call.

Best regards,

Figure 1. Before and After Versions of the Same Letter. *The "Before" version is writer centered and not well organized. The "After" version focuses on the reader (customer) and uses a variety of emphasis techniques. See EMPHASIS.*

AFTER

Ann Devi
Manager, Information Systems
TuffMax, Inc.

Subject: **Invitation to Discuss Improved TuffMax Network Links**

Ann, in our discussion we determined three challenges we can help you meet. Please consider a visit from our new local representative to explore these challenges further:

- TuffMax's need to link networks in different locations
- Field employees' need to to access network information by modem
- TuffMax's need to ensure data security while offering remote access

Linking TuffMax Networks
You mentioned your desire for all TuffMax networks to operate as one big network. The advantage is rapid exchange of information in the office and in the field. The WebWare family of products permits this kind of bridging.

Accessing TuffMax Networks from the Field
Your field engineers and sales representatives need to enter, retrieve, and manipulate data remotely. With WebWare, all they will need is a modem and a piece of access software.

Ensuring Security
With remote access you always worry about security. With WebWare, you can design several levels of security, restricting access to certain databases.

Our local representative will call you next week to arrange a meeting.

Sincerely,

Persuasion

Example 1—Recommendation Document. You might choose to develop a scenario with associated times for troubleshooting a network service problem. This hypothetical example would demonstrate the cost savings to your customers.

Example 2—Research Report. You may have limited discretion to change the information you include. Certain figures, data, and analysis procedures would likely be required for the discussion of any new surgical procedure. You might decide, however, to present before-and-after pictures of the typical patient. You make this decision based on your estimate of your customers' needs for a visualization of the benefits of your procedure.

As examples 1 and 2 show, no rules exist about which examples or details would be most effective and most desirable. You can only choose appropriate ones if you have profiled your customers. For example, if your customers were raised in the 1950s, you can refer to incidents during the presidencies of Harry Truman and Dwight Eisenhower. For customers a generation younger, you might use allusions to later presidents.

5. Maintain a credible position so customers have reasons for agreeing with you and your ideas.

You will be establishing and maintaining your credentials from your first discussion with your customers to the writing of your final document. Your persuasive case stands or falls depending upon your customers' perception of your credibility.

Do the customers see you as honest? knowledgeable? professional? a good listener? sympathetic? In other words, should the customers trust what you have to say or to recommend?

From a personal standpoint, honesty and trust are the basis of any persuasive relationship. Without these virtues, you will have no success mustering reasons or developing a logical case. No questions about your ethics should ever arise. If they do, you will have damaged your own persuasive case. See ETHICS.

Don't rely on purely personal facts about yourself or your organization to help maintain your credibility. You can occasionally refer to your background or your prior business experiences. But these references will not buy you any credibility if you can't, for instance, produce a professionally appearing document or sound analyses of the problems at hand.

From what the clients see in your documents, you also establish your persuasive credibility by providing the following features or information:

—Careful, well-designed format— one that is professional and excellent

—Clear, persuasive organization and examples (see rule 4 above)

—Technically sound, valid analyses of data and examples

—No slips in spelling or punctuation

Photographs convey realism and authenticity. In the past, photos were especially persuasive because readers trusted their exactness and realism. Today, photos are still persuasive, but readers now know that a photograph often does not portray reality. Visual scanners, computer enhancements, and virtual reality techniques mean that the images in a photo or on a computer screen may never have existed except in someone's imagination.

Choose a photograph if you want to show your readers what is (or, perhaps, what could be). Choose a diagram or an illustration if you want to convey a concept, not realism. See ILLUSTRATIONS.

The following discussion presents a few principles for you to use in selecting and placing photographs in your documents and presentations. Techniques of how to take a photograph are beyond the scope of this discussion. Several of the rules, however, mention principles that would help you take effective photographs.

For related information about graphics, see GRAPHICS FOR DOCUMENTS and GRAPHICS FOR PRESENTATIONS. See also COLOR, ILLUSTRATIONS, and PAGE LAYOUT.

Photographs

1. Before choosing (or taking) a photograph, visualize its role by deciding exactly what your message is.

2. Survey different sources of photographs so that you have a rich array of photos to choose from.

3. Remove or adjust the features in a selected picture to complement the purpose of your document or of your presentation.

4. Choose a photo with a simple, yet interesting composition.

5. Select photographs with lighting that enhances the subject and reinforces the message.

6. Choose a photograph with an angle that best shows your subject and reinforces your purpose.

7. Use a color photograph, if appropriate, to provide additional information or to increase the effectiveness of your document or presentation.

8. Establish the size, scale, and orientation of the objects in a photograph.

1. Before choosing (or taking) a photograph, visualize its role by deciding exactly what your message is.

A document or a presentation should have a clear, forceful message. Graphics and any photographs you choose must support this message.

Identifying your readers (viewers) is the first step in deciding what your message should be. What do you want readers to do, to know, to feel, and to remember? Answering these questions is especially important if your readers are clients or customers. You must strive to view each photograph as your readers or your clients would view it.

Assume, for instance, that you are preparing a brochure describing services you could provide to the health care industry. You have done your homework by talking to medical doctors, nursing supervisors, hospital directors, and others within the health care industory. As they explained their needs, they said their highest goal was to provide quality patient care.

This marketing situation is exactly the situation Franklin Covey Consulting Group faced in designing a marketing brochure for the health care industry. Figure 1 (actually two pages with a single photo) shows how Franklin Covey solved its marketing challenge. The right side of figure 1 is the cover for the Franklin Covey brochure. The left side of figure 1 is the back cover of the brochure, so the two halves are continuous if a reader opens up the brochure and looks at both halves at the same time.

The photograph in this figure shows a doctor talking to the concerned mother while the patient sleeps in the bed behind the doctor. The mother is holding her young daughter (a human interest touch), who seems very interested in whatever the doctor is showing to the mother. The intent of the photograph is to make quality patient care visible and concrete because it deals with actual patients and their concerned family members.

Figure 1 illustrates the rich options we have today for creating layouts and presentations that are visually effective. In this figure, the underlying photograph supports the overlaid text and the two panels flow together to convey a single message: high-quality patient care.

Photographs

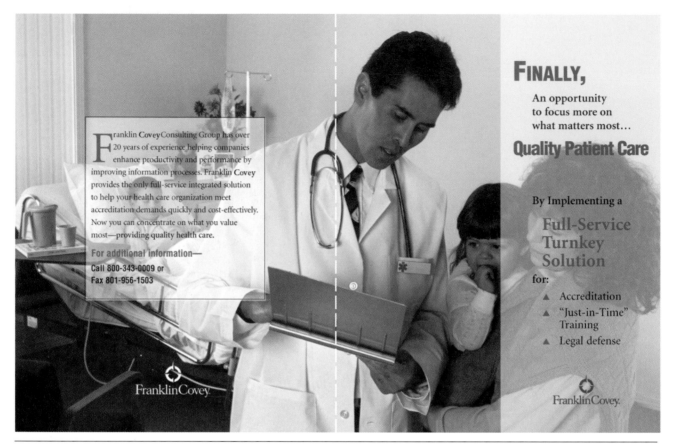

Figure 1. The Front and Back Covers for a Brochure. *The horizontal photograph links the front cover (the right side of the figure) with the back cover (the left side). As in this example, the creative use of a photograph enhances the message in the text.*

As in the preceding health care example, each photograph (image) you choose must capture your readers' interest and convey the message you want to send. Choosing the right photograph should be an early step in the design of an effective document. See EMPHASIS and WRITING AND REVISING.

2. Survey different sources of photographs so that you have a rich array of photos to choose from.

In the past, using photographs in publications was expensive and bothersome. Photographs were costly, both to acquire and then to print, especially if you wanted them to be in color. And you often had to

go to a graphics specialist for help with the layout and typesetting of your document, including photographs and their captions.

Today, however, professional photographs are widely available, and the costs are rapidly decreasing.

A very inexpensive option today is to buy a CD-ROM collection of stock photographs. A single CD-ROM often contains dozens of pictures selected to illustrate a theme—such as business architecture or coins and money.

Remember, however, that all photographs are protected by copyright, as are other graphics. You may not use someone else's photograph without permission and, often, the payment of a fee. So

if you buy a CD-ROM collection, check the accompanying vendor information for any applicable fees or licensing agreements.

Also, when you request permission, you should ask if you are restricted from changing the photo to suit your purposes. For example, some photographers will not grant permission for someone to print a black-and-white version of a color photograph. Other photographers want to know what size of reproduction you intend to make. See INTELLECTUAL PROPERTY.

If you decide to shoot your own photographs, be sure to get a signed release from anyone appearing in your photos. Such a release allows you to publish and distribute the photos.

3. **Remove or adjust the features in a selected picture to complement the purpose of your document or of your presentation.**

This rule expands on rule 1 because, after you have identified a document's message, you may find that no available photograph conveys your exact message.

In the past, graphics specialists could adjust photographs by cropping or cutting out part of the picture. In figure 2, for example, the dark border surrounding the Lincoln Memorial overwhelms the lighted area with the statue of Lincoln. Figure 3, a cropped and enlarged version of figure 2, emphasizes the statue of Lincoln and its relation to the columns framing the statue. Notice that the standing figure in figure 3 shows how large the statue and the memorial are.

Nowadays, techniques for choosing or adjusting a picture are common and are increasingly easy and inexpensive to use. Once a picture is electronically copied or scanned into a computer file, a graphics specialist can adjust the light, the texture, or even add or subtract images to fit the intended purpose.

Figure 4 is an example of a computer-designed image. In this photograph, the unseen scent from the bottle moves through the nasal passage, activating key sectors of the brain. Viewers can easily see that this photograph is not realistic even though some of its components began as realistic images.

If you are taking a picture for a document, you should eliminate distracting details before you even shoot the picture. You might move a person or subject to a different site so that the background is not distract-

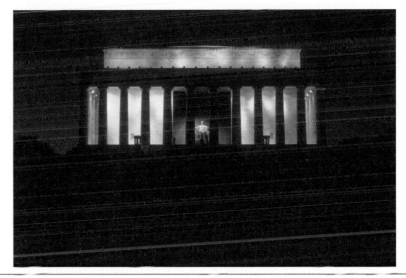

Figure 2. A Night View of the Lincoln Memorial. *This large-angle photo captures the entire front side of the Lincoln Memorial. The image of Lincoln is, however, lost because it is so small, almost indistinguishable. An optional format would be to enlarge the area directly around Lincoln, cutting out the wide dark foreground area. See figure 3 for an example of this optional format.*

Figure 3. A Night View of Lincoln's Statue in the Lincoln Memorial. *In this photograph, the emphasis is directly on the massive, awe-inspiring size of the Lincoln statue. The standing figure shows the massive scale of the statue. Notice also that the back lighting makes any details in the columns indistinct, throwing the emphasis on the statue instead.*

ing. Or, you can adjust your camera angle or direction of the shot so that a distracting image is not part of the picture. Figure 5 is an example of a picture with a distracting image. The people standing to the left of the red arch are likely a distraction to most viewers, so you would want to remove the people either by changing the camera angle (while the picture is being taken) or by cropping the picture, as in figure 3.

Whether you are using someone else's photographs or taking your own pictures, you are responsible for the final images your readers will see. Choosing the proper image is just one step in the design of a document. See EMPHASIS and GRAPHICS FOR DOCUMENTS.

Photographs

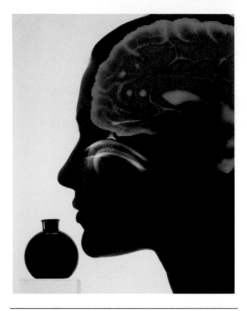

Figure 4. Even Faint Scents Can Trigger Responses in the Brain. *A scent initially passes through the nasal passage. As soon as a scent makes contact with the lining of the nasal passages, nerves trigger a response in the key sectors of the brain.*

4. Choose a photo with a simple, yet interesting composition.

Ensure that your subject is the principal point of interest in the photo, but a subject in the center of a photo often results in a static, uninteresting picture. Instead, choose a photograph where the main image is a bit off balance or off center.

This off-center arrangement—called the rule of thirds—is a widely accepted principle. Imagine that the picture plane is divided into thirds, vertically and horizontally. See figure 6 for a photograph with a superimposed grid of thirds. This grid shows in its four intersections where the primary points of emphasis or focus would usually be. In this picture, the figure of the worker lies on the vertical marking the left-hand third of the picture. The crossbar on the pole is slightly above but close to the upper horizontal line marking the upper third of the image.

Your goal is to choose a photo that has a balanced and interesting composition. Experimenting with the balance between different points of interest is why photographic professionals often take dozens of shots of the same scene, but from slightly different angles or with variations in the lighting.

Figure 7 has a balanced and interesting composition. The staircase with its converging walls and ascending steps conveys a strong sense of depth and power. The vertical composition is centered (a violation of the rule of thirds), but the upper handrail and the lower edge of the steps would line up horizontally with the upper and lower grids in the rule of thirds.

5. Select photographs with lighting that enhances the subject and reinforces the message.

Photographs, either in color or monochrome, record light in two dimensions, but we see in three dimensions. In a photograph the illusion of three dimensions is created by the reflection of light at various angles off the subject(s). Proper lighting also produces shadows in a photograph, helping to create images and make the photograph more interesting.

Look at photographs with a critical eye. Is the existing light sufficient to provide depth and dimension? Light direction, for instance, is important in how we perceive an object.

Direct light from behind the camera makes colors bright but may reduce detail and texture in the background. Sometimes, objects may seem flat. In Figure 8, the direct light from behind the camera throws the emphasis on the tiger, and the overall impression is more two dimensional rather than three dimensional.

Side light emphasizes shape, texture, and detail, but it also can show surface texture or flaws in close-ups, such a wrinkles on a face. In figure 9, the light coming from the left of the picture highlights dramatically the glass vial and the hands recording on the vial's label. Notice that the side lighting does show some of the skin texture around

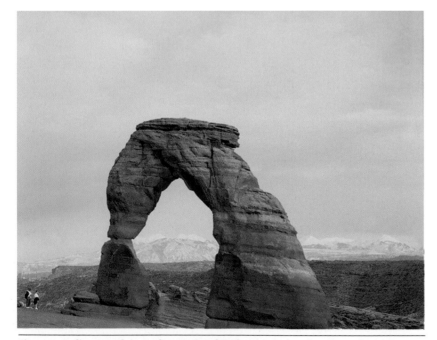

Figure 5. Delicate Arch in Arches National Park. *This arch, a favorite with tourists, appears on many professional postcards. People usually don't appear in such photos even though the people do help viewers realize how large the arch is. (Photo courtesy of Bill Grubbs)*

Figure 6. A Rule-of-Thirds Grid Overlaying a Photograph. *Professional photographers often choose an off-center or off-balance view of a scene. In this case, the figure of the worker is left of center while the sun is right of center. Another, less effective version of this picture might have moved the worker into the vertical center, with the sun nearly out of the picture.*

Figure 7. A Balanced and Formal View of Ascending Steps. *The photograph of these steps effectively uses both the composition (arrangement) of the architectural details and the light coming down from the upper level. As rule 4 says, choose photographs with a simple, yet interesting composition.*

the person's mouth. Also, as in this figure, side lighting often fades out any background details, most of which would likely be irrelevant to the point of this photograph.

Back light is especially dramatic. A subject lit only with a back light is a silhouette. Added side, overhead, or direct light can create a striking

photo. This can be the most difficult lighting to do well because often the photo will be over- or under-exposed. Figure 10 uses back lighting to convert the two standing figures into silhouettes. The interaction between the two figures is the focus of the photograph, as expressed in their body postures and the extended arm of the figure on the right. Notice that the photograph does not include any distracting details, such as their facial expressions or their clothing.

6. Choose a photograph with an angle that best shows your subject and reinforces your purpose.

The angle from which a photograph was taken is often not particularly obvious, but it still affects how viewers interpret the picture.

A **normal** straight-on, frontal shot is often the choice for routine photos. This angle (or lack of an angle) would be appropriate for a control panel or for a static display.

In many other contexts, however, different angles would produce more interesting effects.

Figure 8. A Tiger in Direct Light (from Behind the Camera). *Notice that the light tends to flatten the image of the tiger. The tiger's face, which is offset to the left, illustrates the rule of thirds, as discussed above in rule 4.*

Photographs

Figure 9. Side Light on Hands Holding a Vial. *The light comes from the left of the picture and highlights the hands and their interaction with the vial. Notice that background details vanish into darkness because the side light is falling on the vial and the person's hands.*

A picture taken from a **low camera angle** accents the subject and makes it more impressive, perhaps even dominant. Too obvious an angle, however, will make the subject seem distorted, so be cautious in choosing low-angle shots. Figure 11 is an example of an extremely low-angle shot. Notice that it makes the woman seem to be unrealistically tall. As with any such shot, this lack of realism was likely the photographer's goal, especially if the photographer wanted to show a commanding figure, with implications of control. The woman is also looking at her watch, as if to signal a concern for priorities and goals. As rule 1 suggests, you (and a photographer) must choose photographs to fit your intended message.

A picture taken from a **high camera angle** makes human subjects more abstract and appear less human. The image of the man in figure 12 is overshadowed by the central placement of the equipment; the high angle further de-emphasizes the man.

Figure 10. Back Light for a Business Conference. *The back lighting makes the images of the men dramatic, yet unrealistic. Realistic details, such as the facial features of the man facing the camera, are not the purpose or goal of the photograph. The other man is only a silhouette.*

Figure 11. A Low-Angle Photograph of a Woman. *The extremely low angle makes the figure seem unrealistically tall, yet also powerful and in command of a situation. This message may well have been the photographer's goal in this instance. In other cases, however, this picture might not be acceptable precisely because it is unrealistic.*

Figure 12. Scientist Adjusting Equipment. *Both the high angle and the central position of the equipment de-emphasize the role of the man.*

7. Use a color photograph, if appropriate, to provide additional information or to increase the effectiveness of your document or presentation.

Today's readers (and viewers) increasingly expect to see documents and presentations that use color throughout, especially in photographs. As an example, most major city newspapers now use color, including color photographs, on their front page as well as in color supplements.

Until recently, photographs were rarely used in documents because printing was expensive. Color photos and even high-quality black-and-white photos did not reproduce very well unless they were professionally printed.

Reproduction quality remains an issue even today, whether you are using either color or monochrome photos. Some photocopy machines make photographic images fuzzy or indistinct. In other cases, the final colors may not be true to the original image. So be sure to do a trial version of a photograph using actual production techniques. Validate that the quality is what you or your client expects.

Color photographs provide more information than a black-and-white (monochrome) picture. Colors convey tints, hues, and textures that no monochrome can hope to convey. As figure 13 (the inset color version and its monochrome version) shows, a color photograph has richer details and a sharpness of focus. If you need to print only in one or two colors, either work with monochrome negatives or choose color negatives that have a full range of contrast and color shades. See COLOR.

Sometimes, a photograph can be the background for a page of text. Figure 1 is an example of this technique. If you decide to use a photographic background, experiment with the color balance of the picture. Sometimes, you might shift the main color toward blue or even fade it out toward a neutral tan or even white, rather than a high-contrast black and white.

Figure 13. A Monochrome Version of a Color Photo. *As the small inset photo shows, the original photograph was in color. The monochrome print is still effective even though it has fewer contrasts between light and dark areas and between different hues or shades of color. (Photo courtesy of Bill Grubbs)*

Photographs

8. Establish the size, scale, and orientation of the objects in a photograph.

A photograph can be puzzling to viewers if the size, scale, or orientation of an image is not immediately obvious.

When the size of an image is not obvious, include rulers, a human hand, or common objects in the photograph to make the scale obvious. As options: use a ball-point pen, a key, or a coin next to the main image. This technique is illustrated in figure 14, where the size of the fiber optic strands would have been uncertain without the accompanying figure of a human hand.

For similar reasons, geographical photographs may also be puzzling. Often viewers would need to know from which direction a picture was taken. The freeway interchange in figure 15, for instance, could run either north and south or east and west. If the orientation is important, then, as in figure 15, insert an arrow showing which direction would be north.

Figure 14. Fiber Optic Strands from a Cable. *The strands from the cut end of a fiber optic cable show how tiny each strand of the cable is.*

Figure 15. Freeway Interchange. *The superimposed arrow in the lower right corner shows the north/south orientation of the interstate in the photo.*

Plurals of most nouns and pronouns are signaled by their spelling. Such changes are no problem if they follow the regular pattern: an –s or an –es added to the singular form makes the plural form:

    report + s = reports
    book + s = books
    church + es = churches
    tax + es = taxes

Problems arise when the plural does not follow the regular pattern:

    mouse   mice
    datum   data
    chassis   chassis
    fungus   fungi
    matrix   matrices
    I   we
    he, she, it they

The following discussion covers these and other irregular plurals. The best guide, however, is a good recent dictionary. See REFERENCES, NOUNS, and SPELLING.

1. Check a list of irregular forms to determine the correct plural, especially those plurals borrowed from Latin or other languages:

    addendum, addenda
    agendum, agenda
    alga, algae
    alumnus, alumni (masc. or mixed)
    alumna, alumnae (fem.)
    antenna, antennas (antennae, zoology)
    appendix, appendixes (or appendices)
    axis, axes
    basis, bases
    cactus, cactuses
    calix, calices
    cicatrix, cicatrices
    Co., Cos.
    coccus, cocci
    consortium, consortia
    crisis, crises
    criterion, criteria
    curriculum, curriculums (or curricula)
    datum, data
    desideratum, desiderata
    ellipsis, ellipses
    equilibrium, equilibriums (equilibria, scientific)
    erratum, errata
    executrix, executrices
    focus, focuses

Plurals

1. Check a list of irregular forms to determine the correct plural, especially those plurals borrowed from Latin or other languages.

2. Add the plural ending (usually –s or –es) to the most significant word in compound terms.

3. Add an –es to form the plural of nouns ending in –o with a preceding consonant.

4. Add an –s or sometimes an apostrophe plus an –s to form the coined plurals of abbreviations, titles, figures, letters, and symbols.

5. Plurals of pronouns, when they exist, are very irregular.

---

    folium, folia
    formula, formulas
    fungus, fungi
    genus, genera
    gladiolus (singular and plural)
    helix, helices
    hypothesis, hypotheses
    index, indexes (indices, scientific)
    lacuna, lacunae
    larva, larvae
    larynx, larynxes
    lens, lenses
    locus, loci
    madam, mesdames
    matrix, matrices
    medium, mediums (or media)
    memorandum, memorandums (better memo, memos)
    minutia, minutiae
    nucleus, nuclei
    oasis, oases
    octopus, octopuses
    opus, opera
    parenthesis, parentheses
    phylum, phyla
    plateau, plateaus
    radius, radii
    radix, radixes
    referendum, referendums
    septum, septa
    seta, setae
    stimulus, stimuli
    stratum, strata
    stylus, styluses
    syllabus, syllabuses (or syllabi)
    symposium, symposia
    synopsis, synopses
    terminus, termini
    testatrix, testatrices
    thesaurus, thesauri
    thesis, theses
    thorax, thoraxes
    vertebra, vertebras (vertebrae, zoology)
    virtuoso, virtuosos
    vortex, vortexes

NOTE 1: Many of the above forms now have regular plurals (*appendix, appendixes* or *memorandum, memorandums*). However, some editors still prefer the irregular forms (usually based on the word's origin in Latin or another language: *appendices, memoranda*). The longer a word is in English, the stronger the tendency is to make the plural conform to the regular English pattern (adding an –s or –es to the singular form).

NOTE 2: *Data* (the plural of *datum*) is now used as both a singular and plural form. In everyday conversation or informal writing, the singular is common:

    Data shows that the new . . .

In technical contexts, the plural is usually preferred:

    Test data show that a high correlation exists between . . .

See WORD PROBLEMS.

NOTE 3: Though many of these words come from other languages, they are now sufficiently English words and do not need underlining or italics. See ITALICS and UNDERLINING.

Plurals

2. Add the plural ending (usually −s or −es) to the most significant word in compound terms:

attorneys at law
bills of fare
brothers-in-law
comptrollers general
daughters-in-law
goings-on
grants in aid
lookers-on
reductions in force
surgeons general
assistant chiefs of staff
assistant surgeons general
assistant attorneys
deputy judges
lieutenant colonels
trade unions
hand-me-downs
higher-ups
pick-me-ups

3. Add an −es to form the plural of nouns ending in −o with a preceding consonant:

echo, echoes
potato, potatoes
tomato, tomatoes
veto, vetoes

NOTE: This rule has many exceptions, so if in doubt, check a good dictionary. See REFERENCES. Here are some of the common exceptions:

dynamo, dynamos
Eskimo, Eskimos
ghetto, ghettos
halo, halos
indigo, indigos
magneto, magnetos
octavo, octavos
piano, pianos
sirocco, siroccos
two, twos
zero, zeros

4. Add an −s or sometimes an apostrophe plus an −s to form the coined plurals of abbreviations, titles, figures, letters, and symbols:

ABC's *or* ABCs
COD's *or* CODs
g's
OK's *or* OKs
1 by 4's
SOS's
the three Rs

NOTE: Use the apostrophe only if necessary. Save the apostrophe to show possession, as in *John's hat*. The trend is for the apostrophe to vanish, leaving the simple −s to signal that the item is a plural. See APOSTROPHES.

5. Plurals of pronouns, when they exist, are very irregular:

I	we
you	you
he, she, it	they

See PRONOUNS.

Possessives are those forms of nouns and pronouns that show ownership or, in some cases, other close relationships:

Ownership

IBM's service booklet
Mr. Vaughan's store
his store
Susan's desk
her desk
Lewis' (or Lewis's) report
the engineer's schedule
the Lewises' house

Other relationships

the book's cover
its cover
the corporation's support
his lawyer's consent
the captain's story
a summer's day
a day's absence
a doctor's degree
three years' experience

NOTE: Noun possessive forms routinely require an apostrophe or an apostrophe plus an –s. See APOSTROPHES.

Possessives

1. Distinguish between true possessives and descriptive terms.

2. Add an apostrophe and an –s to form the possessive of singular nouns not ending in –s and for plural nouns not ending in –s.

3. Add only an apostrophe to form the possessive for both plural nouns and singular nouns ending in –s or an –s sound.

4. Use only a single apostrophe plus –s when joint possession is intended.

5. Add an apostrophe plus an –s to the end of personal and organizational names and abbreviations showing possession.

6. Do not use an apostrophe to form the possessives of personal pronouns and of the relative pronoun *who*.

7. Add apostrophes to form the possessives of indefinite pronouns.

8. Be aware that possessives sometimes occur without a following noun.

9. Use a possessive to modify an –ing form of a verb used as a noun.

---

1. Distinguish between true possessives and descriptive terms:

Possessives (whose . . .)

Exxon's reply
the employee's record
Oregon's laws
the Smiths' house

Descriptive terms (what kind of . . .)

an Exxon reply
the employee record
Oregon laws
the Smith house

NOTE 1: Either form of the above phrases is correct, so decide which form you prefer and then be consistent within the same document. See ADJECTIVES.

NOTE 2: The names of countries, governmental units, and organized groups ending in –s usually do not require apostrophes:

the United States plan
a Massachusetts statute
the mineworkers court case
a United Nations publication

---

2. Add an apostrophe and an –s to form the possessive of singular nouns not ending in –s and for plural nouns not ending in –s:

the cat's paw
Anne's statement
a man's coat
men's coats
an accountant's books
the children's payments

---

3. Add only an apostrophe to form the possessive for both plural nouns and singular nouns ending in –s or an –s sound:

General Dynamics' proposal
Sears' 4th Quarter Report
Penneys' reaction
the boss' idea
James' speech
for goodness' sake

NOTE: Some editors and writers prefer to add both an apostrophe and an –s, especially if the new word has an extra syllable:

General Dynamics's proposal
the actress's script
the boss's idea
James's speech

Use of this extra –s is, however, declining.

Possessives

4. Use only a single apostrophe plus –s when joint possession is intended:

> Susan and Harry's proposal
>
> Irene and Sam's book

NOTE: As in the preceding examples, joint possession is usually clear when the two people possess only a single item. But when plural objects or items are involved, the meaning is sometimes ambigious:

> Irene and Sam's books

Do Irene and Sam own all books jointly? From this sentence it is hard to tell, so a clearer version would be this one:

> Irene's and Sam's books
>
> *or*
>
> Irene's books and Sam's books

5. Add an apostrophe plus an –s to the end of personal and organizational names and abbreviations showing possession:

> Sears & Roebuck's policy
>
> Charles F. Shook's decision
>
> the Odd Fellows's initiation (*or* Odd Fellows' initiation)
>
> Dewey, Cheatum, and Howe's corporate policy
>
> HUD's policy
>
> BLM's guidelines

NOTE: Corporate and organizational practices vary, so, if possible, check the letterhead or other correspondence for exceptional cases:

> American Bankers Association
> Steelworkers Union
> Investors Profit Sharing

See APOSTROPHIES.

6. Do not use an apostrophe to form the possessives of personal pronouns and of the relative pronoun *who*:

> My secretary had **mine**.
>
> Your supervisor had **hers**.
>
> The company lost **its** comptroller.
>
> We refused to pay for **ours**.
>
> They lost **theirs** when the market fell.
>
> He mentioned **his**.
>
> **Whose** report is this?

NOTE 1: These are the possessive forms of personal pronouns: *my/ mine, your/yours, his, her/hers, its, our/ours, their/theirs.* In cases with two forms, the first form must come before the noun it possesses and the second form comes after the verb, with its noun implied:

> They were her ideas.
>
> The ideas were hers.

NOTE 2: Distinguish between possessive forms without apostrophes and contractions with apostrophes:

> The pump had lost its cover.
> We decided that it's (*it is*) time to redrill.
>
> He had changed his job recently.
> He's changing his job.
>
> Whose idea was this?
> Who's going to be at the meeting?

See APOSTROPHES.

7. Add apostrophes to form the possessives of indefinite pronouns:

> anyone else's task
>
> one's ideas
>
> the other's notion
>
> the others' schedules
>
> anybody's recommendation
>
> someone else's job

8. Be aware that possessives sometimes occur without a following noun:

> My ideas are like Sue's.
>
> His nose is like a bloodhound's.
>
> I'll be at Jim's.
>
> She was at the doctor's.
>
> IBM's is good, but Apple's is better.

NOTE: Large, established companies sometimes violate the usual rule (singular form plus an apostrophe and an –s):

> We conducted a survey at Macys. (*or* Macys')
>
> Harrods is splitting its stock.

9. Use a possessive to modify an *–ing* form of a verb used as a noun:

> Bill's speaking to my boss helped.
>
> I objected to his working on the rig overnight.
>
> I admired Sue's planning.

Prepositions

Prepositions are words that connect or relate nouns and pronouns to preceding words and phrases:

The engineer moved **from** his desk.

The plans **for** the new substation have yet to be completed.

The case **against** her became even more convincing.

There is truth **in** what you say.

The firm submitted a summary **of** the specifications.

The simple prepositions are *at, by, in, on, down, from, off, out, through, to, up, for, of,* and *with.* More complex, even phrasal, prepositions also exist: *against, beneath, in front of, on top of, on board, according to, on account of, by means of,* etc.

Although they number less than a hundred, prepositions are essential words in English. Most normal sentences contain one or more prepositions.

1. Do not be overly concerned if you end a sentence with a preposition.

For over a thousand years English has had normal sentences that ended with prepositions:

That's something we can't put up with.

The Universal acquisition is the most difficult deal we've gotten into.

This is the report I've been telling you about.

She's the accountant you spoke to.

This project is the one that you objected to.

Winston Churchill was once corrected for ending a sentence with a preposition, and he supposedly replied, "That is the sort of English up with which I will not put."

Prepositions

1. Do not be overly concerned if you end a sentence with a preposition.

2. Omit certain prepositions if you can do so without changing the meaning.

3. Distinguish between the prepositions *between* and *among*.

As Churchill's witty reply indicates, many English sentences sound awkward if you try to avoid ending them with prepositions:

The Universal acquisition is the most difficult deal into which we've gotten.

This is the report about which I told you.

She is the accountant to whom you spoke.

This project is the one to which you objected.

Make your sentences as simple, smooth, and direct as possible, and don't worry about such misconceptions as not ending a sentence with a preposition. The fact is, a preposition is a fine word to end a sentence with.

2. Omit certain prepositions if you can do so without changing the meaning.

In each of the following sentences, the preposition within parentheses is unnecessary. In the last sentence, *at* is both unnecessary and incorrect.

All (of) the engineers visited the site.

We moved the pipe off (of) the loading dock.

The filing cabinet is too near (to) the door.

We met (at) about 8 p.m.

Where are they (at)?

Generally, native speakers of English can be guided by their innate sense of what constitutes smooth and clear uses of prepositions. See MODIFIERS.

---

3. Distinguish between the prepositions *between* and *among*.

Between usually refers to two things, while *among* refers to more than two things. However, *between* can also refer to more than two things if each of the things is compared to all the others as a group:

The judge divided the land between the two parties. (*not* among)

The judge divided the land among a dozen parties. (*not* between)

We had trouble deciding between the two pumps. (*not* among)

We carefully analyzed the differences between the six alternatives. (*or* among)

We had trouble deciding among all the possible small trucks. (*or* between)

See *among/between* in WORD PROBLEMS.

Presentations

Presentations have much in common with documents. Both should have at least one specific purpose and an identified audience. If you want to accomplish the purpose of your presentation and get your audience to know, do, and feel what you want, you must plan your presentation with care and deliver it with confidence.

1. Develop your presentation according to standards of effective design and delivery.

Presentations consist of two equally important elements—design (organization) and delivery.

The design and delivery methods that we recommend in rules 2 through 9 comply with recognized communication standards. However, if you are delivering a presentation for a particular professional society or for a technical organization, you may find that they have special requirements, which you should strive to follow.

Figures 1 through 4 show a sample Presentation Planner form from a Franklin Planner®. This form is a tool for planning an effective presentation.

2. Identify clearly the purpose of your presentation.

Nothing is more important for an effective presentation than having a clear purpose—knowing specifically what you want your audience *to do, to know,* and *to feel*. See figure 1.

Identifying the purpose is important—not only for yourself in the planning phase of the presentation, but for the aid of your audience as well:

> Today I intend to show you the benefits of the proposed Jenkins project and to recommend your support of its acceptance.

> The purpose of my remarks this evening is to encourage you to reject the referendum proposed by my opponent.

Unless you, as a presenter, have a clear understanding of the purpose of your presentation, you cannot expect your audience to know what you hope to achieve with it. See ORGANIZATION.

3. Analyze your audience and plan your presentation to meet their needs.

To be truly effective as a presenter, you must know as much about your audience—their needs, desires, biases, etc.—as you can, even before you plan your presentation.

In addition to general information about audiences (e.g., that the attention span of the average adult is somewhere between 8 and 12 seconds), you would be wise to learn as much as you can about your specific audience. See figure 1.

Many otherwise well-planned presentations have failed simply because the presenter knew too little about the audience.

4. Assess the situation in which you will deliver your presentation.

By "situation," we mean the time, setting, and occasion of the presentation.

If your purpose is to win audience support, for example, you may find that you could do just the opposite—simply by allowing your presentation to run 15 minutes overtime.

The setting can be a major factor in the overall effectiveness of your presentation. If possible, go beforehand to the place where you will deliver your presentation. That will give you a good idea of the advantages and disadvantages of the setting. Consider any possible changes that may contribute to a better situation (room setup, lighting, etc.).

The occasion will often dictate certain elements of your presentation, such as the degree of formality, the use of visual aids, and even the type of clothing you choose to wear. See figure 2.

5. Build the evidence necessary to support your points.

Once you have determined the main points of your presentation, make sure that you provide enough (but not too much) evidence to support those points adequately. Among the types of support available, you may select the following:

Definition

Increased control means that you'll be able to make your own decision about your investments.

Explanation

Each of you will be able to direct your money into 10 available funds.

Example

I divided my money among three different funds and am very pleased with the returns.

Testimony

Our comptroller, Brenda Lewis, estimates your return will be between 10 and 15 percent.

Statistics

Our former plan returned only 8.7 percent last quarter.

See THINKING STRATEGIES.

6. Organize your message logically.

Organization is one of the keys to effective presentations. Unless you can lead your audience logically through your presentation, they may miss the points you are trying to make.

Preview your main points when you present your message. Basically, tell the audience very briefly what you intend to talk about:

I will discuss the three reasons my committee chose Acme Plumbing:

1. Next to lowest price
2. Existing contracts with similar firms
3. Branch office less than 10 minutes away

Figure 1. Franklin Covey Presentation Planner (front page). *As suggested in rules 2 and 3, identify your purpose and analyze your audience.*

Figure 2. Franklin Covey Presentation Planner (back page). *As suggested in rules 4 and 5, assess your situation and build your evidence.*

Presentations

One organizational technique that works very well is what we call the "Triple-S formula."

State your point

Support your point

Summarize your point

Use and even repeat this organization—to ensure a logical flow, a solid format, and a convincing message. See figures 3 and 4. The Triple-S formula will work for your entire presentation or for each main subpoint or subtopic.

7. Design graphics that support your message.

Graphics (graphs, charts, tables, photographs, etc.) can be a valuable means of supporting your message. But avoid the tendency of using them too much. Some suggestions to keep in mind about the use of visuals in presentations:

- Keep the visuals simple, clear, and uncluttered.
- Use no more than you need to convey your message.
- Use informative captions, not just labels.

For additional suggestions regarding the use of graphics, see GRAPHICS FOR PRESENTATIONS, CHARTS, GRAPHS, HEADINGS, ILLUSTRATIONS, LISTS, MAPS, PHOTOGRAPHS, and TABLES.

8. Deliver your presentation engagingly and with confidence.

Delivery is just as important as good organization and design.

Without an effective delivery, even an excellent message may suffer.

Excellent delivery results to a great extent from practicing effective delivery techniques. Among the

Figure 3. Franklin Covey Presentation Planner (inside left page). *As suggested in rules 6 and 7, design your message.*

Figure 4. Franklin Covey Presentation Planner (inside right page). *Conclude your presentation with a strong closing.*

techniques that traditionally contribute to effective presentations are the following:

- Know your material.

- Approach and leave the podium with confidence.

- Begin your presentation with a *relevant* attention-getter (fact, statement, questions, etc.).

- Do not read your presentation (although you may refer to note cards for specific information).

- Speak clearly, confidently, and with enthusiasm.

- Vary your voice in pitch, volume, and rate of speed.

Use appropriate (and natural) gestures, facial expressions, and body movements.

- Maintain good eye contact with your audience.

- End with a powerful closing.

---

9. If appropriate, invite your audience to participate.

Tell your audience when and if you would welcome comments or questions.

In formal situations, you might decide to reserve questions until after your presentation. This strategy allows you to finish all of your prepared content.

In less formal situations, plan to stop to ask for an exchange of ideas. If you have just finished with an example of cost-saving techniques, you might turn to the audience with a question:

What are some cost-saving steps you noticed?

or

What steps would be necessary to implement the cost-saving techniques I just outlined?

Notice that both of the preceding questions are substantive, requiring examples or facts. Avoid dead-end yes/no questions:

Do any of you have ideas?

How many of you here thought the same thing?

Project Management

Project management includes several obvious tasks and skills. A project manager must know how to choose and assign personnel. She must know how to prepare useful schedules and accurate budgets. She must know how to monitor project accomplishments and how to give personnel constructive feedback. She must also know how to report to senior management.

Most important of all, a project manager must know how to record or to document each task and each step in a project.

Intellectual work, including work on any project, requires careful step-by-step documentation. Documents for a typical manufacturing project would include design or engineering plans, marketing surveys, sales brochures, maintenance manuals, and even day-to-day project team records. See MANAGING INFORMATION.

The project team might assert that they are producing a new drug or the latest automotive fuel injection system, but these physical products will not be viable without supporting documents.

Documents, then, are an important product for any project team.

The following rules for project management focus on intellectual processes. These rules are generic and universal because the intellectual processes are themselves universal, not unique to any professional group or academic specialty.

1. Begin by developing a vision of the final product and of its documentation.

Skilled athletes know that if they repeatedly visualize a successful final game or the final winning seconds of a race, they are more likely to be successful in the game or race. Their visualizations guide and strengthen them as they train and practice day by day.

An intellectual vision of a product is similarly a good starting point for a project manager and for a project team. This vision needs to be as comprehensive and as rich as possible. What product features are essential? What questions of technology or science remain to be answered? Who will use this product and how will they use it? What quality features are important?

This vision should also include the dead ends, engineering problems, disputed data, and anything else the project team expects to delay the project.

As early as possible, the team will be making engineering sketches and designs. At some point, the team will even produce a full prototype of the product, often one that works or functions like the final product would.

In a similar way, the team should work early with document prototypes (often called mock-ups). These document prototypes mature and develop as the team members answer questions and make decisions. This evolving prototype is a record of the project team's intellectual activity. See WRITING AND REVISING and PAGE LAYOUT.

Both physical prototypes and document prototypes are essential tools for capturing, as early as possible, a vision of the entire project.

2. Choose a broad, well-balanced project team to help with all phases of the project.

Most projects today are too complex for a single researcher or inventor. One person working alone can't even keep up with the scientific and technical literature for a single field of inquiry. Teams are increasingly replacing the single researcher.

A good project team will include technical and scientific experts, marketing specialists, financial analysts, customers (both internal and external), and managers. Your goal is to include anyone who has a say in how the project will proceed.

If you miss a key contributor, you will wind up redoing phases of the project and, quite likely, wasting valuable time and money.

Project Management

1. Begin by developing a vision of the final product and of its documentation.
2. Choose a broad, well-balanced project team to help with all phases of the project.
3. Identify and record quality standards for the project.
4. Make task assignments and set up an achievable schedule.
5. Provide usability tests for the project products—both the physical products and the documents.
6. Identify and praise each person's contributions to tasks and to project milestones.
7. Develop strategies for improving project management within your department or company.

© 1985–1999 FranklinCovey Co.

3. Identify and record quality standards for the project.

Quality standards establish your expectations as to what the team is to produce and how they will produce it. Often the best practice is to make the team responsible for identifying its own quality standards.

Quality standards apply to three different areas of project management:

—Project Management Standards

—Product Standards

—Document Standards

Project Management Standards. These standards are essentially the seven rules in this discussion of project management. They reflect generic features of any successful project management effort.

Figure 1 presents these project management standards in a checklist format. Use this checklist to guide you as you manage a project or as you help someone else be a successful project manager.

Product Standards. Product standards are physical features and requirements that apply to the product to be produced. Examples would be a new medical drug or a new automotive fuel injection system. In the case of the new medical drug, marketing studies could indicate that it will be successful if taken only once a day (a key sales benefit). The pharmaceutical company's application to the Food and Drug Administration would then have to include studies designed to test the drug's effectiveness if taken only once a day.

As in this example, the physical features and requirements (product standards) of the product require certain levels and types of documents.

Project Management Checklist

Check off each item in this list when you are satisfied that you (and your project team) have completed it. The rules referred to in parentheses relate to rules from this entry on project management.

❏ Begin by developing a vision of the final product and its documentation. (Rule 1)

   —Product prototypes

   —Document prototypes

❏ Choose a broad well-balanced project team to help with all phases of the project. (Rule 2)

   —Technical and scientific experts

   —Marketing and financial representatives

   —Customers (both external and internal)

   —Others?

❏ Identify and record (in writing) quality standards for the entire project. (Rule 3)

   —Product standards

   —Document standards

   —Project Management Standards

❏ Make clear task assignments and set up an achievable schedule. (Rule 4)

❏ Provide for usability tests. If appropriate, repeat these. (Rule 5)

   —Tests for the product

   —Tests for the documents

❏ Identify and praise each person's contributions to tasks and to project milestones. (Rule 6)

❏ Develop strategies for improving project management within your department or company. (Rule 7)

Figure 1. Project Management Checklist. *Use this checklist to monitor your progress, either as a project manager or as a project team member. Remember that project management is complex enough to require your constant efforts to improve and refine its steps.*

Project Management

Document Standards. Document standards begin with the quality of a writer's thoughts. Are major points and conclusions convincingly explored? Is the language (and the thought behind it) credible? Quality documents reflect the intellectual acuity of their writers.

The preceding quality issues are the basis for the quality standards recorded in figure 2. For each quality standard, figure 2 lists common user (reader) questions and the criteria for measuring a document's response to each question.

A new drug application to the Food and Drug Administration (FDA) is an illustration of the role of document standards. As its primary content, an application must describe and analyze clinical trials (tests) of the drug. These data and their analyses must be credible and consistent, but also, data must be arranged and presented to comply with FDA submission requirements (FDA document standards). Besides test data, the application will also include other documents—for example, the proposed drug insert to be included with each bottle of pills.

Each separate document has its own quality standards. Many of these standards are unique, as in the preceding new drug example, but see the rules in the EMPHASIS entry for a list of document standards that are applicable to most documents.

Quality documents, if prepared during the early prototyping phase, can influence the development of the product itself. Early documen-tation forces team members to commit to ideas, and even as they prepare working papers and team records, they will be discovering more ideas.

To return to the new drug example, if the project team prepares an early prototype of the drug insert, the team might discover certain features of the product that need further analysis or attention. The one-a-day requirement may be one such feature. Another might be that the drug should be taken with milk or a dairy product to avoid stomach cramps. If the team writes down such requirements early, they can investigate options. For instance, is a timed-release format medically effective? Or, can the drug be mixed with an antacid so that it need not be taken with milk?

---

4. Make task assignments and set up an achievable schedule.

Staff a project team with achievers and initiators, not passive followers.

The team members should generate their own task assignments and set their own schedules. If a manager or the organization dictates these decisions, the project team will cease to function, and the project will fail.

An achievable schedule is usually based on negotiation. Some people will always overestimate the time needed for a task; others will underestimate. And what is achievable is always uncertain.

As one project manager said about documentation tasks, "Make your best, most reasonable estimate and then double it." The time required will usually match the doubled figure!

---

5. Provide usability tests for the project products—both the physical products and the documents.

Many techniques overlap with or relate to the concept of usability testing: benchmarking, testing the prototype, performing structured walkthroughs, etc.

Testing the physical product is an obvious step. Typically, a sample group of customers receives a version of the product for testing—whether it is a new type of breakfast food or a redesigned electric drill. All the customers have to do is taste the new breakfast food or drill a few test holes. However, parallel testing of the product documentation should also occur.

Figure 3 lists six tests for evaluating the usability of a document. Choose one or more of these tests when usability is an issue.

---

6. Identify and praise each person's contributions to tasks and to project milestones.

Positive, ongoing feedback is a critical success standard in good project management. Feedback also promotes organizational health and growth.

Without good feedback, members of a project team are isolated and tasks performed by the team will be fragmented and often contradictory. If individual team members have a limited grasp of the project features, what they work on will be similarly limited. Much reworking of products and documents will be inevitable.

Good feedback should provide team members with a rich organizational view of their roles and contributions. These team members are part of true learning organizations.

A learning organization (or team) gives everyone broad access to information and the tools for sharing this information. The newest and greenest team member can access the E-mail or voice mail of the most senior member, perhaps even of the company chief executive officer. Such communication links help to flatten and to transform organizational hierarchies.

Document Standards		
Standard	**User Questions**	**Measurement**
Purpose	• Do readers know when they begin what they are going to read and why?	• Each section of the document begins with a statement of purpose. See ORGANIZATION.
Content	• Are regulatory, industry, and experiential standards met? • Can the reader easily identify the main messages?	• The document conforms to standards and guidelines. • Detail and "big picture" are in balance. • The document defines what the reader should do, know, or feel. See ORGANIZATION.
Logic	• Are the message components logically connected?	• In all appropriate places, the document presents conclusions and assesses their significance. • Information is consistent from one portion of the document to another. See REPETITION. • All conclusions clearly evolve from the data presented.
Organization	• Does the reader find key messages in emphatic positions? • Can the reader find information easily?	• Each part of the document begins with a summary overview. See SUMMARIES. • Text is organized deductively, from general to specific. See ORGANIZATION. • Organizational devices guide the reader and improve access to information. See EMPHASIS. • The document has a consistent internal format and organization. See EMPHASIS.
Context	• Can the reader recognize the context of the information being presented?	• Information is placed within a process or industry context. • The relationship between the information in this document and others is clear. See CITATIONS.
Presentation	• Can the reader easily comprehend the information presented? • Are verbal and visual techniques used effectively?	• Information is presented in the most appropriate visual form (text or figure). See GRAPHICS FOR DOCUMENTS. • The graphics are high quality and clearly related to the text. See GRAPHICS FOR DOCUMENTS. • Emphasis techniques help the reader access important information. See EMPHASIS.
Language	• Do language mistakes distract the reader?	• The reader does not have to interpret. • The message is conveyed through good writing techniques and concise language. See STYLE and TONE. • Grammar, spelling, and punctuation are correct.

Figure 2. Document Standards. *These standards are generic guidelines for writers and team members to follow. Team members would need to adjust or expand these standards to match specific writing tasks.*

7. Develop strategies for improving project management within your department or company.

The preceding six rules of project management reflect common sense. Surprisingly, few organizations have consistently applied these rules to their ongoing projects.

These rules will go unheeded unless a project manager makes a conscious effort to adopt them for everyday organizational activities.

Develop your own strategies for working to improve the project management skills within your organization. By way of an illustration, consider some of the following ways to adapt these strategies to your own situation:

—Experiment with different team memberships. Not everyone works well with everyone else.

—Develop personal strategies for organizing and monitoring team accomplishments.

—Structure training and sharing so successful team members can foster team management skills in other employees.

Document Usability Tests

These documentation tests enable you to gauge how a document performs in the hands of a user.

Test 1: Reading Time. How long does it take for the user to read the document in real time?

Method: Time the user on various versions of the document. An alternative: Time how long it takes to access relevant or critical information.

Test 2: Prediction. How easily can the user predict the sequence and content of the message simply by scanning foreground materials?

Method: Limit the user's access only to previews, introductory statements, headings, and visuals. Ask the user to predict the main points of the message.

Test 3: Memory/Summary. How easily and thoroughly can the user give a summary account of the message?

Method: Ask the user to summarize in writing or orally the content of the message.

Test 4: Message Mapping. How easily and thoroughly can the user outline a pattern or map of the message?

Method: Ask the user to sketch an outline of the message and compare it to a standard outline.

Test 5: Performance to Procedure. How helpful is the document in carrying out a procedure?

Method: Monitor both experienced and inexperienced users as they follow the document in actually carrying out the procedure described. Note hesitancies, recursions, confusions, errors, random access, and inferences made.

Test 6: Access and Retrieval. How easily can the user access and retrieve the information?

Method: Evaluate Information Systems protocols for filing and retrieving information. Are file names systematic? Are infobase/database systems in use? Does keyword search enable quick and accurate access?

Figure 3. Document Usability Tests. *Use one or more of these tests to evaluate the usability of a document.*

Pronouns are words that take the place of more specific nouns or noun phrases:

George completed the drawings.
He completed the drawings.

The young engineer spoke up.
She spoke up.

John's survey was efficient.
His survey was efficient.

First State Bank went bankrupt.
It went bankrupt.

John, Sue, Esther, and George left the party early.
They left the party early.

Who completed the drawings?
(Who – *somebody unknown*)

The man hit himself.
We ourselves paid for the damage.

The bid and the interest were issues.
Those were issues.

John, Sue, Esther, George, etc., left the party early.
Everyone left the party early.

As the above examples indicate, pronouns include several types of words: **personal** pronouns (*he, she, his, they*, etc.), **interrogative** and **relative** pronouns (*who, that,* and *which*), **reflexive** and **intensive** pronouns (*himself, ourselves*, etc.), **demonstrative** pronouns (*this, that, these,* and *those*), and **indefinite** pronouns (*everyone, anybody, someone*, etc.).

Personal Pronouns

Personal pronouns are those that commonly replace the names of individuals or objects: *I, we, you, he, she, it,* and *they*:

- *I* and *we* are first-person pronouns—that is, they are used for the person(s) speaking.

- *You* (singular and plural) is the second-person pronoun—that is, it is used for person(s) spoken to.

- *He, she, it,* and *they* are third-person pronouns—that is, they are used for persons or objects spoken about.

Pronouns

1. Use personal pronouns in business and technical documents to establish a personal, human tone.

2. Use subjective case pronouns for the subject of a verb or when the pronoun follows a form of *be* (*am, is, are, was, were, be, been*).

3. Use objective case pronouns when the pronoun is the object of a verb or the object of a preposition.

4. Use possessive cases correctly.

5. Choose pronouns that agree with their antecedents in number, in gender, and in case.

6. For interrogative and relative *who*, use the subjective case (*who*) for subjects and following a form of *be*; use the objective case (*whom*) for objects of verbs and prepositions.

7. Avoid the unnecessary use of intensive/reflexive forms when an ordinary personal pronoun would suffice.

8. Avoid vague uses of demonstrative pronouns (usually when the pronoun is used without the noun it is describing).

9. Indefinite pronouns used as subjects should agree in number with their verbs.

Most personal pronouns also have different forms for the singular and the plural, for different uses in sentences, and for possessives. Table 1 on the next page summarizes these different forms of the personal pronouns.

While the differences between the singular and plural forms are obvious, the differences between the cases are often confusing. Different cases (pronoun forms) have different uses in sentences:

I surveyed the site. (*I is the subjective case.*)

The committee quizzed me. (*Me is the objective case.*)

My report was too long. (*My is the possessive case—the one that comes before its noun.*)

The report is mine. (*Mine is the possessive case—the one that follows its noun.*)

See PLURALS.

1. Use personal pronouns in business and technical documents to establish a personal, human tone.

Pronouns—especially *I* and *you*—establish the identities of the writer and the reader. Such pronouns bring a human tone to a letter or memo:

this

Based on my review, I recommend that you sell your DataDeck stock and buy IBM stock.

not this

Based on a careful review, the sale of your DataDeck stock is recommended. IBM would be a good replacement stock.

See TONE and ACTIVE/PASSIVE.

Pronouns

2. Use subjective case pronouns for the subject of a verb or when the pronoun follows a form of *be* (*am, is, are, was, were, be, been*):

Subject of a verb

Jan and I analyzed the blueprints.

We discussed the design options.

You were omitted from the roll.

He called two colleagues.

She and her employee came to the 11 a.m. meeting.

It was a poor choice.

They and Harold met about the legal problem.

NOTE: In cases where a pronoun and a noun are both subjects of the same verb, you can test the pronoun by removing the noun. In the sentence *She and her employee came to the 11 a.m. meeting,* no one would read it as follows: *Her came to the 11 a.m. meeting.* So *she* is the correct pronoun.

Following a form of be

The engineer chosen was she.

The contractor who won is he.

Was it they who called?

It could have been I.

NOTE: Pronouns following forms of *be* often sound strange:

It is I.

This is she.

Normally, objective case pronouns follow verbs, except the verb *be,* as mentioned above. For that reason people often put objective case pronouns after the various forms of *be*: *It is me* or *This is her.* These sentences may be acceptable in informal speech, which is where they ordinarily would appear anyway. In formal speech and in most writing, the subjective case forms are correct. (Of course, if your sentence sounds stiff or strange,

Table 1. Personal Pronouns

			Subjective Case	Objective Case	Possessive Case
First Person	Singular		I	me	my/mine
	Plural		we	us	our/ours
Second Person	Singular		you	you	your/yours
	Plural		you	you	your/yours
Third Person	Singular	Masculine	he	him	his
		Feminine	she	her	hers
		Non-gendered	it	it	its
	Plural		they	them	their/theirs

rephrase it to avoid the problem. You could say *I am here* instead of *It is I.*)

---

3. Use objective case pronouns when the pronoun is the object of a verb or the object of a preposition:

Object of a verb

The committee chose her.

Carol did not include Jane and him.

The pollution affected them.

The President contacted Harry and me.

NOTE: When a noun and a pronoun both follow a verb, you can check the pronoun by omitting the noun. So, *The President contacted Harry and me* becomes *The President contacted me.* Few people would be comfortable with *I,* which is the wrong pronoun, but many speakers often use *I* when a noun or another pronoun comes before it: *The President contacted Harry and I. The clerk gave it to him and I.* These sentences are incorrect.

Object of a preposition

Frank walked by her.

The team studied with me.

On account of me, the project ended.

The proposed schedule depended on Jane and her.

Acme Inc. worked against Jason and me.

NOTE: In the last two sentences, you can test for the correct pronoun by removing the noun or preceding pronoun that comes between the preposition and the pronoun. (Wrong: *The proposed schedule depended on she. Acme Inc. worked against I.*)

---

4. Use possessive cases correctly:

That was her report.
The report was hers.

The problems were ours, not yours.
They were our problems, not your problems.

I rejected your arguments.
The arguments were yours, not mine.

NOTE 1: In cases where two possessive forms exist for a single pronoun, the simple form (without an -s) comes before the noun; the other form (with an –s) follows a form of *be* (*am, is, are, was, were, be, been*). *His* and *its* have only a single form.

NOTE 2: Do not confuse the possessive pronouns with simple contractions. Possessive pronouns do not have apostrophes; contractions do have apostrophes:

Possessive Pronoun	Contraction
its	it's (it is)
his	he's (he is)
their/theirs	they're (they are)
your/yours	you're (you are)

See POSSESSIVES and CONTRACTIONS.

5. Choose pronouns that agree with their antecedents in number, in gender, and in case:

Agreement in Number

The men worked on the design plan all night, but they were unable to finish. (men [antecedent] = plural; they = plural)

Cheryl Higgins prepared a revised safety procedure, but she failed to get managerial approval. (Cheryl Higgins [antecedent] = singular; she = singular)

Agreement in Gender

Sidney Brown was eager to take his first actuarial exam. (Sidney [antecedent] can be either male or female, so the pronoun is a key sign of which is intended. Often the female spelling is Sydney.)

NOTE: When the antecedent is an indefinite pronoun, writers often don't know whether to use a singular or plural pronoun, much less a masculine or feminine pronoun:

Everyone should arrange their (his or her?) desk before leaving.

Everybody is responsible for their (his or her?) own time cards.

The forms with *their* have become more acceptable in speech, even though *everyone* and *everybody* are usually considered singular pronouns. To avoid any sexist language and to eliminate the clumsy *his or her*, the best option would be to rewrite the sentences as plurals:

All employees should arrange their desks before leaving. (*or simply*, Employees . . .)

All clerks and secretaries are responsible for their own time cards.

See AGREEMENT, BIAS-FREE LANGUAGE, and the discussion below of indefinite pronouns.

Agreement in case

Betty argued with them—especially Susan and him. (them = *objective case*; him = *objective case*)

Interrogative and Relative Pronouns

Interrogative and relative pronouns are similar in their uses, and some interrogative pronouns are identical to the main relative pronouns: *who, whom, whose,* and *which.* Relative pronouns also include *that, whoever,* and *whomever.* Interrogatives also include *what, why,* and *where.*

Many interrogative and relative pronouns have only one form, but *who* changes its form just as the personal pronouns do:

Subjective case: who, whoever

Objective case: whom, whomever

Possessive case: whose

That and the other relative and interrogative forms do not change to reflect the different cases.

6. For interrogative and relative *who,* use the subjective case (*who*) for subjects and following a form of *be;* use the objective case (*whom*) for objects of verbs and prepositions:

Subjective case

Who is the project engineer?

Whoever writes the report gets all the credit.

The agent who spoke to us was courteous.

The supervisor determined who would be the representative.

The representative is whoever has the most years of service.

Objective case

Whom did you nominate?

Whom did you wish to speak to?

Or: To whom did you wish to speak?

Whomever you nominate, we'll find someone to balance the ticket.

The man whom you spoke to is our president.

NOTE 1: The first two examples under the objective case sound almost too formal, even stiff. Most speakers of English are more comfortable if a subjective *who* begins the sentence or question. For this reason, two other versions of these questions are acceptable in informal, spoken English:

Who did you nominate?

Who did you wish to speak to?

Similarly, even with non-questions, subjective *who* sometimes replaces the more correct *whom:*

Whoever you nominate, we'll find someone to balance the ticket.

These informal forms with *who* or *whoever* are incorrect in writing even though acceptable in informal speech.

Pronouns

NOTE 2: Deciding on the correct case is especially difficult when the relative pronoun is part of a complex sentence. The trick is to isolate only the clause containing the relative pronoun:

> who wants to study chemistry
>
> whom the proposal team chose
>
> whoever is the top candidate

These are correct uses of *who* and *whom*, so you can insert them into any sentence, and they'll be correct:

> John, who wants to study chemistry, is our lab technician.
>
> We left with Sandra, whom the proposal team chose.
>
> Whoever is the top candidate will be our speaker.
>
> We planned to interview whoever is the top candidate.

So, to decide on the case of a troublesome use of *who* or *whom*, try to isolate the clause containing the relative pronoun (underlined below):

> We decided to abandon the direction established by the geologist <u>who/whom we first talked to</u>.

The proper form then is *whom*, used as the object of the preposition *to*.

NOTE 3: Adjective clauses introduced by a relative pronoun are often difficult to punctuate. The simplest rule is to enclose such clauses with commas when they are nonessential:

> Jack Craven, who is our project coordinator, has been with the company for 15 years.
>
> We presented the proposal to the team from AirFlo Inc., which is a firm based in Denver.

When the clauses are essential, no commas are required:

> The proposal that we sent to the Department of Transportation has been canceled. (*Without the clause* that we sent to the Department of Transportation, *the sentence would not be clear to most readers, especially if more than one proposal were possible.*)

The Governor proposed banning all autos that did not have a safety inspection. (*The* clause that did not have a safety inspection *is essential to the meaning.*)

See COMMAS and *that/which* in WORD PROBLEMS.

Reflexive and Intensive Pronouns

Reflexive and intensive pronouns are identical in appearance: Both end in *–self* (singular) or *–selves* (plural). Personal pronouns have reflexive and intensive forms: *myself, ourselves, yourself, yourselves, himself, herself, itself,* and *themselves.*

Reflexive pronouns "reflect" back to a noun mentioned earlier in the same sentence:

> George injured himself.
>
> The team quarreled among themselves.
>
> Amy cut herself.
>
> The dog licked itself.

Intensive pronouns usually follow the nouns they intensify:

> George himself was injured.
>
> The team themselves were arguing.
>
> Amy herself ran the errand.
>
> I myself checked on the data.

---

7. Avoid the unnecessary use of intensive/reflexive forms when an ordinary personal pronoun would suffice:

> With our permission, Jeff became the spokesman for Jim and myself. (*better:* Jim and me)
>
> John and myself are both uncomfortable with the proposal. (*better:* John and I)

Demonstrative Pronouns

Only four demonstrative pronouns exist:

	Singular	**Plural**
"near"	this	these
"far"	that	those

Demonstrative pronouns sometimes appear before a noun and sometimes they can replace the noun or noun phrase entirely:

> This design plan has problems.
>
> This has problems. (*This sentence assumes that the reader or listener knows what the word* this *refers to.*)
>
> That proposal for the DOE demonstrates effective graphics.
>
> That demonstrates effective graphics.

---

8. Avoid vague uses of demonstrative pronouns (usually when the pronoun is used without the noun it is describing):

> This is something to consider. (*better:* This shortfall in payments is something to consider.)
>
> These are difficult. (*better:* These exercises are difficult.)

NOTE: Such vague sentences are particularly annoying when, for example, a *this* refers back to an entire sentence or several things in a sentence:

> *not this*
>
> The travel plans were a jumble and even turned out to be beyond our budget. This meant that we could not make connections as planned.
>
> *this*
>
> The travel plans were a jumble and even turned out to be beyond our budget. The jumble (*or* This jumble) meant that we could not make connections as planned.

Indefinite Pronouns

Indefinite pronouns include a number of words that have unspecified or vague meanings, usually because the writer or speaker does not want to identify or can't identify the person(s) or thing(s) referred to. These sentences illustrate some of the common indefinite pronouns:

Everyone should proofread the report before we send it out.

We cleaned out **everything** before vacating the office.

Both were involved in the design tests last summer.

We determined that **somebody** had changed the entry code in the computer.

The procedures required that **anyone** leaving the security area sign and note the date and time.

Nobody had a pass to be on the construction site after normal work hours.

A list of indefinite pronouns

everyone	everything
everybody	every
each	all
both	
someone	something
somebody	somewhere
some	another
one	

anyone	anything
anybody	anywhere
either	any
no one	nothing
nobody	nowhere
none	neither
many	few
several	others
more	most

NOTE: Many of these indefinite pronouns can act very much like adjectives:

Several books were stolen from our library.

Most participants would want to attend the final session.

or

Several were stolen from our library.

Most would want to attend the final session.

---

9. Indefinite pronouns used as subjects should agree in number with their verbs:

Anyone likes to receive a positive performance review. (Anyone = *singular*; likes = *singular*)

Several were contacted before we chose a final candidate. (Several = *plural*; were = *plural*)

All of the sugar was tainted. (All of the sugar = *singular*; was = *singular*)

All of the employees were notified of the new vacation policy. (All of the employees = *plural*; were = *plural*)

NOTE: Sometimes the indefinite pronoun, even though considered grammatically singular, requires a plural pronoun:

Everyone should abandon their attempt to discover the error.

Strict editors would argue that *everyone* is singular and *their* is plural, so traditionally the correct form has been this version:

Everyone should abandon his attempt to discover the error.

Feminists and others have criticized this version as being sexist because females are ignored. One option would be to replace *his* with *his or her*. A more reasonable option is to rewrite the sentence so that it is clearly plural:

All engineers should abandon their attempts to discover the error.

See AGREEMENT and BIAS-FREE LANGUAGE. Also see the discussion above on personal pronouns.

Punctuation

Punctuation marks are as much a part of language as words. Like words, punctuation is a code that allows writers to communicate with readers who know the code.

Like words, punctuation rules (conventions) are not firm, fixed, and unchanging. The rules are evolutionary, but about 95 percent of the rules are relatively fixed and not debated as, for instance, the rule that requires the comma in *June 15, 1997*.

Punctuation rules are subject to tradition and local usage. The rules differ slightly from industry to industry and from publication to publication. The punctuation style that one publisher prefers might differ slightly from the style of another publisher.

Writers who use every permissible mark of punctuation follow a **mandatory** (formal) style. Writers who omit optional punctuation follow an **optional** (informal) style. Other terms can be and have been used to describe these two styles of punctuation: conservative vs. liberal and closed (close) vs. open.

The following examples illustrate the differences between the mandatory and optional styles.

Example 1: Commas in a Series

Writers following the optional style usually omit the comma before the *and* joining the last two items in a series:

> We requested employment figures for 1994, 1995 and 1996.

> The report analyzed the possible market in 1994–1996, the projected labor costs and the supply of raw materials.

Writers following the mandatory style always include the comma before the *and* joining the last two items in a series.

In some sentences, the comma before the *and* is not necessary, but in some sentences, omitting the comma can create ambiguity:

> The maintenance people replaced the rocker arm bracket, hinge pin and wheel assembly.

Are the hinge pin and the wheel part of the same assembly? A comma after *pin* clearly signals that the three items are separate:

> The maintenance people replaced the rocker arm bracket, hinge pin, and wheel assembly.

Because clarity and precision are so important in technical and scientific writing, we recommend that writers adopt the mandatory style and retain the comma before the *and* in a series.

Example 2: Commas in Dates

Punctuating the day, month, and year is usually simple and straightforward. A comma separates the day and the year:

> June 15, 1997

What happens, however, when the date appears in the middle of a sentence?

> We moved on June 15, 1997 into our new office.

Writers following the optional style would not insert a comma after *1997*. Writers following the mandatory style would add a comma after *1997*:

> We moved on June 15, 1997, into our new office.

Both versions are "correct." Both are acceptable because the presence or absence of the comma after *1997* does not affect clarity.

1. Use the mandatory style for most technical, scientific, and legal documents.

The mandatory style allows for more precision and can help you avoid ambiguity, so we recommend it.

We also recommend it for any formal or critical documents. In letters and memos to familiar readers, however, you might wish to follow the optional, less formal style.

Mandatory Punctuation

The following rules are those that allow for optional punctuation. Writers following the optional style might omit punctuation in the cases cited below except when clarity would suffer. If omitting punctuation would make the writing less clear, more ambiguous, or at all confusing, then use the appropriate mark of punctuation.

—Use an apostrophe and an *–s* to form the singular possessive of words of more than one syllable ending in *–s*:

> Harris's report

> Davis's plan

OPTIONAL STYLE: These possessive forms would be *Harris'* and *Davis'*. Note that the apostrophe is not optional.

—Use a comma before a coordinate conjunction to separate two independent thoughts, even when they are quite short and simple:

The plan was finished, and the budget calculated.

OPTIONAL STYLE: You would omit the comma after *finished*.

—Use a comma before the *and* that joins the last two items in a series:

We ordered two water pumps, a fan, and three replacement belts.

OPTIONAL STYLE: You would omit the comma after *fan*.

—Use a comma to enclose parenthetical expressions, even very short ones such as *thus*:

He was, thus, surprised by the answer.

OPTIONAL STYLE: You would omit both commas around *thus*.

—Use a comma after introductory phrases and clauses, even when they are very short and simple:

After we wrote the report, we submitted it.

OPTIONAL STYLE: You would omit the comma after *report*.

—Use a comma after the year in a date and the state in an address when either appears in the middle of a sentence:

The time sheets for July 6, 1997, show no overtime.

His speech in Joplin, Missouri, was most forgettable.

OPTIONAL STYLE: You would omit the commas after *1997* and *Missouri*.

—Use hyphens to form compound words that modify other words:

We will install a high-tension line above the Bradley overpass.

OPTIONAL STYLE: You would omit the hyphen between *high* and *tension*.

—Use periods after all abbreviations, including the names of government agencies, colleges and universities, and private organizations:

I.B.M.
S.U.N.Y. (State University of New York)
N.A.A.C.P.

OPTIONAL STYLE: You would omit the periods in these and most other abbreviations.

—Use a semicolon along with a coordinate conjunction to join independent clauses or complete thoughts that already contain a comma, even if they are clear without the semicolon:

Although new rain gauges helped us monitor total precipitation, we could not have anticipated the heavy spring runoff; and the resulting floods caused considerable damage to the watershed.

OPTIONAL STYLE: You would use a comma after *runoff*, not a semicolon.

For further information on commas, periods, semicolons, colons, dashes, and other marks of punctuation, see the alphabetical entries elsewhere in this *Style Guide*.

Question Marks

Question marks in English, unfortunately, are placed at the end of sentences. Spanish, to make reading easier, places an upside-down question mark at the beginning and a right-side-up question mark at the end of question sentences.

1. Use question marks to indicate direct questions:

Will analysis modeling be required?

NOTE 1: Use a separate question mark for each in a series of incomplete or elliptical questions:

When will the preliminary targeting studies be due? In 30 days? 60? 90?

NOTE 2: Use question marks at the end of statements written as declarations but intended as questions:

These are the final figures?

Regulating the supply pressure was the only realistic solution?

NOTE 3: Do *not* use question marks for indirect questions or for statements written as questions but intended as courteous requests:

During our preliminary design studies, we asked <u>whether the weapon parameters would be an integrated part of the overall system requirements</u>. (*The underlined clause is an indirect question. Its phrasing is not identical to a direct question.*)

Will you please forward five copies of DD Form 1425.

See PERIODS.

2. Use question marks to indicate questions within a sentence:

Your project managers have the authority, don't they, to reallocate resources based on changing needs?

The payment is always late, isn't it?

NOTE 1: When the question follows an introductory statement, capitalize the first word of the question and use a question mark:

The remaining question is, Can shortfalls in determining performance results be quantified with the Phase 2 synthesis procedure?

Today's manufacturer asks, How can Q&A expenses be distributed across project and functional lines?

NOTE 2: If the question precedes a concluding sentence remark, the question mark goes after the question, and the sentence remark begins with a lowercase word:

Which mission would prove most productive? was the remaining question.

3. Use question marks within parentheses to indicate doubt:

CAD/CAM was first investigated at MIT in 1964(?).

Question Marks with Other Punctuation

4. Place question marks inside quotation marks, parentheses, or brackets only when they are part of the quoted or parenthetical material:

During the preproposal conference, an Allied representative asked, "Does the Statement of Work represent a minimal subset of requirements?"

What did the contracting officer mean when she said, "The Statement of Work is the minimal subset of requirements"?

When did she ask, "Who is the project manager?" (*not* manager?"?)

The engineering program includes analysis, design, testing (fabrication?), and integration of the unit into the helicopter.

Doesn't the Program Plan call for Task F completion no later than 75 days ARO (August 17)?

See PARENTHESES, BRACKETS, and QUOTATION MARKS.

Quotation marks have multiple uses. The most common use (enclosing direct quotations) gives them their name. In earlier centuries, quotation marks did not exist and the reader could not tell easily the writer's words from the quoted words. Today, the conventions for using quotation marks are well established. See QUOTATIONS.

Quotation Marks

1. Use quotation marks to enclose direct quotations.

2. Use quotation marks to indicate the title of an article, section, volume, and other parts of a longer document.

3. Use quotation marks to indicate that a word is used in a special or abnormal sense.

4. Always place periods and commas inside of closing quotation marks.

5. Always place semicolons and colons outside of closing quotation marks.

6. Place dashes, exclamation marks, and question marks inside of quotation marks if they are part of the quotation; otherwise, place them outside of quotation marks.

1. Use quotation marks to enclose direct quotations:

> The RFP says, "All pages in the proposal must be numbered."

Direct quotations include the actual words and phrases from a document or from a person speaking.

Indirect quotations do **not** take quotation marks:

> The RFP says that all pages in the proposal have to be numbered.

Indirect quotations do not give every word and phrase in the direct quotation. Often an indirect quotation is only a paraphrase:

> The RFP says that we should number all pages in the proposal.

See QUOTATIONS.

NOTE 1: Long quotations have two equally acceptable conventions: (1) They may be enclosed by quotation marks, or (2) they may be indented from both the left and right margins (in which case they do **not** require quotation marks). If quotation marks are used and the quotation extends for more than one paragraph, quotation marks should appear at the beginning and ending of the entire quotation and at the beginning of each new paragraph within the quotation.

NOTE 2: Single quotation marks are used to indicate a quotation within a quotation:

> According to the NASA report, "National Aerodynamics argued for a 'differential scale of evolution.'"

NOTE 3: In most British publications, single quotes replace the double quotes used in U.S. publications:

> The RFP says, 'All pages in the proposal must be numbered.'

In British publications, double quotations are used to indicate a quotation within a quotation:

> According to the NASA report, 'National Aerodynamics argued for a "differential scale of evaluation."'

2. Use quotation marks to indicate the title of an article, section, volume, and other parts of a longer document:

> The contracting officer must approve all items specified under "Special Equipment" in the cost proposal.

> This volume must include a completed and signed Standard Form 33, "Solicitation, Offer, and Award."

See TITLES.

3. Use quotation marks to indicate that a word is used in a special or abnormal sense:

> The 1994 study suggested that NASA's definition of "suitability" contradicts the goals of the program.

> Only in English do "thin chance" and "fat chance" mean the same.

NOTE: Italics (or underlining) can replace quotation marks when you want to refer to a word as a word:

> In the contract, *boundaries* refers only to those property lines surveyed after July 1995.

See ITALICS and UNDERLINING.

Quotation Marks with Other Punctuation

4. Always place periods and commas inside of closing quotation marks:

We have completed the section entitled "Representations, Certifications, and Acknowledgments."

The logarithmic decrease of the differential threshold is sometimes mistakenly called "Fechner's law."

NOTE: This convention seems illogical, but it is now standard in the United States. The convention developed because printers wanted to put the smaller periods and commas inside of the closing quotation marks for a cleaner appearance on the page.

British usage places commas and periods inside or outside the quotation marks, depending on whether they are or are not part of the quotation:

The logarithmic decrease of the differential threshold is sometimes mistakenly called 'Fechner's law'.

A phrase on the cover, 'Recommended by the Royal Academy', caught her eye.

5. Always place semicolons and colons outside of closing quotation marks:

The corporation's experience belongs under "Related Experience"; the project manager's experience belongs under "Resumes of Key Personnel."

Include the following under "Manhours and Materials":

a. Work statement tasks
b. Estimated completion schedule
c. Materials/equipment required

6. Place dashes, exclamation marks, and question marks inside of quotation marks if they are part of the quotation; otherwise, place them outside of quotation marks:

The section entitled "Personnel Qualifications"—the only part of the proposal where we can address the team's APL experience—is restricted to five pages.

He said, "Can we improve the unload utilities without losing the language interface?"

See QUESTION MARKS and SPACING.

Quotations are an effective tool when you have to refer persuasively to data and conclusions from another document.

When you quote from another document, be careful not to misrepresent the content and the intent of the original passage. The following rules are suggestions. You must judge for yourself if you are accurately representing the original document.

Quotations

1. Quote only the key or relevant passages.

2. Cite the sources for any quoted material—from words and phrases to whole sentences and paragraphs.

3. Distinguish carefully between direct and indirect quotations.

4. Use brackets to insert comments or corrections in quoted material.

---

1. Quote only the key or relevant passages:

> Your letter made an excellent case for the "procedural lapse" that caused the double billing to your account.

> In the analysis of the data, Jameson (1995) argues for three "equally persuasive hypotheses."

NOTE 1: Sometimes a two- or three-word phrase is sufficient to capture the flavor of the original document. Rarely do you need to quote whole sentences or paragraphs from the original document.

Long quotes distract the reader and often signal that the writer has not done the work necessary to boil the quotation down to its essentials.

NOTE 2: As illustrated in the two examples above, all quoted words, phrases, and sentences should normally be enclosed by quotation marks. See QUOTATION MARKS.

NOTE 3: In cases where words are omitted from the middle of quoted material, an ellipsis signals material has been omitted. See ELLIPSES.

> Your letter made an excellent case for the "procedural lapse . . . and the sloppy record keeping" that caused the double billing of your account. (*The original read:* ". . . the procedural lapse when my account was opened and the sloppy record keeping ever since.")

2. Cite the sources for any quoted material—from words and phrases to whole sentences and paragraphs.

Inexperienced writers sometimes are careless in their citations.

No material from another source, especially copyrighted material, should ever appear in another document without full and adequate credit being given to the original author(s). See ETHICS and INTELLECTUAL PROPERTY.

No reader should ever have to guess what is original and what the writer is borrowing. Accurate citations and accurate use of quotation marks and ellipses can remove uncertainties. See CITATIONS and FOOTNOTES.

---

3. Distinguish carefully between direct and indirect quotations.

Direct quotations contain only the original words and phrases of the document being quoted.

Indirect quotations are a summary of someone else's words. Some minor words may come from the original, but the writer has made significant changes. Even then, key words should appear within quotation marks.

Below is an original passage. Following are examples of a direct quotation and an indirect quotation:

Original passage

Hank Stevens was over 30 minutes late three times during the week of November 3. He called in on one of these mornings, but we received no calls on the other two mornings. Although it is now November 15, he has given no satisfactory excuse or explanation of his lateness.

Direct quotation

According to Hank Stevens' supervisor, Hank has failed to give a "satisfactory excuse or explanation of his lateness" on three mornings during the week of November 3. Hank did call in one of the mornings, but he did not call in the other two mornings.

Indirect quotation

According to Hank Stevens' supervisor, Hank has not explained adequately his three instances of lateness during the week of November 3. Hank was over 30 minutes late in each case, and he only called in one time.

NOTE 1: As this example illustrates, the direct quotation is often embedded in a passage that contains some indirect quotations. As rule 1 above indicates, you should quote only the pertinent words and phrases.

NOTE 2: Often changing from direct to indirect quotations involves changing syntax and wording (especially in the pronouns):

Direct quotation

"We need to receive your response by no later than January 15, 1997."

Indirect quotation

MOGO Oil said that they must have our written response by January 15, 1997.

Direct quotation

"I have been unable to locate the original data collected in 1989. The files seem not to have been moved when we moved in 1994 from the old building to our present building."

Indirect quotation

Gene Sayers has been unable to find the original 1989 data. He suspects that the files were not moved in 1994 when we moved into our present building.

---

4. Use brackets to insert comments or corrections in quoted material:

"The measured length [8.35 feet] differs from the length specified in the specification."

"Ralph Stevenson [Stephenson] was the representative elected from Curry County."

See BRACKETS.

Redundant Words

Redundant words or phrases unnecessarily qualify other words or phrases.

For instance, in the expression *basic fundamentals*, the word *basic* is unnecessary because, by definition, all fundamentals are basic.

Past experience is redundant because for experience to be experience, it must have been acquired in the past. *Past history* is redundant for the same reason. You can't have present or future history. All history is past. However, *ancient history* and *recent history* are acceptable because they both refer to specific parts of the past.

Redundant words or phrases are not the same as deliberate repetition. Repetition occurs when writers choose to repeat key words and phrases throughout a document. These key words and phrases usually appear in major headings or in summaries. See REPETITION.

1. Eliminate redundant words.

A fundamental of good writing style is to eliminate unnecessary words. Do not say *main essentials*. Just say *essentials*. Do not speak of the *final conclusion*. It is simply the *conclusion*. Documents are not *attached together*. They are simply *attached*. See WORDY PHRASES.

2. Use redundant words to emphasize or dramatize a situation or condition:

> Mailing the ramjet study by Friday is absolutely essential.

The only proper use of redundancies in writing is to emphasize. The expression *absolutely essential* is redundant because nothing can be

more essential than *essential*. If you need to heighten the sense of urgency in a situation by exaggerating, then redundant words are acceptable. However, do **not** overuse redundancies for emphasis. The effect diminishes quickly. You can become so exaggerated in your style that readers pay less attention to your ideas. Too much emphasis becomes no emphasis. See EMPHASIS and GOBBLEDYGOOK.

A List of Redundancies

The following list of redundancies will help you identify those you habitually use. The redundant expression appears in the left column; in the right column are possible substitutes:

Absolutely complete	complete
absolutely essential	essential
absolutely nothing	nothing
accidentally stumbled	stumbled
a.c. current	a.c./alternating current
actual experience	experience
adequate enough	adequate/enough
advance forward	advance
advance planning	planning
aluminum metal	aluminum
and etc.	etc.
any and all	any/all
arrive on the scene	arrive
ask the question	ask
assembled together	assembled
attached hereto	attached
attach together	attach
Basic fundamentals	fundamentals
before in the past	before/in the past
betwixt and between	between
blue in color	blue
brief in duration	brief/quick/fast
Check up on	check
circle around	circle
close proximity	proximity
collect together	collect
combine together	combine

completely destroyed	destroyed
completely opposite	opposite
connect together	connect
consensus of opinion	consensus
consequent results	results
consolidate together	consolidate
continue on	continue
continue to remain	remain
contributing factor	factor
cooperate together	cooperate
couple together	couple
Desirable benefits	benefits
diametrically opposite	opposite
disappear from sight	disappear
disregard altogether	disregard
Each and every	each/every
early beginnings	beginnings
empty cavity	cavity
enclosed herewith	enclosed
endorse on the back	endorse
end product	product
end result	result
entirely destroyed	destroyed
equally as good	as good/equally good
exactly identical	identical
expired and terminated	expired/terminated
extremely immoderate	immoderate
Fast in action	fast
few in number	few
filled to capacity	filled
final completion	completion
final conclusion	conclusion
finally ended	ended
first beginnings	beginnings
following after	following/after
funeral obsequies	obsequies
fused together	fused
Heat up	heat
hidden pitfall	pitfall
hopeful optimism	hope/optimism
Important essentials	essentials
Joint cooperation	cooperation
join together	join
joint partnership	partnership
just exactly	just/exactly
Large in size	large
large-sized	large
lift up	lift
living incarnation	incarnation

Redundant Words

Main essentials	essentials	Qualified expert	expert	Ten miles distant from	ten miles from
melt down	melt			three hours of time	three hours
mingle together	mingle	Really and truly	really	throughout the entire	throughout
mix together	mix	reason is because	reason is that/because	throughout the whole	throughout
more preferable	preferable	recur again	recur	total of ten	ten
mutual cooperation	cooperation	red in color	red	to the northward	north/northward
		reduce down	reduce	traverse across	traverse
Necessary requisite	requisite	regress back	regress	true fact	fact
new innovation	innovation	remand back	remand		
		repeat again	repeat	Ultimate end	end
One and the same	the same	resultant effect	effect	universal the world over	universal
one definite reason	one reason			unsolved problem	problem
one particular example	one example	Same identical	same		
one specific case	one case	seems apparent	seems/is apparent	Visit with	visit
		separate and distinct	separate/distinct		
Part and parcel	part	shuttle back and forth	shuttle	Ways and means	ways/means
past experience	experience	single unit	unit	where you are at	where you are
period of time	period	skirt around	skirt	where are you at	where are you
personal friend	friend	small in size	small		
personal opinion	opinion	small-sized	small		
pervade the whole	pervade	specific example	example		
plan ahead	plan	still continue	continue		
plan for the future	plan	still remains	remains		
plan in advance	plan	suddenly collapsed	collapsed		
postponed until later	postponed	summer months	summer		
presently planned	planned	surprising upset	upset		
prolong the duration	prolong	surrounding circumstances	circumstances		
		surround on all sides	surround		

References

References are essential because writers must constantly choose between different styles and different ways of saying something. References help writers make proper choices.

This *Style Guide* will answer many of your stylistic questions and will help you to become a more effective writer. However, for further information, including far more exhaustive treatments of some stylistic issues, refer to the books listed below. These references are among the finest available in their special areas. Some of the references listed might not be in print currently, but are available in libraries. Often books go out of print while a new edition is in preparation.

Dictionaries

An up-to-date dictionary is an essential writer's tool. Besides providing correct spellings, a dictionary gives definitions, pronunciations, word origins, synonyms, and guidance on word division and usage.

Most of the dictionaries listed below are abridged dictionaries written for general readers as well as readers in colleges and universities. The exception is *Webster's Third New International Dictionary of the English Language, Unabridged;* this dictionary was completed in 1961 and has been reprinted and updated many times since. This dictionary is still the best reference for American English.

Some general dictionaries are directed toward specific users. For example, the *Oxford Student's Dictionary of American English* has been prepared for non-English-speaking students. The entries are brief and very clear, and special attention is given to simple idioms (phrases) that have special meanings.

References

Dictionaries
    Specialized Dictionaries
Online References
    Public Online References
    Private Online References
Spelling Guides

Thesauruses
General Style Guides
    Specialized Style Guides
Grammar and Usage Handbooks
Books on Writing

The American Heritage Dictionary. 1983. 2d college ed. New York: Houghton Mifflin Company.

Hornby, A. S. *Oxford Student's Dictionary of American English.* 1986. New York: Oxford University Press.

Random House College Dictionary. 1989. New York: Random House, Inc.

Webster's Tenth Collegiate Dictionary. 1995. 10th ed. Springfield, Massachusetts: G. & C. Merriam.

Webster's New World Dictionary. 1988. 2d college ed. New York: World Publishing Company.

Webster's Third New International Dictionary of the English Language, Unabridged. 1986. Springfield, Massachusetts: G. & C. Merriam.

Specialized Dictionaries

In addition to those dictionaries listed above, many professional groups or disciplines have specialized dictionaries that list the technical terms and jargon particular to their professional area. Following are a few of these specialized dictionaries.

Black's Law Dictionary. 1990. 6th ed. Henry Campbell Black. St. Paul, Minnesota: West Publishing Co.

Dictionary of Geological Terms. 1984. 3d rev. ed. Garden City, New York: Anchor Press.

Glossary of Geology. 1990. 3d ed. Ed. by Robert L. Bates and Julia A. Jackson. Falls Church, Virginia: American Geological Institute.

The Illustrated Petroleum Reference Dictionary. 1985. 3d ed. Ed. by R. D. Langenkamp. Tulsa, Oklahoma: PennWell Publishing Company.

Langenkamp, R. D. 1984. *Handbook of Oil Industry Terms and Phrases.* 4th ed. Tulsa, Oklahoma: PennWell Publishing Company.

Mathematics into Type. Rev. ed. 1987. Providence, Rhode Island: Mathematical Society.

McGraw-Hill Dictionary of Scientific and Technical Terms. 1989. 4th ed. Ed. by Sybil P. Parker. New York: McGraw-Hill Book Company.

Macmillan Visual Desk Reference. 1993. Prepared by the Diagram Group. New York: Macmillan Publishing Company.

Webster's New Geographical Dictionary. 1988. Springfield, Massachusetts: G. & C. Merriam.

Online References

Online references are services for retrieving information via computer. They consist of groups of computers capable of transferring information by telephone lines. Some online references are public and some are private commercial networks.

Users can access an immense range of business and financial information through online services. University library catalogs are often open, as well as government information centers. The United States government servers, for example, provide lists of current publications, personnel, contracts up for bid, and so forth.

Public Online References

Internet. A consortium of private companies, government agencies, and universities. Accounts can be obtained through universities that belong to the Internet or through private firms called "servers."

Biznet. American Business Network, the online database of the U.S. Chamber of Commerce.

Private Online References

CompuServ specializes in providing business and technical support to business users.

America Online and *Prodigy* are aimed at the home computer market, providing services like online newspapers, financial market information, and so forth.

Spelling Guides

Spelling guides are alphabetized lists of words meant primarily for persons who need to check spelling or word division.

10,000 Medical Words: Spelled and Divided for Quick Reference. 1972. New York: McGraw-Hill Book Company.

20,000 Words: Spelled and Divided for Quick Reference. 1985. 8th ed. New York: McGraw-Hill Book Company.

Webster's Instant Word Guide. 1980. Springfield, Massachusetts: Merriam-Webster, Inc.

Webster's Medical Speller. 1987. 2d ed. Springfield, Massachusetts: Merriam-Webster, Inc.

Thesauruses

A thesaurus provides synonyms and often antonyms. Use a thesaurus when you need to find optional ways of expressing an idea, when you can't think of a word but know the word exists, or when the only word you can think of is not exactly correct and you need to find a more precise alternative. Do not use a thesaurus to find bigger words than the ones you can think of. In other words, don't try to sound impressive by finding and using big words. See GOBBLEDYGOOK.

The New Roget's Thesaurus in Dictionary Form. 1989. Ed. by Philip D. Morehead. New York: New American Library.

The Random House Thesaurus. 1993. Ed. by Jess Stein and Stuart B. Flexner. New York: Random House.

Roget's II: The New Thesaurus. 1989. New York: Houghton Mifflin Company.

Webster's New Dictionary of Synonyms. 1984. 2d ed. Springfield, Massachusetts: Merriam-Webster, Inc.

General Style Guides

This *Style Guide* is a general style guide. However, it differs from those listed below in that it provides much more information about effective writing techniques and the writing process, and it provides models of effective letters, memos, and other documents.

General style guides are, next to an up-to-date dictionary, the best resources for writers. They usually cover punctuation, abbreviations, spelling problems, capitalization, and special signs and symbols. In addition, each of those listed below has special features. *The Chicago Manual of Style*, for instance, has a long discussion of printing and binding. The *United States Government Printing Office Style Manual* has special guidelines for Congressional publications and a fine chapter on word compounds.

The Chicago Manual of Style. 1994. 14th ed. Chicago: The University of Chicago Press.

Chicago Guide to Preparing Electronic Manuscripts for Authors and Publishers. 1987. Chicago: The University of Chicago Press.

DeVries, Mary A. 1993. *Complete Secretary's Handbook.* 7th ed. Englewood Cliffs, New Jersey: Prentice Hall.

The Economist Style Guide. 1993. London: The Economist Books Ltd.

Garner, Diane L., and Diane H. Smith. 1993. *The Complete Guide to Citing Government Resources: A Manual for Writers and Librarians.* Betheseda, Maryland: American Library Association.

The Gregg Reference Manual. 1992. 7th ed. Ed. by William A. Sabin. Westerville, Ohio: Glenroe Division, McMillan/McGraw-Hill Book Company.

Jaderstrom, Susan, Leonard Kruk, and Joanne Miller. 1992. *Professional Secretaries International® Complete Office Handbook.* New York: Random House.

The McGraw-Hill Style Manual: A Concise Guide for Writers and Editors. 1989. Ed. by Marie Longyear. New York: McGraw-Hill Book Company.

References

The New York Public Library Writer's Guide to Style and Usage. 1994. New York: New York Public Library and The Stonesong Press, Inc.

The Secretary's Handbook. 1988. 10th ed. Revised by Margaret D. Shertzer. New York: Macmillan Publishing Company.

United States Government Printing Office. 1984. *Style Manual.* Washington, D.C.: United States Government Printing Office.

Wired Style: Principles of English Usage in the Digital Age. 1996. From the Editors of *Wired.* Ed. by Constance Hale. San Francisco, California: Hardwired.

Words into Type. 1989. 3d ed. Ed. by M. Skillin and R. Gay. Englewood Cliffs, New Jersey: Prentice-Hall, Inc.

Specialized Style Guides

Specialized style guides are those intended for a particular professional group. Despite their special audience, they usually also cover basic punctuation and other items of general interest.

American Chemical Society. 1997. *The ACS Style Guide: A Manual for Authors and Editors.* 2nd ed. Washington, D.C.: American Chemical Society.

American Psychological Association. 1994. *Publication Manual.* 4th ed. Washington, D.C.: American Psychological Association.

Council of Biology Editors. 1994. *CBE Style Manual.* 6th ed. Cambridge, UK: Cambridge University Press for the: Council for Biology Editors, Inc.

Swanson, Ellen. 1987. *Mathematics into Type: Copyediting and Proofreading of Mathematics for Editorial Assistants and Authors.* Rev. ed. Providence, Rhode Island: American Mathematical Society.

U.S. Geological Survey. 1978. *Suggestions to Authors of the Reports of the United States Geological Survey.* 6th ed. Washington, D.C.: Government Printing Office.

Zweifel, Frances W. 1988. 2d ed. *A Handbook of Biological Illustration.* Chicago: University of Chicago Press, Phoenix Books.

Grammar and Usage Handbooks

Grammar handbooks, especially those intended for college students, survey the principles of English grammar and provide many do's and don'ts for writers. The Harbrace and Random House grammar books listed below are only two of the many such current books available in bookstores.

Usage handbooks provide rules for the proper use of words. Such rules quite often reflect the authors' prejudices, so keep that in mind as you use such handbooks. The best and most comprehensive usage reference is *Webster's Dictionary of English Usage.*

The American Heritage® Book of English Usage. 1996. New York: Houghton Mifflin Company.

Fowler, Henry Watson. 1987. *Dictionary of Modern English Usage.* 2d rev. Ed. by Sir Ernest Gowers. Oxford: Oxford University Press.

The Handbook of Nonsexist Writing for Writers, Editors, and Speakers. 1988. Casey Miller and Kate Swift. 2d ed. New York: Harper & Row Publishers, Inc.

Harbrace College Handbook. 1986. 10th ed. Ed. by John C. Hodges and Mary E. Whitten. New York: Harcourt Brace Jovanovich, Inc.

Quirk, Randolph, Sidney Greenbaum, Geoffrey Leech, and Jan Svartvik. 1985. *A Comprehensive Grammar of the English Language.* New York: Longman, Inc.

Random House Handbook. 1988. 5th ed. Ed. by Frederick Crews. New York: McGraw-Hill Book Company.

Webster's Dictionary of English Usage. 1989. Springfield, Massachusetts: Merriam-Webster, Inc.

Books on Writing

The following books cover writing, both as a process and as a final product. Strunk and White's book is perhaps the most famous and the most readable book of those listed, but the others are also valuable.

Flesch, Rudolf. 1986. *Art of Readable Writing.* Rev. ed. New York: Macmillan.

Strunk, W., Jr., and E. B. White. 1979. *The Elements of Style.* 3d ed. New York: Macmillan.

Tichy, H. J. and Sylvia Fourdrinier. 1988. *Effective Writing for Engineers, Managers, Scientists.* 2d ed. New York: John Wiley & Sons.

Williams, Joseph M. 1989. *Style: Ten Lessons in Clarity and Grace.* 3d ed. Glenview, Illinois: Scott, Foresman and Company.

Zinsser, William Knowlton. 1985. *On Writing Well: An Informal Guide to Writing Nonfiction.* 3d ed. New York: Harper & Row Publishers, Inc.

Repetition is sometimes considered a trait of poor writing. Actually, repetition can be a valuable emphasis technique. It can enhance the impact and readability of a document.

Effective repetition of a fact or idea reinforces it in the reader's mind. See ORGANIZATION, EMPHASIS, and KEY WORDS.

---

1. Repeat key words and phrases throughout a document without changing them in any way.

Paraphrasing an idea, no matter how well done, is not as good as exact repetition. In technical and business documents, exact repetition should be the goal.

For example, if you open a document with a list of topics to be discussed, the wording of this list should be identical to the wording of subheads in the document.

In the Introduction on page 1:

Strategies for the Control of Costs

Subhead 3 on page 5:

3.0 Strategies for the Control of Costs

---

2. Design documents with clear and deliberate repetition in mind.

As you design a document and organize your ideas, build in effective repetition. Consider repeating (1) key requests or recommendations, (2) major conclusions, and (3) most important or most convincing facts.

Repetition

1. Repeat key words and phrases throughout a document without changing them in any way.

2. Design documents with clear and deliberate repetition in mind.

3. Use the inherent repetition in formal report structure to reinforce major ideas and to strengthen logic and impact.

4. Use repetition when you want to emphasize the logic behind a discussion, especially when details are parallel in their intent.

5. Be careful not to repeat an idea too soon after stating it the first time. The rule applies to more traditional text, where one paragraph flows into another.

Most professionals in the world of work have more documents crossing their desks than they have time to read. Research shows that the majority of intended readers skim through the documents they receive. Rarely do they read the documents in depth, and almost never will they read something more than once.

Consequently, you must convey your important ideas quickly and emphatically. Repeating key requests, recommendations, conclusions, and facts helps to ensure that readers who skim will not miss the most important ideas in your documents.

---

3. Use the inherent repetition in formal report structure to reinforce major ideas and to strengthen logic and impact.

Technical and other formal reports are structured for deliberate repetition. The writer's conclusions, for instance, typically appear in these sections of the report: abstract, executive summary, conclusions, and discussion. The recommendations will appear one way or the other in the abstract, executive summary, and perhaps the discussion. They will also appear in their own section.

Repetition in reports is deliberate. It allows readers to read selectively. Some readers will read the abstract and will not need to read further. Others will read the executive summary and perhaps the conclusions and recommendations sections. Still others will glance at the results section and then read through the discussion.

Because reports are deliberately repetitive, all of these readers will have encountered the major conclusions and recommendations. Those who read the major conclusions and recommendations more than once will have had those ideas reinforced. See REPORTS.

---

4. Use repetition when you want to emphasize the logic behind a discussion, especially when details are parallel in their intent.

Repetition of a key word or phrase indicates that a sequence of ideas is parallel:

> Skillful writers have a clear sense of purpose. Skillful writers are aware of their readers' wants, needs, and concerns. Skillful writers can choose between many stylistic options. In short, skillful writers focus their task and use the right techniques to create the right effect.

This kind of repetition is effective in emphasizing key points and limiting sentence length. (Imagine how difficult this passage would be to read if it were a single sentence.) Beware of using this kind of repetition too often, however. With much repetition, the effect diminishes and the writing begins to sound unnatural. See Parallelism, Key Words, and Emphasis.

5. Be careful not to repeat an idea too soon after stating it the first time. The rule applies to more traditional text, where one paragraph flows into another.

Consider the following example:

> *this*
>
> In my opinion, the Rothskeller algorithm will not alleviate error detection inaccuracies. The mathematical model proposed does not adequately account for errors introduced by migrant electrons. These electrons interact randomly with bits and can change bit patterns in fundamental and disastrous ways. Superior error detection techniques not only must minimize the mushrooming effect of errors compounded by repetition of a bit sequence (which Rothskeller does very effectively) but also must account for random errors that may inadvertently be replicated hundreds of times.
>
> The Rothskeller algorithm for random error detection identifies logical bit pattern inconsistencies and applies logic correction.
>
> However, its identification strategies assume that errors will be of predictable types. Nonpredictable logic errors, caused by random migrant electrons, can go undetected. Therefore, I do not believe that the Rothskeller algorithm will alleviate error detection inaccuracies.

The repeated idea (first and last sentences) is separated by lengthy discussion. Someone reading the preceding passage will be less likely to find the repetition obtrusive.

> *not this*
>
> In my opinion, the Rothskeller algorithm will not alleviate error detection inaccuracies. The mathematical model proposed does not account for errors introduced by migrant electrons. Therefore, I do not think that the Rothskeller algorithm will alleviate error detection inaccuracies.

This is poor repetition because the repeated idea (first and last sentences) is repeated too quickly.

Reports cover a broad range of business and technical documents, including formal reports, scientific reports (often published), corporate technical reports (following internal guidelines), progress reports, trip reports, laboratory and research reports, accident reports, memorandum reports, and financial reports.

Many of these reports are periodic documents that convey the status of a program, project, task, study, or other organizational effort. Other reports are written in response to specific needs and situations.

Some reports are more informal than others, but readers of reports generally expect to find certain information (summaries, conclusions, recommendations, analyses, supporting facts, etc.), and they expect the report's tone to be businesslike—not officious or bureaucratic, but objective, factual, and honest. See TONE.

Formal reports have traditional components, which are discussed below. For further information relevant to reports, see MEMOS, ORGANIZATION, and GRAPHICS FOR DOCUMENTS.

Scientific Reports

Scientific reports are tightly controlled by scientific convention and tradition. Many scientific reports are published by professional groups and conferences, and many appear in technical or scientific journals. These professional organizations usually have explicit editorial guidelines that writers must follow.

The tradition of the scientific method dictates the format of most scientific reports:

Abstract
Introduction
Materials and Methods

Reports

```
Results and Discussion
    Fact 1
    Fact 2
    Fact 3
    (therefore)
Conclusions
Recommendations (if any)
Summary (optional)
```

This format is roughly chronological—moving from the problem to be solved, to the test design (including materials as well as methods), to the test results, to an analysis of the results, and finally to the conclusions.

This logical pattern roughly duplicates the process the scientist used while conducting the study. Ideally, readers should be able to duplicate the process themselves and reach the same conclusions.

In scientific reports, the process of arriving at the conclusions is generally as important as the conclusions themselves. And the pattern of the scientific report tends to reinforce the equal importance of process and conclusions. In doing so, however, it delays the conclusions, which many readers would consider the most important ideas in the report.

The logic behind scientific reports is inductive: *fact, fact, fact (therefore) conclusions.* This pattern is effective, but it is also suspenseful—and that's the major drawback to the scientific format. See ORGANIZATION.

Most business and technical readers are too busy to be held in suspense. They want to know what's important right away. If they want to read a good mystery, they'll read Agatha Christie.

So, avoid the scientific format unless you are a scientist writing for other scientists.

In fairness, we should note that reports of all kinds are typically divided into clearly marked sections, and most readers never read the entire report anyway. They read selected sections, depending upon their needs. If readers of scientific reports want to know the conclusions first, they go to the section entitled "Conclusions."

Reports

The inductive mode of thought behind the scientific format is contrary to the way most readers want to encounter information. For most readers you should use the far more common format found in standard technical reports.

Technical Reports

Technical and scientific reports often share many features, but technical reports usually differ from scientific reports in several crucial respects:

—They are distributed within an organization and are generally not formally published.

—They are intended for internal use only (many are even proprietary) or have a very limited distribution outside the parent organization.

—Their readers are decision makers and others who need to have all the important information (key findings, conclusions, and recommendations) right away. They may not be at all interested in how the writer arrived at that important information.

Technical report formats usually follow a managerial format, which emphasizes the conclusions and recommendations by placing them at the beginning of the report and subordinates the results and discussion:

```
Executive Summary
Introduction
Materials and Methods (Optional)
Conclusions
Recommendations (if any)
    (because of)
Results and Discussion
    Fact 1
    Fact 2
    Fact 3
Summary (optional)
```

The managerial format opens with a summary (often called an executive summary) that presents a distillation of the report's most important ideas. Following the summary, writers often provide a list of conclusions and recommendations so that busy managers and supervisors have to read no further to discover the essence of the report.

The managerial format follows an inverted logic: *conclusion (based on) fact, fact, fact.* If readers wish, they can read the facts to determine how the writer arrived at the conclusion. But they don't have to. They can read the conclusion alone and then go on to something else. See ORGANIZATION.

Decision makers are almost always part of the audience for technical reports, and they are usually the primary readers. So, most technical reports should follow the managerial format.

Memorandum Reports

Memorandum reports are less formal and usually shorter versions of technical reports, although both types of reports may be very similar in content. Memorandum reports almost always follow the managerial format, but they usually do not include all of the components of a standard technical report. They do not, for instance, have covers, title pages, tables of contents, lists of figures, abstracts, and other formal sections required for either scientific or technical reports. These formal sections are necessary only when reports are widely circulated or published. See MEMOS.

Parts of Reports

Scientific, technical, and some memorandum reports might include the following:

```
Letter of Transmittal
Cover
Abstract
```

```
Title Page
Preface or Foreword
Table of Contents
List of Figures
Body
Bibliography or List of References
Appendix
```

Letter of Transmittal

A letter of transmittal accompanies and introduces a report. It might explain what the report is about, why it was written, how it relates to previous reports or projects, what problems the writer encountered, why the report includes or excludes particular data, and what certain readers may find of interest.

A letter of transmittal can provide information that would not be appropriate in the report itself, especially sensitive or confidential information. Hence, different letters of transmittal may be written for different readers of the same report.

Letters of transmittal are usually brief. They tend to be less formal than the reports they transmit. However, the more formal the report, the more formal the letter of transmittal is likely to be.

Cover

Covers are appropriate on formal reports and on those intended for widespread or public distribution. The information on the cover is usually similar to the information found on the title page (see below). However, covers are usually well designed and often include artwork.

Abstract

An abstract is a very brief distillation of a report's content. It is intended to describe the report's content and sometimes to provide information about key findings, conclusions, and recommendations.

Some abstracts, especially those for published scientific reports, are primarily useful in data banks and library catalogues. Such abstracts will be printed in catalogues or bibliographies. Prospective readers should be able to determine from reading the abstract whether they would profit from reading the entire report.

Less formal abstracts often function as one-page summaries of corporate technical reports.

Actual summaries may be longer and include more information. In addition, summaries are part of the report and should not be separated from it. Abstracts, on the other hand, are not considered part of the report and should always be understandable in and of themselves.

Abstracts are usually either **descriptive** or **informative**. In either case, they present the key information in a brief paragraph or two (usually no more than about 250 words).

Descriptive Abstracts

Descriptive abstracts describe the content of the report but do not include interpretive statements, conclusions, or recommendations:

> The report analyzes the effects of caffeine on three groups of heart patients: (1) those with diagnosed hypertension and initial signs of heart trouble, (2) those using blood pressure medication but who have not had surgery, and (3) those having had heart surgery. The report discusses the correlation between caffeine and variations in blood pressure for these three groups.

This abstract describes the general scope of the research but does not provide results or conclusions.

Informative Abstracts

Informative abstracts are generally longer and more comprehensive than descriptive abstracts. Typically, they describe the research or project and summarize key results and conclusions:

> Caffeine, in moderate amounts (no more than two cups of coffee per day), has no significant impact on patients with heart problems (ranging from those with diagnosed hypertension to those having had actual heart surgery). Beyond two cups, however, the impacts become increasingly severe. Patients with recent heart surgery showed the most effects, including very high blood pressure and chest pains. Patients on blood pressure medication could cancel the effects of the medication by drinking more than two cups of coffee. Patients with diagnosed hypertension showed elevated blood pressure for up to 3 hours after drinking over two cups of coffee. In conclusion, the effects of caffeine increased substantially with every cup of coffee beyond the two-cup threshold.

In this (fictitious) informative abstract, readers interested in the subject can determine if they would want to read the full report. Informative abstracts provide key results and conclusions. Consequently, if the research techniques are obvious, knowledgeable readers may need no more than the abstract.

If you have a choice, always write an informative abstract. See SUMMARIES.

Title Page

The title page can contain the following information:

—The title of the report

—The name of the person(s) writing the report

—The name of the person(s) for whom the report is prepared

—The date of submission

—The name of the division, group, or department, as well as the name of the organization

—A research number or other documentation aid

—A list of key words for cataloguing or for a computer search

—A copyright notice and other special notations (such as *SECRET* or *PROPRIETARY INFORMATION*)

Preface or Foreword

Prefaces or forewords (they are the same) generally appear only in formal or published reports—and often not even there. Informal and memorandum reports rarely include a preface or foreword. If used, a preface or foreword can include the following:

—References to other researchers or reports to which the author is indebted

—Background information regarding the origin of the report—such as who requested it, who funded it, what the goals were, and so on

—Acknowledgment of contributors, including other researchers, managers, technicians, reviewers, editors, proofreaders, and so on

—Financial implications

—Observations regarding unusual conclusions or recommendations

—Miscellaneous personal comments about the contents, including areas for future study

Table of Contents

The table of contents is an outline of the report.

It helps readers understand the structure of the report and locate particular sections. It helps writers organize their thoughts (or check their organization).

A table of contents should contain enough second- and third-level headings to capture the actual content and approach of the chapters. Chapter headings by themselves are often too cryptic:

not this

I. Introduction

II. Preliminary Conditions

III. Governmental Controls

this

I. Introduction

   A. Corporate Policy on Experiments with Animals

   B. Precedents for this Research

   C. Guidelines and Goals of this Research

II. Preliminary Conditions

   A. Physiological Profiles of the Test Animals

   B. Structure of Control and Experimental Groups

   C. Checks and Balances in the Research Procedures

III. Governmental Controls

   A. Documentation Needed for Report to the FDA

   B. External Verification of Results

   C. Legal Penalties for Failure to Report

See TABLES OF CONTENTS.

List of Figures (or Tables or Maps)

A list of figures (or tables or maps) is necessary only if the report is extensive and contains many of these or other visual aids. See GRAPHICS FOR DOCUMENTS.

If used, the list of figures appears on a separate page following the table of contents. (NOTE: The table of contents should include the list of figures and its page number.) See TABLES OF CONTENTS.

Tables and figures are usually listed separately, so if you list tables, do so in a List of Tables.

Figures include charts, graphs, maps, photographs, and diagrams. If you have a large number of any particular type of figure, you can list them as separate types of visuals:

List of Maps
List of Charts
List of Photographs

Number tables and figures (and other specific types of visuals) separately, and number them sequentially as they appear in the report. See CAPTIONS.

NOTE: If your report has large separate sections, you can number visuals sequentially within each section. See CAPTIONS.

Body

The body of a report can follow either the scientific format or the managerial format. (See the opening section of this discussion of REPORTS, and also see ORGANIZATION.)

We recommend the managerial organization for most internal reports and many external reports.

Scientific Organization

Abstract
Introduction
Materials and Methods
Results and Discussion
Conclusions
Recommendations (if any)
Summary (optional)

Managerial Organization

Executive Summary
Introduction
Conclusions
Recommendations
Materials and Methods (optional)
Results and Discussion
Summary (optional)

See ORGANIZATION and SUMMARIES.

Summary and Executive Summary

Traditionally, the summary appeared at the end of the report. In the scientific format, the summary still appears at the end (if it appears at all). Its purpose at the end of a report is to "sum up" the major ideas presented, and to remind readers what was important about what they read—the key findings, the conclusions, and any recommendations.

Summaries at the beginning of a report are becoming more common. They are highly desirable in reports directed to managers and supervisors.

Quite often, this opening summary is called an "executive summary." The title indicates clearly how this summary is meant to be read and who is meant to read it. It opens the body of a report written in the managerial format. If well done, the executive summary includes everything a busy manager or supervisor needs to know to make a decision. The detailed results and data often appear only as an appendix. Consequently, a good executive summary in effect makes the rest of the report superfluous—and it should be. If you are writing well, readers should not have to read beyond your summaries unless they have a particular need for the detail that follows.

The information in a summary must be consistent with information appearing throughout the body of the report. Furthermore, you should have nothing in the summary that does not also appear elsewhere in the report.

Summaries are always part of the body of a report. Abstracts, on the other hand, should always be able to stand by themselves. See SUMMARIES.

Introduction

The introduction sets the stage. It normally includes the historical background of the report (and the project or program being reported) and establishes the scope of the report. The introduction may also define special terms and discuss the report's relation to other reports or research efforts.

Introductions also discuss the content and organization of the report. In other words, the introduction tells readers what the report contains and where to find it. In essence, the introduction is a road map.

If the report does not contain a preface, some of the items covered in the preface may also appear in the introduction:

—Person or group authorizing the research

—Contributors, especially other researchers

—Financial implications

—Noteworthy points about the conclusions and recommendations

—Other special items of interest

One major difference between an introduction and a summary is that the introduction does not contain the conclusions and recommendations. Another major difference is that a summary does not provide background information or lay out the structure of the report. See INTRODUCTIONS.

Materials and Methods

This section includes the materials and methods used during the experiment, study, or project. Limit this section to those materials and methods unfamiliar to knowledgeable readers. If the materials and methods are standard, you can mention them briefly in the introduction and then omit this section.

Results and Discussion

This section presents relevant data, discusses the meaning and significance of the data, makes inferences, and states the conclusions. If you have a lot of raw data to present, place it in an appendix and extract only the most important data to present in this section.

In some reports, especially formal scientific reports, the results are separate from the discussion.

Conclusion

This section brings together everything in the report and states your convictions. Every conclusion should grow out of information elsewhere in the report. Without such logical support, readers will justifiably feel that you have failed to accomplish the goals of the research.

Recommendations

Recommendations are suggestions for future actions—either managerial action or future research. Recommendations are almost always present in reports directed to corporate managers and supervisors.

In some cases, conclusions and recommendations are presented in a single section.

Bibliography or List of References

A bibliography or list of references is necessary only in more formal reports or in reports with a number of references.

If you have only two or three references, cover them fully in the text:

> As George Stevens established in "The Life Cycle of the Toad" (*Animal Physiology*, X [March 1983] 234–237), toads have very low metabolic levels.

See CITATIONS and BIBLIOGRAPHIES for full information on the use of parenthetical citations and for different ways to list bibliographic entries.

Appendix

The appendix is for information that is not properly part of the text or is too lengthy to be included in the text (voluminous data, computer programs, lengthy descriptions of methods, etc.).

If information in the appendix is of more than one kind, use two or more appendices, each identified by letter and title:

> Appendix A—Graphs
> Appendix B—Photographs
> Appendix C—Programs

Ensure that you always mention the appendices in the text. Where a reference to an appendix would help readers, identify which appendix is appropriate and what the reader can expect to find there:

> Appendix E presents raw distillation data.
>
> For further information regarding these formulas, see appendix B.
>
> The names and addresses of all of those who responded are listed in appendix H.

See APPENDICES.

Resumes

Resumes are sales documents. An effective resume must convince prospective employers that hiring you will benefit their businesses. As a sales document, your resume should be as well written and professional as you can make it. See EMPHASIS.

A cover letter is an option, but we recommend that you use a cover letter in most cases when you submit a resume. See rule 8 for further information on cover letters.

Don't forget to indicate both in your resume and in your cover letter if the prospective employer should not call you where you currently work. Also, you should tell potential employers if they can contact your current employer directly.

Resume is derived from a French term, which uses accents: *résumé*. Increasingly in English, the accents are considered unnecessary. We omit them in this discussion.

Resumes and Cover Letters

1. Choose a resume format that emphasizes your skills and abilities. If possible, limit resumes to one page.

2. Draft a specific employment objective or goal statement for the opening of the resume.

3. Prepare a detailed working list of all positions, activities, or other experiences that can validate your skills and abilities.

4. For each job, activity, or experience you decide to include in your resume, list tasks or skills using an action verb and specifics.

5. List job information and education as accurately as possible, and include specifics.

6. Omit references from your resume, but prepare a separate list of references for submission when requested.

7. Review your resume a final time before submitting it to verify the completeness and accuracy of the information and to avoid inappropriate information.

8. Use a cover letter when you submit a resume by mail. Optionally, attach a cover letter even when you submit the resume during an interview.

---

1. Choose a resume format that emphasizes your skills and abilities. If possible, limit resumes to one page.

Two resume formats are common: the **chronological (traditional) format** and the **functional format**. We recommend that you use the functional format. See figure 1 on the next page for a contrastive view of these two formats.

A functional format uses your skills and abilities as subheadings so that your skills and abilities are immediately visible to readers. See the model functional resume and cover letter in the model documents section of the *Style Guide*.

A chronological format often uses the dates of employment as headings. The dates can demonstrate the continuity in your work history, but they fail to emphasize your skills and abilities. Even if you decide to use a chronological format, add boldface and other emphasis techniques to help make the resume more effective. See the model chronological resume and cover letter in the model documents section of the *Style Guide*.

---

2. Draft a specific employment objective or goal statement for the opening of the resume.

The employment objective usually comes just after your name, address, and phone number, but before the body of the resume.

Some people don't recommend using an employment objective, but our view is that an objective allows you to tailor your resume to specific jobs or, in some cases, to a specific company.

Your objective should be as informative and as focused as you can make it:

this

To be a shift manager, with responsibilities for all production personnel and production records.

not this

To obtain a job as a manager.

nor this

To work in manufacturing in some capacity.

If you are responding to a specific advertisement, tailor the objective to the ad and the company that placed the ad. Most ads, for example,

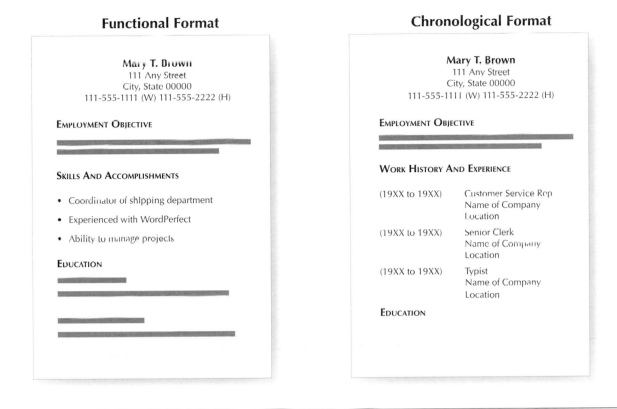

Figure 1. *Choose a functional format when you want to emphasize your skills and accomplishments. Choose a chronological format if you have a sequence of jobs to support and lead up to the employment objective.*

mention both a job and some of the responsibilities. So, frame your objective accordingly:

this

To be a senior retail sales clerk for Fashion Flair, Inc., with responsibility for the departmental sales display and inventory tracking.

not this

To be a retail sales clerk.

3. Prepare a detailed working list of all positions, activities, or other experiences that can validate your skills and abilities.

This list is merely a preliminary source of information. Later you can choose and refine items to emphasize in your resume.

Positions are only the beginning. Especially if you have a limited job history, you need to consider any non-job activities or experiences:

—Have you been active in a local club—maybe even served as an officer?

—Do you sew and tailor your own clothes?

—Do you make routine repairs on automobiles?

—Can you speak, read, or write a foreign language?

—Are you an amateur photographer?

—With which computer programs are you experienced?

In each of these activities you will have used or developed skills. These skills will be highlights in your resume.

4. For each job, activity, or experience you decide to include in your resume, list tasks or skills using an action verb and specifics.

This write-up of tasks or skills is where you really begin to sell yourself.

Each version of your resume will likely have a different list of tasks or skills. We recommend that you prepare several resumes, each targeting a different job or industry. If possible (and you are working on a computer), prepare a separate resume for each job you are applying for.

As an example of how to develop skill descriptions, assume that you were the treasurer for a local sports club. You could initially list this fact as follows:

Treasurer, Loma Linda Sports Club, 1994–1995.

Resumes

Unfortunately, the title of the position and the name of the club are not really informative. So, to beef up the preceding information, you should add specifics, especially numbers, if they would apply:

- Collected and kept account records for over 100 members.

- Prepared the club's 1994–1995 annual budget ($3,000).

- Wrote checks and prepared financial reports for monthly meetings.

NOTE 1: The preceding three phrases begin with an action verb—that is, a verb that suggests actions or accomplishments. Phrases of this sort are both more forceful and shorter than a full-sentence narrative. You can also use these phrases in a displayed list in your resume.

not this

- As club treasurer, I worked to prepare the club's annual budget for 1994–1995, which was roughly $3,000.

nor this

- In 1994–1995 I was responsible for planning and preparing the annual club budget, which provided roughly $3,000.

Both of the preceding are wordy, and they each bury key points in the middle of the sentences.

NOTE 2: Most action verb phrases on resumes will begin with the past tense verb, but if you are still performing the task or you still hold the job, then use a present tense verb:

- Collect and record dues for over 100 members.

- Prepare the club's 1994–1996 annual budget ($3,000).

5. List job information and education as accurately as possible, and include specifics.

Both your list of jobs and your list of education should be complete and accurate. Usually, you should explain any obvious gaps or other unusual information.

Lying or omitting information would be grounds for dismissal later if your employer discovers the problem. See ETHICS.

List both your jobs and your education in reverse order, with the current or latest one first and so on. This upside-down order allows readers to see and remember your latest.

When appropriate (considering the job you are applying for), add specific skills or accomplishments:

> B.S. (1995), Business Administration, University of Maryland—(Emphasis: International Financial Markets and Exchange Rates). London Internship, Spring 1993, Barclays Bank.

6. Omit references from your resume, but prepare a separate list of references for submission when requested.

Most resumes nowadays don't list references. Even mentioning in a resume the availability of references is now unnecessary. Every employer assumes that applicants are prepared to provide references when requested.

Always ask references for permission to use their names. Sometimes, a person would rather not be listed. The person might not know enough about you or might feel that they can't be positive about your skills.

Usually, the list of references includes one or more recent job supervisors, as well as perhaps one non-job reference, who can talk about your character.

7. Review your resume a final time before submitting it to verify the completeness and accuracy of the information and to avoid inappropriate information.

A final review is an essential step when a single error or unintentional omission in your resume may eliminate you from consideration for a job.

If possible, ask one or more friends to review your resume, both for content and for mere mechanics (spelling, punctuation, and consistency). Someone else's eyes will see your errors more readily than your eyes would.

One priority is to check all company names and personal references to verify that you have names correctly spelled, any titles accurately listed, and current addresses and telephone numbers.

A second priority is to avoid mentioning information that is now illegal. Under current federal and many state laws, you should not provide any information about your race, age, sex, religion, ethnic background, or family situation. You should also not mention your physical condition unless you have a problem that would limit your ability to perform a certain job.

The best way to handle topics that you should avoid is to remove some specifics from your application. If your age might be a decision factor, you might choose not to list the graduation dates for your academic degrees. If you need to mention a church activity, do so without mentioning the name of the denomination:

this

Social Chair for Church Adult Forum (over 100 active members) 1992–1995. Planned monthly socials and three annual spring weekend retreats.

not this

Social Chair for the Presbyterian Adult Forum (over 100 active members) 1992–1995. Planned monthly socials and three annual spring weekend retreats.

---

8. Use a cover letter when you submit a resume by mail. Optionally, attach a cover letter even when you submit the resume during an interview.

The cover letter is your best opportunity to tailor and personalize your application.

Before writing a cover letter, read carefully the job ad or job description. What precisely is the employer looking for?

Sometimes the ad may only say "attention to detail" when the task is actually developing and maintaining a computer database. In your review of the job ad, you need to look for such implications. If possible, call the personnel director for clarification or expansion on the implications.

Use the information in the job ad (and the phone call, if applicable) to structure your letter. First of all, mention where you located the job ad or job description (usually a newspaper or other published source).

Next, structure your discussion to parallel the job ad. If the ad mentioned "attention to detail," "hard working," and "team player," then use these three phrases in your letter as headings in the body of the letter. See LETTERS.

If, for example, you are addressing the "team player" phase, you might have a brief paragraph like this one:

Team Player

I work well with people and can coordinate activities effectively. My job as a retail clothing buyer (at Meyers Clothing) required me to work closely with retail sales clerks, with management, and with the financial planners. My last performance review at Meyers rated my team skills as excellent.

In a cover letter you might also include personal details that would set your application apart from the dozens of other applications. Here, for example, is a possible closing with a personal comment:

In our phone conversation, you mentioned that Ajax employees set their own working hours. My current job—at Hoffmann's Condiments—allows us to work flexible hours. I usually get in by 6:45 a.m. so that I can be home by late afternoon for quality time with my family.

Ajax sounds like a great place to work. Please call me at 445-3396 (my home) if you would like me to come in for an interview.

NOTE: In most instances do not use your current employer's letterhead paper or envelopes. And never use your current employer's metering machine to pay for the postage.

Scientists and technical specialists write and speak a different language. They do use many of the words and sentence patterns that nontechnical writers use, but their language is sufficiently different to be called a scientific or technical style. See STYLE.

Most obviously, scientists and technical specialists use technical terms: *joule, volt, electron, ion, protozoa, electroencephalogram, uterine tube, ethyl ethers, hypochlorous acid*, etc. Such terms have specific meanings and are generally foreign to lay readers. Often, lay readers consider such technical terms to be jargon because they do not readily know and perhaps cannot easily understand them. See JARGON.

Less obviously, scientists and technical specialists sometimes use common words in uncommon ways. Often, such uses are more confusing to lay readers than technical words, which lay readers expect to be foreign to their experience. Here are two examples of uncommon uses of common words:

> A continuous function in an *n*-dimensional vector space is considered **smooth** when the function has certain well-defined features.

> We were unable to calculate the **work** because the granite outcrop would not budge, even after a standard charge exploded in a hole drilled into its base produced a hairline fracture evident throughout the circumference of the **neck**.

In the first example, mathematicians have borrowed the intuitive notion of smoothness to describe an abstract mathematical concept. In the second example, physicists define *work* to be the effect when a force moves an object a certain distance. Without movement, work (according to the

definition) has not taken place. Similarly, *neck* describes that portion of an outcropping where the base of the outcropping most clearly resembles the border between the outcropping and the mass of rock from which the outcropping protrudes. The resemblance to a human neck is clear, but lay readers may not make the connection as readily as geologists.

Both technical terms and common words used in uncommon ways complicate scientific and technical writing. In both cases, lay readers may become lost, even when the writing is clear, concise, and logical. Therefore, if you are writing a scientific or technical document that is intended, at least in part, for lay readers, try to define technical terms (or don't use them), and avoid using common terms in uncommon ways.

If you are writing for scientific or technical readers, you must still try to make the writing as clear, concise, and logical as you can. Technical word usage may not hinder technical readers, but writing that is poorly organized, clumsily phrased, and inaccurately conceived will still be difficult if not impossible to read.

1. Make your use of technical and scientific terms appropriate for your readers.

Avoid unusual or overly technical terms if possible. If you cannot avoid them, and if your readers will not understand them, then define the terms. Do not use unfamiliar abbreviations unless your readers will understand them or unless you carefully explain the abbreviations first. See ABBREVIATIONS and ACRONYMS. Once you have established the terms and abbreviations, be consistent in your usage throughout the document.

Do not assume that your readers (**all** of your readers) know and understand your terms as you are using them. This is a trap.

First, rarely do all readers of a document have the same kind and level of technical background. You should usually write for the lowest common denominator—that is, for the least technically sophisticated reader.

Second, even well-established technical terms, concepts, and abbreviations may be subject to dispute, so you may have to stipulate definitions so that your readers know exactly what you intend when you use a particular word.

One of the easiest ways to handle difficult or unfamiliar technical terms is to provide an informal definition when the terms first appear.

> A further health problem in many African countries results from filariasis, which means that the blood contains small threadlike worms.
>
> *or*
>
> The presence of small threadlike worms in the blood (called filariasis) is a further health problem in many African countries.

Third, writers sometimes use different words to describe essentially the same thing, and this creates substantial confusion, even among scientific readers. Do not speak of *aspects* of a procedure in one paragraph, and then refer to the same concept as *elements* or *features* later.

---

2. Use concise, direct sentences.

Sentences are the building blocks of effective writing of any kind. However, they are especially important in writing that is inherently complicated and includes jargon. So, strive to make your sentences clear, direct, and concise. See SENTENCES.

The principles of writing direct, concise sentences are summarized below. Elsewhere in this *Style Guide*, you will find each topic discussed in depth.

- **Choose active rather than passive sentences:**

  this

  We determined that the coefficient of friction varied most at extremely cold temperatures.

  not this

  It was determined that the coefficient of friction varied most at extremely cold temperatures.

  See ACTIVE/PASSIVE.

- **Avoid wordiness:**

  this

  Our revised proposal presented further justification for development costs while offering to reduce our profit fee by 20 percent.

  not this

  Further justification for development costs, along with an offer for the 20 percent reduction of our profit fee, was presented in our revised proposal.

  See WORDY PHRASES.

- **Use strong verbs:**

  this

  After lengthy study, we adjusted the effluent guidelines to accommodate projected economic hardships.

  not this

  After lengthy study, we made an adjustment of the effluent guidelines to effect greater accommodation with projected economic hardships.

  See STRONG VERBS.

- **Avoid false subjects:**

  this

  Five-spot pattern recoveries are probably less efficient in sand trap reservoirs that have been depleted to within 15 percent of recoverable reserves.

  not this

  It is probable that five-spot pattern recoveries are less efficient in sand trap reservoirs that have been depleted to within 15 percent of recoverable reserves.

  See FALSE SUBJECTS.

- **Use pronouns to make your writing more personal and direct:**

  —Pronouns are appropriate when a scientific or technical writer is recommending something, drawing conclusions, or conveying deliberate decisions or choices:

  > The evidence suggests that this species is in fact indigenous to the Everglades. Therefore, I recommend broadening the scope of the USDA's habitat study before it writes the Los Puertos EIS.

  > The globule had a specific density of 6.78, more than twice what the OCS recovery team had estimated, so we concluded that zinc, not iron, was its major constituent.

  > Once we had analyzed the data from the pilot tests, we determined how to control temperature variations in succeeding tests.

  —Some technical and scientific writing does not lend itself to first person pronouns. The historical description of a laboratory procedure, for instance, should not mention the person who performed the procedure unless the focus of the discussion is on that person and not the procedure. If the procedure itself is more important, do not use personal pronouns:

  > The ore sample is washed in a weak solution of hydrochloric acid. Next, the ore is cleansed thoroughly in a water bath and then dried in a heat chamber.

  NOTE: If this passage appeared in a set of instructions, second person pronouns and imperative sentences would be appropriate:

  > Wash the ore sample in a weak solution (no more than 5 percent) of hydrochloric acid. Then you should clean the sample thoroughly in a water bath and dry it in a heat chamber.
  >
  > *or*
  >
  > Wash the ore sample in a weak solution (no more than 5 percent) of hydrochloric acid. Then clean the sample thoroughly in a water bath and dry it in a heat chamber.

The use of pronouns in technical writing has become more common in the last several decades, but don't overuse pronouns. Most scientific and technical writing is meant to convey information objectively, not to establish the writer's personality. If you are writing for the general public, however, use more pronouns and try to convey both clarity and warmth. For an example, read anything by Carl Sagan, Isaac Asimov, or Arthur C. Clarke, three successful scientific writers whose readers are primarily nontechnical. See PRONOUNS.

3. Design scientific and technical documents for visual impact and readability.

Visual appearance has become more and more important as a feature of good scientific and technical style. Well-conceived charts, graphs, tables, photographs and illustrations are essential if a document is to look fully professional.

In essence, the text supports the graphics, not the reverse. So, time spent planning and designing graphics is critical for successful scientific and technical documents.

Below are some key principles of using graphic aids. For a much more complete discussion, see GRAPHICS FOR DOCUMENTS, GRAPHICS FOR PRESENTATIONS, CAPTIONS, CHARTS, GRAPHS, ILLUSTRATIONS, TABLES, MAPS, and PHOTOGRAPHS.

- Create your graphics before you write your text.

- Select graphics that are appropriate for your readers.

- Focus your graphics on key points and keep them simple and uncluttered.

- Introduce graphics before they appear in the text.

- Use clear, interpretive captions on your graphics.

- Use emphatic devices (<u>underlining</u>, *italics*, **boldface**, shading, etc.) to emphasize important ideas in your graphics as well as your text.

4. Above all, be as accurate as possible.

Good scientific and technical writing is precise and accurate—in its facts, its references, its procedures, and its analyses.

Check every detail. If your document mentions that the site of the project is southwest of Dry Gulch, then the map should not show the site to be northwest of Dry Gulch. Similarly, if you mention production data in the text, the same figures (rounded to the same significant figures) should appear in accompanying tables. Every detail in the document should be as accurate and consistent as the writer can humanly guarantee.

A single inaccurate figure or fact can destroy the credibility of a document and its writer.

NOTE: Some writers defend weasel wording or hedging by stating that we can't know anything for sure; therefore, we can make no absolute statements. According to them, we can never state a fact because we can't be sure that anything is irrevocably true. The words typically used to hedge are *generally, usually, likely, possibly, notion, surmise, speculation, conjecture, indicate, suggest, appear, seem, believe,* etc.

If necessary, use such words to indicate honest doubt or uncertainty, but do not overdo them. If you are certain of something, say so. Weasel wording weakens your document and your image:

this

Malodin can be effective as a maintenance therapy for osteoarthritis.

not this

We believe that the evidence favors an interpretation that Malodin is likely to be a potential maintenance therapy for osteoarthritis.

Semicolons have two primary functions—linking thoughts and separating thoughts.

1. Use semicolons to link complete thoughts that could otherwise stand alone as separate sentences:

> Western Aeronautics has completed more than 15 avionics contracts in the last 5 years; in 11 of those contracts we used CAD/CAM techniques to minimize development costs and improve both reliability and performance.

Typically, the complete thoughts linked by a semicolon are equal in structure and importance. Writers could separate the complete thoughts with a period and create two sentences; however, the semicolon shows a closer relationship between the thoughts than a period does. The semicolon says, "These thoughts are closely related."

NOTE 1: Semicolons used to link complete thoughts do not require conjunctions (transitional or connecting words like *however, consequently, furthermore,* and *thus*):

> Detailed trade studies helped us determine the relative importance of the various technologies in designing a supersonic cruise fighter; similar performance studies helped us evaluate the trade study findings in air-to-air operations in a simulated combat environment.

> High maneuverability was our primary design consideration; our secondary considerations included short take-off and large payloads.

NOTE 2: The following transitional words and phrases can be used with semicolons if the writer needs to indicate or clarify the relationship between the thoughts before and after the semicolon: *accordingly, consequently, for example, for instance, further, furthermore, however, indeed, moreover, nevertheless, nonetheless, on the contrary, on the other hand, therefore, thus.* See CONJUNCTIONS.

> We use aircraft geometry to generate survivability parameters such as radar signature; furthermore, we add performance, weapons, and avionics characteristics from the developed aircraft design to evaluate military effectiveness.

> The SDC is a multiterminal facility dedicated to a variety of projects; however, its size and flexibility, coupled with strict management controls, guard against fragmentation and crossover. (*Note the comma following* furthermore *and* however.)

NOTE 3: Do **not** use the shorter conjunctions (*and, but, or, for, nor, so,* and *yet*) with semicolons; use these simple conjunctions only when linking two complete thoughts with a comma.

However, if the complete thoughts are lengthy and already contain commas, then use a semicolon with these shorter conjunctions to join the two complete thoughts:

> The committee began its scrutiny of the preliminary design study, which General Avionics submitted upon just 2 weeks' notice; and they found that the transformational analyses, although obviously hurried, were still superior to those of other designers who had had much more time.

See COMMAS, CONJUNCTIONS, and TRANSITIONS.

---

2. Use semicolons to separate items in series when one or more of the items has a comma:

> Our cost breakdown demonstrates our cost consciousness; our commitment to low overhead, especially through our direct contract-costing procedures; and our desire to minimize risk by using proven resources.

Without the semicolons to separate each major item in the series, readers might not understand how many items the series contains. The need for clarification varies from sentence to sentence. Sometimes it is not crucial; sometimes it is:

> Our avionics designs incorporate state-of-the-art subcomponents, including dual Intel 86000 microprocessors; Marquette frequency stabilizers, the most advanced anti-ECM devices currently available; and Barnett Industries' redesigned RFX regulators.

If the three items in this series had been separated with commas, the purpose of the phrase *the most advanced anti-ECM devices currently available* would not be clear. It would seem to be a fourth item in the series, although its true purpose is to describe the Marquette frequency stabilizers. The semicolons clarify its purpose in the sentence.

NOTE: With a longer and complex series of items, the more desirable option would be a displayed list:

> Our avionics designs incorporate state-of-the-art subcomponents, including:
>
> - Dual Intel 86000 microprocessors
> - Marquette frequency stabilizers, the most advanced anti-ECM devices currently available
> - Barnett Industries' redesigned RFX regulators

See LISTS.

Semicolons

1. Use semicolons to link complete thoughts that could otherwise stand alone as separate sentences.

2. Use semicolons to separate items in series when one or more of the items has a comma.

Sentences are the building blocks of thought. Without sentences and the context in which they appear, communication would be impossible.

Sentences are fundamental to language, yet they are hard to define. *Webster's New Collegiate Dictionary* says that a sentence is a "grammatically self-contained speech unit." Many teachers would call it "a complete thought" and perhaps add that it usually contains, at a minimum, a subject and a verb. That definition would seem to rule out the following, all of which are sentences:

> Yes.
> No.
> Maybe.
> Stop.
> Hello.
> Me?
> When?
> Where?
> Why?
> How?
> OK.
> Oh!

All written sentences begin with a capital letter and end with a mark of punctuation, usually a period but sometimes a question mark or exclamation mark. This convention applies to all sentences, even those with only one word and those in which words that are understood have been left out.

Most sentences are longer than one word and do include both the subject and the verb:

> The invoice was late.
>
> Because the invoice was late, we could not include it in accounts payable for November.
>
> When did the invoice arrive?
>
> It arrived late.
>
> The invoice, which was late, missed the deadline for November accounts payable.

Sentences

1. Use declarative sentences to make statements of fact and opinion. Usually such sentences follow the subject-verb word order, and they end with a period.

2. Use interrogative sentences to ask questions. Interrogative sentences usually begin with a question word *(who, which, where, when, why,* and *how)* or with a verb.

3. Use exclamatory sentences to make strong assertions or surprising observations. Exclamatory sentences usually end with an exclamation mark.

4. Use imperative sentences to give directions or commands. Imperative sentences usually begin with a verb and end with a period (although an exclamation point is also occasionally possible).

5. Limit average sentence length to about 20 words for typical business and technical writing.

6. Use a variety of sentence types and sentence lengths.

7. Strive to make all sentences direct.

> The invoice was late, so we could not include it in November accounts payable.
>
> Next time, send us the invoice promptly.
>
> What happened with the late invoice was that we could not include it in November accounts payable.

In some cases, parts of the sentence are understood but not stated:

> Too late. (The invoice was too late.)
>
> Late again! (The invoice was late again!)

These examples reveal several things about sentences. First, they are self-contained, although they might rely heavily on something said earlier (or later) for readers to fully comprehend them. Second, they consist of a meaningful word or group of words. A word constituting a sentence does not have to be a particular kind of word, nor does it have to be meaningful in normal contexts. *OK* and *Yes* are clearly self-contained expressions, but *String* could also be a sentence:

> What did you use to secure the box?
>
> String. (I used string. *The* I used *is* understood.)

Single verbs can also function as sentences:

> What do you suggest I do during lunch?
>
> Run. (I suggest that you run.)

So, must sentences express complete thoughts to be sentences? Yes, although the completeness of the thought usually depends on the context in which the sentences appear. For an utterance to be a sentence, it must either state or imply a complete thought, given its context.

Must sentences contain a subject and a verb to be sentences? Yes and no. Sentences do have a grammatical structure, including a subject and a verb, but either or both can be understood:

> When should I leave?
>
> Now. (You should leave now. *In this sentence, the subject* [you] *and the verb* [should leave] *are both understood.)*

Sometimes the subject and/or verb are complicated and don't convey the primary meaning or central thought in the sentence:

> What happened with the late invoice was that we could not include it in November accounts payable.

The subject is *What happened with the late invoice*. The verb is *was*. The subject is a complicated noun clause, and the main meaning is not in the main verb, but in the final clause: *that we could not include it in November accounts payable*.

Still, in most business and technical writing, sentences do have a subject and verb, even if these grammatical slots are filled with many words and have complex grammatical relationships.

Perhaps because sentences are difficult to define, most grammar handbooks settle for two fairly simple, yet practical, systems for cataloguing sentences:

- Purpose or Intent
  - —Declarative Sentences
  - —Interrogative Sentences
  - —Exclamatory Sentences
  - —Imperative Sentences
- Grammatical Structures
  - —Simple Sentences
  - —Compound Sentences
  - —Complex Sentences
  - —Compound-Complex Sentences

Purpose or Intent of Sentences

1. Use declarative sentences to make statements of fact and opinion. Usually such sentences follow the subject-verb word order, and they end with a period:

> We reviewed the report
>
> Because of the detailed analyses involved, our review of the report is likely to take several days.
>
> The report is only five pages long.
>
> The report, which is only five pages long, will still take several days to review because the analyses are lengthy.

See PERIODS.

2. Use interrogative sentences to ask questions. Interrogative sentences usually begin with a question word *(who, which, where, when, why, what,* and *how)* or with a verb:

> Who is the engineer in charge?
>
> Which plan is likely to be approved?
>
> When will the construction project end?
>
> How often do they propose to inspect the site?
>
> Have you filled in all the necessary forms?
>
> Were the construction specifications adequate?

See QUESTION MARKS.

3. Use exclamatory sentences to make strong assertions or surprising observations. Exclamatory sentences usually end with an exclamation mark:

> What a surprising conclusion!
>
> That's wrong!
>
> What a field day for the lawyers that will be!
>
> Oh, I doubt that!

NOTE: Exclamatory sentences often have grammatical structures very different from normal declarative sentences. In fact, they may be only a word or two long:

> No!
>
> How surprising!
>
> A shame!

See EXCLAMATION MARKS.

4. Use imperative sentences to give directions or commands. Imperative sentences usually begin with a verb and end with a period (although an exclamation mark is also occasionally possible):

> Check the Internet for additional information.
>
> Adjust the flange on the steam connection to prevent leakage.
>
> Do not submit the pink copy of this form!
>
> Stop. *(or Stop!)*

Grammatical Structures of Sentences

Sentences have four grammatical structures—simple, compound, complex, and compound-complex. These four structures, however, can be formed into an infinite number of unique sentences.

Simple Sentences

Simple sentences are sentences that express one complete thought. Essentially, they contain a single subject and a single verb, although both subject and verb may be compound:

> The pump failed. *(single subject and verb)*
>
> The new steam pump failed after only 3 weeks of service. *(single subject and verb)*
>
> We analyzed the blueprints. *(single subject and verb)*

Sentences

James Hawkins and I analyzed the blueprints for the new maintenance facility. *(compound subject, single verb)*

James Hawkins and I analyzed and revised the blueprints for the new maintenance facility. *(compound subject and compound verb)*

NOTE 1: As indicated above, simple sentences can contain compound subjects, such as *James Hawkins and I*, and compound verbs, such as *analyzed* and *revised*. Although compound, such subjects and verbs form a single unit, at least for the purpose of the sentence in question, so the sentence is still considered simple.

NOTE 2: A quick test for a simple sentence is that you cannot logically break the sentence at any point and come up with two other simple sentences. For example, the following simple sentence, even with compound subject and compound verb, cannot be broken into two simple sentences, so the sentence is a single, simple unit:

My supervisor and I joked about the assignment and then worked on ways to accomplish it.

Compound Sentences

Compound sentences are a union of two or more simple sentences. These simple sentences are usually linked by one of the simple coordinating conjunctions: *and, but, or, nor, for, yet,* and *so.*

The project was expensive, and management still hadn't decided to proceed with it.

Our supervisor wanted to increase office productivity, but the turnover in personnel made such an increase unlikely.

See COMMAS and CONJUNCTIONS.

Sometimes the simple sentences are linked by a semicolon or by a semicolon and a conjunctive adverb:

The data confirmed our initial assumptions about the problems in prototype production; with these problems, the project will almost certainly exceed the budget.

The surveying was to have been completed by October 15; however, construction must start on or before November 15.

See SEMICOLONS and CONJUNCTIONS.

NOTE 1: A quick test for a compound sentence is to see if you can divide the sentence into two or more simple sentences:

The surveying was to have been completed by October 15. Construction must start on or before November 15.

NOTE 2: Sometimes three or more simple sentences can combine into a compound sentence:

The site was ready, the construction crew was ready, and the materials were ready, but the weather was not cooperative.

Complex Sentences

A complex sentence is a simple sentence with a dependent (subordinate) clause attached to it. The dependent clause can appear in front of the main clause (the otherwise simple sentence), in the middle of the main clause, or behind the main clause.

Here are some dependent clauses:

Although our bid was the lowest . . .

. . . who was the most expensive candidate . . .

. . . because the tailings pile is virtually inert.

Adding a simple sentence to each of these dependent clauses forms a complex sentence:

Although our bid was the lowest, another contractor had more experience.

Cameron Blake, who was the most expensive candidate, did have the most impressive credentials.

Reclamation of the mine site will be difficult because the tailings pile is virtually inert.

NOTE 1: A test for a complex sentence is to separate the dependent clause and the main clause (simple sentence). This test will work for the sentences above, but not for this sentence:

What Jack wanted to discuss with us became clear once the meeting got under way.

What Jack wanted to discuss with us is a noun clause that functions as the subject of the sentence. Trying to separate it from the rest of the sentence would result in two sentence fragments, neither of which can stand alone. Although this sentence fails the test, it is still a complex sentence.

NOTE 2: Dependent clauses are usually introduced by these words:

Subordinate conjunctions

Because, since, although, even though, after, before, so that, while, when, etc.

See CONJUNCTIONS.

Relative pronouns

Who, whom, whose which, that, whoever, whomever, why, when, where, etc.

See PRONOUNS.

Compound-Complex Sentences

Compound-complex sentences are a combination of the two previous sentence types. They are both compound and complex. Therefore, a compound-complex sentence has two attached independent clauses— a compound sentence (two simple sentences attached to each other)— and at least one dependent clause:

Because the firm's manufacturing capacity could not be increased rapidly enough, they were unable to fill their orders; consequently, competitors gained a significant foothold on the market.

NOTE: Because this sentence is compound, the semicolon separates two independent clauses, each of which could stand alone as a complete thought. The introductory dependent clause beginning with *because* makes the sentence complex.

Sentence Length and Readability

All readability formulas include average sentence length as one measure of the readability of a piece of writing. Some authorities argue that average sentence length for any level of reader should be kept below some maximum (15 to 20 words). For younger or less sophisticated readers, the average sentence length should be even less (8 to 12 words, depending on how young the readers are).

Sentence length is one important factor in readability. Readers have to read, comprehend, remember, and interpret information sentence by sentence. The longer a sentence, the more they have to hold in their minds to comprehend, remember, and interpret the thought being expressed. Long sentences place an unnecessary burden on readers.

Another factor in readability is sentence syntax (structure). Long sentences can still be easily readable if they are constructed so that the sentence is easy to follow and easy to understand:

We accepted the bid from the Cranston Construction Company—although it was the highest bidder—because (1) it has the manpower and equipment to start the project immediately, (2) its personnel are experienced in this type of construction, (3) it has the necessary permits in hand, (4) it is a local company using local resources, and (5) its management was willing to post a substantial performance bond.

This 67-word complex sentence is long but readable because it states its central point immediately: *We accepted the bid from Cranston.* The dependent clause enclosed by dashes clearly states a fact contrary to our expectations: Cranston was the highest bidder. We don't expect the contract to go to the highest bidder, and we wonder why Cranston received the award. So the numbered list provides the rationale for the decision. The numbering of the list helps clarify the syntax.

However, long sentences must be written this clearly to be readable. If your average sentence becomes too long and you do not have the skill to structure each sentence with great clarity, then your writing will be difficult, if not impossible, to read. See STYLE.

5. Limit average sentence length to about 20 words for typical business and technical writing.

The 20-word average is based on readability experiments and studies that reinforce the discussion of sentence length presented above. Obviously, in arriving at a 20-word average, you will have some longer sentences and some shorter sentences.

Longer sentences were acceptable many years ago. Writers in the 19th century produced some mammoth sentences. Today, the trend is toward short, concise sentences intended for busy readers who don't have the time for or the interest in long-winded prose. The short sentence is the better sentence.

6. Use a variety of sentence types and sentence lengths.

Writing that is uniform is tedious. Make some sentences long and some short. Make most of them moderate in length. Remember that long sentences are useful for presenting involved concepts and for elaborating on a point that requires some thought. Short sentences are useful for stating clear, crisp thoughts.

Create variety, too, in your choice of sentence types. Use mostly simple sentences, but do not avoid the compound, complex, and compound-complex sentences. Compound and complex sentences are very useful for expressing related ideas. If you use only simple sentences, you will be producing Dick-and-Jane writing.

7. Strive to make all sentences direct.

Keep the syntax (structure) of the sentence as uncomplicated as possible. You can do this by keeping the subject as close as possible to the verb; by keeping modifiers as close as possible to the words they modify; and by using conjunctions and transitions to show progress, sequence, connection, and contrast. See TRANSITIONS, PRONOUNS, MODIFIERS, ADJECTIVES, ADVERBS, NOUNS, VERBS, and CONJUNCTIONS.

Signs and symbols are increasingly important in today's visually oriented world. Television stations use visual images (and accompanying theme music) as identifying signs for a particular video production. Corporations spend great sums of money designing logos that symbolize the corporation's mission or image.

Internationally, signs and symbols have crossed national boundaries. For example, the dashboards of automobiles, wherever produced, now use international symbols for the horn, the lights, and so on. A less obvious example are the internationally recognized symbols of distress when the crew of a downed aircraft wish to communicate with a plane overhead. If the crew need food and water, the symbol is a block capital F, which can be recorded in snow, in vegetation, or with rocks. As in this example, many international standards ultimately derive from English, which has become the international language of trade and business.

Within sciences and technology, many symbol systems are now international—for example, the symbols used for an electronic schematic, the astronomical symbols for the planets, or the chemical symbols for the elements.

For a valuable source of information on visual signs and symbols, as well as the names for visual objects or features, see The Diagram Group, *The Macmillan Visual Desk Reference* (New York: Macmillan Publishing Company, 1993).

The following rules are general guidelines about the use of signs and symbols. If you need specific information about signs and symbols

for a single technical area, refer to a publication that covers that area. If you merely need to identify a sign or symbol, check a recently published collegiate dictionary, such as *Merriam-Webster's Collegiate Dictionary*, 10th Edition (Springfield, Mass.: Merriam-Webster, Inc., 1993). See REFERENCES.

1. Choose standard signs and symbols and ensure that readers understand them.

Some symbols are so well known that you don't need to explain them, regardless of where they appear: $=$, $+$, $-$, \$, %, x, $\pm$, and $\div$.

Remember that some symbols may be obvious to you—for example, the K for Potassium—but to a layperson, the connection between K and Potassium will be far from obvious.

So, if you doubt that **all** of your readers (or viewers) will be familiar with a sign or symbol, explain it either in parentheses within the text or in a footnote. Consider including a glossary of signs and symbols in your document if you think readers would find such a glossary helpful.

2. Use the written-out version of signs and symbols in text unless the nature of the text is such that readers would expect to see signs and symbols:

Poisoning from lead or other heavy metals was common among the ancient Romans and Greeks.

not

Poisoning from Pb or other heavy metals was common among the ancient Romans and Greeks.

Most commercial textbooks are routinely copyrighted.

not

Most commercial textbooks are routinely ©.

The examples above come from non-technical contexts and from ordinary text, not from graphics or equations. Therefore, symbols are not appropriate.

The symbol Pb would be appropriate in a chemical equation or in a graphic. But even within the text of a chemical report, the symbol Pb would not usually appear.

Similarly, the © would be appropriate in the copyright information on the back of a title page or as in the copyright notice at the bottom of this page, but not within ordinary text.

Signs and Symbols

1. Choose standard signs and symbols and ensure that readers understand them.

2. Use the written-out version of signs and symbols in text unless the nature of the text is such that readers would expect to see signs and symbols.

3. Repeat a symbol when you have a series of numerical values and the symbol would appear without a space between it and the numerical values.

NOTE: Some symbols, such as the percent sign (%), do appear in ordinary text within such documents as economic surveys, accounting reports, or internal banking reports:

> First State Bank offers to finance the proposed mall at 9.2%, which is 0.8% less than the rate currently offered by Home Savings Bank.

These uses of the percent sign probably reflect a desire to avoid having to spell out the full word a dozen times per page. As is often the case, the purpose and readability of a document are the best indicators of whether or not to use signs and symbols in ordinary text.

3. **Repeat a symbol when you have a series of numerical values and the symbol would appear without a space between it and the numerical values:**

$10 to $15 per visit (*or* $10–$15 per visit)

from 6′ to 8′ sections (*not* 6–8′ sections)

18% to 20%

but

18 to 20 percent (for *non-financial* text)

38 to 45°C

NOTE: Editors sometimes differ in how to handle such repeated symbols. For instance, some editors would prefer to use this version of the temperature example:

38° to 45°C

In cases where usage seem to be mixed, check with some of the common references. See REFERENCES. Then decide what pattern you wish to use, and be consistent throughout your document. See EDITING AND PROOFREADING.

Slashes (/) have several meanings:

And
Or
Both
To
End of a line in poetry
Mathematical division
Per (mathematical division again)

Be careful when you use a slash. Your readers might not understand the meaning of this apparently simple little symbol.

NOTE 1: The slash sometimes is called a solidus and sometimes a virgule.

NOTE 2: A backslash (\) is now common in computer languages. Its special uses there do not carry over into ordinary text.

1. Use a slash when a season or a time period extends beyond a single year:

winter 1989/1990

fiscal year 1989/90

425/424 B.C.

NOTE: An en dash sometimes replaces the slash:

Winter 1989–1990

425–424 B.C.

See DASHES.

> ## Slashes
>
> 1. Use a slash when a season or a time period extends beyond a single year.
>
> 2. Use a slash to replace *per*.
>
> 3. Use a slash in mathematical division when an equation appears on a single line.
>
> 4. Use a slash to separate lines of quoted poetry presented in prose form.
>
> 5. Avoid using *and/or* in most contexts.

2. Use a slash to replace *per*:

yards/mile

feet/second *or* ft/sec

3. Use a slash in mathematical division when an equation appears on a single line:

$$x/a - y/c = 1 \text{ for } \frac{x}{a} - \frac{y}{c} = 1$$

$$(C/D)/(C+2D)^3 \text{ for } \frac{\frac{C}{D}}{(C+2D)^3}$$

See MATHEMATICAL NOTATION.

4. Use a slash to separate lines of quoted poetry presented in prose form:

As Shakespeare so aptly noted: "There is a tide in the affairs of men, / Which, taken at the flood, leads on to fortune."

See QUOTATION MARKS.

5. Avoid using *and/or* in most contexts:

We asked for a rebate and/or an explanation.

Writers and editors object to all uses of *and/or,* arguing that the expression is ambiguous. In the above example, the meaning includes *a rebate and an explanation* as well as *rebate or an explanation.* Many editors would rewrite the sentence:

We asked for a rebate or an explanation or both.

See *and/or* in WORD PROBLEMS

Spacing decisions range from the arrangement of text and graphics on the page to the space left after each paragraph and the number of spaces following the final period in a sentence. Proper, even creative, spacing can help guarantee that a final document looks professional and is easy to read.

Page Formats

Decide early in the writing process how you want your pages to look. Options, especially with word processing, include variable margins, a variety of typefaces, and variable line spacing. For important writing projects, you might consult professional designers before writing the text. Sometimes design considerations affect how much and what you write. See PAGE LAYOUT, EMPHASIS, and WORD PROCESSING.

---

1. Leave ample white space on your pages, especially around important ideas or data.

Writers often cram too much writing onto a page, trying to stay within page limits or adhering to custom, an arbitrary format, or just plain myth about how pages ought to look. Some writers ignore the appearance of the document because they have never had to think about it.

Without careful and early attention to the desired page layout, the text might not fit within prescribed limits, and the tables, figures, and other graphics might not complement the text.

Although every page layout is different, here are some principles to follow as you work with available space:

> **Spacing**
>
> 1. Leave ample white space on your pages, especially around important ideas or data.

- Adjust the margins in letters and memos so that the top and bottom margins are roughly equal and the left and right margins are also equal. Your goal is to center the letter or memo on the page. See LETTERS and MEMOS.

- In single-spaced text, double-space between paragraphs. Even triple-spacing might be desirable for extra space on a page or for highlighting key paragraphs.

- Avoid excessively long paragraphs or a series of short, choppy paragraphs. See PARAGRAPHS.

- Add lists, tables, figures, or other graphics to break up long stretches of text. See LISTS and GRAPHICS FOR DOCUMENTS.

- Design a system of headings that allows you to divide the text frequently and to highlight key ideas. See HEADINGS, EMPHASIS, and WORD PROCESSING.

NOTE: A rough prototype of your document is an excellent planning aid. A prototype typically consists of a series of blank pages, one for each page in the proposed document, with titles, headings, lists, graphics, and perhaps paragraphs sketched in. The prototype suggests where and how long each of the major textual units will be. See WRITING AND REVISING.

You should produce the prototype well before writing the actual text.

A variation of the prototype is to prepare a style sheet prior to writing the text. A style sheet would contain guidance on the margins, the number of columns, the typefaces, and the

spacing of all levels of headings. Such style sheets are especially valuable when teams of writers are working on a document. See WRITING AND REVISING, PAGE LAYOUT, and WORD PROCESSING.

Spacing and Punctuation

Standard and consistent spacing are signs of quality in any well-produced document. The following conventions reflect current desktop publishing/word processing programs, which routinely use proportional spacing. These conventions differ from those that many writers learned who gained their typing skills on typewriters, not personal computers.

- Leave one space after any mark of punctuation that ends a sentence.

NOTE: Documents printed with proportionally spaced typefaces, as most are today, should not have two spaces following ending punctuation. For consistency, therefore, we recommend that organizations use a single space after ending punctuation regardless of how the document will be printed. Following this recommendation means that someone will not have to go through your draft of a document removing one of the two spaces after each mark of ending punctuation.

- Place colons, semicolons, and dashes outside quotation marks. Place question marks and exclamation marks inside or outside quotation marks, depending on whether they are or are not part of the quotation.

- Always place commas and periods inside quotation marks.

Spacing

NOTE: British usage places commas and periods inside or outside quotation marks, depending on whether they are or are not part of the quotation. See QUOTATION MARKS and BRITISH ENGLISH.

- Leave no space before a semicolon and one space after it.

- Leave no space before or after dashes. Most word processing programs have a code to allow for a solid dash, not two hyphens typed together. Use this code whenever possible so that your dashes are solid and do not have a space before or after them:

  The plan—a method for extracting iron ore—is cost effective.

  See DASHES.

- Leave no space before a colon and one space after it within a sentence.

- Leave one space before an opening or left parenthesis within a sentence. Leave one space when the opening parenthesis follows another sentence; if it is a complete sentence, the parenthetical material opens with a capital and the final punctuation comes before the final parenthesis. See PARENTHESES.

- Leave no space before a closing or right parenthesis and one space after it within a sentence. When an entire sentence is enclosed within parentheses, the final parenthesis goes outside of the closing punctuation and one space follows the right parenthesis.

- Leave one space before and after each of the three periods in an ellipsis. If an ellipsis concludes a sentence, use three spaced periods followed by the end punctuation mark for a sentence. See ELLIPSES.

NOTE: Each of the punctuation marks discussed in this section has its own entry in this *Style Guide*. Refer to those entries if you have questions or wish to see additional examples.

Spelling every word correctly is the final step in writing any professional document—from formal report to everyday letter or memo.

Spelling is important for the sake of both clarity and credibility. Most misspellings do not cause readers to misinterpret the sentence in which the misspelling occurs. But the misspelled word draws attention to itself, which slows down readers and diverts their attention away from the ideas being expressed.

Language is a medium. When the medium draws attention to itself, it detracts from the message.

Misspelled words may also cause readers to question the writer's competence, intelligence, and credibility. How much confidence would you have in this writer's engineering abilities?

> Raw seewater has been considured as a posible alternet sorce for the consentrater principle water supply. However, bench scale tests indacate that the high consentration of disolved salts in seewater interfeer in the eficenct recovary of minaral from the ore.

Misspellings in a document make the writer and the writer's organization look incompetent, sloppy, careless, and potentially untrustworthy.

However, spelling in English is far from simple. Roughly 90 percent of the words in English are regular, but the other 10 percent are demons. Which words in the following pairs are correct?

> accomodate/accommodate
> committment/commitment
> concientious/conscientious
> changable/changeable
> imperceptable/imperceptible
> indispensible/indispensable
> inevitible/inevitable
> irresistable/irresistible
> occurence/occurrence
> offerred/offered

Spelling

1. Challenge the spelling of every word in your document, especially those words you have difficulty with.

2. Keep a list of the words you have trouble spelling.

3. Use those spelling rules that you find helpful.

4. Form plurals carefully. Many irregular forms exist.

> preceed/precede
> prefered/preferred
> prevalant/prevalent
> privlege/privilege
> seperate/separate
> similiar/similar
> transfered/transferred
> truely/truly

If you are like most people, you had to pause on at least two or three of the above pairs. Perhaps you still aren't sure. Did you look up any of them in a dictionary?

English is a hybrid language. It evolved over centuries of influence from the languages of the armies that invaded England: the Romans, the Saxons, the Normans, the Vikings, and so on. English is "impure" in this regard and consequently has many inconsistent words. That's why English pronunciation and spelling are inconsistent.

---

1. Challenge the spelling of every word in your document, especially those words you have difficulty with.

The best proofreaders and editors challenge every word, especially those that are known to be difficult (such as those listed above).

If the word is common enough, you can trust yourself to recognize correct spelling. If you are unsure, however, check a dictionary or spelling dictionary. See REFERENCES.

---

2. Keep a list of the words you have trouble spelling.

Remembering spelling rules and their exceptions is difficult. A simpler and nearly foolproof method for improving your spelling is to keep a list of the words you commonly misspell. Look up the correct spellings and list the words alphabetically.

When you see that you have misspelled a word, add it to your list. Then refer to the list when you need to use one of those words. Over time, your mind will come to recognize the look of the word with its correct spelling, and you will no longer need the list.

Until you no longer need it, keep the list in a convenient place: tucked inside your dictionary, on the wall in front of your desk or writing area, under the glass on top of your desk, or taped inside your notebook. Keep it where you can see it easily as you write.

---

3. Use those spelling rules that you find helpful.

Spelling rules are difficult to remember, and most have many exceptions. If you take the time to memorize the rules, you should probably also memorize the exceptions. At some point, the exercise becomes tedious, and the rewards are questionable.

Spelling

However, you should use those rules that you have found helpful and that you remember well enough to apply.

Probably the most well-known and most useful rule is "*i* before *e* except after *c*." Here are some of the exceptions:

> counterfeit
> foreign
> freight
> height
> neighbor
> sleigh
> weigh
> weight

Some of the other common rules are briefly summarized below:

- Change a final *y* to *i* before adding a suffix to a word, but keep the *y* before *–ing*:

activity	activities
deny	denies, denying
happy	happily, happier, happiest, happiness
likely	likelihood
study	studies, studied, studying

- Drop a silent final *e* before suffixes beginning with a vowel but not before suffixes beginning with a consonant:

age	aging
desire	desirable
mobile	mobility
notice	noticing
scarce	scarcity
care	careful
manage	management
safe	safety
wife	wifely

Exceptions

> acreage
> argument
> changeable
> courageous
> judgment
> lineage
> mileage
> ninth
> truly
> wholly

- Double a final consonant before a suffix beginning with a vowel (1) if the consonant ends a stressed syllable (or a single-syllable word) and (2) if the consonant is preceded by a single vowel:

bag	bagged
brag	bragged
gun	gunned
shop	shopped, shopper
stop	stopped
begin	beginning
occur	occurred
prefer	preferred
regret	regretting, regretted

4. Form plurals carefully. Many irregular forms exist:

man	men
ox	oxen
analysis	analyses
matrix	matrices
potato	potatoes
piano	pianos

See PLURALS for a discussion of these irregular forms as well as a list of the most common irregular plurals.

A List of Common Spelling Demons

Below is a list of some of the most common spelling demons. These words, interestingly enough, are not technical ones because most of us learn to spell technical words as we learn our technical subjects.

Common words are the problem because their irregularities are often difficult to predict and almost impossible to remember. Also, we often see common words misspelled, so we remember the look of the misspelling, not the look of the correct spelling.

absorb
acceptable
accessible
accommodate
accompanied
accuracy
accustomed
acetic *(acid)*

achievement
acoustic
acquire
acreage
adapter
adsorb
aegis
affect *(usually a verb)*
affected
aggression
aging
aid *(help)*
aide *(assistant, helper)*
aisles
all ready *(all prepared)*
all right
all together *(all those in group)*
all ways *(by every means)*
a lot of
already *(previously)*
altogether *(entirely)*
aluminum
always *(all the time)*
amateur
analogous
announcement
anonymous
antibiotics
any one *(any specific person or object)*
anyone *(any person)*
appall, appalled
apparent
appearance
appraise *(estimate value)*
apprise *(inform)*
appropriate
aquatic
archaeology
artisan
ascetic *(austere)*
aspirin
athletics
attendance
authentic
a while *(noun)*
awhile *(adverb)*

bargain
basically
beneficial
benefited
beside *(next to)*
besides *(in addition)*
beveled
biased
breath *(noun)*
breathe *(verb)*
bulletin
bureaucracy
business

Caffeine
calendar
caliber
caliper
calk
calorie
canceled, canceling
cancellation
candor

canvas (cloth)
canvass (solicit)
capital (city)
capitol (building)
carat (gem weight)
carot (arrow mark)
category
cemetery
census
challenge
changeable
channel
characteristic
chisel, chiseled
choose (present tense)
chose (past tense)
coarsely
commitment
committee
competent
competition
complement (complete)
compliment (praise)
conceited
conceive
condemn
confidant (person)
confident (sure)
conscience
conscientious
consensus
consistent
continuous
controlled
controversial
councilor (of council)
counselor (advisor)
courteous
criticism
criticize
curiosity
curious

deceive
decision
definitely
descend
descendant
description
desirable
despair
desperate
despicable
device (noun)
devise (verb)
dietitian
disappoint
disapprove
disastrous
discipline
discreet (prudent)
discrete (distinct or separate)
disease
distill, distilled

distinct
doctor
dyeing (coloring)
dying (death)

easily
ecstasy
effect (usually a noun)
efficient
eighth
elaborately
elicit (to draw)
embarrass
emigrate (go from)
employee
enroll, enrolled
ensure (guarantee)
entirely
envelop (verb)
envelope (noun)
environment
equipment
equipped
especially
every day (each day)
everyday (ordinary)
evidently
exaggerate
except
exhaust
existence
experiment
explanation
eying or eyeing

familiar
farther (distance)
fascinate
favorite
February
fiber
finally
financially
flammable (not inflammable)
fluorescent
fluorine
foreign
foresee
foretell
forgo (relinquish)
forego (precede)
forty
forward (ahead)
foreword (preface)
fulfill, fulfilled
further (degree)
fuselage

gauge
generally
glamour
government
governor
grammar
guaranteed
guerrilla

happened
harass
heard
height
heroes
hindrance
hoping
humane
humorous
hurriedly
hypocrisy
hypocrite

ideally
idiosyncrasy
ignorant
illicit (illegal)
illogical
imaginary
imagine
imitate
immediately
immensely
immigrate (go into)
incalculable
incidentally
incredible
indispensable
inequity
influential
initiative
innocuous
insurance
insure (guarantee financially)
integrate
intelligent
interference
interrupt
irrelevant
irresistible
irritated

jealousy
jewelry
judgment

kilogram
knowledge

laboratory
laid
lath (wood)
lathe (machine)
led
leisure
length
lenient
leukemia
liable
library
license
lightning
likelihood
liquefy
liveliest
logistics
loose (adjective)
lose (verb)
luxury
lying

Spelling

magazine
magnificent
maintenance
manageable
management
maneuver
mantel *(shelf)*
mantle *(cloak)*
margarine
marijuana
marriage
material *(goods)*
materiel *(military goods)*
mathematics
meant
medicine
meteorology
mileage
miniature
minor
mirror
mischievous
missile
morale
mortgage
mucous *(adjective)*
mucus *(noun)*
muscle
mysterious

naturally
necessary
nevertheless
nickel
niece
nineteen
ninety
ninth
noticeable
nowadays
nuclear
nuisance
numerous

Occasion
occasionally
occurred
occurrence
occurring
off
offense
official
omission
omitted
omitting
oneself
opponent
opportunity
opposite
oppression
optimism
ordinance *(law)*
ordnance *(military)*
ordinarily
originally

pamphlet
parallel
paralleled
parole
particle
particularly
pastime
peaceable
peculiar
penetrate
perceive
performance
perhaps
permanent
perquisite *(privilege)*
personal *(individual)*
personnel *(employees)*
perspective *(viewpoint)*
persuade
pertain
phosphorous *(adjective)*
phosphorus *(noun)*
physical
picnicking
pigeon
poison
politician
pollute
possession
possibly
practical
practically
precede
precedence *(priority)*
precedents *(prior instances)*
predominant
preferred
prejudice
prerequisite *(requirement)*
prevail
prevalent
preventive (not *preventative*)
principal *(chief* or *main)*
principle *(theory* or *idea)*
prisoner
privilege
probably
procedure
proceed
processes
professor
programmed
programmer
programming
prominent
pronounce
pronunciation
propaganda
prophecy *(noun)*
prophesy *(verb)*
prospective *(expected)*
psychology
publicly
pursue
pursuing
pursuit

quandary
quarreled
quarreling
questionnaire
quiet
quite
quizzes

rarefy
rarity
rebel
receipt
receive
recession
recipe
recommend
reconnaissance
reconnoiter
recyclable
referring
regular
regulate
rehearsal
reinforce
relief *(noun)*
relieve *(verb)*
religious
remembrance
reminisce
repellant *(noun)*
repellent *(adjective)*
repetition
resemblance
resistance
restaurant
rhythm
ridiculous

Sacrifice
safety
salvage *(save)*
satellite
scarcity
scenery
schedule
secede
secretary
seismology
seize
selvage *(edging)*
separate
sergeant
sheriff
shining
shrubbery
signaled
signaling
significant
similar
sincerely
sizable
some time *(some time ago)*
sometime *(formerly)*
sometimes *(at times)*
souvenir
spacious *(space)*
specious *(deceptive)*

sponsor
stationary *(fixed)*
stationery *(paper)*
statistics
stepped
stopped
straight
strategy
strength
strenuous
stretch
studies
studying
subpoena
subpoenaed
subtlety
suburban
succeed
succession
suicide
sulfur
superintendent
supersede
suppress
surely
surreptitious
surround
surveillance
susceptible
suspicious
synonymous

technical
technique
temperature
temporary
their *(pronoun)*
themselves
there *(adverb)*
therefore
thorough
though
through
tie, tied, tying
tobacco
too
totaled, totaling
tragedy
transferable
transferred
traveled
traveling
tremendous
truly
twelfth
typical
tyranny

Unanimous
unconscious
undoubtedly
until
usage
usually

Vacuum
various
vengeance
villain
violence
visible
vitamin

Warrant
warring
weather
Wednesday
where
wherever
whether
whichever
whiskey
wholly
woman *(singular)*
women *(plural)*
writing
written

Yacht
yield
yogurt *or* yoghurt

Zenith
zephyr
zodiac

Strong Verbs

Strong Verbs

1. Use strong verbs.

Strong verbs shorten sentences and usually convey direct, memorable messages.

A common stylistic problem is using weak, rather than strong, verbs. Weak verbs are those simple verbs that occur so frequently in our language that they have little impact: *is, are, was, were, can, could, has, had, have, do, did, done, make, use, come.* See VERBS.

Obviously, these verbs are essential to English. Using them, either as primary or auxiliary sentence verbs, is inescapable. However, writers often use them unnecessarily to create wordy, weak sentences:

> The system has wide applicability for a variety of industrial cogeneration situations. *(12 words)*

In this sentence, the writer has transformed *apply,* a much stronger verb than *has,* into an awkward, bureaucratic noun, *applicability,* and used the weaker verb as the sentence verb. Using *apply* as the sentence verb creates a shorter, stronger sentence:

> The system applies to a variety of industrial cogeneration situations. *(10 words)*

See SCIENTIFIC/TECHNICAL STYLE.

1. Use strong verbs.

Strong verbs are less common; therefore, readers tend to pay more attention to them. They have more impact in a sentence, and they help writers avoid long, bureaucratic nouns:

> *this*
>
> Since 1965, our Basic Development Department has studied membranes for the separation and enrichment of gas mixtures. (17 words)
>
> *not this*
>
> Membranes for the separation and enrichment of gas mixtures have been under study by our Basic Development Department since 1965. (20 words)

> *this*
>
> We have vastly improved our reaction mechanisms. (7 words)
>
> *not this*
>
> We have made vast improvements in our reaction mechanisms. (9 words)

> *this*
>
> We would like to investigate further the pilot program before proposing a factory location. (14 words)
>
> *not this*
>
> We would like to conduct further investigations into the pilot program before giving a proposed factory location. (17 words)

> *this*
>
> We will emphasize evaluating plating techniques for depositing amorphous or glassy metal coatings. (13 words)
>
> *not this*
>
> We will give special emphasis to the evaluation of plating techniques for the deposition of amorphous or glassy metal coatings. (20 words)

> *this*
>
> Before developing the catalyst, we would assess the technical and economic advantages of the source materials. (16 words)
>
> *not this*
>
> Before proceeding with catalyst development, we would make technical and economic assessments of the advantages of the source materials available. (20 words)

Style is the sum of the choices, both conscious and unconscious, that writers make while planning, designing, writing, and editing documents.

These choices include the type of document, the words chosen, the structure and length of sentences, the length and type of paragraphs, the document's organization, the use of emphatic devices (headings, lists, white space), the use and kind of graphics, the typeface and type size, the paper, and so on. See PAGE LAYOUT.

Such choices give each document a unique style, tone, and feeling. Each fax, field note, business letter, quick memo, formal report—they are all unique because they differ in tone, attitude, perspective, and style from every other fax, note, letter, memo, and report.

Style and Tone

Style and *tone* are often confused. The terms are similar, and some speakers use them interchangeably. However, style is the cause and tone is the effect:

- **Style** refers to those choices writers make that create the tone conveyed to readers.

- **Tone** refers to the feeling or impression a document conveys to its readers. See TONE.

Style is often categorized as being either **formal** or **informal**. These distinctions typically depend on the type of document being written, the intended readers, the writer's relationship to the readers, the document's purpose, and the message being conveyed.

> ### Style
>
> Style and Tone
> Word Choice and Style
> Sentences and Style
>   Sentence Length
>   Sentence Structure
>
> Other Stylistic Choices
> Individual Style
> Style and Ineffective Writing

Formal documents, such as legal agreements, technical reports, and many letters, are written for readers with whom the writer has no personal relationship. Therefore, familiarity or humor is generally unacceptable. It would seem inappropriate to the circumstance and would interfere with the message. Formal documents are usually written to convey information objectively to readers who may not know (or care to know) the author.

The tone of formal documents tends to be impersonal, objective, restrained, deliberate, and factual. Formal documents that are intended to convince readers to do or accept something are often also forceful, dynamic, and perhaps intensive. Most documents that convey negative or unpleasant information are formal.

Informal documents, such as personal letters, newsletters, trip reports, and most memos, are generally written for people the writer knows or feels comfortable with, perhaps only through employment in the same organization. Familiarity, humor, and wit are often acceptable. The informality creates a more relaxed atmosphere, which makes the message warmer and more easily accepted. Informal documents are often informative, friendly, and subjective.

The tone of informal documents is generally relaxed, informative, helpful, casual, personal, positive, nonthreatening, and perhaps cheerful. Informal documents may be persuasive, but they are rarely forceful or aggressive. When writers need to be aggressive and when they need to convey negative or unpleasant information, they generally become more formal in their approach. See TONE.

Style also refers to styles associated with particular disciplines: geologic style, geophysical style, legal style, medical style, engineering style, auditing style, academic style, scientific style, social science style, bureaucratic style, and so on. See SCIENTIFIC/TECHNICAL STYLE.

In each of these styles, the writer uses jargon particular to the discipline and writes according to a long tradition of document preparation and appearance. We are perhaps most familiar with the legal and bureaucratic styles, but all disciplines have a set of standards and traditions that affect the way people communicate in writing. See JARGON.

Word Choice and Style

Each word you choose helps establish the style of your writing. Words are one of the most visible traits of style.

Style

You may, for instance, wish to discuss the effects of a decision. The word *effects* is a fairly neutral choice. Instead of *effects,* you might speak of *impacts, consequences,* or *results. Impacts* suggests some negative connotations, as does *consequences,* which is more formal sounding (perhaps because of its length) than *impacts. Results,* on the other hand, has a positive feeling to it: *We're going to get results.*

You have other less common choices: *aftermath, corollary, end product, eventuality, outcome, sequel, upshot. Aftermath* has definite negative implications, besides being almost dramatic in its tone. *Corollary* has limited usefulness, if for no other reason than its mathematical echoes (and hence almost too educated tone). *End product* seems plain, yet still wordy when compared to *effects* or *results. Eventuality* implies some final or ultimate result; again, its length makes it sound more formal. *Outcome* is about as neutral as any of the words in this list, but it may have negative connotations, as in the outcome of a medical test. *Sequel* implies a second follow-up event, not a real effect. And *upshot* suggests surprise, even chaos. Even more words are possible: *development, fruit, outgrowth, ramification, repercussion, conclusion.*

Part of the richness of English is its large vocabulary, which offers multiple possibilities for expressing any idea. Yet no two words mean exactly the same thing, so when you choose one word rather than another, you change the style of the document, if only slightly. Within a few lines, then, you will make dozens of choices, all of which combine to establish the style (and resulting tone) of the document.

Obviously, some word choices make a bigger difference than others. Selecting *effects* rather than *results* changes the style very little. But if you use *impacts, consequences,* or *aftermath,* the document may shift in tone and effect:

> What is the effect of altering course in midflight?
>
> What are the consequences of altering course in midflight?

> What were the effects of the pipeline installation on the salmon in Little Middle River?
>
> What was the aftermath of the pipeline installation on the salmon in Little Middle River?

As you can see, some word choices are important stylistic signals. Others are inconsequential:

> What is the effect of altering course in midflight?
>
> What is the result of altering course in midflight?

Writers in various technical professions have a body of technical words that affect the style:

Legal

tort, legatee, real property, contract, conveyance, *amicus curiae,* party, sue, brief, witness, jurisdiction, plaintiff, etc.

Medical

curette, mammillary, uvulae, amoebic, gastric hernia, leucoplast, dermatitis, proboscis, etc.

Computer

batch processing, cursor, default, field, file, logon, real time, sign off, etc.

Construction

sill, head, transom, fascia, neoprene spaces, support mullion, jamb, seat board, glazing gasket, butt glazed, hopper sash, soffit, rowlock, etc.

Such specialized scientific and technical terms are unavoidable given today's complex technologies. See JARGON. The presence of this jargon is the most visible sign to readers that a document reflects a particular style.

Sentences and Style

Writers have virtually an infinite number of ways to express ideas. Even in an ordinary 15- to 30-word sentence, the possibilities run into the millions, both in terms of word choice and sentence structure. The sheer range of possibility means that every sentence except the shortest and most trivial is potentially unique (never having been written or said before).

Sentence options—**length** and **structure**—are the most important features of a writer's style. However, these options are often less obvious to readers than the choice of a particular word or technical term. Readers notice the style of sentences only when something goes wrong, as in an awkward sentence or one where something is deliberately unusual:

> That is something up with which I shall not put.

or

> Turning into the wrong driveway, a tree was hit by me which I don't have.

Sentence Length

Sentence length by itself normally will not establish a definite style, but it will contribute to style. Most sentences average anywhere from 12 to 25 words. Readers are accustomed to those lengths, so they are likely to notice only those sentences that are either extremely short or extremely long:

> We refuse.

or

> Science is nothing but trained and organized common sense, differing from the latter only as a veteran may differ from a raw recruit: and its methods differ from those of common sense only as far as the guardsman's cut and thrust differ from the manner in which a savage wields his club. (From Thomas Huxley's *Collected Essays*)

An individual sentence, even if potentially noteworthy, won't be noteworthy unless it stands out from the sentences surrounding it. So **average sentence length** is probably more of a direct indication of style than the length of a single sentence. Readability formulas always include average sentence length as a measure of readability because length is a good indicator of the difficulty of a document. See SENTENCES.

Long sentences can reflect different styles (and tones), depending on other features within them. Long, well-structured sentences with a sophisticated vocabulary usually convey an educated or thoughtful quality. But if the sentence seems longer than necessary for the ideas being expressed, and if the vocabulary is more sophisticated than necessary, then the sentence may seem stuffy, extravagant, or pompous:

> If biological populations or habitats that may require additional protection are identified by the DCMOFO (Deputy Conservation Manager, Offshore Field Operations) in the leasing area, the DCMOFO will require the lessee to conduct environmental surveys or studies, including sampling, as approved by the DCMOFO, to determine existing environmental conditions, the extent and composition of biological populations or habitats, and the effects of proposed or existing operations on the populations or habitats that might require additional protective measures.

This sentence's length—77 words—is surely excessive, but other features contribute to its bureaucratic, stiff, faintly legal style:

- The use of the unfamiliar acronym *DCMOFO* gives the sentence a bureaucratic touch, especially with its repetitions of the acronym.

- The repetition within the sentence, especially of the phrase *populations or habitats,* reinforces the bureaucratic, even stuffy, tone.

- The delay of the main subject and verb *(the DCMOFO will require)* until after the long introductory *if* clause forces readers to absorb, comprehend, and remember too much information at once. Consequently, the sentence is more difficult to read than it should be.

- Some of the phrasing is clumsy and ill-placed. The phrase *in the leasing area* comes so late in the opening clause that its meaning is fuzzy. Is the DCMOFO in the leasing area? Are the populations and habitats in the leasing area? Have any or all of these been identified in the leasing area?

For an example of a well-structured long sentence, see SENTENCES.

Sentence Structure

Sentence structure—including grammatical structure, the sequence of ideas, and the various repeated word patterns—all contribute to the style of a sentence or passage. The following versions of the same basic sentence say much the same thing, but their different structures create different tones:

1. We considered how best to present the conflicting data and our interpretations of these conflicts.

2. How to present the conflicting data, as well as our interpretations of these conflicts, was under consideration.

3. Because of conflicting data and differing interpretations, we were considering different presentation strategies.

4. We were considering different strategies for presenting the conflicting data and our interpretations of the data.

5. It was difficult to decide on strategies for presenting the conflicting data and the differing interpretations of the data.

Sentences 1 and 4 are the most direct (and they happen to be the ones that most closely follow normal English word order). Sentence 2 is formal, even stuffy, because its opening clause is so long that the verb *was* is almost lost. Sentence 3 is fairly ordinary, even though it opens with the conditional *because* clause. Sentence 5 is perhaps the most stuffy; it opens with a false subject (see FALSE SUBJECTS), and it avoids all pronouns. See PRONOUNS.

The structural patterns for a single sentence present a broad range of possibilities. Putting sentences together increases the possibilities exponentially.

A string of formal, oddly structured sentences not only slows down readers but also conveys a tone of formality or stuffiness. A string of short, direct sentences can sound clean and efficient (or abrupt and efficient, depending on the context).

Other Stylistic Choices

Many other features in a document besides words and sentences can convey a particular style.

The basic format of a document is usually significant. A document with narrow margins, single-spaced text, and long paragraphs conveys a dense, information-packed but potentially dull image. Readers may consider the language heavy and ponderous. A document with generous margins and lots of open space makes readers feel that the writing is open and inviting, easier to read. See PAGE LAYOUT.

Besides format choices, many other features influence a reader's perception of a document:

- The typeface used for the text

- The type of paper—both weight and texture

Style

- The number and quality of the graphics

- The care with which the proofreading and editing has been done

- The professionalism of the binding and the quality of the printing

- The presence or absence of color

Individual Style

We all have styles of speaking and writing that are unique to us, regardless of the circumstances in which we write. This fact reflects the basic and pervasive nature of style.

In speech, an individual's style is easy to identify. Most of us can recognize a close friend, not only from the sound of the friend's voice, but also from the structure and content of the speech, from the words chosen, and from the sentence patterns used. We know our friends as talkative, quiet, abrupt, cheerful, depressed, thoughtful, humorous, or tactful. In writing, an individual's style may be harder to identify, and yet it exists in each choice the individual has made to produce a document.

Style and Ineffective Writing

Ultimately, style **is** the writer. We can't describe a universally preferable style because the decisions writers make depend on the context: on the subject or content, the purpose of the document, the readers, previous or related documents, and the situation or climate in which the document is produced.

Nevertheless, good writing is distinguishable from bad writing, and you should never confuse bad writing with style.

Good writing is clear, emphatic, well organized, and concise. Bad writing is often vague or confusing, unemphatic, chaotic, and wordy.

Good writers obey the principles of effective writing—regardless of subject matter, purpose, readers, context, style, or tone.

For a review of those principles, see this *Style Guide*, particularly the sections on SENTENCES, PARAGRAPHS, ORGANIZATION, EMPHASIS, ACTIVE/ PASSIVE, STRONG VERBS, FALSE SUBJECTS, and KEY WORDS.

For information on writing specific types of documents, see LETTERS, MEMOS, REPORTS, and SUMMARIES.

Summaries are abridgments or compendiums of the important points in a document. Summaries are essential for readers who don't have time to read the entire document, are not interested in reading the entire document, or need to review the important points without reading the entire document.

Traditional summaries appear at the end of documents, especially those organized scientifically. See ORGANIZATION. These summaries present the main points from the preceding discussion.

Executive summaries appear at the beginning of documents, especially in documents organized according to the managerial format. See ORGANIZATION. These summaries preview the main points that will appear in the discussion that follows.

Traditional Summaries

Traditional summaries briefly repeat the major ideas, especially conclusions and recommendations. These summaries include little, if any, background information and no supporting data or detail of any kind. They are typically shorter than executive summaries, which may include some background and supporting information.

Traditional summaries should not be separated from the rest of the document. They are a final summation, so they depend on information presented earlier in the document. Everything in them must already have been stated earlier.

The writer of a traditional summary often assumes that readers will use the summary after having read the rest of the document.

Executive Summaries

Executive summaries—also known simply as summaries—appear at the beginning of documents. They usually include the following:

- **Background/introduction to the document.** Although very brief, this section gives readers enough information so they will understand the reason for the document, the key problems addressed, and any special conditions or situations that the reader should be aware of. See ORGANIZATION and INTRODUCTIONS.

- **Main conclusions.** These may be a little longer than in traditional summaries because they are not repeated from conclusions presented earlier. Therefore, in addition to the conclusion itself, you may need a little explanation or elaboration. Just keep them short.

- **Recommendations, if any.** Again, you are not repeating recommendations presented earlier, so each recommendation might require some explanation. If appropriate, tie each recommendation to the specific conclusion or conclusions that prompted it.

- **A review of data (optional).** This section is limited to pertinent items, not all the data. The complete data usually appear in an appendix. However, you may need to present key data in an executive summary so that readers are aware of the key supporting information that your document presents. Remember that readers may read only the executive summary, not the entire document. Give them enough detail to substantiate your conclusions, but not so much that the rest of the document becomes unnecessary.

In some instances, business and technical documents may consist only of an executive summary, with supporting or explanatory material located in appendices or attachments. Such documents reflect the attempt of many businesses to limit documentation to the essentials.

Summaries versus Abstracts

Scientific and technical writers often include abstracts with their reports. Abstracts are condensations of a document, usually written so that readers can preview the content of the document to determine whether they are interested in reading the entire document. In a sense, abstracts are extended titles.

Summaries

Abstracts may contain much of the same information found in summaries, but abstracts are meant to be detached from their documents. Frequently, abstracts are published separately, in an online catalog or list of abstracts. Sometimes, journals request that potential authors submit abstracts of their articles. The editors read the abstracts to determine which articles they want to read in full.

Summaries, on the other hand, are an integral part of the documents they belong to, and they are not normally detached.

By convention, abstracts are rarely longer than one paragraph (about 250 words). Summaries have no conventional length restrictions. They should be concise, of course, but summaries may range from 50 to 5,000 words, depending on the length of the parent document. An extensive report or multi-volume proposal could very well have an executive summary of 20 or 30 pages. See REPORTS and ORGANIZATION.

How to Write Summaries

You may wish to produce a preliminary summary of a long or complicated document before you have written the whole document. A preliminary summary will help you organize your thoughts and determine your most significant points. However, the final summary (the one appearing in your document) should be written last. Here is a procedure for writing good summaries (especially executive summaries):

1. Read through the entire document. Ensure that you have a firm grasp of the document's purpose, scope, point of view, and major ideas.

2. Identify the major ideas and data. You can underline or circle major ideas, or put stars beside them, or highlight them with a highlighting pen. Identify all of the major statements: observations, conclusions, recommendations, key supporting data, key facts, etc.

3. Pull the major ideas together and note how they are developed sequentially throughout the document. If necessary, refer to details in the text to clarify any points not absolutely clear.

4. Condense by combining sentences, generalizing, eliminating unnecessary supporting information, and eliminating unnecessary words and phrases. Use simple, direct sentences, and eliminate all unnecessary jargon and big words. Keep your writing simple and straightforward.

5. Use transitional words and phrases to link ideas and provide a smooth flow of thought from one sentence to the next.

6. Test the result by challenging every word, phrase, sentence, and idea. If something isn't pulling its weight, get rid of it.

7. Challenge the overall summary. Does it accurately reflect the content of the whole document? Have you left out major ideas? Does the summary distort any facts, relationships, conclusions, or recommendations? Does the summary provide ample information for readers to comprehend the ideas without reading the whole document? Can the summary stand by itself? If readers read nothing but the summary, will they be adequately informed?

Remember that the purpose of the summary is not to convey everything. Summaries convey the essentials. If readers want additional support or proof, they should read the rest of the document. But make sure that the summary provides readers with a firm grasp of the major ideas.

Tables are information displays organized by rows and columns. Three types of information displays are common:

- Formal data tables
- Matrix (text) tables (see rule 16)
- Run-in tables (see rule 17)

Formal data tables, as traditionally used, present precise data: *3.1415, 9.8690, 31.0035,* etc. Such data cannot be presented as precisely in any other type of graphic aid. See GRAPHICS FOR DOCUMENTS. Tables allow for quick and accurate comparisons and can also depict trends and relationships, although not as well as charts and graphs. See CHARTS and GRAPHS.

Use formal data tables when you must present a large amount of information, when you need to give readers the exact figures, or when you want readers to be able to compare figures or other information presented in different rows and columns.

For a much more elaborate discussion of formal tables, including printing considerations, see the *United States Government Printing Office Style Manual.* See REFERENCES.

Matrix (text) tables. A popular variation of the formal table is a matrix that presents textual information, not precise data. This type of table often looks like a hybrid between formal tables and more informal run-in tables. A matrix table may have column and row labels just like a formal table. The matrix will also have data in some of its squares. Other squares, however, may have words, phrases, or even short paragraphs.

A matrix table can often replace several pages of text. See rule 16 for an example of a matrix table.

Tables

1. Keep tables as simple as possible.

2. Place important tables in the body of the document; place unimportant tables in appendices or attachments.

3. Use table numbers and captions to identify tables and to help readers understand the information presented.

4. Orient tables horizontally on the page.

5. Clearly label tables that extend beyond one page, and use continuation headings on continued pages.

6. Use white space, boxes, or lines to separate tables from surrounding text.

7. Logically organize rows and columns so that they reflect the purpose of the table and make the table easy to read.

8. Use row headings (in the stub) and column headings (in the boxhead) to identify the information listed in each row and column.

9. Use rules to separate the boxhead from the field, and, as necessary, use rules to separate groups of data columns or rows from each other.

10. Where space is limited, use abbreviations.

11. Base comparable numerical amounts on the same unit of measurement, and convert all fractions to decimals.

12. Align decimals vertically within columns.

13. Use zeros, dashes, ellipses, or *NA* to indicate that information is missing or not applicable.

14. Use footnotes to explain or clarify table headings and entries.

15. Identify all data sources.

16. Use a matrix (text) table to present complex textual information.

17. Use informal or run-in tables to replace ordinary text, especially lengthy paragraphs.

Run-in tables are increasingly useful ways to break up dense text. The simplest run-in table has no number, no caption, and may be only two or more columns inserted into a passage of ordinary text. The sentences preceding such a table introduce the information. See rule 17 for an example of a run-in table.

Parts of Tables

The standard parts of formal tables are the following: the **table number** and **caption,** the **boxhead** (containing column headings), the **stub** (containing row headings), the **field** (**body**), **rules, footnotes,** and the **source line.** See figure 1 for a sample table layout.

Tables

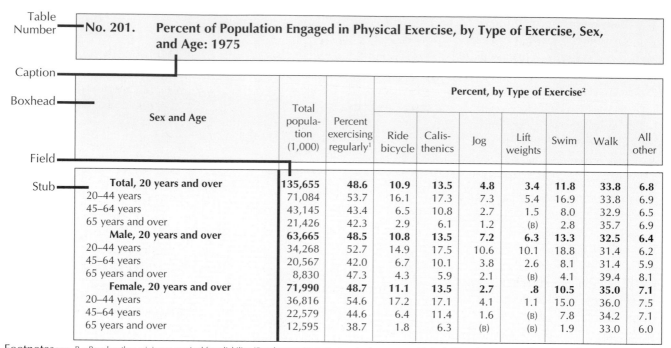

Table Number — **No. 201.** **Percent of Population Engaged in Physical Exercise, by Type of Exercise, Sex, and Age: 1975**

Caption

Boxhead

Field

Stub

Sex and Age	Total population (1,000)	Percent exercising regularly[1]	Percent, by Type of Exercise[2]						
			Ride bicycle	Calisthenics	Jog	Lift weights	Swim	Walk	All other
Total, 20 years and over	**135,655**	**48.6**	**10.9**	**13.5**	**4.8**	**3.4**	**11.8**	**33.8**	**6.8**
20–44 years	71,084	53.7	16.1	17.3	7.3	5.4	16.9	33.8	6.9
45–64 years	43,145	43.4	6.5	10.8	2.7	1.5	8.0	32.9	6.5
65 years and over	21,426	42.3	2.9	6.1	1.2	(B)	2.8	35.7	6.9
Male, 20 years and over	**63,665**	**48.5**	**10.8**	**13.5**	**7.2**	**6.3**	**13.3**	**32.5**	**6.4**
20–44 years	34,268	52.7	14.9	17.5	10.6	10.1	18.8	31.4	6.2
45–64 years	20,567	42.0	6.7	10.1	3.8	2.6	8.1	31.4	5.9
65 years and over	8,830	47.3	4.3	5.9	2.1	(B)	4.1	39.4	8.1
Female, 20 years and over	**71,990**	**48.7**	**11.1**	**13.5**	**2.7**	**.8**	**10.5**	**35.0**	**7.1**
20–44 years	36,816	54.6	17.2	17.1	4.1	1.1	15.0	36.0	7.5
45–64 years	22,579	44.6	6.4	11.4	1.6	(B)	7.8	34.2	7.1
65 years and over	12,595	38.7	1.8	6.3	(B)	(B)	1.9	33.0	6.0

Footnotes — B = Base less than minimum required for reliability. [1]Regular exercise is any exercise done on a weekly basis. [2]More than one type of exercise can be reported per person.

Source Line — Source: U.S. National Center for Health Statistics, *Health, United States, 1976–1977.*

Figure 1. Sample Table Layout. *A clear, correct table layout assists readers to understand and interpret the data.*

Table Number and Caption

Number tables sequentially as they appear in the document, and number them separately from figures.

Unless you are presenting uninterpreted data, make the table caption both a title and an informative caption (see tables 1 through 5). The table caption should clearly identify the table and tell readers how to read or interpret the table:

Table 1. *The industrial gas shipment decline since 1980.*

Table 2. Wood Panel Products (1975–84). *Production has more than doubled in 10 years.*

Table 3. *Increasing arsenic concentrations in groundwater, Sonoma County, California, 1985.*

These captions indicate both what the tables are about and how readers should interpret them.

If you are presenting a large amount of uninterpreted data and your purpose is to present, not interpret, the data, then use shorter, title-like captions:

Table 1. Industrial Gas Shipments (1976–84)

Table 2. Wood Panel Product Production (1975–84)

Table 3. Arsenic concentrations in groundwater, Sonoma County, California, 1985

Most table titles and their associated captions should appear above tables, especially when, as in the preceding examples, the titles/captions are little more than a brief phrase. In some instances, editors place short titles (and brief captions) above a table and then include a detailed explanation under the table. *Scientific American* uses this pattern occasionally, both for tables and figures. Their short title above a table or a graphic becomes a headline; detailed interpretations then appear under the table or figure.

Whichever pattern you choose for placing the titles/captions, be consistent throughout a document. See CAPTIONS.

If a unit of measurement applies throughout the table, you may state the unit of measurement in the caption or within parentheses beneath the caption. If the unit of measurement appears below the caption, you can subordinate it by printing it in a smaller type size. See CAPTIONS.

Boxhead

The boxhead contains the stub heading and the column headings (see figure 1). Place a rule (line) above and beneath the boxhead to separate it from the table number and caption and from the field. Make column and stub headings as concise as possible. Use more than one line, if necessary, to state a column heading, but try not to exceed three lines for any heading. Orient the headings horizontally.

If appropriate, include units of measurement in the headings or enclose the units of measurement within parentheses below the headings. If the column headings require more than one line and you place units of measurement below the headings, separate the headings and units with a thin rule (see tables 2 and 3). Use thicker rules around the boxhead itself.

Stub

The stub is the left column. Use it to label the rows. Make the row headings as concise as possible. As necessary, put row units of measurement either within parentheses following the row heading or in another column beside the stub (see table 4).

If the rows consist of major and subordinate items, place the major items flush left and indent the subordinate items (see table 1).

Field

The field (body) consists of the data rows and columns below the boxhead and to the right of the stub. If necessary for clarity, use leaders (rows of periods) between rows to facilitate reading (see tables 2 or 3). Align the data presented in each column by placing words flush left within columns, integers (e.g., *40*) right flush by digit, and real numbers (e.g., *40.0* or *40.068*) vertically by decimal point.

Rules

Rules are horizontal or vertical lines that separate parts of the table. Always place rules between the boxhead and the field. Also, place a rule above the boxhead to separate the boxhead from the table number and caption. If you use footnotes or a source line, place a rule between them and the bottom of the field. See PAGE LAYOUT.

If your table is large, you might need to place rules between groups of rows. Typically, the rules appear between groups of five. These rules help readers follow information down large tables.

The rules surrounding the box head should be thicker than those appearing within the field.

NOTE 1: Instead of placing rules between every fifth row, you may leave an extra line to separate groups of rows.

NOTE 2: Some authorities also use vertical rules to separate the stub from the field and groups of columns from each other. The trend today is to eliminate all vertical rules.

Footnotes

Use footnotes to clarify the headings, to identify unfamiliar abbreviations and units of measurement, and to explain the data appearing within the field.

Use superscripted footnote numbers or letters (^{1}, ^{2}, ^{3} or ^{a}, ^{b}, ^{c}) or symbols (*, **, ***) to link the footnoted information in the table and its explanation (see tables 2 through 4). If the footnote applies to the entire table, you do not need a footnote symbol (see the note beneath table 1).

The footnotes should appear below the table, beginning flush left. If a footnote extends across the table and you have many footnotes, break the footnote references into two columns and print them in a smaller type size, if possible (see table 4).

Table 1. U.S. Machine Tool Consumption, for Selected Numerically Controlled Machines, 1979–1982. *Imports as a share of consumption increased more rapidly during 1980 and 1981 than during 1982.* [In millions of dollars.]

Item	1979	1980	1981	1982
Machining Centers				
Production	356.5	413.0	482.6	339.5
Exports	45.4	56.7	53.4	34.0
Imports	39.6	93.4	195.7	188.9
Consumption	350.7	449.7	624.9	494.4
Imports as share of consumption	11.3%	20.8%	31.3%	38.2%
Horizontal Spindle Turning Machines				
Production	284.4	321.7	346.6	238.6
Exports	NA	20.5	20.4	30.4
Imports	NA	159.8	278.0	194.1
Consumption	NA	461.0	604.2	402.2
Imports as share of consumption	NA	34.7%	46.0%	48.2%
Punching and Shearing Machines				
Production	82.5	110.6	97.1	59.0
Exports	NA	13.2	28.3	8.3
Imports	NA	16.5	32.5	25.5
Consumption	NA	113.9	101.3	76.2
Imports as share of consumption	NA	14.5%	32.1%	33.4%

NA = *Not Available*

Note: *Data in this table differ from those in other tables due to different source of production data and exclusion of data on machine tool parts.*

Sources: Bureau of the Census, *"Current Industrial Report for Metalworking Machinery,"* MQ-35W; *"U.S. Imports for Consumption,"* IM146; and *"U.S. Exports,"* EM522.

Tables

Source Line

The source line identifies the source of the information presented in the table. Source lines always appear below footnotes and should be aligned with the footnote references (see tables 1 through 4). See INTELLECTUAL PROPERTY.

Rules for Using Tables

1. Keep tables as simple as possible.

Tables can become complicated quickly, so simplify them as much as possible. If the information you are trying to present becomes too complicated, break it up into two or more tables.

2. Place important tables in the body of the document; place unimportant tables in appendices or attachments.

Tables conveying critical information must appear in the text. However, if you are presenting tables of uninterpreted data, consider placing them in an appendix or attachment. Do not force readers to ponder uninterpreted data unless they want to. See APPENDICES and EMPHASIS.

3. Use table numbers and captions to identify tables and to help readers understand the information presented.

Table numbers help readers track tables through a document and help them find important tabular information.

Captions label the information found in a table and can tell readers how to read the table. The caption is your opportunity to influence the reader's perception of the information you present. You should take advantage of that opportunity and write an informative caption. See CAPTIONS.

4. Orient tables horizontally on the page.

Try to orient tables horizontally so that readers do not have to reorient the page to read the table. This means that most tables can be longer than they can be wider (that is, they can have more rows than columns). If you need to have more columns than rows, consider redesigning your table or breaking it into two tables. As a last resort, orient the table sideways with the boxhead toward the left side of the page.

5. Clearly label tables that extend beyond one page, and use continuation headings on continued pages.

If you must continue a table from one page to another, write *continued* on the bottom right corner of the table on each page to be continued. Then on the top of each new page where the table has been continued, write, for instance, *Table 4, continued*.

Finally, repeat the boxhead on each continued page.

Table 2. Production and Imports of Crude Oil—1960 to 1984. *The production and import of crude oil increased significantly from 1960 to 1970; however, the volume remained relatively level during the 1970s and the early 1980s.*

Year	Production				Gross Imports	
	Crude oil[1]	Natural gas[2]	Natural gas plant liquids	Total	Crude oil	Natural gas
	(billions of barrels)	(trillions of cu ft)	(billions of barrels)	(quadrillions of Btu's)	(billions of barrels)	(trillions of cu ft)
1960	2.575	12.23	0.340	29.05	0.373	0.16
1970	3.517	21.01	0.606	44.58	0.482	0.82
1972	3.455	21.62	0.638	44.85	0.813	1.02
1973	3.361	21.73	0.634	44.25	1.183	1.03
1974	3.203	20.71	0.616	42.25	1.270	0.96
1975	3.057	19.24	0.596	39.74	1.497	0.95
1976	2.976	19.10	0.587	39.07	1.936	0.96
1977	3.009	19.16	0.590	39.35	2.413	1.01
1978	3.178	19.12	0.572	40.17	2.321	0.97
1979	3.121	19.66	0.578	40.47	2.380	1.25
1980	3.146	19.60	0.576	40.42	1.925	0.98
1981	3.129	19.40	0.587	40.15	1.605	0.90
1982	3.157	17.75	0.566	38.55	1.273	0.93
1983[3]	3.161	16.28	0.562	37.26	1.278	0.86
1984[4]	3.126	17.41	0.567	38.23	1.636	0.90

[1]Includes lease condensate
[2]Net dry natural gas, including nonhydrocarbon gases
[3]Estimated
[4]Forecast

Source: Energy Information Administration.

Table 3. Prices and Price Indexes for U.S. Imported and Domestically Produced Crude Oil, 1972 to 1984. *The 7 to 9 percent cost increase of crude oil from 1972 to 1984 was passed on to consumers. (Price in dollars per barrel; index of 100 for 1972.)*

Year	Refiner acquisition cost of U.S.-imported crude		Refiner acquisition cost of U.S.-produced crude		Wellhead price of U.S.-produced crude	
	Price	Index	Price	Index	Price	Index
1972	3.22	100.0	3.67	100.0	3.39	100.0
1973	4.08	126.7	4.17	113.6	3.89	114.7
1974	12.52	388.8	7.18	195.6	6.87	202.7
1975	13.93	432.6	8.39	228.6	7.67	226.3
1976	13.48	418.6	8.84	240.9	8.19	241.6
1977	14.53	451.2	9.55	260.2	8.57	252.8
1978	14.57	452.5	10.61	289.1	9.00	265.5
1979	21.67	673.0	14.27	388.8	12.64	372.9
1980	33.89	1,052.5	24.23	660.2	21.59	636.9
1981	37.05	1,150.6	34.33	935.4	31.77	937.2
1982	33.55	1,041.9	31.22	850.7	28.52	841.3
1983	29.13	904.7	28.97	789.4	26.37	777.9
1984	29.00	900.6	29.00	790.2	27.15	809.6

NA = not available

Source: Energy Information Administration.

6. Use white space, boxes, or lines to separate tables from surrounding text.

Tables are graphics and should be placed as thoughtfully as any other graphics. Separate them from surrounding text by leaving three lines above and below tables (more white space on the page), by placing the tables within boxes (or frames), or by using thin rules above and below the tables to separate them from the text. See EMPHASIS and PAGE LAYOUT.

7. Logically organize rows and columns so that they reflect the purpose of the table and make the table easy to read.

The arrangement of rows and columns depends on the information being presented and on the purpose of the table.

Use a chronological order for information presented by time, date, or sequence. Use a whole-to-parts pattern for major and subordinate items. Use logical grouping for items that should appear together because of type, size, or relationship. See ORGANIZATION.

Place information that you want readers to compare in adjacent rows or columns. As much as possible, avoid forcing readers to compare or contrast information separated by other rows or columns.

Place information that must be numerically tallied or compared in columns. Performing mathematical operations across rows is much more difficult than performing the same operations down columns.

When time is one of the variables, you can arrange it along rows or columns. However, time is traditionally displayed on the horizontal or x-axis of charts, so display time across columns (see table 1). (Note, however, that tables 2 and 3 are also easy to read. Time is displayed in rows in these tables because displaying time in columns would create wider, rather than longer, tables. See rule 4 above.)

8. Use row headings (in the stub) and column headings (in the boxhead) to identify the information listed in each row and column.

Tables without adequate headings are often incomprehensible. Ensure that your headings are concise and yet descriptive. If necessary, use footnotes to explain or fully describe the headings.

9. Use rules to separate the boxhead from the field, and, as necessary, use rules to separate groups of data columns or rows from each other.

Complex tables are much easier to read and to follow when the information is separated by rules. Use thicker rules to separate the boxhead and the stub from the field and thinner rules to separate groups of rows and columns.

10. Where space is limited, use abbreviations.

Abbreviations are appropriate in tables (as well as other graphics). Use them where space is limited. If the abbreviation is uncommon, explain it in a footnote. See ABBREVIATIONS.

11. Base comparable numerical amounts on the same unit of measurement, and convert all fractions to decimals.

Numbers that readers will want or need to compare must be presented in the same unit of measurement. Do not present some numbers in meters and similar numbers in centimeters, and some data in feet and comparable data in yards.

Tables

Further, convert all fractions to decimals and use real numbers (numbers with decimals) as necessary for accuracy. However, do not make numbers more precise than accuracy allows. In other words, do not give more than the significant digits in a real number. If you do, you will convey a false sense of accuracy. See DECIMALS and FRACTIONS.

12. Align decimals vertically within columns.

Except where you are mixing types of numbers, ensure that decimals are aligned vertically. The exception occurs in columns containing different types of real numbers, as in table 1. The percentage figures are distinct from the production figures and should not be aligned, although both sets of data contain decimals. Note that the percent signs clearly distinguish the percentages from the production figures.

13. Use zeros, dashes, ellipses, or NA to indicate that information is missing or not applicable.

Do not leave entries in rows or columns blank where the information is unavailable or not applicable (NA). Readers will not know whether the blank entry was intentional.

Instead, indicate missing or inapplicable information by entering a dash, a zero, an ellipsis mark, the abbreviation NA, or a comment like undetermined (see table 4).

NOTE: Use the abbreviation do (for ditto) where a data entry in a column is the same as the data entry directly above it.

14. Use footnotes to explain or clarify table headings and entries.

Tabular information is governed as much by space limitations as it is by content necessity, and you may not be able to explain fully a table heading or entry in the space available. So use footnotes where necessary for clarification. See GRAPHICS FOR DOCUMENTS.

Footnotes belong below the table and are usually flush left. Footnotes usually have the following format: superscripted reference number or letter indented, second or additional lines flush with the left margin, etc. See tables 2, 3, and 4.

If you are referencing numerical entries located within the field, use footnote letters or symbols rather than numbers, which some readers may confuse with the number being referenced. However, use a consistent system of reference. If you establish a system of footnote letters, then use that system throughout all of your tables. See the example tables within this section. See also FOOTNOTES.

15. Identify all data sources.

For the sake of clarity, as well as substantiation, identify all data sources. The source line may follow the standard bibliographic format (see table 1) or may identify the source by name alone (tables 2 through 4). See BIBLIOGRAPHIES and CITATIONS.

Whether you provide full source information depends on the nature of the source documents, the extent to which you have summarized from the

Table 4. Minimum Viable Population Levels for Management Indicator Species for the Targhee National Forest.

(Unless marked, population numbers reflect the total number of individual birds or animals.)

Species	Habitat Unit	Total Acres Habitat on Forest	Potential[1] Population	Minuimum[2] Viable Population
Grizzly Bear	Variable	340,000[3]	Undetermined	Undetermined
Bald Eagle	500 ac/nest site	25,000	50 pairs	Undetermined
Williamson's Sapsucker	20/ac/territory	467,000	23,350 pairs	9,340 pairs
Pika	1 ac/territory	53,000	53,000 pairs	21,200 pairs
Brewers Sparrow	5 ac/territory	121,000	24,200	9,680 pairs
Goshawk	15 sq mi/territory	870,000	90 pairs	36 pairs
Aquatic Invertebrates	per/sample[4]	25,000	Undetermined	Undetermined
Beaver	2 colonies/sq mi	46,000	144 colonies	58 colonies
Trout	lb/ac	25,000	Undetermined	18 lb/ac
Antelope	1/25 ac	77,000	4,000	1,000
Elk	6,000 ac	1,329,000	11,075	5,000[5]
Bighorn Sheep	Undetermined	77,000	600	150[6]
Mountain Goat	Undetermined	77,000	400	50[6]

[1]Within multiple use constraints and using currently available acres.

[2]40 percent of the potential is considered minimum viable population level on nongame species. Game species is the population at which a general hunt can be sustained.

[3]Situation 1 habitat and the occupied portion of Situation 2.

[4]Species diversity will be the measure of habitat quality.

[5]This level with about 40 bulls/100 cows preseason and 20 bulls/100 cows postseason.

[6]Idaho Fish and Game will begin to hunt a population at this level in any given herd area.

Source: *Final Environmental Impact Statement for the Land Management Plan for the Targhee National Forest.*

original, the purpose of your document, and the purpose of the table. If readers will want to examine the original sources, then provide full source information. However, if you have gathered data from a variety of sources or documents, you might not be able to identify specific documents.

If you have examined a number of EPA documents, for instance, and collated data from many of those documents, your source line should not list every single source. Instead, you should simply indicate:

Source: Environmental Protection Agency.

Begin source lines with the word *Source* or *Sources*, followed by a colon. End the source line with a period.

16. Use a matrix (text) table to present complex textual information.

A matrix is a visual tool for reproducing information that needs to be matched or tracked. For example, a manager wanting to consider three

sites for a new plant might decide to construct a summary matrix. Table 5 is an example of what such a summary matrix might look like.

Matrices similar to table 5 are especially common in environmental reports, where the writers want to compare or assess the feasibility of various alternatives. These environmental matrices usually have alternatives listed along one axis and environmental factors (or criteria) listed along the other axis.

17. Use informal or run-in tables to replace ordinary text, especially lengthy paragraphs.

Paragraphs are the weakest of format options, so we recommend using any and all emphasis techniques to replace or break up lengthy paragraphs. See PARAGRAPHS.

An informal or run-in table is just one such emphasis technique. A run-in table appears without all the columns, rows, and headings used in

formal tables. A run-in table is also unnumbered.

The sentences immediately preceding a run-in table introduce the table and, as in the following example, tell readers what they are supposed to see in the table.

Since World War II, only two presidents, both Republicans, have won two elections and then completed two full terms in office. As the following table indicates, all other presidents served fewer years. Truman came the closest to serving two full terms, but he was elected only once after completing Roosevelt's term when Roosevelt died in office.

Truman (D)	1945–1953
Eisenhower (R)	1953–1961
Kennedy (D)	1961–1963
Johnson (D)	1963–1969
Nixon (R)	1969–1974
Ford (R)	1974–1977
Carter (D)	1977–1981
Reagan (R)	1981–1989
Bush (R)	1989–1993
Clinton (D)	1993–

Table 5. Three Potential Sites. *Each site has its strengths, so a decision will likely depend on possible tax incentive packages for each site.*

	A—Omaha, Nebraska	B—Joplin, Missouri	C—Ft. Worth, Texas
Total Construction Cost, Including Site Preparation	$4.385M. Full site prep is necessary.	$3.9 M. Site is already prepared; costs are minimal.	$4.450 M. Full site prep is necessary.
Accessible to Major Transportation (Rail) Lines	Omaha is a major rail hub with connections both north/south and east/west.	Joplin has good north/south connections, but east/west connections are not as well developed.	Ft. Worth has good east/west connections. Southern location makes connections to northern states less convenient.
Airline Connections	Direct connections to major cities, but not a hub airport.	Flights must connect through St. Louis or Tulsa—a clear weakness.	Major hub airport with excellent national and intl. connections.
Quality of Life	Moderate-sized urban area with good schools and many recreational opportunities, esp. Missouri River.	Small-town setting with access to rural areas and associated opportunities. Many streams/reservoirs nearby. Branson is about 40 miles to the southeast.	Large urban center with all its advantages. Dallas/Ft. Worth area is highly desirable place to live.
Cost of Living Base = $100 *Market Basket Survey*	$102.80	$96.30 (This figure parallels a depressed real estate market.)	$105.20 (This figure reflects higher transportation costs.)

Tables of Contents

Tables of contents help readers in two ways: (1) They outline the structure of the document and thus provide insight into the document's organization, and (2) they provide the page numbers for all sections and subsections, thus helping readers to locate parts of the document.

Editors often choose to shorten *Table of Contents* to merely *Contents*. We retained the full phrase as the title of this entry, but we recommend simply *Contents* when you are labeling a page in a document.

Creating a preliminary table of contents is a useful writing technique because writers have to think carefully about the document's organization. Gaps, illogical order, and misplaced emphasis become more apparent when the writer is forced to clarify and complete a preliminary table of contents.

The final table of contents cannot be prepared until the document is finished and the pages numbered.

1. Use a table of contents for any report longer than 10 pages.

The 10-page figure is arbitrary, but remember that a table of contents helps readers to see the overall organization of the document as well as to find key sections. Documents under 10 pages are generally short and uncomplicated enough for readers to determine the structure by skimming through the document before reading. However, skimming through longer documents may not provide an adequate sense of structure because the reader's mind is being asked to comprehend too much information spread over too great a distance.

2. Include major divisions (often chapter headings) and the next level of subdivisions in the table of contents.

Major divisions and the next level subdivisions are essential if readers are to comprehend the document's structure. Make the division titles as specific as possible:

this

2.   Testing for Flammability

       2.1 Temperatures

       2.2 Duration

       2.3 Flash Points

not this

2.   Testing

NOTE: Ensure that all of the divisions and subdivisions that appear in the table of contents also appear in the body of the document. See HEADINGS.

3. Use letters and numbers with division and subdivision titles in the table of contents only if you also use them in the text.

A table of contents can resemble an outline with page numbers, but such an outline structure (*I, A, 1, a,* etc.) is not necessary unless the chapter or section titles and the headings in the document reflect the same numbering system. Tables of contents often have a decimal numbering system (*1.1.1, 1.1.2, 1.1.3,* etc.) in place of the standard outline system. Either system is acceptable. See OUTLINES and NUMBERING SYSTEMS.

4. Use blank lines, indentation, and leader dots to lay out the table of contents and help readers find page numbers.

Leave **blank lines** between major entries, and ensure that the spacing reflects the logical structure of the document. For instance, you may want to leave two lines between major divisions (first-level

---

Tables of Contents

1. Use a table of contents for any report longer than 10 pages.

2. Include major divisions (often chapter headings) and the next level of subdivisions in the table of contents.

3. Use letters and numbers with division and subdivision titles in the table of contents only if you also use them in the text.

4. Use blank lines, indentation, and leader dots to lay out the table of contents and help readers find page numbers.

5. Include preliminary material and appendices or attachments in the table of contents.

6. If appropriate, supplement your table of contents with a matrix or checksheet showing how and where you have dealt with key requirements or issues.

headings) and one line between major subdivisions (second-level headings). Readers should be able to tell where major divisions occur simply by noting the number of lines between entries.

Use **indentation** to show levels of subordination. Major divisions (first-level headings) should be flush left. Major subdivisions (second-level headings) should be indented five spaces. Minor subdivisions (third-level headings) should be indented 10 spaces, and so on.

Finally, consider using **leader dots** (a row of unspaced periods) to connect entries with their page numbers. Leader dots allow readers' eyes to trace the connection across the page.

To emphasize major divisions or subdivisions, you might also use all capital letters, boldface type, and other emphatic techniques. See EMPHASIS.

The table of contents example in figure 1 shows one method of displaying the organizational structure of a document and of providing page numbers to help readers locate the document's parts. For another example, see the table of contents to this *Style Guide*.

5. Include preliminary material and appendices or attachments in the table of contents.

Some writers ignore the preliminary material such as the preface or foreward and attachments when they construct their tables of contents. However, a table of contents should reflect the structure of the entire document, so include all of the document's parts.

6. If appropriate, supplement your table of contents with a matrix or checksheet showing how and where you have dealt with key requirements or issues.

Such matrices or checksheets do not replace the standard table of contents or an index, but they can help guide readers to see how you have organized your document. They are especially valuable when you need to show readers that you have met all legal or procedural requirements. See TABLES.

These matrices or checksheets have various formats, but as figures 2 and 3 on the next page show, most requirements or issues are usually listed vertically down the left with the document sections or chapters horizontally across the top. Page numbers (or subsection numbers) appear in the matrix.

Place a matrix where readers can easily use it to track content questions. Often the most obvious placement is for a matrix to follow the contents page(s). As an option, consider printing the matrix on a foldout sheet positioned at the end of the document. Readers can open the foldout and use it to track points as they read.

CONTENTS

Figure 1. Sample Table of Contents. *This table of contents includes second-level headings so that readers can easily find the relevant sections.*

Tables of Contents

Statement of Work Requirements	Proposal Section Numbers
3. Survivability	4.4, 8.2, and 9.
3.1 Stress Resistance	4.4.1 and 8.2.2
3.2 Temperature Constraints	4.4.2 and 8.2.3
3.3 Humidity	4.4.3 and 8.2.4
3.4 Electromagnetic Pulse	4.5 and 9.

Figure 2. A Matrix from a Proposal. *A two-column matrix may be sufficient to track the way the document responds to each requirement listed in a client's statement of work. An option would be to list all section titles and numbers across the top and then fill in the matrix with page numbers.*

		Chapters (page numbers)					
Issues	Summary	I. Purpose and Need	II. Alternatives	III. Affected Environment	IV. Environmental Consequences	Appendix A Public Involvement	Appendix B
1. Soil Stability	2	4–5	8, 10–11	18–21	49–52	A–3, A–5	B–6, B–11
2. Water Quality	2–3	5	8, 11–12	21–24	53–57, 68–69	A–3, A–5, A–14, and A–20	B–5, B–8, and B–20
3. Wildlife	3	5–6	8, 13	27–30	60–64, 69–70	A–5, A–14 A–20, and A–24	B–1, B–2, B–7, and B–15

Figure 3. A Matrix from an Environmental Document. *The issues are crucial to the organization (and legality) of the document. By showing that each issue appears in each chapter, the writer is able to show readers that all issues have been consistently addressed. In a sense, a matrix like this could replace the index. See* INDEXES *and* TABLES.

Thinking is the tool we use to turn facts, data, and examples into information. Without thought and careful analysis, collections of facts and raw data are not information in any useful sense. See MANAGING INFORMATION.

The following discussion shows how common strategies (actually common patterns of thinking) can help a writer or speaker marshal facts and data into a cogent and convincing message. For example, the strategy of listing pros and cons will often help someone to get their thoughts organized so that they can write an effective document.

Writing down or practicing each strategy is the key to its success. Thought does not survive well or long purely as brainwaves. And multiple thoughts vanish far too rapidly from the mind. So, as you practice each strategy, we recommend that you work with pen and paper, a marker and flipchart, or, if you prefer, on your computer.

The essential task is that you record in language and in accompanying visualizations each new thought, its implication, and its significance.

Recording and visualizing are important whether you are working alone or in a team. Your goal, either alone or in a team, is to discover the implications, the connections, the significance of the facts and data.

You have to discover what matters most, what controls the issues, what will guide your conclusions. These points, once discovered, are useful and productive information.

Thinking Strategies

1. Choose one or more thinking strategies to help you address a problem or resolve an issue.

2. Brainstorm schematically or visually your answers to each chosen question.

3. Retain (or record) for later use the thoughts you captured in rule 2 above.

4. Use your visualization patterns to guide your writing if you decide to publish your findings.

1. Choose one or more thinking strategies to help you address a problem or resolve an issue.

What are the possible strategies? In ancient Greece, rhetoricians listed strategies that allowed them to discover what they needed to say. Their goal was to develop a rich source of ideas so that, in turn, their orations were as rich and as persuasive as possible.

Speakers and writers today surely have nearly the same goal as the ancient Greeks. Therefore, the questions listed in figure 1 are merely an updated version of the techniques known and practiced by the ancient Greeks.

When you are dealing with an issue or a problem, begin by surveying the questions in figure 1. Which ones might be helpful? Often you will find that several of them have promise.

As an example of how to use the strategy questions, assume that you need to decide whether to close a branch office. In this instance, you decide that questions 2, 5, and 11 might be helpful.

2. Brainstorm schematically or visually your answers to each chosen question.

Working alone or in teams, brainstorm answers to a given question. Be sure to record your ideas in writing.

Use pad and pencil, a white board, or multiple flipchart pages. Even a computer can serve to record your ideas, especially if you have software that allows you to share ideas on a network.

To help you record your ideas, we recommend a schematic approach or a visualization, not merely a list of words. Also, don't try to write connected text, which can come later. Instead, your goal is to capture as many of your ideas as rapidly as possible.

Figure 2 shows several common visual patterns that you might use as you develop your ideas. Pick one and flesh it out until the flow of ideas dries up. Then, if you still need more information, try a second pattern. Use separate sheets, and as you fill a sheet, post it on the wall so that you can review what you have previously recorded.

Thinking Strategies

Strategy Questions. Choose one or more of these strategy questions when you need help thinking about a problem or issue. Often, you will find that you need to work through several strategies before you find one that will help you generate productive ideas.

1. What causes led to the existing problem? (cause and effect)

2. What effects will occur from option A? Option B? Option C? (cause and effect)

3. What category would the problem or issue fit into? (classification)

4. What are the constituent parts or steps? (division)

5. Who or what will be affected?

6. How important are the effects? (ranking or prioritization)

7. What steps or options would permit an event to occur? (process)

8. How feasible—with pros and cons—is one or more of the options?

9. What situations are analogous to the problem? (analogy)

10. How do these situations compare (or contrast)? (comparison/contrast)

11. What objections exist to the problem or proposed solutions? (argument)

12. How reasonable or convincing are these objections? (argument)

13. What is the history of the problem or issue?

14. How much will options cost?

15. What scenarios are likely to occur? (examples)

Figure 1. Strategy Questions. *Ancient Greeks used similar questions in their search for powerful and proper information to include in their orations.*

3. Retain (or record) for later use the thoughts you captured in rule 2 above.

Recording and retrieval are crucial steps, especially given the increasing amount of information available. See MANAGING INFORMATION.

As figure 3 shows, you might decide to record your visualizations on a page from the Franklin Day Planner®. Or, you might decide merely to fold up and retain the flipchart pages. And if you worked on a computer, you would save the file.

Whatever way you decide to retain or record information, you should add the following facts, as appropriate:

- Who teamed with you to generate the ideas

- When and where you generated and recorded the ideas

- What comes next and who is responsible for this next step

- How the information should be filed or cross-referenced for retrieval and later use (or expansion)

As in figure 3, these can be a standard heading on sheets that you use for recording information in your planner. In other instances, as with flipchart pages, you may need to write in the information as space allows.

Your goal should be to identify sources for any information you choose to retain. See MEETINGS MANAGEMENT.

4. Use your visualization patterns to guide your writing if you decide to publish your findings.

Visualizations should drive every step in the thinking process. Early in the process, visualization helps you discover ideas. Visualization should also guide you as you publish your memo, report, or findings. See WRITING AND REVISING.

The early visualization often becomes a macro visual for what you intend to write. See GRAPHICS FOR DOCUMENTS and GRAPHICS FOR PRESENTATIONS.

For example, if you have spent time analyzing the effects of a proposal, you might decide to use as a primary graphic a cause-and-effect flow chart (example 5 in figure 2).

Or to consider another example, if you are analyzing the root causes for a problem, such as the delivery of the wrong food in a hospital, you might choose to list these causes as reasons arranged around a circle with the problem stated in the middle.

Even if you don't choose to use an actual graphic in your document, the form of the early visualization should help you design and organize your document. If you determined that the solution to a problem required four steps or remedies, you would want to design a document with four major chapters or subheadings.

In each of the preceding examples, you will be using the initial visualization to channel your final documentation into a schematic or visual type of presentation. Good documents must be well-designed visual constructs if they are to communicate effectively and memorably. See EMPHASIS, GRAPHICS FOR DOCUMENTS, and ORGANIZATION.

1

Pros	Cons
More.	Poor
Less $	Longer
Flexible	Restricted
Innovative	

2

Related Issue — Related Issue — Related — Central Issue or Question — Related — Related Issue

3

Main Idea — Key Word — Key Word/Idea — Key Word — Key Idea — Key Words — Key Words — Key Word — Key Words — Key Idea — and Ideas

4

Class/Group → Sub Division → Sub Division → Sub . . . → Sub . . .

5

Event (Cause) —— Effect 1 —— Effect 2 . . . .

Action/Event
- Effect 1
- Effect 2 → Effect 2a — Effect 2b
- Effect 3 → Effect 3a
- Effect 4
- Effect 5

Figure 2. Visualization Patterns. *As you record your answers and thoughts relating to the strategy questions, use one or more of these visualization patterns. Or create your own visualization to fit your specific data.*

One must be poor to know the luxury of giving.
—George Eliot

15
Friday
January

- Consultations Exchanged
- Journal Entry
- Thoughts & Ideas
- Agenda (telephone, meetings)
- Conversations

Daily Record of Events   week 2 15th Day 350 Left

Who: Susan James (Strategy, Inc.), Harold Rose (Huff Bros.), and Cheryl Larkin (Huff Bros.)

Where/When: Strategy Conf. Room 309, 3/15/97

Cross Ref: Strategy Accnt #2445

Next Step/Assignments: Harold to prepare formal minutes for Susan to Review.

Configuration A		Configuration B	
Pros	Cons	Pros	Cons
----	----	----	----
----	----	----	----
----	----	----	----
----	----	----	----

Configuration C	
Pros	Cons
----	----
----	----
----	----
----	----

Conclusion(s)

1.

2.

3.

4.

©1999 Franklin Covey Co.

Figure 3. Sample Record Sheet. *This sheet, prepared for use with the Franklin Planner®, shows one example of how a visualization can aid in recording information. The page opens with information about the meeting and its attendees. The pro and con visuals are not complete, but show how a team could assess the pros and cons of several configurations.*

Titles of people, organizations, governments, and publications often require special capitalization, punctuation, and other format conventions. See NOUNS and CAPITALS.

---

1. Capitalize the first letter of titles when they immediately precede personal names, but do not capitalize the first letter when they follow personal names:

Mrs. Robert T. Evans

Mr. Edward Johnson

Miss Sylvia Smead

Ms. Josephine Kukor

President Amy Kaufmann

Assistant Professor Ned Davies

Mayor-elect Boon Hollenbeck

General Laswell Hopkins

Lieutenant Cynthia Wagner

the Reverend John Tyler

Rabbi Tochterman

Amy Kaufmann, the president of Union College, spoke to the press.

Ned Davies is an assistant professor at Columbia University.

We voted for Boon Hollenbeck, who is now mayor-elect.

Laswell Hopkins was our general for only 2 months.

Our lieutenant was Cynthia Wagner. (*Here* was *separates the title from the name.*)

NOTE 1: The titles of high-ranking international, national, and state officials often retain their capitalization, even when the name of the individual is either absent or does not follow the title:

The President spoke before the Congress.

We wrote the Vice President.

The Pope toured South America.

The Governor still had 2 years to serve.

The Prime Minister of Ghana was invited to the White House.

Titles

1. Capitalize the first letter of titles when they immediately precede personal names, but do not capitalize the first letter when they follow personal names.

2. Capitalize the first letter of names of companies, schools, organizations, and religious bodies.

3. Capitalize the first letter of names of government bodies.

4. Capitalize and italicize (or underline) the titles of books, magazines, newspapers, plays, movies, television series, and other separately published works.

5. Capitalize and use quotation marks for chapters of books, articles in magazines, news stories or editorials, acts within a play, episodes of a television series, or other sections of something separately produced or published.

NOTE 2: Titles of company or corporation executives as well as titles of lesser federal and state officials are sometimes capitalized. Such capitalization is unnecessary, but you should follow company or agency practice:

The Mayor announced an end to the New York transit strike. (*or* The mayor)

The Vice President for Finance is resigning Monday, September 18.

The Superintendent refused to approve our budget request.

NOTE 3: Titles used in a general sense are not capitalized:

a U.S. representative

a king

a prime minister

an ambassador

2. Capitalize the first letter of names of companies, schools, organizations, and religious bodies:

the Johnson Wax Company

the University of Oregon

the Young Men's Christian Association

the Urban League of Detroit

the Republican Party

St. John's Lutheran Church

NOTE: The words capitalized are those normally capitalized in any title. See CAPITALS. In contrast with book titles, an initial *the* in most such titles is not capitalized unless the company, school, organization, or religious body has established *the* as part of its legal name: *The Johns Hopkins University, The Travelers Insurance Company.* See CAPITALS.

---

3. Capitalize the first letter of names of government bodies:

the United Nations

the Cabinet

the Bureau of the Budget

the California Legislature

the Ohio Board of Education

the Davis County Commission

the House (*for* House of Representatives)

the Department (*for* Department of Agriculture)

the Court (*for* the U.S. Supreme Court)

NOTE 1: Except for international and national bodies, shortened forms of these government bodies or common terms are not capitalized.

the police department

the county council

the board of education

NOTE 2: As explained in rule 2, initial uses of *the* do not require a capital *T*.

4. Capitalize and italicize (or underline) the titles of books, magazines, newspapers, plays, movies, television series, and other separately published works:

Oliver Twist (book or movie)

Newsweek

The New York Times

West Side Story

Superman

NOVA

See CAPITALS, ITALICS, and UNDERLINING.

5. Capitalize and use quotation marks for chapters of books, articles in magazines, news stories or editorials, acts within a play, episodes of a television series, or other sections of something separately produced or published:

The last chapter was called "The Final Irony."

"The Colombian Connection" was the lead article in last week's *Time*.

We supported his editorial, "A Streamlined Election System."

We watched "The Fatal Circle" last night on *Chicago Hope*.

See QUOTATION MARKS, UNDERLINING, and ITALICS.

Tone

Tone reflects your attitude toward your subject and your readers. Your writing may strike your readers as personal or impersonal, friendly or distant. You may sound warm and engaging or cold and abrupt.

Tone and *style* are often confused. Some people use the terms interchangeably, but one is the cause and the other the effect:

- **Tone** refers to the feeling or impression a document conveys to its readers. It is one of the products of the writer's style.

- **Style** refers to the writer's choices that create the tone readers perceive. Style is the writer's "manner of speaking," the way the writer uses language to express ideas.

See STYLE and SCIENTIFIC/TECHNICAL STYLE.

Tone, then, is the impression readers receive from your writing and the attitude conveyed in your treatment of the subject. We usually describe the tone of a piece of writing with these words:

abrasive	formal
aggressive	forthright
assertive	friendly
authoritative	impersonal
blunt	informal
bureaucratic	informative
casual	objective
cold	officious
condescending	personal
courteous	polite
demanding	sincere
discourteous	stiff
distant	subjective
earnest	threatening
engaging	warm

Tone

1. Use pronouns to establish a personal, human tone in letters and memos.

2. Make your letters and memos sound very much like the language you would choose if you actually talked with the readers.

3. Choose sentence structures that reflect a friendly, conversational tone.

4. Include personal information and personal references.

5. Choose your paper, typeface, and format to reflect a personal, friendly tone.

Desirable Business Tone

Most of the time, your business documents should be:

courteous	informative
forthright	personal
friendly	polite
helpful	sincere
informal	warm

The extent to which your documents are personal will depend on your relationship with the reader. But never fail to be courteous, polite, informative, sincere, and helpful—especially when you don't know the reader.

If you need to convey negative information, as in a poor performance appraisal or reprimand, or in a document threatening legal action, your document may need to be:

assertive	impersonal
formal	objective

However, you should never write documents that are:

abrasive	blunt
discourteous	cold
bureaucratic	officious
condescending	

Good business documents—no matter how tough or adversarial they are—should **never** be discourteous.

Below are the stylistic choices that will help you write business letters and memos that have an effective tone. Not coincidentally, these are the same rules that make writing clear, concise, and easy to read.

---

1. Use pronouns to establish a personal, human tone in letters and memos.

Probably no single language choice is as effective in making business documents sound human and personal as well-chosen pronouns. Of the pronouns possible, *you* is the most important. You should always be aware of your readers and address them directly:

this

During the discussion of your April bill, you mentioned that you had called your local service representative at least three times during the month. Do you remember the representative's name and the dates when you called?

not this

Concerning the April bill, the local service representative may have been called, but these calls cannot be verified unless the representative's name and the dates when the representative was called are provided to this office.

The ineffective version has no personal pronouns; consequently, the reader is ignored. Omitting personal pronouns makes the letter cold and informal. The passive verbs contribute to the impersonal tone and make the letter sound unfriendly at best. See ACTIVE/ PASSIVE.

Next to *you*, the pronouns *I* and *we* are essential for effective letters and memos. Some people argue that the writer should not be mentioned in documents. They argue that documents should not reflect personal opinions or the personality of the author. This argument fails to distinguish between personal opinions and personal responsibility for one's actions. Contrast these two examples:

> *this*
>
> Based on the data, I (*or* we) conclude that MOGO should plug and abandon the Gilbert Ray Well 3.
>
> *not this*
>
> Based on the data, it is concluded that MOGO should plug and abandon the Gilbert Ray Well 3.

The second version is mechanical, almost robotic. No person seems to have acted. The conclusion simply occurred, like something out of the twilight zone. The result is a faceless, anonymous tone, one calculated to avoid responsibility and perhaps to confuse readers or keep them deliberately in the dark.

---

2. Make your letters and memos sound very much like the language you would choose if you actually talked with the readers.

Read your document aloud. Would you be comfortable saying those words to someone in person? If you delivered the message to readers orally, would you express yourself this way?

The tone of a good business document is a natural one. It isn't full of slang or homey conversational expressions (*Well shucks, I reckon we ought to drill anyways*), but it should sound natural, not forced or contrived. If the document does not sound natural, if it is stiff and complex, if it is formal and faceless, you should rethink your tone. See LETTERS AND MEMOS.

A business document is not a transcription of your actual words, pauses, corrections, and other verbal lapses (*Well, uh, I think that, uh, if we, uh . . .*). It should, however, be similar to the way you talk. Even contractions are useful in letters and memos but not in more formal reports. See APOSTROPHES and CONTRACTIONS.

The words, phrases, and sentences you use should be simple and direct, even though you have edited and revised them:

> *this*
>
> I recommend that we immediately replace the roof on the Bradley building.
>
> *not this*
>
> It is recommended that the roof on the Bradley building be replaced forthwith.

> *this*
>
> Before leaving the room, turn out the lights.
>
> *not this*
>
> Prior to evacuating the premises, ensure that the illumination has been terminated.

The simplest remedy for overly stiff, bureaucratic writing is to write like a human being. Don't write like an official, faceless bureaucrat. Just be yourself. Imagine that you're talking to other people in person. Try to sound human, not mechanical.

Using personal pronouns will help considerably. Here are some other suggestions:

- **Keep your sentences short and direct.** Challenge any sentence that is longer than 30 words, and try to limit average sentence length to about 20 words. You can often break a long sentence into two shorter sentences. Ensure that each sentence, whatever its length, is as clear and direct as possible. See SENTENCES.

- **Avoid long, unnecessarily complex words and unnecessary technical terms.** See GOBBLEDYGOOK and JARGON. Never use words because you think those words are impressive. The writer who struggles to sound intelligent and educated (often by using a thesaurus) winds up sounding silly:

> *this*
>
> We think your water pipes have corroded so much that only a trickle of water can flow through them.
>
> *not this*
>
> Our hypothesis is that your water supply system has undergone severe corrosion and reached the debilitating point where water normally available is unavailable in the quantity and at the pressure provided for in the original specifications for your domicile.

Leaving aside the laughable words (*debilitating* and *domicile*), the second version still suffers from terminal wordiness. Isn't *pipes* better than *water supply system*? And *corroded* so much better than *undergone severe corrosion*? What do the inexact references to quantity and pressure accomplish that the word *trickle* doesn't do more vividly? The idea being expressed does not require technical terms, especially if the primary reader is a homeowner, not an engineer.

Tone

Legal documents often suffer from the same kind of wordiness and unnecessary complexity:

this

According to the procedure outlined above, please sign all three copies of the conveyance and have your signature notarized. Then return the completed forms to this office by Friday, May 23.

not this

In accordance with the provisions of the aforementioned procedure, the attached conveyance should be executed by you in triplicate, with the signature duly witnessed and attested to by a Notary Public, and the executed set of conveyance forms should then be returned to this office on or before, and no later than, Friday, May 23.

---

3. Choose sentence structures that reflect a friendly, conversational tone.

- **Avoid passive sentences:**

  this

  Our review of your claim indicates that you should receive a refund of $72. This refund would apply to 1996 charges.

  not this

  Your claim has been reviewed, and it has been determined that $72 should be refunded to you for the period January to December 1996.

  ---

  this

  We analyzed the data entries for the sources of the discrepancies. Over 90 percent of the discrepancies turned out to be simple errors in daily recording.

  not this

  The data entries have been analyzed to determine the source of the discrepancies. It is concluded that over 90 percent of the discrepancies were caused by simple errors in daily recording.

  See ACTIVE/PASSIVE.

- **Avoid false subjects:**

this

Unless we address these issues during this quarter, they will distort our financial report for the entire year.

not this

There are certain issues that we should address during this quarter that will distort our financial report for the entire year.

---

this

Under Pharmtech's policies, we will not acquire additional laboratory equipment until the beginning of the new fiscal year.

not this

It is likely that, given Pharmtech's policies, it will be impossible to acquire additional laboratory equipment until the beginning of the new fiscal year.

See FALSE SUBJECTS.

---

4. Include personal information and personal references.

Readers like to know that you have addressed their needs. So, if appropriate, include information from previous letters, memos, or discussions in your document. Or include information they have either requested or will need:

I recommend that you file a complaint with the Federal Trade Commission. Your review of the relevant correspondence with the company persuaded me that you have a case.

A mechanical, yet easy, way to make a letter or memo personal is to include the reader's name in the body of the letter:

So, Beth, if you have any more suggestions, please call me at ext. 3578.

or

If we proceed, Cal, you should ask Product Research for a copy of their assessment form. I think you'd find it helpful.

NOTE: As in the preceding example, an occasional contraction (*you'd*)

makes the tone conversational and informal. See APOSTROPHES and CONTRACTIONS.

---

5. Choose your paper, typeface, and format to reflect a personal, friendly tone.

Even physical concerns can affect the tone of a letter or memo.

Choose quality paper (usually 20-pound rag paper) and a pleasing typeface. Now with word processors and computers, the typeface options are growing. Know your options. Your goal is to capture the personal, friendly quality of the content of your letter (consider Helvetica or Optima). Some typefaces are too rigid and stark (American Typewriter). Others are too strange (Script, which attempts to look like cursive writing). See PAGE LAYOUT.

Next, design your document so that it has a lean and open look, one conveying a personal, friendly tone. This design usually means using generous margins, short paragraphs (on the average), headings, lists, and lots of white space. See EMPHASIS.

Transitions

Transitions are words or phrases that connect ideas and show how they are related. Occurring between two sentences or paragraphs, a transition shows how the sentences or paragraphs are connected, thus making the writing smoother and more logical. A transition creates a point of reference for readers, allowing them to see how the writing is organized and where it is heading.

Following is a list of transitions and their functions.

A List of Transitions

Addition

additionally, again, also, besides, further, furthermore, in addition, likewise, moreover, next, too, what is more

Comparison or contrast

by contrast, by the same token, conversely, however, in contrast, in spite of, instead, in such a manner, likewise, nevertheless, otherwise, on the contrary, on the one hand, on the other hand, rather, similarly, still, yet

Concession

anyway, at any rate, be that as it may, even so, however, in any case, in any event, nevertheless, of course, still

Consequence

accordingly, as a result, consequently, hence, otherwise, so, then, therefore, thus

Diversion

by the way, incidentally

Generalization

as a rule, as usual, for the most part, generally, in general, ordinarily, usually

Illustration

for example, for instance

Place

close, here, near, nearby, there

Restatement

in essence, in other words, namely, that is

Summary

after all, all in all, briefly, by and large, finally, in any case, in any event, in brief, in conclusion, in short, in summary, on balance, on the whole, ultimately

Time and sequence

after a while, afterward, at first, at last, at the same time, currently, finally, first (second, third, etc.), first of all, for now, for the time being, immediately, instantly, in conclusion, in the first place, in the meantime, in time, in turn, later, meanwhile, next, presently, previously, simultaneously, soon, subsequently, then, to begin with

See CONJUNCTIONS, ORGANIZATION, and PARAGRAPHS.

1. Use commas to separate transitions from the main body of a sentence:

However, uncontrolled R&D efforts that do not design quality into the product, process, or service may be of dubious value.

Consequently, areas of future focus will include software design, packaging enhancements, and marketing efforts in the Pacific Rim.

The regulator poppet is, however, normally held open by the regulating spring.

Transitions interrupt and are generally not part of the main thought of the sentence; therefore, you should separate them from the rest of the sentence. When a transitional word occurs where two complete thoughts are joined, as in

the following sentence, use a semicolon where the two complete thoughts join (usually in front of the transition) and a comma after the transition:

The scope of this study will not permit a review of all technologies; however, we believe our experience in advanced ship design will allow us to maximize the study of those areas with greater operational potential.

See SEMICOLONS and COMMAS.

2. If the transition interrupts the flow of a sentence, place commas on both sides of the transitional word or phrase:

Upon examination, for instance, the clinical monitor considered 10 patients to have significant findings.

The sensor probe, on the other hand, contains thermistor sensing elements.

3. If a transitional word occurs at the beginning of a sentence and is essential to the meaning of the sentence, do *not* separate it with a comma:

However warm air enters the cabin, the conditioned temperature will not rise above the nominal range.

NOTE: Such sentences can be confusing, so you should consider rephrasing the sentence:

Regardless of how warm air enters the cabin, the conditioned temperature will not rise above the nominal range.

Transitions

1. Use commas to separate transitions from the main body of a sentence.

2. If the transition interrupts the flow of a sentence, place commas on both sides of the transitional word or phrase.

3. If a transitional word occurs at the beginning of a sentence and is essential to the meaning of the sentence, do *not* separate it with a comma.

Underlining

Underlining can replace italics as a tool for highlighting certain unusual words and phrases. See ITALICS. You can also underline words, phrases, and sentences to emphasize them.

Underlining is becoming less common because most word processing programs provide italics.

So, in rules 1 to 4 below, italics would be preferred if it is available. In rule 5, underlining, not italics, would still be preferred. See ITALICS and WORD PROCESSING.

Editors differ as to whether to underline words and the spaces between them or only the words. Given the influence of word processing, which allows writers to highlight a block of text and then underline it, the pattern of continuous underlining is more common:

> <u>The Making of a President</u>
>
> *not*
>
> The <u>Making</u> of <u>a</u> <u>President</u>

1. Underline words used as examples of words:

> The words <u>affect</u> and <u>effect</u> are often confused.
>
> The contract stipulated that monitoring must be continuous, but during negotiation they stated that periodic monitoring would suffice. Should the contract read <u>continual</u> or <u>periodic</u> rather than <u>continuous</u>?

NOTE: Single letters, words, and even phrases should be underlined to separate them from the ordinary words within a sentence:

> The phrase <u>come hell or high water</u> has a long and interesting history.

> ### Underlining
>
> 1. Underline words used as examples of words.
>
> 2. Underline foreign words and phrases that have not been absorbed into English.
>
> 3. Underline the titles of separate publications and productions.
>
> 4. Underline the names of aircraft, vessels, and spacecraft.
>
> 5. Underline words and phrases for emphasis:

Some editors prefer to use quotation marks for words and phrases used unusually within a sentence. However, quotation marks clutter up a sentence if several words are being talked about:

> The forms "am," "is," "are," "was," and "were" don't even resemble "be," which is the principal form of the verb.

---

2. Underline foreign words and phrases that have not been absorbed into English:

> After a <u>coup d'oeil</u>, the detective was ready to question the suspect. (<u>Coup d'oeil</u> means "a quick survey.")

NOTE: Contrast *coup d'oeil,* which is clearly not part of English, with *ad hoc,* which is now so familiar that no underlining is necessary. Many modern dictionaries fail to specify whether a word should be considered foreign or not, so you may have to use your own judgment.

---

3. Underline the titles of separate publications and productions:

> I bought a copy of <u>The Wall Street Journal</u>.
>
> Have you read the novel <u>All Quiet on the Western Front</u>?
>
> <u>The Sunshine Patriot</u> is a pamphlet being circulated by the Republican Party.

> We attended a preview of <u>The Story of the Bell System</u>.
>
> We have tickets for the opening night of <u>Aida</u>.

NOTE: Underline separately published or produced items, but use quotation marks for book chapters, articles in magazines, and sections of the separate works:

> The latest issue of the <u>Oil and Gas Journal</u> contained an article entitled "Shearing Problems with Sucker Rods."
>
> <u>The Salt Lake Tribune</u> had an editorial entitled "A Bold Proposal."

See QUOTATION MARKS and TITLES.

---

4. Underline the names of aircraft, vessels, and spacecraft:

> U.S.S. <u>Constitution</u>
>
> H.M.S. <u>Bounty</u>
>
> <u>Gemini</u> 4

---

5. Underline words and phrases for emphasis:

> Please send two copies to us by <u>Friday, October 13</u>, at the latest.
>
> Unscrew the fitting by turning it <u>clockwise</u>, not counterclockwise.

NOTE: Use underlining for emphasis sparingly. Underlined text is difficult to read, and the effect diminishes quickly if you overuse it. See EMPHASIS.

Units of measurement include either English units (also called the U.S. customary system) or metric units. Many U.S. firms still favor English units, but metric units are now widely used by scientists and engineers. See Metrics.

> ## Units of Measurement
> 1. Use common English units to measure length and area.
> 2. Use common English units for volume or capacity and weight.

1. Use the following common English units to measure length and area.

Note: The abbreviations for these units of measurement usually appear only in tables, charts, graphs, and other visuals. See Abbreviations.

LENGTH

English Unit	U.S. Equivalents	Metric Equivalents
inch	0.083 foot	2.54 centimeters
foot	$\frac{1}{3}$ yard, 12 inches	30.48 centimeters
yard	3 feet, 36 inches	0.914 meter
rod	$5\frac{1}{2}$ yards, $16\frac{1}{2}$ feet	5.029 meters
mile (statute, land)	1,760 yards, 5,280 feet	1.609 kilometers
mile (nautical, international)	1.151 statute miles	1.852 kilometers

AREA

English Unit	U.S. Equivalents	Metric Equivalents
square inch	0.007 square foot	6.452 square centimeters
square foot	144 square inches	929.030 square centimeters
square yard	1,296 square inches, 9 square feet	0.836 square meter
acre	43,560 square feet, 4,840 square yards	4,047 square meters
square mile	640 acres	2.590 square kilometers

2. Use the following common English units for volume or capacity and weight.

VOLUME OR CAPACITY

English Unit	U.S. Equivalents	Metric Equivalents
cubic inch	0.00058 cubic foot	16.387 cubic centimeters
cubic foot	1,728 cubic inches	0.028 cubic meter
cubic yard	27 cubic feet	0.765 cubic meter

English Liquid Measure	U.S. Equivalents	Metric Equivalents
fluid ounce	8 fluid drams, 1,804 cubic inches	29.573 milliliters
pint	16 fluid ounces, 28.875 cubic inches	0.473 liter
quart	2 pints, 57.75 cubic inches	0.946 liter
gallon	4 quarts, 231 cubic inches	3.785 liters
barrel	varies from 31 to 42 gallons established by law or usage	

VOLUME OR CAPACITY (continued)

English Dry Measure	U.S. Equivalents	Metric Equivalents
pint	$\frac{1}{2}$ quart, 33.6 cubic inches	0.551 liter
quart	2 pints, 67.2 cubic inches	1.101 liters
peck	8 quarts, 537.605 cubic inches	8.810 liters
bushel	4 pecks, 2,150.420 cubic inches	35.239 liters

WEIGHT

English Avoirdupois Unit	U.S. Equivalents	Metric Equivalents
grain	0.036 dram, 0.002285 ounce	64.798 milligrams
dram	27.344 grains, 0.0625 ounce	1.772 grams
ounce	16 drams, 437.5 grains	28.350 grams
pound	16 ounces, 7,000 grains	453.592 grams
ton (short)	2,000 pounds	0.907 metric ton (1,000 kilograms)
ton (long)	1.12 short tons, 2,240 pounds	1.016 metric tons

Apothecary Weight Unit	U.S. Equivalents	Metric Equivalents
scruple	20 grains	1.295 grams
dram	60 grains	3.888 grams
ounce	480 grains, 1.097 avoirdupois ounces	31.103 grams
pound	5,760 grains, 0.823 avoirdupois pound	373.242 grams

Note: Although the British Commonwealth and the United States both use the same names for units and their abbreviations, the two systems do differ, so be cautious in interpreting publications using these units. Here, for example, are the equivalents between the British Imperial units and the U.S. English or customary units:

British Imperial Liquid and Dry Measure	U.S. English Equivalents	Metric Equivalents
fluid ounce	0.961 U.S. fluid ounce, 1.734 cubic inches	28.413 milliliters
pint	1.032 U.S. dry pints, 1.201 U.S. liquid pints, 34.678 cubic inches	568.245 milliliters
quart	1.032 U.S. dry quarts, 1.201 U.S. liquid quarts, 69.354 cubic inches	1.136 liters
gallon	1.201 U.S. gallons, 277.420 cubic inches	4.546 liters

Verts

Verbs are the key action words in most sentences. They tell what the subject has done, is doing, or will be doing, and they indicate the subject's relationship to the object or complement. Because verbs also signal time through their different tenses (forms), they are potentially the most important words in a sentence. For instance, varying only the verb in a sentence produces major shifts in the meaning:

> She shows us her report.
> She showed us her report.
> She will show us her report.

> She has shown us her report.
> She had shown us her report.
> She will have shown us her report.

> She is showing us her report.
> She was showing us her report.
> She will be showing us her report.

These nine sentences only begin to illustrate all the possible verb forms. If we include more complex verb phrases, the possibilities multiply:

> She is going to be showing us her report.
> She must have been showing us her report.

Principal Verb Forms

Verbs commonly have several standard forms (called principal parts) from which all the other verb forms are built:

base form	call
	eat
	cut
–s form (third person singular present— he, she, it)	calls
	eats
	cuts
past form	called
	ate
	cut
–ed participle (past participle)	called
	eaten
	cut
–ing participle (present participle)	calling
	eating
	cutting

> ### Verbs
>
> 1. Check a recent dictionary to determine the correct forms for any verb you are unsure of.
>
> 2. Vary your verb tenses to reflect the varying timing of events in your writing.
>
> 3. Ensure that your verbs agree with your subjects.
>
> 4. Use a subjunctive verb in *if* clauses to state a situation that is untrue, impossible, or highly unlikely.
>
> 5. Use subjunctive verbs in sentences making strong recommendations or demands, or indicating necessity.

Regular verbs, like *call*, routinely require only an *–s*, *–ed*, or *–ing* to change the base form. If a dictionary does not supply any forms except the base form, the verb is regular, like *call*.

Irregular verbs, like *eat* and *cut*, are unpredictable, so writers have to know the different forms, not just follow the regular pattern. Dictionaries include these irregular forms in their entries for these verbs.

NOTE: Unfortunately, not all verbs are clearly regular or irregular. The following verbs, for example, have two different forms of the past participle, one regular, the other irregular:

> mow, mowed, mown (*or* mowed)
> show, showed, showed (*or* shown)
> swell, swelled, swollen (*or* swelled)

---

1. Check a recent dictionary to determine the correct forms for any verb you are unsure of.

Here, for instance, are the main forms for some of the common irregular verbs:

> buy, bought, bought
> cost, cost, cost
> drink, drank, drunk
> freeze, froze, frozen

> keep, kept, kept
> lead, led, led
> lie, lay, lain
> light, lighted/lit, lighted/lit
> rise, rose, risen
> sell, sold, sold
> sit, sat, sat
> speak, spoke, spoken
> spoil, spoilt/spoiled, spoilt/spoiled
> take, took, taken
> tear, tore, torn
> think, thought, thought
> wet, wet/wetted, wet/wetted
> write, wrote, written

NOTE: Where two forms exist, the regular forms (with *–ed*) are becoming more common. Over time, many irregular verbs have changed and are changing into regular verbs.

Verb Tenses

Verbs have the following basic tenses or times:

Basic Verb Tenses

Present:	They study.
Past:	They studied.
Future:	They will study.
Present Perfect:	They have studied.
Past Perfect:	They had studied.
Future Perfect:	They will have studied.

In addition, a parallel set of progressive forms exists, which indicates that the action is continuing:

Progressive Verb Tenses

Present:	They are studying.
Past:	They were studying.
Future:	They will be studying.
Present Perfect:	They have been studying.
Past Perfect:	They had been studying.
Future Perfect:	They will have been studying.

Finally, a parallel set of passive verb tenses also exists:

Passive Verb Tenses

Present:	The report is studied.
Past:	The report was studied.
Future:	The report will be studied.
Present Perfect:	The report has been studied.
Past Perfect:	The report had been studied.
Future Perfect:	The report will have been studied.

NOTE: As in the above sentences, passive verb sentences highlight the object or thing receiving the action, not the person or thing performing the action. The passive sentences above do not identify the person who is, was, or will be studying the report. In most cases, you should favor the active verb and avoid the passive. See ACTIVE/PASSIVE.

2. Vary your verb tenses to reflect the varying timing of events in your writing.

This rule contradicts what you may have learned in high school: "Don't mix your tenses." Actually, you can and should vary your tenses to reflect the often diverse time relationships of your subject:

> Yesterday, we analyzed *(past)* the samples for any traces of zinc ore. We found *(past)* none. Today, however, we were reexamining *(past progressive)* the sample when we found *(past)* two promising pieces of rock. They have *(present)* veins like zinc ore, although their color is *(present)* not quite right. Our report will therefore show *(future)* the potential presence of zinc.

Most writers choose their tenses unconsciously, but several basic conventions exist for selecting tenses in technical writing:

— Record in the past tense experiments and tests performed in the past:

> The second run produced flawed data because the heating unit failed. We failed to detect the failure until the run was almost over.

— Use the present tense for scientific facts and truths:

> Water freezes at 32°F, unless a chemical in the water changes its freezing point.
>
> Newton discovered that every action has an equal and opposite reaction.

— Use the present tense to discuss data within a published report:

> The slope of the temperature curve decreases sharply at 20 minutes. The figures in table 3–14 document this decrease.

— Shift from present to past tense as necessary to refer to research studies and prior papers. When you are discussing an author and his or her research, use the past tense:

> Jones (1976) studied a limited dose of the drug. He concluded that no harmful side effects occurred.

— When you are discussing different current theories, use the present tense:

> Jones (1976) argues that limited doses of the drug produce no harmful side effects. His data, however, are flawed because he failed to distinguish between the natural and synthetic versions of the drug.

Auxiliary Verbs

Auxiliary verbs are the most common verbs in English: *is, are, was, were, be, been, can, could, do, did, has, have, had, may, might, shall, should, will, would, must, ought to,* and *used to.* See STRONG VERBS.

Auxiliaries are crucial to many of the tenses presented above, but auxiliaries also can function by themselves as main sentence verbs:

> The tests are complete.
> He did the primary drawings.
> They have no budget.

See STRONG VERBS.

Verbs and Agreement

The verb should agree in number with its subject. So, a plural subject requires a plural verb, and a singular subject requires a singular verb:

> The geologist has completed the tests. *(singular)*
> The geologists have completed the tests. *(plural)*
>
> A test was completed last week. *(singular)*
> Several tests were completed last week. *(plural)*
>
> The investigator has completed the medical tests. *(singular)*
> The investiagtors have completed the medical tests. *(plural)*

See AGREEMENT.

Verbs

3. Ensure that your verbs agree with your subjects.

The only circumstance in which verbs change their forms to adjust to different numbers is in the third person forms of the present tense:

> She works every day. *(singular)*
> They work every day. *(plural)*
>
> She is the candidate. *(singular)*
> They are the candidates. *(plural)*
>
> He has the answer. *(singular)*
> They have the answer. *(plural)*
>
> It is broken. *(singular)*
> They are broken. *(plural)*

NOTE 1: Third person singular verbs have an –*s* ending, as in *works* above. The third person plural verbs have no –*s*, as in *work*. So the rule for verbs is the opposite of nouns: The forms with –*s* endings are the singular forms.

NOTE 2: The verb *be* is exceptional because it changes in the present tense to agree with different pronouns:

> I am studying.
> You are studying. *(singular)*
> He, she, it is studying.
>
> We are studying.
> You are studying. *(plural)*
> They are studying.

Subjunctive Verbs

Subjunctive verbs are special verb forms that signal recommendations or conditions contrary to fact. Centuries ago, subjunctives were very common verb forms, but today they are limited to the instances covered in the following two rules.

4. Use a subjunctive verb in *if* clauses to state a situation that is untrue, impossible, or highly unlikely:

> If I were (*not* was) the candidate, I would not agree to a debate.
>
> If it were (*not* was) raining, we couldn't conduct the experiment.
>
> If I were (*not* was) you, I would change banks.

NOTE 1: The above sentences require *were* rather than normal *was*, which would appear to agree with the subjects. This use amounts to a historical survival, so it doesn't fit our modern expectations. (Actually, other verbs in *if* clauses are subjunctive, but only the *were/was* pattern looks or sounds exceptional.)

NOTE 2: Subjunctive verbs are especially useful when a writer has to make recommendations. The *if* clause presents the hypothetical condition, and then the main clause indicates what would, could, or might happen:

> If the Accounting Department were reorganized, overall efficiency could increase by perhaps 50 percent.
>
> If rainfall were 40 inches a year or more, most dirt roads would be impassable.

See *would* in WORD PROBLEMS.

NOTE 3: If the *if* clause states something that is possible or likely, then do not use a subjunctive:

> If he leaves this job, he'll get $500 in severance pay.
>
> If it was an error, and I suspect it was, then we'll have to pay you damages.

5. Use subjunctive verbs in sentences making strong recommendations or demands, or indicating necessity:

> I recommend that the case <u>be settled</u> by Tuesday.
>
> He demands that the money <u>be refunded</u>.
>
> The court has resolved that the witness <u>be found</u> in contempt of court.

> It is essential that he <u>leave</u> by noon.
>
> They urge that she <u>return</u> the money.
>
> They resolved that Dan <u>write</u> the termination letter.

NOTE 1: As the first three sentences show, if the verb in the *that* clause would normally be *am, is,* or *are,* then its subjunctive form is *be*.

NOTE 2: As the last three sentences show, if the verb in the *that* clause is normally a third person singular verb, then its subjunctive form does not take the usual –*s* ending.

Words are symbols representing persons, places, things, actions, qualities, characteristics, states of being, and abstract ideas. Words are the substance of language.

A major writing problem can occur if you use the wrong word for the context. Which of the words within parentheses in the following sentences are correct?

(You're, Your) supposed to call the manager before leaving.

The (principal, principle) problem with this alternative is its reliance on a second wash cycle between chemical baths.

The plan will (affect, effect) residents living south of the city.

In all three cases, the first word is correct. Using the wrong word might not prevent readers from understanding the sentences. But many readers might begin to wonder if you are literate. And if you seem illiterate, then even the facts in a document might appear questionable. So using correct words is important.

You should be aware, however, that using incorrect or imprecise words in legal documents (or in any document that can potentially be subject to interpretation in a courtroom) is very dangerous. Courts tend to support the word on the page, not what the author claims to have intended.

Sometimes, using the incorrect word causes serious confusion and potential misinterpretation:

Please ensure that the third production cycle is stopped continuously for quality-assurance testing.

Continuously means "uninterrupted or constant." *Continually* means "recurring often." If the production cycle is stopped continuously, then it never runs. If the cycle is stopped

---

Word Problems

Guidance on individual word problems (often called usage problems) appears alphabetically under each word discussed. Thus, guidance on using *affect* versus *effect* appears initially under *affect/effect*. Readers looking up *effect* will find a cross reference back to the discussion under *affect/effect*.

---

continually, it is stopped frequently, but not constantly. Some readers might not make this distinction. For the sake of clarity, the writer would be better off issuing a more specific order:

Please ensure that the third production cycle is stopped every half hour for quality-assurance testing.

Some words are clearly correct or incorrect. You can't write *it's* when you mean *its*, and vice versa. However, some distinctions are more difficult to make. Even the dictionaries do not offer clear-cut distinctions in some cases:

(Since, Because) we had not received payment, we decided to close the account.

They proposed to publish a (bimonthly, semimonthly) newsletter for all employees.

The proposal (that, which) you prepared has turned out to be very profitable.

In the first example sentence, both choices do include the notion of causality, but *since* primarily means "before now" or "from some time in the past until now." Only secondarily does *since* suggest causality. Thus, strict editors consider *because* less ambiguous.

In the second sentence, *bimonthly* is unclear because the ambiguous *bi–* can mean either twice within a time period (twice a month) or every other time period (every 2 months). *Semimonthly*, which has always meant twice a month, has suffered because of the confusion over

bimonthly. Given the confusion between the two terms, you should avoid both terms and just say *twice a month* or *every 2 months*.

In the third sentence, both words are acceptable to many writers and editors. According to strict editors, however, *that* is more correct because the clause it introduces is essential to the sentence and cannot be removed; if the clause were nonessential, *which* would be the more correct word and the nonessential clause would be separated from the main clause by commas. Many educated writers and speakers violate this distinction, some using *that* and *which* almost interchangeably. So, insisting that *that* is the only correct choice for the third sentence is difficult.

Language and usage rules cannot be and never have been independent from the living language they describe. The spoken and written language that people use is always the final arbiter in disputes over word correctness. And a living language is always changing, so today's correct choice might be tomorrow's error. Good writers must remain alert to changes in a word's meaning and the acceptability of those changes.

The following list of problem word choices reflects some of the main choices facing today's writers. You should supplement this list and update it as necessary to remain current.

Word Problems

For information about words not in the following list, or if you want more detailed information, see *Webster's Dictionary of English Usage* (Springfield Massachusetts: Merriam-Webster, Inc. 1989).

Word Problems

accent/ascent/assent. *Accent* is both a verb meaining "to emphasize or stress" and a noun meaning "emphasis." *Ascent* (noun) means "a going up or rising movement." *Assent* means "to agree" or "an agreemetn":

> He accented the word *demotion*.
>
> His accent on the word *demotion* betrayed his true feelings.
>
> His ascent up the corporate ladder has been rapid.
>
> The trustee's assent is necessary before we sign the agreement.

accept/except. *Accept* is a verb meaning "to receive." *Except* is a preposition meaning "to the exclusion of":

> Did she accept your explanation for the overpayment?
>
> We completed everything except the two proposals for Acme, Inc.

A.D. and B.C. *A.D.* stands for the Latin *anno Domini* (in the year of the Lord). Using *A.D.* is simple—place it before a year and after a century:

> Pope Julius II, whose fertile partnership with Michelangelo produced many fine works of art, reigned from A.D. 1503 to 1513.
>
> Arabians borrowed coffee from the Abyssinians about the twelfth century A.D.

B.C. stands for "before Christ." Using *B.C.* is also simple—place it after the year and after the century:

> King Priam's Troy fell near the end of the Bronze Age, around 1200 B.C.
>
> The high point of ancient Greek civilization, the Periclean Age, was during the fifth century B.C.

Some writers, however, have qualms about using *A.D.* and *B.C.*, which are connected to the birth of Jesus Christ. They use other systems, such as *B.C.E.* (before the common era) for B.C. or *C.E.* (common era) for A.D. and place them after the date.

adapt/adept/adopt. *Adapt* means "to adjust to a situation." *Adept* means "skillful." *Adopt* means "to put into practice or to borrow":

> Within a week she adapted to the new billing procedure.
>
> She won the promotion because she was so adept at her job.
>
> Just last year we adopted a new method for maintaining inventory.

adjacent/contiguous/conterminous. *Adjacent* is the most general word, usually meaning "close to and nearby" and only sometimes "sharing the same boundary":

> Burger King is adjacent to the Cottonwood Mall.
>
> The adjacent lots were both owned by the same construction company.

Contiguous usually means "sharing the same boundary" even though it includes the notion of "adjacent" in most of its uses:

> The two mining claims turned out to be contiguous once the survey was completed; the owners had originally believed that a strip of state land separated the claims.

Conterminous (also *coterminous*) is the most specific of the terms and also the rarest. Its most distinctive meaning is "contained within one boundary" even though it also includes the senses of "sharing the same boundary" and quite rarely of being "adjacent." Its most distinctive use, however, is as follows:

> The conterminous United States includes only 48 of the 50 states.

These three words are a problem because they share a common meaning: "close to or nearby each other." At the same time, they each have more specific meanings, as illustrated. As with any confused words, writers should choose other phrasing if they wish to be as precise as possible:

> *better*
>
> Our two lots shared a common boundary on the north.
>
> *or with a different meaning*
>
> Our two lots fell entirely within the city boundary.
>
> *not*
>
> Our two lots were adjacent. (*neither* contiguous, *nor* conterminous)

adverse/averse. *Adverse* is an adjective meaning "unfavorable." *Averse* is an adjective meaning "having a dislike or a distaste for something." The two also contrast in how they are used in sentences. *Averse* appears only after the verb *be* or occasionally *feel*:

> We studied the adverse data before making our decision to plug and abandon the well.
>
> An adverse comment destroyed the negotiations.
>
> The President was averse to cutting the Defense budget.
>
> We felt averse to signing for such a large loan given the adverse economic forecasts.

advice/advise. *Advice* is a noun meaning "recommendations." *Advise* is a verb meaning "to make a recommendation":

> My advice was to meet with the client about the service problem.
>
> Did someone advise you to hire a lawyer?

affect/effect. *Affect* is usually a verb meaning "to change or influence." *Effect* is usually a noun meaning "a result or consequence":

> Temperature variations will affect the test results.
>
> The technician analyzed the effects of the new sample on the data.

NOTE: *Affect* can also be a noun meaning "the subjective impression of feeling or emotion," and *effect* can also be a verb meaning "to bring about or cause":

> His strange affect (*noun*) caused the psychiatrist to sign the committal order.

> The general manager's directive effected (*verb*) an immediate restructuring of all senior staff operations.

aid/aide. *Aid* is both a verb meaning "to help" or "assist" and a noun meaning "the act of helping someone." *Aid*, as a noun, also means "the person or group providing the assistance":

> He aided us by carrying furniture out of the burning building. (*verb*)

> U.S. aid included three emergency evacuation flights. (*noun*)

> A nursing aid helped to care for my hospitalized mother. (*noun*)

Aide is a noun meaning "a person who acts as an assistant," especially in a military or governmental situation:

> The admiral's aide was in charge of all of the admiral's appointments.

Aid and *aide* are frequently confused because of their similar meanings. Remember to limit *aide* to military or governmental contexts.

all right/alright. *All right* is the standard spelling; *alright* is an informal or nonstandard spelling and is not considered correct. Never use *alright*.

allusion/illusion/delusion. *Allusion* means "a reference to something." *Illusion* means "a mistaken impression." *Delusion* means "a false belief":

> His allusion to Japanese management techniques was not well received, but he made his point.

> Like the old magician's illusions of the floating lady, the bank manager created an illusion of solvency that fooled even seasoned investors.

> The patient had delusions about being watched by the FBI.

alternate/alternative. Confusion comes from competing adjective uses. *Alternate* as an adjective means "occurring in turns" or "every other one." *Alternative* as an adjective means "allowing for a choice between two or more options":

> Winners were chosen from alternate lines rather than from a single line.

> The alternative candidate was a clear compromise between the two parties.

Sometimes these two adjective meanings almost merge, especially when an alternative plan is viewed as a plan that replaces another:

> An alternate/alternative plan provided for supplementary bank financing. (*Either is correct.*)

NOTE: Strict editors attempt to restrict *alternative* (in its noun and adjective uses) to only two options:

> Life is the alternative to death.

Actual (correct) usage, however, has broadened *alternative* to include any number of options:

> The planning commission analyzed five alternative sites. (*or* The planning commission analyzed five alternatives.)

altogether/all together. *Altogether* means "completely or entirely." *All together* means "in a group":

> We had altogether too much trouble getting a simple answer to our question.

> The spare parts lists are all together now and can be combined.

a.m./p.m./m. The abbreviations *a.m.*, *p.m.*, and *m.* sometimes appear in printed text with small caps: A.M., P.M., and M. In most word processing text, lowercase versions are preferred.

Use *a.m.* for times after *midnight* and before *noon*:

12:01 a.m.	(1 minute after midnight)
6:00 a.m.	(early morning)
11:59 a.m.	(1 minute before noon)

Use *p.m.* for times after *noon* and until *midnight*:

12:01 p.m.	(1 minute after noon)
6:00 p.m.	(early evening)
12:00 p.m.	(midnight)

Noon remains a problem. Some guides continue to list *12 m.* as *noon*. However, using *m.* (Latin for *meridies*) for *noon* with readers who do not know this abbreviation is unwise. They might well read *m.* as *midnight*. *Noon* and *midnight* will never be misunderstood; use them in place of *12 m*, *12:00 a.m.*, and *12:00 p.m.*:

> The conference will be at noon on July 25.

among/between. *Among* refers to more than two choices. *Between* usually refers to two choices only, but it can refer to more than two:

> We had difficulty deciding among the many options—over 200 colors

> The contracting officer has eliminated three bidders, so the Source Selection Authority must choose between us and Universal Data.

Strict editors do try to restrict *between* to two choices only. But occasionally, you can use *between* instead of *among*, especially where *among* would not sound right:

> The research group analyzed the differences between the five alternatives.

See PREPOSITIONS.

and/or, or, and. Avoid using *and/or*. This term is usually difficult and sometimes impossible to read with surety. See SLASHES.

In one court case, three judges ruled three different ways as to the meaning of *and/or*. Courts in different cases have ruled that *and* means *or*, and that *or* means *and*. Be careful when using these three troublesome words. See CONJUNCTIONS.

Word Problems

Try to avoid using *and/or*. If you do use it, make sure that the situation you describe has at least three possibilities:

> The road will be made of sand and/or gravel.

This road could be (1) an all-sand road (2) an all-gravel road, or (3) a road made from both sand and gravel.

You can make reading even more difficult by adding other possibilities:

> The road will be made from asphalt, concrete, sand, *and/or* gravel.

The road now has far more construction combinations. Rather than using the shorthand *and/or*, change the sentence to explain to your readers your exact meaning:

> The road will be made from asphalt, concrete, sand, and gravel. *(Implies a combination of all four—with the percent composition variable.)*
>
> The road will have an asphalt and concrete surface, with fill being a mixture of sand and gravel. *(More specific and less ambiguous.)*

Or has two meanings: inclusive and exclusive. For the most precise use of this word, use only the **exclusive** meaning:

> Use the blue pen or the black pen.
>
> Use either the blue pen or the black pen.

Do not use *or* in its **inclusive** sense:

> Limestone or calcium carbonate is used to neutralize the effects of acid rain.

Readers who do not know that limestone is calcium carbonate might think that two substances can be used. They cannot tell whether *or* is being used in its inclusive or its exclusive sense. See CONJUNCTIONS.

Readers who know that limestone is calcium carbonate know that *or* is being used in its inclusive sense, but these knowledgeable readers do not need the reminder that limestone is calcium carbonate.

Write the sentence, eliminating *or* and using parentheses:

> Limestone (calcium carbonate) is used to neutralize the effects of acid rain.

See PARENTHESES.

ante–/anti–. *Ante–* is a prefix meaning "comes before" as in *antebellum* ("coming before a war") or *antedate* ("coming before a specified date"). *Anti–* is also a prefix, but with the meaning of "in opposition or against" as in *antiacademic* or *antismoking*. Occasionally *anti* appears as a word, not as a prefix:

> He turned out to be anti to our proposal.

anyone/any one. *Anyone* means "any person." *Any one* means "a specific person or object":

> Anyone who wants a copy of the Camdus report should receive one.
>
> We were supposed to eliminate any one of the potential mine sites.

appraise/apprise. *Appraise* is a verb meaning "to give the value or worth of something." *Apprise* is a verb meaning "to tell or notify":

> Before the auction, the auto was appraised for over $100,000.
>
> The defendant's lawyer apprised the court that the defendant had been declared bankrupt a year earlier.

as regards. See in regard to/as regards/in regards to.

assure/insure/ensure. All three words mean "to make certain or to guarantee." *Assure* is limited to references with people:

> The doctor assured him that the growth was nonmalignant.

Insure is used in discussing financial guarantees:

> His life was insured for $150,000.
>
> The company failed to insure the leased automobile.

Much of the time, *insure* and *ensure* are confusingly interchangeable. For example, in one Federal document in the late 1970s, *insure* and *ensure* both appeared numerous times with the same meaning; chance seems to have guided which spelling appeared in which sentence. To try to end such confusion, the *U.S. Government Printing Office Style Manual* (March 1984) defines *insure* as "protect" and *ensure* as "guarantee":

> Your life insurance will insure (protect) your family from financial ruin.
>
> To ensure (guarantee) that the drill bit does not overheat as it penetrates through the rock layer, keep the drilling fluid flowing at a maximum rate.

Reality suggests that despite such tidy distinctions, *insure* and *ensure* will continue to be confused. Try, however, to be consistent within a single document by choosing *insure* or *ensure* and then sticking with your choice.

bad/badly. B*ad* is primarily used as an adjective, but in informal English it is also an adverb. *Badly* is an adverb. Now, however, *badly* has begun to function in a few sentences the same way *bad* has. This overlap is a problem when you use the verbs of the senses (*feel, look, smell,* etc.):

Originally and currently acceptable

Harold felt bad *(adjective)* all day from the blow on his head.

The machine worked badly *(adverb)* despite the overhaul.

or

The machine worked bad *(adverb)* despite the overhaul.

Currently acceptable

Harold felt badly all day from the blow on his head.

NOTE: Only the verb *feel* allows for either *bad* or *badly*, as in the preceding sentence. Other confusions between the adjective (*bad*) and the adverb (*badly*) are not acceptable, especially in written English:

Not acceptable

He looked badly after the bachelor party. (*correct form:* bad)

The lab smelled badly after the drainage samples arrived. (*correct form:* bad)

B.C. See A.D. and B.C.

between. See among/between.

biannually/biennially. *Biannually* means "two times a year." *Biennially* means "every 2 years":

Because we meet biannually, we will have 10 meetings over the next 5 years.

Our long-range planning committee meets biennially—on even-numbered years.

bimonthly/semimonthly. *Bimonthly* can mean either "every 2 months" or "twice a month." *Semimonthly* means "twice a month." Because of the potential confusion surrounding *bimonthly*, you should avoid the word and write *every 2 months* or *twice a month*. *Semimonthly* has only one meaning and should not be confusing. Still, it has suffered from the ambiguity of *bimonthly*:

Our bimonthly newsletter appears in January, March, May, July, September, and November. (*better:* Our newsletter appears every 2 months, beginning in January.)

We proposed semimonthly meetings of the legislative committee. (*better:* We proposed meetings twice a month of the legislative committee.)

can/may. *Can* means (1) "ability," (2) "permission," and (3) "theoretical possibility." *May* means (1) "permission" and (2) "possibility":

Ability

She can speak German, but she can't write it very well.

Permission

Can I help you with your project?

May I help you with your project?

NOTE: *May* sounds more formal than *can*, so if you wish to sound formal, use *may*.

Possibility

George can make mistakes if he's rushed. (*or* may)

The project can be stopped if necessary. (*or* may)

The trail may be blocked, but we won't know until later.

Your objection may be reasonable, but we still don't agree.

capital/capitol. *Capital* means "the central city or site of government," "invested money," and "an uppercase letter." *Capitol* means "the main government building":

Paris is the capital of France.

The necessary capital for such an elegant restaurant is $1.5 million, but I doubt that investors will put up that much.

THIS SENTENCE IS WRITTEN IN CAPITALS.

The legislature authorized a complete renovation of the capitol dome.

carat/caret/karat. *Carat* means "the weight of a gem." *Caret* means "a mark showing an insertion." *Karat* means "a unit for the purity of gold":

The ring had a 2.2-carat diamond.

I've used a caret to indicate where to insert the new sentence.

The ring is made of 18-karat gold.

cite/sight/site. *Cite* means "to quote." *Sight* means "vision." *Site* means "a location":

During the trial, our attorney cited earlier testimony.

Most of the tunnel was out of sight, so we could not estimate the extent of the damage.

The contractor prepared the site by bulldozing all the brush off to the side.

complement/compliment. *Complement* means "completing or supplementing something." *Compliment* means "an expression of praise":

The report's recommendations complement those made by the executive committee last year.

The manager passed on a compliment from the vice president, who was impressed with the proposal team's efforts.

comprise/compose. Strict editors carefully distinguish between these two words—that is, *comprise* means "to include or contain" and *compose* means "to make up from many parts":

The U.S. Congress comprises the House of Representatives and the Senate.

The House of Representatives and the Senate compose the U.S. Congress.

Such sentences, especially those with *comprise*, are beginning to sound stiff and overly formal, and passive alternatives are more and more common, although not accepted by all editors:

The U.S. Congress is comprised of the House of Representatives and the Senate.

As with other disputed word uses, choose an alternate version whenever possible:

The House of Representatives and the Senate constitute the U.S. Congress.

contiguous. See adjacent/contiguous/conterminous.

continual/continuous. *Continual* means "intermittent, but frequently repeated." *Continuous* means "without interruption":

Because the pipes are so old, continual leaks appear despite our repair efforts.

Because of a short in the wiring, the horn sounded continuously for 10 minutes.

contractions. Do not use contractions (*don't, couldn't*) in formal documents. However, when you want to create a personal tone, do

Word Problems

use contractions in informal documents such as letters and memos:

> John, don't forget that you must finish this work by Tuesday; otherwise, Bill can't get your figures into his report, which must be done for Vice President Stern by Thursday.

See STYLE and CONTRACTIONS.

council/counsel/consul. *Council* means "a group of people." *Counsel* means "to advise" (verb), "advice" (noun) or "an attorney." *Consul* means "a foreign representative":

> The safety council passed a motion to ban smoking in shaft elevators.
>
> The consultant counseled us in ways to improve our management of ID team efforts.
>
> His counsel was to rewrite the proposal.
>
> MOGO's counsel made the opening statement in the hearing.
>
> The French consul helped us obtain an import license.

councilor/counselor. *Councilor* means "a member of council." *Counselor* is "an advisor or lawyer":

> The councilors decided to table the motion until the next meeting.
>
> Our staff medical counselor has a PhD in clinical psychology.

could. See would/probably would/could/might/should.

credible/creditable/credulous. *Credible* means "believable." *Creditable* means "praiseworthy." *Credulous* means "gullible":

> His revised report was more credible, chiefly because the manpower estimates were scaled to match the price.
>
> In spite of some short cuts, the proposal team wrote a creditable proposal; in fact, they won the contract.
>
> He was so credulous that anyone could fool him.

data. *Data* (the plural of *datum*) is now often used as both the singular and plural forms of the word. In some technical and scientific writing, however, *data* is still traditionally plural only. If the convention in your discipline or organization is to use *data* as a plural, then be sure that your sentences reflect correct agreement of subject and verb:

> Our production data are being examined by the EPA because a citizen complained about excessive emissions from our plant.
>
> The data have been difficult to analyze, chiefly because of sloppy recordkeeping.

These sentences may sound strange or awkward to many readers. Consequently, some technical writers avoid phrasing that calls attention to the plural meaning of *data*. The two sentences above, for instance, could read as follows:

> EPA is examining our production data because a citizen complained about excessive emissions from our plant.
>
> We found the data difficult to analyze, chiefly because of the sloppy recordkeeping.

delusion. See allusion/illusion/delusion.

different from/different than. These two forms can and should be used interchangeably. Strict editors, however, may insist that *different from* is somehow better than *different than*. Actually, well-educated writers and many editors have used both forms for well over 300 years. The argument over these two forms is an example of a preference being mistaken for a rule. In fact, no clear distinction between the two forms has ever existed:

> The results were far different from those we expected. (*or* different than)
>
> The study is different than we had been led to expect. (*or* different from the one we had been led to expect)

disburse/disperse. *Disburse* is the verb meaning "to pay out." *Disperse* is the verb meaning "to scatter":

> The payroll clerk disburses the petty cash funds as needed.
>
> The reserved top soil was dispersed over the site after the project was completed.

discreet/discrete. *Discreet* means "tactful or prudent." *Discrete* means "separate or individual":

> The counselor was so discreet that no one learned we had been meeting with him.
>
> The testing included three discrete samples of the ore body.

disinterested/uninterested. Originally, *disinterested* meant "neutral or unbiased," and *uninterested* meant "without interest." Careful writers and editors still maintain this distinction:

> The judge was appointed because he was clearly disinterested in the dispute.
>
> The President was so uninterested in the problem that he failed to act.

effect. See affect/effect.

e.g./i.e. Both *e.g.* and *i.e.* are Latin abbreviations. Most of the time avoid them and use the equivalent English phrases.

E.g. is the abbreviation for *exempli gratia*, meaning "free examples." *I.e.* is the abbreviation for *id est*, meaning "that is." The two have similar, but still slightly different uses:

> Many appliances (e.g., clothes washers, dryers, and dishwashers) are so common that they have been standard in all new homes. (*The list consists of several free examples.*)
>
> Most first-time house buyers should be aware of this one principle, i.e., let the buyer beware. (*I.e. introduces a restatement of an idea, not a list of examples.*)

In the preceding examples, *for example* could replace *e.g.* in the first sentence. A simple *that is* could replace *i.e.* in the second sentence. Use the English versions unless you are writing for a publication that prefers *e.g.* and *i.e.*

Both abbreviations use periods in the U.S. style: *e.g.* and *i.e.* In British English, the periods usually are not used, with no space between the letters: *eg* and *ie.* Notice also that both abbreviations are enclosed in commas or by another mark of punctuation. See BRITISH ENGLISH.

elapse/lapse. *Elapse* is a verb meaning "to pass by or to slip"; it usually refers to time. *Lapse* is a verb with many meanings, most derived from the sense of "to drift, to discontinue, or to terminate":

> Two weeks elapsed before we heard from the Internal Revenue Service.

> The speaker lapsed into silence after the embarrassing question.

> Our contract lapsed before we could negotiate its renewal.

emigrate/immigrate and **emigration/immigration.** *Emigrate* (verb) means "to leave one's home or residence—to go out." *Immigrate* (verb) is the opposite: "to come into a town or country."

> Peter and his family emigrated from Poland over 10 years ago.

> When he first immigrated into the United Sates, he had difficulty finding work as a doctor because of his poor English skills.

The similar distinction holds for the two parallel nouns: *emigration/immigration.* The only difference is in the point of view:

> Over 10,000 emigrants left Haiti last year for the United States.

> The U.S. policy on Haitian immigrants is becoming increasingly restrictive.

eminent/imminent. *Eminent* means "outstanding or prestigious." *Imminent* means "impending or soon to happen":

> Only eminent researchers will win Nobel prizes.

> The dam's collapse was imminent, so we evacuated downstream communities.

ensure. See assure/insure/ensure.

envelop/envelope. *Envelop* is the verb meaning "to enclose or to encase." *Envelope* is the noun meaning "something that contains or encloses":

> They proposed to envelop the storage tank with the fire-retardant foam.

> We placed in the envelope both the final report and the backup surveys.

etc. Avoid using *etc.* in most of your writing. *Etc.* is the abbreviation for *et cetera,* which is Latin for "other items or persons of the same sort":

> She wrote letters to many governmental figures: the President, Secretary of Defense, Army Chief of Staff, her senator, etc.

As in the preceding sentence, we can only guess about how many people received a letter from her. The use of *etc.* is usually an evasion of the responsibility for listing all the exact facts or details. So avoid using *etc.* in most business or technical writing.

except. See accept/except.

extemporaneous/impromptu. These two words are widely confused, and even some dictionaries have definitions of them that overlap. *Extemporaneous,* especially among speech teachers, means "a speech that is carefully planned and practiced, but not memorized." So its delivery is an extemporaneous action. The common meaning, however, is closer to *impromptu,* as defined below.

Impromptu means that "something that arises without notice or preparation." So an impromptu speech is made without practice or preparation.

As with many confused words, either avoid the two words or use them in contexts where their meanings will be clear:

> During his tour of the plant, the President unexpectedly asked one of the workers to answer impromptu questions from reporters.

> President Clinton is an excellent extemporaneous speaker, as illustrated when his teleprompter broke and he didn't have a printed copy of his speech. He still delivered a good speech.

farther/further. As far back as Shakespeare these words have been confused, and in some contexts they are clearly interchangeable—e.g., *farther/further from the truth.*

Strict editors still maintain that *farther* should be restricted to senses involving distance, while *further* includes other senses:

> The assembly site was farther from the testing area than we wished.

> A further consideration was the inflation during those years.

fewer/less. *Fewer,* the comparative form of *few,* usually refers to things that can be counted. *Less,* one comparative form of *little,* refers to mass items, such as sugar or salt, which cannot be counted, and to abstractions:

> We analyzed fewer well sites than the government wanted us to analyze.

> Less sodium chloride in the water meant that we had fewer problems with corrosion.

> Fewer teachers, less education.

See NOUNS and ADJECTIVES.

flammable/inflammable. Avoid using *inflammable* because it has two contradictory meanings: "able to burn" and "not able to burn." Dictionaries usually list the first of these two meanings as the proper one, but the other meaning is too common to ignore. These two meanings arise from two different interpretations of the prefix *in–;* one means "not" while the other signals

Word Problems

a "presence or possible" (as in "a flame is present"). So never use *inflammable*, but use *not flammable* or *non-flammable* or other phrases:

> The pajamas are non-flammable at temperatures up to 240 °F. (*not* "are inflammable")

> These treated roofing shingles will not catch fire even if glowing coals land on them from a nearby fire. (or non-flammable)

Flammable means "able to burn," or "burns easily," so using it is no problem:

> Even the fumes from a gasoline can be flammable.

forward/foreword. *Forward* is an adjective and an adverb, both meaning "at or near the front." *Foreword* is the noun meaning "the introduction to a book":

> The hopper moves forward when the drying phase is nearly finished.

> The foreword to the book was two pages long.

he/she, s/he, (s)he. Avoid these created new words. If possible, recast your sentence so that it is plural:

> *this*

> All engineers must bring their reports to the meeting. (*plural*)

> All new employees should complete the health forms before beginning work. If they have not done so, their insurance will not be in effect.

> *not this*

> Every engineer must bring his/her report to the meeting. (*singular*)

> Each new employee must complete the health forms before beginning work. If (s)he has not done so, his/her insurance will not be in effect.

These newly coined words, which have not been widely accepted, are attempts to create a singular pronoun other than the word *it* because *it* in many sentences is too odd and too impersonal to refer to people. See BIAS-FREE LANGUAGE and AGREEMENT.

i.e. See e.g./i.e.

illusion. See allusion/illusion/delusion.

immigrate. See emigrate/immigrate.

imminent. See eminent/imminent.

imply/infer. *Imply* means "to suggest or hint." *Infer* means "to draw a conclusion or to deduce":

> The report implies that the break-even point may be difficult to reach, but it fails to give supporting data.

> Based on our comments, she inferred that we would not give our wholehearted support to her project.

impromptu. See extemporaneous/impromptu.

infinitives. See split infinitives.

inflammable. See flammable/inflammable.

in regard to/as regards/in regards to. The first two forms are acceptable. By convention, the third form (*in regards to*) is unacceptable. Do not use *in regards to*.

> In regard to your report, our firm is still busy analyzing it.

> As regards your second question, we have taken all of the steps necessary to acquire mineral rights on the Bruneau lease.

A better choice in most sentences is to use the shorter and simpler *regarding*:

> Regarding your second question, we have taken all of the steps necessary to acquire mineral rights on the Bruneau lease.

insure. See assure/insure/ensure.

irregardless/regardless. *Irregardless* is an unacceptable version of *regardless*. Do not use *irregardless* in either speech or writing:

> We decided to fund the project regardless of the cash flow problems we were having.

its/it's. *Its* is the possessive pronoun. *It's* is the contraction for *it is*:

> Its last section was unclear and probably inaccurate.

> It's time for the annual turnaround maintenance check.

See PRONOUNS.

karat. See carat/caret/karat.

lapse. See elapse/lapse.

later/latter. *Later*, the comparative form of *late*, means "coming after something else." *Latter* is an adjective meaning "the second of two objects or persons":

> Later in the evening a fire broke out.

> In our analysis of the Lankford and Nipon sites, we finally decided that the latter site was preferable.

NOTE: *Latter* (and its parallel *former*) are sometimes confusing, so rewrite to avoid them:

> We finally decided that the Nipon site was preferable to the Lankford site.

lay/laid/laid. These three words are the principal parts of the verb *lay*. The verb itself means "to put or to place." It must have an object:

> The contractor promised to lay the sod before the fall rains began. (*object:* sod)

> The manager laid his plan before his colleagues. (*object:* plan)

> Our recent talks with the Russians have laid the groundwork for control of nuclear weapons in space. (*object:* groundwork)

less. See fewer/less.

lie/lay/lain. These three forms are the principal parts of the verb *lie*. *Lie* means "to rest or recline." In contrast with *lay*, *lie* cannot have an object:

> The main plant entrance lies south of the personnel building.

> The new access road lay on the bench above the floodplain.

> That supply has lain there for over a decade.

marital/martial. These two are confused because they look similar and can, on occasion, be mispronounced.

Marital refers to "marriage or its conditions." *Martial* refers to "war or warriors." So their uses are distinctly separate:

> The marital agreement established a not-to-exceed alimony amount.

> The martial sound of drums and bagpipes encouraged the Scottish soldiers to fight and, supposedly, frightened their enemies.

may. See can/may.

maybe/may be. *Maybe* is the adverb meaning "perhaps." *May be* is a verb form meaning "possibility":

> Maybe we should analyze the impacts before going ahead with the project.

> Whatever happens may be beyond our control, especially if inflation is unchecked.

might. See would/probably would/could/might/should.

or. See and/or, or, and.

p.m. See a.m./p.m./m.

practical/practicable. These two words mean much the same thing, and dictionaries disagree on their distinctions. Given this confusion, writers should stay with the common form *practical* and avoid *practicable.*

Strict editors do maintain that the difference between *practical* and *practicable* is similar to the difference between *useful* and *possible. Practical* means "not theoretical; useful, proven through practice." *Practicable* means "capable of being practiced or put into action; feasible":

> Despite the uniqueness of the problem, the contractor developed a practical method for shoring up the foundation.

Although technically practicable, the solution was not practical because it would have put us over budget.

The last sentence says that we were technically capable of achieving the solution but that this solution was not feasible because of financial constraints.

Similarly, building a house on top of Mt. St. Helens is probably possible (it is practicable), but doing so is not feasible (it is not practical) for obvious reasons.

precede/proceed. *Precede* means "to go ahead of or in front of," so it implies an order or sequence of some kind. *Proceed* simply means "start" or "go on." The two are probably confused because they have similar spellings.

> A dentist's deadening the nerve should precede any drilling or other painful processes.

> The guide proceeded carefully along the bank because the wet soil seemed unstable.

Occasionally *proceeding* appears in a sentence where *preceding* is the correct form:

> The preceding speaker ran over her allotted time, so we got off schedule. (*not* the proceeding speaker)

precedence/precedents. *Precedence* is the noun meaning "an established priority." *Precedents* is the plural form of the noun meaning "an example or instance, as in a legal case":

> The Robbins account should take precedence over the Jackson account; after all, Robbins gives us over 50 percent of our business.

> The Brown decision was the precedent for many later decisions involving racial issues and education.

principal/principle. *Principal* is a noun or adjective meaning "main or chief." *Principle* is a noun meaning "belief, moral standard, or law governing the operation of something":

The principal technical problems we faced were simply beyond current technologies.

The principles of electricity explain the voltage drop in lines.

If we act according to our principles, we will not allow the transaction to proceed.

NOTE: Some writers are confused by *principal* because it also means "the head of a school" and "the money borrowed from a bank." These are noun forms of a word that used to be only an adjective. The noun forms of *principal* come from noun phrases: *the principal teacher* and *the principal amount.* Over time, the nouns *teacher* and *amount* were dropped, and *principal* assumed the full meaning of the original phrases. Now, *principal* is a noun as well as an adjective.

probably would. See would/probably would/could/might/should.

raise/raised/raised. These three forms are the principal parts of the verb *raise. Raise* means "to move (something) upward." *Raise* always requires an object:

> They will raise the funds by January 1, 1990. (*object:* funds)

> We raised the water level some 20 feet to accommodate the changing use patterns. (*object:* water level)

> They had raised the amount to cover the travel costs. (*object:* amount)

rational/rationale. *Rational* is an adjective meaning "logical or well thought out." *Rationale* is a noun meaning "the supporting facts or proof." Confusion arises because the two words are so similar in their spelling.

> The business team followed a rational seven-step process for evaluating each potential site for the new plant.

> His rationale for selling the franchise rested more with his time constraints than with financial considerations.

Word Problems

regardless. See irregardless/regardless.

respectfully/respectively. *Respectfully* means "with deference and courtesy." *Respectively* means "in the sequence named":

> Our representatives were not treated very respectfully.

> According to production data for March, May, July, and September, the number of cases were, respectively, 868, 799, 589, and 803.

NOTE: *Respectively* often makes sentences difficult to interpret, so avoid *respectively* whenever you can.

rise/rose/risen. These three forms are the principal parts of the verb *rise*. *Rise* means "to stand up or move upward." *Rise* does not take an object:

> The balloon rises (*or* will rise) once the air heats up.

> Because the water rose, we had to evacuate the ground floor.

> The moisture level in the gas has risen substantially over the last week.

said. The word *said* often becomes a shorthand term for a document or item previously mentioned:

> We have examined said plans and can find no provisions for the clay soils on the site.

Such uses of *said* are not appropriate in normal business and technical writing. Only in legal writing (and maybe not even there) should writers ever use *said* in this way. The above sentence could be rewritten as follows:

> We have examined the plans and can find no provisions for the clay soils on the site. (*Readers will usually know from the context what plans the writer is referring to.*)

semimonthly. See bimonthly/semimonthly.

set/set/set. These three forms are the principal parts of the verb *set. Set* means "to put or to place (something)." *Set* must have an object:

> They set the surveying equipment in the back of the truck. (*object:* equipment)

> Yesterday we set up the derrick so that drilling could start at the beginning of today's shift. (*object:* derrick)

> After we had set the flow, we began to monitor fluctuations from changes in pressure. (*object:* flow)

shall/will. Use *will* for the simple future with all of the personal pronouns:

> I/We will leave.

> You will leave.

> He/She/It/They will leave.

Shall is rarely used for simple future, at least in American English, but it does retain some sense of extra obligation or force, as in legal contexts:

> The vendor shall provide 24-hour security at the site.

Shall (or *should)* is also used for some questions:

> Shall/Should I stop by your office tomorrow?

> Shall/Should I sign the document now?

Neither *will* nor *would* can replace *shall/should* in these questions.

Some grammarians, beginning in the seventeenth century, formulated a supposed rule for *shall* and *will:* For simple future, use *shall* with *I* and *we; will* with *he, she, it,* and *they.* For obligation and permission, reverse the choices: *will* with *I* and *we; shall* with *he, she, it,* and *they.*

This rule was not accurate in the seventeenth century, and it has never been true of actual English sentences. British English does use *shall* somewhat more frequently for the simple future than American English, but even in England, the seventeenth-century rule is not consistently followed.

she. See he/she, s/he, (s)he.

should. See would/probably would/could/might/should.

sic. *Sic*, from the Latin, means "thus." Use *sic* when you are quoting something and want to show that, yes, I have copied this ungrammatical or odd language as it was originally written or spoken:

> The computer experts in their memorandum stated: "We took for granite [sic] that everyone knew about their [sic] weekend changes to the system."

> The stationary [sic] bus was coming from the opposite direction.

Do not use *sic* to embarrass someone by highlighting harmless mistakes, which we all make.

sight/site. See cite/sight/site.

sit/sat/sat. These three forms are the principal parts of the verb *sit. Sit* means "to rest or to recline." *Sit* does not take an object:

> The well sits at the foot of a steep cliff.

> The committee sat through the long session with very few complaints.

> The oil drums must have sat on the loading dock all weekend.

split infinitives. Many people who often can't even recognize a split infinitive still believe a split infinitive is a grammatical crime. Perhaps because of its memorable name, a split infinitive has become part of the folklore about what good writers should avoid.

Actually, split infinitives have been acceptable in English for hundreds of years. Only in fairly recent times have editors even worried whether sentences like the following should be accepted because they contain split infinitives:

> The company's goal was **to rapidly retire** its investment debt before moving into new markets.

To totally avoid splitting infinitives, the writer decided to eliminate all infinitives from the document.

In the first of these examples, rephrasing to move *rapidly* before or after the infinitive *to retire* is easy: *rapidly to retire* or *to retire rapidly.* Strict editors would choose one of these rephrasings and thus eliminate the split infinitive, but the sentence is actually correct with or without the split infinitive.

In the second example, however, moving *totally* behind the infinitive *to avoid* changes the sentence:

> To avoid totally splitting infinitives, the writer decided to eliminate all infinitives from the document. *(Is the splitting being done totally or does* totally *continue to modify* avoid?)

In this second example, a writer would have to either retain the split infinitive or recast the entire sentence.

To conclude, split infinitives are not worth worrying about. Leave them in your document when the context seems to require a split infinitive.

stationary/stationery. *Stationary* is an adjective meaning "fixed in one spot, unmoving." *Stationery* is a noun meaning "paper for writing on":

> Because the boiler was bolted to the floor, it remained stationary despite the vibration.

> The new letterhead on our stationery made our company seem more up to date.

than/then. *Than* is used in comparisons. *Then* is an adverb meaning "at that time":

> George's report was shorter than Mary's.

> We then decided to analyze the trace minerals in the water samples.

that/which. After centuries of competition (and confusion), the two words continue to be often interchangeable:

> The connecting rod that failed delayed us for two days

or

> The connecting rod which failed delayed us for two days.

In both of these correct sentences, the clauses *that failed* and *which failed* identify which specific rod— that is, the rod that failed, not the other rods. So these clauses are both identifying (restricting) the meaning. As in these two sentences, the restrictive clause is not set off by commas. When *that* and *which* introduce restrictive clauses, the choice between them is merely stylistic—that is, choose the one that sounds the best.

Which is the proper choice, however, for nonrestrictive clauses:

> The Evans report, which took us several months to finish, is beginning to attract attention.

> The U.S. Senate, which many consider the most exclusive club in the world, does follow some quaint rules of decorum.

In both of these examples, the *which* clauses provide additional but unnecessary information about the Evans report and the Senate. Both *which* clauses are thus nonrestrictive because neither helps to identify the report or the Senate. An informal test is if the *which* clauses were deleted, the basic meaning of each sentence would not change. Note, also, that such nonrestrictive clauses are enclosed with commas. See Commas.

Strict editors argue that because *which* is clearly the choice to introduce nonrestrictive clauses, *that* should be used for all restrictive clauses. The tidy distinction is not true of spoken English, and many careful writers continue to use *that* and *which* interchangeably for restrictive clauses

This is another case where a supposed rule (actually part of a rule) is best ignored. To summarize, use either *that* or *which* to introduce restrictive clauses (with no enclosing commas). Use *which* for nonrestrictive clauses (with enclosing commas).

their/there/they're. *Their* is a possessive pronoun. *There* is an adverb meaning "at that place." *They're* is the contraction for *they are*:

> The engineers turned in their reports for printing.

> The well site was there along the base of the plateau.

> They're likely to object if we try to include those extra expenses in the invoice.

to/too/two. *To* is the preposition or infinitive marker. *Too* is both an adverb meaning "excessively" and a conjunctive adverb meaning "also." *Two* is the numeral:

> The proposal went to the Department of the Interior for approval.

> She wants to revise the proposal.

> The design was too costly considering our budget. (too = *excessively*)

> The issue, too, was that technology is only now beginning to cope with these low-temperature problems. (too = *also*)

toward/towards. *Toward* and *towards* are merely different forms of the same word. *Toward* is the preferred form in American English. In British English, *towards* is more common than *toward.*

uninterested. See disinterested/uninterested.

which. See that/which.

while. *While* is best used as only a

Word Problems

time word to show simultaneity— "at the same time as another event":

> While the wash water flows over the screening plates, measure the water's temperature.

> Check the level of the car's transmission fluid while the engine is running.

In other instances, *while* can mean "though," "although," "even though," "but," or "and." These meanings are particularly common in spoken English. In written English, however, replace *while* with its equivalent word:

> *this*

> Although windmills are economical, they are too often destroyed by severe storms, and in calm weather, they produce no electrical power.

> At some places the coal layer is 4 feet wide, but at other places it narrows to 10 inches.

> *not this*

> While windmills are economical, they are too often destroyed by severe storms, while in calm weather, they produce no electrical power.

> At some places the coal layer is 4 feet wide, while at other places it narrows to 10 inches.

who/whom. See the discussion of interrogative and relative pronouns in PRONOUNS.

who's/whose. *Who's* is the contraction for *who is. Whose* is the possessive form of the pronoun *who*:

> Who's the contractor for the site preparation work?

> She was the supervisor whose workers had all that overtime.

will. See shall/will.

would/probably would/could/ might/should. Today these words are usually used as one form of the subjunctive mood, stating future probability. Long ago, *would* and *could* were used as past tense verbs.

These words, except for *would*, never convey an exact probability. The context in which these words are used gives the reader a sense of the probability:

- Would = certain, 100 percent

> If we were to drill the well, we would get 100 barrels of oil per day.

- Probably would = very high, 80 percent

> If we were to drill the well, we probably would get 100 barrels of oil per day.

- Could = reasonably high, 50 percent

> If we were to drill the well, we could get 100 barrels of oil per day.

- Might = moderate, 30 percent

> If we were to drill the well, we might get 100 barrels of oil per day.

Do not use *should* for "high probability." Use *should* in its principal meaning—"an ethical or moral obligation":

> You should not allow your graph to have an appearance of precision greater than your data allow.

> This final part of the president's speech should not be quoted out of context.

See the discussion of subjunctives in VERBS.

your/you're. *Your* is the possessive form of *you. You're* is the contraction for *you are*:

> Your letter arrived too late for us to adjust the original invoice.

> If you're interested, we can survey the production history of that sand over the last decade or so.

See PRONOUNS.

Word processing is the writing, editing, and printing of documents using computers and computer printers. Workers using word processing equipment type (input) text, move it around, revise it at will, paste in pieces of other documents, and file and retrieve their work—all electronically.

Word processing is different from typing—so much so that the term *typing* now seems old-fashioned. In the world of word processing, typing is now called keyboarding or inputting, which includes the original writing of text as well as the typing in of existing text. Once text has been input, word processing allows the writer or editor to experiment freely with different formats and to revise and edit the text easily.

Format options include margins, typefaces, line lengths, tabs, boxes, shaded areas, italics, boldface, and graphics. These format options used to be available only in professionally typeset documents.

Now, a sophisticated word-processed document can be very professional appearing. Word-processed documents are especially sophisticated if they have been prepared using software with desktop publishing features. See PAGE LAYOUT.

Revising with word processing software is especially easy. All word processing programs have a menu of commands: **save, print, delete, search, replace, cut, copy, paste, sort,** etc. With these commands, writers and editors can rearrange sentences, paragraphs, or whole sections; can delete single words or whole sentences; and can replace with a single command a specific word or phrase throughout an entire document.

Word processing makes writing and editing easier and more flexible than they have ever been.

Word Processing

1. Learn to save often and, for important documents, to save on a second (backup) disk.

2. Be flexible (and patient!) when your computer refuses to respond to a command.

3. Save your work using intelligible file names.

4. Decide on a format for your document before you begin writing.

5. Plan your document before you begin to write (input).

6. Brainstorm your content.

7. Organize your content.

8. Use word processing techniques to simplify drafting your document.

9. Revise (edit) efficiently by setting priorities and sticking to them.

10. Use word processing techniques to help you proofread your document.

This ease and flexibility can, however, be a trap. Clients, supervisors, and editors begin to believe that everything can be changed and made better within a few seconds by pushing a single key. They believe change is easy, and it is, but it is also time consuming, and often frustrating to the person doing the changes. In the workplace, efficient word processing means knowing when the document is okay as it is—when enough changes are enough!

Part of learning to use word processing involves becoming comfortable looking at a computer monitor. Many of today's writers and editors are more comfortable with a hard (printed) copy of a document than with a document on a monitor. To them, the computer monitor prevents them from perceiving the overall organization and structure of a document—the "feel" of the document. They find it hard to proofread on a monitor.

Change in the word processing environment has been rapid. Many workers, especially those who have grown up using computers, are now accustomed to seeing documents or data on the computer monitor. They often find it easier to work on a monitor than to proofread and edit on a hard copy.

Such differences in background and experience mean that no single set of rules (suggestions) about word processing techniques will work for everyone.

Whatever your own comfort level with computers, take time to learn how to use your computer's word processing features. It will be time well spent.

Short classes are readily available at many schools and colleges or even from computer retailers, who include training as part of their customer support. Don't overlook the individual computer tutorial that likely came with your word processing software. Also,

Word Processing

review the software documentation manual so you'll know where to find answers quickly when problems occur. If nothing else helps, try calling the software company's customer service department.

When Problems Occur

1. Learn to save often and, for important documents, to save on a second (backup) disk.

Remember that the computer's memory is temporary and may vanish whenever the power goes off or the hardware or software fails. Therefore, the cardinal rule of word processing is to **save often**.

When you command your machine to save, everything you have written up to that point (including all corrections, changes, and even errors) will be recorded on a diskette or hard disk.

Certain word processing programs or networks are programmed to save your copy automatically every few minutes—assuming you want it saved! Usually, the automatic save function can be set to save your work at whatever interval you choose. Some systems signal you with a bell or a flashing notice to remind you to save your work.

For important documents, save your work on a second (backup) disk in case problems develop with the hard disk or disk drive. Some word processing programs and networks automatically back up (save) everything that has been written on a given day so that nothing will be lost if the whole network fails (crashes).

In any case, if you lose something, don't panic. Your work might have been preserved somewhere on a network system that provides backup

possibilities. Many word processing programs also permit you to "undo" the last editing function performed. Be sure to check your word processing program for such an "undo" command.

2. Be flexible (and patient!) when your computer refuses to respond to a command.

Even the most sophisticated computer system has its quirks and lapses. Sometimes problems develop within hardware or software, but more often, you are asking the machine to do something it isn't programmed to do.

Occasionally, such problems cause computers to freeze, crash, or otherwise fail. When this happens, you have probably lost all of the text input since you last saved the document, if your program does not have an auto-save feature.

Repeating a command will sometimes solve the problem. If not, **copy your work to a new file** and try the command again.

If after trying everything you still can't get a command to work, call the technical support group for your word processing software, often an 800 number. They can tell you how to check to see if you have a system conflict, hardware conflict, virus, or other problem.

As You Get Started

3. Save your work using intelligible file names.

As rule 1 suggested, **save often**. Almost as important is how you name your files so that material saved will be accessible to you or a colleague days, weeks, even months later.

Electronic word processing files are similar to the files in a filing cabinet. Well-organized, clean files are a pleasure to work with; messy, chaotic files are a disaster.

Each word processing file should have its own name (code), including, as appropriate, alphabetical or numerical indications of its subject, its writer, and the version saved. For example, you might choose to label a file on *word processing* with the abbreviation*wrdpro*. If different writers work on the same subject, you could add the writer's initials: *wrdprost*.

Most software programs have a feature that indicates the date and time when the file was last opened, but this information might not always help you, especially if you have multiple versions of the same document with the same title. After all, you may have opened an early version of a document while you were trying to find the current version; this early version will automatically carry the most recent date. Consider, therefore, some system for identifying the version or draft—A, B, C, or 1, 2, 3, etc.

File Names for a Team Document. File names are crucial if a number of writers and editors are working as a team on a document. Teams usually share electronic drafts for review and revision. The more sharing, the more a recent revision is likely to be lost or replaced with an earlier version. Remember also that computers are very literal; they will replace an early draft with the new draft if the two drafts have the same title.

Also, agree as a team on how to manage access to the files. Consider privacy issues and the problems of handling client and proprietary information. Decide beforehand who will know passwords and have access privileges.

4. Decide on a format for your document before you begin writing.

The simplest format is usually the one that is already set for your computer by your software program. This basic format will have certain standards (default settings)—for example, default margins, typeface, and tabs. Use this format for routine documents or change the default settings to reflect your own or your company's standards and preferences. These changes will become the default settings.

The more sophisticated your document, however, the more you will want to develop your own format—such as wider margins, two-column format, different typeface, etc. Word processing software allows you to program such style variations so you can insert them with a single key stroke. See PAGE LAYOUT.

You can also develop templates with special styles to use whenever you prepare a standard document such as a proposal, newsletter, marketing flyer, etc. Preparing a template for each type of document will allow you to begin writing immediately without having to worry about what format styles you used last time.

Consider also creating a primary or boilerplate file with merge codes for regularly used documents instead of generating a new document each time. A primary or boilerplate file is a standardized document or preset form (e.g., memo, sales letter, proposal, customer service letter, invoice, manual, procedure, report) that you change or update frequently. To update such a file, you create a secondary or merge file attaching the same merge codes used in your primary to the new information.

These codes permit you to jump immediately to your preselected points of insertion (names, addresses, dates, particular responses or new text, personalized closings).

Often your software will bring up these files as a new document rather than using the original file name. If not, remember to save the changed text under a new file name to avoid confusion when retrieving the standardized document.

Format Decisions for a Team. If a team is working on a document, the earlier the team members can agree on a format, the more efficient will be the writing.

A simple team technique is to develop a single printed style sheet for everyone to use. A style sheet can be as complex as you wish to make it. In essence, it shows how your page will be laid out (margins, spacing, etc.), which typeface to use, and when to use special features (boxes for visuals, shaded quotations, etc.). Figure 1 presents a simple style sheet, which would be easy to construct using most word processing software. See PAGE LAYOUT for an example of a more complex style sheet.

If You Write on Your Computer

Writing a new document directly on your computer is becoming easier as word processing tools become more user friendly and accessible.

Word processing equipment now represents a fourth or even fifth upgrade of electronic equipment for writing. In less than a generation, writers and writing have moved from manual typewriters to electric typewriters with interchangeable type balls, and finally to computers using updated word processing software. Of course, some holdouts still argue that nothing helps the writer more than sitting down with a yellow legal pad and a favorite pen or pencil.

The changes in writing technology have even changed how we write.

The most obvious change is that writers can write much faster. If your fingers unconsciously know the keyboard, you can now input (write) your text probably two or three times faster than you could type on a manual typewriter and four or five times faster than you could scratch your text on a legal pad. You can now write your text with a speed that more closely mirrors the speed of speech. Your thoughts will still run ahead of the words your fingers are typing, but the faster you write, the better your chance of catching an insight or an implication before your mind moves on.

Writing is still a mystery, however. Even the computer cannot reveal just how someone comes up with a particular organization or a certain train of logical thought.

The following rules are suggestions about how to write using word processing. As suggestions, they are necessarily provisional and tentative. You need to ask yourself what works for you and what doesn't. You might still need, for example, to plan on paper before turning to the keyboard. Or you might decide that you can only proofread effectively if you have a hard (printed) copy in front of you.

As you write using word processing, test the following suggestions. Be alert for shortcuts. Try to make your writing efficient, even pleasant. See WRITING AND REVISING.

First-level Heading will be 14-pt. Helvetica Bold, centered; 6-pt. space after

Second-level Headings will be 12-pt. Helvetica Bold, flush left; 6-pt. space after

Third-level headings will be 10-pt. Times Bold and will lead into paragraph. Body text will be 10-pt. Times.

Paragraphs will be single line space with 6-pt. space after, flush left, no indent on first line.

1. Primary lists will be numbered with a .25-inch hanging indent from the margin on the left and a tab set at .5 inch; and a .5-indent from the right margin.

    • Secondary lists will be bulleted with a .5-inch hanging indent from the margin on the left and a tab set at .125 from indent. Right indent will remain at .5-inch from margin.

    — Any remaining lists will be dashed with an em dash. Hanging indent will be .625-inch from the left margin with the paragraph indent set at .75-inch from the left margin. Right indent will remain .5-inch from the margin.

Figure 1. A Basic Style Sheet. *Even a basic style sheet as simple as this one will help teams of writers submit text with uniform features. See* PAGE LAYOUT *for a more complex style sheet.*

5. Plan your document before you begin to write (input).

Planning is important to avoid false starts or dead ends. Try to identify a few of the givens about the document before you begin to write.

Do you have your task or assignment clearly in mind?

• What is your main purpose?

• What do you want your readers to do, to know, and to feel?

• Who will read your document and what are their goals and priorities?

• What sort of document (length, format, content) do you expect to write?

These and similar questions will surely be in the back of your mind as you are writing. Do you need to write them down before beginning—perhaps on a pad or on a whiteboard?

Will writing down some of these givens help you focus your efforts? Do what you must to make your writing as efficient as possible. See WRITING AND REVISING.

6. Brainstorm your content.

Your computer can be a valuable brainstorming tool. Don't be afraid of writing down something you feel is stupid or something that you think won't fit. After all, you can move ideas around at will, and you can later delete anything you don't need with the touch of a key.

Experiment with a brainstorming phase before you actually begin to write the text—that is, **before** you try to write complete sentences and fleshed-out paragraphs.

Such a brainstorming phase might be a rapid inputting of key words and phrases without any order or sequence. Let your mind race as fast as it will, and don't block even the dumb ideas. Don't worry about spelling or punctuation. See THINKING STRATEGIES.

Brainstorming is most applicable to documents that are not regular and routine. For routine documents, you already know much of the content, and you may even have a format (template) to start with. See rule 4 above.

After you finish brainstorming, you have to choose what you want to do next. You might, for example, print a copy of your brainstorming and use it as a guide for writing your draft. Your software may even display your brainstorming notes in a window on the screen while you are writing your text.

7. Organize your content.

The more complex the document, the more you will need to organize your brainstorming notes.

This process might be merely a sequencing or tidying up of your brainstorming notes. Or, you might decide to work up a fairly complete outline.

Many word processing programs have an outlining function. This function usually gives you a standard outline format to work with, and once you finish your outline, you can usually view the outline in a window on your screen while you are writing your text. See OUTLINES and ORGANIZATION.

If you have always liked to outline before writing, you will probably want to continue using an outline as part of word processing. If you never liked writing from an outline, you might want to move directly from your brainstorming notes to the writing of your draft.

8. Use word processing techniques to simplify drafting your document.

Writing rough drafts used to be a more daunting task before word processing software. Now you can write, tweak, move text around, insert, and delete ideas at any point in the writing process.

The computer can help you overcome "writer's block." If you write quickly, not trying to be perfect the first time, the computer can cut your writing time. You can also avoid anxiety about having something with errors, misspellings, and other "warts."

Nevertheless, ease of editing on the computer means you will be tempted to rework sections or whole drafts before you finish writing the initial version.

Try not to allow such revision work to interrupt your thinking or cause you to forget ideas you should record.

Keep these things in mind while writing on a computer:

- Remember, you can always change text later, so avoid editing grammar, spelling, and punctuation before you have all your ideas on the screen.

- Make on-screen notes of ideas that occur to you but may not be relevant to the passage you're working on. Some word processing programs permit you to make "text notes," i.e., text that is invisible to the printer but appears on-screen.

- Code or mark points in the text where missing data needs to be inserted or more work needs to be done. For example, you can insert a non-word symbol like < > or ~. Then with your SEARCH feature, you can tell the computer to search for places where this symbol appears.

Team Writing of a Draft. Recognize that rough drafting is not a group activity. Instead, assign each team member a section to write, and remind them of the style they should follow. See rule 4 above. When team members finish with their drafts, assign a single person to integrate the drafts so that the team can review the whole document.

9. Revise (edit) efficiently by setting priorities and sticking to them.

Take care of the big issues such as purpose, content, and emphasis before you begin to polish sentences and mold your paragraphs. See WRITING AND REVISING.

Proofreading comes last.

Setting priorities makes sense because it forces you to address the more global issues rather than spending too much time on trivial details when the document has failed to achieve its main purpose.

Revision (editing) begins when you reread what you've written. Decide, first, if you need to see the document in hard copy. If so, print a copy, preferably with double spacing and wide margins.

Next, review the whole document with these major questions in mind:

- Is my main purpose clear and up-front?

- Have I emphasized my key ideas?

- What else should I tell my readers?

- Is my tone and approach appropriate and effective?

After you have asked these hard questions (and fixed any problems), begin working on your paragraphs and sentences.

Here is where the computer is a boon. You can rewrite, move, or delete text so easily that you can experiment with different ways to say the same thing. For example, you might make a second copy of a paragraph and rewrite the copy. After rewriting, you can return to the original to see if you have improved it. Finally, you can delete the version you decide not to use.

To help with rewriting, some word processing programs have an electronic thesaurus. Consider using it if you are stumped for an appropriate word or phrase.

Also, during rewriting, you might want to code words or phrases that you wish to appear in your index or in a table of contents. Then when you finish editing, you can command

Word Processing

your software to sort the words and phrases and to prepare the table of contents or the index. See INDEXES and TABLES OF CONTENTS.

A Final Caution About Revision. No text is ever finished or perfect, at least in the minds of most writers. Word processing often lures writers into spending excessive time revising and polishing their drafts. The secret is to know when to quit revising.

Decide when the draft is adequate, even good, but not necessarily perfect, and then stop.

10. Use word processing techniques to help you proofread your document.

Although the computer makes writing and especially editing much more flexible and easier than ever before, it also adds new possibilities for errors. The ease of changing things makes consistency of content, data, grammar, and spelling a major problem. See EDITING AND PROOFREADING.

Proofreading becomes even more essential after a writer has tinkered with a text for hours and hours because for every change the writer has made, probably 10 others should have been made for consistency with the single change.

Follow these general suggestions for proofreading on a computer:

- **Proofread on the Screen.** An advantage of the computer is that you don't have to print a hard copy to proofread or to review your text. But even experienced editors have trouble proofreading using only the screen. The text is often too small, and it is sometimes awkward to check the document for overall consistency when you can see only a dozen or so lines of text at a time.

If you do proofread on the screen, consider changing the text to larger, more readable type and adjusting the line spacing to double spaces. Both of these changes will help you identify proofreading problems.

- **Proofread a Hard Copy.** Some people find it difficult to proofread on a screen because screens do not always show entire pages, and the visual resolution of characters on a screen is not always clear and sharp. Actually, reviewing a hard copy will give you a second chance to catch things you've already missed on the screen.

- **Check for Consistency.** When you change your text at some point, odd problems may appear elsewhere in the text. Some subjects no longer agree with verbs, spellings become inconsistent, and pronouns no longer agree with their antecedents.

Be particularly careful about global search and replace commands; if you order all the *threes* in your document to become *fives*, you had better be sure that you mean **all** the *threes*. When you insert new information or update boilerplate, be careful that the old text is consistent in every way with the new.

- **Run a Spelling Check.** Most word processing programs are equipped with spellcheck features. When you command the computer to check your spelling, it matches every word in your text with words in its internal dictionary, flagging those it doesn't recognize. Then the machine gives you the option of changing the questionable word or leaving it as is.

Spellcheckers are wonderful for finding typographical errors and plain old misspellings—but be careful. The spellchecker may overlook words that are spelled right but are wrong for the context (e.g., *there* instead of *their*), so proofreading is still necessary. Often, you can add words from your professional vocabulary to the computerized dictionary; make sure you spell them correctly when you do.

- **Run a Grammar Check.** Grammar checkers are designed to catch grammar and punctuation errors by comparing your writing with lists of common phrases that often present problems.

For example, most grammar checkers can identify whether you have used a passive or an active verb in a sentence. The checker cannot, however, tell you whether the passive is the correct choice or whether you should change it to an active verb. See ACTIVE/ PASSIVE.

Grammar programs are not very advanced in their ability to point out errors in grammar, punctuation, or word usage. They may flag only a small percentage of the errors in your copy, and what they flag may not even be errors.

Some grammar checkers also purport to analyze style. Such style checkers measure sentence length and word length to determine a "reading level" for your text. These levels may be expressed in terms of an index of readership or grade level in school terms. Often, style checkers can help you gauge whether your sentences are short enough and your word choice simple enough to make your point effectively. See SENTENCES and GOBBLEDYGOOK. Style checkers will not really identify basic problems of inconsistent or incoherent sentence structure.

Special Word Processing Features for Writers

Bibliographic Databases. Scientific and technical researchers who must work with or provide reference lists in reports may find bibliography programs helpful. These programs permit you to enter information about references and then to format the information according to any bibliographical style you choose (e.g., for formal reports, catalogs, journals, conference proceedings, or dissertations). Professionals who use online databases can transfer reference information directly into the bibliographic database. See BIBLIOGRAPHIES, CITATIONS, and FOOTNOTES.

Remember to proofread reference lists just the same as you proofread text.

Mathematical Expression Checkers. Aimed at technical professionals who present mathematical proofs in their writing, these programs enable them to pull mathematical symbols into their copy; to highlight equations, making editing easier; and to work within templates that provide preset mathematical structures for many common equations. See MATHEMATICAL NOTATIONS.

Graphics Programs. Professional-looking graphics are becoming standard in business and technical reports. Many sophisticated, easy-to-use programs exist for generating graphics. You can create your own graphs, diagrams, and charts with a painting or drawing program, and then paste them into your copy. Or you can use one of the many programs that contain predesigned graphics and just plug them into your copy (be careful here—the quality of these images ranges widely). Finally, you can transfer an image printed on paper into your computer by using a scanner, which turns a picture into digital codes and then displays it on the computer screen. You can then manipulate its size, orientation, and position on the page. See GRAPHICS FOR DOCUMENTS and GRAPHICS FOR PRESENTATIONS.

If you need to use colored or complex and eye-catching graphics, you may want to step from word processing to desktop publishing, which involves more sophisticated page layout and graphics opportunities. See PAGE LAYOUT.

Wordy Phrases

Wordy Phrases

1. Avoid wordy phrases.

Wordy phrases are phrases that use too many words to express an idea. Many of them incorporate or are similar to redundancies, and many wordy phrases have been overused so much they've become cliches:

    all of a sudden
    at a later date
    beyond a shadow of a doubt
    in light of the fact that
    in the environment of
    in the neighborhood of
    kept under surveillance
    on two different occasions
    reported to the effect
    the fullest possible extent

None of these phrases is necessary, but many writers use them habitually, so they seem "natural" somehow. In informal speech and writing, these phrases may in fact be preferable, depending on your audience. In technical and business writing, however, you should avoid them. See REDUNDANT WORDS, CLICHES, GOBBLEDYGOOK, and SCIENTIFIC/TECHNICAL STYLE.

1. Avoid wordy phrases.

A fundamental of good writing style is to avoid unnecessary words. Do not say *all of a sudden.* Just say *suddenly.* Instead of *at a later date,* say *later. In light of the fact that* simply means *because of.*

The shorter, simpler words or expressions make your writing more concise and, consequently, make it look and sound more professional.

A List of Wordy Phrases

The following list of wordy phrases will help you identify those you habitually use. The wordy phrase appears in the left column; in the right column are possible substitutes.

According to the law	legally
add an additional	add
add the point that	add that
afford an opportunity	permit/allow
a great deal of	much
a greater number of	more
a great number of times	often/frequently
a large number of	many
a little less than	almost
all of a sudden	suddenly
along the lines of	like
a majority of	most
a number of	several/many/some
any one of the two	either
a period of several weeks	several weeks
as a general rule	usually/generally
as a matter of fact	in fact
a small number of	a few
as of now	now
as of this date	today
as regards	about
as related to	for/about
assuming that	if
as to	about
a sufficient number	enough
at a later date	later
at all times	always
at an early date	soon
at hand	here
at present	now
at regular intervals of time	regularly
at that time	then
at the conclusion of	after
at the present time	now
at the rear of	behind
at the same instant	simultaneously
at this time	now
at which time	then
Based on the fact that	due to/because
beyond a shadow of a doubt	doubtless
brought to a sudden halt	halted
by means of	by
by the time that	when
by the use of	by
by way of illustration	for example
Called attention to the fact	reminded/noted
came to a stop	stopped

cannot be possible	impossible
come to an end	end
cost the sum of	cost
Despite the fact that	although
detailed information	details
draw to a close	end
due to the fact that	because
during the course of	during
during the time that	when/while
during which time	while
Estimated at about	estimated at
estimated roughly at	estimated at
exactly alike	identical
except in a small number of cases	usually
exhibit a tendency to	tend to
expose to elevated temperature	heat
Few in number	few
for a short space of time	for a short time
for the purpose of	for/to
for the reason that	because/since
for this reason	so
from the point of view of	for
from time to time	occasionally
Having reference to this	for/about
If and when	if/when
if at all possible	if possible
if that were the case	if so
in accordance with	by/under
in addition (to)	also/besides
in a number of cases	many/some
in a position to	can/may
in a satisfactory manner	satisfactorily
inasmuch as	because/since/as
in back of	behind
in case of	if
in close proximity	near/close
in conjunction with	with
in consideration of the fact	because
in excess of	more than
in favor of	for
in few cases	seldom
in few instances	seldom
in lieu of	instead of/in place of
in light of the fact that	because

Phrase	Replacement
in many cases	often
in most cases	usually
in order to	to
in other words	or/that is
in rare cases	rarely
in (with) reference to	about/concerning
in regard to	about/concerning
in relation to	with
in respect to	about/concerning
in short supply	scarce
in terms of	according to
in the absence of	without
in the amount of	of/for
in the case of	for/by/in/if
in the course of	during
in the environment of	around/near
in the event of	if
in the event that	should/if
in the first place	first/primarily
in the instance of	for
in the majority of cases	usually
in the matter of	about
in the nature of	like
in the near future	soon
in the neighborhood of	about/near
in the proximity of	near/nearly/about/close to
in the vicinity of	around/near/close to
introduced a new	introduced
in view of the fact that	considering
involve the necessity of	requires
is/are in the possession of	has/have
is defined as	is
is in the process of making	is making
is of the opinion that	believes
is representative of	typifies
it is apparent that	apparently
it is clear that	clearly
it is evident that	evidently
it is obvious that	obviously
it is often the case that	often
it is plain that	plainly
it is unquestionable that	unquestionably
it would appear that	it seems/apparently
Kept an eye on	watched
kept under surveillance	watched
Last of all	last
leaving out of consideration	disregarding
Made an investigation of	investigated
major portion of	most of
make application to	apply
make a purchase	buy
make contact with	meet/contact
more and more	increasingly
Notwithstanding the fact that	although
Of considerable magnitude	big/large/great
off of	off
of no mean ability	capable
of small diameter	fine/thin
of very minor importance	unimportant
on account of	because
on a few occasions	occasionally
on an ongoing basis	continually
on a stretch of road	on a road
on behalf of	for
once in a great while	seldom/rarely
one after another	alternately
one by one	singly
one part in a hundred	one percent
on the basis of	by
on the grounds that	because
on the part of	by/for
on two different occasions	twice
ought to	should
outside of	except/outside
owing to the fact that	since/because
Period of time	interval/period
pertaining to	about
possibly might	might
prior to	before
probed into	probed
proceed to investigate, control, study	analyze/study/investigate
provide a continuous indication of	show continuously
pursuant to	following
Range all the way from	range from
reduced to basic essentials	simplified
refer back	refer
relative to	about
repeat again	repeat
reported to the effect	reported
revise downward	lower/decrease
Seldom if ever	rarely
separate into two equal parts	halve/divide
since the time when	since
started off with	started with
subsequent to	after/following
Take appropriate measures	act
taking this factor into consideration	therefore
that is to say	that is
the foregoing	the/this/that/these/those
the fullest possible extent	mostly/fully completely
the only difference being that	except that
there is no doubt that	doubtless/no doubt
there is no question that	unquestionably
through the use of	by
to be cognizant of	to know
to summarize the above	in summary
total operating costs	operating costs
turn up	turn
two by two	paired/in pairs
Until and unless	unless
until such time as	until
up to now	formerly
Went on to say	added/continued
when and if	if
with a view to	intending to
with full approval	approved
within the realm of possibility	possibly/possible
without variation	constant/stable
with reference to	about
with regard to	about/regarding
with respect to	about/respecting
with the exception of	except
with the object of	to
with the result that	so that

Writing has always been a challenging personal intellectual skill; it is also now increasingly an organizational activity. Organizations now rely on teams of experts and writers to make sense of complex, often puzzling data.

As a personal intellectual skill, writing proficiencies vary from person to person. Many people find writing difficult and intimidating. They procrastinate often and they apologize frequently for what they've written. Others write more willingly because they find satisfaction in completing a document—despite hard work and long hours.

Each person approaches writing differently because each person's intellectual skills are unique.

Some people prefer to plan, to discuss, and to think out their entire content before writing a word of text. With today's computers, many others begin writing the text while ideas are growing and changing. Computers make it easy for them to move language around and to edit as their thoughts flow.

No matter how you personally approach the task of writing, you likely will find it cyclic, even chaotic. For most writers, writing is an unruly, unpredictable intellectual skill. Unpredictable ideas and implications surface as you struggle to form ideas into words.

Using your own approach is okay, assuming that you are writing efficiently.

As an organizational activity, writing is a new and changing skill. Writers within organizations now confront different communication problems. Online documents, data files, and computer runs are increasingly complex and extensive.

Writing and Revising

Front Loading

1. Determine the givens for a document as early as possible.

Prototyping

2. Develop an evolving prototype of your potential document and use this prototype to monitor your progress on the document.

3. Build prototypes collaboratively and with brainstorming techniques.

4. Use the prototype to define content issues that need to be resolved.

5. Integrate ongoing reviews into each prototyping session.

Drafting

6. Develop your own personal strategies for making the writing of a draft a comfortable, repeatable task.

Reviewing

7. Provide for early and frequent reviews from a broad sample of reviewers (including managers).

8. Use an oral (face-to-face) meeting for most reviews, but record the results of such a meeting in writing.

9. Develop strategies for who will work on document defects and who will research content issues.

Revising

10. Set revision priorities both for yourself and for others who can help you revise and edit.

11. Use up-to-date references to guide your revision decisions.

12. Know when to stop revising.

For example, sensing data from orbital satellites have become so extensive and complex that less than five percent of the data is ever analyzed and explained.

The overwhelming scope and complexity of today's data mean that a single person cannot efficiently analyze and then record all available data for a given task or project. See WORD PROCESSING .

Writing—Linear Process or Separate Activities?

Those who believe in the linear process theory believe writing and writers follow a sequence of steps as illustrated in figure 1. If people learn these steps, they'll know how to write.

This view of writing as a linear sequence of steps will work for short, routine letters and memos. Writers of short documents often move step by

Figure 1. A Simple, Linear Writing Process. *This process works well for short, routine documents. For example, a routine six-line memo or letter would require only the four steps listed above. Writing such a memo might take 20 minutes or less. Usually, one person plans, designs, drafts, and revises the memo.*

step, with few if any iterations to pick up unexpected information.

A simple, linear process does not work if the written document is complex and non-routine.

Instead of staying with a strict linear model, the following guidelines focus on several skill sets or techniques:

- Front loading (Planning)
- Prototyping (Designing)
- Drafting
- Reviewing
- Revising

As shown in figure 2, successful writers usually will draw on each skill set several times during their work on a document. The exact nature and sequence of the steps, however, will vary. Even a single writer will vary the steps for a repeated type of document after becoming accustomed to writing it.

As you write and edit, ask yourself what works and what doesn't. Be alert for shortcuts. Work to discover ways to avoid time-consuming and costly false starts. Every rewritten document is a costly step in the documentation process. Current quality initiatives view extensively rewritten documents as an

unacceptable waste of organizational resources. See PROJECT MANAGEMENT.

Front Loading

Front loading means providing as much input to the process as possible from as many concerned people as possible as early as possible.

Front loading combines traditional ideas about project planning with a new and fairly different assumption about the writing of documents.

The assumption is that the writer's goal is to produce the best possible document the first time it's written— even though everyone involved in the process expects the document to face changes and revisions.

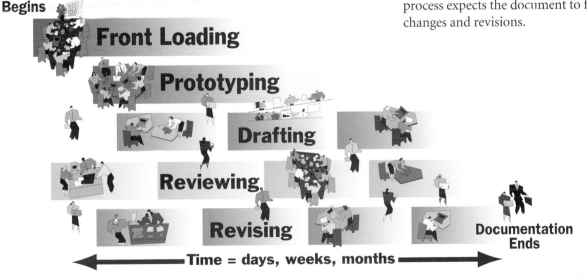

Figure 2. Writing Process for Non-Routine, Complex Documents. *Non-routine, complex documents are usually long and data rich. They usually require multiple contributors and reviewers. The process for such documents requires overlapping, concurrent steps, and often steps will be repeated when new givens (constraints) appear.*

Writing and Revising

Current discussions of quality processes focus on doing something right the first time. If properly designed, for example, the pump in an automobile can be installed only the right way, not upside down or backward.

In a similar fashion, if you use front loading to plan a projected document, then what you write should need little revision and certainly no major late-stage rethinking of content, format, and organization.

1. Determine the givens for a document as early as possible.

This step is more inclusive than the traditional notion of document planning. Yes, in this step you'll ask questions and set assignments, but you should also begin to visualize your document even before you've written a word.

This initial visualization is a provisional target, one that will evolve and change as you work on the document. With an early visualization in your mind's eye, your text will grow from and yet be constrained by the format and appearance of your final document. If you are preparing a two-column, four-sided newsletter, the format will limit the sorts of articles and graphics you can include.

As in this newsletter example, format and appearance affect and limit the content. This approach reverses the traditional model, where content comes first and is then formatted and polished later on.

To begin your front loading of the document, ask the following questions:

—What is your main point? (What do you want readers to do? to know? to feel?)

—Who will read your document and what are their priorities?

—What sort of document (length, format, graphics, and content) do you intend to write?

—What organizational goals (or constraints) exist?

—Who inside or outside the organization can help you meet these goals?

If you are working alone, check to see if you have answered each of the preceding questions. The more complex the writing task, the more desirable you'll find the habit of answering such questions in writing, either in a formal checklist or an informal list of reminders.

Don't assume that because you are working alone you needn't address these front-loading questions.

If your writing is an organizational activity, you, your colleagues, and your manager(s) need to agree on answers to the front-loading questions. The longer you delay involving these key participants, the more likely you'll face costly rewrites. As early as possible, convene a team with as many contributors as feasible. If possible, include both internal and external customers. See WORD PROCESSING.

Be sure to record answers in writing and circulate these answers to all the contributors. What you will find is that you have already begun the writing because material in your answers will likely flow directly into the document you are planning.

Prototyping

Prototypes are full-scale visualizations of a document. Often document prototypes are called mock-ups or storyboards. Regardless of the terminology used, a document prototype has these features:

—A full page-to-page correspondence between the prototype and the final document

—A page layout (or style sheet) to guide how text is written (See PAGE LAYOUT.)

—Headings and subheadings that show the organization and scope of the text to be written

—Graphics and captions to highlight key points

A document prototype differs from an engineering prototype, which is full-scale working model. A document prototype is not full or complete, so it is not a "working" model in the engineering sense. The document prototype is, however, a full visualization of the final document.

2. Develop an evolving prototype of your potential document and use this prototype to monitor your progress on the document.

A document prototype evolves gradually, through iterations. A document prototype should be a team activity although a single writer sometimes prepares a prototype for discussion or team review.

A document prototype will save time and money if it guides all later stages of document preparation, including the writing of text. A document prototype is an evolving and maturing tool as a team's vision of the final document evolves and matures.

The **initial prototype** is very skeletal—perhaps little more than blank pages with a few key headings and several key graphics sketched in. The initial prototype is a visualization of the document to come. This visualization functions as a working hypothesis. See figure 3 for a few pages from an initial prototype.

Several iterations later, an **interim prototype** will contain most headings and subheadings, as well as sketches of most graphics. But this prototype still has little text. See figure 4 for an example of an interim prototype.

A **mature prototype**—which may be the product of weeks of teamwork—begins to look like a rough draft. A mature prototype has full headings and subheadings, versions of all graphics, and even some text. Some pages are still blank, however. See figure 5 for an example of a mature prototype.

The mature prototype becomes a rough draft when the text is complete, but not final. The design and scope of the document should be final by the time the rough draft is ready for review.

As in most rough drafts, mature prototypes have a few mispelled words and slips in punctuation. Late-stage, careful revision will correct the errors.

3. Build prototypes collaboratively and with brainstorming techniques.

A prototype should include rich input from all concerned and interested people. Invite input from engineers, scientists, managers, legal staff, fabrication specialists, sales personnel, government regulators, and customers (internal and external).

Early prototyping should be a brainstorming activity—that is, almost a game to be played. Remind yourself and your collaborators not to be too judgmental or too negative.

4. Use the prototype to define content issues that need to be resolved.

Even an initial prototype will allow you to define content issues that need further work.

—What, for example, does the customer want the product to do?

—Which scientific studies are yet to be done?

—Do government regulations require a particular test or sampling approach?

—What financial constraints will govern production decisions?

Your work with the early prototypes raises content issues, not superficial late-stage questions about format or language.

5. Integrate ongoing reviews into each prototyping session.

Make reviewing part of the proto-typing process, not something done after a version of the prototype is finished. (See the reviewing guidelines in rules 7 through 11.)

Ongoing reviews are just one version of team collaboration. You might, for instance, open a follow-on prototyping session by walking through the prototype from an earlier session. Or, you might end a prototyping session by asking a participant to turn pages and review remaining content issues.

Such reviews are different from a late-stage managerial or red-team review.

If possible, include your manager(s) in the early prototyping sessions so they have a stake in the evolving prototype as it is produced. If they don't see the prototype until it is mature, they will often require the team to repeat many of the earlier steps—thus wasting much time and money.

Drafting

Writing the draft begins when you make your first front-loading notes. It continues as you work to flesh out your prototype. It does not end until you make your final revisions.

A key tenet of time management is that you manage a complex task by breaking it up into shorter tasks. Use the same approach in your writing.

6. Develop your own personal strategies for making the writing of a draft a comfortable, repeatable task.

Successful writing is 50 percent psychology, 50 percent skill with words. Ask yourself what most frustrates you about writing. Consider ways to lessen your frustrations and to make your own writing a pleasant task. See WORD PROCESSING.

Your strategies will be necessarily unique, but some possible ones to consider are the following:

—Write the easy stuff first. This will get your creative thoughts flowing.

—Don't worry about writing your draft in one sitting. Instead, work on your draft section by section, sentence by sentence.

—Turn off the internal voice that judges each word you write. Instead, view each word as an accomplishment, not something to immediately delete and rewrite.

—Visualize yourself talking to your readers. Your thoughts and language should be just as natural and as free-flowing as your talk would be.

—When you complete a section, take time to compliment yourself.

Writing and Revising

Outside brochure

5

HEADING: SUCCESSES

CALLOUT
all in solid box—
reverse txt

photo:
petroworker

SAVE $/
PARTNERING
HEADING: WHY
Reasons
testimonial/client
statement

HEADING: WHY
Reasons
testimonial/client
statement

HEADING: WHY
Reasons

4.5 x 8.5 text box

6

Photo: Petrochemical plant.

BACK COVER

About our company—
blah, blah, blah (get frm
Mkt dept.)

address, phone, etc.

Logo

1

Full bleed, ghosted text boxes

FRONT COVER

WHAT
MATTERS
MOST

TEXT,

OFFERING,

SOLUTIONS

Logo

Inside brochure

2

HEADING: CHALLENGES

CALLOUT

Challenges of O&G
industry.
What if:
• problem to solve
• problem to solve
• problem to solve
• problem to solve
• etc.

4 x 5 in. text box

photo: petroworker on
tower or similar photo

3

HEADING: WE CAN HELP

CALLOUT

Text
about system specs
(check with MIS)
4.5 x 2.5 text box

Graphic: Just-in-
time online system
(get from art dept.)

4

HEADING: SOLUTIONS

CALLOUT

Text

Graphic: our JIT
process (from art
dept.)

Description of each
piece of process
•
•
•
•

4.5 x 8.5 text box

Figure 3. Initial Prototype. *Team members prepare an initial prototype using flipchart pages or single sheets of paper. For a brochure such as this, they might tape together three 8.5 x 11 sheets to capture the sequence of pages and to help them visualize the final product. As in this example, text in an initial prototype is often sketchy or missing, and graphics remain to be designed or located.*

Outside brochure

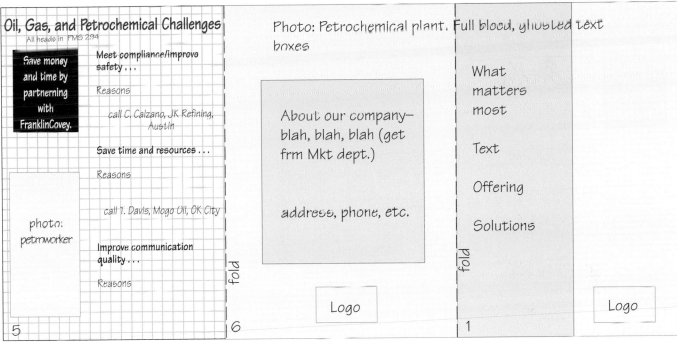

Open dimensions: 25.5 x 11 in.; folded dimensions: 8.5 x 11 in.
100lb. coated stock, full color, varnish

Inside brochure

Figure 4. Interim Prototype. *Days or weeks later, the prototype moves over into a computer format, as in this example. Text is still sketchy, or missing. Graphics are sketched, but not finished. An interim prototype should be complete enough to allow for review by managers or customers.*

Outside brochure

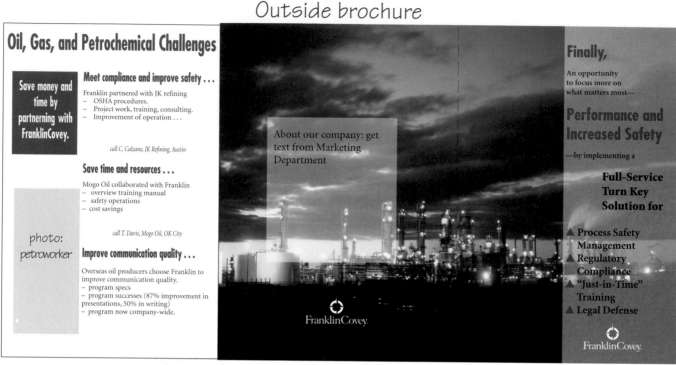

Open dimensions: 25.5 x 11 in.; folded dimensions: 8.5 x 11 in.
100lb. coated stock, full color, varnish

Inside brochure

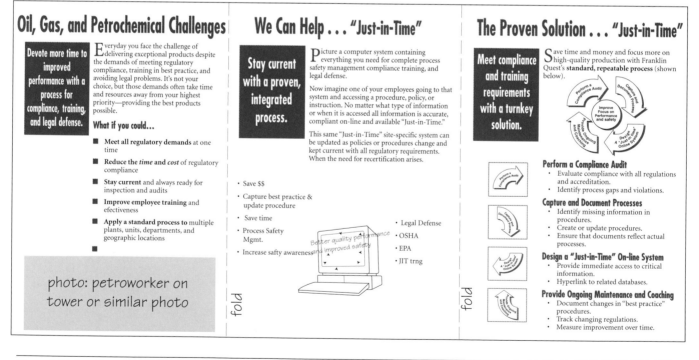

Figure 5. Mature Prototype. *A mature prototype is often the same as a rough draft. Text and graphics are included, even though still rough or unfinished. Color might or might not be used. Revision and editing will change some of the text and, perhaps, even some of the graphics.*

Reviewing

Reviewing provides valuable feedback for organizations to use in guaranteeing the quality of intellectual products. Reviewing was and remains, however, an inefficient and costly tool unless it is well managed.

Two types of review are possible: **peer** and **managerial.** The numbered rules 7 through 9 apply to both peer and managerial reviews.

Peer review occurs when professional and technical colleagues review a document (either a prototype or rough draft) for its content or its presentation of the content. Peers, by definition, are colleagues who have no managerial authority over the writer(s). Their suggestions to the writer(s) are not binding.

Managerial review occurs when managers within an organization exercise their authority to review and approve or disapprove a document. Their responses to a document are binding unless they choose to allow for negotiations and adjustments.

---

7. Provide for early and frequent reviews from a broad sample of reviewers (including managers).

Schedule reviews during the development of the initial prototype. Continue to schedule reviews until the final draft is ready to be printed and shipped.

Both peer reviews and managerial reviews should occur early if they are to be effective. Early reviews give reviewers a stake in how an evolving document looks and what it says.

Mid-project or late reviews are

wasteful and costly when reviewers change the whole scope and direction of the document. Such mid-project or late reviews are frequently the only time a manager sees the document. Managerial review comments at these later stages are costly to the organization and frustrating to the writer(s).

Include managers, if possible, especially in the early review sessions. Managerial input is essential if you want to head off last-minute adjustments based on managerial preferences that you failed to identify in the early stages of your work on a key document.

The broader your reviewers' backgrounds, the more likely they are to catch all problems or inconsistencies. Include reviewers who are not familiar with the project as well as those who are familiar with it. Consider including customers, especially external ones.

---

8. Use an oral (face-to-face) meeting for most reviews, but record the results of such a meeting in writing.

A face-to-face meeting between reviewers and the writer(s) is efficient and productive, if properly conducted. Such a meeting works well, whether the review is between peers or with a manager.

Written comments on draft materials are time consuming to write, not to mention being difficult to read and collate, especially if several reviewers disagree about points. Written comments are often even insulting! An efficient oral review has the features shown in the checklist on the following page.

9. Develop strategies for who will work on document defects and who will research content issues.

Either during or after the oral review session, prepare a list of content issues, the names of people responsible for resolving the issues, and due dates.

Circulate this list to all participants, including reviewers, and schedule a follow-up session.

Subsequent review sessions should always address these content issues. Some issues, however, will require several follow-up discussions as new information becomes available.

Revising

Traditional advice was to leave revising until you had finished the full draft. Creating the draft supposedly required a different mental approach than revising.

With today's computers, this advice is less and less true. The computer encourages writers to revise and then revise again as they are working on headings, section introductions, and pieces of the draft.

Revision on the computer is a problem only if a writer bogs down and fails to get a full working draft done on time. Too much revision is the enemy of efficiency. See WORD PROCESSING.

Writing and Revising

Oral Review Checklist

❑ The reviewers have had ample time to review a copy of the prototype or draft before the oral session. This copy is stamped PROTOTYPE or DRAFT.

❑ The writer or writers conduct the review session, setting priorities and monitoring the time. Some reviews deal with broad issues; others properly focus on syntax and writing. Tell reviewers what to expect and what **you** expect!

❑ Time devoted to the review is strictly limited, by agreement with the participants.

❑ Reviewers give their comments and observations briefly, with no explanations of details or their rationale unless the writer asks for clarification.

❑ Comments are as constructive and as positive as possible.

❑ Comments need not be repeated unless reviewers disagree about a point. Discussions of the disagreement are not allowed unless the writer asks for clarification.

❑ One person records comments. If appropriate, this person prepares and circulates a summary of comments or items to be researched.

10. Set revision priorities both for yourself and for others who can help you revise and edit.

Revision priorities mean that neither reviewers nor revisors attempt to do everything at once. Most people cannot read and revise everything in a single reading. Instead, plan to use multiple readings, each reading directed toward a different reviewing/revision priority.

The three broad levels of potential revision are as follows:

- **Macro revision.** Rework the overall content, design, and organization of the document. Revise or expand conclusions and recommendations. Tinker with headings and subheadings to make them more informative. Rework or add graphics.

- **Medium revision.** Rewrite data and information for consistency and logical effectiveness. Control the flow of old and new information from sentence to sentence. Your goal is to make sure the language flows logically and smoothly.

- **Micro revision.** Proofread and edit individual sentences and phrases for correctness, including word choice, spelling, punctuation, and grammar.

11. Use up-to-date references to guide your revision decisions.

No one can or should remember all the rules and guidelines of document preparation and language correctness.

Maintain next to your computer or on a nearby bookshelf a set of basic and up-to-date reference books. At the least, obtain and use the following:

—A recent dictionary from a major publisher

—One or more general style guides

  This *Style Guide* is an illustration of the sort of guide to acquire. For additional suggestions, see REFERENCES.

—Specialized professional guides or glossaries

  Geologists, mathematicians, chemists—these and every professional group have their own guides. Be sure you know what these are and acquire the latest editions.

12. Know when to stop revising.

Know when enough is enough.

Many writers are tempted to revise more than necessary, especially given the editing tools in word processing software. Hours spent revising and reworking low-priority items are costly. Many writers today waste 20 percent, 30 percent, or even more of their time revising. They move text around, rewrite passages, and then repeatedly print hard copies for review.

Efficient writing means limiting revisions to the essentials.

Model
Documents

Using Model Documents

The following models illustrate both effective document design and the best in current business and technical English.

As you survey these models, you will notice that they all use headings, informative subject lines, lists, short paragraphs, color, and, whenever appropriate, graphics. The goal of these emphasis techniques is to make the information in these documents 100 percent unambiguous to any and all readers.

This goal is, of course, not achievable. Not all readers read accurately, nor consistently. Still, writers of documents must do everything they can to assist readers both to discover accurately the information in a document and then to remember this information for later use.

Well-designed documents are the single best tool for making sure that readers receive unambiguous information. See EMPHASIS.

The following suggestions should help you use these models to improve your own documents.

• Use these models as a source for document design ideas, not for exact words and phrasing. Most of the time, you will find that your own topic or content will not match the words and phrases in a given model.

• Choose words and phrases that sound like you, not like someone else. The best business or technical style is usually the one that is natural, even conversational. See STYLE, TONE, SCIENTIFIC/TECHNICAL STYLE, and LETTERS.

• Refer frequently to the Reference Glossary section in this *Style Guide*. As in the preceding suggestion, all models cross-reference entries in the Reference Glossary.

• Begin your own collection of models, ones that reflect your own professional content and organizational conventions. Then refine or polish these models each time you use them, referring, as necessary, to the principles illustrated in the *Style Guide* entries and models.

The setup is short but essential. It explains why John Smythe isn't writing and, coupled with the subject line, immediately presents the purpose of the letter. See ORGANIZATION.

The straightforward response directly follows the short setup and clearly states what Mrs. Lantham is to do. See ORGANIZATION.

Listing the requirements emphasizes them and provides a ready checklist for Mrs. Lantham to accomplish the necessary prerequisites. See EMPHASIS and LISTS.

Using a bulleted list makes every item equally important. The listed items do not end in periods because none of them is a complete sentence. See LISTS and PARALLELISM.

The closing summarizes the to do. See ORGANIZATION.

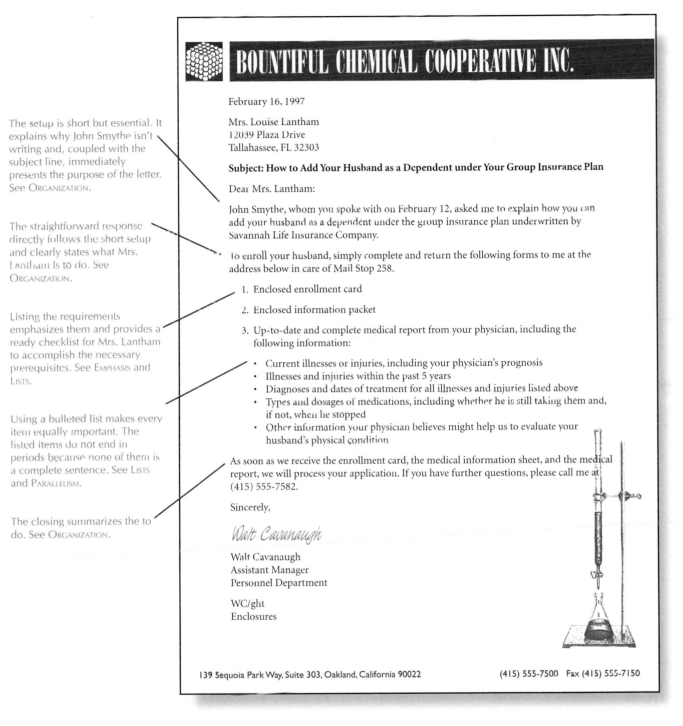

BOUNTIFUL CHEMICAL COOPERATIVE INC.

February 16, 1997

Mrs. Louise Lantham
12039 Plaza Drive
Tallahassee, FL 32303

Subject: How to Add Your Husband as a Dependent under Your Group Insurance Plan

Dear Mrs. Lantham:

John Smythe, whom you spoke with on February 12, asked me to explain how you can add your husband as a dependent under the group insurance plan underwritten by Savannah Life Insurance Company.

To enroll your husband, simply complete and return the following forms to me at the address below in care of Mail Stop 258.

1. Enclosed enrollment card

2. Enclosed information packet

3. Up-to-date and complete medical report from your physician, including the following information:

   • Current illnesses or injuries, including your physician's prognosis
   • Illnesses and injuries within the past 5 years
   • Diagnoses and dates of treatment for all illnesses and injuries listed above
   • Types and dosages of medications, including whether he is still taking them and, if not, when he stopped
   • Other information your physician believes might help us to evaluate your husband's physical condition

As soon as we receive the enrollment card, the medical information sheet, and the medical report, we will process your application. If you have further questions, please call me at (415) 555-7582.

Sincerely,

Walt Cavanaugh

Walt Cavanaugh
Assistant Manager
Personnel Department

WC/ght
Enclosures

139 Sequoia Park Way, Suite 303, Oakland, California 90022   (415) 555-7500 Fax (415) 555-7150

The bulleted list may not be essential if the attachments or enclosures are clear. See ORGANIZATION and LISTS.

The writer provides all necessary information to ease cooperation in the response— for example, the appropriate mail stop number (paragraph 2) and a personal phone number (closing paragraph).

To a Concerned Customer

When you don't know the addressee's gender, use no courtesy title, such as *Mr., Ms.,* and *Mrs.,* in the inside address or salutation. See LETTERS.

The first paragraph establishes the context of the response and attempts to develop rapport with the customer.

Acronyms are good shorthand devices, but be cautious about overloading the text with unfamiliar acronyms that hinder reading. When you introduce a new or unfamiliar acronym, use the acronym and then, in parentheses, spell out the name or expression. See ACRONYMS.

Graphics are the best devices for emphasizing information. Because this graphic is highly visual, it provides emphasis and is more memorable than the written text around it. The advantages of the cheese substitute are immediately identified without reading any supplemental text. See GRAPHICS.

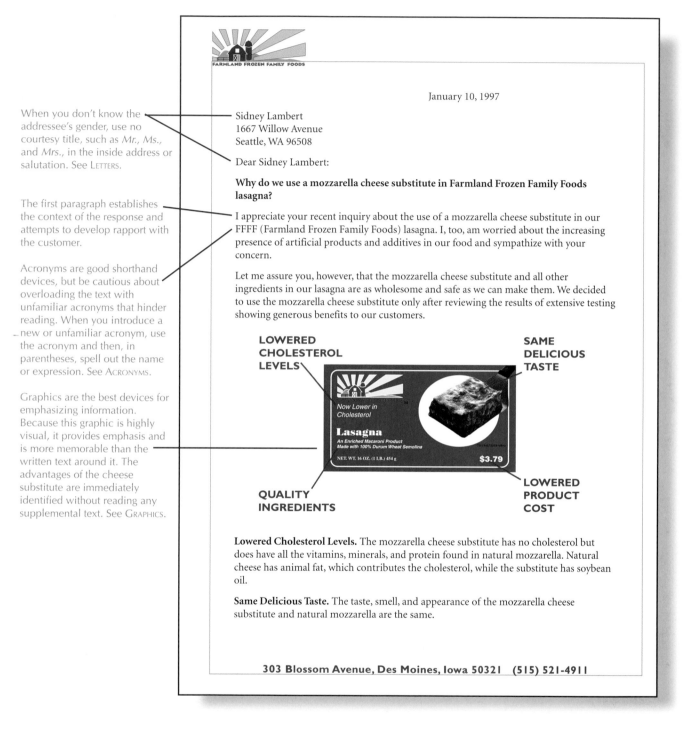

Letters responding to customer complaints should be as personal and direct as possible. The writer must address all questions or grievances in the reader's earlier letter and must do so in a friendly, sympathetic, and courteous manner.

This letter illustrates the modified block style, which is not commonly used in business today. The date, complimentary closing, and signature block appear right of center; everything else is flush left. The paragraphs are not indented.

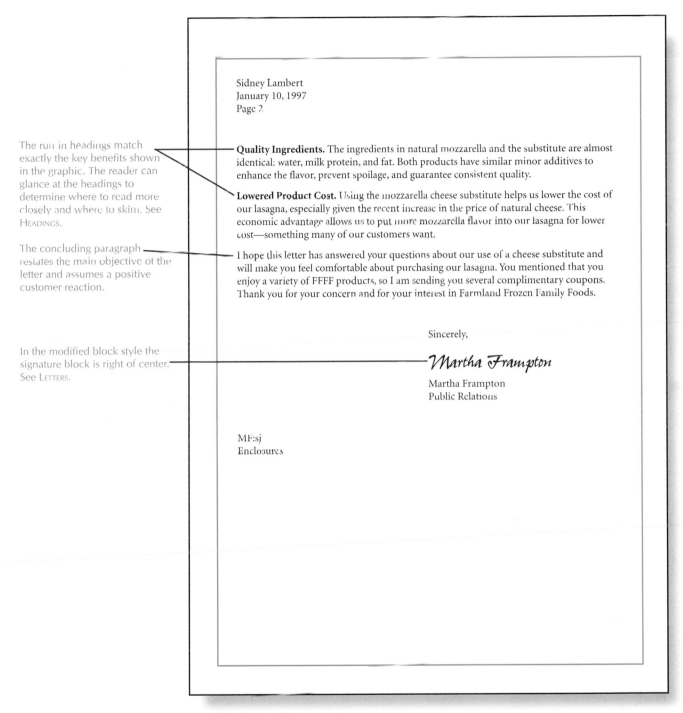

Sidney Lambert
January 10, 1997
Page 2

The run in headings match exactly the key benefits shown in the graphic. The reader can glance at the headings to determine where to read more closely and where to skim. See HEADINGS.

Quality Ingredients. The ingredients in natural mozzarella and the substitute are almost identical: water, milk protein, and fat. Both products have similar minor additives to enhance the flavor, prevent spoilage, and guarantee consistent quality.

Lowered Product Cost. Using the mozzarella cheese substitute helps us lower the cost of our lasagna, especially given the recent increase in the price of natural cheese. This economic advantage allows us to put more mozzarella flavor into our lasagna for lower cost—something many of our customers want.

The concluding paragraph restates the main objective of the letter and assumes a positive customer reaction.

I hope this letter has answered your questions about our use of a cheese substitute and will make you feel comfortable about purchasing our lasagna. You mentioned that you enjoy a variety of FFFF products, so I am sending you several complimentary coupons. Thank you for your concern and for your interest in Farmland Frozen Family Foods.

Sincerely,

Martha Frampton

Martha Frampton
Public Relations

In the modified block style the signature block is right of center. See LETTERS.

MF:sj
Enclosures

Although this letter is a response to a concerned customer, it also presents an opportunity to sell a product. The writer designs a message that speaks clearly, effectively, and persuasively to the customer. See PERSUASION.

The personal pronoun *I* is appropriate even though the writer is speaking for FFFF. She shifts to the collective *we* when she speaks for the company as a whole. Such shifts in pronouns are natural and acceptable. See TONE, LETTERS, and PRONOUNS.

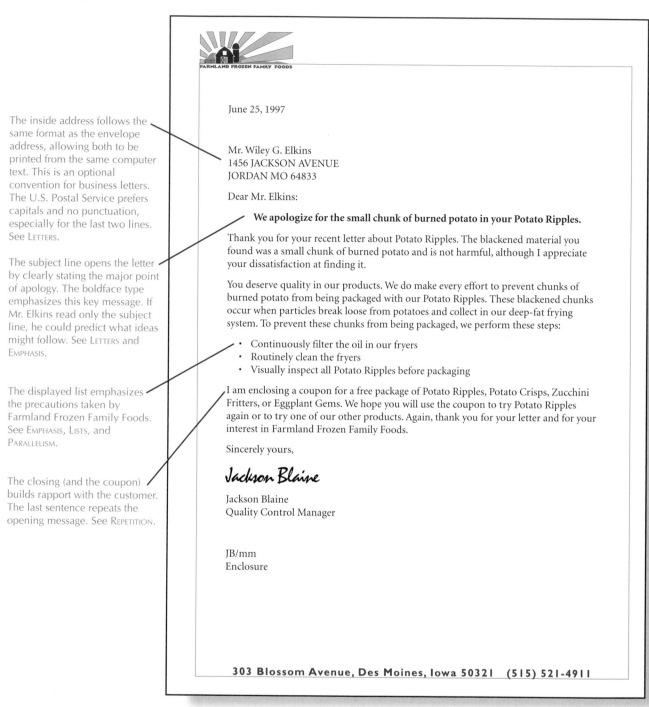

The inside address follows the same format as the envelope address, allowing both to be printed from the same computer text. This is an optional convention for business letters. The U.S. Postal Service prefers capitals and no punctuation, especially for the last two lines. See LETTERS.

The subject line opens the letter by clearly stating the major point of apology. The boldface type emphasizes this key message. If Mr. Elkins read only the subject line, he could predict what ideas might follow. See LETTERS and EMPHASIS.

The displayed list emphasizes the precautions taken by Farmland Frozen Family Foods. See EMPHASIS, LISTS, and PARALLELISM.

The closing (and the coupon) builds rapport with the customer. The last sentence repeats the opening message. See REPETITION.

FARMLAND FROZEN FAMILY FOODS

June 25, 1997

Mr. Wiley G. Elkins
1456 JACKSON AVENUE
JORDAN MO 64833

Dear Mr. Elkins:

We apologize for the small chunk of burned potato in your Potato Ripples.

Thank you for your recent letter about Potato Ripples. The blackened material you found was a small chunk of burned potato and is not harmful, although I appreciate your dissatisfaction at finding it.

You deserve quality in our products. We do make every effort to prevent chunks of burned potato from being packaged with our Potato Ripples. These blackened chunks occur when particles break loose from potatoes and collect in our deep-fat frying system. To prevent these chunks from being packaged, we perform these steps:

- Continuously filter the oil in our fryers
- Routinely clean the fryers
- Visually inspect all Potato Ripples before packaging

I am enclosing a coupon for a free package of Potato Ripples, Potato Crisps, Zucchini Fritters, or Eggplant Gems. We hope you will use the coupon to try Potato Ripples again or to try one of our other products. Again, thank you for your letter and for your interest in Farmland Frozen Family Foods.

Sincerely yours,

Jackson Blaine

Jackson Blaine
Quality Control Manager

JB/mm
Enclosure

303 Blossom Avenue, Des Moines, Iowa 50321 (515) 521-4911

Tact and a personal touch are crucial in letters to disgruntled customers. Personal pronouns help establish a tactful tone, and the details include specific references to Mr. Elkins' letter without repeating the negative events verbatim. See PRONOUNS and TONE.

The writer avoids technical complexity and jargon (he might have called the chunk of potato a "carbonized carbohydrate particle"). See JARGON, GOBBLEDYGOOK, and SCIENTIFIC/ TECHNICAL STYLE.

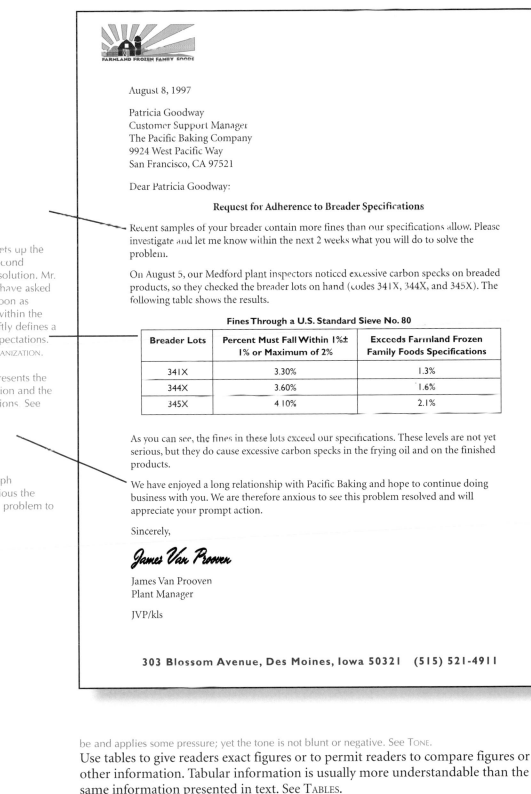

The lead sentence sets up the problem, and the second sentence asks for a solution. Mr. Van Prooven could have asked for the solution as soon as possible. Instead, "within the next two weeks" softly defines a deadline and his expectations. See LETTERS and ORGANIZATION.

The table quickly presents the supporting information and the approved specifications. See EMPHASIS.

The closing paragraph establishes how serious the writer considers the problem to

---

FARMLAND FROZEN FAMILY FOODS

August 8, 1997

Patricia Goodway
Customer Support Manager
The Pacific Baking Company
9924 West Pacific Way
San Francisco, CA 97521

Dear Patricia Goodway:

Request for Adherence to Breader Specifications

Recent samples of your breader contain more fines than our specifications allow. Please investigate and let me know within the next 2 weeks what you will do to solve the problem.

On August 5, our Medford plant inspectors noticed excessive carbon specks on breaded products, so they checked the breader lots on hand (codes 341X, 344X, and 345X). The following table shows the results.

Fines Through a U.S. Standard Sieve No. 80

Breader Lots	Percent Must Fall Within 1%± 1% or Maximum of 2%	Exceeds Farmland Frozen Family Foods Specifications
341X	3.30%	1.3%
344X	3.60%	1.6%
345X	4.10%	2.1%

As you can see, the fines in these lots exceed our specifications. These levels are not yet serious, but they do cause excessive carbon specks in the frying oil and on the finished products.

We have enjoyed a long relationship with Pacific Baking and hope to continue doing business with you. We are therefore anxious to see this problem resolved and will appreciate your prompt action.

Sincerely,

James Van Prooven

James Van Prooven
Plant Manager

JVP/kls

303 Blossom Avenue, Des Moines, Iowa 50321   (515) 521-4911

---

be and applies some pressure; yet the tone is not blunt or negative. See TONE.

Use tables to give readers exact figures or to permit readers to compare figures or other information. Tabular information is usually more understandable than the same information presented in text. See TABLES.

As in this letter, complaint letters usually start with a concise statement of the problem followed by a request for action or resolution. The problem statement should be as brief as possible but long enough to make the request understandable. See the discussion of setups in ORGANIZATION.

With a Tactful Request for Aid

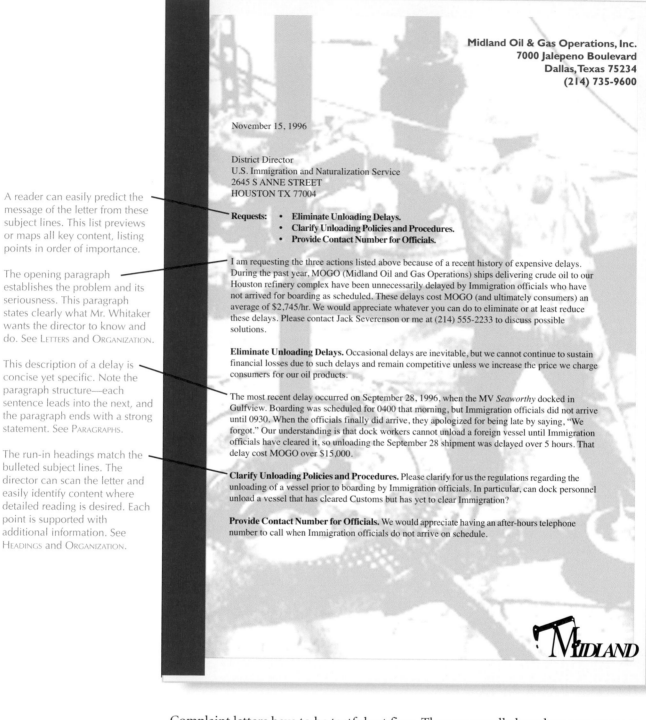

A reader can easily predict the message of the letter from these subject lines. This list previews or maps all key content, listing points in order of importance.

The opening paragraph establishes the problem and its seriousness. This paragraph states clearly what Mr. Whitaker wants the director to know and do. See LETTERS and ORGANIZATION.

This description of a delay is concise yet specific. Note the paragraph structure—each sentence leads into the next, and the paragraph ends with a strong statement. See PARAGRAPHS.

The run-in headings match the bulleted subject lines. The director can scan the letter and easily identify content where detailed reading is desired. Each point is supported with additional information. See HEADINGS and ORGANIZATION.

Midland Oil & Gas Operations, Inc.
7000 Jalepeno Boulevard
Dallas, Texas 75234
(214) 735-9600

November 15, 1996

District Director
U.S. Immigration and Naturalization Service
2645 S ANNE STREET
HOUSTON TX 77004

Requests:
- **Eliminate Unloading Delays.**
- **Clarify Unloading Policies and Procedures.**
- **Provide Contact Number for Officials.**

I am requesting the three actions listed above because of a recent history of expensive delays. During the past year, MOGO (Midland Oil and Gas Operations) ships delivering crude oil to our Houston refinery complex have been unnecessarily delayed by Immigration officials who have not arrived for boarding as scheduled. These delays cost MOGO (and ultimately consumers) an average of $2,745/hr. We would appreciate whatever you can do to eliminate or at least reduce these delays. Please contact Jack Severenson or me at (214) 555-2233 to discuss possible solutions.

Eliminate Unloading Delays. Occasional delays are inevitable, but we cannot continue to sustain financial losses due to such delays and remain competitive unless we increase the price we charge consumers for our oil products.

The most recent delay occurred on September 28, 1996, when the MV *Seaworthy* docked in Gulfview. Boarding was scheduled for 0400 that morning, but Immigration officials did not arrive until 0930. When the officials finally did arrive, they apologized for being late by saying, "We forgot." Our understanding is that dock workers cannot unload a foreign vessel until Immigration officials have cleared it, so unloading the September 28 shipment was delayed over 5 hours. That delay cost MOGO over $15,000.

Clarify Unloading Policies and Procedures. Please clarify for us the regulations regarding the unloading of a vessel prior to boarding by Immigration officials. In particular, can dock personnel unload a vessel that has cleared Customs but has yet to clear Immigration?

Provide Contact Number for Officials. We would appreciate having an after-hours telephone number to call when Immigration officials do not arrive on schedule.

MIDLAND

Complaint letters have to be tactful yet firm. They are usually based on one or more incidents, which must be established before you can request a remedy. The opening sentences of the first paragraph provide background information to establish the nature and seriousness of the problem. The request that follows is therefore understandable and reasonable. See ORGANIZATION and LETTERS.

Tone in complaint letters is important. Such letters should not sound shrill, angry, or unreasonable. In this letter, the author writes calmly but directly. He presents a specific case and then makes several understandable requests. The letter ends with a plea for cooperation. See TONE.

U.S. Immigration and Naturalization Service
November 15, 1996
Page 2

Please call Jack Severenson or me at (214) 555-2233 to discuss solutions to the unloading delays. I can also be contacted at fwwhitak@somogo.com on the Internet. We want to do everything we can to cooperate with the U.S. Immigration and Naturalization Service.

Frank W. Whitaker

Frank W. Whitaker
Shipping Operations Coordinator

FWW:dfe

The closing paragraph repeats the purpose of the letter. The telephone and Internet address strengthen the pleasant yet direct closing. See LETTERS, ORGANIZATION, and REPETITION.

Reference initials are always flush with the left margin. The writer's initials, *FWW*, can be separated from the secretary's initials, *dfe*, by a colon, as shown here, or a slash (/). See LETTERS.

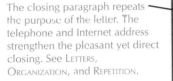

This letter illustrates the simplified format. The simplified format omits the salutation and the complimentary closing. This format is appropriate in cases where you don't have a name for the addressee, or the addressee is a title or a company department.

Internet addresses are used by individuals to communicate through computer-accessed mail or E-mail. The beginning letters, *fwwhitak*, indicate the host or person's name (Frank Whitaker). The symbol and letters *@somogo.com* represent the physical location or site. In this case, they represent the division and company name (Frank Whitaker is at Shipping Operations, Midland Oil and Gas Operations). The letters *com* indicate the type of domain—a commercial company.

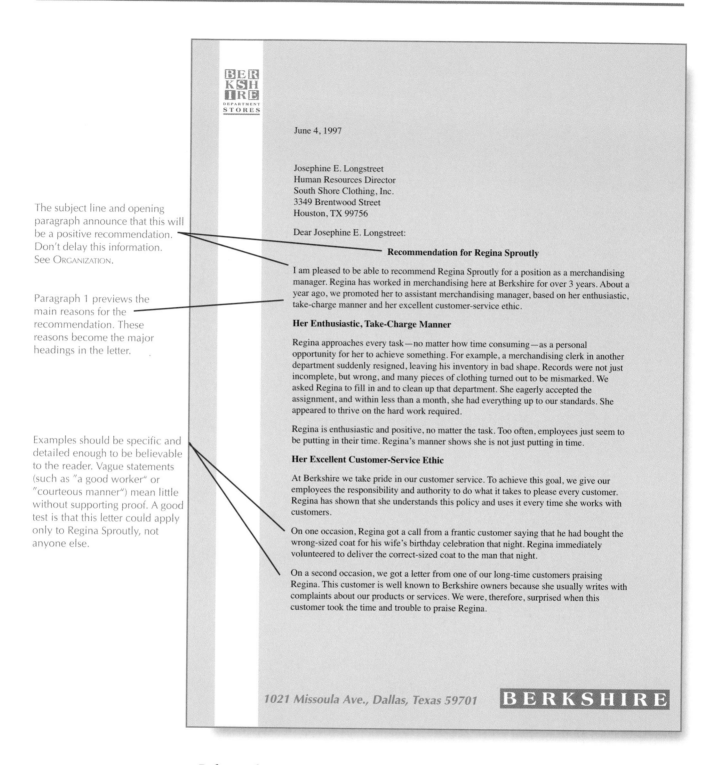

The subject line and opening paragraph announce that this will be a positive recommendation. Don't delay this information. See ORGANIZATION.

Paragraph 1 previews the main reasons for the recommendation. These reasons become the major headings in the letter.

Examples should be specific and detailed enough to be believable to the reader. Vague statements (such as "a good worker" or "courteous manner") mean little without supporting proof. A good test is that this letter could apply only to Regina Sproutly, not anyone else.

BERKSHIRE
DEPARTMENT
STORES

June 4, 1997

Josephine E. Longstreet
Human Resources Director
South Shore Clothing, Inc.
3349 Brentwood Street
Houston, TX 99756

Dear Josephine E. Longstreet:

Recommendation for Regina Sproutly

I am pleased to be able to recommend Regina Sproutly for a position as a merchandising manager. Regina has worked in merchandising here at Berkshire for over 3 years. About a year ago, we promoted her to assistant merchandising manager, based on her enthusiastic, take-charge manner and her excellent customer-service ethic.

Her Enthusiastic, Take-Charge Manner

Regina approaches every task—no matter how time consuming—as a personal opportunity for her to achieve something. For example, a merchandising clerk in another department suddenly resigned, leaving his inventory in bad shape. Records were not just incomplete, but wrong, and many pieces of clothing turned out to be mismarked. We asked Regina to fill in and to clean up that department. She eagerly accepted the assignment, and within less than a month, she had everything up to our standards. She appeared to thrive on the hard work required.

Regina is enthusiastic and positive, no matter the task. Too often, employees just seem to be putting in their time. Regina's manner shows she is not just putting in time.

Her Excellent Customer-Service Ethic

At Berkshire we take pride in our customer service. To achieve this goal, we give our employees the responsibility and authority to do what it takes to please every customer. Regina has shown that she understands this policy and uses it every time she works with customers.

On one occasion, Regina got a call from a frantic customer saying that he had bought the wrong-sized coat for his wife's birthday celebration that night. Regina immediately volunteered to deliver the correct-sized coat to the man that night.

On a second occasion, we got a letter from one of our long-time customers praising Regina. This customer is well known to Berkshire owners because she usually writes with complaints about our products or services. We were, therefore, surprised when this customer took the time and trouble to praise Regina.

1021 Missoula Ave., Dallas, Texas 59701   **B E R K S H I R E**

Reference letters are a vanishing custom in the business world. Because of possible legal questions, many companies now have policies that prevent any manager from writing a reference letter. At the most, a manager or human resources specialist will write a letter verifying a person's employment status, but making no statements about the person's skills or abilities. (See the verification letter following this reference letter.)

Also, be aware that if you write a reference letter, the person discussed in the letter may have a legal right to see the letter. So do not consider your letter confidential or privileged.

Employment Reference Letter

Josephine E. Longstreet
June 4, 1997
Page 2

Our Loss, Your Gain

You'll probably have gathered that we are sorry to see Regina leave Berkshire. Unfortunately, we have to close two of our five stores in the Dallas area and can only retain workers with a good deal of seniority. So our loss will be your gain.

Please call me if you would like further information about Regina's abilities. I can be reached at (214)□883-9991 (the number at our central Dallas warehouse).

Sincerely,

Lee S. Baskett

Lee S. Baskett
Merchandising Manager
LSB:cv

The letter ends with a summary section reinforcing the recommendation. See REPETITION.

If you need to write a reference letter, be honest and be specific. You should honestly cite specific examples of the person's abilities and accomplishments. If you do not have positive examples, we recommend that you tell the applicant to find another person to write the recommendation letter. Also, if you praise someone falsely, you open yourself and your company to legal liability if that person is hired based on your letter and then has problems in the new job. See ETHICS.

This letter illustrates the full block format, with all parts of the letter flush left. See LETTERS.

BOUNTIFUL CHEMICAL COOPERATIVE INC.

May 31, 1996

Harold O. Seythe
Loan Officer
Westside State Bank
1413 LaSalle Street
Detroit, MI 34825

Dear Mr. Seythe:

Subject: Letter of Employment Verification for Jason Stoutwell

Jason Stoutwell has been employed as a shipping clerk for Bountiful Chemical since August 18, 1994.

Jason's responsibilities include:

- Packaging items
- Preparing shipping labels
- Entering shipping information on a computerized tracking system
- Assisting team members with back orders

If you need further information about Jason's responsibilities, please contact me at (801) 555-3343.

Sincerely,

Annette Zimmer

Annette Zimmer
Human Resource Director

139 Sequoia Park Way, Suite 303, Oakland, California 90022   (415) 555-7500   Fax (415) 555-7150

List the key job responsibilities. These should be non-judgmental descriptions of essential job tasks.

As a courtesy, provide your telephone number and extension.

Use an employment verification letter when employees need you to verify their position(s) and their dates of employment. Banks often request such letters. Also, insurance companies often request such information when they are verifying insurance status (especially when an employee has double coverage or the employee's spouse has overlapping coverage).

A verification letter is not a reference or a recommendation letter in the traditional sense. See the preceding model in this *Style Guide* for an example of a reference letter.

Sky Aviation
822 Ocean View Drive, Long Beach, Caifornia 90802 (714) 332-3978

April 24, 1997

Mr. James Quirk
Wizard Machine Tools, Inc.
Flatbush Boulevard
Montrose Island, IL 44572

Subject: Invitation to Bid for Delta Q Indicators

Sky Aviation is soliciting bids for Delta Q indicators for our Foxx 176 business jets. Please examine the enclosed drawing and specifications and submit your quote to Ernestine Gonzales in our Purchasing Department by May 16. Bid requirements are shown in the following table.

Bid for Delta Q Indicators

Date Due	Friday, May 16, 1997
Production Number	1,980 Delta Q Indicators
Delivery Rate	55 per month for 36 months
Date Delivery Begins	November 4, 1997

I understand that the indicators you already provide for our Windstream 88 fixed-wing aircraft are similar to the proposed Delta Q indicators. This similarity should make design and fabrication of the new indicators relatively easy and should therefore reduce development and manufacturing costs.

Please submit your quote so it arrives no later than Friday, May 16. If you have any questions, please call me or Jim Booth at (714) 332-3984.

Arnold Madsen

Arnold Madsen
Manager, Engineering
E-mail: amadsen@skyavia.com

AM/mm
Enclosures
1. Drawing DQI-514-B
2. Attachment A (Specifications)

The first paragraph concisely states the letter's purpose and indicates that the letter has enclosures. See ORGANIZATION.

The table quickly presents the support information, with essential details available at a glance. See EMPHASIS and TABLES.

This paragraph is an effective though not entirely subtle appeal to the reader to keep the bid price low.

The closing paragraph repeats the deadline date given in the table. See ORGANIZATION and REPETITION.

This letter features a classic letter design: a concise opening that clearly indicates the letter's purpose (to solicit bids); a crisp middle with details appearing in table form and a short, well-designed paragraph; a courteous closing that repeats the deadline and ends with an offer of assistance. See LETTERS and ORGANIZATION.

Some company letterheads display Internet or E-mail numbers as part of the address line. But most frequently, the number is placed in the text of the letter or just below the signature block, as shown above.

This letter illustrates the simplified format. See LETTERS.

With a Soft Sell

An attention line is used when the inside address does not contain either the name of an individual or the name of a department. The attention line allows the writer to identify a person or department to review the letter as soon as it arrives. See LETTERS.

The opening is positive yet low-key, and the writer establishes the purpose of the letter in the first paragraph. See ORGANIZATION.

The bulleted list and run-in headings highlight key points. See HEADINGS, LISTS, and LETTERS.

RFP (Request for Proposal) is an abbreviation that will be familiar to the readers. Therefore, the writer does not have to spell it out. See ABBREVIATIONS.

The displayed list emphasizes Sky Aviation's production strengths. See LISTS and EMPHASIS.

Sky Aviation

822 Ocean View Drive, Long Beach, Caifornia 90802 (714) 332-3978

June 18, 1996

Attention Mr. Boon Hollenbeck
International Aeronautics
PO BOX 1149
GALVESTON TX 41504

Proposal to Assist in Designing the Cabin Pressurization System for the K-38

We are delighted to hear that IA (International Aeronautics) won the contract to develop the K-38 Heavy Cargo Helicopter. As you initiate design studies, we hope you will consider basing cabin pressurization on our patented flowback valve, the VA-321-E, and allowing us to assist in cabin pressurization design.

Choosing to use the VA-321-E would bring the following benefits to IA's K-38 development program:

- VA-321-E meets or exceeds IA's design requirements.
- VA-321-E increases operational efficiency.
- Sky Aviation's industry track record shows we deliver on time and within budget.

VA-321-E Meets or Exceeds IA's Design Requirements. According to the RFP, the K-38 will require an 8-lb/min valve capable of maintaining a delta P of 0.3 to 0.5 psi. Valve VA-321-E meets and exceeds these requirements. The enclosed drawing (DRA-321-E) shows the standard SA configuration for the VA-321-E valve, including the outflow, check, and solenoid subsystems. The control modes within this configuration are listed on Attachment A.

VA-321-E Increases Operational Efficiency. The VA-321-E valve is more efficient than any other valve currently used in aircraft pressurization systems. No other valve regulates differential pressure as accurately as the VA-321-E.

Sky Aviation's Industry Track Record Shows We Deliver on Time and within Budget.
Each of the following production steps is carefully monitored by SA's Production Team.

✓ Accurate sizing of the outflow valve-return spring to match your design specifications. This design and test phase would take no more than 4 weeks—less than half the time required by other valve manufacturers.

✓ Customized detailing to your design specifications to assure integration with other design components and to eliminate costly rework.

✓ Careful attention to quality assurance in production to decrease waste, reduce time, and increase cost efficiency.

The attention line has traditionally been placed two spaces below the inside address. Instead of this traditional placement on envelopes, the U.S. Postal Service prefers that the attention line be placed above the company name, the street address, and the city and state. To be consistent in the letter, the attention line is placed as the first line of the inside address. See LETTERS.

This letter illustrates the simplified format. See LETTERS.

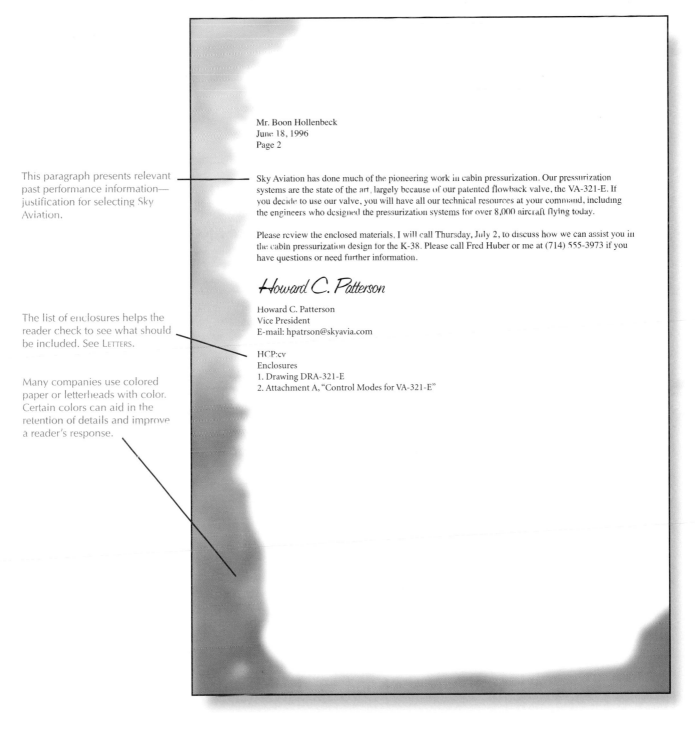

This paragraph presents relevant past performance information—justification for selecting Sky Aviation.

The list of enclosures helps the reader check to see what should be included. See LETTERS.

Many companies use colored paper or letterheads with color. Certain colors can aid in the retention of details and improve a reader's response.

Mr. Boon Hollenbeck
June 18, 1996
Page 2

Sky Aviation has done much of the pioneering work in cabin pressurization. Our pressurization systems are the state of the art, largely because of our patented flowback valve, the VA-321-E. If you decide to use our valve, you will have all our technical resources at your command, including the engineers who designed the pressurization systems for over 8,000 aircraft flying today.

Please review the enclosed materials, I will call Thursday, July 2, to discuss how we can assist you in the cabin pressurization design for the K-38. Please call Fred Huber or me at (714) 555-3973 if you have questions or need further information.

Howard C. Patterson

Howard C. Patterson
Vice President
E-mail: hpatrson@skyavia.com

HCP:cv
Enclosures
1. Drawing DRA-321-E
2. Attachment A, "Control Modes for VA-321-E"

A sales letter is a blend of fact and sales pitch. Presenting information positively is essential, but sincerity and realism are also necessary ingredients of successful sales letters. See PERSUASION. This letter opens and closes with a soft sales pitch. The technical information in the middle is emphasized by boldface headings. The writer's goal is to make the technical information seem substantial and convincing. See EMPHASIS, SCIENTIFIC/TECHNICAL STYLE, and TONE.

Sales Letter

With a Soft Sell—Attachment

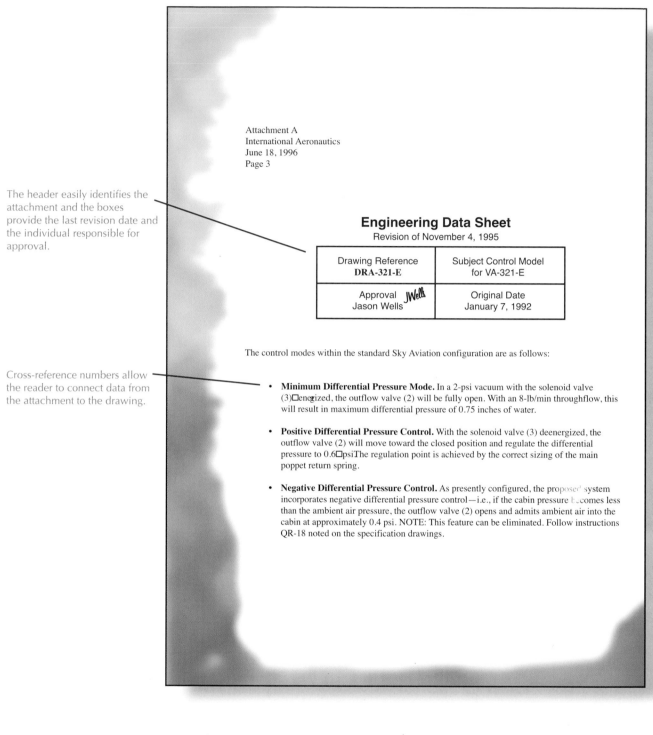

The header easily identifies the attachment and the boxes provide the last revision date and the individual responsible for approval.

Cross-reference numbers allow the reader to connect data from the attachment to the drawing.

Attachment A
International Aeronautics
June 18, 1996
Page 3

Engineering Data Sheet
Revision of November 4, 1995

Drawing Reference **DRA-321-E**	Subject Control Model for VA-321-E
Approval *JWells* Jason Wells	Original Date January 7, 1992

The control modes within the standard Sky Aviation configuration are as follows:

- **Minimum Differential Pressure Mode.** In a 2-psi vacuum with the solenoid valve (3) deenergized, the outflow valve (2) will be fully open. With an 8-lb/min throughflow, this will result in maximum differential pressure of 0.75 inches of water.

- **Positive Differential Pressure Control.** With the solenoid valve (3) deenergized, the outflow valve (2) will move toward the closed position and regulate the differential pressure to 0.6 psi. The regulation point is achieved by the correct sizing of the main poppet return spring.

- **Negative Differential Pressure Control.** As presently configured, the proposed system incorporates negative differential pressure control—i.e., if the cabin pressure becomes less than the ambient air pressure, the outflow valve (2) opens and admits ambient air into the cabin at approximately 0.4 psi. NOTE: This feature can be eliminated. Follow instructions QR-18 noted on the specification drawings.

Drawing DRA-321-E and Attachment A come from the engineering design team. The drawing and attachment provide necessary information to the sale. To determine if an attachment is justified, ask the following question: "Would a knowledgeable reader need the information in the attachment(s) to interpret the conclusions and recommendations?" If the answer to that question is yes, the attachment is justified. See APPENDICES.

NOTE: Drawing DRA-321-E is omitted.

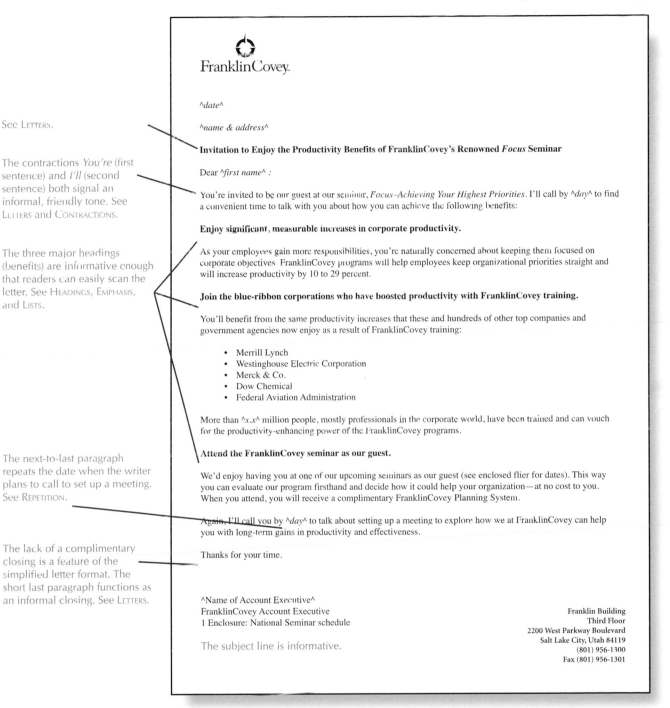

See LETTERS.

The contractions *You're* (first sentence) and *I'll* (second sentence) both signal an informal, friendly tone. See LETTERS and CONTRACTIONS.

The three major headings (benefits) are informative enough that readers can easily scan the letter. See HEADINGS, EMPHASIS, and LISTS.

The next-to-last paragraph repeats the date when the writer plans to call to set up a meeting. See REPETITION.

The lack of a complimentary closing is a feature of the simplified letter format. The short last paragraph functions as an informal closing. See LETTERS.

The subject line is informative.

FranklinCovey.

^date^

^name & address^

Invitation to Enjoy the Productivity Benefits of FranklinCovey's Renowned *Focus* Seminar

Dear ^first name^ :

You're invited to be our guest at our seminar, *Focus–Achieving Your Highest Priorities*. I'll call by ^day^ to find a convenient time to talk with you about how you can achieve the following benefits:

Enjoy significant, measurable increases in corporate productivity.

As your employees gain more responsibilities, you're naturally concerned about keeping them focused on corporate objectives. FranklinCovey programs will help employees keep organizational priorities straight and will increase productivity by 10 to 29 percent.

Join the blue-ribbon corporations who have boosted productivity with FranklinCovey training.

You'll benefit from the same productivity increases that these and hundreds of other top companies and government agencies now enjoy as a result of FranklinCovey training:

- Merrill Lynch
- Westinghouse Electric Corporation
- Merck & Co.
- Dow Chemical
- Federal Aviation Administration

More than ^x.x^ million people, mostly professionals in the corporate world, have been trained and can vouch for the productivity-enhancing power of the FranklinCovey programs.

Attend the FranklinCovey seminar as our guest.

We'd enjoy having you at one of our upcoming seminars as our guest (see enclosed flier for dates). This way you can evaluate our program firsthand and decide how it could help your organization—at no cost to you. When you attend, you will receive a complimentary FranklinCovey Planning System.

Again, I'll call you by ^day^ to talk about setting up a meeting to explore how we at FranklinCovey can help you with long-term gains in productivity and effectiveness.

Thanks for your time.

^Name of Account Executive^
FranklinCovey Account Executive
1 Enclosure: National Seminar schedule

Franklin Building
Third Floor
2200 West Parkway Boulevard
Salt Lake City, Utah 84119
(801) 956-1300
Fax (801) 956-1301

A template is a document model or shell that writers can tailor to their own specific needs. Most software programs allow you to copy a template and then rewrite or revise it to fit your needs. Other software programs, similar to the pattern illustrated above, have blanks (usually numbered) for you to provide information. This information, once typed in, merges into the letter, so you don't have to do any revising or rewriting.

OS^GE GAS & ELECTRICAL COMPANY INC.

February 1, 1997

Miller Door & Gate Company
2000 E. Lake Street
Davenport, IA 54882-2345

**Gain Significant Electric Power Cost Savings
by Applying for the Interruptible Supply Rate**

You can reduce your electric power costs by up to 10 percent through our new Interruptible Supply Program. The reduced rate applies if you permit us to interrupt part of your power supply, in rare cases when emergencies or maintenance needs arise. Please send us a letter of application by March 1, 1997, if you'd like to participate.

Let me explain how to apply for the reduced rate and how the program affects you.

How to Apply for the Interruptible Supply Rate

To apply, simply send a letter to me by March 1, 1997, with the following information:

- A formal request to apply for the Interruptible Supply Rate
- The load to be interrupted (presumably a low-priority area for you)
- The method of interruption
- Proposed circuitry to be interrupted

How the Interruptible Supply Program Affects You

How Much Will the Program Save You? You should save from *$18,000 to $21,500* a year, depending on the size of the interruptible load and your past electricity costs.

How Much Power Will Be Subject to Interruption? You should be able to do without 50 kilowatts and up to 2 megawatts temporarily, in the area you designate.

How Long Do Interruptions Last? At no time would your power be interrupted for more than 8 hours a day, or for more than 500 hours a year. We will help you define in advance where and how much power you can afford to have interrupted. (The attached Interruptible Supply Rate tariff sheet contains further information.)

4239 E. Jennings Avenue, Cedar Rapids, Iowa 54336

The subject line is lengthy, but informative. See LETTERS.

The focus on *you* in the opening paragraph sets a good customer-service tone for the letter. See LETTERS and TONE.

Paragraph 2 previews the two content subjects to be covered in the letter. See ORGANIZATION.

The displayed list (with bullets) needs no final periods because the listed items are not sentences. See LISTS.

The subheadings are questions, so they are parallel. See PARALLELISM and HEADINGS.

This customer letter is a combination of service information and an indirect sales request for companies receiving it to apply for the reduced rate. As such, it is more factual than persuasive, although some sentences highlight sales benefits. See PERSUASION and TONE.

The MPSC abbreviation in parentheses follows the full name of the commission. Other editors would reverse the order, using the initials before the full name in parentheses. See ABBREVIATIONS.

Parentheses contain additional information. In this example, they are optional; the text would be fine without them. See PARENTHESES.

The closing paragraph reemphasizes the need for timely action.

Miller Door & Gate Company
February 1, 1997
Page 2

Why the Interruptible Supply Program? Uninterruptible power supplies are very expensive to maintain. We don't want you to pay high prices for emergency power at peak use times, and occasionally we must cut power to maintain our system. Therefore, the Michigan Public Service Commission (MPSC) permits us to reduce your power costs if you permit us to interrupt a predetermined portion of your supply when these needs arise. (To help with your planning, you should know that the MPSC will authorize 5 more megawatts of interruptible power each year.)

Apply Early for Reduced Rates

To take advantage of these reduced rates, send me a request letter with the information above by March 1. Apply early because we anticipate that requests will far exceed the limited capacity authorized by the MPSC. I have enclosed my business card if you wish to call for more information.

Elizabeth Johnston

Elizabeth Johnston
Manager
Corporate Power Management

EJ:tm

Attachment: Tariffs Sheet for Interruptible Supply Rates

The letter follows the 4-box letter organization. Box 1 (paragraph 1) opens with a request or a statement of purpose. Box 2 (paragraph 2) summarizes or lists the points to be covered. Box 3 (the remaining paragraphs, except for the final one) expands on the points listed in box two. Box 4 (the final paragraph) closes with a review of the content and a final request for action. See ORGANIZATION.

The letter follows a simplified format. See LETTERS.

The subject line and the opening sentence clearly establish the purpose of the memo. See LETTERS and ORGANIZATION.

The side comments, or callouts, provide supplemental information. See PAGE LAYOUT.

Items in the bulleted list are parallel in structure. See LISTS and PARALLELISM.

Use of graphics in procedures aids the reader's understanding of the information being presented. Graphics can emphasize important data and ideas in ways that text cannot. See GRAPHICS.

The split-screen or double-column format makes the text more readable. A 0.5-point divider line separates the main procedure text from the side comments. See PAGE LAYOUT.

Sky Aviation

To: All Department Heads
From: Susan Hall
Date: December 28, 1997
Subject: Procedures for Storing Records at Trolley Street Warehouse

Please comply with the following procedures when you ship records for storage at the Trolley Street Warehouse:

Call 287-9009 to order the transmittal boxes. Each empty box contains a blank records transmittal slip.

Duplicate copies of the R-23 policy are available from Susan Jameson in Corporate Services (call 287-9106).

Box numbers are selected consecutively from the location log at the Trolley Street receiving desk. The numbers indicate the box storage location at Trolley Street Warehouse.

1. Obtain a standard records transmittal box and a records transmittal slip.

2. Include the following information on each records transmittal slip:

   • Date of records sent to Trolley Street
   • Description of the contents
   • Name of the responsible supervisor
   • Department number (and extension)
   • Destruction date according to policy R-23
   • Records transmittal box number

   Central Records

   Date _____
   Contents _____
   _____
   _____
   _____
   _____
   Supervisor _____
   Dept No. _____
   Destruction date _____
   Box No. _____

3. Separate the white and yellow copies of the records transmittal slip.

4. Attach the white copy of the records transmittal slip to the outside spine of the records transmittal box within the marked space.

The imperative (command) verbs in the numbered list are essential in procedures. They highlight actions the reader should take, and they allow writers to condense their directions. For the sake of parallelism, state all directions or steps using imperative verbs. See SENTENCES and VERBS.

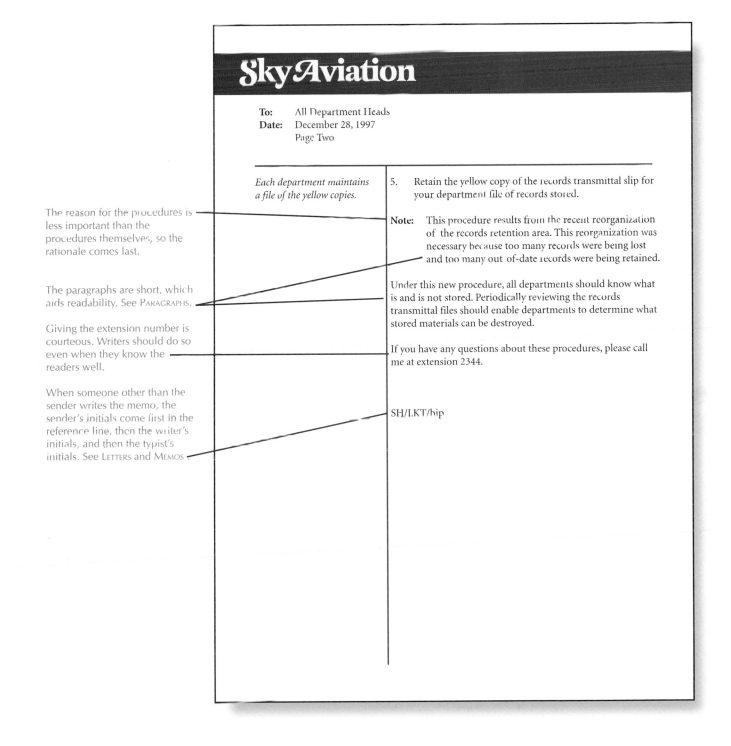

Sky Aviation

To: All Department Heads
Date: December 28, 1997
Page Two

Each department maintains a file of the yellow copies.

5. Retain the yellow copy of the records transmittal slip for your department file of records stored.

Note: This procedure results from the recent reorganization of the records retention area. This reorganization was necessary because too many records were being lost and too many out of-date records were being retained.

Under this new procedure, all departments should know what is and is not stored. Periodically reviewing the records transmittal files should enable departments to determine what stored materials can be destroyed.

If you have any questions about these procedures, please call me at extension 2344.

SH/LKT/hip

The reason for the procedures is less important than the procedures themselves, so the rationale comes last.

The paragraphs are short, which aids readability. See PARAGRAPHS.

Giving the extension number is courteous. Writers should do so even when they know the readers well.

When someone other than the sender writes the memo, the sender's initials come first in the reference line, then the writer's initials, and then the typist's initials. See LETTERS and MEMOS.

A clear format is essential in procedures. In this memo, the numbered and bulleted lists are crucial if the procedure is to be clear and readable. Each logical step must be complete and documented. Information or data gaps leave the reader unsure of what action to take.

See EMPHASIS and LISTS; also see the more formal procedures illustrated elsewhere in these model documents.

Request Memo

For Clarification of a Problem

The specific subject line simplifies cross-referencing and filing. See HEADINGS.

The opening paragraph conveys the purpose of the memo and immediately presents the action requested. See ORGANIZATION.

The second paragraph establishes a definite deadline and leads into the details. See ORGANIZATION.

Displayed lists are naturally emphatic, so main points are highlighted. Note that listed items are grammatically parallel. See EMPHASIS, LISTS, and PARALLELISM.

Compound modifiers, such as *1-inch*, must be hyphenated. See HYPHENS, MODIFIERS, and NUMBERS.

---

memorandum

TO   Howard Deedy

FROM   Charlotte Smart

DATE   November 24, 1997

SUBJECT   Request to Investigate Improper Repairs on the Barrett-Woodward Rotary Car Dumper and Positioner

I understand that the recent repairs on the BW (Barrett-Woodward) rotary car dumper and positioner did not follow the recommended procedure and are therefore inadequate. I would appreciate your investigating to determine why the repairs were not made according to BW's recommendations and who was responsible.

Please contact me by next Tuesday, December 1, with a report of your findings. Here are the facts as I understand them.

Problems Discovered

Early in November, John Sturgees reported many problems with the BW rotary car dumper and positioner as a result of a routine safety inspection. He called the BW Customer Service Engineering Group for assistance.

Repairs Recommended

The BW consulting engineer analyzed the problems and recommended the following:

1. Replacing the 3/8-inch steel rails with l-inch rails

2. Installing the 1-inch rails by grouting under them and continuously welding the AR (abrasion resistant) plate to the rails

3. Installing reinforcing cross beams at 30-inch intervals

Repairs Improperly Completed

Management authorized the repairs on November 9. Before the repairs were completed, the BW consulting engineer discovered that the AR plate had been stitch welded, not continuously welded. He claims that he reported this to Howard Beale. However, I learned of the improper welding only after John Sturgees conducted another safety inspection and discovered it more or less by accident.

BOUNTIFUL CHEMICAL COOPERATIVE INC.

While basically a request for information, this memo is potentially critical of the reader or people working for the reader. In such politically sensitive matters, tone is important. The writer must be forceful without being aggressive, direct but not blunt, businesslike but not inhuman. See TONE.

The headings basically provide a chronological list of events. The reader can easily glance at the headings and determine where he needs to read more closely and where he can skim. See HEADINGS.

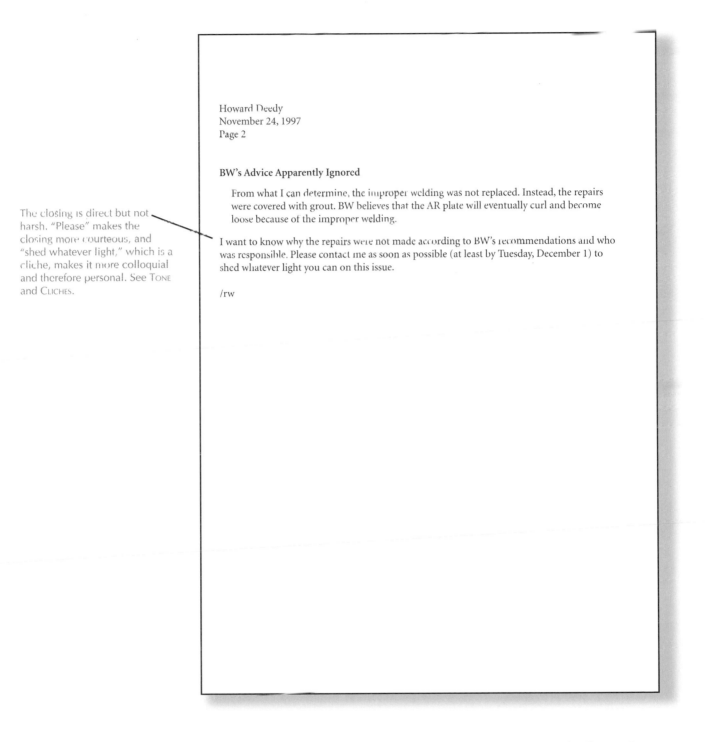

Howard Deedy
November 24, 1997
Page 2

BW's Advice Apparently Ignored

From what I can determine, the improper welding was not replaced. Instead, the repairs were covered with grout. BW believes that the AR plate will eventually curl and become loose because of the improper welding.

I want to know why the repairs were not made according to BW's recommendations and who was responsible. Please contact me as soon as possible (at least by Tuesday, December 1) to shed whatever light you can on this issue.

/rw

The closing is direct but not harsh. "Please" makes the closing more courteous, and "shed whatever light," which is a cliche, makes it more colloquial and therefore personal. See TONE and CLICHES.

The deadline date is repeated in the closing paragraph. Restating a deadline or key point reinforces or emphasizes that key point in the reader's mind. As you design your document and organize your ideas, build in effective repetition of your most important ideas. See EMPHASIS, KEY WORDS, REPETITION, and ORGANIZATION.

Summary Memo

For an Executive Audience

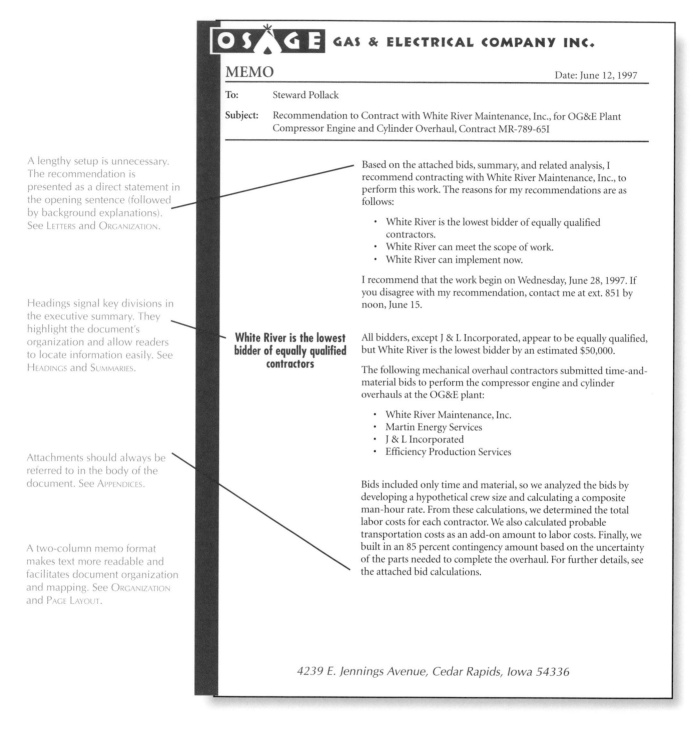

OSAGE GAS & ELECTRICAL COMPANY INC.

MEMO

Date: June 12, 1997

To: Steward Pollack

Subject: Recommendation to Contract with White River Maintenance, Inc., for OG&E Plant Compressor Engine and Cylinder Overhaul, Contract MR-789-65I

A lengthy setup is unnecessary. The recommendation is presented as a direct statement in the opening sentence (followed by background explanations). See LETTERS and ORGANIZATION.

Based on the attached bids, summary, and related analysis, I recommend contracting with White River Maintenance, Inc., to perform this work. The reasons for my recommendations are as follows:

- White River is the lowest bidder of equally qualified contractors.
- White River can meet the scope of work.
- White River can implement now.

I recommend that the work begin on Wednesday, June 28, 1997. If you disagree with my recommendation, contact me at ext. 851 by noon, June 15.

Headings signal key divisions in the executive summary. They highlight the document's organization and allow readers to locate information easily. See HEADINGS and SUMMARIES.

White River is the lowest bidder of equally qualified contractors

All bidders, except J & L Incorporated, appear to be equally qualified, but White River is the lowest bidder by an estimated $50,000.

The following mechanical overhaul contractors submitted time-and-material bids to perform the compressor engine and cylinder overhauls at the OG&E plant:

- White River Maintenance, Inc.
- Martin Energy Services
- J & L Incorporated
- Efficiency Production Services

Attachments should always be referred to in the body of the document. See APPENDICES.

Bids included only time and material, so we analyzed the bids by developing a hypothetical crew size and calculating a composite man-hour rate. From these calculations, we determined the total labor costs for each contractor. We also calculated probable transportation costs as an add-on amount to labor costs. Finally, we built in an 85 percent contingency amount based on the uncertainty of the parts needed to complete the overhaul. For further details, see the attached bid calculations.

A two-column memo format makes text more readable and facilitates document organization and mapping. See ORGANIZATION and PAGE LAYOUT.

4239 E. Jennings Avenue, Cedar Rapids, Iowa 54336

Many memos are actually summaries of attached materials. Such summary memos are similar to executive summaries, which open long, more-involved reports. Readers of summaries are often managers and supervisors who already know something about the subject but who do not need extensive background information before making a decision. See SUMMARIES and REPORTS.

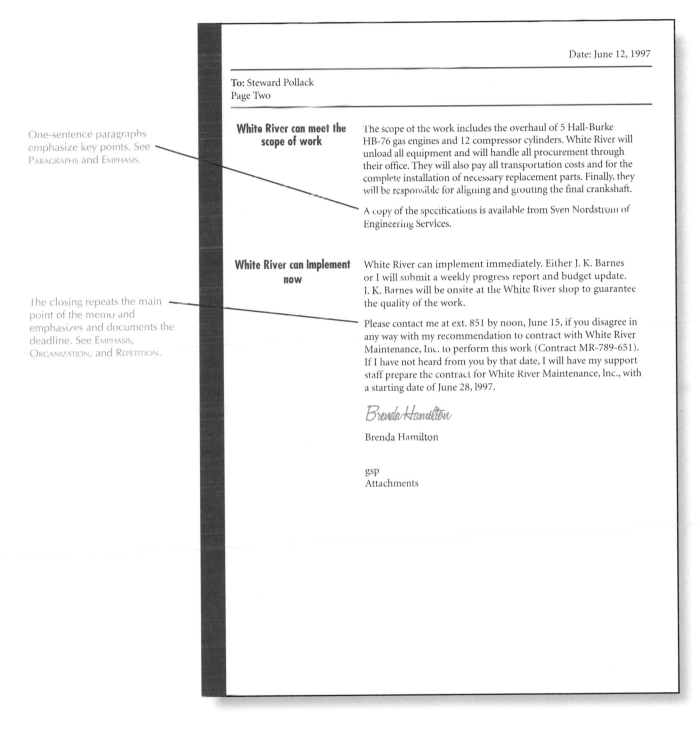

One-sentence paragraphs emphasize key points. See PARAGRAPHS and EMPHASIS.

The closing repeats the main point of the memo and emphasizes and documents the deadline. See EMPHASIS, ORGANIZATION, and REPETITION.

Date: June 12, 1997

To: Steward Pollack
Page Two

White River can meet the scope of work

The scope of the work includes the overhaul of 5 Hall-Burke HB-76 gas engines and 12 compressor cylinders. White River will unload all equipment and will handle all procurement through their office. They will also pay all transportation costs and for the complete installation of necessary replacement parts. Finally, they will be responsible for aligning and grouting the final crankshaft.

A copy of the specifications is available from Sven Nordstrom of Engineering Services.

White River can implement now

White River can implement immediately. Either J. K. Barnes or I will submit a weekly progress report and budget update. J. K. Barnes will be onsite at the White River shop to guarantee the quality of the work.

Please contact me at ext. 851 by noon, June 15, if you disagree in any way with my recommendation to contract with White River Maintenance, Inc. to perform this work (Contract MR-789-651). If I have not heard from you by that date, I will have my support staff prepare the contract for White River Maintenance, Inc., with a starting date of June 28, 1997.

Brenda Hamilton

Brenda Hamilton

gsp
Attachments

This memo (as in most executive summaries) does not need to contain extensive background data, calculations, supporting documents, and references. Such information should remain as attachments. See APPENDICES.

Proposal Memo

To an Antagonistic Audience

The arrangement of these items varies from memo to memo. Some memos, as in this case, omit the *From* line, opting instead for a typed name and signature at the end of the memo. See MEMOS.

Because the readers are antagonistic, the memo proposes a meeting, not a solution, and the language is deliberately conciliatory. Note the inclusive *we*. See TONE.

The writer prepares the layout to facilitate note taking, and suggests a dual use of the memo—as an agenda. See PAGE LAYOUT.

The headings act as a map to additional information presented in the preview of key content—the bulleted list. See HEADINGS and LISTS.

OG&E (Osage Gas and Electric Company) is an acronym the readers will be familiar with, so it does not need to be spelled out. See ACRONYMS.

The *My Suggestions* box is smaller than the open *Your Ideas* box, giving emphasis to the readers' ideas and implying their importance. See PAGE LAYOUT.

OSAGE GAS & ELECTRICAL COMPANY INC.

MEMO
Date: August 23, 1997

To: Jack Ladda and Harvey Smith

Subject: Invitation to Discuss Upgrading Substation Testing and Maintenance

---

As we found in Tuesday's meeting, we can agree on a number of current problems regarding upgrading substation testing and maintenance. Let's collaborate to discover ways to solve these problems. Could you meet at 2 p.m. on Wednesday, September 6, in my office to discuss ideas and solutions?

During Tuesday's meeting we identified and agreed upon several specific test and maintenance areas needing improvement. Here are my notes taken at the meeting, and as a starting point, I've included a few preliminary suggestions. I've left enough space for your ideas. Please jot them down through the week and bring this memo with you to the meeting. I'd like to use it as the agenda for discussion.

- Overall commitment to maintenance as a priority responsibility
- Tests between maintenance intervals
- Maintenance intervals
- Adherence to maintenance procedures

Overall Commitment to Maintenance as a Priority Responsibility

Maintenance is not a high priority in many substations (although it should be, given the complex and expensive equipment in the OG&E electrical system).

MY SUGGESTIONS

1. Jack could issue E-mail messages from management to increase awareness and stimulate adherence to maintenance procedures.

2. Harvey, test requests could be issued on a *PRIORITY 1* routine schedule.

YOUR IDEAS

4239 E. Jennings Avenue, Cedar Rapids, Iowa 54336

Because of the antagonistic audience, the writer deliberately makes his memo more tentative than it would ordinarily need to be. The opening paragraph is conciliatory, and the writer's ideas are called preliminary suggestions, not proposals. See TONE.

Some companies provide printed memo forms, others allow employees to design and type the format for their interoffice correspondence. Continuation pages usually contain the following elements: date, who the memo is to, and the page number. See MEMOS.

Using the readers' names and the pronoun *we* help make the tone friendly and personal. Consequently, this memo will be easier for the readers to accept. See PRONOUNS and TONE.

Date: August 23, 1997

To: Jack Ladda and Harvy Smith
Page Two

Tests Between Maintenance Intervals	Testing should be performed on a routine schedule, not just when a problem is noted. Currently, company regulations state that testing must be performed once a quarter, but no department is named as a responsible party—Operations has just assumed the task.
MY SUGGESTIONS	**YOUR IDEAS**
1. Jack, as manager, could be accountable for and issue a 1-year schedule with specific dates assigned for testing and for routine maintenance each quarter. 2. Harvey, as supervisor of Engineering, could be responsible for and track the testing following Jack's schedule.	
Maintenance Intervals	Maintenance should be performed on a routine schedule. However, maintenance personnel who leave are not being replaced, so many substations have inadequate staff. Consequently, some of the routine procedures have not been completed regularly.
MY SUGGESTIONS	**YOUR IDEAS**
1. Jack could be accountable for and issue a 1-year schedule with specific dates assigned for testing and for routine maintenance each quarter (same as above). 2. We could make a comprehensive manpower and equipment forecast based on present maintenance needs and use this forecast as a basis to hire additional maintenance personnel.	

Even the way a memo looks can affect the tone of a memo. Design your document with a lean and open look. See TONE and PAGE LAYOUT.

Proposal Memo

To an Antagonistic Audience

This double-column format allows separation of the writer's and readers' ideas, yet facilitates and implies collaboration. See PAGE LAYOUT.

Date: August 23, 1997

To: Jack Ladda and Harvy Smith
Page Three

---

3. As supervisor of Operations, I could be responsible for and track all routine maintenance following Jack's schedule.

4. We could contract with Noble Engineering to perform key testing and to inspect and maintain power circuit breakers. Noble personnel could be on call 24 hours a day but used only to catch up during crises.

5. We could establish a troubleshooting maintenance crew in the Central Office. This crew would have special responsibilities for high-voltage equipment.

Adherence to Maintenance Procedures	Many personnel are not properly trained, and maintenance procedures are not posted. Some maintenance crews spend too much time on nonessential tasks.

MY SUGGESTIONS	YOUR IDEAS

1. We could train existing personnel to meet the above forecasts.

2. We could develop work aids containing basic procedures.

3. We could use contract or construction personnel, not maintenance personnel, for all constrction work.

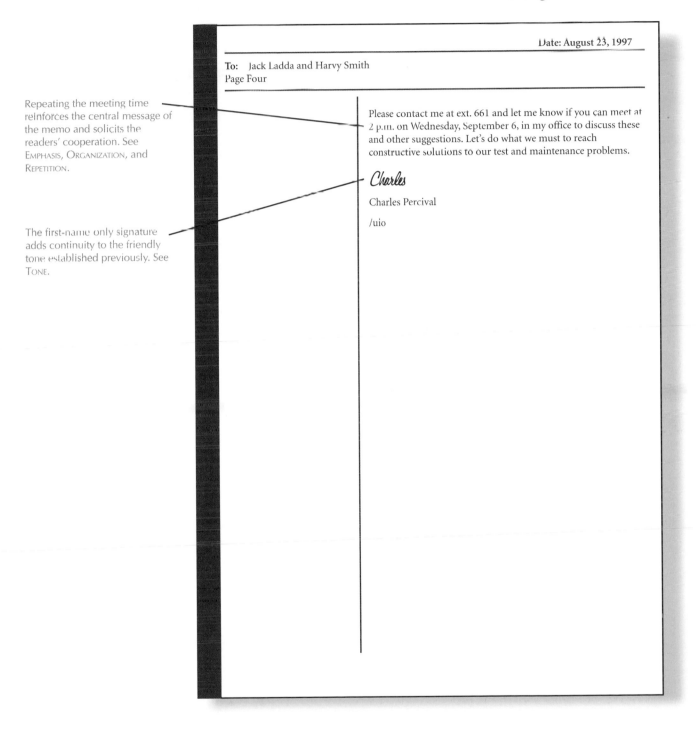

Repeating the meeting time reinforces the central message of the memo and solicits the readers' cooperation. See EMPHASIS, ORGANIZATION, and REPETITION.

The first-name only signature adds continuity to the friendly tone established previously. See TONE.

Date: August 23, 1997

To: Jack Ladda and Harvy Smith
Page Four

Please contact me at ext. 661 and let me know if you can meet at 2 p.m. on Wednesday, September 6, in my office to discuss these and other suggestions. Let's do what we must to reach constructive solutions to our test and maintenance problems.

Charles

Charles Percival

/uio

Make your closing as simple and direct as your opening lines. You could close with a restatement of your main point, as shown in this memo, or you could refer to questions or problems, such as "Please call or write Neil Thornbush at (415) 555-01234 if you have any questions about the proposed manufacturing schedule."

With Informal Instructions

The list of managers and supervisors is usually standard, so it need not be attached. If necessary, however, the list could be attached as a distribution list at the end of the memo. See MEMOS.

Paragraph 1 sets up the request in paragraph 2. Setups are optional, but in this case the managers and supervisors might not understand why the request is being made, so the setup is retained. See LETTERS and ORGANIZATION.

The major points in paragraph 2 contain the exact wording of the subheadings in the document. This exact repetition is a good strategy in any document, but especially in longer memos and reports. See REPETITION and ORGANIZATION.

Bullets introduce the displayed list because numbering would be unnecessary, even distracting. See LISTS and NUMBERING SYSTEMS.

Bullet 3 references the attachment, as does subheading 2. Using an attachment keeps this cover memo short and to the point. See APPENDICES.

---

memorandum

TO   All Managers and Supervisors

FROM   Jacqueline Burrows

DATE   April 7, 1997

SUBJECT Request to Prepare for Air-Conditioning Systems Review and Balance, April 15–April 26

We have contracted with Constant Air, Inc., an air-conditioning specialist, to review and balance the air-conditioning systems in Buildings 3 and 4 between April 15 and April 26. The objective is to ensure that all departments can independently maintain the temperatures appropriate for their areas.

Please complete the following three assignments **before 8:00 a.m., April 10:**

1. Appoint someone from your department as a monitor to assist Constant Air, Inc.
2. Place completed, detached top half of the attachment "Monitor to Assist Constant Air, Inc., April 15–26" in Ned Grumer's mailbox.
3. Instruct all employees to remove materials from the ventilation grills.

1. Appoint someone from your department as a monitor to assist Constant Air, Inc.

- Carefully select this individual. (A monitor must have time available to promptly complete all tasks as listed on the attached sheet.)
- Notify the selected individual. (Confirm their availability to meet with the Constant Air representative at 1:00 p.m., April 10, and to be working on site April 15–26.)
- Fill in all information requested on the attachment, "Monitor to Assist Constant Air, Inc., April 15–26."
- Detach and give to the monitor the bottom half of the attachment, "Duties of the Air-Conditioning Monitor."

2. Place completed, detached top half of the attachment "Monitor to Assist Constant Air, Inc., April 15–26" in Ned Grumer's mailbox.

3. Instruct all employees to remove materials from the ventilation grills.

Many employees have tried to control the temperature in their offices by blocking the vents. Please ask all employees to remove cardboard, Styrofoam, tape, and other material from the ventilation grills. Constant Air will not be able to draw valid conclusions about the current system unless the vents are clear.

BOUNTIFUL CHEMICAL COOPERATIVE INC.

This memo and its attachment are typical of internal communications within a company or division. In this memo, the writer chose to keep the basic memo as short as possible, using the attachment sheet to provide additional information to the appointed monitors. Many long memos (and letters) would be easier to write if they were similarly designed: a cover memo/letter outlining the basics, with details provided in one or more attachments. See LETTERS and APPENDICES.

The subheading "NOTE" and the boldface in the following sentence signal a key reminder. As an option, this reminder could come earlier (toward the beginning of page 1). Notice that the reminder also appears at the bottom of the attachment sheet shown on p. 390. See EMPHASIS and ORGANIZATION.

All Managers And Supervisors
April 7, 1997
Page 2

NOTE: Only Constant Air, not Building Services, should adjust the air-conditioning systems between April 15 and April 26.

Your monitor will be meeting with the Constant Air representative in the Murri conference center at 1:00 p.m. on April 10. Please call me (ext. 4556) or Ned Grumer (ext. 4559) before the meeting if you or your monitor have any questions about these assignments.

asd
Attachment

The memo follows the 4-box organization. Box 1 (paragraphs 1 and 2) contains the request and some background information. Box 2 (the list in paragraph 2) presents the requested steps. Box 3 (the listed subheadings and text) expands on the steps. Box 4 (the final paragraph) closes the memo and reminds the managers of the deadline (the meeting date and time). See ORGANIZATION.

Request Memo

With Informal Instructions—Attachment

The continuation block identifies the general subject and the date of the main memo. This information on attachments helps identify attachments if they become separated from the main memo.

The top section allows managers to respond without generating additional memos.

The bottom half is essentially a numbered list of procedures or duties. The appointed monitor would receive this list and, optionally, the cover memo, which does provide some background information. See Lists.

Items in the list are parallel in their structure. See Parallelism.

Attachment
Air-Conditioning Memo
April 7, 1997

Monitor to Assist Constant Air, Inc., April 15–26

Name:	
Extension:	
Position Title:	
Department/Section:	

Detach here and return the top section to Ned Grumer

- -

DUTIES OF THE AIR-CONDITIONING MONITOR

Questions? Contact Constant Air at 555-3421.

1. Meet with the Constant Air representative in the Murri conference center at 1:00 P.M. on April 10.

2. Inspect your department before your scheduled tour to locate all ventilation grills and ensure that all cardboard, Styrofoam, tape, or other material blocking ventilation grills has been removed. NOTE: A tour schedule will be given to you when you meet with the Constant Air representative on April 10.

3. Tour your department with the Constant Air representative. Assist in identifying all ventilation grills.

4. Keep an hourly log of temperatures at selected points in your department from April 15 through 26. The Constant Air representative will identify these points during the tour of your department. NOTE: The Constant Air representative will provide log sheets at the initial meeting on April 10.

5. Survey employees (in your department) at least once a day from April 15 through 26 to determine their satisfaction with room temperatures. Log their responses.

6. Contact the Constant Air representative each day with any problems so the system can be balanced.

7. Prepare a weekly report summarizing gathered data. NOTE: The Constant Air representative will provide forms for these reports at the initial meeting on April 10.

8. Deliver all reports to Ned Grumer before noon on Monday, April 29.

NOTE: Only Constant Air, not Building Services, should adjust the air-conditioning system between April 15 and April 26. Do not call Building Services with requests related to air-conditioning during this time. Constant Air's number is 555-3421.

A tear-off sheet is a handy option and allows the sender of the memo to check off those who have returned the sheets by the deadline. Nowadays, some (maybe most) managers might choose to reply by E-mail (or voice mail); the writer might have mentioned this option, but such information is optional. See Electronic Mail.

With a Recommendation

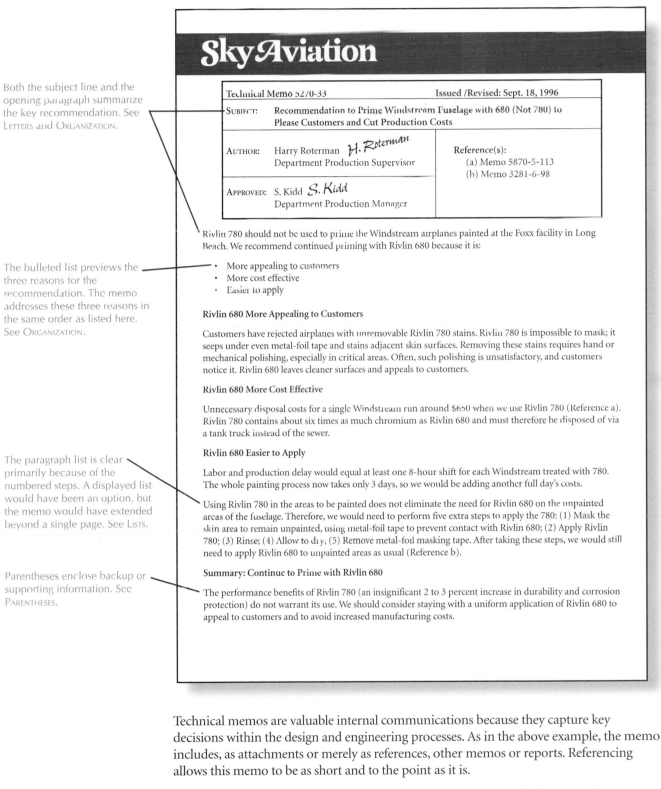

Both the subject line and the opening paragraph summarize the key recommendation. See LETTERS and ORGANIZATION.

The bulleted list previews the three reasons for the recommendation. The memo addresses these three reasons in the same order as listed here. See ORGANIZATION.

The paragraph list is clear primarily because of the numbered steps. A displayed list would have been an option, but the memo would have extended beyond a single page. See LISTS.

Parentheses enclose backup or supporting information. See PARENTHESES.

SkyAviation

Technical Memo 5270-33	Issued /Revised: Sept. 18, 1996

SUBJECT: Recommendation to Prime Windstream Fuselage with 680 (Not 780) to Please Customers and Cut Production Costs

AUTHOR: Harry Roterman *H. Roterman*
Department Production Supervisor

Reference(s):
(a) Memo 5870-5-113
(b) Memo 3281-6-98

APPROVED: S. Kidd *S. Kidd*
Department Production Manager

Rivlin 780 should not be used to prime the Windstream airplanes painted at the Foxx facility in Long Beach. We recommend continued priming with Rivlin 680 because it is:

- More appealing to customers
- More cost effective
- Easier to apply

Rivlin 680 More Appealing to Customers

Customers have rejected airplanes with unremovable Rivlin 780 stains. Rivlin 780 is impossible to mask; it seeps under even metal-foil tape and stains adjacent skin surfaces. Removing these stains requires hand or mechanical polishing, especially in critical areas. Often, such polishing is unsatisfactory, and customers notice it. Rivlin 680 leaves cleaner surfaces and appeals to customers.

Rivlin 680 More Cost Effective

Unnecessary disposal costs for a single Windstream run around $650 when we use Rivlin 780 (Reference a). Rivlin 780 contains about six times as much chromium as Rivlin 680 and must therefore be disposed of via a tank truck instead of the sewer.

Rivlin 680 Easier to Apply

Labor and production delay would equal at least one 8-hour shift for each Windstream treated with 780. The whole painting process now takes only 3 days, so we would be adding another full day's costs.

Using Rivlin 780 in the areas to be painted does not eliminate the need for Rivlin 680 on the unpainted areas of the fuselage. Therefore, we would need to perform five extra steps to apply the 780: (1) Mask the skin area to remain unpainted, using metal-foil tape to prevent contact with Rivlin 680; (2) Apply Rivlin 780; (3) Rinse; (4) Allow to dry; (5) Remove metal-foil masking tape. After taking these steps, we would still need to apply Rivlin 680 to unpainted areas as usual (Reference b).

Summary: Continue to Prime with Rivlin 680

The performance benefits of Rivlin 780 (an insignificant 2 to 3 percent increase in durability and corrosion protection) do not warrant its use. We should consider staying with a uniform application of Rivlin 680 to appeal to customers and to avoid increased manufacturing costs.

Technical memos are valuable internal communications because they capture key decisions within the design and engineering processes. As in the above example, the memo includes, as attachments or merely as references, other memos or reports. Referencing allows this memo to be as short and to the point as it is.

The memo follows the 4-box letter organization. Box 1 (paragraph 1) opens with a request or a statement of purpose. Box 2 (paragraph 1, second sentence) summarizes or lists the points to be covered. Box 3 (the remaining paragraphs, except for the final one) expands on the points listed in Box 2. Box 4 (the final subheading and paragraph) closes with a review of the content and a final request for action. See ORGANIZATION.

Recommendation Memo

The handwritten initials confirm that the writer has read and approved the contents of the memo before distribution.

The subject line is very specific. Even though the reader will be averse to the request, the subject block should not be coy, misleading, or vague.

The opening paragraph sets up the request by providing sound support for it. The reader is being asked to do something he does not want to do; therefore, the writer must validate the request. See LETTERS and ORGANIZATION.

Repeating the 20 percent figure is helpful because it reinforces the writer's major point. See EMPHASIS and REPETITION.

Sky Aviation

TO: Bob Conners   DATE: June 10, 1996

FROM: Denise Van Horn *DVH*

SUBJECT: Recommendation to Test the Toggles on Only 20 Percent of the Nose Landing Gear Transducers

Please authorize a decrease in toggle testing from 100 percent to 20 percent of the nose landing gear transducers. Testing 100 percent of the transducers adds 12.5 hours to the production time of each lot.

Reasons for the Recommendation

1. Recent tests (100 percent of the transducers in each lot) have shown them to be of excellent quality. Tom Rogers has compiled the following test data. I believe he called you yesterday to summarize the data.

Lot Number	Transducers Tested	Transducers Passed
4	32	30
5	32	32
6	32	31

2. The three transducers that did not pass were only slightly outside the specification limits. The tests showed that none of the three failed to work, so they would not have caused a failure of the nose landing gear.

3. Quality fabrication and installation procedures are now our highest priority. We believe that doing things right during production makes final testing less and less necessary. The decrease to 20 percent now is a prudent decision; this level of testing will screen for any unexpected decrease in production quality.

By return memo, please authorize a decrease in toggle testing from 100 percent to 20 percent of the nose landing gear transducers. If I can provide further information, please let me know (ext. 6380).

Whenever possible, writers should open their memos by clearly stating their request.

In this case, Bob Conners has been adamant about 100 percent toggle testing, so Denise knows that she must follow her request immediately with solid evidence to support it. An optional approach would be for Denise to delay the request until later in the letter. We do not recommend this option. See MEMOS, LETTERS, and ORGANIZATION.

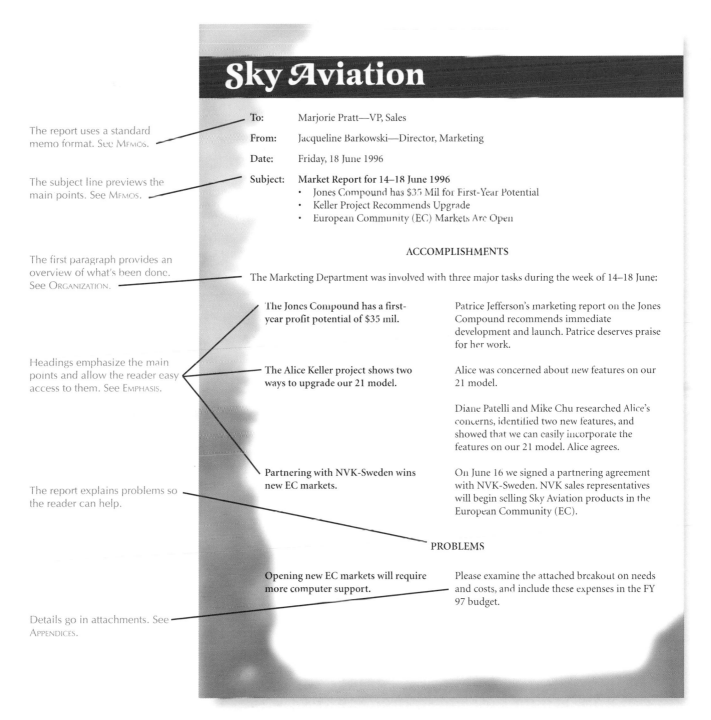

The report uses a standard memo format. See MFMOS.

The subject line previews the main points. See MFMOS.

The first paragraph provides an overview of what's been done. See ORGANIZATION.

Headings emphasize the main points and allow the reader easy access to them. See EMPHASIS.

The report explains problems so the reader can help.

Details go in attachments. See APPENDICES.

Sky Aviation

To: Marjorie Pratt—VP, Sales

From: Jacqueline Barkowski—Director, Marketing

Date: Friday, 18 June 1996

Subject: **Market Report for 14–18 June 1996**
- Jones Compound has $35 Mil for First-Year Potential
- Keller Project Recommends Upgrade
- European Community (EC) Markets Are Open

ACCOMPLISHMENTS

The Marketing Department was involved with three major tasks during the week of 14–18 June:

The Jones Compound has a first-year profit potential of $35 mil.

Patrice Jefferson's marketing report on the Jones Compound recommends immediate development and launch. Patrice deserves praise for her work.

The Alice Keller project shows two ways to upgrade our 21 model.

Alice was concerned about new features on our 21 model.

Diane Patelli and Mike Chu researched Alice's concerns, identified two new features, and showed that we can easily incorporate the features on our 21 model. Alice agrees.

Partnering with NVK-Sweden wins new EC markets.

On June 16 we signed a partnering agreement with NVK-Sweden. NVK sales representatives will begin selling Sky Aviation products in the European Community (EC).

PROBLEMS

Opening new EC markets will require more computer support.

Please examine the attached breakout on needs and costs, and include these expenses in the FY 97 budget.

The report focuses on outcomes and action. It includes both accomplishments and problems so the reader has a complete picture and can help as needed. The format clearly identifies the main points and allows the reader to scan the document.

Response Memo (E-Mail)

With Instructions

Using the reader's first name (*Diane*) is a good way to personalize your message. Optionally, you might insert the name in the initial sentence, enclosed by two commas. See ELECTRONIC MAIL and COMMAS.

Paragraph 1 provides the background for paragraph 2, which summarizes the enrollment procedures. See ELECTONIC MAIL and ORGANIZATION.

The list in paragraph 2 previews the information to follow. Screen 2 then follows the same sequence of topics. See ORGANIZATION.

D. Bianchi /ID234-4098 [E-Mail]

Via:	Mailbox 50, DBIANCHI
Date:	Tues/Mar 7, 1996/9:31 p.m. MST
From:	L. Kim / ID:987-5789
To:	D. Bianchi / ID:234-4098
Subject:	Procedure for Enrolling Spouse in SAVMED

Diane,

You asked how to enroll your spouse in the new SAVMED Insurance program.

Please sign and return by March 31 the enrollment card you received, because no new enrollments will be accepted for 90 days after that.

To complete the enrollment card you will have to:

- Obtain a full record of dependents' medical histories over the last 5 years.

- List all current medications.

- Fully disclose any other insurance program your spouse may be participating in.

The format of the headings and the short paragraphs help make this page readable. Such readability features are just as important in E-mail as in printed documents. See ELECTRONIC MAIL.

In the last paragraph, "To conclude" signals that the message is at an end, so the reader should not have to look at additional screens. Optionally, you could use an informal closing like "Thank you" or "Have a good day." See ELECTRONIC MAIL.

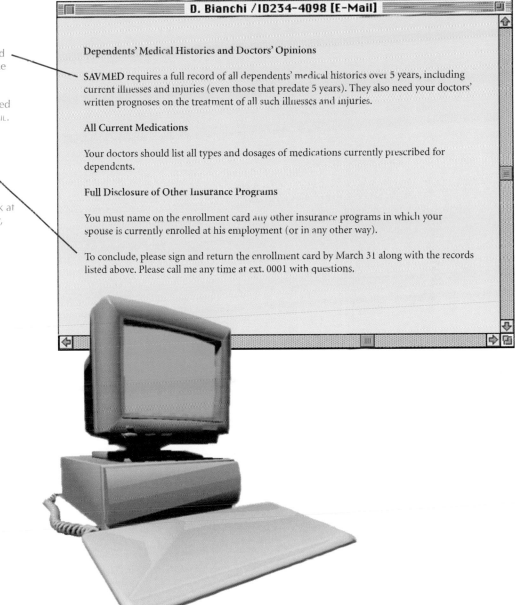

D. Bianchi /ID234-4098 [E-Mail]

Dependents' Medical Histories and Doctors' Opinions

SAVMED requires a full record of all dependents' medical histories over 5 years, including current illnesses and injuries (even those that predate 5 years). They also need your doctors' written prognoses on the treatment of all such illnesses and injuries.

All Current Medications

Your doctors should list all types and dosages of medications currently prescribed for dependents.

Full Disclosure of Other Insurance Programs

You must name on the enrollment card any other insurance programs in which your spouse is currently enrolled at his employment (or in any other way).

To conclude, please sign and return the enrollment card by March 31 along with the records listed above. Please call me any time at ext. 0001 with questions.

Electronic mail (E-mail) needs to be just as clear and as well written as printed documents. Often, you might be tempted to dash off an E-mail message without taking time to check it for accuracy or completeness. If you don't check your message, you may find yourself sending a follow-up E-mail to cover missing facts or information. See ELECTRONIC MAIL.

Transmittal Memo

For Attachments

Both the subject line and the opening line of the first paragraph focus on the key point—the recommendation of the Alka-Seltzer field test. See MEMOS and ORGANIZATION.

The opening paragraph states the author's position and lists two key reasons for that position.

The table boxhead contains the column headings. See TABLES.

Courteous writers give their telephone or extension numbers when they offer to provide more information. See LETTERS.

The NOTE acts as a closing paragraph, restating the purpose of the memo. It also introduces and emphasizes a necessary caution. See EMPHASIS and REPETITION.

INTEROFFICE MEMO

TO Distribution

FROM Clarence Hough

DATE February 27, 1996

SUBJECT **Recommendation of the Alka-Seltzer® Field Test for Determining the Presence of Sulfides in Effluents**

I recommend the Alka-Seltzer® field test for determining the presence of sulfides in the effluents we release into the county water system for two reasons:

- It is faster and simpler than our current tests.

- It has been used successfully by the Dade County Sanitation District for the past 3 years.

Attached are the detailed procedures for the Alka-Seltzer field test. Briefly, this test uses half an Alka-Seltzer tablet in one cup of sample. The liberated gases pass through a test paper.

If . . .	Then . . .
Sulfides are present (a positive reaction)	The test paper turns brown.
The Alka-Seltzer test is positive	The Hamilton test will usually give a positive reading.
The Hamilton test and the Alka-Seltzer disagree	Use the Alka-Seltzer test results to test determine whether to release effluents into the county water system.
You need further information about this test	Please call Steve Hankin (ext. 589) or me (ext. 591).

NOTE: I recommend the Alka-Seltzer test because it is fast and simple, but it does not reveal the concentration of the sulfides present. Samples with a positive reaction must go to the laboratory for further testing.

CH

nm
Attachment: "Alka-Seltzer Field Test Procedures"

Distribution: Alex Lerner
Matt Decker
Elisha Milborn
Rick Warner
Gonzalo Feliz

MIDLAND

Attachment notations remind readers that one or more documents are to be included with the memo. In this case, the writer specified the title of the attachment (not included with this model), making a replacement request easier should the attachment become separated from the memo. See MEMOS.

Memos sent to a large number of readers often have a distribution list instead of a courtesy copy list. See MEMOS.

Always include a current address and telephone number. See LETTERS.

A statement of your career goal is helpful.

List first the information you want to emphasize most. See ORGANIZATION.

Arrange chronologically, beginning with the most recent experiences.

List information applicable to the position. Avoid lengthy lists of interests or outside activities.

DOUGLAS A. BOWEN

1862 South Elm Avenue, Lincoln, NE 48298 *(302) 531-2468*

Objective

A challenging, responsible position in human resource management

Experience

- **1989 to present.** Personnel Supervisor for Western Electronics, Lincoln, Nebraska

  —Supervise currently the Human Resource Department in a 1,500-employee facility. Responsible for all personnel activities, including labor/management relations.

  —Coordinated a plant-wide Total Quality Management (TQM) program in a manufacturing environment. Member of President's Quality Council.

- **1985 to 1989.** Human Resource Coordinator, Lesco, Inc., Kansas City, Kansas

  —Designed a performance planning and review system for all hourly and exempt workers, including a career enhancement program for clerical employees.

- **1982 to 1985.** Benefits Administrator, Lincoln General Hospital, Lincoln, Nebraska

  —Developed and conducted management skills training courses for 200 mid-level managers.

Education

- M.A., Human Resource Management, University of Nebraska, 1990
- B.S., Sociology (major), Accounting (minor), Kansas State University, 1984

Other Qualifications

- Member, American Society of Personnel Administrators (ASPA)
- Member, American Society for Training and Development (ASTD)

Interests

- Water skiing, snow skiing, camping, woodworking

References *(available on request)*

October 8, 1996

Keep your resume short and concise—a single page if you can. The above content is standard, but you might include military service, special skills (e.g., facility with a foreign language), and licenses or accreditation. Avoid personal information, such as age, marital status, national origin, religion, or physical features. See RESUMES.

Layouts for resumes may vary, but spacing should always be neat and uncluttered. Readability and the ease of finding important information are critical. See EMPHASIS.

Resume

Functional Format

Resume for **Douglas A. Bowen**
1862 South Elm Avenue
Lincoln NE 48298
(302) 531-2468

Objective · A managerial role in human resources for a growing firm in the medical technologies field

Major Accomplishments

The bulleted points are like headlines, with the explanations (in smaller type) giving positive results or benefits.

- **Supervise currently the Human Resource Department in a 1,500-employee facility at Western Electronics.**

  I am responsible for all personnel activities, including labor/management relations, wage and salary administration, hiring, and Affirmatives/EEO requirements. My staff and I have been credited with avoiding two threatened strikes during the past 3 years.

- **Coordinated a plant-wide TQM (Total Quality Management) program for Western Electronics.**

  Member of the President's Quality Council. Our TQM program is credited with reducing our in-plant rejects from 12 percent to 8 percent and our customer returns from 4 percent to 0.2 percent.

- **Designed a performance planning and review system for all hourly and exempt workers, including a career enhancement program for clerical employees.**

  This program at Lesco, Inc., has reduced significantly the legal challenges of disciplined and terminated employees.

- **Developed and conducted management skills training courses for 200 mid-level managers.**

  These training courses at Lincoln General Hospital are now a regular part of the curriculum. The course materials have been separately printed and are being used under contract by other companies.

Job History

List jobs chronologically beginning with your current position.

- 1989 to present—Personnel Supervisor for Western Electronics, Lincoln, Nebraska

- 1985 to 1989—Human Resource Coordinator, Lesco, Inc., Kansas City, Kansas

- 1982 to 1985—Benefits Administrator, Lincoln General Hospital, Lincoln, Nebraska

Education and Professional Memberships

Prepare a separate list of references for use at the interview or for sending later to an interested prospective employer. (Only use people's names after you've received their permission.)

- M.A., Human Resource Management, University of Nebraska, 1990

- B.S., Sociology, Kansas State University, 1984

- Member of ASPA (American Society of Personnel Administrators) and ASTD (American Society for Training and Development). Program chair in 1987–1988 for ASTD.

References available on request

October 8, 1996

A resume need not follow the traditional chronological format (as illustrated in the previous example). Instead, resumes can be designed to highlight (sell) the person's qualifications, as the above resume does in its list of accomplishments. You should still keep your resume short; one page is ideal. Do not include information on your religion, national origin, marital status, age, or physical features. See RESUMES.

1862 South Elm Avenue
Lincoln, NE 48298
October 9, 1996

Ms. Carolyn Myers
Human Resources Director
Healthtronics, Inc.
500 Research Parkway
Denver, CO 80014

Dear Ms. Myers:

Subject: Job Application for Regional Human Resources Manager

My qualifications closely match your advertisement in today's *Wall Street Journal*.

According to your job profile, you need a human resource generalist in the electronics industry. As the current personnel supervisor for Western Electronics, I have broad experience in human resource activities:

- Wage and salary administration
- Labor contract negotiation and administration
- Hiring and outplacement
- Affirmative action and EEO guidelines

My prior work at Lesco, Inc., provided me with practical experience in design, performance measurement, and succession planning. In addition, I have held positions in local ASPA and ASTD chapters.

As this letter and my resume indicate, I am a dedicated professional with the skills and experience necessary for a human resource generalist in a growing industry. I am available to discuss this position; please call me at (302) 531-2468.

Sincerely,

Douglas A. Bowen

Douglas A. Bowen

Always use the person's name and title in the salutation if the advertisement gives the name. See LETTERS.

Make your opening direct, and refer to the position and the source for your information. See LETTERS and ORGANIZATION.

Focus on the need you can fill.

Organize for readability and emphasis. See LISTS and EMPHASIS.

Include related experience.

Use a strong closing statement with positive language. See LETTERS.

The cover letter should expand or amplify the information contained in the resume. Your letter should also mention specific qualifications or requirements from the advertisement for the position. See RESUMES.

Be creative and be direct about your qualifications and suitability for the job. Always follow any interviews with a thank-you letter.

September 16, 1996

**MINUTES OF THE SEPTEMBER 15 MEETING ON THE SHUTTLE SYSTEM
FROM GREEN BRIAR TO LAKEVIEW CENTER**

The subject line is quite specific.
See HEADINGS and MEMOS.

Attending: George Benson, Frank Houck, Martha Memmert, and Jeanne Skorut

An accurate record of
participants is essential.

Absent: Fred Householder

Action items emphasize the
participants (with names
boldfaced), their responsibilities,
and the due dates. See BOLDFACE,
EMPHASIS, and ORGANIZATION.

ACTION ITEMS

Martha Memmert   Obtain bids from several other transportation companies. (Due
                            October 1.)

Jeanne Skorut   Develop an estimate of what it would cost for us to lease our own
                            vans and hire drivers. (Due October 1.)

Frank Houck   Study the feasibility of eliminating air-conditioning from the buses.
                            (Due October 5.)

George Benson   Discuss our work on the criteria with Fred Householder, who
                            originally drafted the criteria. (Due October 1.)

This overview supplies necessary
background information (much
as corrections to prior minutes
would do).

AN OVERVIEW OF THE SHUTTLE SYSTEM CRITERIA

George Benson opened the meeting with a review of the criteria:

The numbered list helps to
highlight key information. See
LISTS.

1. Buses must make one round trip every 2 hours (two buses to operate simultaneously), with
   trips starting at 7 a.m. and ending at 6 p.m. (Travel time is estimated to be about 50 minutes
   one way.)

2. Buses must be comfortable and attractive—ones that convey a good image for our
   company.

3. Buses must carry at least 12 passengers.

4. Buses must be economical to operate and maintain.

BOUNTIFUL CHEMICAL COOPERATIVE INC.

Minutes should highlight (1) actions during the meeting and (2) actions needed in
the future (usually before the next meeting). Minutes should not attempt to capture
everything that was discussed, and they deliberately do not record the meeting in
strict chronological order. See ORGANIZATION and MEETINGS MANAGEMENT.

The bid information is necessary background to the following motions.

MLT Bus System's Preliminary Bid

Frank Houck reviewed the preliminary bid from MLT Bus System. They proposed using two vehicles at a cost per hour of $37 (including the buses, their drivers, and maintenance).

If we maintained the proposed schedule of 11 hours a day, our weekly, monthly, and yearly rates would be as follows:

Weekly Fee	$2,035
Monthly Fee	$8,954
Yearly Fee	$107,448

This motion highlights the name of the person making the motion, but the heading could identify the issue: Other Busing Systems. See HEADINGS.

George Benson's Motion

> That we investigate other arrangements, given the costs of the MLT Bus System. Martha volunteered to investigate other companies, and Jeanne will develop an estimate of costs for leasing buses and hiring drivers.

Possible Changes to the Criteria

These headings highlight the content of the motion, but the person's name is included in parentheses.

Number of Trips (motion by Martha Memmert)

> That we use a single bus for most trips, with double buses on the trips at 7 a.m. and at noon. The motion passed, so Martha and Jeanne will include this new criterion in their reports.

Painting of the Buses (informal motion)

> That we not paint the yellow MLT buses maroon (BCC's corporate color). Motion passed, saving a one-time cost per bus of $1,000.

Elimination of Air-Conditioning (motion by Frank Houck)

> That we eliminate air conditioning (also recommended in the MLT proposal). Initial installation costs would be $2,500 per bus, with weekly costs of $250 per bus (because of fuel, maintenance, etc.). Frank will investigate the problem and report no later than October 5.

Report to Fred Householder

> George Benson agreed to report recommended criteria revisions to Fred, who originally developed the criteria. George will report on Fred's response by October 1.

Respectfully submitted,

Jeanne Skorut

Jeanne Skorut

BOUNTIFUL CHEMICAL COOPERATIVE INC.

The headings, lists, short paragraphs, and brief sentences all contribute to the overall readability, but motions and action items are potentially lost. See EMPHASIS.

Some repetition is inevitable at times, especially if the meeting is long and the issues complex. See REPETITION.

Job Title:	Administrative Assistant	Job Code:	1380
Department:	Operations	Job Grade:	24
Revision Date:	March 3, 1997	FLSA:	Non-Exempt

Position Overview

Provide administrative and secretarial support for division managers. Create, edit, and produce written documentation. Establish division documentation standards.

Essential Job Functions

- Answer and screen incoming calls; take and deliver accurate messages.
- Write, edit, proofread, and publish all correspondence, reports, proposals, and other documents.
- Represent managers in their absence.
- Coordinate travel arrangements.
- Create presentation visuals using PowerPoint or other similar software.
- Create and maintain spreadsheets and generate weekly, monthly, and custom reports.
- Coordinate division meetings and functions.
- Coordinate internal and external speaking engagements.
- Complete all pre-and post-engagement paperwork.

Non-Essential Job Functions

- Assist with department budgeting.
- Prepare division purchase orders.
- Coordinate building maintenance and housekeeping.
- Schedule A/V equipment.

Requirements

- Thorough understanding of and ability to use Windows '97; Microsoft Office programs, including Word, Excel, and PowerPoint; and page layout programs such as PageMaker or QuarkXpress.
- Minimum 5 years' secretarial experience.
- Excellent writing, editing, and proofreading skills.
- Type 70 wpm.
- Proven organization skills.
- Proven ability to work under pressure, meet aggressive deadlines, and make effective decisions.
- High school graduate.

Other Skills/Abilities

- Dictaphone and shorthand experience preferred.
- Post high school secretarial/business courses preferred.
- Background in accounting preferred.

NOTE: This job description is not intended to be all-inclusive. Employee may perform other related duties as required to meet the ongoing needs of the organization.

Margin notes:

Essential job functions describe the core of each position. These are the functions that must be done; the incumbent must be able to perform each function.

The non-essential job functions are the "nice-to-haves." These functions may be eliminated or modified for people with different skill sets or for those employees requesting an accommodation due to a disability.

The functions or requirements in each section may be listed with bullets or numbers. Generally, numerical systems imply that the items are listed in order of importance. See Lists.

Well-written job descriptions should become the basis for internal job postings and external job advertisements. Keep job descriptions up to date and use them as a tool in shared expectation reviews or performance reviews between employees and supervisors.

Companies have quite different policies about how and when to do performance reviews (often called shared expectation reviews). Because policies are so different, we do not provide any written examples of a performance review.

For a Proposal (Financial Services)

The bulleted list identifies the three major benefits covered in the proposal. The listed items reflect the organization both for the executive summary and for the main text of the proposal. See ORGANIZATION.

Each subheading ends with a section number in parentheses. These section numbers are cross-references to sections in the text of the proposal.

The marginal callouts highlight with sales language why Save-a-Lot Rental should be interested in Waterfall's assistance with management of their taxes. See PERSUASION.

Waterfall Financial Services iii

A PROPOSAL FOR SAVE-A-LOT RENTAL

Save Taxes with Tailored Solutions from Waterfall Financial Services (WFS)

"We always know exactly what we're saving on taxes. There are no surprises when you work with WFS."

—Kim Lee
CFO, Thomas Corp

With WFS, Save-a-Lot can:

- Save taxes through proper planning
- Enhance executive income through tailored tax planning
- Enjoy tailored national and international tax solutions

Save taxes through proper planning (Section 2.0)

You'll be in the best possible tax position consistent with proper business, personal, and financial planning with WFS. We believe taxpayers should pay only what the law requires.

Save-a-Lot can minimize federal, state, and foreign taxes on business transactions with WFS continuous tax planning. You will get regular advice for maximizing credit (on, say, research activity and other areas), anticipating problems, and planning for opportunities, rather than just reacting to past events.

As Save-a-Lot expands (through acquisitions or mergers, for example), you'll need the timely, efficient tax planning we can give you as a result of our size and extensive practical experience with a large clientele.

Enhance executive income through tailored tax planning (Section 3.0)

Save-a-Lot executives can enhance their income and benefits with a tailored program to help them build capital through income tax savings, while you benefit from favorable funding arrangements and executive retention.

Minimize all taxes with across-the-board strategic tax planning.

Enjoy tailored national and international tax solutions (Section 4.0)

Get specialized tax counsel and quick solutions for your particular situation.

Save-a-Lot will benefit from our frequent contact with national and district IRS offices as we obtain early answers to tax questions and rulings on tax aspects of proposed transactions. You'll avoid tax controversy and cut time and costs because of our expertise in resolving tax disputes efficiently and informally.

In a constantly changing tax environment, you need the specialized knowledge of our Washington WFS Office, specializing in more than 30 tax areas. Also, we have an international presence and experience in worldwide tax planning.

Our offices throughout the world would like to help Save-a-Lot with a full range of business, tax, and accounting services.

WATERFALL FINANCIAL SERVICES   214 BAYWAY BOULEVARD   ORLANDO, FLORIDA 32862-7201

Both federal and commercial (non-governmental) proposals usually include a well-written executive summary. Usually, as in this example, the executive summary highlights key benefits to the customer. Also, the summary introduces with cross-references key content in the main text of the proposal.

The many references to Save-a-Lot help tailor the proposal to Save-a-Lot readers, even though much of the text would be generic and usable for any client.

For a Proposal (Training)

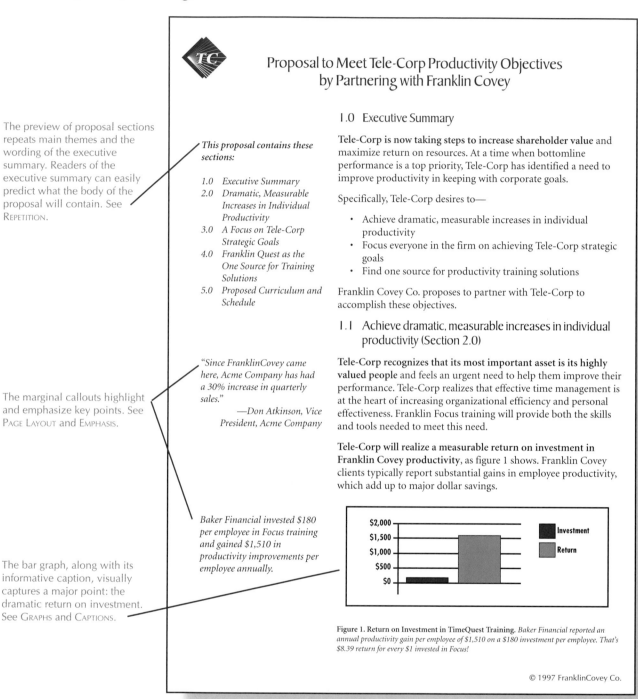

The preview of proposal sections repeats main themes and the wording of the executive summary. Readers of the executive summary can easily predict what the body of the proposal will contain. See REPETITION.

The marginal callouts highlight and emphasize key points. See PAGE LAYOUT and EMPHASIS.

The bar graph, along with its informative caption, visually captures a major point: the dramatic return on investment. See GRAPHS and CAPTIONS.

Proposal to Meet Tele-Corp Productivity Objectives by Partnering with Franklin Covey

1.0 Executive Summary

Tele-Corp is now taking steps to increase shareholder value and maximize return on resources. At a time when bottomline performance is a top priority, Tele-Corp has identified a need to improve productivity in keeping with corporate goals.

Specifically, Tele-Corp desires to—

- Achieve dramatic, measurable increases in individual productivity
- Focus everyone in the firm on achieving Tele-Corp strategic goals
- Find one source for productivity training solutions

Franklin Covey Co. proposes to partner with Tele-Corp to accomplish these objectives.

1.1 Achieve dramatic, measurable increases in individual productivity (Section 2.0)

Tele-Corp recognizes that its most important asset is its highly valued people and feels an urgent need to help them improve their performance. Tele-Corp realizes that effective time management is at the heart of increasing organizational efficiency and personal effectiveness. Franklin Focus training will provide both the skills and tools needed to meet this need.

Tele-Corp will realize a measurable return on investment in Franklin Covey productivity, as figure 1 shows. Franklin Covey clients typically report substantial gains in employee productivity, which add up to major dollar savings.

This proposal contains these sections:

1.0 *Executive Summary*
2.0 *Dramatic, Measurable Increases in Individual Productivity*
3.0 *A Focus on Tele-Corp Strategic Goals*
4.0 *Franklin Quest as the One Source for Training Solutions*
5.0 *Proposed Curriculum and Schedule*

"Since FranklinCovey came here, Acme Company has had a 30% increase in quarterly sales."

—Don Atkinson, Vice President, Acme Company

Baker Financial invested $180 per employee in Focus training and gained $1,510 in productivity improvements per employee annually.

Figure 1. Return on Investment in TimeQuest Training. *Baker Financial reported an annual productivity gain per employee of $1,510 on a $180 investment per employee. That's $8.39 return for every $1 invested in Focus!*

© 1997 FranklinCovey Co.

A brief, highly readable executive summary has become the standard opening for most proposals. An executive summary combines persuasive sales information with a preview of the contents of the proposal. Often, as in the above example, each subhead in the executive summary parallels a section in the proposal.

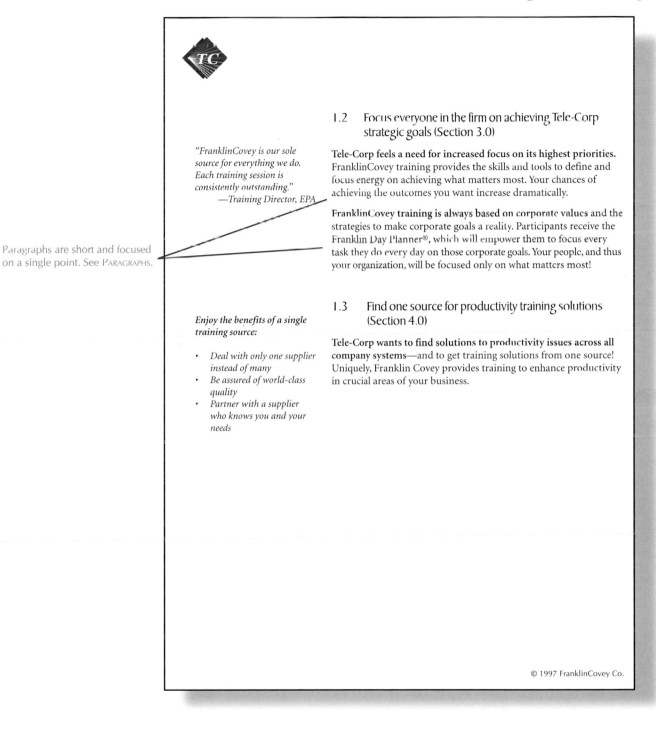

1.2 Focus everyone in the firm on achieving Tele-Corp strategic goals (Section 3.0)

Tele-Corp feels a need for increased focus on its highest priorities. FranklinCovey training provides the skills and tools to define and focus energy on achieving what matters most. Your chances of achieving the outcomes you want increase dramatically.

FranklinCovey training is always based on corporate values and the strategies to make corporate goals a reality. Participants receive the Franklin Day Planner®, which will empower them to focus every task they do every day on those corporate goals. Your people, and thus your organization, will be focused only on what matters most!

1.3 Find one source for productivity training solutions (Section 4.0)

Tele-Corp wants to find solutions to productivity issues across all company systems—and to get training solutions from one source! Uniquely, Franklin Covey provides training to enhance productivity in crucial areas of your business.

"FranklinCovey is our sole source for everything we do. Each training session is consistently outstanding."
—*Training Director, EPA*

Paragraphs are short and focused on a single point. See PARAGRAPHS.

Enjoy the benefits of a single training source:

- *Deal with only one supplier instead of many*
- *Be assured of world-class quality*
- *Partner with a supplier who knows you and your needs*

© 1997 FranklinCovey Co.

Executive Summary

For an Audit

The major finding opens the summary, rather than coming at the end. See ORGANIZATION.

Paragraph 1 provides the essential background and references the full report, which is attached. This brief background is all that is necessary before a reader sees the recommendations in the matrix table.

The matrix table is an excellent tool for capturing the logic behind some crucial content. This table replaces three, four, or more paragraphs of text. See TABLES and EMPHASIS.

The conclusion totals the proposed financial savings and repeats the recommendation for a third time. Repetition is an essential feature of unambiguous text. See WRITING AND REVISING and REPETITION.

OSAGE GAS & ELECTRICAL COMPANY INC.

Major Account Servicing Audit MA41

1.0 Executive Summary

Major Finding: *Unsatisfactory Contracting and Collection Practices Expose Osage G&E to Significant Financial Losses.*

We have concluded our audit of the internal controls over the major account contracting and collection functions for the year 1996 (final report attached). A random sampling of 150 deliveries was examined. Account management is unsatisfactory and exposes Osage G&E to a loss of as much as $2.5 million in fiscal 1997.

We recommend management's immediate attention to these principal concerns. Section references refer to sections in the final audit report.

Management should . . .	To improve controls over these unsatisfactory account servicing practices
1. Motivate on-time payments with automatic discounts on future deliveries	*Aging Accounts* A significant number (47 percent) of major account deliveries show more than 90 days past due for payment. Projected interest losses to Osage G&E over the next year: $1.1 million. (Section 3.2)
2. Instruct delivery directors to make no deliveries unless contracts are in hand first	*Deliveries without Contracts* Contracts were not issued in 8 percent of power deliveries to major accounts. Potential loss from payment defaults over one year: $1 million. (Section 3.3)
3. Require Financial Office to approve all discounts in advance	*Non-Compliance with Discounting Guidelines* Discounts of between 10 percent and 50 percent were given to selected major accounts where sales volume did not warrant them. Actual loss over the past year: $400,000. (Section 3.4)

Conclusion

Osage G&E might lose as much as $2.5 million in fiscal 1997 if control objectives are not met. We recommend immediate attention to the detailed findings and recommendations in the attached report.

4239 E. Jennings Avenue, Cedar Rapids, Iowa 54336

This executive summary opens with the major finding and the supporting recommendations. We recommend using this organization instead of the more traditional organization. Traditional audit reports often mirror the audit process, which begins with the collection of data, interviews with key employees, the collection of more data, and finally some interpretations. Following that sequence, the traditional report would present the audit findings on page 20, page 30, or later. See ORGANIZATION and SUMMARIES.

This initial page contains some cross-references to later sections of the audit report. These references would help readers to search and find information more efficiently. (We have not included these additional pages from the audit report.)

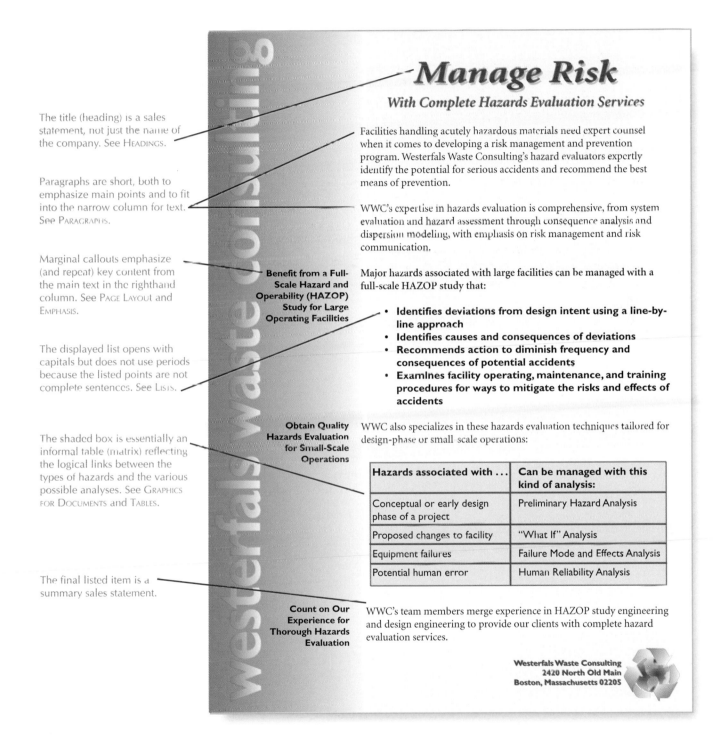

The title (heading) is a sales statement, not just the name of the company. See HEADINGS.

Paragraphs are short, both to emphasize main points and to fit into the narrow column for text. See PARAGRAPHS.

Marginal callouts emphasize (and repeat) key content from the main text in the righthand column. See PAGE LAYOUT and EMPHASIS.

The displayed list opens with capitals but does not use periods because the listed points are not complete sentences. See LISTS.

The shaded box is essentially an informal table (matrix) reflecting the logical links between the types of hazards and the various possible analyses. See GRAPHICS FOR DOCUMENTS and TABLES.

The final listed item is a summary sales statement.

Manage Risk

With Complete Hazards Evaluation Services

Facilities handling acutely hazardous materials need expert counsel when it comes to developing a risk management and prevention program. Westerfals Waste Consulting's hazard evaluators expertly identify the potential for serious accidents and recommend the best means of prevention.

WWC's expertise in hazards evaluation is comprehensive, from system evaluation and hazard assessment through consequence analysis and dispersion modeling, with emphasis on risk management and risk communication.

Benefit from a Full-Scale Hazard and Operability (HAZOP) Study for Large Operating Facilities

Major hazards associated with large facilities can be managed with a full-scale HAZOP study that:

- **Identifies deviations from design intent using a line-by-line approach**
- **Identifies causes and consequences of deviations**
- **Recommends action to diminish frequency and consequences of potential accidents**
- **Examines facility operating, maintenance, and training procedures for ways to mitigate the risks and effects of accidents**

Obtain Quality Hazards Evaluation for Small-Scale Operations

WWC also specializes in these hazards evaluation techniques tailored for design-phase or small-scale operations:

Hazards associated with . . .	Can be managed with this kind of analysis:
Conceptual or early design phase of a project	Preliminary Hazard Analysis
Proposed changes to facility	"What If" Analysis
Equipment failures	Failure Mode and Effects Analysis
Potential human error	Human Reliability Analysis

Count on Our Experience for Thorough Hazards Evaluation

WWC's team members merge experience in HAZOP study engineering and design engineering to provide our clients with complete hazard evaluation services.

Westerfals Waste Consulting
2420 North Old Main
Boston, Massachusetts 02205

This marketing fact sheet deliberately uses text. Other versions might be more graphic, with only a few bulleted headline statements. This fact sheet could be sent to prospective clients as part of an information packet.

The format is designed to be open and inviting, and the text focuses on the two key benefits a client would gain from using Westerfals for waste management problems.

The mission sentence—actually an informative heading—is an effective, visual emphasis technique. See EMPHASIS and HEADINGS.

Each phrase in the mission sentence is broken out for separate analysis. This format breaks up what might have been a lengthy traditional paragraph. See PARAGRAPHS.

FranklinCovey.

WE HELP PEOPLE THINK AND COMMUNICATE MORE PRODUCTIVELY

We help clients improve their intellectual productivity by helping them discover, define, and communicate valuable ideas and information.

We Help People . . .

Helping people is a simple, elegant approach, and in line with Franklin's focus on helping people—individuals, teams, and organizations—gain control and be more productive. The focus on helping people, as opposed to customers, makes Franklin Covey Professional Services Group a service-oriented company open to future service ideas.

. . . Think and Communicate . . .

This is our discriminator concept. The word *think* is a point of departure for raising issues with clients about leveraging intellectual resources, maximizing brain capital, and enhancing knowledge work. The link between thinking and communicating is backed by research on the nature of cognition and the fact that, in business, knowledge has no value unless it's shared. Furthermore, we benefit from the current interest in collaborative thinking and how to facilitate it.

. . . More Productively

This is our value. The issue for Franklin, and for most clients, is increased productivity. The services we provide produce measurable results in terms of productivity. We help people think and communicate better, faster, and less expensively.

The Opportunity

Franklin Covey Professional Services Group has the opportunity to provide significant value to people and organizations by helping them think and communicate better in accomplishing their critical goals. By helping people move beyond original ways of thinking and communicating, Franklin Covey Professional Services Group can provide a breakthrough service to individuals, teams, and large organizations.

Franklin Building, Third Floor
2200 West Parkway Boulevard
Salt Lake City, Utah 84119
(801) 956-1300
Fax (801) 956-1301

Mission statements are increasingly important because businesses and other organizations need a clear view of their core values and goals. Otherwise, employees will often waste time and money on peripheral tasks.

Successful mission statements must be brief (only one or two pages, at most). They should also be organized around a slogan or key sentence, as in the mission sentence that is the heading above.

Mission Statement
Franklin Covey Professional Services Group
Page 2

Repetition of the mission sentence is proper, especially if page 2 was printed on the back of page 1. See REPETITION.

The Approach

We Help People Think and Communicate More Productively

Franklin Covey Professional Services Group identifies market needs and trends to establish where it can provide significant value. Next, it designs consulting, training, projects, and product support to meet these needs. Finally, it organizes around these market needs.

The Benefits, as Seen by Our Clients

The numbered list, the boldface openings, and the short paragraphs produce a readable list of benefits. See EMPHASIS.

1. **Increase productivity.**

   Sky Aviation reduces costs 35 percent, improves sales quality. Franklin Covey Professional Services Group partnered with this client in consulting and training to improve processes and internal capability to win new business more productively. The company increased their win rate on proposals from 50 percent to 73 percent, an increase of 23 percent. They also reduced their costs by 35 percent.

2. **Discover and leverage valuable ideas and information.**

   Bountiful Chemical Corporation, Inc., saves $900,000 by clarifying communication. Franklin Covey Professional Services Group partnered with this customer to clarify critical ideas and procedures. Franklin facilitated a team process that allowed employees to design and leverage written policies and procedures. These procedures improve the thinking of employees, reduce risk and cost, and increase safety.

3. **Communicate the right message to the customers.**

   Midland Oil and Gas Operations, Inc., sharpens its message—customer wins up 300 percent. The Franklin Covey Professional Services Group process of training and consulting was transferred into this client's environment. Franklin trained 300 Midland Oil people to understand their customers' needs and to match their message directly in documents and presentations. The customer approval rate went from 20 percent to 80 percent over 3 years.

4. **Improve processes that facilitate collaboration and teamwork.**

   Osage Gas and Electrical Company's Franklin-trained team outperforms others threefold. Osage contracted with Franklin Covey Professional Services Group to instill processes and tools that brought a team together to productively solve critical issues. The Franklin Covey Professional Services Group process brought simple, but powerful standards for thinking, writing, and presenting.

Page 2 of this mission statement shifts to four success stories from actual clients. This shift to marketing or sales information is especially appropriate if the mission statement will be circulated to customers.

Procedure

For a Business Process

The heading block provides the title, SOP (Standard Operating Procedure) number, date, and the number of pages. This format allows easy updating and quick reference.

The purpose of the procedure appears in the first paragraph.

The scope defines the applicability of the procedure.

The policy statement describes the intent behind the procedure and establishes the policy's basic goals.

The content description previews the rest of the procedure and functions as a table of contents.

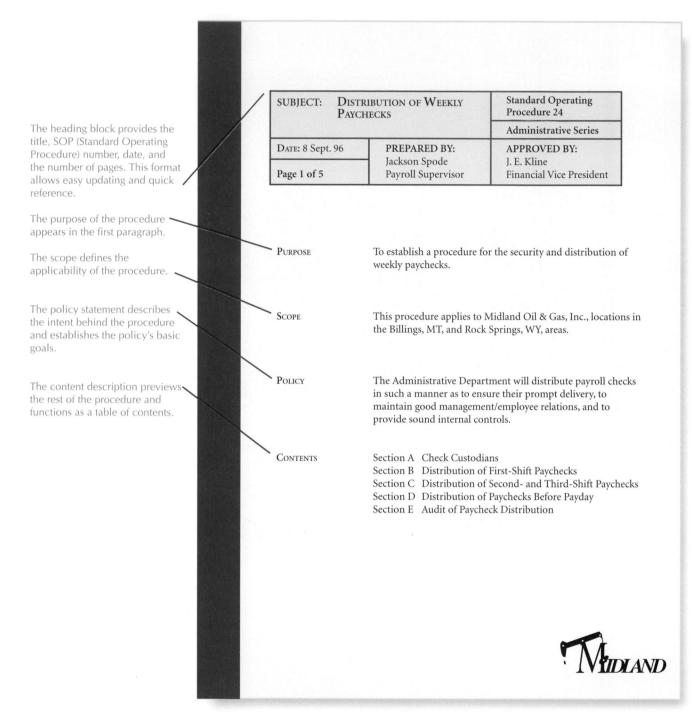

SUBJECT:	DISTRIBUTION OF WEEKLY PAYCHECKS	Standard Operating Procedure 24
		Administrative Series
DATE: 8 Sept. 96	PREPARED BY: Jackson Spode Payroll Supervisor	APPROVED BY: J. E. Kline Financial Vice President
Page 1 of 5		

PURPOSE   To establish a procedure for the security and distribution of weekly paychecks.

SCOPE   This procedure applies to Midland Oil & Gas, Inc., locations in the Billings, MT, and Rock Springs, WY, areas.

POLICY   The Administrative Department will distribute payroll checks in such a manner as to ensure their prompt delivery, to maintain good management/employee relations, and to provide sound internal controls.

CONTENTS
Section A   Check Custodians
Section B   Distribution of First-Shift Paychecks
Section C   Distribution of Second- and Third-Shift Paychecks
Section D   Distribution of Paychecks Before Payday
Section E   Audit of Paycheck Distribution

*M*IDLAND

Procedures should be as schematic as possible, with headings, lists, and imperative statements. These format techniques enhance readability and allow readers to find their particular responsibilities and actions.

Inevitably, procedures must be updated, so the numbering system, date of creation, and any revision date need to appear on each page.

Procedure

For a Business Process

SUBJECT: DISTRIBUTION OF WEEKLY PAYCHECKS	SOP 24

SECTION A. CHECK CUSTODIANS

RESPONSIBILITY	ACTION

EACH DEPARTMENT

A-1. Appoint a check custodian for the department by signed memo to the CDS (Check Distribution Section) giving name, dept. number, and signature of check custodian.

Boxed-in notes in the callout left margin are more emphatic and accessible.

> **NOTE:**
> In no instance does the check distribution section appoint as the check custodian a supervisor/manager who approves time cards.

CHECK DISTRIBUTION OFFICE

A-2. Assign a specified time for each check custodian to pick up checks at the Check Distribution Office.

A-3. Forward checks to outlying check custodians via MOGO courier, using locked bags.

Quotation marks enclose titles of forms. See QUOTATION MARKS.

CHECK CUSTODIAN

A-4. Pick up checks at the assigned time, signing the pick-up log for the checks. If assigned time to pick up checks has passed, pick up checks as soon as possible.

A-5. Prepare Form C82-974, "Notification of Personnel Transfer" (see attachment A), whenever employees are transferred to other departments or locations, and forward it to the CDS no later than noon on the Wednesday before payday.

MIDLAND

The most common problem with procedures is the passive voice. Writers list actions passively, and readers often don't know who is supposed to do what. A procedure that says "checks must be examined before delivery" does not indicate who is supposed to do the examining. Therefore, all steps in procedures must identify not only the action but also the person or the department responsible. See ACTIVE/PASSIVE.

Each step in the procedure opens with the person or department responsible for the step. Next comes the action associated with the step. Note that the action is stated in imperative sentences. See SENTENCES, and ACTIVE/PASSIVE.

Procedure

For a Business Process

Using boldface, underlining, or capital letters emphasizes key warnings and cautions. See BOLDFACE, EMPHASIS, and UNDERLINING.

SUBJECT: DISTRIBUTION OF WEEKLY PAYCHECKS	SOP 24

NOTE:
Under no circumstances give paychecks to anyone other than the employee whose name appears on the check

A-6. Deliver paychecks to payees only.

SECTION B. DISTRIBUTION OF FIRST-SHIFT PAYCHECKS

RESPONSIBILITY	ACTION
EACH DEPARTMENT	
FIRST-SHIFT CHECK CUSTODIAN	B-1. Pick up checks each Friday at the assigned time.
	B-2. Deliver checks to the employees after pickup and safeguard undelivered checks. Return checks not picked up by employees by 2:30 p.m. to the Check Distribution Section (CDS) by 2:45 p.m. DO NOT HOLD CHECKS UNTIL THE FOLLOWING DAY.
FIRST-SHIFT EMPLOYEE WHO DID NOT RECEIVE A PAYCHECK	B-3. Pick up undelivered check at the CDS on the following day.

MIDLAND

NOTE: This procedure would have two more pages. Because the other pages would add little to the model, we have omitted them.

The heading gives both the procedure number and the date when it was written or last revised.

A summary profiles for users the essential tasks. It serves as a content preview for the detailed steps. See ORGANIZATION.

Both the matrix listing requirements and the information under IMPORTANT are crucial, so one uses a graphic matrix and the other a marginal icon. See GRAPHICS FOR DOCUMENTS.

Warnings (or sometimes less-important cautions) flag key safety or procedural problems. Again, the marginal icon should ensure that readers don't overlook the warning.

WORLD◆AUTOMOTIVE◆MANUFACTURING

DIAGNOSTIC PROCEDURE: 23-89A

24 NOVEMBER 1997
PAGE 1 of 4

Subject   Solenoid and Wiring Tests on Transmissions for Model Z Trucks (1996, 1997, and 1998 model years)

Applicability   All 1996–1998 Model Z Trucks with 8-cylinder engines (for 6-cylinder Z models, see Procedure 23-90B)

SUMMARY   Procedure 23-89A tests the solenoid and third clutch shift wiring using an operational truck. It is not a bench test procedure. The test involves the following:

1. Removing the terminal housing cover.

2. Attaching an ohmmeter.

3. Taking readings both while the motor is idling and while the motor is in third gear.

4. Repairing and replacing the solenoid and associated wiring.

REQUIREMENTS	ITEMS
Equipment	Meter or scale-type ohmmeter Standard wrenches
Document	Transmission Repair Manual 5–96/98–4 (Reference pp. 28–33)

IMPORTANT   Use the following procedure to test the solenoid and associated circuits as installed in the truck. This test is not a bench test.

WARNING   All bench tests of the solenoid using a 12V battery will burn out the solenoid. See Test Procedure 1595-K for bench test procedure.

A technical procedure must be both accurate and very readable. If possible, it should be 100 percent unambiguous—that is, its graphics and its text should present steps that no reader can misinterpret. See WRITING AND REVISING.

Procedure

For a Technical Process

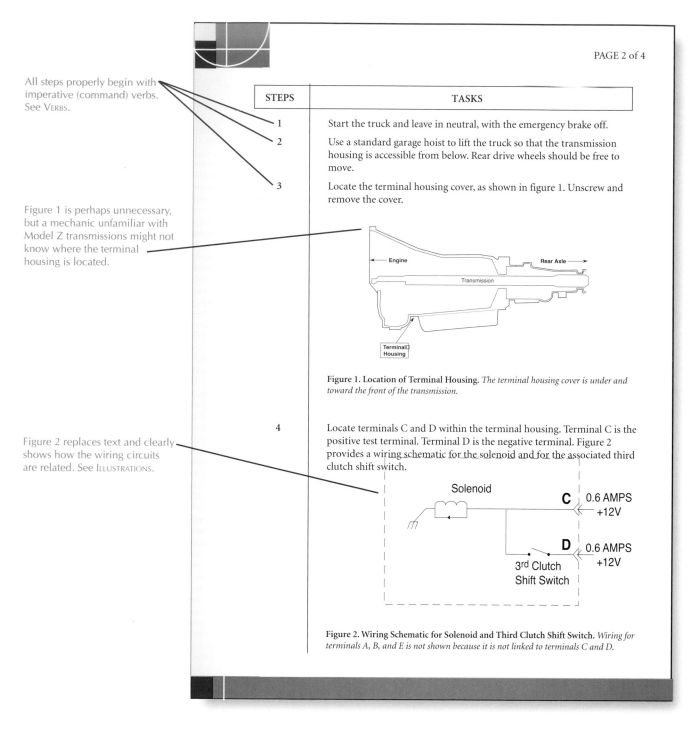

All steps properly begin with imperative (command) verbs. See VERBS.

Figure 1 is perhaps unnecessary, but a mechanic unfamiliar with Model Z transmissions might not know where the terminal housing is located.

Figure 2 replaces text and clearly shows how the wiring circuits are related. See ILLUSTRATIONS.

STEPS	TASKS
1	Start the truck and leave in neutral, with the emergency brake off.
2	Use a standard garage hoist to lift the truck so that the transmission housing is accessible from below. Rear drive wheels should be free to move.
3	Locate the terminal housing cover, as shown in figure 1. Unscrew and remove the cover.

Engine — Rear Axle —

Transmission

Terminal
Housing

Figure 1. Location of Terminal Housing. *The terminal housing cover is under and toward the front of the transmission.*

STEPS	TASKS
4	Locate terminals C and D within the terminal housing. Terminal C is the positive test terminal. Terminal D is the negative terminal. Figure 2 provides a wiring schematic for the solenoid and for the associated third clutch shift switch.

Solenoid

C 0.6 AMPS +12V

D 0.6 AMPS +12V

3rd Clutch
Shift Switch

Figure 2. Wiring Schematic for Solenoid and Third Clutch Shift Switch. *Wiring for terminals A, B, and E is not shown because it is not linked to terminals C and D.*

For clarity, each step in the procedure reflects a single task, and the tasks are carefully sequenced. The numbering of the steps allows for easy referencing and recall if one or more need to be repeated. See LISTS and NUMBERING SYSTEMS.

Procedure

For a Technical Process

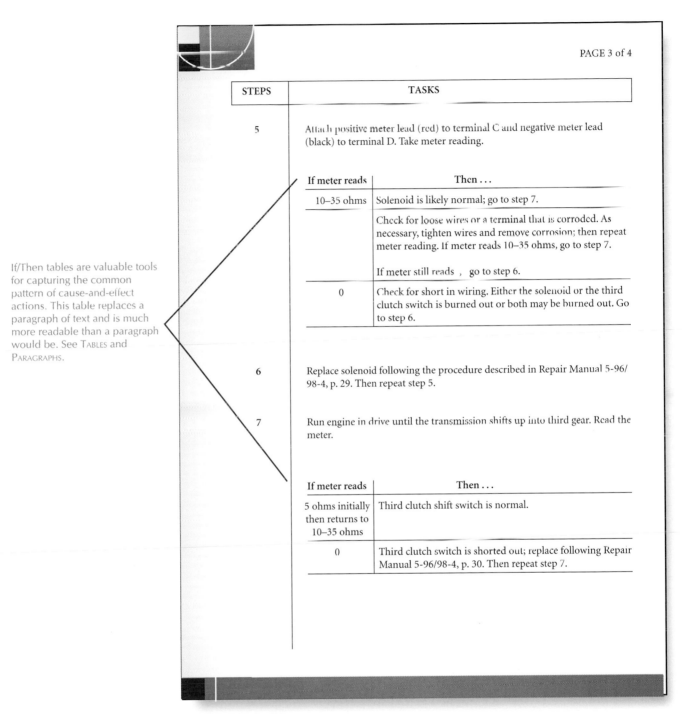

STEPS	TASKS

5 — Attach positive meter lead (red) to terminal C and negative meter lead (black) to terminal D. Take meter reading.

If meter reads	Then ...
10–35 ohms	Solenoid is likely normal; go to step 7.
	Check for loose wires or a terminal that is corroded. As necessary, tighten wires and remove corrosion; then repeat meter reading. If meter reads 10–35 ohms, go to step 7. If meter still reads , go to step 6.
0	Check for short in wiring. Either the solenoid or the third clutch switch is burned out or both may be burned out. Go to step 6.

6 — Replace solenoid following the procedure described in Repair Manual 5-96/98-4, p. 29. Then repeat step 5.

7 — Run engine in drive until the transmission shifts up into third gear. Read the meter.

If meter reads	Then ...
5 ohms initially then returns to 10–35 ohms	Third clutch shift switch is normal.
0	Third clutch switch is shorted out; replace following Repair Manual 5-96/98-4, p. 30. Then repeat step 7.

If/Then tables are valuable tools for capturing the common pattern of cause-and-effect actions. This table replaces a paragraph of text and is much more readable than a paragraph would be. See TABLES and PARAGRAPHS.

Procedure

For a Technical Process

STEPS	TASKS
8	Disconnect the meter and reverse the leads. Attach positive lead (red) to terminal D and negative lead (black) to terminal C. Then let the engine idle in drive. Take meter reading.

If meter reads	Then . . .
5–15 ohms	Solenoid is normal.
0	Solenoid is shorted out; repeat steps 6, 7, and 8.

STEPS	TASKS
9	Disconnect the meter and replace the terminal housing cover. See step 3 above.

The title and associated data allow for careful cross-referencing and document storage and retrieval. The page notation (*1 of 3*) helps readers keep track of pages.

The one-page summary, although not asking for executive action, is almost an executive summary. See REPORTS and SUMMARIES.

The recommendations and their potential cost savings begin the summary.

This paragraph establishes the purpose as well as the original line of investigation. See MEMOS, LETTERS, and ORGANIZATION.

The listed findings are concise. The sentences are deliberately short. See SENTENCES and SCIENTIFIC/TECHNICAL STYLE.

Sky Aviation

RESEARCH AND DEVELOPMENT DEPARTMENT

Title	RECOMMENDED MODIFICATIONS TO PREVENT HOLE ELONGATION WHEN DRILLING THE G-175 STRUT FITTING		RDD Number 8795-3
Routing Status Routine	Charge Number 3-T3743-8042-286444	Model Number(s) G-175	Page Number 1 of 3

SUMMARY

We recommend a larger clamp foot (CF-8765-54-A) and a new Skylube application system (LA-5767-87) for use with all Acme 570 drills now being used. We estimate that these changes will save about $6,000 per year by eliminating the need to rework poorly drilled holes.

We have investigated the cause of the hole elongation in the drilling of the G-175 strut fitting. Three Acme Model 570 drills are currently used for this operation. We originally thought that improper sequencing of the feed and clamp-up system caused the elongation problem. In investigating this problem, we found the following:

1. Laboratory tests showed that one drill motor was unclamping with the drill still in the hole. We rebuilt the feed and clamp-up system to remedy this problem.

2. Further tests showed that the area of the clamp foot was too small to prevent the motor from rocking on its axis during drilling, so we designed a larger clamp foot.

3. Tests indicated that the drill motor feed rates were excessive. We corrected the feed rates on all three Acme drills.

4. The drill motors tended to stall right at the breakout of the drill, so we fabricated a Skylube application system. This modification prevents stalling.

Please see the attached discussion for a detailed report of our investigation.

Diane Metcalf   5/30/97
PREPARED BY   DATE

Wallace Petersen   6/10/97
APPROVED BY   DATE

Randall H. Volgel   6/12/97
APPROVED BY   DATE

The summary (likely limited to one page) is a powerful technique for limiting documentation and for making technical reports more accessible. Many readers will not want or need to read more than the summary. If the summary contains the important details, these readers will be able to determine whether they need to read further. See REPORTS, SUMMARIES, and ORGANIZATION.

Technical Report

The brief introduction establishes the reason for and purpose of the investigation. As appropriate, relevant prior work and other background information might also appear in the introduction. See INTRODUCTIONS and REPORTS.

The displayed list highlights the proposed test and redesign program. This list actually repeats information covered under Tests. See REPETITION and LISTS.

The headings are not specific, but they are probably standard. All research/investigation reports in this company have the same headings. The consistent format helps readers of many similar reports find information easily. See HEADINGS and ORGANIZATION.

The body of the report follows a scientific format rather than a managerial format. Thus, the conclusions and recommendations appear at the end rather than at the beginning. In most cases, the sequence and specificity of the headings in the body are almost irrelevant. Most readers will not read carefully beyond the summary, and readers familiar with the report format will already understand the content and organization of ideas appearing in the body. See ORGANIZATION.

Sky Aviation

The tests are explained in the chronological order in which they were performed. The chronological pattern helps readers follow the test sequence and therefore its logic. Note that each step ends with a conclusion or recommendation for further study.

To solve this problem, we designed a new clamp foot (CF-8765-54-A) with 57 percent greater surface area. Then we subjected the new clamp to 140 drill tests. During these tests, the drill did not migrate as before, nor did the hole elongate significantly, although some imperfections in the drilling holes were observable to the naked eye. (See attached figure 1.)

We next checked the feed rate on the drill motor for drilling the 0.309 holes. The standard rate (4,300 rpm) produces a uniform drilling shaft so long as the drill bit is aligned precisely in the drill. But if the bit is not aligned precisely, the bit produces excessive vibration and hole elongation.

To determine an optimal drill speed, we tested the drive at five speed ranges: 2,000; 2,500; 3,000; 3,500; and 4,000 rpm. Rates below 3,000 rpm were unsatisfactory because the reduced speed created more friction and thus more heat. Rates above 3,500 rpm produced excessive vibration and hole elongation with drill bits not precisely aligned. So we repeated this test using another four speed ranges: 3,100; 3,200; 3,300; and 3,400 rpm.

Most paragraphs are organized chronologically, from problem to result or finding. This pattern is common in technical and scientific reports. See PARAGRAPHS and SCIENTIFIC/TECHNICAL STYLE.

Of these ranges, 3,400 rpm proved to be optimal. Further adjusting revealed that 3,460 rpm (±30 rpm) is the best compromise rate. Accordingly, we adjusted the driving speed to 3,460 rpm. (See Ref. 5Y114-87, Drilling and Reaming Feeds and Speeds.)

Finally, we noticed that the drill tended to stall just before the drill finished the hole. We designed a Skylube application system (LA-5767-87) to lubricate the bit (see attached figure 2). This system eliminated stalling problems. For further information on this application system, see RDD NO. 8799-6.

CONCLUSIONS AND RECOMMENDATIONS

The conclusions and recommendations can be brief because they have already been covered first in the summary and later in the Tests section. See ORGANIZATION and REPORTS.

The Acme 570 drill was returned to the Production line in mid-April. It had a new clamp foot, a correct feed rate, and the Skylube application system. We are continuing to monitor the performance of this drill, but preliminary results are promising.

We sent a recommendation memo (56984-76) to B. Worth recommending that all Acme 570 drills be modified with a larger clamp foot (CF-8765-54-A) and the new Skylube application system (LA-5767-87).

No. 8795-3
Page 3 of 3

Attached figures 1 and 2 are not included.

Index

Using the Index

Indexes are often more annoying than useful. They omit key cross-references, or they refer readers to pages where the indexed word or phrase is missing. To address these problems, we have provided detailed cross-references. We have also tried to eliminate inaccurate or "ghost" references.

We used the following conventions as we compiled the index. Please take a moment to familiarize yourself with these conventions:

- Main entries from the Reference Glossary are printed in a large capital and small capitals. For example, ABBREVIATIONS, ACRONYMS, and ACTIVE/PASSIVE.

- Following the title of a main entry, the page number(s) in boldface refer to the main alphabetically arranged entries, as in this example: ADJECTIVES, **12–14.**

- Cross-references with only *See* and a page number indicate that what you are looking up appears under the *See* reference. For example, if you look up *adept*, you will find the following *See* reference: See *adapt*, 330. On p. 330 you will find a discussion of *adapt*, which includes information about *adept*.

- Cross-references with *Also see* and a page number indicate that you will find extra information on the pages listed, but that this information is not the main discussion. For example, under ADVERBS appears this reference: *Also see* ADJECTIVES, 12. Thus, you will find that the entry for ADJECTIVES discusses adverbs on p. 12, even though the main discussion of adverbs appears on p. 15.

- Model documents on pp. 359–421 are not indexed in detail. They are only listed once and then only by their title. These single references appear in boldface followed by a page number, as in this example: **Technical Report (model), 419–421.**

Index

Index

Index

Index

Index

Index

Index